Guide to Higher Education in Africa

third edition

Association of African Universities
Association des Universités africaines

International Association of Universities
Association internationale des Universités

 IAU/UNESCO INFORMATION CENTRE ON HIGHER EDUCATION
CENTRE AIU/UNESCO D'INFORMATION SUR L'ENSEIGNEMENT SUPERIEUR

palgrave

Whilst every care has been taken in compiling the information contained in this publication, neither the publisher nor the editor can accept any responsibility for any errors or omissions therein.

Prepared by the International Association of Universities,
IAU/UNESCO Information Centre on Higher Education
Editor: Claudine Langlois
Assistant Editor: Geneviève Rabreau

IAU ISBN 92–9002–172–1

First published 2004 by
PALGRAVE MACMILLAN
Houndmills, Basingstoke, Hampshire RG21 6XS and
175 Fifth Avenue, New York, N. Y. 10010
Companies and representatives throughout the world

PALGRAVE MACMILLAN is the global academic imprint of the Palgrave Macmillan division of St. Martin's Press, LLC and of Palgrave Macmillan Ltd. Macmillan® is a registered trademark in the United States, United Kingdom and other countries. Palgrave is a registered trademark in the European Union and other countries.

ISBN 1–4039–3674–9

This book is printed on paper suitable for recycling and made from fully managed and sustained forest sources.

Cataloguing-in-publication data

A catalogue record for this book is available from the British Library

A catalogue record for this book is available from the Library of Congress.

10   9   8   7   6   5   4   3   2   1
13   12   11   10   09   08   07   06   05   04

Printed in China

CONTENTS

GUIDE TO HIGHER EDUCATION IN AFRICA

THIRD EDITION

FOREWORD

The current edition of the *Guide to Higher Education in Africa* continues the effort of the Association of African Universities (AAU) in collaboration with the International Association of Universities (IAU) to make reliable and updated information on tertiary education in Africa available and easily accessible. Our objectives are to promote interchange, contact and cooperation among university institutions in Africa; to encourage increased contact between African higher education institutions and the international academic world; and to disseminate information on higher education and research in Africa.

The first two editions, published in 1999 and 2002, received positive comments and suggestions for improvement as well as additional information for entries, particularly from our Member institutions.

As with previous editions, this *Guide* contains details on the educational systems of 47 African countries, their institutions of higher education and, for each country, the national bodies concerned with higher education. It is the result of collaboration between the Association of African Universities (AAU) and the International Association of Universities (IAU) to collect and disseminate information on higher education on the African continent.

The *Guide* has been produced from the computerized database maintained at the AAU Secretariat in Accra and the global database maintained at the IAU/UNESCO Information Centre on Higher Education in Paris. Institutional entries have been updated and revised for this edition. Where information was not available in time for inclusion, entries are based on data already in the database or on documentation available at the AAU's Information and Communication Section and the IAU/UNESCO Information Centre on Higher Education.

The AAU and IAU are indebted to the many universities, governmental agencies and academic bodies that have provided material for this *Guide*.

It is our hope that the *Guide* will continue to meet the need and interest of our readers, particularly our Member institutions, whose comments and suggestions have been invaluable as we strive to improve the quality and relevance of AAU and IAU publications.

We are also grateful to our partners for contributing financially to the publication of the *Guide* and for their interest in the promotion of higher education in Africa.

January 2004

Prof. Akilagpa Sawyerr
AAU Secretary-General

Ms Eva Egron-Polak
IAU Secretary-General/Executive Director

GUIDE TO THE ENTRIES

This Third Edition of the *Guide to Higher Education in Africa* comprises entries for over 900 institutions of higher education, university and non-university level in 47 African countries, as well as background information on their educational system, qualifications and higher education agencies. Depending on the country, the information provided is generally based on the academic year 2002-2003 (except for staff and student statistics).

COUNTRY PROFILES

The descriptions of education systems are based on entries in the current version of the *World Higher Education Database* CD-Rom. Each profile includes the following:
- main diplomas and degrees awarded;
- description of primary and secondary education;
- description of higher education system (vocational-technical studies and the different stages of university level studies);
- teacher education;
- non-formal higher education;
- grading system;
- admissions to higher education (including requirements for foreign students);
- recognition of studies and qualifications;
- student services, expenses and financial aid;
- international cooperation;
- national bodies and agencies dealing with higher education.

Information for this section has either been provided by the competent authorities in the country or has been compiled by the IAU/UNESCO Information Centre on Higher Education from authoritative sources.

INSTITUTIONAL ENTRIES

Institutional entries in the *Guide* are of two types :
- Institutions of university level;
- Other institutions of higher education.

Institutions of university-level

For the first category, the International Association of Universities (IAU) and the Association of African Universities (AAU) have sent questionnaires to those degree-granting institutions communicated by competent authorities in each country as being of "university level". The inclusion or omission of an institution, in consequence, does not imply any judgement by the IAU or the AAU as to the status of that institution. Similarly, the designations employed for countries and territories are those in use in the United Nations system and do not imply any expression of opinion with regard to their status or the delimitations of their frontiers.

Individual entries for university-level institutions are generally listed within Public and Private sections, where relevant, with postal address and telecommunication information. The name of each institution is systematically given first in English, followed by the name in the national language(s), where appropriate. The names and full communication details of the Academic Head, the Chief Administrative Officer, and the Director of International Relations are given, where available.

The lists of faculties, colleges, departments, schools, institutes, etc., are intended primarily as a general guide to the academic structure of the institutions of which they form a part. They normally include the various fields of study offered (standardized list). The names of heads at that level are provided whenever possible and are followed by brief descriptions of the history and structure of the institution and, where applicable, by information on cooperation programmes with institutions in other countries. The name of the agency accrediting or recognizing the institution is also given when available.

Admission requirements are usually listed for courses leading to a first degree or similar qualification. Special requirements for admission to studies leading to higher degrees and specialized diplomas are indicated where appropriate.

The names of degrees, diplomas and professional qualifications are generally given in the language of the country concerned. The duration of studies, indicated in years or semesters, is normally the required minimum period. Translations into English of fields of study are included where they are likely to be helpful.

Overall academic staff and student enrolment statistics complete the entry and include a breakdown of numbers for foreign students, evening students and students by correspondence

Other institutions of higher education

Entries for the "other institutions of higher education" (institutions which have not been classified as "university level" establishments by the competent national bodies) comprise institutions offering terminal degrees after three to four years of higher education. Usually less detailed, they include:

- name in English and, where relevant, in the language of country;
- postal and telecommunication details, with the introduction of E-mail and Website addresses, where available;
- names of the Academic Head, Administrative Officer and Director of International Relations and, where available, their telecommunication details;
- listing of the Main Divisions of Study by Faculties, Colleges, Schools, Departments, Institutes and/or study areas, etc.; and
- date(s) of foundation.

It should be noted that neither seminaries and schools of theology, if they only train ministers or religious leaders, nor military academies only preparing for military careers are included in the *Guide*. Newly created online-only institutions of higher education are not listed either.

Institutions marked with a dot (•) are members of the Association of African Universities.

Institutions and agencies marked with an asterisk (*) are members of the International Association of Universities.

AAU – THE ASSOCIATION OF AFRICAN UNIVERSITIES

HISTORICAL BACKGROUND

The *Association of African Universities* (AAU) is an international non-governmental organization set up by the universities in Africa to promote cooperation among themselves and between them and the international academic community.

The AAU, whose headquarters is in Accra, Ghana, was formed in November 1967 at a founding conference in Rabat, Morocco, attended by representatives of 34 universities who adopted the constitution of the Association. This followed earlier consultations among Executive Heads of African universities at a UNESCO Conference on Higher Education in Africa in Antananarivo, Madagascar, in 1962, and at a Conference of Heads of African Universities in 1963 in Khartoum, Sudan.

The AAU is the apex organization and principal forum for consultation, exchange of information and cooperation among the universities and other higher education institutions in Africa, with a membership of 178 institutions from 43 African countries.

OBJECTIVES

The constitutional objectives of AAU are the following:
- to promote interchange, contact and cooperation among university institutions in Africa;
- to collect, classify and disseminate information on higher education and research, particularly in Africa.
- to promote cooperation among African Institutions in curriculum development, and in the determination of equivalence of degree;
- to encourage increased contacts between its Members and the international academic world;
- to study and make known the educational and related needs of African university institutions and, as far as practicable, to coordinate the means whereby those needs may be met;
- to encourage the development and wider use of African languages;
- to organize, encourage and support seminars and conferences between African university teachers, administrators and others dealing with problems of higher education in Africa.

ORGANIZATIONAL STRUCTURE

The AAU governing bodies are the General Conference, the Executive Board, the Conference of Rectors, Presidents and Vice-Chancellors (COREVIP), and the Secretariat.

The **General Conference** is an assembly of Vice-Chancellors, Presidents and Rectors of all Member institutions or their representatives that meets every four years with the purpose of:
- assessing the activities implemented in the past four years against the background of a programme and a budget approved at the previous Conference;
- approving the core programme of activities and budget for the following four-year period;
- electing the governing bodies of the Association including election of one President and three Vice-Presidents from among the Vice-Chancellors, Presidents and Rectors of the Member universities.

The **Executive Board** and its standing Committees on Administration and Finances and on Membership and Programmes, comprise one President, three Vice-Presidents and eleven Vice-Chancellors elected form among the African sub-regions. The Executive Board meets once every year and approves the annual programme and budget of the AAU. It also appoints the Secretary-General and approves the appointment of other professional staff to a permanent Secretariat based in Accra, Ghana.

The **Conference of Rectors, Vice-Chancellors and Presidents** (COREVIP) is an assembly of the chief executive officers of Member institutions or their representatives that meets every two years with the purpose of:
- examining collectively themes identified as common concerns and priorities for the development of higher education in Member Institutions;
- making recommendations primarily to Members, as well as to the Executive Board and to the Secretariat;
- acting as a Mid-term Conference and taking stock of the implementation of the decisions of the General Conference and recommending corrective measures.

The **Secretariat**, headed by the Secretary-General, currently comprises six senior professional staff, three junior professional staff and sixteen support staff. It is situated in an office of the Secretary-General with three Sections, namely Research and Programmes, Communication and Services and Finance, and one special unit which is the Coordination of Working Groups on Higher Education.

The current President of the Association elected at the 10th General Conference in February 2001 for a four-year term is Prof. George Eshiwani, former Vice-Chancellor of the Kenyatta University, Kenya, and the current Secretary-General is Prof. Akilagpa Sawyerr, former Rector of the University of Ghana.

CORE PROGRAMME 2000–2004

For the more effective attainment of its objectives, the Association has, for some time now, directed its effort at formulating a coherent Core Programme of activities aimed at:
- contributing more effectively to capacity building in African Universities;
- creating a framework within which its partners can contribute more effectively to the funding of the Core Programme as a whole;
- ensuring improved utilization of resources.

The first two Core Programmes (1993–1997 and 1997–2000) were approved at the 8th and 9th General Conferences of the AAU, respectively. As in the past, the Core Programme for 2001–2004 aims broadly at assisting African universities to respond effectively both to specific needs expressed by their communities, and to the rapidly changing national and global environment within which they operate. To address this general objective, the AAU has prepared a programme under the general theme: ***African Universities and the Challenge of Knowledge Creation and Application in the New Century***.

The Core Programme covers the following Sub-Themes:
- Leadership and Management;
- Quality of Training and Research;
- Information and Communication Technologies;
- Women in African Tertiary Institutions;
- Improving Management and Access to African Scholarly Work;
- Education for Peace and Conflict Avoidance;
- HIV/AIDS and the African University.

SPECIAL MEMBERSHIP SERVICE TO PROMOTE ACADEMIC MOBILITY AND QUALITY ENHANCEMENT

In addition to activities planned to fit within these sub-themes, the AAU will continue to provide special Membership services aimed at promoting academic mobility and quality enhancement.

Currently these services cover:
- Staff Exchange: the staff exchange scheme is to foster inter-university cooperation through exchange of external examiners, staff exchange for teaching, participation in seminars and conferences, and research cooperation.
- Fellowships and Scholarships: AAU makes available fellowships and scholarships on a competitive basis to citizenship or normal residence.

OTHER MEMBERSHIP SERVICES

On and off Campus Special Issues Workshops
Over the years, the AAU has carried out a number of studies and conducted workshops and seminars on critical issues of higher education in Africa. In the process, considerable expertise on these issues has been accumulated both among personnel of the AAU Secretariat as well as among resources persons in Member Universities. On the invitation of a Member University, the AAU can arrange to send to the university campus, at the AAU's expense, a resource person or a member of the Secretariat to conduct a seminar or workshop on an issue related to AAU programmes.

Information Exchange
The AAU publishes a *Newsletter* three times each year in English and French. The *Newsletter* carries news about African universities and features articles on higher education in Africa. It is circulated widely to universities and university libraries throughout Africa. Member Universities are encouraged to send information about their activities for inclusion in the *Newsletter*.

Guide to Higher Education in Africa
This is published every two years and contains:
- listing of Member Universities;
- information about their executive officers;
- programmes offered in the universities;
- description of higher eduction systems.

AAU Website
This represents the AAU's presence on the Internet. It provides information about the AAU and Member Universities, and some useful Internet resources as well as links to partner organisations.

Reports
Research reports and reports of workshops and seminars conducted by the Association are also occasionally published.

COOPERATION WITH OTHER ORGANIZATIONS

The AAU collaborates with African Governments, national and international organizations. It is member of the International Association of Universities (IAU), the Permanent Council of International Congress of African Studies (ICAF), and UNESCO and is accorded observer status by the Organization of African Unity (OAU). Collaborative linkages are maintained with: African and Malagasy Council for Higher Education (CAMES); United Nations University (UNU); Commonwealth Higher Education Support Scheme (CHESS); Commonwealth of Learning (COL); Commonwealth Secretariat (ComSec); African Virtual University and the United Nations Economic Commission for Africa (UNECA).

FINANCIAL RESOURCES

Funding of AAU programmes derives from the following sources:
*   membership subscriptions;
*   grants from developed countries, international and other donor agencies;
*   grants from OAU;
*   income from services provided and from publications.

AAU ONGOING PROGRAMMES 2001–2004

The following projects are being implemented:
*   Study Programme on Higher Education Management in Africa;
*   Academic Mobility (staff exchange, small grants, scholarships);
*   Senior University Management Workshops;
*   Developing Quality Assurance Systems in African Universities;
*   Regional Cooperation in Graduate Training and Research;
*   Use and application of ICTs in Higher Education in Africa;
*   Database on African Thesis and Dissertation (DATAD);
*   Ford Foundation International Fellowship Programme (IFP);
*   HIV in African Universities.

HEADQUARTERS

Association of African Universities
Aviation Road Extension, Airport Residential Area,
P. O. Box 5744, Accra-North, Ghana
Tel: +233-21-774495/761588; Fax: +233-21+774821
E-mails: secgen@aau.org; info@aau.org
Website: www.aau.org

OFFICERS OF THE ASSOCIATION OF AFRICAN UNIVERSITIES (AAU)

Executive Board 2001-2004 (Elected at the 10th General Conference, February 2001, Nairobi, Kenya)

President

Prof. George Eshiwani   Former Vice-Chancellor, Kenyatta University, Kenya

Vice-Presidents

Dr. Dorothy L. Njeuma   Vice-Chancellor, University of Buea, Cameroon
Prof. Lamine Ahmadou Ndiaye   Ancien Recteur Fondateur, Université Gaston Berger, Sénégal
Prof. Abdulkabir Saied Al-Fahry   President of Popular Committee University of Sebha, Libya

Members of the Executive Board

Prof. Peter Katjavivi   Vice-Chancellor, University of Namibia
Prof. John Melamu   Former Vice Chancellor, University of North-West University of Botswana
Dr. Thikhoi L. Jonathan   Deputy Vice-Chancellor, National University of Lesotho
Prof. Ndjabulo Ndebele   Vice-Chancellor, University of Cape Town, South Africa
Prof. John Sefa K. Ayim   Vice-Chancellor Kwame Nkrumah University of Science & Technology (KNUST), Ghana
Prof. Moussa Ouattara   Recteur, Université Polytechnique de Bobo-Dioulasso, Burkina Faso
Dr. Emile Rwamasirabo   Recteur, Université Nationale de Rwanda
Prof. Matthew Luhanga   Vice-Chancellor, University of Dar-es-Salaam, Tanzania
Prof. Matthew A. Aduol   President, University of Bahr El Ghazal, Sudan

Alternate Members

Prof. Mutale Chanda, Vice-Chancellor, University of Zambia; Prof. Mazula Brazao, Rector, Eduardo Mondlane University, Mozambique; Prof. M. Ramashala, Vice-Chancellor, University of Durban-Westville, South Africa; Dr. M. Takalo, Campus Principal, Vista University, South Africa; Prof. Amer Mohammed, President, Zagazig University, Egypt; Prof. Mohammed Alaoui, Rector, Mohammed V University, Morocco; Prof. Raymond Bening, Vice-Chancellor, University of Development Studies, Tamale, Ghana; Prof. Ginigeme Mbanefoh, Vice-Chancellor, University of Nigeria, Nigeria; Prof. Boubacar Cisse, Recteur, Université du Mali, Mali; Prof. Daouda Aidara, Président, Université d'Abobo-Adjamé, Côte d'Ivoire; Prof. Silas Lwakabamba, Rector, Kigali Institute of Science & Technology, Rwanda; Prof. Jean Tabi Manga, Recteur, Université de Yaoundé I, Cameroon; Prof. Ratemo Michieka, Vice-Chancellor, Jomo Kenyatta University of Agriculture & Technology, Kenya; Prof. Mogessie Ashenafi, President, Addis Ababa University, Ethiopia; Prof. A. B. Lwoga, Vice-Chancellor, Sokoine University of Agriculture, Tanzania

IAU – THE INTERNATIONAL ASSOCIATION OF UNIVERSITIES

The *International Association of Universities* (IAU) is a UNESCO-based, international non-governmental organization, which was formally established in 1950 to encourage links between institutions of higher education throughout the world. It brings together universities and higher education institutions, as well as organizations of universities from some 130 countries, including in Africa, for debate, reflection and action on topics of shared interest and common concern. Its permanent Secretariat, the International Universities Bureau, is located at UNESCO, Paris, and it provides a wide variety of services to Members and to the international higher education community at large.

MEETINGS

The IAU provides a forum for higher education leaders to discuss major current trends and issues in higher education and higher education policy. Heads of all Member Institutions and Organizations or their representatives are invited to the IAU quadrennial General Conferences as well as to annual international events, such as Colloquiums, Seminars and Round Tables. These events are organized by the Association either alone or in co-operation with other academic bodies and provide unique opportunities for the exchange of experience and ideas on issues of international interest and importance. The Eleventh General Conference was held in Durban, South Africa, in August 2000, and discussed the theme "*Universities – Gateway to the Future*". The Twelfth General Conference will be held in São Paulo, Brazil, on 25–29 July 2004 and will focus on "*The Wealth of Diversity – the Role of Universities in Promoting Dialogue and Development*".

PUBLICATIONS

Services traditionally offered to Member Institutions and Organizations include the right to receive, either on a complimentary basis or at considerably reduced rates, the Association's publications. These include two major reference works the *International Handbook of Universities* and the *World List of Universities and Other Institutions of Higher Education* (both published biennially), the *World Higher Education Database* (WHED) CD-Rom (annually), the quarterly journal *Higher Education Policy*, the bimonthly *IAU Newsletter* and a monograph series *Issues in Higher Education*. The two reference works are long-established, invaluable tools for all those concerned with international cooperation in higher education, providing detailed information on thousands of higher education institutions worldwide. The CD-Rom is a more recent addition which provides, apart from the information above, data on higher education systems and credentials, and many search facilities. In addition, in cooperation with the AAU, the *Guide to Higher Education in Africa* was launched by the IAU in 1999. All four publications are prepared from the IAU's computerized database, WHED. *Higher Education Policy* and *Issues in Higher Education* focus on policy issues and the role of higher education in society today, offering a comparative platform for the exchange and sharing of information and debate within the world community of higher education. (See list of IAU Publications p. xv - xvi)

INFORMATION SERVICES

Also available to Member Institutions and Organizations is the vast body of information housed in the specialized IAU/UNESCO Information Centre on Higher Education. The Centre, managed by the IAU, contains over 50,000 volumes on higher education worldwide. Staff of the Centre also coordinate HEDBIB, the Higher Education Bibliographical Database. Different types of information services (topical bibliographies, institutional and statistical data, credential evaluation and advice, and address labels) are also provided. HEDBIB can be consulted online at www.unesco.org/iau/hedbib.html. The IAU website www.unesco.org/iau is an important source of information, updated regularly and offering the most recent news on IAU priorities and its Members.

COOPERATION

The IAU, through its unique networking capacity, provides an important clearing-house function to Members for academic exchange and cooperation, implying active involvement and participation of Member universities in the important mission of bringing a real international perspective to the life of universities. Among the major areas retained for cooperation are Higher Education and Sustainable Human Development, Universities and Information Technologies, Internationalization and Globalization of Higher Education, and Inter-Cultural Dialogue.

SECRETARIAT

International Association of Universities
1, rue Miollis
75732 Paris Cedex 15, France
Telephone: +33 1-45-68-48-00
Fax: +33 1-47-34-76-05
Telex: 270602
E-Mail: iau@unesco.org
Website: www.unesco.org/iau

PRESIDENT

Hans Van Ginkel, Former Rector of Utrecht University and Rector of the United Nations University (UNU), Japan

SECRETARY-GENERAL/EXECUTIVE DIRECTOR

Eva Egron-Polak

OFFICERS OF THE INTERNATIONAL ASSOCIATION OF UNIVERSITIES

MAIN AAU PUBLICATIONS 1995–2004

- Demand, Access and Equity Issues in African Higher Education, 1995
- Enhancing Linkages between African Universities, the Wider Society, the Business Community and Governments, 1995
- Governance Issues in African Universities: Improving Management and Governance to make
- African Universities viable in the 1990s and beyond, 1995
- Universities in Africa: Challenges and Opportunities of International Cooperation, 1995
- Adequate and Sustainable Funding of African Universities, 1995
- Quality and Relevance: African Universities in the 21st Century, 1995
- The Emerging Role of African Universities in the Development of Science and Technology, 1995
- The Future Missions and Roles of the African Universities, 1995
- Strategic Planning at Selected African Universities, 1996
- The African Experience with Higher Education, 1996
- The Political Economy of Development, An African Perspective (2 Volumes), 1999
- Higher Education Leadership in Africa: A Casebook, 1999
- Towards the Introduction and Application of Information and Communication Technologies in
- African Universities, 2001
- Guide to Higher Education in Africa (Directory)

Occasional Papers

- Women in Higher Education and Research in Africa, 1999
- North-South Cooperation to Strengthen Universities in Africa, 1999
- The Role of University Libraries in African Universities, 1999
- Post-Genocide Restructuring of Higher Education in Rwanda, an Overview, 2001

Research Papers

- Statistical Data: The Underestimated Tool for Higher Education Management. The Case of Makerere University, 1998
- Revitalizing Financing of Higher Education in Kenya: Resource Allocation in Public Universities, 1998
- The Social Background of Makerere University Students and the Potential for Cost Sharing, 1998
- Modeling for Resource Allocation to Departments and Faculties in African Universities, 1998
- An Innovative Approach to Undergraduate Education in Nigeria, 2000
- The Stories We Tell and the Way We Tell Them: An Investigation into the Institutional Culture of the University of the North, South Africa, 2000
- Etude sur le Suivi des Diplômés de l'Université Cheikh anta Diop de Dakar (UCAD-Sénégal) dans le Milieu du Travail, 2001
- Knowledge and Skills of B.Com Graduates of the Faculty of Commerce and Management, University of Dar-es-Salaam in the Job Market, 2001
- A Comparative Study of Makerere University Graduates of the Faculties of Arts and Sciences, 2001
- L'Evaluation de la Formation Universitaire: Le Point de Vue des Diplômés, 2001
- Management Styles in Nigerian Universities under Military Rule and the Challenges of Democracy, 2002
- Perceptions Concerning Academic Workload among South African Academics, 2002
- Quality Assurance and Management and Equitable Access: Hard Choices in Phases, 2003
- The Politics of Participatory Decision Making in Campus Governance, 2003

MAIN IAU PUBLICATIONS 1995–2004

For a worldwide Association, sharing information, expertise and experience amongst leaders and decision-makers on the central issues facing higher education, is key. IAU has made – and continues to make – a very substantial input to informed debate on public policy. It maintains databases and produces reference works on higher education systems, institutions and credentials and brings out state of the art research on vital issues that concern higher education. By doing so, it serves the academic community and its leadership, stimulating discussion and advancing action. Major publications resulting from this commitment are:

REFERENCE WORKS

- **International Handbook of Universities**, Seventeenth Edition, 2003, Palgrave Macmillan, Basingstoke, 2761pp.,ISBN: 0–333–92265–4; 92–9002–170–5 (IAU)

- **World List of Universities and Other Institutions of Higher Education**, Twenty-fourth Edition, 2004, Palgrave Macmillan, Basingstoke, ISBN: 1–4039–0687–4; 92–9002–173–X (IAU)

- **Guide to Higher Education in Africa**, Third Edition, 2004, Palgrave Macmillan, Basingstoke, xxxpp ISBN: 1–4039–3674–9; 92–9002–172–1 (IAU)

- **World Higher Education Database 2003-2004 CD-Rom**, combines information from the latest editions of the *International Handbook of Universities* and the *World List of Universities* (more than 15,000 institutions) and offers descriptions of the higher education systems and qualifications in over 180 countries. Palgrave Macmillan, Basingstoke, ISBN: 1–4039–0685–8

PUBLISHED GLOBALLY BY: Palgrave Macmillan, Houndmills, Basingstoke, Hampshire RG21 6XS and 175 Fifth Avenue, New York, N.Y. 10010, www.palgrave.com

RECENT ISSUES IN HIGHER EDUCATION SERIES (IHES)

Higher Education and the Nation State: the International Dimension of Higher Education. Edited by Jeroen Huisman, Peter Maassen and Guy Neave (Centre for Higher Education Policy Studies, University of Twente, Enschede, The Netherlands). Oxford, Pergamon/IAU Press, 2001. 237pp. ISBN: 0–08–042790–1

Access to Knowledge: New Information Technologies and the Emergence of the Virtual University. Edited by F. T. Tschang (United Nations University, Institute of Advanced Studies, Tokyo, Japan) & T. Della Senta (United Nations University, Institute of Advanced Studies, Tokyo, Japan). Oxford, Pergamon /IAU Press, 2001. 411pp. ISBN: 0–08–043670–6

Abiding Issues, Changing Perspectives: Visions of the University Across a Half-Century. Edited by Guy Neave (International Association of Universities, Paris). IAU Press, 2000. 320pp. ISBN: 92–9002–166–7

The Universities' Responsibilities to Society: International Perspectives. Edited by Guy Neave (International Association of Universities, Paris). Oxford, Pergamon /IAU Press, 2000. 289pp. ISBN: 0–08–043569–6 (Report of IAU Fourth Mid-Term Conference, Bangkok, 1997).

Local Knowledge and Wisdom in Higher Education. Edited by G. R. (Bob) Teasdale (Flinders University Institute of International Education, Adelaide, Australia) and Zane Ma Rhea (National Centre for Gender and Cultural Diversity, Swinburne University of Technology, Melbourne, Australia). Oxford, Pergamon/IAU Press, 2000. 264pp. ISBN: 0–08–043453–3

Higher Education Research: Its Relationship to Policy and Practice. Edited by Ulrich Teichler (Centre for Research on Higher Education and Work, University of Kassel, Germany) and Jan Sadlak (UNESCO). Oxford, Pergamon/IAU Press, 2000. 192pp. ISBN: 0–08–043452–5

Challenges Facing Higher Education at the Millennium. Edited by Werner Z. Hirsch and Luc E. Weber – Oxford, Pergamon /IAU Press, 1999. 199pp. ISBN: 0–08–042817–7

Distance and Campus Universities: Tensions and Interactions. A Comparative Study of Five Countries. Edited by S. Guri-Rosenblit (The Open University of Israel, Israel). Oxford, Pergamon /IAU Press, 1999. 290pp. ISBN: 0–08–043066–X

Creating Entrepreneurial Universities: Organizational Pathways of Transformation. Edited by Burton R. Clark (University of California, Los Angeles, USA). Oxford, Pergamon /IAU Press, 1998, 160pp. ISBN: 0–08–043342–1

Organising Innovative Research: The Inner Life of University Departments. Edited by Li Bennich-Björkman (Uppsala University, Sweden). Oxford, Pergamon /IAU Press, 1997. 250pp. ISBN: 0–08–043072–4

The Mockers and Mocked: Comparative Perspectives on Differentiation, Convergence and Diversity in Higher Education. Edited by V. Lynn Meek (University of New England, Australia), L. Goedegebuure (Centre for Higher Education Policy Studies (CHEPS), University of Twente, The Netherlands), O. Kivinen and R. Rinne (University of Turku, Finland). Oxford, Pergamon /IAU Press, 1996. 236pp. ISBN: 0–08–042563–1

Emerging Patterns of Social Demand and University Reform: Through a Glass Darkly. Edited by David D. Dill (University of North Carolina, USA) and Barbara Sporn (Vienna University of Economics and Business Administration, Austria). Oxford, Pergamon/IAU Press, 1995.

244pp. ISBN: 0–08–042564–X

East Asian Higher Education: Traditions and Transformations. By Albert H. Yee (Division of Academic Affairs, Florida International University, Miami, USA). Oxford, Pergamon/IAU Press, 1995. 213pp. ISBN: 0–08–042385–X

HIGHER EDUCATION POLICY

The Quarterly Journal of the International Association of Universities
Editor: Guy Neave, International Association of Universities

Recent issues have focused on the following themes:

• **Sciences, Training and Career**	Vol. 17, no. 2, 2004
• **The Business of University Research: Cross National Perspectives**	Vol. 17, no. 1, 2004
• **Higher Education Policy in China and Far East**	Vol. 16, no. 4, 2003
• **Africa: Reform or Collapse?**	Vol. 16, no. 3, 2003
• **Europe: Higher Education in Transition**	Vol. 16, no. 2, 2003
• **Perspectives on Higher Education in North America**	Vol. 16, no. 1, 2003
• **Academic Freedom in a Globalising World**	Vol. 15, no. 4, 2002
• **Research Management: Cross National and Regional Perspectives**	Vol. 15, no. 3, 2002
• **Sustainability and Higher Education: Initiatives and Agendas**	Vol. 15, no. 2, 2002
• **General Education: New Rationales, New Thinking**	Vol. 15, no. 1, 2002
• **Dimensions of Comparison**	Vol. 14, no. 4, 2001
• **Policy Making: Perspectives from Eastern Europe**	Vol. 14, no. 3, 2001
• **Out of Africa: Planning Change and Reform**	Vol. 14, no. 2, 2001
• **The Changing Frontiers of Autonomy and Accountability**	Vol. 14, no. 1, 2001

AVAILABLE FROM:
Both *Issues in Higher Education** and *Higher Education Policy* are available from Palgrave Macmillan.
North America Palgrave Macmillan, 175 Fifth Avenue, New York, NY 10010, USA, Tel.: +1-212-982-3900 or 1-800-221-7945, Fax: +1-212-777-6359
Rest of the World: Palgrave Macmillan, Houndmills, Basingstoke, Hampshire RG21 6XS, UK, Tel.: +44(0)1256 329242, Fax: +44(0)1256 357268

* For *Issues in Higher Education,* publications prior to 2003 may be ordered from:

Elsevier Books Customer Services
Linacre House Jordan Hill
Oxford OX2 8DP
United Kingdom
Email: amstbkinfo@elsevier.com
Website: www.elsevier-international.com/newcustomerservice/
Tel: +44(0)1865 474140
Fax: +44(0)1865 474141

IAU NEWSLETTER / NOUVELLES DE L'AIU

The bimonthly Newsletter of the International Association of Universities

AVAILABLE FROM:
International Association of Universities
UNESCO House
1, rue Miollis, 75732 Paris Cedex 15, France
Tel: +33-1-45 68 25 45 - Fax: +33-1-47 34 76 05 - E-mail: iau@unesco.org
Website: http://www.unesco.org/iau

Country Entries

Algeria

INSTITUTION TYPES AND CREDENTIALS

Types of higher education institutions:

Université (University)
Centre universitaire (University Centre)
Ecole nationale (National School)
Institut national (National Institute)
Ecole normale supérieure (Higher Teacher Training College)
Ecole polytechnique (Polytechnic)

School leaving and higher education credentials:

Baccalauréat de l'Enseignement secondaire
Baccalauréat technique
Certificat de Capacité en Droit
Diplôme de Technicien supérieur
Diplôme d'Etudes universitaires appliquées (DEUA)
Diplôme
Diplôme d'Etudes supérieures (DES)
Diplôme d'Ingénieur
Licence
Diplôme de Docteur
Magister
Doctorat d'Etat

STRUCTURE OF EDUCATION SYSTEM

Pre-higher education:

Duration of compulsory education:

Age of entry: 6
Age of exit: 15

Structure of school system:

Basic
Type of school providing this education: Ecole fondamentale
Length of programme in years: 9

Age level from: 6 to: 15
Certificate/diploma awarded: Brevet d'Enseignement fondamental

General Secondary
Type of school providing this education: Lycée d'Enseignement général, lycées polyvalents
Length of programme in years: 3
Age level from: 15 to: 18
Certificate/diploma awarded: Baccalauréat de l'Enseignement secondaire

Technical Secondary
Type of school providing this education: Lycées d'Enseignment technique (technicum)
Length of programme in years: 3
Certificate/diploma awarded: Baccalauréat technique

School education:

Basic education (Enseignement fondamental) lasts for nine years and leads to the Brevet d'enseignement fondamental. Secondary education is compulsory and consists of a three-year cycle of study provided in secondary schools and technicums. There are two branches of secondary education: general and specialized and technical/vocational. Students in general secondary and specialized secondary education study for three years. Successful students are awarded the Baccalauréat de l'Enseignement secondaire in one of the various streams offered. The Baccalauréat gives access to higher education but some institutions require it to be of a certain type (science, arts, etc.). The objective of technical and vocational secondary education is to prepare students for active life and industry (technicians and qualified workers). Studies last between one and four years, according to the type of training undertaken and can also lead to the Baccalauréat technique and higher education.

Higher education:

Higher education is provided by universities, university centres, national schools and institutes, and higher teacher training institutes (Ecoles normales supérieures), which fall under the responsibility of the Ministry of Higher Education and Scientific Research, as well as by institutes run by other ministries. The specific degrees awarded are determined by the field of study, not the institution. The Ministry of Higher Education approves the curriculum, which is standardized for each field of study. Algerian institutions also award graduate degrees (Diplômes de Postgraduation) in most fields in which a Licence or DES is awarded. A National Conference of Universities was created in 2000. It is a coordinating and evaluation body.

Main laws/decrees governing higher education:

Decree: Loi n°99-05 d'Orientation sur l'Enseignement supérieur   Year: 1999
Concerns: Higher Education

Decree: Décret exécutif n° 98-253   Year: 1998
Concerns: Status of Universities

Decree: Décret exécutif n° 98-254   Year: 1998
Concerns: Doctorate, postgraduation and habilitation

Academic year:

Classes from: September *to:* June

Long vacation from: 1 July *to:* 31 August

Languages of instruction:

Arabic, French

Stages of studies:

Non-university level post-secondary studies (technical/vocational type):

The technological institutions are national Institutes under the responsibility of one of the main ministries. They offer a variety of courses at the higher and graduate levels and students are trained in specific skills. Recruitment is at Baccalauréat level, and studies lead to a Diplôme d'Ingénieur after a five-year course, which is considered of university level. At the lower level, students who have reached Baccalauréat level but not passed the examination may follow a two-and-a-half-year course leading to the Diplôme de Technicien supérieur. This Diplôme is not recognized as a qualification for university entrance. However, a Technicien supérieur with five years' experience may continue to study for the Diplôme d'Ingénieur.

University level studies:

University level first stage:

At undergraduate level, higher education is divided into a short (three-year) cycle, leading to a Diplôme d'Etudes universitaires appliquées (DEUA), and a long (four to six-year) cycle, leading to the Licence or the Diplôme d'Etudes supérieures in Science or, in technological institutions, to the Diplôme d'Ingénieur. In most cases, the two cycles are parallel rather than consecutive programmes. Courses for the Diplôme in Engineering, Dental Surgery, Pharmacy, Architecture and Veterinary Medicine last for five years while the title of Doctor in Medicine is awarded after seven years' study.

University level second stage: Postgraduation:

After the main stage, the best students undertake postgraduate studies (Diplôme de Postgraduation). Studying for the Magister requires a minimum of four semesters after the DES or Licence and the defence of a thesis. The Magister is conferred by the major universities and replaces the Doctorat de 3ème cycle.

University level third stage: Doctorat d'Etat:

The last stage leads to the Doctorat d'Etat. Usually lasting three to five years, studies involve individual research work and submission of a substantial thesis.

Teacher education:

Training of pre-primary and primary/basic school teachers

Primary school teachers are trained at Ecoles normales supérieures. They obtain the Diplôme de Maître d'Enseignement fondamental (1st and 2nd stage) after three years after the Baccalauréat and the Diplôme de Professeur de l'Enseignement fondamental after four years.

Training of secondary school teachers

Secondary school teachers are trained at the Ecoles normales supérieures where they obtain the

Diplôme de Professeur de l'Enseignement secondaire (general or technical) five years after the Baccalauréat.

Training of higher education teachers

Teaching at the university level requires at least a Magister. Technological institutes outside the purview of the Ministère de l'Enseignement supérieur recruit teachers who hold the Ingéniorat d'Etat, Licence or Diplôme d'Etudes supérieures, depending on the specialization and the function the teacher is to serve. Experience in the relevant field of study is also taken into consideration.

Non-traditional studies:

Lifelong higher education

L'Université de la Formation Continue (UFC) opened in 1989. UFC is a network composed of ten regional institutes which is open to workers having at least five years' professional experience and who successfully completed the final secondary year but failed the Baccalauréat exam. Study consists of a preparatory year to enable a transition to "university" studies in Natural Science, Maths, Letters and Law, followed by three years' (short cycle) or four years' (long cycle) study. In 1990, the Université du Soir was created for people who do not hold the Baccalauréat or want to resume their studies after several years of professional life.

NATIONAL BODIES

Responsible authorities:

Ministry of Higher Education and Scientific Research (Ministère de l'Enseignement supérieur et de la Recherche scientifique)

Minister: Rachid Harraoubia

Secretary-General: Abdelatif Baba Ahmed

International Relations: Arezki Saidani

11 Chemin Doudou Mokhtar

Ben-Aknoun

Alger

Tel: +213(21) 91-18-86 +213(21) 91-47-69

Fax: +213(21) 91-18-23 +213(21) 91-21-41

EMail: mesrs@ist.cerist.dz

WWW: http://www.mesrs.edu.dz/

Role of governing body: Coordinates higher education.

ADMISSIONS TO HIGHER EDUCATION

Admission to non university higher education studies

Name of secondary school credential required: Baccalauréat de l'Enseignement secondaire

Name of secondary school credential required: Baccalauréat technique

Alternatives to credentials: At the lower level of the technological institutions, students who have reached Baccalauréat level but not passed the examination may follow a two-and-a-half-year course leading to the Diplôme de Technicien supérieur. This diploma, added to five years' experience, allows them to study for the Diplôme d'Ingénieur.

Admission to university-level studies

Name of secondary school credential required: Baccalauréat de l'Enseignement secondaire

Alternatives to credentials: Specific competitive examinations give access to certain streams (filières) to candidates having attended third-year classes without obtaining the Baccalauréat. Postsecondary programmes in sports, fine arts, music and youth affairs admit students on the basis of an aptitude test rather than Baccalauréat results.

Foreign students admission

Admission requirements: Students must hold the Baccalauréat or an equivalent qualification.

Entry regulations: Foreign students must hold a visa or copy of agreement between their country and Algeria (e.g. proof of an equivalence agreement).

Language requirements: Students must have good knowledge of Arabic. Arabic language courses are compulsory for specialized studies

Recognition of studies and qualifications:

Studies pursued in foreign countries (bodies dealing with recognition of foreign credentials):
Commission nationale d'Equivalences, Ministère de l'Enseignement supérieur et de la Recherche scientifique
  11 Chemin Doudou Mokhtar
  Ben Aknoun
  Alger
  Tel: +213(21) 91-17-96
  Fax: +213(21) 91-46-01
  Telex: 61381/67446DZ
  EMail: mesrs@ist.cerist.dz;allia@wissal.dz
  WWW: http://www.mesrs.edu.dz/english

Deals with credential recognition for entry to: University and Profession

Special provisions for recognition:

For access to university level studies: All necessary prerequisites and documents required are listed in the Ministry of Higher Education Website with forms to be downloaded.

Multilateral agreements concerning recognition of foreign studies

Name(s) of agreement(s): Convention on the Recognition of Studies, Certificates, Diplomas and Degrees in Higher Education in Arab and European States Bordering on the Mediterranean
Year of signature: 1976

Convention on the Recognition of Studies, Certificates, Diplomas, Degrees and Other Academic Qualifications in Higher Education in the African States
Year of signature: 1981

Convention on the Recognition of Studies, Diplomas and Degrees in Higher Education in the Arab States
Year of signature: 1978

References to further information on foreign student admissions and recognition of studies

Title: Guide de l'Enseignement supérieur et de la Recherche scientifique en Algérie (on-line)
Author: Ministry of Higher Education and Scientific Research
Publisher: http://www.mesrs.edu.dz/

STUDENT LIFE

Main student services at national level

Office national des Oeuvres universitaires
    Route de Dely-Brahim
    Wilaya d'Alger

Student expenses and financial aid

Bodies providing information on student financial aid:

Ministère de l'Enseignement supérieur et de la Recherche scientifique
    11 Chemin Doudou Mokthar, Ben-Aknoun
    Alger
    Tel: +213(2) 91-18-86
    Fax: +213(2) 91-18-23
    WWW: http://www.mesrs.edu.dz

    Deals with: Grants
    Category of students: Students from all countries with Baccalauréat & knowledge of Arabic & French.

Publications on student services and financial aid:

    Title: Study Abroad 2004-2005, 32nd Edition
    Author: UNESCO
    Publisher: UNESCO Publishing
    Year of publication: 2003

INTERNATIONAL COOPERATION AND EXCHANGES

Principal national bodies responsible for dealing with international cooperation and exchanges in higher education:

Agence de Coopération internationale, Ministère des Affaires étrangères (International Cooperation Agency, Ministry of Foreign Affairs)

Rue Shakespeare El-Mouradia
Wilaya d'Alger

Ministry of Higher Education and Scientific Research (Ministère de l'Enseignement supérieur et de la Recherche scientifique)
Director of Cooperation: Arezki Saidani
11 Chemin Doudou Mokhtar
Ben-Aknoun
Alger
Tel: +213(21) 91-15-16
Fax: +213(21) 91-15-16
EMail: ares_saidani@yahoo.fr
WWW: http://www.mesrs.edu.dz/english

GRADING SYSTEM

Usual grading system in secondary school

Full Description: 0-20: 16-20 très bien; 14-15 bien; 12-13 assez bien; 10-11 passable; 0-9 insuffisant
Highest on scale: 16-20 Très-Bien (Excellent)
Pass/fail level: 10-11 pass
Lowest on scale: 0-9 poor

Main grading system used by higher education institutions

Full Description: 0-20: 15-20 très bien; 13-14 bien; 12 assez bien; 11 passable; 10 sans mention
Highest on scale: 15-20 very good
Pass/fail level: 11-Pass
Lowest on scale: 0-10

NOTES ON HIGHER EDUCATION SYSTEM

Data for academic year: 2002-2003
Source: International Association of Universities (IAU), updated from Algerian Ministry of Higher Education website, 2003 (www.mesrs.edu.dz)

INSTITUTIONS OF HIGHER EDUCATION

UNIVERSITIES

UNIVERSITY OF ADRAR
Université d'Adrar
Rue 11 décembre, Adrar 1960
Tel: +213(49) 96-85-32
Fax: +213(49) 96-75-71

Faculties
Arts and Humanities (Arts and Humanities; Literature)
Science and Engineering (Engineering; Natural Sciences)
Social Sciences and Islamic Studies (Islamic Studies; Social Sciences)

History: Founded 2001.
Academic Staff *2001-2002:* Total: c. 35
Student Numbers *2001-2002:* Total: c. 1,030

• UNIVERSITY OF ALGIERS
Université d'Alger
2, rue Didouche Mourad, Alger 16000
Tel: +213(21) 64-69-70
Fax: +213(21) 63-53-03
EMail: rectorat@mail.univ-alger.dz
Website: http://www.univ-alger.dz

Recteur: Tahar Hadjar

Faculties
Economics and Management (Business and Commerce; Economics; Management)
Humanities and Social Sciences (Archaeology; Archiving; Arts and Humanities; Educational Sciences; Library Science; Philosophy; Physical Education; Psychology; Social Sciences; Sociology; Speech Therapy and Audiology)
Islamic Studies (Arabic; Islamic Law; Islamic Studies; Law; Religious Studies)
Law (Law; Private Law; Public Law)
Letters and Languages (Arabic; Communication Studies; English; French; German; Information Sciences; Italian; Linguistics; Literature; Oriental Languages; Slavic Languages; Spanish; Translation and Interpretation)
Medicine (Dentistry; Medicine; Pharmacy)
Political and Information Sciences (International Relations; Journalism; Media Studies; Political Science)

History: Founded 1859 as a School of Medicine and Pharmacy, followed in 1879 by schools of Law, Science, and Letters. Formally established as University 1909. Acquired present status 2001.
Academic Year: October to June (October-December; January-April; April-June)

Admission Requirements: Secondary school certificate (baccalauréat) or recognized equivalent or entrance examination
Main Language(s) of Instruction: Arabic, French
Accrediting Agencies: Ministry of Higher Education and Scientific Research
Degrees and Diplomas: *Certificat de Capacité en Droit*: 2 yrs; *Diplôme*: Midwifery (Professional Qualification), 3 yrs; Dentistry, 4 yrs; Pharmacy, 5 yrs; Medicine, 6 yrs; *Licence*: 4 yrs; *Magister*: 2 yrs following Licence; *Doctorat d'Etat*: by thesis
Student Residential Facilities: Yes
Special Facilities: Musée du Bardo; Musée national des Beaux-Arts; Musée Savorgnan de Brazza; Musée Stéphane Csell; Musée Franchet d'Esperey
Publications: Majalatou Koulyat el Adab; Revue africaine; Errihla el Maghribia; Revue Lybica; Bulletin d'Information historique; Sciences médicales de Constantine
Academic Staff *2001-2002:* Total: c. 2,540
Student Numbers *2001-2002:* Total: c. 73,370

• UNIVERSITY OF SCIENCE AND TECHNOLOGY 'HOUARI BOUMEDIÈNE' ALGIERS
Université des Sciences et de la Technologie 'Houari Boumediène' (USTHB)
BP 32, El Alia, Bab-Ezzouar, Alger 16123
Tel: +213(21) 24-79-12
Fax: +213(21) 24-79-65
EMail: webmaster@usthb.dz
Website: http://www.usthb.dz

Recteur: Benali Benzagliou
Secrétaire général: Reda Djellid
International Relations: Mehrez Drir

Faculties
Biological Sciences (Biological and Life Sciences)
Chemistry
Civil Engineering
Earth Sciences, Geography and Regional Planning (Earth Sciences; Geography; Geology; Geophysics; Regional Planning) *Dean*: H. Benhallou
Electronic and Computer Engineering (Computer Engineering; Electronic Engineering) *Dean*: A. Aissani
Mathematics
Mechanical and Process Engineering (Mechanical Engineering; Systems Analysis)
Physics

History: Founded 1974.
Governing Bodies: Scientific Council

Academic Year: September to June (September-December; January-April; April-June)

Admission Requirements: Secondary school certificate (baccalauréat)

Main Language(s) of Instruction: Arabic, French

Accrediting Agencies: Ministry of Higher Education and Scientific Research

Degrees and Diplomas: *Diplôme d'Etudes universitaires appliquées (DEUA):* 3 yrs; *Diplôme d'Etudes supérieures (DES):* 3-4 yrs; *Diplôme d'Ingénieur:* 5 yrs; *Magister, Doctorat d'Etat*

Student Services: Academic Counselling, Social Counselling, Employment Services, Cultural Centre, Sports Facilities, Health Services, Canteen

Special Facilities: Earth Sciences Museum. Biological Garden. Experimental Station (In Sahara, Beni Abbes)

Libraries: Central Library, c. 30,000 vols; libraries of the institutes

Academic Staff *2001-2002:* Total: **1,370**

Student Numbers *2001-2002:* Total: **19,400**

• BADJI MOKHTAR UNIVERSITY, ANNABA

Université Badji Mokhtar de Annaba
BP 12, Annaba 23000
Tel: +213(38) 87-24-10
Fax: +213(38) 87-24-36
EMail: info@univ-annaba.org
Website: http://www.univ-annaba.org

Recteur: Mohamed Tayeb Laskri
Tel: +213(38) 87-24-10 +213(38) 87-26-78
EMail: mtlaskri@wissal.dz

Secrétaire général: Saïd Arabi Tel: +213(38) 87-15-19
Fax: +213(38) 87-15-19

Faculties

Arts, Humanities and Social Sciences *(Annaba)* (Arabic; Arts and Humanities; Modern Languages; Psychology; Sociology; Translation and Interpretation) *Dean:* Mohamed Aïlane

Earth Sciences and Agronomy *(Sidi-Amar)* (Agronomy; Earth Sciences; Geology; Mining Engineering; Regional Planning) *Dean:* Tayeb Serradj

Economics and Management *(Sidi-Achour)* (Communication Studies; Economics; Finance; Management) *Dean:* Mahfoud Benosmane

Engineering *(Sidi Amar)* (Civil Engineering; Computer Science; Electronic Engineering; Hydraulic Engineering; Materials Engineering; Mechanical Engineering; Production Engineering) *Dean:* Nasr-Eddine Debbache

Law *(Annaba)* (Law; Political Science; Private Law; Public Law) *Dean:* Djamel Abdelnacer Mana

Medicine *(Annaba)* (Medicine; Pharmacy; Stomatology) *Dean:* Abdesslem Kaïdi

Science *(Annaba)* (Biochemistry; Biology; Chemistry; Marine Science and Oceanography; Mathematics; Physics) *Dean:* Faouzia Rebbani

Research Centres
Entrepreneurial Training (Management)
Environment and Pollution (Environmental Studies; Sanitary Engineering)
Industrial Health (Occupational Health)
Materials Science (Materials Engineering)

History: Founded 1975 as Institute of Mining and Metallurgy, acquired present status 1998.

Governing Bodies: Conseil d'Université; Conseil Scientifique

Academic Year: September to July (September-February; March-July)

Admission Requirements: Secondary school certificate (baccalauréat) or foreign equivalent

Fees: (Dinars): c. 65 per annum

Main Language(s) of Instruction: Arabic, French

Accrediting Agencies: Ministry of Higher Education and Scientific Research

Degrees and Diplomas: *Diplôme d'Etudes universitaires appliquées (DEUA):* 3 yrs; *Diplôme d'Etudes supérieures (DES):* 4 yrs; *Diplôme d'Ingénieur:* 5 yrs; *Licence:* 4 yrs; *Magister:* a further 2 yrs; *Doctorat d'Etat:* a further 4 yrs

Student Services: Cultural Centre, Sports Facilities, Handicapped Facilities, Health Services, Canteen

Libraries: Central Library, c. 200,000 vols; libraries of the faculties and departments

Publications: El - Tawassol; Synthèse (biannually)

Academic Staff *2002*	TOTAL
FULL-TIME	1,475
PART-TIME	400
TOTAL	**1,875**
STAFF WITH DOCTORATE	
FULL-TIME	170
PART-TIME	20
TOTAL	**190**

Student Numbers *2002*	TOTAL
All (Foreign Included)	**38,000**
FOREIGN ONLY	100

HADJ LAKHDAR UNIVERSITY OF BATNA

Université Hadj Lakhdar de Batna
1, rue Chahid Boukhlouf Mohamed El Hadi, Batna 05000
Tel: +213(33) 81-47-07
Fax: +213(33) 81-24-80
EMail: webmaster@univ-batna.dz
Website: http://www.univ-batna.dz

Recteur: Mohamed Khezzar Tel: +213(33) 81-24-80
EMail: recteur@univ-batna.dz

Secrétaire général: Ali Lahouel

Head Librarian: Khadidja Charhabil

Faculties

Economics and Management (Economics; Management) *Dean:* Fares Boubakour

Engineering (Architecture; Civil Engineering; Computer Engineering; Electronic Engineering; Engineering; Hydraulic

Engineering; Hygiene; Industrial Engineering; Mechanical Engineering; Safety Engineering) *Dean*: Noureddine Bouguechal
Humanities (Arts and Humanities) *Dean*: Abdelmadjid Amrani
Law *Dean*: Mabrouk Ghodbane
Medicine (Health Sciences; Medicine; Pharmacy) *Dean*: Hachemi Makhloufi
Science (Agronomy; Biology; Chemistry; Earth Sciences; Mathematics; Natural Sciences; Physics; Veterinary Science) *Dean*: Tahar Bendaikha
Social Sciences and Islamic Sciences (Islamic Studies; Social Sciences) *Dean*: Saïd Fekra

History: Founded 1977 as university centre. Acquired present status 2001.

Degrees and Diplomas: *Diplôme d'Etudes universitaires appliquées (DEUA)*; *Diplôme d'Ingénieur*; *Licence*; *Diplôme de Docteur*: Veterinary Medicine, 5 yrs; Medicine, 6 yrs; *Magister*

Libraries: Central University Library

Press or Publishing House: University of Batna Press

Student Numbers *2001-2002:* Total: c. 14,000

UNIVERSITY CENTRE OF BÉCHAR
Centre Universitaire de Béchar
BP 417, Béchar 08000
Tel: +213(7) 81-55-81
Fax: +213(7) 81-52-44
EMail: cub@ist.cerist.dz

Institutes
Exact Sciences (Arabic; Architecture; Economics; Law; Literature; Management; Physics)
Mechanical Engineering (Electrical and Electronic Engineering; Mechanical Engineering)

History: Founded 1992.
Academic Staff *2001-2002:* Total: c. 150
Student Numbers *2001-2002:* Total: c. 3,345

ABDERRAHMANE MIRA UNIVERSITY OF BÉJAÏA
Université Abderrahmane Mira de Béjaïa
Route de Targua Ouzemour, Béjaïa 06000
Tel: +213(34) 21-43-33
Fax: +213(34) 21-43-32
EMail: infobej@univbei.dz;infobej@mail.wissal.dz
Website: http://www.univbej.dz

Recteur: Djoudi Merabet
Secrétaire général: Brahim Mira

Faculties
Arts and Humanities (Arabic; Arts and Humanities; English; French; Literature; Modern Languages; Oriental Languages) *Dean*: Farida Boualit
Law and Economics (Business and Commerce; Economics; Law; Management) *Dean*: Farid Yaici

Natural and Life Sciences (Biological and Life Sciences; Food Science; Microbiology; Natural Sciences) *Dean*: Mohamed Chibane
Science and Engineering (Biological and Life Sciences; Biology; Chemistry; Civil Engineering; Computer Science; Demography and Population; Electronic Engineering; Food Science; Hydraulic Engineering; Mathematics; Mechanical Engineering; Operations Research; Physics; Production Engineering) *Dean*: Boualem Saidani

History: Founded 1983 as Centre universitaire de Béjaia. Acquired present status 2001.

Degrees and Diplomas: *Diplôme d'Etudes universitaires appliquées (DEUA)*; *Diplôme d'Etudes supérieures (DES)*; *Diplôme d'Ingénieur*; *Licence*

Student Numbers *2000-2001:* Total: c. 3,900

MOHAMED KHIDER UNIVERSITY OF BISKRA
Université Mohamed Khider de Biskra
BP 145, Biskra 07000
Tel: +213(33) 73-20-53
Fax: +213(33) 74-61-62

Faculties
Arts, Humanities and Social Sciences (Arabic; Arts and Humanities; Demography and Population; English; Literature; Social Sciences; Sociology)
Law and Economics (Economics; Law)
Science and Engineering (Architecture; Civil Engineering; Computer Science; Electrical and Electronic Engineering; Engineering; Hydraulic Engineering; Mathematics; Mechanical Engineering)

History: Founded 1998.
Academic Staff *2001-2002:* Total: c. 300
Student Numbers *2001-2002:* Total: c. 11,285

SAAD DAHLAB UNIVERSITY OF BLIDA
Université Saad Dahlab de Blida
BP 270, Blida 09000
Tel: +213(3) 43-36-25
Fax: +213(3) 43-38-64
EMail: Contact@univ-blida.edu.dz
Website: http://www.univ-blida.edu.dz
Rectrice: Nadia Mimoun

Faculties
Agro-Veterinary Science (Agronomy; Biology; Veterinary Science)
Economics
Engineering (Aeronautical and Aerospace Engineering; Architecture; Civil Engineering; Electronic Engineering; Engineering; Industrial Chemistry; Mechanical Engineering)
Exact Sciences (Chemistry; Computer Science; Mathematics; Physics)
Law

Medicine (Medicine; Stomatology)
Sociology and Modern Languages (Arabic; English; French; Italian; Modern Languages; Sociology)

History: Founded 1981.
Publications: Revue de l'Université
Academic Staff *2001-2002:* Total: c. 770
Student Numbers *2001-2002:* Total: c. 24,585

UNIVERSITY CENTRE OF BORDJ BOU ARRERIDJ
Centre Universitaire de Bordj Bou Arreridj
Bordj Bou Arreridj
Tel: +213(35) 66-65-17
Fax: +231(35) 66-65-21

Institutes
Computer Science
Electronics (Electronic Engineering)

History: Founded 2001.
Academic Staff *2001-2002:* Total: c. 25
Student Numbers *2001-2002:* Total: c. 900

M'HAMED BOUGUERRA UNIVERSITY OF BOUMERDÈS
Université M'Hamed Bouguerra de Boumerdès
Avenue de l'Indépendance, Boumerdès 35000
Tel: +213(24) 81-69-01
Fax: +213(24) 81-69-01
Website: http://www.umbb.dz

Recteur: Rafika Kesri Tel: +213(24) 81-64-20
Fax: +213(24) 81-63-73 EMail: rectorat@umbb.dz
Secrétaire général: Ahmed Boufellah
Tel: +213(24) 81-69-29 EMail: secr-gener@umbb.dz
International Relations: Abdelaziz Tairi, Vice-Rector
Tel: +213(24) 81-99-87 EMail: vrpgr@umbb.dz

Faculties
Engineering (Energy Engineering; Engineering; Environmental Engineering; Food Technology; Industrial Engineering; Industrial Maintenance; Materials Engineering; Mechanical Engineering) *Dean:* Mohamed-Seghir Zaoui
Hydrocarburates and Chemistry (Automation and Control Engineering; Chemical Engineering; Economics; Engineering Management; Geophysics; Industrial Management; Marketing; Mining Engineering; Petroleum and Gas Engineering; Safety Engineering) *Dean:* Noureddine Abdelbaki
Law and Commercial Sciences (Arabic; Business Education; Finance; Law; Literature; Management; Marketing) *Dean:* Boudjema Souilah
Science (Biology; Chemistry; Computer Science; English; Mathematics; Physics) *Dean:* Kamel Badari

History: Founded 1998. Acquired present status 2002.
Admission Requirements: Baccalauréat

Fees: None
Main Language(s) of Instruction: Arabic, French, English
Degrees and Diplomas: *Diplôme d'Etudes universitaires appliquées (DEUA)*: 3 yrs; *Diplôme d'Ingénieur*: Electrical Engineering; Computer Science, 5 yrs; *Licence*: Electrical Engineering; Computer Science, 4 yrs; *Magister*: Electrical Engineering; Computer Science, a further 2 yrs; *Doctorat d'Etat*: a further 4 yrs following Magister
Student Services: Employment Services, Nursery Care, Cultural Centre, Sports Facilities, Language Programmes, Health Services
Student Residential Facilities: Five residences
Libraries: Faculty libraries

Academic Staff *2001-2002*	MEN	WOMEN	TOTAL
FULL-TIME	379	124	503
PART-TIME	381	292	673
TOTAL	**760**	**416**	**1,176**
STAFF WITH DOCTORATE			
FULL-TIME	64	5	69
PART-TIME	49	8	57
TOTAL	**113**	**13**	**126**

Student Numbers *2001-2002*	MEN	WOMEN	TOTAL
All (Foreign Included)	11,780	9,130	**20,910**
FOREIGN ONLY	193	47	240

HASSIBA BEN BOUALI UNIVERSITY, CHLEF
Université Hassiba Ben Bouali, Chlef
BP 151, Chlef 02000
Website: http://www.univ-chlef.dz/

Faculties
Earth Sciences and Agronomy (Agronomy; Earth Sciences)
Humanities and Social Sciences (Arabic; Arts and Humanities; Literature; Social Sciences)
Science and Engineering (Civil Engineering; Construction Engineering; Electrical and Electronic Engineering; Hydraulic Engineering; Mechanical Engineering)

History: Founded 2001.
Academic Staff *2001-2002:* Total: **167**
Student Numbers *2001-2002:* Total: **11,024**

• EMIR ABDELKADER UNIVERSITY OF ISLAMIC SCIENCES , CONSTANTINE
Université des Sciences Islamiques Emir Abdelkader
BP 137, Constantine 25000
Tel: +213(31) 93-92-92
Fax: +213(31) 93-80-73
EMail: usieak1@ist.cerist.dz
Website: http://www.univ-emir.dz

Recteur: Abdullah Boukhelkhal (1998-)
Secrétaire général: A. Krada

Faculties

Arts and Humanities (Administration; Arabic; Arts and Humanities; Economics; Koran; Literature)

Oussoul Eddine, Shariah and Islamic Civilization (Islamic Law; Islamic Studies; Islamic Theology)

History: Founded 1984. Acquired present status 1998.

Academic Year: September to June (September-February; February-June)

Admission Requirements: Secondary school certificate (baccalauréat)

Fees: None

Main Language(s) of Instruction: Arabic

Degrees and Diplomas: *Licence*: 4 yrs; *Magister*: a further 2 yrs; *Doctorat d'Etat*: a further 2 yrs

Student Residential Facilities: Yes

Libraries: University library, c. 10 000 vols

Publications: Revue de l'Université (biannually)

Press or Publishing House: Emir Abdelkader University Press

Academic Staff *2001-2002:* Total: **101**

Student Numbers *2001-2002:* Total: **1,985**

• MENTOURI CONSTANTINE UNIVERSITY

Université Mentouri de Constantine
Route de Aïn-El-Bey, Constantine 25000
Tel: +213(31) 61-43-48
Fax: +213(31) 61-43-49
EMail: Université-mentouri@umc.edu.dz
Website: http://www.umc.edu.dz

Recteur: Abdelhamid Djekoune (1992-)
EMail: constantine@ist.cerist.dz

Secrétaire général: Fodil Belaouira Tel: +213(31) 92-57-79

International Relations: Fouzia Bensouiki
Tel: +213(31) 92-61-81 Fax: +213(31) 92-52-57

Faculties

Earth Sciences and Regional Planning (Architecture; Earth Sciences; Regional Planning; Town Planning) *Dean*: Salaheddine Cherad

Economics and Management (Economics; Management)

Engineering (Civil Engineering; Computer Engineering; Electronic Engineering; Industrial Chemistry; Mechanical Engineering; Meteorology) *Dean*: Abdelmadjid Benghalia

Humanities and Social Sciences (Arts and Humanities; History; Library Science; Philosophy; Psychology; Social Sciences; Sociology; Sports) *Dean*: Abdelhamid Khrouf

Languages and Literature (Arabic; French; Literature; Modern Languages; Translation and Interpretation) *Dean*: Youssef Ghioua

Law (Law; Political Science; Private Law; Public Law) *Dean*: Abdelmadjid Guemouh

Medicine (Medicine; Pharmacy; Stomatology)

Science (Chemistry; Mathematics; Natural Sciences; Nutrition; Physics; Veterinary Science) *Dean*: Djamel Hamana

Further Information: Also Audiovisual Centre

History: Founded 1969 as University Centre, acquired present status 1998.

Governing Bodies: Conseil universitaire

Academic Year: September to June (September-January; February-June)

Admission Requirements: Secondary school certificate (baccalauréat)

Main Language(s) of Instruction: Arabic, French, English

Accrediting Agencies: Ministry of Higher Education and Scientific Research

Degrees and Diplomas: *Diplôme d'Etudes universitaires appliquées (DEUA)*: 3 yrs; *Diplôme d'Etudes supérieures (DES)*: 4 yrs; *Diplôme d'Ingénieur*: Architecture; *Licence*; *Magister*: a further 2 yrs; *Doctorat d'Etat*: 4 yrs; Veterinary Medicine, 5 yrs

Student Residential Facilities: Yes

Libraries: Central Library, 260,000 vols

Academic Staff *2001-2002:* Total: **1,979**

Student Numbers *2001-2002:* Total: **42,610**

ZIANE ACHOUR UNIVERSITY CENTRE OF DJELFA

Centre Universitaire Ziane Achour de Djelfa
BP 3117, Cité Ain Chih, Djelfa
Tel: +213(27) 87-10-82
Fax: +213(27) 87-13-78

Institutes

Agro-pastoral (Accountancy; Agronomy; Fiscal Law; Law; Management)

Electronics (Electronic Engineering)

Law

History: Founded 2000.

Degrees and Diplomas: *Diplôme d'Etudes universitaires appliquées (DEUA)*: Computer Science; Electronic Engineering; Agronomy; Management; Accountancy and Fiscal Law, 6 sem.; *Diplôme d'Ingénieur*: Electronic Engineering, 5 yrs; *Licence*: Agronomy; Law, 4 yrs

Academic Staff *2001-2002:* Total: c. **60**

Student Numbers *2001-2002:* Total: c. **1,550**

UNIVERSITY CENTRE OF EL OUED

Centre Universitaire d'El Oued
BP 789, El Oued
Tel: +213(32) 24-41-81
Fax: +213(32) 24-47-67

Institutes

Commerce (Business and Commerce)

Law

Literature and Languages (Literature; Modern Languages)

History: Founded 2001.

UNIVERSITY CENTRE OF EL TARF
Centre Universitaire El Tarf
El Tarf
Tel: +213(38) 60-09-43
Fax: +213(38) 60-14-17

Institutes
Agronomy (Agronomy; Arabic)
Arabic and Arab Literature (Arabic; Literature)
Biology
Veterinary Science

History: Founded 2001.
Degrees and Diplomas: *Licence*: Agronomy, 4 yrs; *Magister*;
Doctorat d'Etat
Academic Staff *2001-2002:* Total: c. 45
Student Numbers *2001-2002:* Total: c. 970

8 MAY 1945 UNIVERSITY OF GUELMA
Université du 8 mai 1945 Guelma
BP 401, Guelma
Tel: +213(37) 20-49-80
Fax: +213(37) 20-72-68

Faculties
Economics and Management (Accountancy; Economics; Management; Taxation)
Law, Humanities and Social Sciences (Arts and Humanities; English; Law; Social Sciences)
Science and Engineering (Chemistry; Civil Engineering; Computer Engineering; Electrical and Electronic Engineering; Industrial Engineering; Mechanical Engineering; Physics)

History: Founded 2001.
Academic Staff *2001-2002:* Total: **137**
Student Numbers *2001-2002:* Total: **6,716**

ABDELHAK BENHAMOUDA UNIVERSITY OF JIJEL
Université Abdelhak Benhamouda de Jijel
BP 98, Ouled Aissa, Jijel
Tel: +213(34) 49-80-16
Fax: +213(34) 49-55-78
Website: http://www.univ-jijel.dz

Faculties
Engineering (Architecture; Automation and Control Engineering; Civil Engineering; Computer Engineering; Electronic Engineering; Engineering; Environmental Engineering; Industrial Chemistry; Materials Engineering; Mechanical Engineering)
Law
Management
Science (Biochemistry; Chemistry; Ecology; Geology; Mathematics; Microbiology; Physics)

History: Founded 1998.
Degrees and Diplomas: *Diplôme d'Etudes universitaires appliquées (DEUA)*: Computer Science; Biology; International Trade, 6 semesters; *Diplôme d'Ingénieur*: Biology; Electrical and Electronic Engineering; Civil Engineering; Chemical Engineering; Automation; Computer Science; Agronomy; Geology; Regional Planning, 5 yrs; *Licence*: Mathematics; Physics; Chemistry; Management; Law, 4 yrs; *Magister*
Libraries: 60,000 vols
Academic Staff *2001-2002:* Total: **137**
Student Numbers *2001-2002:* Total: **3,757**

UNIVERSITY CENTRE OF KHEMIS MILIANA
Centre Universitaire de Khemis Miliana
Khemis Miliana
Tel: +213(27) 66-42-32
Fax: +213(27) 66-48-63

Institutes
Economics
Natural and Earth Sciences (Earth Sciences; Natural Sciences)

History: Founded 2001.

UNIVERSITY CENTRE OF KHENCHELA
Centre Universitaire de Khenchela
Khenchela
Tel: +213(32) 31-46-71
Fax: +213(32) 31-74-76

Institutes
Computer Management (Computer Science; Management)
Economics
Law
Literature and Languages (Literature; Modern Languages)

History: Founded 2001.

AMAR TLEDJI UNIVERSITY OF LAGHOUAT
Université Amar Tledji de Laghouat (UATL)
BP 37 G, route de Ghardaia, Laghouat
Tel: +213(29) 93-17-91
EMail: biblio@mail.lagh-univ.dz
Website: http://www.lagh-univ.dz
Recteur: Aissa Benhorma (2002-) Tel: +213(29) 93-10-24
Fax: +213(29) 93-26-98
Secrétaire général: Khelifa Megoussi
Tel: +213(29) 93-26-94

Faculties
Economics *Dean*: Mokhadam Abirat
Law and Social Sciences (Law; Social Sciences) *Dean*: Larbi Rezkallah
Technology *Dean*: Lakdar Azzouz

15

Departments

Arab Literature (Arabic; Literature) *Head*: Brahim Chouaeb
Architecture *Head*: Ahmida Benchikh
Biology (Biology; Chemistry; Geology; Physics) *Head*: Mohamed Ouinten
Civil Engineering *Head*: Mustapha Gafsi
Computer Science *Head*: Rachid Ben hacen Derragi
Data Processing Management (Data Processing) *Head*: Moradj Houari
Electrical Engineering *Head*: Abdelkrim Ben Abdelkrim
Industrial Chemistry *Head*: Mokhtar Bealia
Law *Head*: Lakhdar Zaza
Management and Economy (Economics; Management) *Head*: Abdallah Brahimi
Psychology *Head*: Daoud Bourghiba
Technology *Head*: Mohamed Ferhat

Institutes

Civil Engineering
Economics
Electrical Engineering
Mechanical Engineering *Head*: Mohamed Mechikel

History: Founded 1986 as a high school for technical teaching. Became university centre 1997. Acquired present status 2001.

Governing Bodies: Conseil d'orientation

Admission Requirements: Secondary school certificate (baccalauréat)

Fees: None

Main Language(s) of Instruction: Arabic and French

International Co-operation: With universities in France

Degrees and Diplomas: *Diplôme d'Etudes universitaires appliquées (DEUA)*: 3 yrs; *Diplôme d'Ingénieur*: Engineering, 5 yrs; *Licence*: 4 yrs

Student Services: Sports Facilities, Health Services

Libraries: Yes

Publications: El Ichara

Academic Staff *2001-2002*	MEN	WOMEN	TOTAL
FULL-TIME	163	20	**183**

Student Numbers	MEN	WOMEN	TOTAL
All (Foreign Included)	3,527	2,773	**6,300**
FOREIGN ONLY	27	6	33

MUSTAPHA STOMBOULI UNIVERSITY CENTRE WILAYA DE MASCARA
Centre Universitaire Mustapha Stombouli
BP 763, Route de Mamounia, Mascara 29000
Tel: +231(45) 80-41-68
Fax: +231(45) 80-41-64
Website: http://www.cuniv-mascara.edu.dz

Institutes

Agronomy
Biology
Biology *(short cycle)*
Computer Science

History
Hydraulics (Hydraulic Engineering)
Law and Administration (Administration; Law)
Management
Management Informatics (Computer Science; Management)
Mechanical Engineering

History: Founded 1986. Acquired present status 1994.

Degrees and Diplomas: *Diplôme d'Etudes universitaires appliquées (DEUA)*: Computer Science; Biology; Business Computing, 6 sems; *Diplôme d'Ingénieur*: Biology; Hydraulics; Mechanical Engineering; Computer Science; Agronomy, 5 yrs; *Licence*: Economics; Management; Law, 4 yrs; *Magister*

Academic Staff *2001-2002*: Total: c. 95

Student Numbers *2001-2002*: Total: c. 2,690

YAHIA FARÈS UNIVERSITY CENTRE OF MÉDÉA
Centre Universitaire Yahia Farès de Médéa
Quartier Ain D'heb, Médéa
Tel: +213(25) 58-16-87
Fax: +213(25) 58-28-09

Institutes

Engineering (Civil Engineering; Electrical and Electronic Engineering; Industrial Chemistry)
Languages (Modern Languages)
Law and Administration (Administration; Law)
Management (Business and Commerce; Law; Management)

History: Founded 2000.

Degrees and Diplomas: *Diplôme d'Etudes universitaires appliquées (DEUA)*: Electrical and Electronic Engineering; Business Computing, 3 yrs; *Diplôme d'Ingénieur*: Electrical and Electronic Engineering; Civil Engineering; Industrial Chemistry, 5 yrs; *Licence*: Commerce; Law, 4 yrs; *Magister*

Academic Staff *2001-2002*: Total: c. 70

Student Numbers *2001-2002*: Total: c. 2,495

UNIVERSITY OF MOSTAGANEM
Université de Mostaganem
BP 227, Route Belahcene, Mostaganem
Tel: +213(45) 26-54-55
Fax: +213(45) 26-54-52
EMail: webmaster@univ-mosta.dz
Website: http://www.univ-mosta.dz

Recteur: Si Kadi Mahi **EMail:** rector@univ-mosta.dz

Faculties

Arts and Letters (Arabic; Arts and Humanities; English; Fine Arts; French; Literature; Spanish)
Law and Commerce (Business and Commerce; Law)
Science and Engineering (Agronomy; Biology; Chemistry; Civil Engineering; Computer Science; Electronic Engineering;

Mathematics; Measurement and Precision Engineering; Mechanical Engineering; Natural Sciences; Physics)
Social Sciences and Physical Training and Sports (Physical Education; Social Sciences; Sports)

History: Founded 1978 as Centre universitaire de Mostaganem. Acquired present status and title 1998.

Degrees and Diplomas: *Diplôme d'Etudes universitaires appliquées (DEUA)*: 3 yrs; *Diplôme d'Ingénieur*: 5 yrs; *Licence*: 4 yrs

Libraries: Central Library, c. 80,000 vols; 22 periodical subscriptions

Publications: Revue des Sciences de l'Ingénieur

Academic Staff *2001*: Full-Time: c. 340 Part-Time: c. 430 Total: c. 770

Staff with doctorate: Total: c. 60

Student Numbers *2001:* Total: c. 14,000

UNIVERSITY OF M'SILA
Université de M'sila
BP 166, Draa El Hadjar, M'sila
Tel: +231(35) 55-09-06
Fax: +231(35) 55-04-11
EMail: cubmsila@ist.cerist.dz

Faculties
Arts and Social Sciences (Arabic; Arts and Humanities; Literature; Social Sciences; Sociology)
Economics, Management and Commercial Sciences (Business and Commerce; Economics; International Business; Management)
Law
Science and Engineering (Biology; Chemical Engineering; Civil Engineering; Computer Science; Mathematics; Mechanical Engineering; Physics; Town Planning)

History: Founded as Centre Universitaire de M'sila. Acquired present status 2001.

Academic Staff *2001-2002:* Total: **246**
Student Numbers *2001-2002:* Total: **10,355**

• MOHAMED BOUDIAF UNIVERSITY OF SCIENCE AND TECHNOLOGY OF ORAN
Université Mohamed Boudiaf des Sciences et de la Technologie d'Oran
BP 1505, El M'Naouer, Oran 31000
Tel: +213(41) 42-25-61
Fax: +213(41) 45-15-81
Website: http://www.univ-usto.dz
Recteur: Djamel Eddine Kerdal
Secrétaire général: Iouadi Dergham

Faculties
Architecture and Civil Engineering (Architecture; Civil Engineering; Hydraulic Engineering) *Dean:* Kouider Kouider
Electrical Engineering (Electrical Engineering; Electronic Engineering) *Dean:* Abdelhamid Midoun

Mechanical Engineering (Marine Engineering; Mechanical Engineering; Metallurgical Engineering; Mining Engineering) *Dean:* Omar Imine
Science (Biotechnology; Chemistry; Computer Science; Mathematics; Natural Sciences; Physics) *Dean:* Mohamed Benyettou

History: Founded 1975. Acquired present status 1998.

Academic Year: September to June

Admission Requirements: Secondary school certificate (baccalauréat) or equivalent

Main Language(s) of Instruction: French

Accrediting Agencies: Ministry of Higher Education and Scientific Research

Degrees and Diplomas: *Diplôme d'Etudes universitaires appliquées (DEUA)*; *Diplôme d'Ingénieur*; *Magister*

Student Residential Facilities: Yes

Academic Staff *2001-2002:* Total: **512**
Student Numbers *2001-2002:* Total: **111,108**

• UNIVERSITY OF ORAN ES-SENIA
Université d'Oran Es-Sénia
BP 1524, El-M'naouar, Oran 31000
Tel: +213(41) 41-61-55
Fax: +213(41) 41-60-21
Website: http://www.univ-oran.dz
Recteur: Abdelkader Derbal
Secrétaire général: Abdelkader Bekada
International Relations: Abdelbaki Benziane

Faculties
Earth Sciences, Geography and Regional Planning (Earth Sciences; Geography; Regional Planning)
Economics, Management and Commerce (Business and Commerce; Economics; Management)
Humanities and Islamic Civilization (Arts and Humanities; History; Islamic Studies; Library Science)
Law (Law; Political Science; Private Law; Public Law)
Letters, Languages and Arts (Arabic; English; French; German; Italian; Literature; Modern Languages; Russian; Spanish; Translation and Interpretation)
Medicine (Medicine; Pharmacy; Stomatology)
Science (Chemistry; Computer Science; Industrial Maintenance; Maintenance Technology; Mathematics; Natural Sciences; Physics)
Social Sciences (Demography and Population; Philosophy; Psychology; Social Sciences; Sociology)

History: Founded 1961 as Centre universitaire d'Oran attached to the University of Algiers. Became University 1967 and acquired present status and title 1998.

Academic Year: October to July (October-February; March-July)

Admission Requirements: Secondary school certificate (baccalauréat)

Main Language(s) of Instruction: Arabic, French

Degrees and Diplomas: *Certificat de Capacité en Droit*: 2 yrs; *Diplôme*: Pharmacy, 5 yrs; Medicine, 6 yrs; *Licence*: 4 yrs; *Magister*; *Doctorat d'Etat*

Academic Staff *2001-2002:* Total: c. 1,275

Student Numbers *2001-2002:* Total: c. 36,670

OUARGLA UNIVERSITY
Université de Ouargla
Route de Ghardaia, Ouargla
Tel: +213(29) 71-24-68
Fax: +213(29) 71-51-61
Website: http://www.ouargla-univ.dz
Directeur: Mohamed El-Khames Tidjani

Faculties
Arts and Humanities (Literature; Modern Languages; Psychology) *Director*: Salah Khennour
Law and Economics (Economics; Law; Management; Political Science) *Dean*: Nasreddine Semar
Science and Engineering (Agronomy; Biology; Chemical Engineering; Civil Engineering; Computer Science; Engineering; Hydraulic Engineering; Mechanical Engineering; Natural Sciences) *Dean*: Belkheir Dada Moussa

History: Founded 1987 as Ecole Nationale Supérieure. Became University Centre 1997. Acquired present status 2001.

Academic Year: September to June

Admission Requirements: Baccalauréat

Fees: (Dhiram) 200 per annum

Main Language(s) of Instruction: Arabic and French

International Co-operation: With universities in France

Degrees and Diplomas: *Diplôme d'Ingénieur*: 5 yrs; *Licence*: 4 yrs; *Magister*: 6 yrs

Student Residential Facilities: Yes

Academic Staff 2001-2002	MEN	WOMEN	TOTAL
FULL-TIME	20	–	20
PART-TIME	25	5	30
TOTAL	**45**	**5**	**50**
STAFF WITH DOCTORATE			
FULL-TIME	215	15	230
PART-TIME	210	25	235
TOTAL	**425**	**40**	**465**

Student Numbers 2001-2002	MEN	WOMEN	TOTAL
All (Foreign Included)	4,617	5,501	**10,118**
FOREIGN ONLY	33	3	36

Evening Students, 1,500

LARBI BENMHIDI UNIVERSITY CENTRE OF OUM EL BOUAGHI
Centre Universitaire Larbi Benmhidi d'Oum El Bouaghi
BP 358 , Route de Constantine, Oum El Bouaghi 04000
Tel: +213(32) 42-33-54
Fax: +213(32) 42-10-36
Directeur général: Mohamed Guerras (2002-)
Secrétaire général: Mostepha Amokrane

Colleges
Teacher Training

Institutes
Electrotechnology (Electronic Engineering)
Exact Sciences (Natural Sciences)
Mechanical Engineering
Natural Sciences

History: Founded 1983.

UNIVERSITY CENTRE OF SAIDA
Centre Universitaire de Saida
BP112, Route de Mascara, Saida
Tel: +213(48) 51-74-05
Fax: +213(48) 51-89-13

Institutes
Electrical Technology (Electrical and Electronic Engineering; Technology)
Exact Sciences (Arabic; Business Computing; Chemistry; Law; Literature; Mathematics; Physics)
Hydraulics (Hydraulic Engineering)

History: Founded 1998.

Degrees and Diplomas: *Diplôme d'Etudes universitaires appliquées (DEUA)*: Computer Science; Electronic Engineering; Electrical Technology; Hydraulics; Business Computing, 6 sems; *Diplôme d'Ingénieur*: Electrical Technology; Electronic Engineering; Hydraulics, 5 yrs; *Licence*: Mathematics; Physics and Chemistry; Law; Arab Literature, 4 yrs; *Magister*

Academic Staff *2001-2002:* Total: c. 70

Student Numbers *2001-2002:* Total: c. 2,130

FERHAT ABBAS UNIVERSITY , SÉTIF
Université Ferhat Abbas, Sétif
Cité Mabouda, Sétif 19000
Tel: +213(36) 90-88-93
Fax: +213(36) 90-38-79
EMail: webmaster@univ-setif.dz
Website: http://www.univ-setif.dz
Recteur: Smaïl Debeche **EMail:** recteur@univ-setif.dz

Faculties
Economics, Management and Commerce (Business and Commerce; Economics; Management)
Engineering (Architecture; Civil Engineering; Computer Science; Electronic Engineering; Engineering; Industrial Chemistry; Measurement and Precision Engineering)
Law (Law; Private Law; Public Law)
Medical Sciences (Medicine; Pharmacy)
Science (Biology; Chemistry; Mathematics; Physics)
Social Sciences and Letters (Arabic; Arts and Humanities; Modern Languages; Psychology; Social Sciences; Sociology)

History: Founded 1978 as Centre Universitaire, acquired present status and title 1992. The institutes are financially autonomous but maintain a joint structure presided over by a Conseil de Coordination.

Academic Year: September to June (September-January; March-June)

Admission Requirements: Secondary school certificate (baccalauréat)

Main Language(s) of Instruction: Arabic, French

Accrediting Agencies: Ministry of Higher Education and Scientific Research

Degrees and Diplomas: *Diplôme d'Etudes supérieures (DES)*: 4 yrs; *Diplôme d'Ingénieur*: 5 yrs; *Licence*: 4 yrs; *Magister*: 2 yrs after Licence

Student Residential Facilities: Yes

Libraries: c. 100,000 vols

Academic Staff *2000-2001:* Total: c. 800

Student Numbers: Total: c. 18,500

DJILLALI LIABES UNIVERSITY, SIDI BEL ABBÈS
Université Djillali Liabes, Sidi Bel Abbès
BP 89, Sidi-Bel-Abbès 22000
Tel: +213(48) 54-30-18
Fax: +213(48) 54-11-52
EMail: webmaster@univ-sba.dz
Website: http://www.univ-sba.dz

Recteur: A. Tadjer **EMail:** rectorat@univ-sba.dz

Secrétaire générale: A. Toumi

Faculties
Economics *Dean*: M. Dani Elkbir
Engineering (Civil Engineering; Engineering) *Dean*: A. Khalfi
Humanities (Arts and Humanities; Literature) *Dean*: N. Sebbar
Law *Dean*: B. Mekelkel
Medicine *Dean*: A. Djadel
Science (Biology; Chemistry; Mathematics; Natural Sciences; Physics) *Dean*: M. Benyahya

History: Founded 1978. Acquired present status 1989.

UNIVERSITY OF SKIKDA
Université de Skikda
BP 26, Route El-Hadaiek, Skikda 21000
Tel: +213(38) 70-10-32
Fax: +213(38) 70-10-04
EMail: univskikda@wissal.dz
Website: http://www.univ-skikda.dz

Recteur: Mohamed Taibi

Vice-Recteur à la Planification: Allaoua Bendif

Head Librarian: Azzeddine. Moundes

Faculties
Engineering (Agronomy; Civil Engineering; Computer Engineering; Electronic Engineering; Mechanical Engineering; Natural Sciences) *Dean*: Mounir Hamami
Law and Social Sciences (Law; Literature; Sociology) *Dean*: Said Mouats
Management and Economics (Economics; Management) *Dean*: Omar Mecheoud

History: Founded 2001.

UNIVERSITY CENTRE OF SOUK-AHRAS
Centre Universitaire de Souk-Ahras
Souk-Ahras
Tel: +213(37) 32-62-62
Fax: +213(37) 32-65-65

Institutes
Law and Administration (Administration; Law)
Science and Engineering (Engineering; Natural Sciences)

History: Founded 2001.

LARBI TEBESSI UNIVERSITY CENTRE OF TEBESSA
Centre Universitaire Larbi Tebessi de Tebessa
BP 289, Route de Constantine, Tebessa
Tel: +213(37) 49-00-62
Fax: +231(37) 49-02-68
EMail: cutebessa@ist.cerist.dz

Institutes
Civil Engineering
Earth Sciences
Industrial Chemistry
Mining Engineering (Geography; Geology; Mining Engineering)

History: Founded 1992.

Academic Staff *2001-2002:* Total: c. 215

Student Numbers *2001-2002:* Total: c. 5,620

IBN KHALDUN UNIVERSITY OF TIARET
Université Ibn Khaldoun de Tiaret (UIKT)
BP 78, Zaaroura, Tiaret 14000
Tel: +213(46) 42-42-13
Fax: +213(46) 42-47-10
EMail: direction@mail.univ-tiaret.dz
Website: http://www.univ-tiaret.dz

Recteur: Nasredine Hadj-Zoubir (1997-)
Tel: +213(46) 42-41-47 EMail: hadj_zoubir@univ-tiaret.dz

Secrétaire général: Messouad Bensaadi
Tel: +213(46) 42-56-83 Fax: +213(46) 42-56-83
EMail: bensaadi@mail.univ-tiaret.dz

International Relations: Sahraoui Hadj-Ziane
Tel: +213(46) 42-46-07 Fax: +213(46) 42-46-07
EMail: hadj_ziane@mail.univ-tiaret.dz

Faculties
Agronomy and Veterinary Science (Agronomy; Biology; Veterinary Science)

Humanities and Social Sciences (Accountancy; Arabic; Business Administration; Business and Commerce; Fiscal Law; French; Law; Literature; Management)
Science and Engineering (Chemistry; Civil Engineering; Computer Science; Electrical Engineering; Hydraulic Engineering; Mechanical Engineering; Organic Chemistry; Physics)

History: Founded 1980 as Centre Universitaire de Tiaret, acquired present status and title 2002.

Admission Requirements: Baccalaureate

Fees: (Dinars) 20,000 per annum

Main Language(s) of Instruction: Arabic, French

International Co-operation: With universities in France, United Kingdom and Jordan

Accrediting Agencies: Ministry of Higher Education and Scientific Research

Degrees and Diplomas: *Diplôme d'Etudes universitaires appliquées (DEUA)*: Computer Science; Mechanics; Electrical Engineering; Hydraulics; Veterinary Science; Biology; Accountancy; Fiscal Law, 3 yrs; *Diplôme d'Etudes supérieures (DES)*: Physics; Chemistry; Biology, 4 yrs; *Diplôme d'Ingénieur*: Agronomy; Mechanics; Electrical Engineering; Rural Engineering; Nutrition (DIE), 5 yrs; *Licence*: Law and Administration; Commerce and Management; French Literature and Language; Arabic Language and Literature, 4 yrs; *Diplôme de Docteur*: Veterinary Medicine, 5 yrs; *Magister*: Physical Engineering; Chemistry and Environment; Mechanics; Ecology, 6 yrs

Student Services: Academic Counselling, Social Counselling, Nursery Care, Cultural Centre, Sports Facilities, Health Services, Canteen, Foreign Student Centre

Student Residential Facilities: Yes

Special Facilities: Veterinary Science Museum

Libraries: 8 libraries

Publications: Bulletin de l'Université Ibn Khaldoun (monthly)

Academic Staff *2002-2003*	MEN	WOMEN	TOTAL
FULL-TIME	195	42	237
PART-TIME	56	44	100
TOTAL	**251**	**86**	**337**
STAFF WITH DOCTORATE			
FULL-TIME	43	11	54
PART-TIME	15	8	23
TOTAL	**58**	**19**	**77**

Student Numbers *2002-2003*	MEN	WOMEN	TOTAL
All (Foreign Included)	4,726	5,767	**10,493**
FOREIGN ONLY	123	2	125

MOULOUD MAMMERI UNIVERSITY TIZI-OUZOU
Université Mouloud Mammeri Tizi-Ouzou (UMMTO)
Oued Aissi, Tizi-Ouzou
Tel: +213(26) 40-56-51
Fax: +213(26) 21-29-68

Recteur: Rabah Kahlouche
Vice-Recteur: Idir Ahmed Zaid

Faculties
Arts and Humanities

Biology and Agronomy (Agronomy; Biology)
Construction Engineering (Construction Engineering; Engineering)
Economics and Management (Economics; Management)
Electrical and Computer Engineering (Computer Engineering; Electrical Engineering)
Law
Medicine
Science (Mathematics; Natural Sciences)

History: Founded 1977 as University Centre of Tizi-Ouzou. Became university 1989 and acquired present status 2001.

Academic Year: September to June (September-January; February-June)

Admission Requirements: Secondary school certificate (baccalauréat) and entrance examination

Main Language(s) of Instruction: Arabic, French

Accrediting Agencies: Ministry of Higher Education and Scientific Research

Degrees and Diplomas: *Diplôme d'Etudes supérieures (DES)*; *Diplôme d'Ingénieur*; *Licence*; *Magister*; *Doctorat d'Etat*: Medicine

Libraries: Central Library; libraries of the institutes

Academic Staff *2001-2002:* Total: **829**

Student Numbers *2001-2002:* Total: **25,733**

ABOUBEKR BELKAID UNIVERSITY, TLEMCEN
Université Aboubekr Belkaid
BP 119, 22 rue Abi Ayed Abdelkrim, Faubourg Pasteur, Tlemcen 13000
Tel: +213(43) 20-23-36
Fax: +213(43) 27-15-03
Telex: 18971-18034
Website: http://www.univ-tlemcen.dz

Recteur: Zoubir Chaouche-Ramdane (1990-)

Secrétaire général: Abdeldjellil Sari-Ali
Tel: +213(43) 20-64-32 Fax: +213(43) 20-64-32

International Relations: Sidi-Mohamed Bouchnak Kheladi
Tel: +213(43) 20-16-31 Fax: +213(43) 20-16-31

Faculties
Arts, Humanities and Social Sciences (Arabic; Archaeology; Arts and Humanities; English; French; History; Literature; Modern Languages; Sociology)
Economics and Management (Accountancy; Business and Commerce; Economics; Management)
Engineering (Civil Engineering; Computer Engineering; Electronic Engineering; Engineering; Hydraulic Engineering)
Law
Medicine (Medicine; Pharmacy; Stomatology)
Science (Agronomy; Biochemistry; Biology; Chemistry; Ecology; Environmental Studies; Forestry; Geology; Mathematics; Microbiology; Physics; Plant and Crop Protection)

History: Founded as Centre universitaire de Tlemcen 1974, acquired present status and title 1998.

Governing Bodies: Scientific Council

Academic Year: September to July (September-December; January-March; April-July)

Admission Requirements: Secondary school certificate (baccalauréat) or equivalent

Fees: (Dinars): 50 per annum

Main Language(s) of Instruction: Arabic, French

Accrediting Agencies: Ministry of Higher Education and Scientific Research

Degrees and Diplomas: *Diplôme d'Etudes universitaires appliquées (DEUA)*: 3 yrs; *Diplôme d'Etudes supérieures (DES)*: 4 yrs; *Diplôme d'Ingénieur*: 5 yrs; *Licence*: 4 yrs; *Diplôme de Docteur*: Medicine, 6 yrs; *Magister*: 2-3 yrs and thesis; *Doctorat d'Etat*: by thesis

Student Services: Sports Facilities, Health Services, Canteen

Student Residential Facilities: For c. 5 300 students

Libraries: Libraries of the Institutes

Publications: Arabic Literature Magazine (biannually); Popular Culture Magazine

Academic Staff *2001-2002:* Total: c. 630

Student Numbers *2001-2002*: All (Foreign Included): c. 11,400 Foreign Only: c. 100

OTHER UNIVERSITY LEVEL INSTITUTIONS

ECOLE NATIONALE D'ADMINISTRATION (ENA)
13 Chemin Gadouche Hydra, Alger
Tel: +213(21) 60-14-16
Fax: +213(21) 60-49-41
EMail: ena@wissel.dz
Website: http://www.cerist.dz/ena

Programmes
Economics and Finance (Economics; Finance)
International Institutions (International Relations)
Law (Private Law; Public Law)
Public Administration

History: Founded 1964. Acquired present status 1987.

ECOLE NATIONALE POLYTECHNIQUE (ENP)
10, Avenue Hassen Badi , El Harrach, Alger
Tel: +213(21) 52-14-94
Fax: +213(21) 52-29-73
EMail: ENP@ist.cerist.dz
Website: http://www.enp.edu.dz

Departments
Basic Science (Mathematics; Physics) *Head*: M. Ouadjaout
Chemical Engineering *Head*: Toudert Ahmed Zaïd
Civil Engineering *Head*: Saadi Lakhal
Electrical Engineering *Head*: Abdelouahab Mekhaldi

Electronics (Electronic Engineering; Information Management; Microwaves; Telecommunications Engineering) *Head*: Mohamed Trabelsi

Environmental Engineering *Head*: Djazia Arar

Hydraulics (Hydraulic Engineering) *Head*: Saadia Benmamar

Industrial Engineering *Head*: Nacéra Aboun

Languages (English; Modern Languages) *Head*: C. Larbes

Mechanical Engineering

Metallurgical Engineering *Head*: Med Lamine Djeghlal

Mining Engineering *Head*: Salima Chabou

History: Founded 1925 as Institut Industriel d'Algérie. Acquired present status 1966.

Degrees and Diplomas: *Diplôme d'Ingénieur*, *Magister*, *Doctorat d'Etat*

ECOLE NATIONALE SUPÉRIEURE DE L'HYDRAULIQUE DE BLIDA (ENSH)
BP 31, Blida 09000
Tel: +213(25) 39-94-47
Fax: +213(25) 39-94-46
EMail: miah@ensh.edu.dz
Website: http://www.ensh.edu.dz

Directeur: Tahar Khettal

Programmes
Hydraulic Engineering and Environment (Environmental Engineering; Hydraulic Engineering)
Irrigation and Draining (Irrigation)
Non-conventional Water Re-use (Water Management; Water Science)
Urban Hydraulics (Hydraulic Engineering)
Urban Techniques (Urban Studies)

History: Founded 1972. Acquired present status 1998.

Degrees and Diplomas: *Diplôme d'Ingénieur*, *Doctorat d'Etat*

ECOLE NATIONALE DES TRAVAUX PUBLICS (ENTP)
1, rue Sidi Garidi, Vieux Kouba, Alger 16051
Tel: +213(21) 28-66-97
Fax: +213(21) 28-87-61
EMail: entp@wissal.dz
Website: http://www.entp.edu.dz

Directeur: Berriche Yacine

Programmes
Civil Engineering
Computer Science
Economics and Management (Economics; Management)
Hydraulics (Hydraulic Engineering)
Transport (Transport and Communications)

History: Founded 1966. Acquired present status 1998.

Degrees and Diplomas: *Diplôme d'Ingénieur*, *Magister*

ECOLE NORMALE SUPÉRIEURE DES LETTRES ET SCIENCES HUMAINES D'ALGER
93 Rue Ali Remli-Bouzaréah, Alger
Tel: +213(21) 94-13-57
Fax: +213(21) 94-18-65
EMail: enslsh@ensb.dz

Programmes
Arabic and Arab Literature (Arabic; Literature)
English
French
History and Geography (Geography; History)
Philosophy
Teacher Training

History: Founded 1984.

ECOLE NORMALE SUPÉRIEURE DES LETTRES ET SCIENCES HUMAINES DE CONSTANTINE
Plateau de Mansourah, Constantine
Tel: +213(31) 61-22-40
Fax: +213(31) 61-43-60

Programmes
Humanities (Arts and Humanities)
Literature

History: Founded 1984.

INSTITUT NATIONAL D'AGRONOMIE (INA)
10, avenue Hassen Badi , El-Harrach, Alger
Tel: +213(21) 76-19-87
Fax: +213(21) 75-95-47
Directeur: Mohand Mouloud Bellal

Programmes
Agronomy (Agronomy; Forestry; Hydraulic Engineering; Nutrition; Plant and Crop Protection; Zoology)

History: Founded 1905, acquired present title 1966.
Degrees and Diplomas: *Diplôme d'Ingénieur; Magister; Doctorat d'Etat*

INSTITUT NATIONAL D'ENSEIGNEMENT SUPÉRIEUR EN COMMERCE
11 chemin Doudou Mokhtar, Ben Aknoun, Alger
Tel: +213(21) 91-11-76
Fax: +213(21) 91-54-51
Website: http://www.inc.edu.dz

Departments
International Commerce (Business and Commerce; International Business)
Management
Marketing

History: Founded 1998.

Degrees and Diplomas: *Licence; Magister.* Also specialized post-graduate courses

INSTITUT NATIONAL D'ENSEIGNEMENT SUPÉRIEUR DE SCIENCES COMMERCIALES ET FINANCIÈRES
1 Rampe Salah Gharbi, Alger
Tel: +213(21) 42-32-35
Fax: +213(21) 42-37-32

Departments
Commerce (Business and Commerce)
Finance

History: Founded 1985.
Degrees and Diplomas: *Licence; Magister; Doctorat d'Etat*

INSTITUT NATIONAL D'INFORMATIQUE (INI)
BP 68M, Oued Smar El Harrach, Alger
Tel: +213(21) 51-60-77
Fax: +213(21) 51-61-56
Website: http://www.ini.dz
Directeur: Abderrazak Henni **EMail:** henni@ini.dz
Secrétaire générale: Hassina Brahimi
EMail: h_brahimi@ini.dz

Programmes
Computer Science

History: Founded 1969.
Degrees and Diplomas: *Diplôme d'Ingénieur; Magister; Doctorat d'Etat*

INSTITUT NATIONAL DE LA MAGISTRATURE (INM)
Boulevard du 11 Décembre 1960 El Biar, Alger
Tel: +213(21) 91-51-92
Fax: +213(21) 91-52-01
EMail: inm@inm-dz.org
Website: http://www.inm-dz.org

Programmes
Law (Administrative Law; Commercial Law; Law; Maritime Law)

History: Founded 1990.
Admission Requirements: Licence de droit

INSTITUT NATIONAL DE LA PLANIFICATION ET DES STATISTIQUES (INPS)
11 chemin Doudou Mokhtar, Ben Aknoun, Alger
Tel: +213(21) 91-21-39
Fax: +213(21) 91-21-39

Departments
Planning and Statistics (Statistics)

History: Founded 1983 as Institut des Sciences de la Planification et d'Economie appliquée. Acquired present title and status 1987.

Degrees and Diplomas: *Licence*; *Magister*; *Doctorat d'Etat*

INSTITUT DES SCIENCES DE LA MER ET DE L'AMENAGEMENT DU LITTORAL (ISMAL)
BP 19, Campus universitaire de Delly Brahim, Alger
Tel: +213(2) 37-68-06
Fax: +213(2) 37-70-76
EMail: info@ismal.net
Website: http://www.ismal.net

Programmes
Aquaculture
Coast Planning (Coastal Studies)
Environment (Environmental Studies)
Fishery

Degrees and Diplomas: *Magister*

OTHER INSTITUTIONS

ECOLE NATIONALE POLYTECHNIQUE D'ARCHITECTURE ET D'URBANISME (EPAU)
10 Avenue Hassen Badi, El-Harrach, Alger
Tel: +213(21) 52-17-57
Fax: +213(21) 52-58-89
Founded: 1970

Programmes
Architecture; Town Planning

ECOLE NATIONALE VÉTÉRINAIRE
10 Avenue Hassen Badi, El Harrach, Alger
Tel: +213(21) 52-41-09
Fax: +213(21) 52-51-32
Founded: 1965

Programmes
Veterinary Science

ECOLE NORMALE SUPÉRIEURE DE KOUBA
BP 92, Kouba
Tel: +213(21) 29-86-58
Fax: +213(21) 28-20-67
Website: http://www.ens-kouba.dz
Founded: 1964, 2002

Programmes
Education
Teacher Training

ECOLE NORMALE SUPÉRIEURE D'ENSEIGNEMENT TECHNIQUE D'ORAN (ENSET)
BP 1523, El-M'naouer, Oran 31000
Tel: +213(41) 41-97-19
Fax: +213(41) 41-64-30
Website: http://www.enset-oran.dz
Directeur: Abdelbaki Benziane

Founded: 1970, 1984

Departments
Civil Engineering
Electrical Engineering
Exact Sciences (Mathematics; Physics)
Mechanical Engineering

History: Founded 1970 as Ecole Normale Supérieure d'Enseignement polytechnique, became Ecole Normale Supérieure de l'Enseignement technique 1984.

ECOLE SUPÉRIEURE DE BANQUE (ESB)
BP 156, Route de Baïnem Bouzaréah, Alger
Tel: +213(21) 90-29-29
Fax: +213(21) 90-43-16
Website: http://www.esb.edu.dz
Founded: 1995

Programmes
Banking

INSTITUT DE TÉLÉCOMMUNICATIONS D'ORAN
Es-Senia, Oran
Founded: 1971

Programmes
Telecommunications Engineering

Note: Also Ecole militaire polytechnique de Bordj El-Bahri (http://www.emp.edu.dz)

Angola

INSTITUTION TYPES AND CREDENTIALS

Types of higher education institutions:

Universidade (University)
Instituto (Institute)

School leaving and higher education credentials:

Habilitações Literárias
Bacharel
Licenciado

STRUCTURE OF EDUCATION SYSTEM

Pre-higher education:

Duration of compulsory education:

Age of entry: 6
Age of exit: 10

Structure of school system:

Primary
Type of school providing this education: Primary School
Length of programme in years: 6
Age level from: 6 to: 12

First Cycle Secondary
Type of school providing this education: Ensino medio
Length of programme in years: 3
Age level from: 12 to: 15

Second Cycle Secondary
Type of school providing this education: Ensino Medio
Length of programme in years: 3
Age level from: 15 to: 18
Certificate/diploma awarded: Habilitações Literárias (Secondary School Leaving Certificate)

Vocational Secondary
Length of programme in years: 3
Age level from: 12 to: 15

Technical
Type of school providing this education: Ensino medio tecnico
Length of programme in years: 4
Age level from: 15 to: 19

School education:

The education law of 2001 established a primary education system lasting for six years and a secondary education system divided into two cycles of three years each culminating in the Habilitaçãos Literárias. The second cycle of secondary education replaces the specialized pre-university courses. Parallely there is a technical education system divided into three years of vocational education (after primary school) and four years of middle technical education lasting for four years (after class 9)

Higher education:

There is one State university, the Universidade Agostinho Neto. Founded in 1962 as Estudios Gerais Universitarios, it became the University of Luanda in 1968, the University of Angola in 1976, and acquired its present title 1985. It is closely ruled by the government. The Rector is appointed by the President of the Republic and the directors of faculties and schools are appointed by the Minister of Education on the Rector's recommendation. The University is financially supported by public funds and its management follows the public administration pattern. It is autonomous and is responsible to the Ministry of Education and Culture. Its governing body is the University Council. Recently, a private institution, the Universidade Católica de Angola, has been established. There are also teacher training institutes.

Main laws/decrees governing higher education:

Decree: Lei de Base do Sistema de Educação   Year: 2001
Concerns: All educational levels

Decree: No. 3/92   Year: 1991
Concerns: Management of higher education institutions

Academic year:

Classes from: October *to:* July

Languages of instruction:

Portuguese

Stages of studies:

University level studies:

University level first stage: *Bacharelato*:
The title of Bacharel is obtained after three years' study. It is a terminal degree which may be followed by two years' study leading to the Licenciatura.

University level second stage: *Licenciatura*:
The title of Licenciado is obtained after five years' study, or two years after the Bacharel. In Medicine, it is conferred after six years. The proposed reform foresees a two-cycle programme leading to a Bacharelato after three years and to the title of Licenciado after two more years.

University level third stage: Postgraduate:
The proposed reform foresees a postgraduate level in two stages leading to the Mestre and the Doctorate

Teacher education:

Training of pre-primary and primary/basic school teachers
Primary school teachers are trained in four years after the ninth year of Ensino Medio in Institutos Medios Normales (IMN). They must have the title of Magistério Primário and a pedagogical Agregação in order to teach.

Training of secondary school teachers
Secondary school teachers are trained at the Instituto Superior de Ciências de Educação (ISCED) of the University. The last year (estagio) is spent in classroom practice and writing a dissertation. Secondary school teachers must hold a Bachalerato or Licenciatura and a pedagogical Agregação.

Training of higher education teachers
Higher education teachers are trained at the University. Studies last for five years and lead to the Licenciatura.

Non-traditional studies:

Distance higher education
There are distance education programmes to upgrade unqualified teachers offered by the Instituto Superior de Ciências de Educação. Students sit for examinations at the University.
Teachers can also follow distance education courses to upgrade their professional training.

NATIONAL BODIES

Responsible authorities:

Ministry of Education and Culture (Ministério da Educação y Cultura)
    Minister: António Burity da Silva Neto
    Caixa postal 1451
    Rua Comandante Gika
    Luanda
    Tel: +211(2) 32-33-26
    Fax: +244(2) 32-15-92   +244(2) 32-11-18
    WWW: http://mineduc.snet.co.ao

ADMISSIONS TO HIGHER EDUCATION

Admission to university-level studies

Name of secondary school credential required: Habilitações Literárias

Entrance exams required: Entrance examination

Other admission requirements: Period of State employment or pre-university education

Foreign students admission

Admission requirements: Secondary-school-leaving certificate equivalent to the Habilitações Literárias and success in the entrance examination

Language requirements: Good knowledge of Portuguese

STUDENT LIFE

Main student services at national level

Service d'Accueil et d'Information
Ministry of Education and Culture
Caixa postal 1451 Rua Comandante Gika
Luanda
Tel: +211(2) 32-33-26

GRADING SYSTEM

Usual grading system in secondary school

Full Description: 0-20
Highest on scale: 20
Pass/fail level: 10
Lowest on scale: 0

NOTES ON HIGHER EDUCATION SYSTEM

Data for academic year: 2002-2003
Source: International Association of Universities (IAU), updated from IBE website, 2003
(www.ibe.unesco.org/International/Databanks/Wde/profilee.htm)

INSTITUTIONS OF HIGHER EDUCATION

UNIVERSITIES

*• AGOSTINHO NETO UNIVERSITY
Universidade Agostinho Neto
Caixa postal 815, Avenida 4 de Fevereiro 7, Luanda
Tel: +244(2) 332-089
Fax: +244(2) 330-520
Telex: (0991) 3076 univela an
Website: http://www.uan.ao
Reitor: João Sebastião Teta (2002-)

Faculties
Agrarian Sciences *(Huambo)* (Agriculture)
Economics (Accountancy; Economics; Finance)
Engineering (Architecture; Chemical Engineering; Civil Engineering; Electronic Engineering; Engineering; Mining Engineering)
Jurisprudence (Law)
Medicine
Sciences (Biology; Chemistry; Engineering; Geophysics; Mathematics; Physics)

Higher Institutes
Educational Sciences *(Benguela)*
Educational Sciences *(Luanda)*
Educational Sciences *(Lubango)* (Biology; Chemistry; Educational Sciences; English; French; Geography; Mathematics Education; Modern Languages; Pedagogy; Philosophy; Physics; Portuguese; Psychology)

Centres
National Scientific Investigation

History: Founded 1963 as Estudos Gerais Universitários, became University of Luanda 1968, University of Angola 1976 and acquired present title 1985. An autonomous State institution.
Governing Bodies: Conselho Universitário
Academic Year: October to June (October-February; March-June)
Admission Requirements: Secondary school certificate and entrance examination
Main Language(s) of Instruction: Portuguese
Degrees and Diplomas: *Bacharel*: 3 yrs; *Licenciado*: 5 yrs; Medicine, 6 yrs

Student Residential Facilities: Yes
Special Facilities: Geology Museum; Archaeology Museum
Libraries: Central Library, c.8000 vols; libraries of the faculties
Academic Staff *2001-2002:* Total: c. 700
Student Numbers *2001-2002:* Total: c. 6,800

CATHOLIC UNIVERSITY OF ANGOLA
Universidade Católica de Angola (UCAN)
Caixa postal 2064, Rua N. Sra da Maxima 29, Luanda
Tel: +244(2) 331-973
Fax: +244(2) 398-759
EMail: info@ucan.edu
Website: http://www.ucan.edu
Reitor: Damiao Antonio Franklin
EMail: damiaofranklin@ucan.edu
Vice-Reitor: Filomeno Vieira Dias

Faculties
Computer Science
Economics
Law
Management

History: Founded 1997.

OTHER INSTITUTIONS

INSTITUT NATIONAL D'ADMINISTRATION PUBLIQUE (INAP)
BP 6852, Estrago do Futungo, Luanda
Tel: +244(2) 35-11-60
Fax: +244(2) 35-45-55

Programmes
Economics
Law
Political Science
Public Administration
Social Sciences

Benin

INSTITUTION TYPES AND CREDENTIALS

Types of higher education institutions:

Université (University)
Ecole (School)
Institut (Institute)

School leaving and higher education credentials:

Baccalauréat de l'Enseignement secondaire
Baccalauréat de l'Enseignement secondaire technique
Certificat d'Aptitude au Professorat de l'Enseignement secondaire
Diplôme d'Etudes techniques supérieures
Brevet d'Aptitude au Professorat de l'Enseignement moyen
Diplôme d'Etudes universitaires générales (DEUG)
Diplôme universitaire d'Etudes littéraires (DUEL)
Diplôme universitaire d'Etudes scientifiques (DUES)
Licence
Diplôme
Diplôme d'Ingénieur agronome
Ingénieur
Maîtrise
Doctorat en Médecine
Diplôme d'Etudes approfondies (DEA)
Diplôme d'Etudes supérieures spécialisées (DESS)

STRUCTURE OF EDUCATION SYSTEM

Pre-higher education:

Duration of compulsory education:

Age of entry: 6
Age of exit: 12

Structure of school system:

Primary
Type of school providing this education: Primary School
Length of programme in years: 6

Age level from: 6 to: 12
Certificate/diploma awarded: Certificat d'Etudes primaires

First Cycle Secondary
Type of school providing this education: Etablissement d'Enseignement secondaire général
Length of programme in years: 4
Age level from: 12 to: 16
Certificate/diploma awarded: Brevet d'Etudes du premier Cycle (BEPC)

Technical Secondary
Type of school providing this education: Ecole technique (Premier cycle)
Length of programme in years: 3
Age level from: 12 to: 15
Certificate/diploma awarded: Certificat d'Aptitude professionnelle

Second Cycle Secondary
Type of school providing this education: Lycée
Length of programme in years: 3
Age level from: 16 to: 19
Certificate/diploma awarded: Baccalauréat de l'Enseignement secondaire

Technical
Type of school providing this education: Lycée technique
Length of programme in years: 3
Age level from: 15 to: 18
Certificate/diploma awarded: Baccalauréat de l'Enseignement secondaire technique; Diplôme de Technicien industriel (DTI)

School education:

Primary education lasts for six years divided into Cours d'Initiation, Cours préparatoire, Cours élémentaire 1ère and 2ème années and Cours moyen 1ère and 2ème années, leading to the Certificat d'Etudes primaires. Secondary education lasts for seven years, divided into two cycles: General First Cycle, which lasts for four years and leads to the Brevet d'Etudes du premier Cycle and Second Cycle, which lasts for three years. At the end of the second cycle, pupils obtain the Baccalauréat. In technical secondary education, the first cycle leads to the Certificat d'Aptitude professionnelle (CAP) after three years and the second cycle to the Baccalauréat technique or Diplôme de Technicien industriel after three years. Agricultural education leads to the Brevet d'Etudes agricoles tropicales at the end of the second cycle.

Higher education:

Higher education is provided by two State universities - including one created in 2001- which group all the institutions of higher education. The universities are responsible to the Ministry of Education and Scientific Research. Institutions of higher education are autonomous as far as management is concerned. The contents of the curricula are prepared by the administrative heads and teaching staff of the institutions.

Main laws/decrees governing higher education:

Decree: Décret n° 93-111   Year: 1993
Concerns: Organization of Ministry of Education and state educational policy

Decree: Loi n° 75-30   Year: 1975
Concerns: Document cadre de Politique éducative

Academic year:

Classes from: October *to:* July

Languages of instruction:

French

Stages of studies:

University level studies:

University level first stage: Premier Cycle:
The first phase of studies lasts for two years and leads to the Diplôme universitaire d'Etudes littéraires (DUEL), the Diplôme universitaire d'Etudes scientifiques (DUES) and the Diplôme d'Etudes universitaires générales (DEUG) in Law and Economics. The DUEL comprises specialized work in Foreign Languages, Philosophy, Linguistics, History and/or Geography. The first year of the DUES offers two main options: Pure Science and Biological Science and Geology. The second year is more specialized. In Agronomy, the Diplôme d'Ingénieur agronome is awarded after six years' study. The Diplôme d'Etudes techniques supérieures is conferred by the Collège Polytechnique Universitaire at the end of a three-year course. The qualification of Ingénieur de Conception is awarded four or five years after the Baccalauréat.

University level second stage: Deuxième Cycle:
Students who hold the DUES, DUEL or DEUG may continue their studies for a further one year to obtain the Licence or two years to obtain the Maîtrise.

University level third stage: Troisième Cycle:
A year beyond the Maîtrise leads to the DEA in Management and Arts and Humanities or to the DESS in Demography and Natural Resources. In Medicine, the Doctorat de Médecine is awarded after seven years of university study.

Teacher education:

Training of pre-primary and primary/basic school teachers
Primary school teachers must hold the Brevet d'Etudes du premier Cycle and sit for an entrance examination. They train at one of the three Ecoles normales intégrées (ENI). The course lasts for three years and leads to the award of the Certificat élémentaire d'Aptitude professionnelle/Certificat d'Aptitude pédagogique (CEAP/CAP). Initial teacher training programmes have been stopped lately at ENIs because of lack of funds.

Training of secondary school teachers
First cycle secondary school teachers are also trained at the Ecoles normales intégrées (ENI). They follow a three-year course leading to the Certificat élémentaire d'Aptitude professionnelle/Certificat

d'Aptitude pédagogique (CEAP/CAP). Initial teacher training programmes have been stopped lately at ENIs because of lack of funds.

Those who train as second-cycle teachers follow a three-year course at the Ecole normale supérieure (ENS) in Porto Novo. The first two years are spent at university where students complete the DUEL or the DUES. First-cycle secondary school teachers follow a three-year course on their return to the ENS leading to the Brevet d'Aptitude au Professorat de l'Enseignement moyen (BAPEM) and are called Professeurs adjoints. Second cycle secondary school teachers returning to the ENS complete a three-year course leading to the award of the Certificat d'Aptitude au Professorat de l'Enseignement secondaire (CAPES) and are called Professeurs certifiés. The Institut national pour la Formation et la Recherche en Education (INFRE) offers distance courses for teachers wanting to obtain credentials in primary education such as the Certificat d'Aptitude pédagogique.

NATIONAL BODIES

Responsible authorities:

Ministry of Higher Education and Scientific Research (Ministère de l'Enseignement supérieur et de la Recherche scientifique)

    Ministre: Osseni Kémoko Bagnan

    Directeur de Cabinet: Roger N'Tia

    International Relations: Zéphirin Tossa

    01 BP 348

    Cotonou

    Tel: +229 30-19-91 +229 30-57-95

    Fax: +229 30-57-95 +229 30-18-48

    EMail: mesrs@intnet.bj;dsossa@yahoo.fr

    WWW: http://www.un.org/french/Depts/dpi/Abidjan99/edu_benin

ADMISSIONS TO HIGHER EDUCATION

Admission to non university higher education studies

Name of secondary school credential required: Baccalauréat de l'Enseignement secondaire technique

Alternatives to credentials: Diplôme de Technicien industriel

Other admission requirements: In professional schools, portfolio and recruitment test in addition to the Baccalauréat.

Admission to university-level studies

Name of secondary school credential required: Baccalauréat de l'Enseignement secondaire

Entrance exams required: Competitive examination in some cases (professional schools)

Other admission requirements: In professional schools, portfolio.

Foreign students admission

Admission requirements: Students should hold a Secondary School Leaving Certificate (Baccalauréat) or its equivalent. For vocational education, the students' files are studied. They may have to sit for an examination.

Language requirements: Good knowledge of French is indispensable.

Application procedures:

Apply to individual institution for entry to: university

Apply to: Direction des Affaires académiques, Rectorat de l'Université nationale du Bénin
    BP 526
    Cotonou
    Tel: +229 36-00-74
    Fax: +229 36-00-28

Recognition of studies and qualifications:

Studies pursued in foreign countries (bodies dealing with recognition of foreign credentials):
Direction de l'Enseignement supérieur, Commission nationale d'Etude des Equivalences de Diplômes (CNEED)
    Director: Marc-Abel Ayedoun
    Permanent Secretary: Constant Houndenou
    02BP1211
    Cotonou
    Tel: +229 30-89-24
    Fax: +229 30-89-25
    EMail: mayedoun@hotmail.com

Services provided and students dealt with: Examination of degrees awarded abroad in order to give them an equivalence in the Benin system. Search for information.

Multilateral agreements concerning recognition of foreign studies

Name(s) of agreement(s): Convention on the Recognition of Studies, Certificates, Diplomas, Degrees and Other Academic Qualifications in Higher Education in the African States
Year of signature: 1981

References to further information on foreign student admissions and recognition of studies

Title: Guide d'information et d'orientation pour s'inscrire à l'Université nationale du Bénin
Publisher: Université nationale du Bénin

STUDENT LIFE

Main student services at national level

Centre national des Oeuvres universitaires (CENOU)
    B.P. 526

Cotonou
Tel: +229 36-00-74
Fax: +229 30-00-28

Category of services provided: Social and welfare services

Service des Etudes et de l'Orientation universitaire (SEOU)
B.P. 526
Campus universitaire d'Abomey-Calavi
Cotonou
Tel: +229 36-00-74
Fax: +229 36-00-28   +229 30-00-96

Category of services provided: Academic and career counselling services

Student expenses and financial aid

Student costs:

Home students tuition fees: Minimum: 6,500 (CFA Franc-O)

GRADING SYSTEM

Usual grading system in secondary school
Full Description: 14-20; 12-13; 10-11; 9; 0-8.
For the Baccalauréat: passable, assez bien, bien, très bien

Main grading system used by higher education institutions
Full Description: 0-20
Highest on scale: 20
Pass/fail level: 10/12
Lowest on scale: 0

NOTES ON HIGHER EDUCATION SYSTEM

Data for academic year: 2002-2003
Source: International Association of Universities (IAU), updated from IBE website, 2003
(www.ibe.unesco.org/International/Databanks/Wde/profilee.htm)

INSTITUTIONS OF HIGHER EDUCATION

UNIVERSITIES

PUBLIC INSTITUTIONS

*• ABOMEY-CALAVI UNIVERSITY

Université d'Abomey-Calavi (UAC)
BP 526, Abomey-Calavi University Campus, Abomey-Calavi
Tel: +229 36-00-74   +229 36-07-14
Fax: +229 30-00-28   +229 30-09-38   +229 30-09-38
Telex: 5010 uac
EMail: uac@intnet.bj

Rector: Salifou Alidou (2001-) Tel: +229 36-00-28
EMail: alidou@bj.refer.org

Secretary-General: Sumanou Toleba Tel: +229 36-00-53
EMail: toleba@bj.refer.org

International Relations: Bienvenu Olory Tel: +229 36-11-19
Fax: +229 30-11-19 EMail: bolory@intnet.bj

Head Librarian: Pascal Gandaho Tel: +229 36-01-01
EMail: pgandaho@bj.refer.org

Faculties

Agronomy and Animal Husbandry (Agronomy; Animal Husbandry; Economics; Environmental Management; Food Technology; Nutrition; Rural Studies; Vegetable Production) *Dean*: Mathurin Nago

Economics and Management (Economics; Management) *Dean*: Fulbert Géro Amoussouga

Health Sciences *Dean*: César Akpo

Law and Political Science (Law; Political Science) *Dean*: Virgile Akpovo

Letters, Arts and Humanities (Archaeology; Arts and Humanities; Communication Studies; English; French; Geography; German; History; Linguistics; Philosophy; Sociology; Spanish) *Dean*: Ascension Boghiaho

Science and Technology (Biochemistry; Biology; Chemistry; Ecology; Geology; Mathematics; Natural Sciences; Physics; Technology) *Dean*: Cyprien Gnanvo

Colleges

Polytechnic (Animal Husbandry; Electronic Engineering; Energy Engineering; Mechanical Engineering; Radiology) *Director*: Marc Kpodékon

Schools

Administration and Law (Administration; Communication Studies; Finance; Law; Management; Secretarial Studies) *Director*: Lydie Pognon

Teacher Training (ENS) *(Porto Novo)* (Teacher Training) *Director*: Moubachirou Gbadamassi

Institutes

Arabic Language and Islamic Culture (Arabic; Islamic Studies) *Director*: Taofiki Aminou

Economics *(Cotonou)* (Accountancy; Banking; Business Administration; Business and Commerce; Computer Science; Demography and Population; Economics; Statistics) *Director*: Siméon Fagnisse

Mathematics and Physics *(Porto-Novo)* (Mathematics; Physics) *Director*: Jean-Pierre Ezin

Public Health *(Cotonou)* *Director*: Khaled Bessaoud

Sports and Physical Education *(Porto-Novo)* (Physical Education; Sports) *Director*: Souaïbou Gouda

Centres

Foreign Languages (Applied Linguistics; English; French; Modern Languages) *Director*: Bienvenu Akoha

History: Founded 1970 as Université du Dahomey incorporating departments of former Institut d'Enseignement supérieur du Bénin, established 1962. Acquired present status 1976 and present title 2000. A State Institution responsible to the Ministry of Higher Education and Scientific Research.

Governing Bodies: Conseil scientifique; Comité de Direction

Academic Year: October to July (October-January; January-March; April-July)

Admission Requirements: Secondary school certificate (baccalauréat) or equivalent

Fees: (Francs CFA): 6,200

Main Language(s) of Instruction: French

International Co-operation: With universities in Africa; Belgium; Canada; France; Germany; Netherlands; United States

Accrediting Agencies: African and Malagasy Council for Higher Education (CAMES)

Degrees and Diplomas: *Certificat d'Aptitude au Professorat de l'Enseignement secondaire*: Teaching Qualification, secondary level (CAP), 2-4 yrs; *Diplôme d'Etudes techniques supérieures*: (DETS); *Diplôme d'Etudes universitaires générales (DEUG)*: Law, Economics, 2 yrs; *Diplôme universitaire d'Etudes littéraires (DUEL)*: Arts, Humanities, 2 yrs; *Diplôme universitaire d'Etudes scientifiques (DUES)*: Science; Technology, 2 yrs; *Licence*: Law, Economics, Arts and Humanities, Science and Technology, 1 further yr following DEUG, DUEL, DUES; *Diplôme*: Administration, 5 yrs; *Ingénieur*: Polytechnics, Agronomy, 5 yrs; *Maîtrise*: Law, Economics, Arts and Humanities, Science and Technology, 1 further yr following Licence; *Doctorat en Médecine*: Health Sciences, 7 yrs; *Diplôme d'Etudes approfondies (DEA)*: Law, Economics, Arts and Humanities, Science and Technology, 1 further yr following Licence; *Diplôme d'Etudes supérieures spécialisées (DESS)*: Demography and Population, Natural Resources Management, 1 further yr following Maîtrise. Also three-year Diplôme Universitaire de Technologie in Banking, Commerce, Management, Computer Science, Statistics

Student Services: Academic Counselling, Sports Facilities, Health Services, Canteen

Student Residential Facilities: For 1782 students

Libraries: Central Library, c. 50,000 vols; Agriculture, c. 10,000; Medicine, c. 7000; Education, c. 5000

Publications: Revue générale des Sciences juridiques, économiques et politiques; Annales de la Faculté des Sciences Agronomiques (quarterly); Bénin Médical (3 per annum); Cahiers d'Etudes linguistiques (biannually); Annales de la Faculté des Lettres (annually)

Press or Publishing House: Services des Publications Universitaires

Academic Staff *2001-2002*: Full-Time: c. 490 Part-Time: c. 170 Total: c. 660

Staff with doctorate: Total: c. 475

Student Numbers *2001-2002*	MEN	WOMEN	TOTAL
All (Foreign Included)	14,870	3,670	**18,540**
FOREIGN ONLY	–	–	700

Note: Also Ecole régionale supérieure de la Magistrature

PARAKOU UNIVERSITY
Université de Parakou (UP)
BP 123, Parakou
Tel: 229 61-07-12
Fax: 229 61-07-12
Website: http://www.cnf.bj.refer.org

Recteur: Gilbert Dossou Avode

Secrétaire général: Sanni Allou Doko

Faculties
Agronomy
Economics and Management (Economics; Management)
Law and Political Science (Law; Political Science)

Schools
Medicine

Institutes
Technology

History: Founded 2001.

Botswana

INSTITUTION TYPES AND CREDENTIALS

Types of higher education institutions:

University
Vocational and Technical Institution

School leaving and higher education credentials:

Botswana General Certificate of Secondary Education
Certificate
Diploma
Bachelor's Degree
Post-Graduate Diploma
Master's Degree
PhD

STRUCTURE OF EDUCATION SYSTEM

Pre-higher education:

Duration of compulsory education:

Age of entry: 7
Age of exit: 15

Structure of school system:

Basic First Stage
Type of school providing this education: Primary School
Length of programme in years: 7
Age level from: 7 to: 14
Certificate/diploma awarded: Primary School Leaving Certificate (PSLE)

Junior Secondary
Type of school providing this education: Junior Secondary School
Length of programme in years: 3
Age level from: 14 to: 17
Certificate/diploma awarded: Junior Certificate Examination (JCE)

Senior Secondary
Type of school providing this education: Senior Secondary School
Length of programme in years: 2

Age level from: 17 to: 19
Certificate/diploma awarded: Botswana General Certificate of Secondary Education; Cambridge Overseas School Certificate (being phased out)

School education:

Primary education lasts for seven years leading to the Primary School Leaving Certificate (PSLE). Secondary education begins at fourteen. It covers five years and is divided into two cycles: Junior Secondary education leading to the Junior Certificate and Senior Secondary education leading to the Botswana General Certificate of Secondary Education, which is a prerequisite for admission to the university. The Cambridge Overseas School Certificate is being phased out.

Vocational and technical education has always been limited because of a lack of training places. A new Botswana Technical Education Programme (BTEP) was launched in 2001 by the Ministry of Education to address the problem. Courses which have been developed at secondary school level will start being developed at Diploma level (tertiary education).

Higher education:

Higher Education refers to all education that stipulates a minimum entry requirement of successful completion of senior secondary school. This refers to Diploma or Degree programmes and other advanced professional courses. Higher Education is provided by the University of Botswana. The governing body of the University is the University Council consisting of 21 members. The Senate formulates and carries out the academic policy, regulates courses and examinations, admits students and supervises research.

Main laws/decrees governing higher education:

Decree: Revised National Policy on Education (RNPE)   Year: 1994
Concerns: Educational planning
Decree: The University of Botswana Act   Year: 1982

Academic year:

Classes from: August *to:* May

Languages of instruction:

English

Stages of studies:

Non-university level post-secondary studies (technical/vocational type):

Three-year Diploma programmes are offered in different broad areas, professional studies, technical, engineering and business studies. The entry requirement is the Botswana General Certificate of Secondary Education with a minimum of a C grade pass. One-year certificates are also offered in broad areas. Entry requirements for these programmes are a minimum of a pass in Junior Certificate plus a working experience in the area to be studied. Botswana Polytechnic used to offer Certificate, Diploma and Degree courses in Engineering. It has been incorporated in the University of Botswana as the Faculty of Engineering.

University level studies:

University level first stage: First Degree:
First degree programmes are carried out over a period of four to five years. First degrees offered are Bachelor of Arts (in Humanities or Social Sciences); Bachelor of Accounting/Business Administration; Bachelor of Education; Bachelor of Science (Agriculture); Bachelor of Science (Computing Science); Bachelor of Science (Urban and Regional Planning); Bachelor of Social Work; Bachelor of Library and Information Studies. They all take four years, except the Bachelor of Laws, which takes five years.

University level second stage: Postgraduate Level:
At postgraduate level, there are one-year postgraduate programmes and one-and-a-half to two-and-a-half years' Master programmes. Postgraduate Diplomas are awarded in Secondary Education Teacher Training; Library and Information Studies; and Counselling Education. The two-year master programme is offered in Arts (in Humanities or Social Sciences); Education; Business Administration; Public Administration; and Science. Entry requirements for postgraduate studies is a first degree pass with a minimum overall average of 65% in the relevant field. A PhD (Doctor of Philosophy) may be obtained after the master's degree and a minimum period of three years' research devoted to preparing a thesis.

Teacher education:

Training of pre-primary and primary/basic school teachers
Primary school teachers are trained in primary teacher training colleges. Programmes last for three years. After completion, students are awarded a Diploma in Primary Education. The entry requirement for this course is the Botswana General Certificate of Secondary Education third class.

Training of secondary school teachers
A two-year Diploma in Secondary Education course is open to those who are training to teach in junior secondary schools. They must hold the Botswana General Certificate of Secondary Education. Senior secondary teachers are trained in four years at the University of Botswana where they obtain a Bachelor of Education or in three years for a Diploma in Education. Technical teachers will be trained at the new College of Technical and Vocational Education.

Training of higher education teachers
MEd and PhD programmes in Education are available.

Non-traditional studies:

Distance higher education
Distance education is currently being developed at Diploma and first degree level.

NATIONAL BODIES

Responsible authorities:
Ministry of Education
    Minister: Pontashego Kedikilwe
    Deputy Secretary-General: Violet Essilfe

Private Bag 005
Gaborone
Tel: +267(31) 365-5471
Fax: +267(31) 365-5458
EMail: moe.webmaster@gov.bw
WWW: http://www.gov.bw/moe/index.html

ADMISSIONS TO HIGHER EDUCATION

Admission to university-level studies

Name of secondary school credential required: Botswana General Certificate of Secondary Education
Minimum score/requirement: Grade B
For entry to: BA (Humanities or Social Sciences)/BSc/BEd/BNS, etc

Alternatives to credentials: Mature entry : students should be 25 years old or more and hold at least the Junior Secondary Certificate (with an entrance examination).

Foreign students admission

Definition of foreign student: All students who are not Botswana nationals.

Quotas: At University level all foreign students are free to apply.

Admission requirements: Candidates must be holders of a Senior Secondary School Certificate or the Cambridge Overseas School Certificate or the General Certificate of Education (GCE), Ordinary ('O') level.

Entry regulations: Visas are required for some countries.

Language requirements: Students must be proficient in English.

Application procedures:

Apply to individual institution for entry to: University (colleges of education admit locals only).

Application closing dates:

   For university level studies: 30 December
   For advanced/doctoral studies: 30 December

Recognition of studies and qualifications:

Studies pursued in foreign countries (bodies dealing with recognition of foreign credentials):
Ministry of Education
   Private Bag 005
   Gaborone
   Tel: +267(31) 365-5471
   Fax: +267(31) 365-5458
   WWW: http://www.gov.bw/moe/index.html

References to further information on foreign student admissions and recognition of studies

Title: University of Botswana Calendar
Publisher: University of Botswana

STUDENT LIFE

National student associations and unions

Student Representative Council (SRC)
   Private Bag 0022
   Gaborone

Health/social provisions

Social security for home students: No

Special student travel fares:

By road: No
By rail: No
By air: No
Available to foreign students: No

Student expenses and financial aid

Student costs:

   Home students tuition fees: Minimum: 4,000 (Pula)
   Maximum: 7,500 (Pula)
   Foreign students tuition fees: Minimum: 8,000 (Pula)
   Maximum: 15,000 (Pula)

INTERNATIONAL COOPERATION AND EXCHANGES

Principal national bodies responsible for dealing with international cooperation and exchanges in higher education:

Ministry of Education
   Private Bag 005
   Gaborone
   Tel: +267(31) 365-5471
   Fax: +267(31) 365-5458
   Telex: 2944 THUTO BD
   WWW: http://www.gov.bw/moe/index.html

GRADING SYSTEM

Usual grading system in secondary school

Full Description: The Botswana General Certificate of Secondary Education is marked on an A-G grade scale with A as the highest grade.
Highest on scale: A
Lowest on scale: G

Main grading system used by higher education institutions

Full Description: 1st class A average; 2nd class 1st division B average; 2nd class 2nd division C average; pass D average; fail E or F average
Highest on scale: A
Pass/fail level: D
Lowest on scale: E-F

NOTES ON HIGHER EDUCATION SYSTEM

Data for academic year: 2002-2003
Source: University of Botswana, Gaborone, 2001, updated from IBE website, 2003
(www.ibe.unesco.org/International/Databanks/Wde/profilee.htm)

INSTITUTIONS OF HIGHER EDUCATION

UNIVERSITIES

*• UNIVERSITY OF BOTSWANA
Private Bag UB 0022, Gaborone
Tel: +267(31) 355-0000
Fax: +267(31) 395-6591
EMail: webadmin@mopipi.ub.bw
Website: http://www.ub.bw

Vice-Chancellor: Bojosi Otlhogile (2003-)
Tel: +267(31) 355-2284 EMail: botlhogile@mopipi.ub.bw
Deputy Vice-Chancellor, Finance and Administration:
Shabani Ndzinge Tel: +267(31) 355-2119
EMail: ndzinges@mopipi.ub.bw
International Relations: Brian Mokopakgosi, Deputy
Vice-Chancellor (Academic Affairs) Tel: +267(31) 355-2032
Head Librarian: H.K. Raseroka Fax: +267(31) 355-2297
EMail: raseroka@mopipi.ub.bw

Faculties
Business (Accountancy; Business Administration; Business
and Commerce; Management) *Dean (Acting):* S. Chinyoka
Education (Adult Education; Education; Educational Sciences;
Home Economics; Nursing; Physical Education; Primary Edu-
cation; Science Education) *Dean:* L. Nyati-Ramahobo
Engineering and Technology (Civil Engineering; Electrical
Engineering; Engineering; Mechanical Engineering; Technol-
ogy) *Head:* T. Oladiran
Humanities (African Languages; Arts and Humanities; English;
French; History; Library Science; Religious Studies; Theology)
Head: J. Tsonope
Science (Biology; Chemistry; Computer Science; Environmen-
tal Studies; Geology; Mathematics; Natural Sciences; Physics)
Dean: S. Mpuchane
Social Sciences (Demography and Population; Economics;
Law; Political Science; Public Administration; Social Sciences;
Social Work; Sociology; Statistics) *Dean:* B. Otloghile

Schools
Graduate Studies S. Weeks

Centres
Academic Development *Director:* A. Morisson
Continuing Education G. Adekanmbi

Research Centres
Harry Oppenheimer Okavango *Director:* L. Ramberg
Research and Development *Director (Acting):* I. Mazonde
Further Information: Also Legal Clinic and Business Clinic.

History: Founded 1964 as University of Basutoland,
Bechuanaland and Swaziland. Acquired present status and title
1982.
Governing Bodies: University Council

Academic Year: August to May (August-December;
January-May)
Admission Requirements: Cambridge Overseas School Certificate (COSC) or General Certificate of Education (GCE) or
recognized foreign equivalent. Direct entrance to second year
on completion of studies in another tertiary Institution
Fees: (Pula): c.4000-7500 per annum; foreign students,
8000-15000
Main Language(s) of Instruction: English
Degrees and Diplomas: *Certificate; Diploma; Bachelor's De-
gree:* Education (BEd), 2 yrs following BA or BSc, or holders of
DipSecEd with credit, 2 yrs; Arts (BA); Commerce (BCom); Ed-
ucation (primary level) (BEd); Library and Information Sciences;
Science (BSc); Social Work (BSocWork), 4 yrs; Law (LLB), 5
yrs; Nursing (BSN), following SRN; *Master's Degree:* Arts (MA);
Education (MEd); Science (MSc), a further 1 1/2-2 1/2 yrs; *PhD*
Student Services: Academic Counselling, Social Counselling,
Employment Services, Sports Facilities, Handicapped Facili-
ties, Health Services, Canteen
Student Residential Facilities: Yes
Libraries: Central Library, c. 270,000 vols, 1200 periodicals,
21,500 pamphlets
Publications: Calendar
Academic Staff *2001-2002:* Total: c. 600
Student Numbers *2001-2002:* Total: **11,500**

BOTSWANA COLLEGE OF AGRICULTURE
PO Bag 0027, Gaborone
Tel: +267(31) 352-381
Fax: +267(31) 3314-253
Website: http://www.bca.bw

Principal: E.J. Kemsley (1991-)
Head Librarian: L. Ramore EMail: lramore@bca.bw

Departments
Agricultural Economics, Education and Extension (Agricul-
tural Economics; Agricultural Education) *Head:* T. B. Seleka
Agricultural Engineering and Land Planning (Agricultural
Engineering; Regional Planning) *Head:* R. Tsheko
Animal Husbandry and Production (Animal Husbandry; Cat-
tle Breeding) *Head:* J. M. Kamau
Basic Sciences (Natural Sciences) *Head:* R. M. Sakia
Crop Science and Production (Crop Production) *Head:* C.
Munthali

Centres
In-service and Continuing Education

History: Founded 1991.
Degrees and Diplomas: *Certificate; Diploma; Bachelor's
Degree*

Burkina Faso

INSTITUTION TYPES AND CREDENTIALS

Types of higher education institutions:

Université (University)
Université polytechnique (Polytechnic University)
Ecole (School)

School leaving and higher education credentials:

Baccalauréat
Baccalauréat technique
Brevet d'Etudes professionnelles
Brevet de Technicien supérieur
Diplôme
Diplôme d'Etudes universitaires générales (DEUG)
Diplôme universitaire de Technologie (DUT)
Certificat d'Aptitude au Professorat de l'Enseignement technique
Certificat d'Aptitude au Professorat des Collèges d'Enseignement général
Diplôme d'Ingénieur des Travaux
Licence
Certificat d'Aptitude au Professorat de l'Enseignement secondaire
Diplôme d'Ingénieur
Maîtrise
Diplôme d'Etudes approfondies (DEA)
Diplôme d'Etudes supérieures spécialisées (DESS)
Doctorat d'Etat en Médecine
Doctorat de troisième Cycle
Certificat d'Etudes spécialisées (CES)
Doctorat d'Etat

STRUCTURE OF EDUCATION SYSTEM

Pre-higher education:

Duration of compulsory education:

Age of entry: 6
Age of exit: 16

Structure of school system:

Primary
Type of school providing this education: Ecole primaire
Length of programme in years: 6
Age level from: 6 to: 12
Certificate/diploma awarded: Certificat d'Etudes primaires

Lower Secondary
Type of school providing this education: Collège d'Enseignement général
Length of programme in years: 4
Age level from: 12 to: 16
Certificate/diploma awarded: Brevet d'Etudes du premier Cycle (BEPC)

Technical Secondary
Type of school providing this education: Collège d'Enseignement technique (CET)
Length of programme in years: 3
Age level from: 12 to: 15
Certificate/diploma awarded: Certificat d'Aptitude professionnelle (CAP)

Upper Secondary
Type of school providing this education: Lycée
Length of programme in years: 3
Age level from: 16 to: 19
Certificate/diploma awarded: Baccalauréat

Technical
Type of school providing this education: Lycée technique
Length of programme in years: 2
Age level from: 16 to: 18
Certificate/diploma awarded: Brevet d'Etudes professionnelles (BEP)

Technical
Type of school providing this education: Lycée technique
Length of programme in years: 3
Age level from: 16 to: 19
Certificate/diploma awarded: Baccalauréat Technique

School education:

Primary education is compulsory and lasts for six years leading to the Certificat d'Etudes primaires. Secondary education lasts for seven years and is divided into four-year lower secondary education (compulsory) followed at a Collège d'Enseignement général or a Lycée. It culminates in the Brevet d'Etudes du premier Cycle (BEPC). The upper cycle lasts for three years and may only be taken at a Lycée. It leads to the Baccalauréat. Short technical secondary education leads to the Certificat d'Aptitude professionnelle (CAP) in Collèges d'Enseignement technique after three years. Completion of the upper cycle in a technical specialization leads to the Baccalauréat technique after three years. On completion of two years of upper cycle in a vocational specialization, candidates sit for the Brevet d'Etudes professionnelles (BEP).

Higher education:

Higher education is provided by two universities and several institutions of higher education. The universities are autonomous institutions under the jurisdiction of the Ministère des Enseignements secondaire, supérieur et de la Recherche scientifique. In 1995-96, the Institut universitaire de Technologie, the Institut de Développement rural and the Ecole supérieure d'Informatique were transferred to Bobo-Dioulasso to constitute the Centre universitaire Polytechnique de Bobo-Dioulasso which is now the Université Polytechnique de Bobo-Dioulasso. In 1996-97, the Institut des Sciences de l'Education was transferred to Koudougou and is now called the Ecole Normale supérieure de Koudougou.

Main laws/decrees governing higher education:

Decree: Loi d'Orientation de l'Education   Year: 1996

Decree: Décret n°91-0346   Year: 1991
Concerns: Université de Ouagadougou

Decree: Décret n°AN/VIII-184   Year: 1991
Concerns: Private education

Academic year:

Classes from: October *to:* June

Languages of instruction:

French

Stages of studies:

Non-university level post-secondary studies (technical/vocational type):

Higher technical and vocational education is offered at the Ecole Inter-Etats des Techniciens supérieurs de l'Hydraulique et de l'Equipement rural, which awards the title of Technicien supérieur after two years' study. Several private higher technical institutions have been founded: the Centre d'Etudes et de la Formation en Informatique de Gestion, which confers a Brevet de Technicien supérieur en Informatique de Gestion after two years; the Ecole supérieure des Sciences appliquées; the Ecole des Sciences et Techniques informatiques du FASO which trains for the Diplôme de Technicien supérieur en Informatique.

University level studies:

University level first stage: *Premier Cycle*:
The first stage of university studies leads to the Diplôme d'Etudes universitaires générales (DEUG) after two years. In Health Sciences, the first stage leads to the Premier Cycle d'Etudes médicales (PCEM) and, at the Institut universitaire de Technologie, it leads to the Diplôme universitaire de Technologie (DUT).

University level second stage: *Deuxième Cycle*:
The second stage leads after one year to the Licence. One year after the Licence, the Maîtrise may

be obtained in some fields. In Medicine, the second stage lasts for four years. In Engineering, it leads after three years' further study to the Diplôme d'Ingénieur. The Ecole Inter-Etats d'Ingénieurs de l'Equipement rural awards a Diplôme d'Ingénieur after three years.

University level third stage: Troisième Cycle:
The third stage leads after one year to the Diplôme d'Etudes supérieures spécialisées (DESS) and to the Diplôme d'Etudes approfondies (DEA), and after two years following the DEA, to the Doctorat de troisième Cycle. After three to five years following the DEA, the Doctorat or the Doctorat d'Etat is conferred in some fields of study. In Medicine, after one further year following the four-year second cycle, the Doctorat d'Etat en Médecine is awarded.

Teacher education:

Training of pre-primary and primary/basic school teachers
Primary school teachers are trained at the Ecole nationale des Enseignants du Primaire (ENEP). Access to the ENEP is by entrance examination open to candidates holding the BEPC. Studies last for two years and lead to the Certificat de Fin d'Etudes des ENEP.

Training of secondary school teachers
General and technical secondary school teachers are trained in the appropriate university department or institute for three years following the Baccalauréat. They either hold a DEUG, a Licence, a Maîtrise, a Doctorat de Troisième cycle or the CAPES. English teachers are trained in the Département de Langues Vivantes by means of a teacher training option in the third year. The Ecole normale supérieure de Koudougou offers secondary teacher training courses preparing for the CAPCEG (Certificat d'Aptitude au Professorat des Collèges de l'Enseignement général), for the CAPES (Certificat d'Aptitude au Professorat de l'Enseignement secondaire) and for the CAPET (Certificat d'Aptitude au Professorat de l'Enseignement technique).

Training of higher education teachers
Higher education teachers must hold a Doctorat.

Non-traditional studies:

Other forms of non-formal higher education
Non-formal studies are provided by the Université populaire africaine. Evening courses are also offered.

NATIONAL BODIES

Responsible authorities:
Ministry of Secondary and Higher Education and Scientific Research (Ministère des Enseignements secondaire, supérieur et de la Recherche scientifique)
Minister: Laya Sawadogo
Secretary-General: Eloi Bambara
BP 7047
Ouagadougou 03
Tel: +226 32-45-52

Fax: +226 30-02-32
EMail: sawadogo_l@yahoo.com

National Centre for Science and Technology Research (Centre national de la Recherche scientifique et technologique) (CNRST)

Délégué général: Michel P. Sedogo
Secrétaire général: Jean Marc Palm
International Relations: Lamourdia Tchiombiano
BP 7047
Ougadougou 03
Tel: +226 32-46-48   +226 32-45-04
Fax: +226 31-50-03
EMail: dg.cnrst@fasonet.bf

ADMISSIONS TO HIGHER EDUCATION

Admission to non university higher education studies

Name of secondary school credential required: Baccalauréat technique

Admission to university-level studies

Name of secondary school credential required: Baccalauréat

Foreign students admission

Admission requirements: Foreign students must hold the Baccalauréat or its equivalent or sit for a special entrance examination. Applications should be sent to the Rector of the Université de Ouagadougou between 15 August and 30 October. Foreign students enjoy the same facilities as nationals with regard to social and welfare services, counselling and scholarships. They may also work on campus.

Entry regulations: Conditions vary according to relations with the country of origin.

Language requirements: Students must have a good command of French.

Recognition of studies and qualifications:

Studies pursued in foreign countries (bodies dealing with recognition of foreign credentials):
Commission nationale d'Equivalence des Titres et Diplômes (National Commission for the Equivalence of Diplomas)

Permanent Secretary: Dafrassi Jean-François Sanou
B.P. 1990
Ouagadougou
Tel: +226 33-34-62

Multilateral agreements concerning recognition of foreign studies

Name(s) of agreement(s): Convention on the Recognition of Studies, Certificates, Diplomas, Degrees and Other Academic Qualifications in Higher Education in the African States
Year of signature: 1981

References to further information on foreign student admissions and recognition of studies

Title: Présentation de l'Université de Ouagadougou
Publisher: Université de Ouagadougou

STUDENT LIFE

Main student services at national level

Centre national des oeuvres universitaires
　　B.P. 1926
　　Ouagadougou
　　Category of services provided: Social and welfare services

Student expenses and financial aid

Student costs:
　　Foreign students tuition fees: Minimum: 200,500 (CFA Franc)

Bodies providing information on student financial aid:

Direction de l'orientation et des bourses
　　B.P. 3419
　　Ouagadougou

GRADING SYSTEM

Usual grading system in secondary school

Full Description: 0-20
Highest on scale: 20
Pass/fail level: 10
Lowest on scale: 0

Main grading system used by higher education institutions

Full Description: 0-20. 16-20 très bien; 14-15 bien; 12-13 assez bien; 10-11 passable
Highest on scale: 20
Pass/fail level: 10-11
Lowest on scale: 0

NOTES ON HIGHER EDUCATION SYSTEM

Data for academic year: 2002-2003

Source: International Association of Universities (IAU), updated from IBE website, 2003
(www.ibe.unesco.org/International/Databanks/Wde/profilee.htm)

INSTITUTIONS OF HIGHER EDUCATION

UNIVERSITIES

*• POLYTECHNIC UNIVERSITY OF BOBO-DIOULASSO
Université Polytechnique de Bobo-Dioulasso (UPB)
B.P. 1091, Bobo-Dioulasso 01
Tel: +226 98-06-35
Fax: +226 97-25-77

Recteur: Akry Coulibaly (2002-) Tel: +226 97-05-57
EMail: akry@univ-ouaga.bf

Secrétaire général: Lazare Ouedraogo

Vice-Recteur: Georges Anicet Ouedraogo
EMail: oga@fasonet.bf

International Relations: Patrice Toe
EMail: ptoe@ifrance.com

Higher Schools
Computer Science *(ESI)* (Computer Science; Mathematics; Statistics) *Director:* Théodore Tapsoba

Institutes
Rural Development *(IDR)* (Agricultural Economics; Agriculture; Cattle Breeding; Economics; Forestry; Rural Studies; Social Studies) *Director:* Chantal Yvette Zoungrana-Kaboré
Technology *(IUT)* (Electrical Engineering; Management; Mechanical Engineering; Mechanical Equipment and Maintenance; Secretarial Studies; Technology) *Director:* Ousmane Kaboré

History: Founded 1997.

Academic Year: October to July

Admission Requirements: Secondary school certificate (baccalaureat)

Fees: (Franc CFA): 8,500 per annum; foreign students 200,500 per annum

Main Language(s) of Instruction: French

International Co-operation: With universities in France, Canada, Sweden, Denmark, Côte d'Ivoire, Niger.

Degrees and Diplomas: *Brevet de Technicien supérieur:* Technology, 2 yrs; *Diplôme universitaire de Technologie (DUT):* Business; Commerce; Finance; Accountancy, 2 yrs; *Diplôme d'Ingénieur des Travaux:* Civil Engineering, 3 yrs; *Diplôme d'Ingénieur:* Computer Science; Rural Development; Agronomy; Animal Husbandry; Forestry; Sociology; Economics, 5 yrs; *Doctorat de troisième Cycle:* Agronomy, 8 yrs

Student Services: Sports Facilities, Health Services, Canteen

Student Residential Facilities: Yes

Academic Staff 2001-2002	MEN	WOMEN	TOTAL
FULL-TIME	48	1	49
PART-TIME	27	2	29
TOTAL	**75**	**3**	**78**

STAFF WITH DOCTORATE			
FULL-TIME	6	–	6
PART-TIME	21	2	23
TOTAL	**27**	**2**	**29**

Student Numbers 2001-2002	MEN	WOMEN	TOTAL
All (Foreign Included)	404	141	**545**
FOREIGN ONLY	24	2	26

• UNIVERSITY OF OUAGADOUGOU
Université de Ouagadougou
03 B.P. 7021, Ouagadougou 03
Tel: +226 30-70-64/65
Fax: +226 30-72-42
EMail: info@univ-ouaga.bf
Website: http://www.univ-ouaga.bf

Président: Joseph Paré Tel: +226 30-38-71

Secrétaire général: Sidiki O. Traoré

International Relations: René François Tall, Vice-Président chargé de la Recherche et de la Coopération internationale

Faculties
Applied and Exact Sciences (Applied Mathematics; Chemistry; Computer Science; Mathematics; Physics)
Economics and Management (Agricultural Economics; Business Administration; Economics; Management)
Health Sciences (Health Sciences; Medical Technology; Medicine; Pharmacy)
Humanities (Archaeology; Arts and Humanities; Geography; History; Philosophy; Psychology; Sociology)
Languages, Arts, and Communication (African Studies; Archaeology; Arts and Humanities; Communication Studies; English; Fine Arts; German; Linguistics; Literature; Modern Languages)
Law and Political Science (International Law; Law; Political Science; Private Law; Public Law)
Life and Earth Sciences (Biochemistry; Biological and Life Sciences; Earth Sciences; Geology; Microbiology; Physiology; Plant and Crop Protection)
Science and Technology (Biochemistry; Biology; Chemistry; Geology; Mathematics; Natural Sciences; Physics; Technology)

Institutes
Arts and Crafts *(Burkinabe)* (Handicrafts)

History: Founded 1965 as Ecole normale supérieure, became Centre d'Enseignement supérieur 1969. Acquired present title and status 1974. Reorganized 1985, 1991 and 1997. An autonomous institution under the jurisdiction of the Ministry of Education and Culture.

Governing Bodies: Conseil d'Administration; Assemblée; Conseil de l'Université

Academic Year: September to June (September-December; January-March; April-June)

Admission Requirements: Secondary school certificate (baccalauréat) or recognized equivalent and entrance examination

Main Language(s) of Instruction: French

Degrees and Diplomas: *Diplôme d'Etudes universitaires générales (DEUG)*: 2 yrs; *Diplôme universitaire de Technologie (DUT)*: 2 yrs; *Certificat d'Aptitude au Professorat de l'Enseignement technique*: 3 yrs; *Certificat d'Aptitude au Professorat des Collèges d'Enseignement général*: 3 yrs; *Licence*: 1 yr following DEUG; *Certificat d'Aptitude au Professorat de l'Enseignement secondaire*: 5 yrs; *Maîtrise*: 1 yr following Licence; *Diplôme d'Etudes approfondies (DEA)*: 1 yr following Maîtrise; *Diplôme d'Etudes supérieures spécialisées (DESS)*: 1 yr following Maîtrise; *Doctorat d'Etat en Médecine*: Medicine, 6 yrs; *Doctorat de troisième Cycle*: Chemistry; Linguistics; Mathematics; Economics, 5 yrs following DEA; *Certificat d'Etudes spécialisées (CES)*: Surgery, 3 yrs following Doctorat d'Etat en Médecine; *Doctorat d'Etat*. Also teaching qualifications, secondary level, 2 yrs

Student Services: Social Counselling, Cultural Centre, Health Services, Canteen

Special Facilities: Experimental Fields at Gampela and Leo

Libraries: Central Library, c. 75,000 vols; libraries of the Faculties, c. 25,250 vols

Publications: Bulletin du Laboratoire universitaire pour la Tradition orale; Journal de l'Université Campus Echos (quarterly); Revue Burkinabe de Droit (biannually); Annales de l'Ecole supérieure des Lettres et des Sciences humaines; Annales de l'Université (Série A: Sciences humaines et sociales, Série B: Sciences exactes) (annually); la Revue du CEDRES

Press or Publishing House: Direction des Presses Universitaires (DPU)

Academic Staff *2001-2002*: Full-Time: c. 270 Part-Time: c. 270 Total: c. 540

Student Numbers *2001-2002*: All (Foreign Included): c. 7,800 Foreign Only: c. 650

OTHER UNIVERSITY LEVEL INSTITUTIONS

ECOLE INTER-ETATS D'INGÉNIEURS DE L'EQUIPEMENT RURAL (EIER)
B.P. 7023, Ouagadougou 03
Tel: +226 30-20-53
Fax: +226 31-74-24
EMail: dir@eier.org;eier@eier.org
Website: http://www.eier.org

Directeur: Philippe Mangé EMail: dir@eier.org

Directeur, Administration et Finances: Jacques Muhet EMail: jacques.andre.muhet@eier.org

Programmes
Agricultural Engineering

Civil Engineering
Computer Engineering
Energy Engineering
Industrial Engineering
Mathematics
Water Management

History: Founded 1968.

Main Language(s) of Instruction: French

International Co-operation: With universities in France, Switzerland

Degrees and Diplomas: *Diplôme d'Ingénieur*: Engineering, 5 yrs; *Diplôme d'Etudes supérieures spécialisées (DESS)*: Hydraulic Engineering; Health; Environment, 1 yr

Student Services: Academic Counselling, Social Counselling, Cultural Centre, Sports Facilities, Health Services

Publications: Sud Sciences et Technologie (2 per annum)

Academic Staff *2001-2002*		TOTAL
FULL-TIME		40
PART-TIME		20
TOTAL		**60**

Student Numbers *2001-2002*	MEN	WOMEN	TOTAL
All (Foreign Included)	270	30	**300**

OTHER INSTITUTIONS

ECOLE INTER-ETATS DES TECHNICIENS SUPÉRIEURS DE L'HYDRAULIQUE ET DE L'EQUIPEMENT RURAL (ETSHER)
BP 594, Ouagadougou 01
Tel: +226 31-92-03
Fax: +226 31-92-34 +226 31-74-24
EMail: dir@etsher.org;etsher@etsher.org
Website: http://www.eier.org/etsher/index.htm

Directeur général: Philippe Mange EMail: dir@etsher.org

Directeur des Études et de la Recherche: Jérôme Makin Djegui Tel: 226 31-92-18 Fax: 226 31-92-03

Founded: 1972

Departments
3D Graphics (Computer Graphics)
Advanced Systems Engineering (Computer Engineering)
Agrarian Sciences (Agriculture)
Agricultural Equipment (Agricultural Equipment; Agriculture)
Concrete Technology (Building Technologies)
Construction Engineering (Building Technologies; Construction Engineering)
Foundation Engineering (Construction Engineering)
Hydrodynamics (Mechanics)
Irrigation
Irrigation Engineering (Irrigation)
Road Engineering (Civil Engineering)
Topography (Surveying and Mapping)

Degrees and Diplomas: *Brevet de Technicien supérieur:* Hydraulics; Rural Equipment, 2 yrs
Student Residential Facilities: Yes
Libraries: Library
Publications: Sud Sciences et Technologies (2 per annum)
Academic Staff *2001-2002:* Full-Time: c. 100

ECOLE NATIONALE D'ADMINISTRATION ET DE MAGISTRATURE
03 B.P. 7024, Ouagadougou
Tel: +226 31-86-88
Fax: +226 30-66-11

Directrice: Haridia Dakouré

Founded: 1966

Programmes
Communication (Communication Studies)
Management
National Economy (Economics)
Political Science
Public Administration
Public Finance (Finance)
Social Sciences

ECOLE NORMALE SUPÉRIEURE DE KOUDOUGOU (ENSK)
BP 376, Koudougou
Tel: +226 44-01-22
Fax: +226 44-01-19
EMail: ensk@fasonet.bf
Founded: 1997

Departments
Educational Sciences
Secondary Education
Teacher Training
Technical and Vocational Education (Vocational Education)

Centres
Research in Education (Educational Research)

INSTITUT NATIONAL DES SPORTS
BP 7035, Ouagadougou

Programmes
Physical Education; Sports

INSTITUT PÉDAGOGIQUE DU BURKINA (IPB)
B.P. 7043, Ouagadougou
Tel: +226 32-47-09
Fax: +226 32-47-10
EMail: ipb@liptinfor.bf

Directeur général: Ouri Sanou (1998-) Tel: +226 32-47-10
EMail: sanououri@liptinfor.bf

Founded: 1965
Teacher Training

Note: Also Grand Séminaire de Koumi and Grand Séminaire Saint Jean de Wayalgé which train future priests.

Burundi

INSTITUTION TYPES AND CREDENTIALS

Types of higher education institutions:

Université (University)

Institut supérieur (Higher Institute)

School leaving and higher education credentials:

Diplôme d'Etat

Technicien

Candidature

Diplôme

Ingénieur technicien

Diplôme d'Ingénieur

Licence

Doctorat en Médecine

Diplôme d'Etudes approfondies (DEA)

Diplôme de Spécialité

Doctorat de Spécialité (3e Cycle)

STRUCTURE OF EDUCATION SYSTEM

Pre-higher education:

Duration of compulsory education:

> Age of entry: 6
> Age of exit: 12

Structure of school system:

> *Primary*
> Type of school providing this education: Ecole primaire
> Length of programme in years: 6
> Age level from: 6 to: 12
> Certificate/diploma awarded: Certificat de Fin d'Etudes primaires (Primary School Leaving Certificate)

> *Lower Secondary*
> Type of school providing this education: Collège
> Length of programme in years: 4

Age level from: 12 to: 16

Certificate/diploma awarded: Certificat du Tronc commun (Lower Secondary Level Certificate)

Technical Secondary

Type of school providing this education: Technical Secondary School (Lower Level)

Length of programme in years: 5

Age level from: 12 to: 17

Certificate/diploma awarded: Technicien (Technician Diploma A3 For Lower Level)

Upper Secondary

Type of school providing this education: Lycée

Length of programme in years: 3

Age level from: 16 to: 19

Certificate/diploma awarded: Diplôme d'Etat

Vocational Secondary

Type of school providing this education: Technical Secondary School (Upper Level)

Length of programme in years: 7

Age level from: 12 to: 19

Certificate/diploma awarded: Technicien (Diploma A2 For Upper Level)

School education:

Primary education lasts for six years leading to the Certificat d'Etudes primaires. Secondary education is divided into lower and upper secondary education. Lower secondary education is available to those who pass the National Entrance Examination and lasts four years. A national test is imposed on all those who complete lower secondary education. Their records are submitted to a National Orientation Commission. Schooling at upper secondary level lasts three years and leads to the Diplôme d'Etat, which gives access to higher education. Technical secondary education lasts seven years. A Diplôme de Technicien A2 sanctions success in technical studies and a Diplôme de Technicien A3 is conferred after a cycle of studies lasting five years following upon primary education.

Higher education:

Higher education is mainly provided by the Université du Burundi. It is largely financed by the State and enjoys administrative and management autonomy. It is administered by a rector appointed by the President of the Republic for four years. Policy-making is the responsibility of a Governing Board appointed by the President of the Republic and representing the major spheres of activity concerning higher education development. Four private universities have been created recently.

Main laws/decrees governing higher education:

Decree: Décret-loi n°1/025   Year: 1989

Concerns: reorganization of educational system

Decree: Décret n° 100/181   Year: 1988

Concerns: Ministry of Education

Academic year:

Classes from: October *to:* June

Long vacation from: 1 July *to:* 1 October

Languages of instruction:

French

Stages of studies:

Non-university level post-secondary studies (technical/vocational type):

Several Ministries organise higher level courses.

University level studies:

University level first stage: Candidature:
The first stage of study in preparation for the Licence lasts for two years and leads to the Candidature.

University level second stage: Licence:
A further two years' study beyond the Candidature leads to the Licence. In Medicine, the professional title of Docteur en Médecine is awarded after a further four years of study following the Candidature. In Civil and Agronomic Engineering, courses last for five years and lead to the award of the professional title of Ingénieur. The Diplôme d'Ingénieur Technicien is conferred after three or four years' training in the technical institutes (within the University).

University level third stage: Diplôme d'Etudes approfondies (DEA), Doctorat de 3ème Cycle:
A Diplôme d'Etudes approfondies is conferred in subjects such as Computing, Physics and Agricultural Planning following the Licence or the Diplôme d'Ingénieur. In Medicine, there are two stages which lead to a professional Doctorat in Medicine after six years and a Special Doctorat after five more years of study and the presentation of a major thesis in Clinical Biology, Paediatrics, Surgery, Gynaecology and Internal Medicine. The University also awards a Doctorat de 3ème Cycle.

Teacher education:

Training of pre-primary and primary/basic school teachers
Primary school teachers are trained in lycées pédagogiques which offer studies divided into two cycles of two years each. In-service training of primary teachers is a regular activity of the Office for Rural Education (BER), a curriculum development agency.

Training of secondary school teachers
Secondary school teachers are trained at the University of Burundi from which they graduate after four years in the various specialities. Some teachers, specifically trained for secondary education, are also trained at the Pedagogical Institute for three to five years. They may also be trained in Ecoles normales supérieures.

Non-traditional studies:

Other forms of non-formal higher education
Non-formal studies consist of in-service courses offered by the Institut supérieur de Gestion d'Entreprise for management professionals. There are two levels of training: short cycle training for holders of the Diplôme d'Etat and long cycle training for holders of degrees in economics or their equivalent. Evening courses are also organized in computer sciences.

NATIONAL BODIES

Responsible authorities:

Ministry of National Education (Ministère de l'Education nationale)
Minister: Prosper Mpawenayo
Conseillère, Département de l'Enseignement supérieur: Alice Museri
PO Box 1990
Bujumbura
Tel: +257(22) 5112 +257(22) 5514
Fax: +257(22) 68-39
EMail: museri2002@yahoo.fr

Role of governing body: Central administration and coordination body.

ADMISSIONS TO HIGHER EDUCATION

Admission to non university higher education studies

Name of secondary school credential required: Diplôme d'Etat
Minimum score/requirement: Varies according to year

Alternatives to credentials: State examination

Admission to university-level studies

Name of secondary school credential required: Diplôme d'Etat
Minimum score/requirement: Varies according to year

Alternatives to credentials: An Examen d'Etat is required for the Higher Technical Institute.

Foreign students admission

Admission requirements: Foreign students must have followed seven years' general education or hold a technician's diploma.

Entry regulations: They must hold a visa and a residence permit.

Language requirements: Good knowledge of French

Application procedures:

Apply to national body for entry to: University

Apply to: Commission nationale d'Orientation à l'Enseignement supérieur
PO Box 1990
Bujumbura
Tel: +257(22) 44-07
Fax: +257(22) 84-77

Recognition of studies and qualifications:

Studies pursued in foreign countries (bodies dealing with recognition of foreign credentials):
Commission Nationale d'Equivalence des Diplômes, Titres Scolaires et Universitaires
   Head: Aaron Barutwanayo
   PO Box 1990
   Bujumbura
   Tel: +257(22) 5112 +257(22) 5514

Special provisions for recognition:

For access to university level studies: The holder of a foreign credential must submit to the "Commission d'Equivalence des Titres et Diplômes universitaires" the following data: curriculum vitae specifying the duration of the training abroad; total number of hours of all the training modules; contents of training programmes; methods of assessment, and certified copy of the original credential.

For access to advanced studies and research: Same as above.

Multilateral agreements concerning recognition of foreign studies

Name(s) of agreement(s): Convention on the Recognition of Studies, Certificates, Diplomas, Degrees and Other Academic Qualifications in the African States
Year of signature: 1981

References to further information on foreign student admissions and recognition of studies

Title: Vademecum de l'Etudiant
Publisher: Université du Burundi

STUDENT LIFE

Main student services at national level

Régie des Oeuvres universitaires (ROU)
   PO Box 1644
   Bujumbura

   Category of services provided: Social and welfare services

Secrétariat du Service académique de l'Université du Burundi
   PO Box 1550
   Bujumbura
   Tel: +257(22) 20-59   +257(22) 34-68
   Fax: +257(22) 32-88

   Category of services provided: Academic and career counselling services

National student associations and unions

Association des Etudiants RUMURI (ASSER)
   PO Box 1644
   Bujumbura

Special student travel fares:

By air: Yes

Student expenses and financial aid

Bodies providing information on student financial aid:

Bureau des Bourses d'Etudes et de Stages (BBES)
  PO Box 1990
  Bujumbura
  Tel: +257(22) 51-12 +257(22) 55-14
  Fax: +257(22) 68-39

GRADING SYSTEM

Usual grading system in secondary school

Full Description: 0-100%: 90-100% excellent; 80-89% la plus grande distinction; 70-79% grande distinction; 60-69% distinction; 50-59% satisfaction; below 50% fail
Highest on scale: 100%
Pass/fail level: 50%
Lowest on scale: 0%

Main grading system used by higher education institutions

Full Description: 0%-100% 90-100% excellent; 80-89% la plus grande distinction; 70-79% grande distinction; 60-69% distinction; 50-59% satisfaction; below 50% fail
Highest on scale: 100%
Pass/fail level: 50%
Lowest on scale: 0%

NOTES ON HIGHER EDUCATION SYSTEM

Data for academic year: 2003-2004
Source: Ministère de l'Education nationale, Département de l'Enseignement supérieur, Bujumbura, 2003

INSTITUTIONS OF HIGHER EDUCATION

UNIVERSITIES

PUBLIC INSTITUTIONS

*• UNIVERSITY OF BURUNDI
Université du Burundi
B.P. 1550, Bujumbura
Tel: +257(22) 0979
Fax: +257(22) 3288
Website: http://www.ub.edu.bi

Recteur: Didace Nimpagaritse (2002-) Tel: +257(21) 9838
Fax: +257(22) 7534 EMail: rectorat@biblio.ub.edu.bi

Directeur Administratif et Financier: Oda Sindayizeruka
Tel: +257(22) 9209 EMail: ondayi@cabinet.ub.edu.bi

International Relations: Firmard Nsabimana
Tel: +257(22) 2852

Faculties
Agronomy
Applied Sciences (Applied Chemistry; Applied Mathematics;
Applied Physics; Natural Sciences)
Arts and Humanities (African Languages; Arts and Humani-
ties; English; French; Geography; History; Literature)
Economics and Administration (Administration; Economics)
Law
Medicine
Psychology and Education (Education; Psychology)
Science (Mathematics and Computer Science; Natural
Sciences)

Institutes
Pedagogy
Physical Education and Sports (Physical Education; Sports)

Higher Institutes
Agriculture (*Gitega*)
Commerce (Business and Commerce)
Technical Studies (Technology)

History: Founded 1960, incorporating the Institut agronomique
du Ruanda-Urundi, previously Faculty of Agriculture of the
Université officielle du Congo Belge founded 1958 and the Centre universitaire Rumuri founded 1960. Title of Université
officielle de Bujumbura adopted 1964, acquired present title
1977. Largely financed by the State.

Governing Bodies: Conseil d'Administration comprising 15
members, appointed by the President of the Republic

Academic Year: October to July (October-December; January-April; April-July)

Admission Requirements: Secondary school certificate
(Certificat d'Humanités complètes) or foreign equivalent

Main Language(s) of Instruction: French

Degrees and Diplomas: *Candidature*: Agriculture; Arts and
Humanities; Economics and Social Sciences; Education and
Psychology; Law; Medical Sciences; Physical Education; Pure
and Applied Sciences, 2 yrs; Civil Engineering, 3 yrs; *Diplôme*:
Commerce; Journalism; Teacher Training, 2 yrs; *Ingénieur
technicien*: Agriculture, 3-4 yrs; *Diplôme d'Ingénieur*: Agron-
omy; Civil Engineering, 5 yrs; *Licence*: Administration; Arts and
Humanities; Economics; Education; Law; Mathematics and
Physics; Physical Education; Psychology; Pure and Applied
Sciences, 2 yrs following Candidature; *Doctorat en Médecine*:
Medicine, 6 yrs; *Diplôme d'Etudes approfondies (DEA)*: Agricul-
tural Planning; Management Systems; Mathematics; Physics;
Diplôme de Spécialité: Medicine; *Doctorat de Spécialité (3e
Cycle)*

Student Residential Facilities: Yes

Libraries: c. 100,000 vols

Publications: Revue de l'Université (Séries: Sciences
humaines; Sciences exactes, naturelles, et médicales)

Academic Staff *2001-2002*: Full-Time: c. 170 Part-Time: c. 45 Total:
c. 215

Student Numbers *2001-2002:* Total: c. 4,500

PRIVATE INSTITUTIONS

LIGHT UNIVERSITY OF BUJUMBURA
Université Lumière de Bujumbura (ULBu)
B.P. 1368, Bujumbura
Tel: +257(23) 5549
Fax: +257(22) 9275
EMail: ulbu@cbinf.com
Website: http://www.ulbu.org

Recteur: Grégoire Njejimana Tel: +257(23) 6800
EMail: gregnjejimana@yahoo.com

Directeur administratif: Parfait Mboninyibuka
EMail: ulbu@cbinf.com

Faculties
Business Administration
Communication Sciences (Communication Studies)
Theology

History: Founded 2000.

Governing Bodies: Board of Directors

Admission Requirements: Secondary school certificate

Fees: (Burundi Francs): 45,000 per annum

Main Language(s) of Instruction: French, English

Accrediting Agencies: Ministry of Education

Degrees and Diplomas: *Candidature*: 2 yrs; *Licence*: 3-4 yrs

Student Services: Academic Counselling, Sports Facilities, Language Programmes

Academic Staff *2001-2002:* Total: **4**

STAFF WITH DOCTORATE	MEN	WOMEN	TOTAL
FULL-TIME	1	–	1
PART-TIME	21	3	24
TOTAL	**22**	**3**	**25**

Student Numbers *2001-2002*	MEN	WOMEN	TOTAL
All (Foreign Included)	260	250	**510**
FOREIGN ONLY	21	4	25

UNIVERSITY OF THE GREAT LAKES
Université des Grands Lacs (UGL)
B.P. 2310, Bujumbura
Tel: +257(24) 3554
Fax: +257(27) 2020

Recteur: Sylvère Suguru

International Relations: Nicodème Niyongabo

Faculties
Administration and Business Management (Administration; Business Administration)
Education

History: Founded 2000.

UNIVERSITY OF LAKE TANGANYIKA
Université du Lac Tanganyika (ULT)
B.P. 5403, Bujumbura
Tel: +257(24) 3645

Recteur: Evariste Ngayimpenda

Faculties
Applied Economics (Economics)
Political and Administrative Studies (Administration; Political Science)
Social Sciences

History: Founded 2000.

UNIVERSITY OF NGOZI
Université de Ngozi
B.P. 137, Ngozi
Tel: +257(30) 2171
Fax: +257(30) 2259
EMail: Ungozi@cbinf.com

Recteur: Théophile Ndikumana

Directeur administratif: Erasme Nzeyimana

Faculties
Arts and Humanities
Higher Education

Paramedical Studies (Paramedical Sciences)

Political Science, Economics and Administration (Administration; Economics; Political Science)

History: Founded 1999.

OTHER INSTITUTIONS

PUBLIC INSTITUTIONS

ECOLE NATIONALE DE POLICE (ENAPO)
Bujumbura

Programmes
Police Studies

ECOLE NORMALE SUPÉRIEURE (ENS)
B.P. 6983, Bujumbura
Tel: +257(24) 2799
Fax: +257(24) 3356
EMail: ENS@cbinf.com

Directeur: Charles Nditije

Chef du Service administratif: Gaspard Habarugira

Founded: 1999

Arts and Humanities; Modern Languages; Natural Sciences; Science Education; Teacher Training

INSTITUT SUPÉRIEUR DE GESTION DES ENTREPRISES (ISGE)
B.P. 2450, Bujumbura
Tel: +257(22) 4698 +257(21) 4875
Fax: +257(22) 1785
EMail: isge@cbinf.com

Directeur général: Damien Karerwa

Founded: 1987

Programmes
Business Administration

PRIVATE INSTITUTIONS

COLLÈGE UNIVERSITAIRE DE BUJUMBURA (CUB)
B.P. 2393, Bujumbura
Tel: +257(24) 3944 +257(9) 20308
Fax: +257(22) 9656
EMail: cub@hotmail.com
Directeur administratif: Gérard Muringa

Founded: 1999
Administration; Business Administration

INSTITUT SUPÉRIEUR DE CONTRÔLE DE GESTION (ISCG)
B.P. 439, Bujumbura
Tel: +257(22) 4418
Fax: +257(24) 2186

Directeur général: André Nkundikije
Directeur administratif: Frédéric Hatungimana

Founded: 1988

Programmes
Management

INSTITUT SUPÉRIEUR DES TECHNOLOGIES (IST)
B.P. 6960, Bujumbura
Tel: +257(21) 6662
EMail: istkana@yahoo.fr
Founded: 1999
Computer Science; Electronic Engineering; Telecommunications Engineering

History: Founded 1999.

Cameroon

INSTITUTION TYPES AND CREDENTIALS

Types of higher education institutions:

Université (University)
Institut (Institute)
Grande Ecole (Higher School)

School leaving and higher education credentials:

Baccalauréat
City and Guilds Part III
General Certificate of Education Advanced Level
Brevet de Technicien
Diplôme de Technicien supérieur
Diplôme d'Etudes universitaires en Sciences sociales (DEUSS)
Diplôme d'Etudes universitaires générales (DEUG)
Diplôme d'Etudes universitaires professionnelles
Diplôme en Soins infirmiers
Diplôme universitaire de Technologie (DUT)
Bachelor's Degree
Diplôme d'Ingénieur des Travaux
Diplôme de Professeur des Collèges d'Enseignement général
Diplôme de Professeur des Collèges d'Enseignement technique
Licence
Bachelor's Degree (Honours)
Diplôme
Diplôme d'Ingénieur
Diplôme de Professeur des Lycées d'Enseignement général
Diplôme de Professeur des Lycées d'Enseignement technique
Maîtrise
Master's Degree
Diplôme d'Etudes approfondies (DEA)
Diplôme d'Etudes supérieures spécialisées (DESS)
Doctorat en Médecine
Postgraduate Diploma
Doctorat de troisième Cycle
Doctorat/Doctorate

STRUCTURE OF EDUCATION SYSTEM

Pre-higher education:

Duration of compulsory education:
Age of entry: 6
Age of exit: 12

Structure of school system:

Primary
Type of school providing this education: Ecole primaire (Francophone system)
Length of programme in years: 6
Age level from: 6 to: 12
Certificate/diploma awarded: Certificat d'Etudes primaires élémentaires (CEPE)

Primary
Type of school providing this education: Primary School (Anglophone system)
Length of programme in years: 7
Age level from: 5 to: 12
Certificate/diploma awarded: First School Leaving Certificate

Lower Secondary
Type of school providing this education: Lower Secondary School (Anglophone system)
Length of programme in years: 5
Age level from: 12 to: 17
Certificate/diploma awarded: Cameroon GCE "O' Level

General Secondary
Type of school providing this education: Collège d'Enseignement général, Collège d'Enseignement secondaire (Francophone system)
Length of programme in years: 4
Age level from: 12 to: 16
Certificate/diploma awarded: Brevet d'Etudes du premier Cycle du second Degré

Upper Secondary
Type of school providing this education: Lycée (Francophone system)
Length of programme in years: 3
Age level from: 16 to: 19
Certificate/diploma awarded: Baccalauréat

Upper Secondary
Type of school providing this education: Upper Secondary School (Anglophone system)
Length of programme in years: 2
Age level from: 17 to: 19
Certificate/diploma awarded: GCE' A' Level

Technical
Type of school providing this education: Technical Secondary School (Anglophone system)
Length of programme in years: 7
Age level from: 12 to: 19
Certificate/diploma awarded: City and Guilds Part III

Technical
Type of school providing this education: Lycée technique (Francophone system)
Length of programme in years: 7
Age level from: 12 to: 19
Certificate/diploma awarded: Brevet de Technicien, Brevet professionnel, Baccalauréat

School education:

Primary education lasts for seven years in the Anglophone system, leading to the First School Leaving Certificate, and six years in the Francophone system, leading to the Certificat d'Etudes primaires élémentaires (CEPE). In the Anglophone system, the first cycle of secondary education lasts for five years and leads to the Cameroon GCE Ordinary level. Higher schools offer two-year courses leading to the GCE Advanced level. In the Francophone system, the first four years of secondary education lead to the Brevet d'Etudes du premier Cycle du second Degré. At the Lycées (upper secondary), three years' study lead to the Baccalauréat. Technical secondary education leads to the City and Guilds Part III and to the Baccalauréat or the Brevet de Technicien respectively, or the Brevet professionnel.

Higher education:

Higher education is mainly provided by universities, specialized institutions and schools. The Minister in charge of higher education takes final policy decisions regarding universities, although each university has a governing council. Councils have responsibility for personnel recruitment. The creation of new departments, degrees, courses and changes in regulations must receive ministerial consent. Each university receives a budget from the State. The University of Buéa is headed by a Vice-Chancellor who is nominated by the government and who, in turn, is chair of the Administrative Council. Other public universities are headed by a Rector. A Catholic University Institute was established in 1990. Several higher education institutions do not fall directly under the Ministry of Higher Education, but the Minister must ascertain that they meet academic standards. Some are directly run by other ministries and offer specialized training in such fields as agriculture, health, post and telecommunications, forestry and public works.

Main laws/decrees governing higher education:

Decree: Loi 005   Year: 2001
Concerns: Higher education

Decree: Decree 99/0055   Year: 1999
Concerns: Higher Education

Decree: Decree n°95/041   Year: 1995
Concerns: Ministry of Education

Decree: 93/026   Year: 1993
Concerns: universities

Academic year:

Classes from: October *to:* July

Long vacation from: 1 August *to:* 31 August

Languages of instruction:

English, French

Stages of studies:

Non-university level post-secondary studies (technical/vocational type):

Higher technical and vocational education is mainly provided by specialized schools and institutes in such fields as Administration, Technology, Social Work, and Public Works. They award diplomas generally recognized as equivalent to a first degree.

University level studies:

University level first stage: *Premier Cycle, Bachelor's Degree*:
In Economics and Management and in Law, the first stage leads to a Diplôme d'Etudes universitaires générales (DEUG) after two years. The Licence and Bachelor's degree are obtained after three years in the Humanities and in the Sciences. In Engineering, the Diplôme d'Ingénieur des Travaux and d'Ingénieur de Conception are conferred after three years' study (up to five years for Ingénieur de Conception). In Medical Sciences, the Diplôme de Technicien supérieur de la Santé is awarded after three years and the Diplôme en Soins infirmiers after two years. In Agronomy, a Diplôme d'Ingénieur agronome is conferred after four years' study at the Ecole nationale supérieure agronomique.

University level second stage: *Deuxième Cycle*:
In Law, Economics and Management, the Licence is conferred after a further year's study following the DEUG. The Maîtrise is conferred after a further two years' study following the Licence in Arts and Sciences. In Law it is conferred after a further year's study beyond the Licence. In Engineering a Diplôme d'Ingénieur is awarded after a total of five years' study. In Medicine, the Diplôme de Docteur en Médecine is conferred after six years. In Anglophone universities, Master's Degrees and Postgraduate Diplomas are conferred at least one year after the first terminal degree.

University level third stage: *Doctoral Cycle*:
A Diplôme d'Etudes approfondies (DEA) and a Diplôme d'Etudes supérieures spécialisées (DESS) are conferred by the Francophone universities one year after the Maîtrise. A Doctorat de troisième Cycle is conferred after two to three years' further study. It is being replaced by the Doctorat unique or PhD, conferred four years after the Maîtrise. Anglophone universities award a Doctor's Degree.

Teacher education:

Training of pre-primary and primary/basic school teachers
Pre-primary and primary school teachers are trained at the Ecoles normales d'Instituteurs (ENI). Holders of the BEPC are trained in three years and holders of the Baccalauréat are trained in one year. They obtain the Certificat d'Aptitude pédagogique d'Instituteur de l'Enseignement maternel et

primaire (CAPIEMP).

Holders of the Primary School Leaving Certificate are trained in three years. Holders of the GCE Ordinary level examinations can complete the course in two years and holders of the GCE Advanced level examinations or those who have at least three years' teaching experience with the Grade II Certificate can complete the same course in one year.

Training of secondary school teachers

Secondary school teachers are trained in three years following secondary high school or two years following a first degree at the Ecoles normales supérieures for collège and lycée teachers or at the Ecole normale supérieure d'Enseignement technique for technical secondary education teachers.

Training of higher education teachers

Higher education teachers are recruited at the doctoral level.

NATIONAL BODIES

Responsible authorities:

Ministry of Higher Education (Ministère de l'Enseignement supérieur)
    Minister: Maurice Tchuente
    Secretary-General: Elie C. Ndjitoyap
    Director of Higher Education Development: François-Xavier Etoa
    International Relations: Anaclet Fomethe
    PO Box 1457
    Yaoundé
    Tel: +237 (223) 3677
    Fax: +237 (223) 2282
    Telex: 8418 mesres ku
    WWW: http://www.minesup.gov.cm

ADMISSIONS TO HIGHER EDUCATION

Admission to non university higher education studies

Name of secondary school credential required: Baccalauréat

Name of secondary school credential required: General Certificate of Education Advanced Level

Alternatives to credentials: Yes

Admission to university-level studies

Name of secondary school credential required: General Certificate of Education Advanced Level

Name of secondary school credential required: Baccalauréat

Name of secondary school credential required: Brevet de Technicien
For entry to: Technical and Vocational School/Faculty

Entrance exams required: Entrance Examination

Foreign students admission

Definition of foreign student: Non-Cameroonian, non-member of CEMAC (Central African Economic Community)

Quotas: No.

Admission requirements: Foreign students must hold a Baccalauréat or its equivalent, a scientific Baccalauréat or a General Certificate of Education Advanced Level or the Higher School Certificate and have passed the competitive examination of one of the schools.

Entry regulations: Visa, residence permit

Health requirements: Medical assistance is offered free of charge at the university.

Language requirements: Good knowledge of French and English. Language and orientation courses are offered.

Recognition of studies and qualifications:

Studies pursued in foreign countries (bodies dealing with recognition of foreign credentials):
Division of Comparative University Systems and of Equivalences, Ministry of Higher Education
   Chief, Division of Comparative University Systems and Equivalences: Ebot Enaw
   Director, Student Assistance and Counselling: Eno Lafon
   PO Box 1457
   Yaoundé
   Tel: +237(223) 1407
   Telex: 8418 KN

   Services provided and students dealt with: Assistance to students of Cameroon nationality

References to further information on foreign student admissions and recognition of studies

Title: L'Annuaire de l'Université de Yaoundé
Publisher: Université de Yaoundé

Title: Livret de l'Etudiant (English and French editions)
Publisher: Université de Yaoundé

STUDENT LIFE

Main student services at national level

Service des oeuvres universitaires
   PO Box 337
   Yaoundé

National student associations and unions

MUSEC

    c/o University of Yaoundé

    Yaoundé

Health/social provisions

Social security for home students: Yes

Social security for foreign students: No

Student expenses and financial aid

Student costs:

    Home students tuition fees: Minimum: 50,000 (CFA Franc)

    Maximum: 825,000 (CFA Franc)

    Foreign students tuition fees: Minimum: 300,000 (CFA Franc)

    Maximum: 2,000,000 (CFA Franc)

Bodies providing information on student financial aid:

Direction de l'Assistance et de l'Orientation

    PO Box 1457

    Yaoundé

    Deals with: Grants and Loans

    Category of students: Scholarships for Cameroon students for Africa, Germany, Belgium, Brazil, Canada, China, Spain, United States, France, India, Italy, United Kingdom, Switzerland and Russia.

INTERNATIONAL COOPERATION AND EXCHANGES

Principal national bodies responsible for dealing with international cooperation and exchanges in higher education:

Division de la Prospective, de la Recherche et de la Coopération, Ministère de l'Enseignement supérieur

    Chef: Anaclet Fomethe

    PO Box 1457

    Yaoundé

    Tel: +237 (223) 3677

    Fax: +237 (223) 2282

    WWW: http://www.minesup.gov.cm

GRADING SYSTEM

Usual grading system in secondary school

Full Description: 0-20 in the Francophone system. 0-9 fail; 10-11 passable; 12-13 assez bien; 14-15 bien; 16-20 très bien

Highest on scale: 20

Pass/fail level: 10
Lowest on scale: 0

Main grading system used by higher education institutions

Full Description: 0-20
Highest on scale: 20
Pass/fail level: 10
Lowest on scale: 0

Other main grading systems

In the Anglophone system grading follows the GCE Ordinary and Advanced level system.
Master's and Doctoral degrees can be awarded with the following classifications: très honorable avec félicitations du jury; très honorable; honorable. The University of Buea uses an A-F scale

NOTES ON HIGHER EDUCATION SYSTEM

Data for academic year: 2002-2003
Source: Ministry of Higher Education, Yaoundé, 2003

INSTITUTIONS OF HIGHER EDUCATION

UNIVERSITIES

PUBLIC INSTITUTIONS

• UNIVERSITY OF BUEA
Université de Buéa (UB)
PO Box 63, Buéa, South West Province
Tel: +237(332) 2134
Fax: +237(343) 2508
Telex: 5155KN

Vice-Chancellor: Dorothy L. Njeuma (1993-)
Tel: +237(332) 2706

Faculties
Arts (Arts and Humanities; Curriculum; Educational Administration; English; French; History; Linguistics; Theatre) *Dean*: Emmanuel Gwan
Education *Dean*: Lydia E. Luma
Health Sciences *Dean*: Theodosia McMoli
Science (Biochemistry; Botany; Chemistry; Environmental Studies; Geology; Mathematics and Computer Science; Microbiology; Natural Sciences; Physics; Zoology) *Dean*: Nzumpe Mesape Ntoko
Social Sciences and Management (Accountancy; Anthropology; Banking; Economics; Finance; Geography; Journalism; Law; Management; Mass Communication; Political Science; Social Sciences; Sociology; Women's Studies) *Dean*: Cornelius Lambi

Schools
Translation and Interpretation *(Advanced, ASTI) Director*: Charles Nama

History: Founded 1977 as University Centre for postgraduate programme in Translation and Interpretation. Acquired present status and title 1992.
Governing Bodies: Conseil d'Administration, comprising 26 members; Senate
Academic Year: October to July (October-February; March-July)
Admission Requirements: Secondary school certificate and competitive entrance examination. Licence (Translation), or recognized equivalent for School of Translation and Interpretation
Fees: (Francs CFA): Foreign students, 300,000-1m. per annum
Main Language(s) of Instruction: French, English
Degrees and Diplomas: *Bachelor's Degree*: Arts (BA); Law (LLB); Science (BSc), 3 yrs; *Bachelor's Degree (Honours)*: 4 yrs; *Master's Degree*: 1-2 yrs; *Postgraduate Diploma*: Education; Interpretation, 1 yr; *Doctorat/Doctorate*: 4 yrs

Student Services: Academic Counselling, Social Counselling, Foreign Student Adviser, Sports Facilities, Handicapped Facilities, Health Services, Canteen
Student Residential Facilities: Yes
Special Facilities: Language Laboratory; Interpretation Laboratory
Libraries: University of Buéa Library, c. 35,000 vols
Publications: Buéa University Newsletter, BUN (quarterly); UBDEF, University of Buéa Development Fund Newsletter; Epasa Moto, Bilingual Journal of Language, Letters and Culture (annually)
Academic Staff *2001-2002:* Total: **260**
Student Numbers *2001-2002:* Total: **4,600**

UNIVERSITY OF DOUALA
Université de Douala (UDLA)
BP 2701, Douala
Tel: +237(340) 6415
Fax: +237(340) 6415
EMail: ud@u-douala.cm
Website: http://www.u-douala.cm

Recteur: Bruno Bekolo Ebé (2003-)
Secrétaire générale: Thérèse B. Wangue
International Relations: Nicole C. Ndoko

Faculties
Arts and Social Sciences *(FLSH)* (African Studies; Arts and Humanities; Bilingual and Bicultural Education; English; French; Geography (Human); German; History; Literature; Philosophy; Psychology; Social Sciences; Spanish) *Dean*: Blaise Moukoko
Economics and Applied Management *(FSEGA)* (Econometrics; Economic and Finance Policy; Economics; Finance; Management; Marketing; Mathematics) *Dean*: Blaise Moukoko
Law and Political Science *(FSJP)* (Law; Political Science; Private Law; Public Law) *Dean*: François Mbome
Science *(FS)* (Biology; Chemistry; Computer Science; Mathematics; Natural Sciences; Physics) *Dean*: Paul Henri Awam Zollo

Institutes
Technology *(IUT)* (Accountancy; Biology; Business Administration; Business and Commerce; Civil Engineering; Computer Science; Electrical and Electronic Engineering; Industrial Engineering; Secretarial Studies; Telecommunications Engineering) *Director*: Charles Awono Onana

Centres
Atomic Molecular Physics and Quantum Optics *(CEPAMOQ)* (Nuclear Physics) *Director*: Kwato Njock

History: Founded 1977 as Centre Universitaire. Previously part of the University of Yaoundé. Acquired present status and title 1993.

Governing Bodies: Conseil d'Administration

Academic Year: October to July (October-December; January-March; April-July)

Admission Requirements: Competitive entrance examination following secondary school certificate (baccalauréat)

Fees: (Franc CFA): c. 50,000 per annnum; foreign students, c. 300,000-1m.

Main Language(s) of Instruction: French, English

Degrees and Diplomas: *Diplôme de Technicien supérieur*: 3 yrs; *Diplôme universitaire de Technologie (DUT)*; *Diplôme de Professeur des Collèges d'Enseignement technique*: 3-5 yrs; *Licence*: 3 yrs; *Diplôme*: Commerce, 4 yrs; *Maîtrise*: 4 yrs

Student Services: Academic Counselling, Cultural Centre, Sports Facilities, Health Services, Canteen

Student Residential Facilities: Yes

Libraries: Central Library, c. 5600 vols; libraries of the Schools, c. 4000

HIGHER SCHOOL OF ECONOMICS AND COMMERCE
ECOLE SUPÉRIEURE DES SCIENCES ÉCONOMIQUES ET COMMERCIALES
BP 1931, Douala, Littoral
Tel: +237(340) 5298 +237(340) 5311
EMail: essecdla@u-douala.cm
Website: http://www.u-douala.cm/essec
Directeur: Emmanuel Kamdem

Departments

Economics, Business and Commerce (Business and Commerce; Economics)
Finance and Accountancy (Accountancy; Finance)
Human Relations Management (Behavioural Sciences)
Information Systems (Information Sciences)
International Management and Commerce (Business and Commerce; International Business)
Marketing

History: Founded 1979. Acquired present status and title 1993.

Degrees and Diplomas: *Diplôme*: Commerce; *Maîtrise*: Management; Business Administration

HIGHER SCHOOL OF TECHNICAL TEACHER TRAINING
ECOLE NORMALE SUPÉRIEURE DE L'ENSEIGNEMENT TECHNIQUE
BP 1872, Douala, Littoral
Tel: +237(340) 4291
Fax: +237(340) 0798
Directeur: John M. O. Ebanja

Education; Technology
Administration Techniques (Administration)
Chemistry
Civil Engineering

Economics
Mechanical Engineering

History: Founded 1979. Acquired present status and title 1993.

• UNIVERSITY OF DSCHANG
Université de Dschang (UDS)
BP 96, Dschang
Tel: +237(345) 1381 +237(345) 1092
Fax: +237(345) 1381
Telex: 970 7013 kn
EMail: udsrect@sdnemr.undp.org
Website: http://www.dschang-online.com/universite.htm

Recteur: Jean Louis Dongmo (2003-)

Secrétaire général: André Mvesso

International Relations: Joseph P. Ayissi

Head Librarian: Micheline Tchouamo Tel: +237(345) 1351 Fax: +237(345) 1381 EMail: matchuamo@yahoo.com

Faculties

Agronomy and Agricultural Sciences *(FASA)* (Agriculture; Animal Husbandry; Forestry; Rural Studies; Soil Science; Veterinary Science; Water Science) *Dean:* Mpoame Mbida
Economics and Applied Management *(FSEGA)* (Agricultural Business; Economics; Management) *Dean:* François Anoukaha
Law and Political Science *(FSJP)* (Law; Political Science; Private Law; Public Law) *Dean:* Samuel Ngongang
Letters and Humanities *(FLSH)* (African Studies; Arts and Humanities; Geography; History; Linguistics; Philosophy; Psychology; Sociology) *Dean:* Kuitcheu Fonkou
Science *(FS)* (Chemistry; Earth Sciences; Mathematics and Computer Science; Natural Sciences; Physics) *Dean:* Remy Minpfoundi

Programmes

Distance Education (Agricultural Management; Animal Husbandry; Crop Production) *Coordinator:* Michel Omoko

Schools

Fine Arts *(Foumban)*

Institutes

Technology *(FOTSO Victor)* (Business and Commerce; Computer Engineering; Electrical and Electronic Engineering; Secretarial Studies; Technology) *Director:* Médard Fogue

Centres

Audiovisual (Cinema and Television)
Computer Science (Computer Science; Statistics) *Head:* Louis-Marie Ngamassi
Continuing Education *Director:* Joseph Djoukam
Forest Wood Agriculture *(Regional)* (Agriculture; Forestry; Wood Technology)
Languages (English; Modern Languages) *Director:* Donatus Ngaba
Research and Phytosanitary Training *(African)*

History: Founded 1977 as Centre Universitaire. Previously part of the University of Yaoundé. Acquired present status and title 1993.

Academic Year: October to July (October-March; March-July)

Admission Requirements: Secondary school certificate (baccalauréat), or foreign equivalent at Advanced 'A' level. General Certificate of Education

Fees: (Francs CFA): Foreign students, 500,000-1m. per annum

Main Language(s) of Instruction: French, English

Degrees and Diplomas: *Diplôme de Technicien supérieur*: Agriculture, 3 yrs; *Diplôme d'Etudes universitaires générales (DEUG)*: 2 yrs; *Licence*: 3 yrs; *Diplôme d'Ingénieur*: Agronomy, 5 yrs; *Maîtrise*: 4 yrs; *Master's Degree*: Social Sciences (MA/Msc); Water Management (MA/Msc), 5 yrs; *Doctorat/Doctorate*: Agronomy

Student Services: Academic Counselling, Employment Services, Cultural Centre, Sports Facilities, Language Programmes, Handicapped Facilities, Health Services, Canteen

Libraries: Central Library, c. 25,000 vols

Publications: Le Flamboyant; Jeune Afrique Economique (monthly)

Academic Staff *2001-2002:* Total: c. 340

Student Numbers 2001-2002	MEN	WOMEN	TOTAL
All (Foreign Included)	7,709	2,809	**10,518**
FOREIGN ONLY	–	–	18

Distance Students, 350

• UNIVERSITY OF NGAOUNDÉRÉ
Université de Ngaoundéré (UNDERE)
BP 454, Ngaoundéré
Tel: +237(225) 2767 +237(225) 2765
Fax: +237(225) 2767 +237(225) 2573 +871 761 330-643 (satellite)
Telex: cundere 970 7645 kn
Recteur: Paul Henri Amvam Zollo (2003-)
Tel: +237(225) 2741 +871 761 330-642 (satellite)
Secrétaire général: Hamadou Adama
International Relations: Joseph Kayem, Vice-Recteur, Recherche et Coopération Tel: +237(764) 4872

Faculties
Arts and Humanities *(FALSH)* (Arts and Humanities; Social Sciences) *Dean*:
Economics and Applied Management *(FSEG)* (Accountancy; Economics; Finance; Management; Marketing) *Dean*: Lucien Kombou
Education
Law and Political Science *(FSJP)* (Law; Political Science; Private Law; Public Law) *Dean*: Victor-Emmanuel Bokally
Science *(FS)* (Mathematics and Computer Science; Natural Sciences) *Dean*: Oumarou Bouba

Schools
Chemical Engineering and Mineral Processing (Chemical Engineering; Materials Engineering)

Geology and Mining Prospecting (Geology; Mining Engineering; Petroleum and Gas Engineering)

Veterinary Medicine and Animal Science (Animal Husbandry; Veterinary Science)

Institutes

Technology *(IUT)* (Computer Science; Electrical and Electronic Engineering; Food Technology; Heating and Refrigeration; Maintenance Technology; Mechanical Engineering; Technology) *Director*: Ali Ahmed

History: Founded 1982 as Centre Universitaire, acquired present status and title 1993. A State Institution.

Governing Bodies: Conseil de l'Université; Conseil d'Administration

Academic Year: October to July (October-February; March-July)

Admission Requirements: Secondary school certificate (baccalauréat), or foreign equivalent at Advanced ('A') level

Fees: (Francs CFA): Foreign students, undergraduate, 300,000-600,000 per annum; postgraduate, 3m.-5m.

Main Language(s) of Instruction: French, English

International Co-operation: With universities in Belgium, Chad, France, Germany, Norway and United Kingdom.

Degrees and Diplomas: *Diplôme d'Etudes universitaires générales (DEUG)*: 2 yrs; *Diplôme universitaire de Technologie (DUT)*: Technology; Food Technology, 2 yrs; *Diplôme d'Ingénieur des Travaux*: Agroindustrial Sciences; *Licence*: 3 yrs; *Diplôme d'Ingénieur*: Food Technology, 5 yrs; *Maîtrise*: a further yr following Licence; *Diplôme d'Etudes approfondies (DEA)*: Management; Food Science; Geography; Process Engineering; Arts and Humanities, a further yr following Maîtrise; *Doctorat/Doctorate*: Management; Food Science; Geography; Process Engineering; Arts and Humanities, 3-5 yrs following DEA. Also Diplôme d'Etudes universitaires professionnelles in Finance and Marketing

Student Services: Academic Counselling, Social Counselling, Sports Facilities, Health Services, Canteen

Student Residential Facilities: Yes

Libraries: Total, c. 50,000 vols

Publications: Annales de la FALSH, Arts and Humanities, Social Sciences (2 per annum)

Academic Staff 2001-2002	MEN	WOMEN	TOTAL
FULL-TIME	174	16	**190**
STAFF WITH DOCTORATE			
FULL-TIME	86	4	**90**

Student Numbers 2001-2002	TOTAL
All (Foreign Included)	**6,800**
FOREIGN ONLY	1,100

NATIONAL SCHOOL OF AGRO-INDUSTRY SCIENCES
ECOLE NATIONALE SUPÉRIEURE DES SCIENCES
AGRO-INDUSTRIELLES
BP 455, Ngaoundéré
Tel: +237(225) 1313
Fax: +237(225) 2573
Website:
http://ensai-iut.minesup.gov.cm/ensai/ensai_departe.htm
Directeur: Carl M. Mbofung (2000-)

Departments
Applied Chemistry
Electrical, Energy and Automation Engineering
Food Sciences and Nutrition
Mathematics and Computer Science
Mechanical Engineering
Process Engineering

History: Founded 1982.

Degrees and Diplomas: *Diplôme d'Etudes approfondies (DEA)*; *Doctorat/Doctorate*

• UNIVERSITY OF YAOUNDÉ I
Université de Yaoundé I (UY I)
BP 337, Yaoundé, Centre
Tel: +237(222) 1320
Fax: +237(222) 1320
EMail: uy.cdc@uninet.cm
Website: http://www.uninet.cm
Recteur: Sammy Beban Chumbow (2003-)

Secrétaire générale: Lisette Elomo Ntonga
Tel: +237(222) 15-23 Fax: +237(222) 05-34

International Relations: Edward O. Ako, Vice-Recteur (Recherche et Coopération) Tel: +237(222) 12-60 Fax: +237(222) 12-60 EMail: tako640@yahoo.ca

Faculties
Arts, Letters and Humanities *(FALSH)* (African Languages; African Studies; Anthropology; Archaeology; Arts and Humanities; English; Fine Arts; Foreign Languages Education; French; Geography; German; History; Philosophy; Psychology; Sociology; Spanish) *Dean:* André Marie Ntsobé Njoh
Medicine and Biomedical Studies *(FSMB)* (Anaesthesiology; Anatomy; Behavioural Sciences; Biology; Biomedicine; Botany; Cardiology; Dentistry; Dermatology; Embryology and Reproduction Biology; Endocrinology; Environmental Studies; Epidemiology; Gastroenterology; Gynaecology and Obstetrics; Haematology; Health Education; Medical Technology; Medicine; Microbiology; Nephrology; Nutrition; Ophthalmology; Otorhinolaryngology; Paediatrics; Parasitology; Pathology; Pharmacology; Physiology; Pneumology; Psychiatry and Mental Health; Radiology; Surgery; Venereology; Virology) *Dean:* Peter Ndumbe
Science *(FS)* (Biochemistry; Biology; Computer Science; Earth Sciences; Inorganic Chemistry; Mathematics; Natural Sciences; Organic Chemistry; Physics; Physiology) *Dean:* Jean Wouafo Kamga

Schools
Polytechnic *(Ecole Nationale Supérieure Polytechnique)* (Chemistry; Civil Engineering; Computer Engineering; Electrical Engineering; Engineering; Industrial Engineering; Mechanical Engineering; Physics; Technology; Urban Studies) *Head:* Max Ayina Ohandja
Teacher Training *(Ecole normale supérieure (ENS))* (Biology; Chemistry; Education; Educational Sciences; English; Foreign Languages Education; French; Geography; History; Mathematics Education; Philosophy; Physics; Teacher Training) *Head:* François Mathurin Minyono Nkodo

Centres
Biotechnology (Biological and Life Sciences; Biotechnology; Pharmacy) *Head:* Denis Omoloko
Information Technology *Head:* Gabriel Nguetseng

History: Founded 1962, replacing the Institut national d'Etudes supérieures, founded 1961. Acquired present status and title 1993. A State Institution responsible to the Ministry of Education.

Governing Bodies: Conseil de l'Université; Conseil d'Administration presided by the Rector (Senate and Council).

Academic Year: October to August (October-February; March-August)

Admission Requirements: Secondary school certificate (baccalauréat) or foreign equivalent, and entrance examination (for Medicine and Engineering)

Fees: (Francs CFA): 50,000 per annum; foreign students, 600,000 per annum for Science and Technology; 300,000 for foreign students in Arts and Education

Main Language(s) of Instruction: French, English

International Co-operation: Participates in the Fulbright Grant programme.

Degrees and Diplomas: *Bachelor's Degree*: Letters (BA); Science (BSc), 3 yrs; *Diplôme de Professeur des Collèges d'Enseignement général*: Teaching Qualification (DIPCEG), 2 yrs; *Licence*: Economics; Law; Letters; Science, 3 yrs; *Diplôme d'Ingénieur*: Engineering (Dip.Ing), 5 yrs; *Diplôme de Professeur des Lycées d'Enseignement général*: Teaching Qualification (DIPES II), 4 yrs; *Maîtrise*: a further 1-2 yrs; *Master's Degree*: (MA; MSc), a further 1-2 yrs; *Doctorat en Médecine*: Medicine (BM; BS), 6-7 yrs; *Doctorat de troisième Cycle*: (Doc. 3e cycle), 2-3 yrs; *Doctorat/Doctorate*: (PhD); (PhD), a further 2-3 yrs

Student Services: Academic Counselling, Social Counselling, Employment Services, Sports Facilities, Language Programmes, Health Services, Canteen

Student Residential Facilities: Yes

Libraries: Central Library, c. 90,000 vols

Publications: Annales des Facultés (annually); Sosongo; Revue Ecriture; Syllabus

Academic Staff *2001-2002:* Full-Time: c. 780 Part-Time: c. 150 Total: c. 930

Student Numbers *2001-2002:* Total: c. 21,000

UNIVERSITY OF YAOUNDÉ II
Université de Yaoundé II (UY II)
BP 48, Yaoundé
Tel: +237(221) 3403
Fax: +237(221) 6553

Recteur: Jean Tabi Manga (2003-)
Secrétaire général: Jean Ongla
International Relations: Georges E. Ekodeck

Faculties
Economics and Management *(FSEG)* (Economics; Management) *Dean*: Touna Mama
Law and Political Science *(FSJP)* (Law; Political Science) *Dean*: Maurice Kamto

Higher Schools
Mass Communication *(ESSTIC)* (Information Sciences; Journalism; Mass Communication; Radio and Television Broadcasting) *Director*: Marc Joseph Ombga

Institutes
International Relations *(of Cameroon, IRIC) Director*: Jean Emmanuel Pondi
Training and Demographic Research *(IFORD)* (Demography and Population) *Director*: Eliwo Akoto

History: Founded 1993.

Academic Year: October to July (October-December; January-March; April-July)

Admission Requirements: Secondary school certificate (baccalauréat) or foreign equivalent, and entrance examination

Main Language(s) of Instruction: French, English

Degrees and Diplomas: *Brevet de Technicien*: Information, 2 yrs; *Licence*: Economics; Law, 3 yrs; *Diplôme*: Journalism, 3 yrs; *Maîtrise*: International Relations; Political Science, 5 yrs; Law, a further 2 yr; Economics, a further 2 yrs; *Doctorat/Doctorate*: Law; Science, 2-4 yrs following Maîtrise; International Relations, 4 yrs

Libraries: Bibliothèque de l'Université

PRIVATE INSTITUTIONS

CATHOLIC INSTITUTE OF YAOUNDÉ-CATHOLIC UNIVERSITY OF CENTRAL AFRICA
Institut catholique de Yaoundé-Université catholique d'Afrique centrale (ICY/UCAC)
Yaoundé, Centre 11628
Tel: +237(223) 7400
Fax: +237(223) 7402
EMail: ucac.icy-nk@camnet.cm

Recteur: Oscar Eone Eone (1999-) Tel: +237(223) 7401
International Relations: Gilles Noudjag

Faculties
Philosophy *Dean*: Gabriel Ndinga
Social Sciences and Management (Accountancy; Computer Science; Economics; Law; Management; Political Science; Social Sciences) *Dean*: Louis De Vaocelles
Theology *Dean*: Antoine Babe

Board of Studies
Accountancy-Finance (Accountancy; Finance) *Coordinator*: Célestin Nenta
Human Rights Research *(GRDH)* (Human Rights) *Director*: Jean-Didier Boukongou
Interdisciplinary Studies on African Theology (African Studies; Theology) *Director*: Antoine Babé
Promotion of Human Dignity in Africa (Ethics; Law) *Director*: Jean Didier Boukongou
Socio-Anthropology *(IRSA)* (Anthropology; Sociology) *Director*: Séverin Cécile Abega

Departments
Canon Law *Director*: Silvia Recchi
Nursing *Director*: Renée Geoffray

Research Groups
Artificial Intelligence and Management Sciences *(GRIAGES)* (Artificial Intelligence; Management) *Director*: Philippe Dubin
Business and Culture *(GREC)* (Business Administration; Cultural Studies) *Director*: Philippe Dubin

History: Founded 1989, opened 1991.

Governing Bodies: Administrative Council; Private Council; Permanent Council; Academic Council

Academic Year: October to June (October-February; March-June)

Admission Requirements: Secondary school certificate (baccalauréat), or foreign equivalent

Fees: (Francs CFA): 365,000-825,000 per annum

Main Language(s) of Instruction: French

Degrees and Diplomas: *Diplôme d'Etudes universitaires en Sciences sociales (DEUSS)* : Social Sciences, 2 yrs; *Diplôme d'Etudes universitaires générales (DEUG)*: Philosophy, 2 yrs; *Diplôme universitaire de Technologie (DUT)*: Management; Commerce; Marketing and Sales, 2 yrs; *Licence*: Management; Commerce; Marketing and Sales; Social Anthropology; Political Science and Law; Human Resource Management (LEG, LICOD, LSS), 3 yrs; *Maîtrise*: 3-5 yrs; Finance and Accountancy; Management; Commerce; Marketing and Sales; Social Anthropology; Political Science and Law; Human Resource Management (MSTCF; MEG; MAGICOI; MSS), 4 yrs; *Diplôme d'Etudes approfondies (DEA)*: 6 yrs; *Diplôme d'Etudes supérieures spécialisées (DESS)*: African Projects Management, 5 yrs

Student Services: Sports Facilities, Health Services, Canteen

Student Residential Facilities: For 215 students

Libraries: 38,850 vols

Publications: Cahiers de l'UCAC (annually)

Press or Publishing House: Presses de l'USAC

Academic Staff 2001-2002	MEN	WOMEN	TOTAL
FULL-TIME	42	14	56
PART-TIME	16	18	34
TOTAL	**58**	**32**	**90**
STAFF WITH DOCTORATE			
FULL-TIME	26	4	30
PART-TIME	56	8	64
TOTAL	**82**	**12**	**94**
Student Numbers 2001-2002	MEN	WOMEN	TOTAL
All (Foreign Included)	806	568	**1,374**
FOREIGN ONLY	167	64	231

Part-time Students, 55 **Evening Students,** 74

COSENDAI ADVENTIST UNIVERSITY

Université Adventiste Cosendai
Nanga-Eboko, Centre

Faculties
Management and Computer Science (Accountancy; Business Administration; Computer Science; Finance; Management; Software Engineering)
Theology

OTHER INSTITUTIONS

PUBLIC INSTITUTIONS

HIGHER INSTITUTE OF PUBLIC MANAGEMENT

Institut supérieur de Management public (ISMP)
B.P. 1280, Yaoundé
EMail: ismp.cba@lom.camnet.cm

Departments
Public Administration

INSTITUTE OF ADMINISTRATION AND FINANCE

Institut des Techniques administratives et financières (ITAF)
BP 23-11-40, Yaoundé
Tel: +237(223) 2013
Administration; Finance

INSTITUTE OF STATISTICS AND APPLIED ECONOMICS

Institut sous-régional de Statistiques et d'Economie appliquée (ISSEA)
BP 294, Yaoundé
Tel: +237(222) 0134
Founded: 1961
Applied Statistics and Economics (Economics; Statistics)

INSTITUTE OF TRAINING AND RESEARCH IN DEMOGRAPHY

Institut de Formation et de Recherche démographiques (IFORD)
BP 1556, Yaoundé
Tel: +237(222) 2471
Founded: 1972
Demography Research (Demography and Population)

INTERNATIONAL INSTITUTE OF INSURANCE

Institut International des Assurances (IIA)
BP 1575, Yaoundé, Centre 1575
Tel: +237(220) 7152
Fax: +237(220) 7151
EMail: iia@syfed.cm.refer.org
Website: http://www.cm.refer.org

Directeur général: Jean Gratien Zanouvi (1996-)
EMail: DG-iia@syfed.cm.org

Directeur Administratif et Financier: Albert Mboko
Mondombélé EMail: DAF-iia@syfed.cm.refer.org

International Relations: Momath Ndao
EMail: DE-iia@syfed.cm.refer.org

Founded: 1972, 1992
Insurance Management and Studies *(International)* (Insurance)

History: Founded 1972. Acquired present status 1992.
Governing Bodies: Conseil des Ministres; Conseil d'Administration
Academic Year: December to November
Admission Requirements: DEUG for cycle II, MSTA; Master for cycle III, DESSA
Main Language(s) of Instruction: French
International Co-operation: CAMES; AUF; Association des Etablissements Francophones de Formation à l' Assurance (AIEFFA)
Degrees and Diplomas: *Diplôme*: Technology, 2 yrs; *Diplôme d'Etudes supérieures spécialisées (DESS)*: Insurance; Management, 2 yrs
Student Services: Foreign Student Adviser, Cultural Centre, Sports Facilities, Health Services, Canteen

Student Residential Facilities: Yes

Publications: Afrique Assurance, Research in the field of Insurance (biannually); 'Assur Echo', Student magazine (annually)

Student Numbers *2001-2002:* Total: c. 60

NATIONAL CENTRE FOR ADMINISTRATION AND MAGISTRACY
Centre national d' Administration et de Magistrature (CENAM)
BP 128, Yaoundé
Tel: +237(222) 2431

Administration
Magistracy (Justice Administration)

NATIONAL HIGHER SCHOOL OF CIVIL ENGINEERING
Ecole nationale supérieure des Travaux publics (ENSTP)
BP 510, Yaoundé, Centre
Tel: +237(222) 0406
Fax: +237(223) 0944
EMail: enstp@iccnet.cm

Directeur: George Elambo Nkeng Tel: +237(222) 1816
Fax: +237(222) 1816 EMail: gnkeng@yahoo.com

Administrative Officer: Biboa Embogo Gatien

Founded: 1982

Departments
Civil Engineering (Civil Engineering; Town Planning) *Head*: Emmanuel Etonde Sosso
Management (Engineering Management; Management) *Head*: Jean Tchami
Rural Engineering (Agricultural Engineering; Surveying and Mapping) *Head*: André Talla

Governing Bodies: Ministère des Travaux Publics

Academic Year: September to June

Admission Requirements: Secondary school certificate (GCE Advanced Level)

Main Language(s) of Instruction: French, English

Degrees and Diplomas: *Diplôme de Technicien supérieur*: Civil Engineering; Rural Engineering, 2 yrs; *Diplôme d'Ingénieur des Travaux*: Civil Engineering; Rural Engineering, 3 yrs; *Master's Degree*: Engineering Management (MSc Engineering Mgt), 2 yrs

Student Services: Academic Counselling, Social Counselling, Sports Facilities, Language Programmes, Health Services

Student Residential Facilities: None

Academic Staff *2001-2002*: Full-Time: c. 60 Part-Time: c. 70 Total: c. 130

Student Numbers *2001-2002:* Total: c. 500

NATIONAL HIGHER SCHOOL OF POLICE STUDIES
Ecole nationale supérieure de Police (ENSP)
BP 148, Yaoundé
Tel: +237(222) 4260

Police Studies

NATIONAL HIGHER SCHOOL OF POST AND TELECOMMUNICATIONS
Ecole nationale supérieure des Postes et Télécommunications (ENSPT)
BP 1186, Yaoundé
Tel: +237(222) 3700
Fax: +237 (223) 5005
EMail: enspt1@camnet.cm
Website: http://www.camnet.cm/enspt/

Post and Telecommunications (Postal Services; Telecommunications Services)

NATIONAL INSTITUTE OF YOUTH AND SPORT
Institut national de la Jeunesse et des Sports (INJS)
BP 1016, Yaoundé

Founded: 1961
Physical Education

NATIONAL SCHOOL FOR ADMINISTRATION AND MAGISTRACY
Ecole nationale d'Administration et de Magistrature (ENAM)
BP 7171, Yaoundé
Tel: +237(222) 3754
Fax: +237(223) 1308

Directeur général: Benjamin Amama Tel: +237(223) 1308
Directeur suppléant: André Abate Messanga
Tel: +237(223) 0931
International Relations: Constantin Abena

Founded: 1959, 1995

Divisions
Accountancy and Taxation (Accountancy; Taxation) *Head*: Jacques Burnouf
Administration (Administration; Labour and Industrial Relations; Social Welfare) *Head*: Abdoulaye Nana
Justice Administration *Head*: Bruno Latastate

Centres
Research and Documentation (Documentation Techniques) *Head*: Constantin Abena

History: Founded 1959. Acquired present status 1995.

Governing Bodies: Conseil d'Administration

Admission Requirements: Secondary school certificate or equivalent and competitive entrance examination

Main Language(s) of Instruction: French, English

Student Services: Sports Facilities, Language Programmes

Publications: Journal de l'ENAM (biannually)

Academic Staff *2001-2002*: Full-Time: c. 70 Part-Time: c. 30 Total: c. 100

Staff with doctorate: Total: c. 10

Student Numbers *2001-2002:* Total: c. 1,070

NATIONAL SCHOOL OF SOCIAL WORKERS
Ecole nationale des Assistantes des Affaires sociales (ENAAS)
Yaoundé

Social Work

PANAFRICAN INSTITUTE FOR DEVELOPMENT IN CENTRAL AFRICA
Institut panafricain pour le Développement en Afrique Centrale (IPD-AC/PAID-CA)
BP 4078, Douala, Littoral
Tel: +237(340) 3770
Fax: +237(340) 3968
Telex: 6048 KN
EMail: ipdac@camnet.cm

Directeur: Ernest Zocli (1996-)

Directeur adjoint: Jacob Ngwa

International Relations: Faya Kondiano, Secrétaire général Tel: +237(342) 1061 Fax: +237(342) 4335

Founded: 1965

Institutes
Panafrican Development (Adult Education; African Studies; Development Studies; Library Science; Natural Resources; Rural Studies) *Director:* Ernest Zocli

History: Founded 1965, IPD-AC contributes to the development of regions through training, research and practical action, counselling, publication and institution development.

Governing Bodies: Conseil d'Administration

Academic Year: October to September

Admission Requirements: Secondary school certificate or equivalent

Main Language(s) of Instruction: French

Degrees and Diplomas: *Diplôme de Technicien supérieur:* Environmental Studies; Business Management; Finance; Natural Resources Management (DCTD), 2 yrs; *Diplôme d'Etudes supérieures spécialisées (DESS).* Also Certificat de fin de Formation, 1-7 months

Student Services: Academic Counselling, Sports Facilities, Health Services, Canteen

Student Residential Facilities: None

Libraries: Main Library

Publications: Nouvelles de l'IPD-AC (biannually)

Academic Staff *2001-2002*: Full-Time: c. 15 Part-Time: c. 10 Total: c. 25

Staff with doctorate: Total: c. 5

Student Numbers *2001-2002*: All (Foreign Included): c. 130 Foreign Only: c. 80

PRIVATE INSTITUTIONS

BTS UNITED PROFESSORS
BTS Professeurs Réunis
BP 5297, Douala
Tel: +237(778) 4573

Programmes
Commerce and Management (Accountancy; Business Administration; Business and Commerce; Business Computing; International Business; Secretarial Studies)

FACULTY OF PROTESTANT THEOLOGY
Faculté de Théologie protestante de Yaoundé
PO Box 4011, Yaoundé, Center Province
Tel: +237(221) 2690
Fax: +237(220) 5324
EMail: unipro@acamnet.cm

Dean: Maurice Kouam

Academic Secretary: Jean-Samuel Zoe-Obianga

International Relations: Friedegard Schneider Owono

Founded: 1962
Protestant Theology *Dean:* Maurice Kouam

History: Founded 1962.

Admission Requirements: Baccalauréat; Licence

Main Language(s) of Instruction: French

Degrees and Diplomas: *Maîtrise:* Theology, 2 yrs; *Doctorat/Doctorate:* Theology, 5 yrs

Student Services: Academic Counselling, Employment Services, Nursery Care, Sports Facilities, Health Services, Canteen

Publications: Marturia, Lettre de la Faculté

Press or Publishing House: Flambeau

Academic Staff *2001-2002*: Full-Time: c. 10 Part-Time: c. 10 Total: c. 20

Student Numbers *2001-2002*: All (Foreign Included): c. 180 Foreign Only: c. 100

FONAB POLYTECHNIC
BP 370, Bamenda
Tel: +237(336) 2750

Programmes
Education and Professional Development (Curriculum; Education; Educational Administration; Pedagogy)

HIGHER INSTITUTE OF TECHNOLOGY AND INDUSTRIAL DESIGN
Institut supérieur des Technologies et du Design Industriel (ISTDI)
BP 3001, Douala
Tel: +237(968) 4612

Programmes
Industrial Design
Technology

HIGHER MANAGEMENT INSTITUTE
Institut supérieur de Management (ISMA)
BP 5739, Douala
Tel: +237(943) 1251
Fax: +237(343) 1259

Programmes
Commerce (Business and Commerce)
Management

HIGHER SAMBA INSTITUTE
Institut Samba Supérieur (INSASUP)
BP 2490, Yaoundé
Tel: +237(997) 7135

Programmes
Accountancy and Business Administration (Accountancy; Business Administration)
Automobile Maintenance (Maintenance Technology)
Commerce (Business and Commerce; International Business)
Electronics (Electronic Engineering)
Hotel and Restaurant
Journalism
Management Computing (Computer Science; Management)
Secretarial Studies
Social and Family Economics (Economics)

HIGHER SIANTOU INSTITUTE
Institut Siantou Supérieur (ISS)
BP 04, Yaoundé
Tel: +237(955) 9141
EMail: siantou@gcnet.cm
Website: http://www.gcnet.cm/siantou

Programmes
Accountancy
Commerce (Business and Commerce)
Communication (Communication Studies; Journalism; Photography)
Economics
Electronic Engineering

Law
Management
Mechanical Engineering

HIGHER SCHOOL OF MANAGEMENT
Ecole supérieure de Gestion (ESG)
BP 12489, Douala
Tel: +237(337) 5059 +237(337) 5060
Fax: +237(342) 8902
EMail: esg@camnet.cm

Programmes
Commerce and Management (Accountancy; Business Administration; Business and Commerce; Business Computing; International Business; Secretarial Studies)
Communication (Communication Studies; Journalism)

HIGHER SCHOOL OF SCIENCE AND TECHNIQUES
Ecole supérieure des Sciences et Techniques (ESSET)
BP 13244, Douala
Tel: +237(343) 3893

Programmes
Commerce and Management (Accountancy; Business Administration; Business Computing; Insurance; International Business; Secretarial Studies)
Industry and Technology (Electrical Engineering; Electronic Engineering; Industrial Engineering; Maintenance Technology; Technology)

NATIONAL POLYTECHNIC BAMBUI
BP 214, Bamenda
Tel: +237(336) 3293 +237(336) 3653
Fax: +237(336) 2033
EMail: napolytechn@bamenda.org

Programmes
Business, Finance and Management (Accountancy; Banking; Finance; Insurance; Management; Marketing)
Engineering and Technology (Electrical and Electronic Engineering; Engineering; Technology; Telecommunications Engineering)
Journalism and Media (Journalism; Media Studies)

TANKOU GROUP OF HIGHER EDUCATION
Groupe Tankou d'Enseignement supérieur (GTES)
BP 1160, Bafoussam
Tel: +237(955) 9141

Programmes
Commerce and Management (Accountancy; Business Administration; Business and Commerce; Business Computing; Secretarial Studies)

Cape Verde

INSTITUTION TYPES AND CREDENTIALS

Types of higher education institutions:

Universidade (University)
Higher Institute

School leaving and higher education credentials:

Certificado da Habilitações Literárias
Bacharelato
Licenciatura
Mestrado
Doutoramento

STRUCTURE OF EDUCATION SYSTEM

Pre-higher education:

Duration of compulsory education:

Age of entry: 6
Age of exit: 12

Structure of school system:

Primary
Type of school providing this education: Primary School
Length of programme in years: 6
Age level from: 6 to: 12
Certificate/diploma awarded: Diploma de Ensino Primário de Segundo Grau

First Cycle Secondary
Type of school providing this education: First Cycle Secondary school (Tronco Comun)
Length of programme in years: 2
Age level from: 12 to: 14
Certificate/diploma awarded: National Examination

Second Cycle Secondary
Type of school providing this education: Second Cycle Secondary School
Length of programme in years: 2
Age level from: 14 to: 16

Certificate/diploma awarded: Certificado de Habilitações Literárias (Secondary School Leaving Certificate)

Third Cycle Secondary
Type of school providing this education: Third Cycle Secondary School
Length of programme in years: 2
Age level from: 16 to: 18

Technical
Type of school providing this education: Technical Secondary School
Length of programme in years: 4
Age level from: 14 to: 18
Certificate/diploma awarded: Technician Diploma

School education:

Primary education lasts for six years and leads to the Diploma de Ensino Primário de Segundo Grau. Secondary education lasts for six years and is divided into three cycles of two years each, leading to the Habilitações Literárias. Access to higher education requires an entrance examination. Technical education is offered in the last two cycles of secondary education.

Higher education:

Higher education is mainly provided by the Universidade Jean Piaget de Cabo Verde and higher institutes (Institutos superiores) offering courses in Education, Marine Science, Engineering, Accountancy, Marketing and Languages .

Main laws/decrees governing higher education:

Decree: Decreto-Lei nº30/2002   Year: 2002
Concerns: Organization of Government and Ministries

Decree: Lei nº 113/V/99 de Bases do Sistema Educativo   Year: 1999
Concerns: Public and Private Education System (including higher education)

Languages of instruction:

Portuguese

Stages of studies:

University level studies:

University level first stage: *Bacharelato*:
The first stage leads to the Bacharelato after 3 years.

University level second stage: *Licenciatura*:
The second stage leads to the Licenciatura following a further two years of study.

University level third stage: *Mestrado*:
The third stage leads to the Mestrado after two years' further study beyond the Licenciatura.

University level fourth stage: *Doutoramento*:
The fourth stage leads to the Doutoramento following four years' further study.

Teacher education:

Training of pre-primary and primary/basic school teachers
Primary school teachers are trained in the Instituto Pedagógico where they obtain the Magistério Primário.

Training of secondary school teachers
Secondary school teachers must hold a degree at the level of a Bacharelado, a Licenciatura or a Mestrado

Non-traditional studies:

Distance higher education
Licenciatura courses in Education and Administration are organized through the Universidade Aberta in Portugal.

NATIONAL BODIES

Responsible authorities:

Ministry of Education and Valorization of Human Resources (Ministério de Educação e Valorização dos Recursos Humanos)
Minister: Victor Manuel Barbosa Borges
C.P. 111
Praía
Tel: +238 61-05-07
Fax: +238 61-27-64
EMail: GEDSE@mail.cvtelecom.cv
WWW: http://www.gov.cv/minedu

ADMISSIONS TO HIGHER EDUCATION

Admission to university-level studies

Name of secondary school credential required: Certificado da Habilitações Literárias
For entry to: Universities and Institutes

Alternatives to credentials: Completion of middle level technician courses may also qualify a student for undergraduate entry.

Entrance exams required: Entrance examination

Recognition of studies and qualifications:

Studies pursued in foreign countries (bodies dealing with recognition of foreign credentials):
Equivalence Commission, General Directorate for Higher Education and Science (Comissão Nacional de Equivalências, Direcção-Geral do Ensino Superior e Ciência)
Ministry of Education

C.P. 111
Praía

NOTES ON HIGHER EDUCATION SYSTEM

Data for academic year: 2002-2003
Source: Cape Verde Permanent Delegation to Unesco, Paris, 2003 and Ministry of Education website, 2004 (www.gov.cv/minedu)

INSTITUTIONS OF HIGHER EDUCATION

UNIVERSITIES

• JEAN PIAGET UNIVERSITY OF CAPE VERDE
Universidade Jean Piaget de Cabo Verde
Campus Universitário da Cidade de Praía, Palmarejo Grande, Cidade da Praía
Tel: +238 62 90 85
Fax: +238 62 90 89
EMail: info@caboverde.ipiaget.org
Website: http://www.caboverde.ipiaget.org

Reitora: Estela Pinto Ribeiro Lamas
EMail: elamas@gaia.ipiaget.pt
Vice-reitor: Jorge Sousa Brito
Administrador Geral: David Ribeiro Lamas

Courses
Architecture
Civil Engineering
Communication Sciences (Communication Studies)
Computer Science
Economics and Management (Economics; Management)
Educational Sciences
English Language and Literature (English; Literature)
Hotel Management and Tourism (Hotel Management; Tourism)
Management Informatics (Computer Science; Management)
Mathematics
Nursing
Pharmacy
Physics and Chemistry (Chemistry; Physics)
Physiotherapy (Physical Therapy)
Portuguese Language and Literature (Literature; Portuguese)
Psychology
Socio-professional Studies
Sociology
Systems Engineering and Computer Science (Computer Science; Systems Analysis)

History: Founded 2001.

Main Language(s) of Instruction: Portuguese

Degrees and Diplomas: *Bacharelato:* Architecture; Communication Sciences; Educational Sciences; Economics and Management; Social Work; Nursing; Civil Engineering; Computer Engineering; Physics and Chemistry; Mathematics; English; Portuguese; Hotel Management and Tourism; Business Computing; Psychology; Sociology, 3 yrs; *Licenciatura:* Architecture; Communication Sciences; Educational Sciences; Economics and Management; Social Work; Nursing; Civil Engineering; Computer Engineering; Physics and Chemistry; Mathematics; English; Portuguese; Hotel Management and Tourism; Business Computing; Psychology; Sociology; Pharmacy; Physical Therapy, a further 2 yrs; *Mestrado:* 2 yrs following *Licenciatura; Doutoramento:* 4 yrs

Libraries: 4872 vols

Student Numbers *2002-2003:* Total: c. 700

OTHER INSTITUTIONS

INSTITUTO DE ENSINO SUPERIOR ISIDORO DA GRAÇA (IESIG)
CP 648, Rua Patrice Lumumba, Mindelo
Tel: +238-326810
Fax: +238-325132
Website: http://www.iesig-cv.org

President: Albertino Graça

Founded: 2002
Anthropology; Computer Science; Education; History; Hotel Management; Sociology; Tourism
Degrees and Diplomas: *Bacharelato; Licenciatura*

INSTITUTO NACIONAL DE INVESTIGAÇÃO E DESENVOLVIMENTO AGRÁRIO (INIDA)
Endereço São Jorge do òrgãos Santiago CP 84, Cidade de Praia
Tel: +238 71-11-47
Fax: +238 71-11-33
EMail: inida@cvtelecom.cv

Presidente: António Luis Evora

Departments
Agriculture

INSTITUTO SUPERIOR DE CIÊNCIAS ECONÓMICAS E EMPRESARIAIS (ISCEE)
Endereço Praça José Lopes, Mindelo
Tel: +238 32-40-70
Fax: +238 323-1075
EMail: iscee@cvtelecom.cv

Coordeenadora: Helena Rebelo Rodrigues

Founded: 1998
Accountancy; Marketing

INSTITUTO SUPERIOR DE EDUCAÇÃO (ISE)

Endereço Ministério da Educação CP 279, Praceta Dr Antonio Lereno, Cidade da Praía
Tel: +238 61-12-68
Fax: +238 61-41-89
EMail: pise@cvtelecom.cv
Presidente: Maria Cãndida Gonçalves

Founded: 1995
Education

INSTITUTO SUPERIOR DE ENGENHARIA E CIÊNCIAS DO MAR (ISECMAR)

Endereço Ribeira de São Julião-S. Vicente CP 163, Mindelo
Tel: +238 32-11-29
Fax: +238 31-18-06
EMail: info@isecmar.cv
Website: http://www.isecmar.cv
Presidente: Elisa Lopes da Cruz Ferreira da Silva

Founded: 1996

Departments

Electronic and Computer Engineering (Automation and Control Engineering; Computer Engineering; Electrical and Electronic Engineering; Telecommunications Engineering) *Director*: Abel Felisberto de Oliveira Almada

Fisheries and Aquatic Resources (Fishery; Marine Biology) *Director*: José Manuel Lima Ramos

Mechanical and Electrical-Mechanical Engineering (Civil Engineering; Electrical Engineering; Marine Engineering; Mechanical Engineering) *Director*: Manuel Eduardo Fortes Tavares de Almeida

Nautical Science (Marine Engineering; Nautical Science) *Director*: Daniel Marcos Sousa Lopes

History: Founded 1996.

Degrees and Diplomas: *Bacharelato*; *Licenciatura*

Central African Republic

INSTITUTION TYPES AND CREDENTIALS

Types of higher education institutions:

Université (University)
Institut (Institute)
Ecole normale (Teacher Training College)

School leaving and higher education credentials:

Baccalauréat
Capacité en Droit
Diplôme
Diplôme de Technicien supérieur de Santé
Diplôme universitaire de Technologie (DUT)
Diplôme d'Etudes économiques générales (DEEG)
Diplôme d'Etudes juridiques générales (DEJG)
Diplôme d'Etudes universitaires générales (DEUG)
Diplôme universitaire d'Etudes littéraires (DUEL)
Diplôme universitaire d'Etudes scientifiques (DUES)
Certificat d'Aptitude pédagogique à l'Enseignement secondaire
Diplôme d'Ingénieur
Diplôme supérieur de Gestion (DSG)
Licence
Maîtrise
Doctorat en Médecine

STRUCTURE OF EDUCATION SYSTEM

Pre-higher education:

Duration of compulsory education:

Age of entry: 6
Age of exit: 12

Structure of school system:

Basic First Stage
Type of school providing this education: Ecole primaire
Length of programme in years: 6

Age level from: 6 to: 12

Certificate/diploma awarded: Certificat d'Etudes fondamentales 1 (CEF)

Basic Second Stage

Type of school providing this education: College d'Enseignement secondaire

Length of programme in years: 4

Age level from: 12 to: 16

Certificate/diploma awarded: Brevet d'Etudes fondamentales 2 (BEF)(formerly Brevet d'Etudes du premier Cycle)

General Secondary

Type of school providing this education: Lycée

Length of programme in years: 3

Age level from: 16 to: 19

Certificate/diploma awarded: Baccalauréat

Technical Secondary

Type of school providing this education: Collège d'Enseignement technique

Length of programme in years: 3

Age level from: 15 to: 18

Certificate/diploma awarded: Certificat d'Aptitude professionnelle (CAP)

Technical

Type of school providing this education: Lycée technique

Length of programme in years: 3

Age level from: 16 to: 19

Certificate/diploma awarded: Baccalauréat de Technicien

School education:

Basic education lasts for ten years divided into six years' basic first stage (compulsory), leading to the Certificat d'Etudes fondamentales 1 and four years' basic second stage, leading to the Brevet d'Etudes fondamentales 2. General secondary school lasts for three years and leads to the Baccalauréat which gives access to higher education.

Technical education at secondary level is offered at two levels: Form 4 school leavers may study for four years in a College d'Enseignement technique and obtain the Certificat d'Aptitude professionnelle (CAP); and Form 3 school leavers may study for three years at a lycée technique and obtain the Baccalauréat de Technicien.

Higher education:

Postsecondary education is offered at the Université de Bangui, which comprises faculties, institutes and a Higher Teacher Training College (Ecole normale supérieure). The Administrative Council, presided over by the Minister of National Education and Higher Education and composed of people nominated by the Minister of Finance, implements the University's development plan set out by the government. The University Council, presided over by the President of the university, approves proposed official documents to be submitted to higher authorities. It is consulted about the regulations, organization and programme of study.

Main laws/decrees governing higher education:

Decree: Loi n° 97/04   Year: 1997
Concerns: Education Policy

Decree: Décret n°85/264   Year: 1985
Concerns: Statutes of the University

Decree: Ordonnance n°69/0063   Year: 1969
Concerns: Université de Bangui

Academic year:

Classes from: September *to:* July

Long vacation from: 30 June *to:* 1 September

Languages of instruction:

French

Stages of studies:

Non-university level post-secondary studies (technical/vocational type):

Technical education is offered at the University of Bangui. Higher vocational education is also offered in a number of new private 2-year institutes.

University level studies:

University level first stage: Premier Cycle:

The first cycle lasts two years. Admission is based on the Baccalauréat. It leads to a degree which bears the name of the specialization in which it is awarded: Diplôme d'Etudes universitaires générales (DEUG), Diplôme universitaire d'Etudes littéraires (DUEL), Diplôme universitaire d'Etudes scientifiques (DUES), Diplôme universitaire d'Etudes juridiques (DUEJ), Diplôme d'Etudes économiques générales (DEEG).

University level second stage: Deuxième Cycle:

The second cycle lasts one year after the Diploma programme and leads to the Licence. In Engineering, the Diplôme d'Ingénieur is conferred after three years' study and a Diplôme d'Ingénieur d'Agriculture is awarded after four years. A further year leads to the Maîtrise (in the University). In Medicine, a Doctorate is awarded after six years. It is the only Doctorate awarded by the University.

Teacher education:

Training of pre-primary and primary/basic school teachers

First stage basic school teachers are trained in two years after the Baccalauréat at the Ecole normale d'Instituteurs. The course leads to the Certificat d'Aptitude pédagogique à l'Enseignement fondamental 1.

Training of secondary school teachers

Second stage basic school teachers are trained in the Ecoles normales in three years leading to the Certificat d'Aptitude pédagogique à l'Enseignement fondamental 2.

Lycée teachers must normally hold a Licence and take a two-year course at the Ecole normale Supérieure de Bangui. They are awarded the Certificat d'Aptitude pédagogique à l'Enseignement secondaire (CAPES). Technical secondary school teachers are awarded the Certificat d'Aptitude au Professorat de l'Enseignement technique (CAPET) after two years' study;

Training of higher education teachers
Higher education teachers must hold a DEA or DESS (Assistants) or a Doctorate and years of experience for Maîtres de Conference and Professors

NATIONAL BODIES

Responsible authorities:

Ministry of National and Higher Education (Ministère de l'Education nationale et de l'Enseignement supérieur (MENES))
    Minister: Timoléon M'baikoua
    PO Box 1583
    Bangui
    Tel: +236(61) 72-19
    Fax: +236(61) 72-19
    Telex: mineduc5333rc bangui

ADMISSIONS TO HIGHER EDUCATION

Admission to non university higher education studies

Name of secondary school credential required: Baccalauréat

Alternatives to credentials: Baccalauréat de Technicien

Admission to university-level studies

Name of secondary school credential required: Baccalauréat

Alternatives to credentials: Completion of seven years study at secondary level is required for entrance to the following programmes: Diplôme d'Aide en Hygiène/Santé/Accoucheuse; Diplôme d'Agent de Développement communautaire.

GRADING SYSTEM

Usual grading system in secondary school

Full Description: 17-20=Très Bien; 14-16=Bien; 12-13=Assez Bien; 10-11=Passable; 0-9=Ajourné.
Highest on scale: 20
Pass/fail level: 10
Lowest on scale: 0

Main grading system used by higher education institutions

Full Description: 17-20=Très Bien; 14-16=Bien; 12-13=Assez Bien; 10-11=Passable; 0-9=Ajourné
Highest on scale: 20
Pass/fail level: 10
Lowest on scale: 0

NOTES ON HIGHER EDUCATION SYSTEM

Data for academic year: 2002-2003
Source: International Association of Universities (IAU), updated from IBE website, 2003
(www.ibe.unesco.org/International/Databanks/Wde/profilee.htm)

INSTITUTIONS OF HIGHER EDUCATION

UNIVERSITIES

PUBLIC INSTITUTIONS

• UNIVERSITY OF BANGUI

Université de Bangui
BP 1450, Avenue des Martyrs, Bangui
Tel: +236(61) 20-00
Fax: +236(61) 78-90
EMail: univ-bangui@yahoo.fr

Recteur: Isaac Benguemalet Tel: +236(61) 17-67
Secrétaire général: Gabriel Ngouandji-Tanga
Tel: +236(61) 64-60

Faculties
Arts and Humanities (Arts and Humanities; English; History; Philosophy; Spanish)
Health Sciences (Biomedicine; Community Health; Education; Health Sciences)
Law and Economics (Economics; Law)
Science and Technology (Building Technologies; Construction Engineering; Mathematics and Computer Science; Natural Sciences; Physics; Science Education; Technology) *Dean*: Jacques Ndemanda-Kamoune

Higher Schools
Teacher Training *(ENS)* (Educational Psychology; Pedagogy; Teacher Training)

Institutes
Applied Linguistics
Business Management (Business Administration)

Higher Institutes
Rural Development (Cattle Breeding; Forestry; Rural Studies)
Technology

Research Institutes
Mathematics Education

Further Information: Also 4 other University and Research Centres (History, Traditional Medicine, Pedagogy)

History: Founded 1969. Formerly Institut d' Etudes juridiques of the Fondation de l' Enseignement supérieur en Afrique centrale. Acquired present status 1985.

Governing Bodies: Conseil d' Administration

Academic Year: September to June (September-December; January-March; April-June)

Admission Requirements: Secondary school certificate (Baccalauréat) or special entrance examination

Main Language(s) of Instruction: French

Degrees and Diplomas: *Capacité en Droit*: Law, 2 yrs; *Diplôme*: Midwifery; Nursing, 3 yrs; *Diplôme de Technicien supérieur de Santé*: 4 yrs; *Diplôme universitaire de Technologie (DUT)*: Computer Science, Mining Engineering and Geology, Civil Engineering, Management, Agriculture, 3 yrs; *Diplôme d'Etudes économiques générales (DEEG)*: Law and Economics, 2 yrs; *Diplôme d'Etudes juridiques générales (DEJG)*: Law and Economics, 2 yrs; *Diplôme d'Etudes universitaires générales (DEUG)*: 2 yrs; *Diplôme universitaire d'Etudes littéraires (DUEL)*: 2 yrs; *Diplôme universitaire d'Etudes scientifiques (DUES)*: Science, 2 yrs; *Diplôme d'Ingénieur*: 3-4 yrs; *Diplôme supérieur de Gestion (DSG)*: Management, 3 yrs; *Licence*: Arts and Humanities; Economics; Law; Mathematics; Natural Sciences; Physics, 3 yrs; *Maîtrise*: Arts and Humanities; Economics; Law, 1 yr following Licence; *Doctorat en Médecine*: Medicine, 7 yrs

Student Residential Facilities: Yes

Libraries: Central Library, 28,000 vols, 600 periodicals; Health Sciences, 5200 vols, 170 periodicals

Publications: Revue d'Histoire et d'Archéologie Centrafricaine; Annales

Academic Staff *2001-2002:* Total: c. 155

Student Numbers *2001-2002:* Total: c. 6,500

OTHER INSTITUTIONS

PUBLIC INSTITUTIONS

ECOLE NATIONALE D'ADMINISTRATION ET DE MAGISTRATURE
BP 1045, Bangui
Tel: +236(61) 08-94
Fax: +236(61) 27-77
EMail: ctenam@intnet.cf

Directeur: Daniel Kosse

Departments
Administration
Magistracy (Justice Administration)

Chad

INSTITUTION TYPES AND CREDENTIALS

Types of higher education institutions:

Université (University)
Ecole nationale (National School)
Institut (Institute)

School leaving and higher education credentials:

Baccalauréat
Baccalauréat de Technicien
Diplôme d'Etudes universitaires générales (DEUG)
Diplôme universitaire d'Etudes scientifiques (DUES)
Licence
Diplôme d'Ingénieur
Maîtrise
Doctorat en Médecine

STRUCTURE OF EDUCATION SYSTEM

Pre-higher education:

Structure of school system:

Primary
Type of school providing this education: Ecole élémentaire
Length of programme in years: 6
Age level from: 6 to: 12
Certificate/diploma awarded: Certificat d'Etudes primaires (CEP)/Concours d'Entrée en sixième

First Cycle Secondary
Type of school providing this education: Collège d'Enseignement général
Length of programme in years: 4
Age level from: 12 to: 16
Certificate/diploma awarded: Brevet d'Etudes du premier Cycle (BEPC)

Technical Secondary
Type of school providing this education: Collège technique
Length of programme in years: 3

Age level from: 13 to: 16
Certificate/diploma awarded: Certificat d'Aptitude professionnelle (CAP)

Second Cycle Secondary
Type of school providing this education: Lycée
Length of programme in years: 3
Age level from: 16 to: 19
Certificate/diploma awarded: Baccalauréat

Technical
Type of school providing this education: Lycée technique commercial/industriel
Length of programme in years: 3
Age level from: 16 to: 19
Certificate/diploma awarded: Baccalauréat de Technicien

School education:

Primary education lasts for six years and leads to the Certificat d'Etudes primaires (CEP). At the same time as the CAP, pupils must pass a Concours d'Entrée en sixième. Secondary education consists of two cycles. The lower cycle, lasting four years, is offered at a Collège d'Enseignement général (CEG) or a Lycée. Completion of the first cycle leads to the Brevet d'Etudes du Premier Cycle. The higher cycle of secondary education, offered by the Lycées, lasts three years and leads to the Baccalauréat, which is usually divided into one of four specializations: Physical or Natural Sciences, Philosophy and Literature, Mathematics, or Economics and Social Sciences. Technical Lycées offer three-year courses on completion of the BEPC that lead to the Baccalauréat de technicien. Technical vocational schools offer courses from the third year of lower secondary school lasting five years and leading to certificates of vocational aptitude.

Higher education:

Higher education in Chad is provided by the only university, the Université de N'Djaména (former Université du Tchad). It is divided into four faculties: Law, Economics, and Business Administration; Letters, Modern Languages, and Human Sciences; Exact and Applied Sciences; Medicine. There are also other institutions of higher education such as the Ecole nationale des Travaux publics and the Institut supérieur des Sciences de l'Education (formerly Ecole normale supérieure). As of 1994, some other institutions have also been conferring the Diplôme d'Etudes universitaires générales.

Main laws/decrees governing higher education:

Decree: Décret no 32/PR/MENCJS/94   Year: 1994
Concerns: Université de N'Djamena

Decree: Ordonnance no 26/PR/71   Year: 1971
Concerns: Université du Tchad

Academic year:

Classes from: October *to:* June
Long vacation from: 30 June *to:* 30 September

Languages of instruction:

French, Arabic

Stages of studies:

Non-university level post-secondary studies (technical/vocational type):

There are a number of professional training institutions at the tertiary level. Students need the Baccalauréat to enter them. In addition, most of these institutions impose a selective entrance examination. These professional training institutions award degrees that are equivalent to the first university cycle. The Institut supérieur de Gestion awards the Brevet de Technicien supérieur (BTS).

University level studies:

University level first stage: *Premier Cycle*:
The first cycle lasts for two years and leads to a Diplôme d'Etudes universitaires générales in Arts and Humanities, Law and Management, and to a Diplôme universitaire d'Etudes scientifiques in Science.

University level second stage: *Deuxième Cycle*:
The second cycle of higher education leads to a Licence after one year's further study in Arts and Humanities, Law and Management, and Science. The Maîtrise is conferred one or two years after the Licence. The University awards a Doctorate in Medicine after seven years of study.

Teacher education:

Training of pre-primary and primary/basic school teachers
Teachers are required to complete a three-year upper secondary course at an Ecole normale d'Instituteurs leading to the title of Instituteur. Those who leave on completion of the first two years obtain the title of Instituteur adjoint. The entry requirement to this course is the Brevet d'Etudes du premier Cycle (BEPC).

Training of secondary school teachers
Students who hold the Baccalauréat can sit for a competitive examination for entry to the Institut supérieur des Sciences de l'Education, N'Djaména, to follow a two-year course leading to the Certificat d'Aptitude professionnelle de l'Enseignement aux Collèges d'Enseignement général (CAPCEG). The CAPCEG entitles the holders to teach at the lower secondary cycle. Since 1989, teachers with the CAPCEG can follow a two-year course at the Institut supérieur des Sciences de l'Education leading to the Certificat d'Aptitude professionelle de l'Enseignement dans les Lycées (CAPEL). Holders of the Licence are required to follow a one-year course at the Institut supérieur des Sciences de l'Education which also leads to the CAPEL.

Training of higher education teachers
For the University, same requirements as in other countries. In the Ecoles normales, teachers must hold a Licence en Sciences de l'Education or the CAPEL. For the Institut supérieur en Sciences de l'Education, teachers must hold the DEA, the Maîtrise en Sciences de l'Education, the DES or the Doctorat.

NATIONAL BODIES

Responsible authorities:

Ministry of Higher Education, Scientific Research and Vocational Training (Ministère de l'Enseignement supérieur, Recherche scientifique et Formation prof.)

Minister: Adoum Guemessou

Secrétaire général: Beyom Malo Adrien

International Relations: Dandjaye Daouna Jules

PO Box 125

N'Djaména

Tel: +235(51) 7624

Fax: +235(51) 9231

EMail: beyomadrien@yahoo.fr

ADMISSIONS TO HIGHER EDUCATION

Admission to non university higher education studies

Name of secondary school credential required: Baccalauréat de Technicien

Admission to university-level studies

Name of secondary school credential required: Baccalauréat

Alternatives to credentials: Special entrance examination to the university instead of secondary school certificate

Foreign students admission

Admission requirements: Foreign students should hold the Baccalauréat or an equivalent qualification or pass the special entrance examination to the University.

Entry regulations: Students should have a visa for entrance to Chad and a residence permit.

Health requirements: None

Language requirements: Good knowledge of French or Arabic is required.

Application procedures:

Application closing dates:

For non-university level (technical/vocational type) studies: 30 September

For university level studies: 30 September

For advanced/doctoral studies: 30 September

Recognition of studies and qualifications:

Studies pursued in foreign countries (bodies dealing with recognition of foreign credentials):

Commission d'Admission de l'Université de N'Djaména

Recteur: Mbaïlad Mbaïguinam

Secrétaire général: Abakar Zougoulou

PO Box 1117
Avenue Mobutu
N'Djaména
Tel: +235(51) 4444
Fax: +235(51) 4033
EMail: rectorat@intnet.td

References to further information on foreign student admissions and recognition of studies

Title: Annuaire de l'Université de N'Djaména
Publisher: Editions Université de N'Djaména

INTERNATIONAL COOPERATION AND EXCHANGES

Principal national bodies responsible for dealing with international cooperation and exchanges in higher education:

Service des Affaires académiques et de la Coopération internationale, Université de N'Djaména
Chef de Service des Affaires académiques et de la Coopération internationale: Gilbert Lawane
PO Box 1117
N'Djaména
Tel: +235(51) 5946 +235(51) 4444
Fax: +235(51) 4033

GRADING SYSTEM

Usual grading system in secondary school

Full Description: 16-20=Très Bien; 14-15.9=Bien; 12-13.9=Assez Bien; 10-11.9=Passable.
Highest on scale: 20
Pass/fail level: 10
Lowest on scale: 0

Main grading system used by higher education institutions

Full Description: 16-20=Très Bien; 14-15.9=Bien; 12-13.9=Assez Bien; 10-11.9=Passable
Highest on scale: 20
Pass/fail level: 10
Lowest on scale: 0

NOTES ON HIGHER EDUCATION SYSTEM

Data for academic year: 2002-2003
Source: Commission nationale tchadienne pour l'UNESCO, N'Djamena, updated by the International Association of Universities (IAU) from IBE website, 2003
(www.ibe.unesco.org/International/Databanks/Wde/profilee.htm)

INSTITUTIONS OF HIGHER EDUCATION

UNIVERSITIES

*• UNIVERSITY OF N'DJAMÉNA
Université de N'Djaména
BP 1117, Avenue Mobutu, N'Djaména
Tel: +235(51) 4444
Fax: +235(51) 4033
Telex: unitchad 53 69 kd
EMail: syfed@intnet.td

Recteur: Mbailao Mbaiguinam (2002-) Tel: +235(51) 4033
EMail: jmbailaou@yahoo.fr

Secrétaire général: Mahamat Barka EMail: syfed@intnet.td

International Relations: Gilbert Lawane
EMail: lawanegilbert@yahoo.fr

Faculties

Arts and Humanities (Arabic; Arts and Humanities; Communication Studies; English; Geography; History; Information Sciences; Linguistics; Modern Languages; Philosophy; Social Sciences) *Dean*: Tchago Bouimon

Exact and Applied Sciences (Biology; Cattle Breeding; Chemistry; Computer Science; Geology; Mathematics; Physics; Technology) *Dean*: Tagui Guelbeye

Health Sciences (Biomedicine; Health Sciences; Medicine; Public Health; Surgery) *Dean*: Ivoulsou Douphang Phang

Law and Economics (Economics; Law) *Dean*: Enoch Nodjigoto

Institutes

Humanities Research (Arts and Humanities; Social Sciences) *Director*: Moukhtar Mahamat

History: Founded 1971 as University of Chad. Comprising institutions that were formerly part of the Fondation de l' Enseignement supérieur en Afrique Centrale. Acquired present status and title 1994.

Governing Bodies: Conseil de l' Université, comprising Government representatives and members of the academic staff and student body

Academic Year: October to June (October-February; March-June)

Admission Requirements: Secondary school certificate (baccalauréat)

Fees: (Francs CFA): 40,000 per annum

Main Language(s) of Instruction: French, Arabic

International Co-operation: With universities in France, Cameroon, Libya, Sudan. Also participates in CAMES

Degrees and Diplomas: *Diplôme d'Etudes universitaires générales (DEUG)*: Arts and Humanities; Law; Management, 2 yrs; *Diplôme universitaire d'Etudes scientifiques (DUES)*: Science, 2 yrs; *Licence*: Arts and Humanities; Law; Management; Science, 3 yrs; *Diplôme d'Ingénieur*: Electromechanics; Stockraising, 4 yrs; *Maîtrise*: Electromechanics, Arts and Humanities, Law, 4 yrs; *Doctorat en Médecine*: Medicine, 7 yrs. Also Certificates.

Student Services: Sports Facilities, Health Services

Libraries: University Documentation Centre, c. 30, 000 vols

Academic Staff *2001-2002*	MEN	WOMEN	TOTAL
FULL-TIME	193	10	**203**
STAFF WITH DOCTORATE			
FULL-TIME	115	7	**122**

Student Numbers *2001-2002*	MEN	WOMEN	TOTAL
All (Foreign Included)	4,517	666	**5,183**
FOREIGN ONLY	–	–	23

HIGHER INSTITUTE FOR EDUCATION

INSTITUT SUPÉRIEUR DES SCIENCES DE L'EDUCATION (ISSED)
BP 473, N'Djaména
Tel: +235(51) 4487
Fax: +235(51) 4550

Directeur: Mayore Karyo Tel: +235(51) 6175
EMail: issed@intnet.td

Departments

Teacher Training for Primary Education (Education; Educational Administration; Educational Psychology; Primary Education) *Head*: Dingamy Djedouboum

Teacher Training for Secondary Education (Administration; Arabic; Biology; Chemistry; Curriculum; Education; Educational Technology; English; French; Geography; Geology; History; Mathematics; Physics; Secondary Education) *Head*: N. Djarangar

Teacher Training for Technical and Professional Education (Accountancy; Administration; Finance; Management) *Head*: Baba Abakoura

History: Founded 1992.

Special Facilities: Workshop; Printing workshop. Computer centre

OTHER INSTITUTIONS

ECOLE NATIONALE D'ADMINISTRATION ET DE MAGISTRATURE
BP 758, N'Djaména
Tel: +235(51) 4097
Fax: +235(51) 4356
EMail: enam@intnet.td

Directeur: Abdoulaye Saleh

Founded: 1963

Programmes
Administration; Finance; Law
Diplomacy Studies (International Relations)
Justice Administration
Technical Studies (Technology)

History: Founded 1963.

ECOLE NATIONALE DES TRAVAUX PUBLICS
BP 60, N'Djaména
Tel: +235(52) 4971
Fax: +235(52) 3420
Telex: 5222 kd

Founded: 1966

Programmes
Civil Engineering (Civil Engineering; Construction Engineering; Rural Planning; Town Planning)

History: Founded 1966.

INSTITUT DE RECHERCHE DU COTON ET DES TEXTILES
Route de Farcha, BP 764, N'Djaména
Tel: +235(51) 2751
Fax: +235(51) 3228

Founded: 1932

Programmes
Textile Technology

History: Founded 1932.

Congo

INSTITUTION TYPES AND CREDENTIALS

Types of higher education institutions:

Université (University)
Institut (Institute)
Ecole (School)

School leaving and higher education credentials:

Baccalauréat
Certificat de Capacité en Droit
Certificat d'Aptitude au Professorat dans les Collèges d'Enseignement Géneral
Certificat d'Aptitude au Professorat de l'Enseignement Technique
Diplôme Universitaire d'Etudes Littéraires (DUEL)
Diplôme Universitaire d'Etudes Scientifiques (DUES)
Certificat d'Aptitude au Professorat d'Education Physique et Sportive
Certificat d'Aptitude au Professorat dans l'Enseignement secondaire
Licence
Diplôme d'Ingénieur
Maîtrise
Diplôme d'Etudes approfondies (DEA)
Diplôme d'Etudes supérieures (DES)
Doctorat en Médecine

STRUCTURE OF EDUCATION SYSTEM

Pre-higher education:

Duration of compulsory education:

Age of entry: 6
Age of exit: 16

Structure of school system:

Primary
Type of school providing this education: Ecole Primaire
Length of programme in years: 6
Age level from: 6 to: 11
Certificate/diploma awarded: Certificat d'Etudes primaires et élémentaires (CEPE)

First Cycle Secondary
Type of school providing this education: Collège d'Enseignement général/Collège d'Enseignement Technique
Length of programme in years: 4
Age level from: 12 to: 16
Certificate/diploma awarded: Brevet d'Etudes du premier Cycle (BEPC)

Technical Secondary
Length of programme in years: 3
Age level from: 16 to: 19
Certificate/diploma awarded: Brevet de Technicien

Second Cycle Secondary
Type of school providing this education: Lycée d'Enseignement général
Length of programme in years: 3
Age level from: 16 to: 19
Certificate/diploma awarded: Baccalauréat

Technical
Type of school providing this education: Lycée technique
Length of programme in years: 4
Age level from: 16 to: 20
Certificate/diploma awarded: Baccalauréat technique

School education:

Primary school education is compulsory and covers six years leading to the Certificat d'Etudes primaires élémentaires (CEPE). It is followed by seven years of secondary school which is divided into a four-year first cycle (6ème to 3ème) and a three-year second cycle (Seconde to Terminale). Access to the first cycle is through a competitive examination and, on completion, pupils take the Brevet d'Etudes du Premier Cycle. Access to technical secondary school education is also through a competitive entrance examination in Form 5 (5ème) and, on completion, pupils obtain the Brevet d'Etudes techniques. The second cycle of secondary education takes place in lycées (general or technical) and leads to the Baccalauréat or to the Baccalauréat technique.

Higher education:

Higher education is provided by the Université Marien Ngouabi and its Instituts and Ecoles ((including the Ecole normale supérieure). The University is a public institution which is responsible to the Ministère de l'Enseignement supérieur et de la Recherche scientifique. Its resources come from a State subsidy as well as its own funds.

Main laws/decrees governing higher education:

Decree: Loi 25/95   Year: 1995
Concerns: Structure of educational system

Decree: Ordonnance No. 29/71   Year: 1971
Concerns: University

Academic year:

Classes from: October *to:* June

Long vacation from: 1 July *to:* 30 September

Languages of instruction:

French

Stages of studies:

University level studies:

University level first stage: *Premier Cycle*:

The first stage of studies leads, after two years, to the Diplôme universitaire d'Etudes littéraires (DUEL) in Arts and Humanities and the Diplôme universitaire d'Etudes scientifiques (DUES) in the Sciences.

University level second stage: *Deuxième Cycle*:

A further year's study after the DUEL or DUES leads to the Licence, a further year leads to the Maîtrise and a further two years leads to the Diplôme d'Etudes supérieures (DES). The Institut de Développement Rural (IDR) provides training in Agricultural Science. At the Institut supérieur des Sciences de la Santé (INSSA), three years' study is required to become a trained nurse (Licence en Sciences de la Santé pour les Infirmiers). INSSA also awards, after six years' study, the State degree of Doctorat en Médecine.

University level third stage: *Troisième Cycle*:

A further year behond the Maîtrise leads to the Diplôme d'Etudes approfondies in some fields of study.

Teacher education:

Training of pre-primary and primary/basic school teachers

Primary school teachers are trained for three years in teacher training colleges (ENI) at secondary level.

Training of secondary school teachers

Secondary school teachers are trained at the Ecole normale supérieure for collège and lycée teachers, at the Ecole Normale supérieure de l'Enseignement technique (ENSET) for technical education teachers, and at the Institut supérieur d'Education physique et sportive (ISEPS) for teachers of physical education and sports. A two-year course leads to the Certificat d'Aptitude au Professorat dans les Collèges d'Enseignement Général (CAP de CEG) and after a further year to the Certificat d'Aptitude au Professorat dans l'Enseignement Secondaire (CAPES). Technical teachers study for the Certificat d'Aptitude au Professorat de l'Enseignement Technique (CAPET). ISEPS offers both training and in-service training courses. A three-year course leads to the assistant teacher qualification and the Certificat d'Aptitude au Professorat d'Education Physique et Sportive (CAPEPS) is awarded on completion of a four-year course.

Training of higher education teachers

Higher education teachers must hold a Doctorat de 3ème cycle, a Doctorat or a Diplôme d'Ingénieur, generally obtained abroad.

NATIONAL BODIES

Responsible authorities:

Ministry of Higher Education and Scientific Research (Ministère de l'Enseignement supérieur et de la Recherche scientifique)

    Minister: Henri Ossebi
    Head of Cabinet: Pierre Ossete
    Brazzaville
    Tel: +242(81) 52-65
    Fax: +242(81) 52-65

Role of governing body: Supervises the higher education system and the institutions

ADMISSIONS TO HIGHER EDUCATION

Admission to university-level studies

Name of secondary school credential required: Baccalauréat

Other admission requirements: Competitive entrance examination for access to the university institutes and portfolio for access to the university faculties.

Foreign students admission

Quotas: 10% of study places are reserved for foreign students.

Application procedures:

Apply to: Division de la Scolarité et des Examens de l'Université Marien Ngouabi

    PO Box 69
    Brazzaville
    Tel: +242(81) 01-41   +242(81) 24-36
    Fax: +242(81) 01-41   +242(81) 42-07

INTERNATIONAL COOPERATION AND EXCHANGES

Principal national bodies responsible for dealing with international cooperation and exchanges in higher education:

Ministère de l'Enseignement supérieur et de la Recherche scientifique

    Brazzaville
    Tel: +242(81) 52-65
    Fax: +242(81) 52-65

GRADING SYSTEM

Usual grading system in secondary school

Full Description: Subjects are marked on a scale of 0-20 (maximum), with no official minimum pass mark. Overall grades in the Baccalauréat are: très bien (very good), bien (good), assez bien (quite good) passable (average).
Highest on scale: 20
Pass/fail level: 10
Lowest on scale: 0

Main grading system used by higher education institutions

Full Description: 0-20 (16-20 : Très bien; 14-15 : Bien; 12-13 : Assez bien; 10-11: Passable)
Highest on scale: 20
Pass/fail level: 10
Lowest on scale: 0

NOTES ON HIGHER EDUCATION SYSTEM

Data for academic year: 2002-2003
Source: International Association of Universities (IAU), updated from IBE website, 2003
(www.ibe.unesco.org/International/Databanks/Wde/profilee.htm)

INSTITUTIONS OF HIGHER EDUCATION

UNIVERSITIES

*• UNIVERSITY MARIEN NGOUABI BRAZZAVILLE

Université Marien Ngouabi
BP 69, Brazzaville
Tel: +242(81) 01-41 +242(81) 18-28
Fax: +242(81) 01-41
Telex: 5331 kg
EMail: unimariengouabi@yahoo.fr

Recteur: Charles Gombe Mbalawa

Secrétaire général: Mocktar Ongomoko

International Relations: Emmanuel Daho

Faculties

Arts and Humanities (African Studies; Arts and Humanities; Communication Studies; English; Geography; History; Linguistics; Literature; Philosophy; Social Sciences; Sociology) *Dean*: Paul Nzete

Economics (Economics; Finance) *Dean*: Hervé Diata

Health Sciences (Embryology and Reproduction Biology; Haematology; Health Sciences; Histology; Medicine; Microbiology; Midwifery; Physiology; Surgery) *Dean*: Georges Moyen

Law (Law; Private Law; Public Law) *Dean*: Bernard Tchicaya

Science *(Dolisie)* (Biology; Chemistry; Earth Sciences; Mathematics; Natural Sciences; Physics) *Dean*: Jean Moali

Schools

Administration and Training for the Magistrature *(ENAM)* (Administration; Commercial Law; Educational Sciences; Law; Management; Private Law; Psychology; Public Law) *Director*: Cyriaque Ayon-Boue

Teacher Training *(ENS) Director*: Rosalie Kama Niamayoua

Technical Education *(ENSET)* (Civil Engineering; Electrical Engineering; Food Technology; Technology Education) *Director*: Bernard Mabiala

Institutes

Management (Justice Administration; Management) *Director*: François Sita

Physical Education and Sport *(INSSA)* (Physical Education; Sports) *Director*: Bernard Packa Tchissambou

Rural Development *(IDR)* (Agricultural Equipment; Botany; Forestry; Rural Studies; Zoology) *Director*: Paul Yoka

History: Founded 1959 as Centre d'Etudes administratives et techniques supérieures. Previously formed part of the Fondation de l'Enseignement supérieur en Afrique centrale. Became Université de Brazzaville 1971, acquired present title 1977.

Governing Bodies: Comité de Direction

Academic Year: October to June (October-December; January-March; April-June)

Admission Requirements: Secondary school certificate (baccalauréat) or equivalent. Competitive entrance examination for schools and institutes and the faculty of health sciences

Fees: (CFA Francs): Foreign students: 149,500

Main Language(s) of Instruction: French

Degrees and Diplomas: *Certificat de Capacité en Droit*: Law; *Certificat d'Aptitude au Professorat dans les Collèges d'Enseignement Général*: Education, 3 yrs; *Certificat d'Aptitude au Professorat d'Education Physique et Sportive*: Sports, 5 yrs; *Licence*: Fundamental Sciences, Arts and Humanities, Law, 3 yrs; *Diplôme d'Ingénieur*: Electrical Engineering, Food Technology, 2-5 yrs; *Maîtrise*: Economics; Fundamental Sciences, Arts and Humanities, Law; Geology, 1 yr following Licence; *Diplôme d'Etudes approfondies (DEA)*: Botany, 1 year following Maîtrise; *Diplôme d'Etudes supérieures (DES)*: Arts and Humanities, 2 yrs following licence; *Doctorat en Médecine*: Medicine. Also Teaching Qualifications

Student Services: Sports Facilities, Health Services

Libraries: Central Library, c.70,000 vols

Publications: Sango (Bulletin) (bimonthly); Mélanges; Dimi; Annales (annually); Revue médicale du Congo

Academic Staff *2001-2002:* Total: c. 1,100

Student Numbers *2001-2002:* Total: c. 16,000

Congo (Democratic Republic)

INSTITUTION TYPES AND CREDENTIALS

Types of higher education institutions:

Université (University)

Institut supérieur (Higher Institute)

School leaving and higher education credentials:

Diplôme d'Etat d'Etudes secondaires du Cycle long

Graduat

Agrégation de l'Enseignement secondaire supérieur

Diplôme d'Ingénieur

Licence

Docteur en Médecine

Docteur en Médecine Vétérinaire

Diplôme d'Etudes supérieures (DES)

Diplôme de Spécialiste

Agrégation de l'Enseignement supérieur en Médecine

Agrégation de l'Enseignement supérieur en Médecine vétérinaire

Doctorat

STRUCTURE OF EDUCATION SYSTEM

Pre-higher education:

Duration of compulsory education:

Age of entry: 6

Age of exit: 12

Structure of school system:

Primary

Type of school providing this education: Primary School

Length of programme in years: 6

Age level from: 6 to: 12

Certificate/diploma awarded: Certificat d'Etudes primaires

General Secondary

Type of school providing this education: Secondary school

Length of programme in years: 6

Age level from: 12 to: 18

Certificate/diploma awarded: Diplôme d'Etat d'Etudes secondaires du Cycle long

Technical Secondary

Length of programme in years: 6

Age level from: 12 to: 18

Certificate/diploma awarded: Diplôme d'Etat d'Etudes secondaires du Cycle long

Vocational

Type of school providing this education: Vocational school

Length of programme in years: 5

Age level from: 12 to: 17

School education:

Primary school lasts for six years leading to the Certificat d'Etudes primaires (CEP) which gives access to secondary education. Secondary education (general or technical) consists of one cycle lasting for six years after which pupils obtain the Diplôme d'Etat d'Etudes secondaires du Cycle Long which gives access to higher education at university and technical institute levels. After primary school, pupils can also begin short technical courses in trade and crafts. Those who complete the long cycle in a technical field and pass the Diplôme d'Etat are eligible for admission to higher education. Vocational education is provided by vocational schools and courses last for five years. It does not give access to higher education.

Higher education:

Higher education has expanded a lot during the 1990's and many new establishments - public and private - have been created. Higher education is mainly provided by universities, higher teacher training institutes and higher technological institutes. It comes under the authority of the Ministère de l' Enseignement supérieur et universitaire. Each institution has a University or Institute Council, an Administrative Committee, faculties (or sections) and departments. The University or Institute Council is the highest authority. It is comprised of the Administration Committee, the deans, a faculty representative, a student representative, a representative of the administrative personnel and the head librarian. This body coordinates the academic and scientific policy of the institution. The Administration Committee is appointed by the central power. The Section or Faculty Council is exclusively concerned with the academic and scientific problems of that faculty or institute. It comprises full professors and department heads. The Department Council is the source of academic life in the universities. It comprises full professors who elect the department head. Several private institutions are also being established.

Main laws/decrees governing higher education:

Decree: Ordonnance-Loi n° 82-004 du 6 février 1982   Year: 1982

Concerns: Academic degrees in technical higher education institutions

Decree: Ordonnance-Loi n° 81-028 du 3 octobre 1981   Year: 1981

Concerns: Higher education and universities

Decree: Ordonnance-Loi n° 81-160 du 7 octobre 1981   Year: 1981
Concerns: University staff

Academic year:

Classes from: October *to:* June

Languages of instruction:

French

Stages of studies:

Non-university level post-secondary studies (technical/vocational type):

Higher technical and vocational education is mainly provided in teacher-training and technological institutes. Studies generally last for three years and lead to the qualification of Gradué.

University level studies:

University level first stage: Premier Cycle:
The first stage of higher education lasts for three years and leads to the title of Gradué.

University level second stage: Deuxième Cycle:
The second cycle lasts for two years and grants the Licence, except in Medicine and Veterinary Medicine where this stage lasts for three years and leads to the title of Docteur en Médecine and Docteur en Médecine Vétérinaire.

University level third stage: Troisième Cycle:
The third cycle mainly consists in a programme of higher studies leading to the Diplôme d'Etudes supérieures (DES). This programme lasts for two years and includes a certain number of courses and seminars, as well as the presentation of a dissertation. After obtaining the DES, the candidate can register in a doctoral programme and prepare the thesis. The next stage leads to the Doctorate which is conferred after a further four to seven years' further study. At the Faculties of Medicine, doctors devote three or four years to a specialization in one of the medical fields, after which they obtain a Diplôme de Spécialiste. Most Spécialistes become practitioners. Those who prefer to teach prepare an Agrégation. Requirements are the possession of the Diplôme de Spécialiste with "distinction" plus three to five years' preparation. The degree is that of Agrégé de l'Enseignement supérieur en Médecine. In Veterinary Medicine, it leads to the Agrégation de l'Enseignement supérieur en Médecine vétérinaire.

Teacher education:

Training of pre-primary and primary/basic school teachers
Pre-primary and primary school teachers holding a Certificat d'Etudes primaires are trained in four to six years at secondary level in Ecoles normales or Ecoles pédagogiques. They obtain the Brevet d'Instituteur or a State Diploma in Pedagogy. Courses include general and educational studies and practical teaching experience.

Training of secondary school teachers
Secondary school teachers are trained at the Instituts supérieurs pédagogiques (ISP), the Instituts supérieurs techniques (ITS) or education faculties. Candidates must hold the Diplôme d'Etat

d'Etudes secondaires du Cycle long. Courses are offered in all subjects taught at secondary level. They last for five years which are divided into two cycles. The first cycle lasts for three years and leads to the qualification of Gradué en Pédagogie appliquée. The second lasts for two more years and culminates in a Licence en Pédagogie appliquée or a Licence plus the Aggrégation. Holders of the title of Gradué are qualified to teach the first four years of secondary school. Holders of the Licence and Aggrégation are qualified to teach the final two years of secondary school. Students who have completed a non-pedagogical first degree course and who wish to teach can qualify by completing a one-year course leading to the Agrégation de l'Enseignement secondaire supérieur.

Training of higher education teachers
There are five ranks of teachers in higher education: assistant, project head, associate professor, professor and full professor. An assistant must hold a Licence or its equivalent and is nominated for a two-year period, twice renewable. A project head needs four years as an assistant and two publications in a scientific journal. An associate professor must hold a first-level Doctorate. Promotion requires four years from the previous level, together with several publications. There is a Service de Pédagogie universitaire which organizes training sessions for higher education teachers.

Non-traditional studies:

Other forms of non-formal higher education
Non-formal studies are offered by the Centre interdisciplinaire pour l'Education permanente which trains adults for their vocational needs and updates their technical knowledge. It has several training centres.

NATIONAL BODIES

Responsible authorities:
Ministry of Higher and University Education (Ministère de l'Enseignement supérieur et universitaire)
    Minister: Emile Ngoy
    10 Avenue du Haut Commandement
    Kinshasa/Gombe

Presidence of the Universities of the Democratic Republic of Congo (Présidence des Universités de la République démocratique du Congo)
    President: Tshibangu Tshishiku Tharcisse
    Permanent Secretary: Mwabila Malela Clement
    International Relations: Matundu Lelo
    PO Box 13399
    Kinshasa 1
    Tel: +243(99) 18198
    Telex: 982-21 216 cau zr

ADMISSIONS TO HIGHER EDUCATION

Admission to non university higher education studies

Name of secondary school credential required: Diplôme d'Etat d'Etudes secondaires du Cycle long

Admission to university-level studies

Name of secondary school credential required: Diplôme d'Etat d'Etudes secondaires du Cycle long

Entrance exams required: Entrance examination.

Foreign students admission

Admission requirements: Students must hold a diploma giving access to higher education in their country of origin.

Entry regulations: Students must ask for a visa at the Embassy of their country.

Language requirements: Students must have a good knowledge of French. Those who wish to improve their knowledge of French may follow courses in learning centres.

STUDENT LIFE

Student expenses and financial aid

Student costs:

    Foreign students tuition fees: Minimum: 250 (US Dollar)
    Maximum: 375 (US Dollar)

GRADING SYSTEM

Usual grading system in secondary school

Full Description: 0-100%
Highest on scale: 100%
Pass/fail level: 50%
Lowest on scale: 0%

Main grading system used by higher education institutions

Full Description: 0%-100%; 90%-100% la plus grande distinction; 80%-89% grande distinction; 70%-79% distinction; 50%-69% satisfaction; 50%
Highest on scale: 100%
Pass/fail level: 50%
Lowest on scale: 0%

NOTES ON HIGHER EDUCATION SYSTEM

Data for academic year: 2002-2003

Source: International Association of Universities (IAU), updated from IBE website, 2003 (www.ibe.unesco.org/International/Databanks/Wde/profilee.htm)

INSTITUTIONS OF HIGHER EDUCATION

UNIVERSITIES

CATHOLIC FACULTIES OF KINSHASA
Facultés catholiques de Kinshasa
BP 1534, Limete, Kinshasa
Tel: +243(88) 46961
Fax: +243(88) 46965
EMail: facakin@ic.cd

Recteur: Hippolyte Ngimbi Nseka (2001-)
EMail: nginseka@yahoo.fr

Secrétaire Général Académique: Richard Mugaruka
Tel: +243(88) 06053

Faculties
Economics and Development (Development Studies; Economics) *Dean:* Félicien Lukoki
Philosophy *Dean:* Georges Ndumba
Social Communication (Communication Studies; Social Studies) *Dean:* Dominique Mwenze
Theology (Christian Religious Studies; Theology) *Dean:* André Kabasele

Centres
African Religions *(CERA)* (African Studies; Religious Studies) *Director:* Théodore Mudiji
Ecclesiastical Archives *(Abbé Stephano (CAEK))* (Religious Studies) *Director:* Faustin Jovite Mapwar

History: Founded 1957.
Admission Requirements: State Diploma (+60%), and recommendation by a member of the Clergy
Fees: (US Dollars): 375 per annum
Main Language(s) of Instruction: French
Degrees and Diplomas: *Licence:* Philosophy, Theology, Development Studies, Journalism, 5 yrs; *Doctorat:* Philosophy, Theology
Publications: Kinshasa Journal of Philosophy; Journal of African Religions; Journal of African Theology (quarterly)
Academic Staff *2001-2002:* Total: **141**
Student Numbers *2001-2002:* Total: **1,066**

• CATHOLIC UNIVERSITY OF BUKAVU
Université catholique de Bukavu (UCB)
BP 285, Bukavu
Tel: +243(888) 7193
Fax: +871(762) 741-134
Website: http://www.ucbukavu.org

Recteur: Joseph Birindwa Gwamuhanya (2002-)
EMail: recteur@ucbukavu.org
Vice-Recteur aux Affaires académiques: Augustin Bashwira
EMail: vracad@ucbukavu.org

Faculties
Agronomy *Dean:* Jean Walangululu
Economics *Dean:* Augustin Mutabazi
Law *Dean:* Séverin Mugangu
Medicine *Dean:* Raphaël Cirimwami

History: Founded 1989.
Governing Bodies: Conseil d'Administration, comprising 19 members; Conseil Académique et Scientifique, comprising 29 members; Comité de Direction, comprising 3 members
Academic Year: October to July (October-December; January-March; April-July)
Admission Requirements: Secondary school certificate and entrance examination
Main Language(s) of Instruction: French
Degrees and Diplomas: *Graduat:* 3 yrs; *Diplôme d'Ingénieur;* *Licence:* Economics; Law; Medicine, a further 2-3 yrs; *Doctorat:* Medicine
Libraries: Central Library, c. 11,000 vols
Academic Staff *2001-2002:* Full-Time: c. 30 Part-Time: c. 90 Total: c. 120
Student Numbers *2001-2002:* Total: c. 1,300

CATHOLIC UNIVERSITY OF THE GRABEN
Université catholique du Graben (UCG)
BP 29, Butembo, Nord-Kivu
EMail: butembo@caramail.com

Recteur: Apollinaire Malu Malu

Faculties
Agronomy
Economics
Human Medicine (Medicine)
Law
Social Sciences
Veterinary Medicine (Veterinary Science)

History: Founded 1989.

FREE UNIVERSITY OF THE 'GREAT LAKES' REGION
Université libre des Pays des Grands Lacs
BP 368, Goma, Nord-Kivu
Tel: +243(88) 85-608
Fax: +243(88) 85-608

Recteur: Léonard Masu-Ga-Rugamika

KONGO UNIVERSITY
Université Kongo (UK)
BP 8443, Kinshasa 1

Recteur: B. Lututala Mumpasi

History: Founded as Université du Bas-Zaïre.

PROTESTANT UNIVERSITY OF CONGO
Université protestante du Congo (UPC)
BP 4745, Kinshasa
Tel: +243(88) 468-12
Fax: +243(88) 461-22
Website: http://www.carey.ac.nz/upc

Recteur: Daniel Boliya Ngoy
Tel: +243(88) 600-44 +243(88) 605-62
EMail: UNIVPROCONGO@MAF.org

Schools
Business and Economics (Business Administration; Economics)
Law
Theology

History: Founded 1959 in Lubumbashi as a Theology Department. Became Free University of the Congo 1963, Protestant University of Zaire 1990. Acquired present name and status 1997.

Governing Bodies: Board

Main Language(s) of Instruction: French

Degrees and Diplomas: *Licence*: 5 yrs

Libraries: 13,000 vols

Student Numbers *2001-2002:* Total: c. 4,400

UNIVERSITY CENTRE OF BUKAVU
Centre universitaire de Bukavu
BP 570, Bukavu

Recteur: Nyakabwa Mutabana

UNIVERSITY OF THE KASAYI
Université du Kasayi (UKA)
Kananga

Recteur: Nyeme Tese

Faculties
Agronomy *(Kabinda)*
Medicine

Centres
Computer Science

History: Founded 1996 by the Episcopal Conference of the province of Kananga.

• UNIVERSITY OF KINSHASA
Université de Kinshasa
BP 190, Kinshasa XI
Tel: +243(12) 27-793
Fax: +243(12) 21-360
Telex: 982 23 068
EMail: centreinfo@ic.cd
Website: http://unikin.sciences.free.fr/

Recteur: Ndelo di Phanzu (2000-) Tel: +243(12) 27-793

Faculties
Agronomy
Economics
Law
Medicine (Dentistry; Medicine)
Pharmacy
Polytechnic (Civil Engineering; Engineering; Technology)
Science (Mathematics and Computer Science; Natural Sciences)

History: Founded 1949 as Université Lovanium, became a campus of the Université nationale du Zaïre 1971. Acquired present status and title 1981. A State institution.

Governing Bodies: Conseil d'Administration d'Université

Academic Year: October to June (October-February; February-June)

Admission Requirements: Secondary school certificate and entrance examination

Main Language(s) of Instruction: French

Degrees and Diplomas: *Graduat*; *Diplôme d'Ingénieur*: Civil Engineering, 5 years; *Licence*: Economics, 4 yrs; Civil Engineering; Law; Science, 5 yrs; *Docteur en Médecine*: Medicine, 6 yrs; *Diplôme d'Etudes supérieures (DES)*: Law (DES); *Diplôme de Spécialiste*: Medicine; *Agrégation de l'Enseignement supérieur en Médecine*: Medicine; *Doctorat*: Economics; Pharmacy; Science

Special Facilities: Musée universitaire

Libraries: c. 300,000 vols

Publications: Bulletin d'Information (monthly); Cahiers économiques et sociaux des Religions africaines (quarterly); Annales of the Faculties of Science, Polytechnic and Pharmacy

Press or Publishing House: Presses universitaires de l'Université de Kinshasa

Academic Staff *2001-2002:* Total: c. 540

Student Numbers *2001-2002:* Total: c. 6,000

• UNIVERSITY OF KISANGANI
Université de Kisangani
BP 2012, Kisangani, Haut Zaïre
Tel: +243(21) 1335

Recteur: Labama Lokwa

Faculties
Education and Psychology (Education; Psychology)
Medicine (Dermatology; Gynaecology and Obstetrics; Medicine; Paediatrics; Stomatology)

Science (Biochemistry; Biology; Ecology; Natural Sciences)
Social Sciences, Administration, and Political Science (Administration; Political Science; Social Sciences; Sociology)

History: Founded 1963 as Université libre du Congo, became a campus of the Université nationale du Zaïre 1971. Acquired present status and title 1981. A State institution.

Governing Bodies: Conseil d'Administration

Academic Year: October to July (October-February; February-July)

Admission Requirements: Secondary school certificate and entrance examination

Main Language(s) of Instruction: French

Degrees and Diplomas: *Graduat*; *Licence*: Administration; Sociology; Education, 4 yrs; Psychology; Science, 5 yrs; *Docteur en Médecine*: 6 yrs; *Diplôme d'Etudes supérieures (DES)*: Pedagogy; Psychology; Science; *Diplôme de Spécialiste*: Medicine; *Agrégation de l'Enseignement supérieur en Médecine*: Medicine; *Doctorat*: Pedagogy; Psychology; Sociology

Student Residential Facilities: Yes

Libraries: c. 46,000 vols

Press or Publishing House: Presses universitaires de Kisangani

Academic Staff *2001-2002*: Full-Time: c. 220 Part-Time: c. 40 Total: c. 260

Student Numbers *2001-2002:* Total: c. 4,000

• UNIVERSITY OF LUBUMBASHI

Université de Lubumbashi
BP 1825, Lubumbashi, Shaba
Tel: +243(22) 5403
Fax: +243(22) 8099
Telex: 40179
EMail: unilu@unilu.net
Website: http://www.unilu.net

Recteur: Kaumba Lufunda

Secrétaire général administratif: Chabu Mumba

Faculties
Agronomy *Dean*: Ngongo Luhembwe
Economics *Dean*: Malangu Mposhy
Law
Letters (Arts and Humanities; English; French; History; Literature; Philosophy) *Dean*: Mabika Nkata
Medicine (Gynaecology and Obstetrics; Medicine; Paediatrics; Surgery) *Dean*: Muteta Wa Pa Manda
Polytechnic (Electronic Engineering; Industrial Chemistry; Mechanical Engineering; Metallurgical Engineering; Mining Engineering) *Dean*: Kalenga Ngoy
Psychology and Educational Sciences (Educational Sciences; Psychology) *Dean*: Fumuni Bikuri
Science (Chemistry; Geography; Geology; Mathematics; Natural Sciences) *Dean*: Byamungu bin Rusangiza
Social, Political, and Administrative Sciences (Administration; Anthropology; International Relations; Political Science; Social Sciences; Sociology) *Dean*: Elengesa Ndunguna

Veterinary Medicine (Veterinary Science) *Dean*: Kashala Kapalwola

Higher Schools
Commerce (Business and Commerce; Finance; Marketing; Secretarial Studies) *Directeur*: Kizobo O'Obweng O.
Engineering (Chemical Engineering; Construction Engineering; Electrical Engineering; Electronic Engineering; Mechanical Engineering; Mining Engineering) *Directeur*: Ngoie Nsenga

Higher Institutes
Medical Techniques (Health Administration; Laboratory Techniques; Nursing) *Directeur*: Malonga Kaj

History: Founded 1955 as Université officielle du Congo, became a campus of the Université nationale du Zaïre 1971, and acquired present status and title 1981. A State institution.

Governing Bodies: Conseil d'administration

Academic Year: October to June (October-February; February-June)

Admission Requirements: Secondary school certificate and entrance examination

Fees: (Francs congolais): 45,000-105,000

Main Language(s) of Instruction: French

Degrees and Diplomas: *Graduat*; *Diplôme d'Ingénieur*: Civil Engineering, 5 yrs; *Licence*: Anthropology; International Relations; Political Science; Letters; Sociology, 4 yrs; Engineering; Science, 5 yrs; *Docteur en Médecine*: Medicine; *Docteur en Médecine Vétérinaire*: Veterinary Medicine, 6 yrs; *Diplôme de Spécialiste*: Medicine; *Agrégation de l'Enseignement supérieur en Médecine*: Medicine; *Doctorat*: Anthropology; International Relations; Letters; Political Science; Science; Sociology

Student Residential Facilities: For 1300 students

Libraries: c. 95,000 vols

Academic Staff *2001-2002:* Total: c. 400

Student Numbers *2001-2002:* Total: c. 13,000

UNIVERSITY OF MBUJIMAYI

Université de Mbujimayi (UM)
BP 225, Avenue de l'Université, Campus de Tshikama, Dibindi, Mbujimayi, Kasaï Oriental
Tel: +243(88) 54890 +243(81) 20905
Fax: +243 (88) 5411 +32(2) 7065818
EMail: univmayi@yahoo.fr;odile_mpemba@yahoo.fr

Recteur: Raphaël Mbowa Kalengayi Tel: +243(99) 57314 Fax: +32(2) 7065818 EMail: ralphka@hotmail.com

Secrétaire général: J. Ntumba Tshibambula Fax: +243(88) 5411

International Relations: P. Reyntjens

Chief Librarian: Charles Tshibanza Monji Tel: +243(88) 5411 EMail: tshikamau@yahoo.fr

Faculties
Applied Science (Polytechnic) (Civil Engineering; Mechanical Engineering; Mining Engineering; Science Education) *Dean*: Charles Tshiula
Economics *Dean*: François Kalala Kabuya

Human Medicine (Biomedicine; Medicine) *Dean*: Ghislain Ntumba Disashi

Law (Law; Notary Studies; Private Law; Public Law) *Dean*: Florent Makanda Kabongo

History: Founded 1990. Acquired present status 1992.

Governing Bodies: Council of Founders; Administration Council; University Council; Executive Committee

Academic Year: November to July

Admission Requirements: Diplôme d'Etat or equivalent secondary school certificate

Fees: (US Dollars) 280-330 per annum

Main Language(s) of Instruction: French

International Co-operation: With universities in Belgium; Germany; Canada; Japan; Italy; Spain

Accrediting Agencies: AUF; FIUC

Degrees and Diplomas: *Graduat*: Biomedical Sciences; Civil Engineering; Mining Engineering; Mechanical Engineering; Law; Economics, 3 yrs; *Licence*: Civil Engineering; Mining Engineering; Mechanical Engineering, a further 2 yrs; *Doctorat*: Medicine, 4 yrs

Student Services: Academic Counselling, Social Counselling, Nursery Care, Cultural Centre, Sports Facilities, Health Services, Canteen

Special Facilities: Research Laboratory; Internet Centre

Libraries: 14,000 vols

Publications: Actes des Journées Scientifiques de l'U.M. (annually)

Academic Staff *2001-2002*	MEN	WOMEN	TOTAL
FULL-TIME	35	1	36
PART-TIME	97	1	98
TOTAL	**132**	**2**	**134**
STAFF WITH DOCTORATE			
FULL-TIME			6
PART-TIME			51
TOTAL			**57**

Student Numbers *2001-2002*	MEN	WOMEN	TOTAL
All (Foreign Included)	755	149	**904**

OTHER INSTITUTIONS

ACADÉMIE DES BEAUX-ARTS
BP 8249, Kinshasa
Tel: +243(12) 68476

Programmes
Fine Arts

INSTITUT DE FORMATION DES CADRES DE L'ENSEIGNEMENT PRIMAIRE
BP 711, Kisangani

Programmes
Teacher Training (Primary Education; Teacher Training)

History: Founded 1971. Acquired present status 1981.

INSTITUT DES BÂTIMENTS ET DES TRAVAUX PUBLICS
BP 4731, Kinshasa

Programmes
Civil Engineering

History: Founded 1961. Acquired present status and title 1971.

INSTITUT FACULTAIRE DES SCIENCES DE L'INFORMATION ET DE LA COMMUNICATION
BP 14998, Kinshasa
Tel: +243(12) 25117

Recteur: Ya Mpiku Mbelolo

Directeur général: Melembe Tamandiak

Founded: 1973, 1997
Information Technology; Journalism; Library Science; Public Relations

History: Founded 1973 as Institut des Sciences et Techniques de l'Information. Acquired present status and title 1997.

INSTITUT NATIONAL DES ARTS
BP 8332, Kinshasa

Programmes
Fine Arts

History: Founded 1971. Acquired present status and title 1981.

INSTITUT PÉDAGOGIQUE NATIONAL
BP 8815, Kinshasa-Binza

Programmes
Teacher Training

History: Founded 1961. Acquired present status and title 1971.

INSTITUT SUPÉRIEUR DES ARTS ET MÉTIERS
BP 15198, Kinshasa-Gombe

Programmes
Fine Arts (Crafts and Trades; Fine Arts)

History: Founded 1968. Acquired present status and title 1975.

INSTITUT SUPÉRIEUR DE COMMERCE
BP 16596, Kinshasa

Programmes
Business and Commerce

History: Founded 1964. Acquired present status and title 1971.

INSTITUT SUPÉRIEUR DE COMMERCE
BP 2012, Kisangani

Programmes
Business and Commerce

History: Founded 1971. Acquired present status and title 1981.

INSTITUT SUPÉRIEUR DE STATISTIQUE
BP 2471, Lubumbashi

Programmes
Statistics

History: Founded 1967. Acquired present status and title 1971.

INSTITUT SUPÉRIEUR DES TECHNIQUES APPLIQUÉES
BP 6593, Kinshasa
Tel: +243(12) 23592

Programmes
Technology

History: Founded 1971. Acquired present status and title 1981.

INSTITUT SUPÉRIEUR D'ETUDES AGRONOMIQUES DE BENGAMISA
BP 202, Kisangani

Programmes
Agronomy

History: Founded 1968. Acquired present status and title 1971.

INSTITUT SUPÉRIEUR D'ETUDES AGRONOMIQUES DE MONDONGO
BP 60, Lisala

Programmes
Agronomy

History: Founded 1972. Acquired present status and title 1981.

INSTITUT SUPÉRIEUR D'ETUDES SOCIALES
BP 2849, Bukavu

Programmes
Social Studies

History: Founded 1971. Acquired present status and title 1981.

INSTITUT SUPÉRIEUR D'ETUDES SOCIALES
BP 1575, Lubumbashi

Programmes
Social Studies

History: Founded 1971. Acquired present status and title 1981.

INSTITUT SUPÉRIEUR PÉDAGOGIQUE
BP 854, Bukavu

Programmes
Teacher Training

History: Founded 1964. Acquired present status and title 1971.

INSTITUT SUPÉRIEUR PÉDAGOGIQUE
BP 340, Bunia

Programmes
Teacher Training

History: Founded 1968. Acquired present status and title 1971.

INSTITUT SUPÉRIEUR PÉDAGOGIQUE
BP 282, Kananga

Programmes
Teacher Training

History: Founded 1966. Acquired present status and title 1971.

INSTITUT SUPÉRIEUR PÉDAGOGIQUE DE GOMBE (ISP-GOMBE)
BP 3580, Kinshasa-Gombe
Tel: +243(12) 34-092 +243(12) 34-094
Directeur général: Robert Mondo Kibwa Tuba (1997-)
Secrétaire général: Shadrack Nsimba-Lubaki

Founded: 1961, 1981

Departments
Biology and Chemistry (Biology; Chemistry; Teacher Training) *Head*: Ifuta Ndey Bibula
Commerce (Business Education) *Head*: Kabemba Assani

115

English and African Civilization (African Studies; English; Regional Studies; Teacher Training) *Head*: Katombe Mukengeshay

French and African Linguistics (African Languages; French; Linguistics; Teacher Training) *Head*: Zandu dia Zulu M'Ndendi

Geography and Natural Sciences (Geography; Natural Sciences; Teacher Training) *Head*: Bakunda Matezo

History and Social Sciences (History; Social Sciences; Teacher Training) *Head*: Kikokula Meno

Hotel Management (Hotel Management; Teacher Training) *Head*: Zongwa Mbangilwa

Psychopedagogy (Educational Psychology; Teacher Training) *Head*: Manwana Mahinga

Teacher Training *Head*: Robert Mondo Kibwa Tuba

History: Founded 1961 by Catholic Sisters to promote the study level of women. Acquired present status and title 1981.

Admission Requirements: Secondary school certificate

Main Language(s) of Instruction: French

Degrees and Diplomas: *Graduat*: (G3); *Licence*: Biology; English; French; Geography; History

Student Services: Academic Counselling, Employment Services, Sports Facilities, Health Services

Student Residential Facilities: For 335 students

Libraries: Main Library

Publications: Les cahiers de l'ISP/Gombe, Pluridisciplinary (2 per annum)

Academic Staff *2001-2002*: Full-Time: c. 110 Part-Time: c. 15 Total: c. 125

Staff with Doctorate: Total: c. 40

Student Numbers *2001-2002:* Total: c. 1,100

INSTITUT SUPÉRIEUR PÉDAGOGIQUE
BP 1514, Kisangani

Programmes
Teacher Training

History: Founded 1967. Acquired present status and title 1971.

INSTITUT SUPÉRIEUR PÉDAGOGIQUE
BP 1796, Lubumbashi

Programmes
Teacher Training

History: Founded 1959. Acquired present status and title 1971.

INSTITUT SUPÉRIEUR PÉDAGOGIQUE
BP 116, Mbandaka
Founded: 1971, 1981

Programmes
Teacher Training

History: Founded 1971. Acquired present status and title 1981.

INSTITUT SUPÉRIEUR PÉDAGOGIQUE
BP 127, Mbanza-Ngungu

Programmes
Teacher Training

History: Founded 1971. Acquired present status and title 1981.

INSTITUT SUPÉRIEUR PÉDAGOGIQUE
BP 682, Mbuji-Mayi

Programmes
Teacher Training

History: Founded 1968. Acquired present status and title 1971.

INSTITUT SUPÉRIEUR PÉDAGOGIQUE TECHNIQUE
BP 3287, Kinshasa-Gombe

Programmes
Technology Education

History: Founded 1976. Acquired present status and title 1981.

INSTITUT SUPÉRIEUR PÉDAGOGIQUE TECHNIQUE
BP 75, Likasi

Programmes
Technology Education

History: Founded 1971. Acquired present status and title 1981.

Côte d'Ivoire

INSTITUTION TYPES AND CREDENTIALS

Types of higher education institutions:

Université (University)
Ecole nationale supérieure (National Higher School)
Centre universitaire (University Centre)
Institut supérieur (Higher Institute)
Ecole normale supérieure (Higher Teacher Training College)

School leaving and higher education credentials:

Baccalauréat
Brevet de Technicien Supérieur
Diplôme d'Infirmier d'Etat
Capacité en Droit
Diplôme d'Instituteur stagiaire
Diplôme universitaire
Diplôme en Pharmacie
Licence
Certificat d'Aptitude au Professorat de l'Enseignement secondaire
Diplôme d'Agronomie générale
Diplôme d'Ingénieur
Maîtrise
Docteur en Médecine
Diplôme d'Etudes approfondies (DEA)
Diplôme d'Etudes supérieures (DES)
Diplôme d'Etudes Supérieures Spécialisées (DESS)
Diplôme de Docteur Ingénieur
Doctorat

STRUCTURE OF EDUCATION SYSTEM

Pre-higher education:

Structure of school system:

    Primary
    Type of school providing this education: Ecole primaire
    Length of programme in years: 6

Age level from: 6 to: 12
Certificate/diploma awarded: Certificat d'Etudes primaires élémentaires (CEPE)

First Cycle Secondary
Type of school providing this education: Collège d'Enseignement général
Length of programme in years: 4
Age level from: 12 to: 16
Certificate/diploma awarded: Brevet d'Etudes du premier Cycle (BEPC)

Technical Secondary
Type of school providing this education: Centre de Formation Professionnelle
Length of programme in years: 4
Age level from: 12 to: 16
Certificate/diploma awarded: Brevet d'Etudes du premier Cycle (BEPC)

Second Cycle Secondary
Type of school providing this education: Lycée
Length of programme in years: 3
Age level from: 16 to: 19
Certificate/diploma awarded: Baccalauréat/Diplôme de Bachelier de l'Enseignement du second Degré

Technical
Type of school providing this education: Lycée technique/Lycée professionnel
Length of programme in years: 3
Age level from: 16 to: 19
Certificate/diploma awarded: Baccalauréat technique

School education:

Primary education lasts for six years and leads to the Certificat d'Etudes primaires élémentaires (CEPE). Secondary schooling is divided into a four-year cycle culminating in the Brevet d'Etudes du premier Cycle (BEPC), and a three-year cycle culminating in the Baccalauréat/Diplôme de Bachelier de l'Enseignement du second Degré. Lower technical and vocational secondary education are available at the Centres de Formation professionnelle which offer four-year courses leading to the Brevet d'Etudes du premier Cycle. After a three-year course at upper secondary level in a Lycée technique/professionnel, students are awarded the Baccalauréat technique.

Higher education:

Since 1996, higher education is offered at three separate universities (formerly the Université nationale de Côte d'Ivoire): the Université de Cocody, the Université d'Abobo-Adjamé and the Université de Bouaké as well as at centres universitaires and at institutions providing higher professional training. The universities and the teacher college are under the auspices of the Ministère de l'Enseignement supérieur. There are also some private institutions.

Academic year:

Classes from: October *to:* June

Long vacation from: 30 June *to:* 30 September

Languages of instruction:

French

Stages of studies:

Non-university level post-secondary studies (technical/vocational type):

Technical and professional education is offered at various institutes and higher schools. Courses usually last for two to three years and lead to such qualifications as the Brevet de Technicien supérieur and the Diplôme d'Infirmier d'Etat. An entrance examination is often required.

University level studies:

University level first stage: Premier Cycle:

Two years of university study lead to the Diplôme universitaire d'Etudes générales (DEUG). In Medicine, the first cycle of studies is devoted to necessary grounding in the relevant sciences. A Capacité en Droit is conferred after two years' study to candidates who do not hold the Baccalauréat. A Diplôme universitaire de Technologie is awarded after three years' study by the Instituts universitaires de Technologie (IUT). A Diplôme en Pharmacie is conferred after three years. A Diplôme d'Agronomie générale is awarded after four years' study.

University level second stage: Deuxième Cycle:

A further year's study leads to the Licence. In engineering schools, studies last for five years and lead to the professional qualification of Ingénieur and the Diplôme d'Ingénieur des Travaux publics. In Agriculture, a Diplôme d'Agronomie générale is conferred after four years and a Diplôme d'Ingénieur agronome is awarded after five years' study with a further year's specialization. The Maîtrise in Arts and Science subjects takes one year after the Licence and includes a mini-thesis.

University level third stage: Troisième Cycle:

The Diplôme d'Etudes supérieures spécialisées (DESS) and the Diplôme d'Etudes approfondies (DEA) are conferred after one year's further study beyond the Licence or Maîtrise. After three more years candidates may be awarded the Doctorat. The qualification of Docteur-Ingénieur is conferred after three years' study and the submission of a thesis to holders of a diploma in Engineering. In Medicine, a professional Doctorate is awarded after seven years and in Dentistry and Pharmacy after five years.

Teacher education:

Training of pre-primary and primary/basic school teachers
Primary school teachers are trained in Centres d'Animation et de Formation Pédagogique (CAFOPs) in a three-year post-Baccalauréat course.

Training of secondary school teachers
At lower secondary level (premier cycle), a three-year course leads to the Certificat d'Aptitude pédagogique pour l'enseignement du premier cycle (collèges modernes)(CAPCM). Holders may go to university for a further year to obtain the Licence. Upper secondary school teachers study for a Licence d'Enseignement or follow a one-year course and a one-year supervised and examined teaching practice if they have a degree. This leads to the Certificat d'Aptitude pédagogique pour

l'Enseignement du Second Degré (CAPES).

For technical secondary education, students follow courses at the Institut Pédagogique national de l'Enseignement technique et professionnel where they obtain the title of Instructeur de Formation professionnelle after two years, of Professeur de Centre de Formation professionnelle after three years, of Professeur de Lycée professionnel after four years and of Professeur certifié de l'Enseignement technique et de la Formation professionnelle after five years.

Training of higher education teachers

University teachers must hold a Doctorat with a high pass mark.

Non-traditional studies:

Lifelong higher education

The Centre Africain et Mauricien de Perfectionnement des Cadres (CAMPC) awards the Diplôme de Direction du Personnel (five-week course), the Diplôme de Formation (six-week course), and the Diplôme de Gestion des Affaires (16-month programme). The Centre Ivoirien de Gestion des Entreprises provides short-term professional development courses for middle- and upper-level managers.

Other forms of non-formal higher education

The broadcast media offers two non-formal education opportunities, which include La Coupe Nationale du Progrès and the Télé Pour Tous. La Coupe Nationale du Progrès is a 15-20 minute daily radio programme that provides agricultural information. The Télé Pour Tous offers televised lectures that are broadcast in French for 30 minutes each week and feature a variety of topics ranging from health care to agricultural practices. Télé Pour Tous is aimed at television classrooms run by lecturers who translate and explain the lectures.

NATIONAL BODIES

Responsible authorities:

Ministry of Higher Education (Ministère de l'Enseignement supérieur)
Minister: Zemogo Fofana
Director of Cabinet: Mokodou Thiam
BP V 151
Abidjan
Tel: +225(20) 21-33-16 +225(20) 21-57-73
Fax: +225(20) 21-49-87   +225(20) 21-22-25
Telex: 26138 rectu ci
WWW: http://www.pr.ci/gouvernement/ministeres/index.html

ADMISSIONS TO HIGHER EDUCATION

Admission to non university higher education studies

Name of secondary school credential required: Baccalauréat

Alternatives to credentials: Baccalauréat technique

Admission to university-level studies

Name of secondary school credential required: Baccalauréat

Foreign students admission

Admission requirements: Foreign students must hold a qualification that is equivalent to the Baccalauréat. Entrance to the Institut national polytechnique Félix Houphouët-Boigny is based on a competitive examination. For universities, students' files are examined.

Entry regulations: They must have a valid passport, a visa and scholarship from their government or an international organization.

Health requirements: Students must be vaccinated against yellow fever.

Language requirements: Knowledge of French is necessary. The University organizes one- to three-year courses for students who are not proficient in French.

Recognition of studies and qualifications:

Studies pursued in foreign countries (bodies dealing with recognition of foreign credentials):
Université de Cocody
   President: Gokou Célestin Téa
   BP V 34
   Abidjan 01
   Tel: +225(22) 44-90-00
   Fax: +225(22) 44-07-14
   Telex: 26138 rectu ci
   WWW: http://www.ucocody.ci

Multilateral agreements concerning recognition of foreign studies

Name(s) of agreement(s): UNESCO Convention on the Recognition of Studies, Certificates, Diplomas, Degrees and Other Academic Qualifications in Higher Education in the African States
Year of signature: 1981

STUDENT LIFE

Main student services at national level

Centre régional des Oeuvres universitaires d'Abidjan
   22 BP42
   Abidjan 22
   Category of services provided: Social and welfare services
Centre régional des Oeuvres universitaires de Bouaké
   01 BPV 18
   Bouaké 01
   Category of services provided: Social and welfare services

Centre régional des Oeuvres universitaires de Daloa
BP 157
Daloa
Category of services provided: Social and welfare services

Student expenses and financial aid

Student costs:

Home students tuition fees: Minimum: 6,000 (CFA Franc-O)
Maximum: 25,000 (CFA Franc-O)
Foreign students tuition fees: Minimum: 200,000 (CFA Franc-O)
Maximum: 500,000 (CFA Franc-O)

Bodies providing information on student financial aid:

Direction des Bourses et Aides, Ministère de l'Enseignement supérieur et de la Recherche scientifique
Abidjan
Tel: +225(20) 21-33-16
Fax: +225(20) 21-49-87

INTERNATIONAL COOPERATION AND EXCHANGES

Principal national bodies responsible for dealing with international cooperation and exchanges in higher education:

Ministry of Higher Education (Ministère de l'Enseignement supérieur)
Minister: Zemogo Fofana
Director of Cabinet: Mokodou Thiam
B.P. V 151
Abidjan
Tel: +225(20) 21-33-16 +225(20) 21-57-73
Fax: +225(20) 21-49-87   +225(20) 21-22-25
Telex: 26138 rectu ci
WWW: http://www.pr.ci/gouvernement/ministeres/index.html

GRADING SYSTEM

Usual grading system in secondary school

Full Description: 16-20=Très Bien; 14-15=Bien; 12-13=Assez bien; 11=Passable; 0-9=Ajourné.
Highest on scale: 20
Pass/fail level: 10
Lowest on scale: 0

Main grading system used by higher education institutions

Full Description: 16-20=Très Bien; 14-15=Bien; 12-13=Assez Bien; 10-11=Passable; 8-9=Ajourné (Fail but allowed to retake exam); 0-7=Ajourné

Highest on scale: 20

Pass/fail level: 10

Lowest on scale: 0

NOTES ON HIGHER EDUCATION SYSTEM

Data for academic year: 2003-2004

Source: Ministère de l'Enseignement supérieur, 2003

INSTITUTIONS OF HIGHER EDUCATION

UNIVERSITIES AND UNIVERSITY LEVEL INSTITUTIONS

PUBLIC INSTITUTIONS

NATIONAL POLYTECHNIC INSTITUTE FÉLIX HOUPHOUËT-BOIGNY

Institut national polytechnique Félix Houphouët-Boigny (INP-HB)
BP 1093, Yamoussoukro
Tel: +225(30) 64-05-41
Fax: +225(30) 64-04-06
EMail: inp@ci.refer.org
Website: http://www.inphb.edu.ci

Directeur général: Ado Gossan Tel: +225(30) 64-03-63
EMail: dg.inp@ci.refer.org

Secrétaire général: Blaise Diegba Kotro
Tel: +225(30) 64-11-36 EMail: sg.inp@ci.refer.org

Schools
Agriculture (Agricultural Economics; Agriculture; Animal Husbandry; Development Studies; Food Technology; Rural Studies; Sociology)
Civil Engineering
Commerce and Business Administration (Business Administration; Business and Commerce)
Industrial Technology (Industrial Engineering)
Lifelong Education and Executive Proficiency
Mines and Geology (Geology; Mining Engineering)

History: Founded 1996, incorporating previously existing institutions, including Ecole nationale supérieure Agronomique, Ecole nationale supérieure des Travaux Publics, and Institut national supérieur de l'Enseignement technique.

Main Language(s) of Instruction: French

Degrees and Diplomas: *Brevet de Technicien Supérieur; Diplôme d'Agronomie générale; Diplôme d'Ingénieur; Diplôme d'Etudes approfondies (DEA)*

*• UNIVERSITY OF ABOBO-ADJAMÉ

Université d'Abobo-Adjamé
BP 801, Abidjan 02
Tel: +225 (20) 37-81-21
Fax: +225 (20) 37-81-18
EMail: abobo-adj@abobo.edu.ci-mes/rs-ci
Website: http://www.abobo.edu.ci

Président: Etienne Ehouan Ehilé Tel: +225(20) 37-74-48
EMail: abobo-adj@abobo.edu.ci

Units
Basic Sciences (Natural Sciences)
Environment Science and Management (Environmental Management; Environmental Studies)
Food Technology
Higher Education *(URES Daloa)*

Programmes
Natural Sciences (Mathematics and Computer Science; Natural Sciences)

Schools
Health Sciences *(Preparatory)*

Institutes
Research

Centres
Advanced Training
Ecology (Ecology; Environmental Studies)

History: Founded 1995 as University Centre.

Main Language(s) of Instruction: French

Degrees and Diplomas: *Diplôme universitaire*: Natural Sciences, 2 yrs; *Maîtrise*: 4 yrs; *Diplôme d'Etudes approfondies (DEA)*: a further 2 yrs

Academic Staff *2000-2001:* Total: c. 50

Student Numbers *2000-2001:* Total: c. 4,300

UNIVERSITY OF BOUAKÉ

Université de Bouaké
BP V 18, Bouaké 01
Tel: +225(31) 63-32-42
Fax: +225(31) 63-25-13
Website:
http://www.ci.refer.org/ivoir_ct/edu/sup/uni/bke/accueil.htm

Président: Aka Landry Komenan Tel: +225(31) 63-48-57

Secrétaire général: Germain Kouassi

Units
Communication, Environment and Society (Communication Studies; Environmental Studies; Social Studies)
Economics and Development (Development Studies; Economics)
Higher Education *(URES, Korhogo)*
Law, Administration and Development (Administration; Development Studies; Law)
Medical Sciences (Health Sciences)

Centres
Development Research (Development Studies)
Lifelong Education

History: Founded 1994 as University Centre.

Main Language(s) of Instruction: French

• UNIVERSITY OF COCODY
Université de Cocody
BP V34, Abidjan 01
Tel: +225(22) 44-90-00
Fax: +225(22) 44-14-07
Telex: 26138 rectu ci
Website: http://www.ucocody.ci

Président: Célestin Téa Gokou Tel: +225(22) 44-08-95
EMail: presidence@ucocody.ci

Units
Bioscience (Biochemistry; Biomedicine; Biophysics) *Director:* Yao Tanoh

Criminology *Director:* Alain Sissoko

Earth Sciences and Mining Resources (Earth Sciences; Mineralogy)

Economics and Management (Economics; Management)

Information, Art and Communication (Communication Studies; Fine Arts; Information Sciences)

Languages, Literature and Civilizations (Cultural Studies; Literature; Modern Languages) *Director:* Bailli Sery

Law, Administration and Political Science (Administration; Law; Political Science) *Director:* Abou Ouraga

Mankind and Society (Geography; History; Sociology)

Mathematics and Computer Science (Computer Science; Mathematics) *Director:* Niango Niango

Medical Sciences (Health Sciences; Medicine) *Director:* Thérèse Ndri Yoman

Odonto-Stomatology (Dentistry; Stomatology) *Director:* S. Touré

Pharmaceutical Sciences (Pharmacy) *Director:* Abe Yapo

Structure of Matter and Technology (Physics; Technology)

Institutes
Mathematics *(IRMA)*

Centres
Economic and Social Research *(CIRES)* (Economics; Social Studies)

Lifelong Education *(CUFOP)*

History: Founded 1995 as University Centre. Acquired present status 1996.

Admission Requirements: Baccalauréat or equivalent

Fees: (Francs CFA): c. 6000-25,000; foreign students, c. 200,000-500,000 (if agreements, foreign students may pay same fees as nationals)

Main Language(s) of Instruction: French

Degrees and Diplomas: *Licence:* 3 yrs; *Maîtrise:* 4 yrs; *Docteur en Médecine:* Medicine, 8 yrs; *Diplôme d'Etudes approfondies (DEA)*; *Diplôme d'Etudes Supérieures Spécialisées (DESS):* Pharmacy, Dentistry; *Doctorat:* 3 yrs following DEA

Student Services: Academic Counselling, Social Counselling, Nursery Care, Sports Facilities, Language Programmes, Handicapped Facilities, Health Services, Canteen

Libraries: Central Library and specialized Libraries per unit (13)

Publications: Revues médicales (quarterly); En-Quête, Letters; Repères, Letters and Human Sciences; Revues sociales (biannually)

Academic Staff *2000:* Total: **1,081**

Staff with doctorate: Total: **1,005**

Student Numbers *2000:* Total: **37,500**

Evening Students, 1,434

PRIVATE INSTITUTIONS

CATHOLIC UNIVERSITY OF WEST AFRICA/UNIVERSITY OF ABIDJAN UNIT
Université Catholique de l'Afrique de l'Ouest/Unité universitaire d'Abidjan (UCAO/UUA)
08 BP 22, Abidjan, Cocody
Tel: +225(22) 40-06-50
Fax: +225(22) 44-15-93
EMail: ucao@aviso.ci
Website: http://www.ucao.fr.fm

Président: Barthélémy Zan Fax: +225(22) 44-15-93

Secrétaire General: Roger Afan

International Relations: Célestin Gnako
EMail: aviso@ucao.ci

Faculties
Law

Philosophy *Dean:* Frédéric Lot

Theology (Religious Studies; Theology) *Dean:* Célestin Gnako

Schools
Theological Training for the Lay (Theology)

Higher Institutes
Christian Religious Studies *(Institut Supérieur de Catéchèse (ISC)) Director:* Barthélémy Zan

Communication Studies *(Institut Supérieur de Communication) Director:* Prosper Akuetey

Pastoral Studies *(Institut Supérieur de Pastorale (ISP)) Director:* Cécé Apollinaire Kolie

History: Founded as Institute (ICAO)1969. Acquired present status and name 2000.

Admission Requirements: Baccalauréat or equivalent

Fees: (Francs CFA): 500,000-700,000 per annum

Main Language(s) of Instruction: French

Degrees and Diplomas: *Diplôme universitaire:* Christian Religious Studies (DENC); Pastoral Studies; Communication Studies; Philosophy (DEUG), 2 yrs; Theology (DUET), 3 yrs; *Licence:* Philosophy; Christian Religious Studies;

Communication Studies, a further 1-2 yrs; *Maîtrise*: Theology; Philosophy, 1-2 yrs following Licence; *Diplôme d'Etudes approfondies (DEA)*: Philosophy; Theology, 1 yr following "Maîtrise"; *Doctorat*: Theology; Philosophy, 3 yrs by thesis

Student Services: Academic Counselling, Employment Services, Nursery Care, Sports Facilities, Health Services, Canteen

Libraries: Central Library c. 50,000 vols

Publications: Ricao, Newspaper (quarterly)

Academic Staff 2001-2002	MEN	WOMEN	TOTAL
FULL-TIME	17	1	18
PART-TIME	65	4	69
TOTAL	**82**	**5**	**87**

Student Numbers 2001-2002	MEN	WOMEN	TOTAL
All (Foreign Included)	126	97	**223**

HIGHER INTERNATIONAL SCHOOL OF LAW
Ecole supérieure internationale de Droit (ESID)
B.P. 825, Abidjan 03
Tel: +225(22) 42-88-10
Fax: +225(22) 42-88-10
EMail: esid@globeaccess.net

Directrice: Anne-Marie Hortense Assi Esso

Departments
Law

History: Founded 1999.

IVORY-CANADIAN UNIVERSITY
Université Ivoiro-Canadienne (UICA)
BP 2875, Abidjan 06
Tel: +225(22) 47-63-16
Fax: +225(22) 47-72-66
EMail: admission@uica.ci
Website: http://www.uica.com

Recteur: Hugues Albert

Programmes
Business Administration
Communication-Multimedia (Communication Studies; Multimedia)
Computer Science

History: Founded 1998.

UNIVERSITY OF THE ATLANTIC
Université de l'Atlantique (UA)
B.P. 6631, 11 rue des Jardins, Abidjan 06
Tel: +225(22) 48-72-55
Fax: +225(22) 44-21-72
EMail: uatl@aviso.ci
Website: http://www.uatl.com

Président: Asseypo Hauhouot

History: Founded 2000.

OTHER INSTITUTIONS

PUBLIC INSTITUTIONS

CENTRE AFRICAIN DE MANAGEMENT ET DE PERFECTIONNEMENT DES CADRES (CAMPC)
08 BP 878, Abidjan 08
Tel: +225(22) 44-43-22
Fax: +225(22) 44-03-78
Telex: 26170 camp-ci

Directeur général: Palaki-Pawi Marcus Palouki Haredema (1995-) **Tel:** +225(22) 44-49-46

Founded: 1970

Programmes
Management
Management Techniques (Management)

CENTRE D' ANIMATION ET DE FORMATION PÉDAGOGIQUE
BP 121, Abengourou
Tel: +225(35) 91-35-02

Founded: 1977

Programmes
Primary Teacher Training (Primary Education)

CENTRE D' ANIMATION ET DE FORMATION PÉDAGOGIQUE
BP 351, Aboisso
Tel: +225(21) 30-40-52

Founded: 1982

Programmes
Primary Teacher Training (Primary Education)

CENTRE D' ANIMATION ET DE FORMATION PÉDAGOGIQUE, BOUAKÉ 1
BP 125, Bouaké 01
Tel: +225(31) 63-35-21

Founded: 1967

Programmes
Primary Teacher Training (Primary Education)

CENTRE D' ANIMATION ET DE FORMATION PÉDAGOGIQUE, BOUAKÉ 2
BP 125, Bouaké 01
Tel: +225(31) 63-03-33
Founded: 1969

Programmes
Primary Teacher Training (Primary Education)

CENTRE D' ANIMATION ET DE FORMATION PÉDAGOGIQUE
BP 135, Dabou
Founded: 1966

Programmes
Primary Teacher Training (Primary Education)

CENTRE D' ANIMATION ET DE FORMATION PÉDAGOGIQUE
BP 1410, Daloa
Founded: 1965

Programmes
Primary Teacher Training (Primary Education)

CENTRE D' ANIMATION ET DE FORMATION PÉDAGOGIQUE
BP 583, Gagnoa
Tel: +225(32) 77-26-88
Founded: 1977

Programmes
Primary Teacher Training (Primary Education)

CENTRE D' ANIMATION ET DE FORMATION PÉDAGOGIQUE
BP 227, Grand-Bassam
Tel: +225(21) 30-12-31
Founded: 1969

Programmes
Primary Teacher Training (Primary Education)

CENTRE D' ANIMATION ET DE FORMATION PÉDAGOGIQUE
BP 123, Katiola
Tel: +225(31) 66-04-88
Founded: 1982

Programmes
Primary Teacher Training (Primary Education)

CENTRE D' ANIMATION ET DE FORMATION PÉDAGOGIQUE
BP 77, Korhogo
Tel: +225(36) 86-06-02
Founded: 1969

Programmes
Primary Teacher Training (Primary Education)

CENTRE D' ANIMATION ET DE FORMATION PÉDAGOGIQUE
BP 493, Man
Tel: +225(33) 79-04-57
Fax: +225(33) 79-04-57
Founded: 1975

Programmes
Primary Teacher Training (Primary Education)

CENTRE D' ANIMATION ET DE FORMATION PÉDAGOGIQUE
BP 612, Odienné
Tel: +225(33) 70-45-85
Founded: 1982

Centres
Primary Teacher Training (Educational Sciences; Primary Education) *Director:* Anvire Oi Anvire Darius

Main Language(s) of Instruction: French

Degrees and Diplomas: *Diplôme d'Instituteur stagiaire*

Student Services: Sports Facilities, Health Services

Student Residential Facilities: Yes

Libraries: Central Library

Academic Staff *2001-2002:* Full-Time: c. 15 Part-Time: c. 10 Total: c. 25

Student Numbers *2001-2002:* Total: c. 160

CENTRE D' ANIMATION ET DE FORMATION PÉDAGOGIQUE
BP 224, Yamoussoukro
Tel: +225(30) 64-03-87

Founded: 1982

Programmes
Primary Teacher Training (Primary Education)

ECOLE NATIONALE D'ADMINISTRATION (ENA)
BP V 20, Abidjan
Tel: +225(22) 41-40-33

Directeur: Irie Dje Bi Tel: +225(22) 44-52-25
Fax: +225(22) 41-49-63

Secrétaire général: Mameri Diaby Tel: +225(22) 41-52-31

Founded: 1960

Schools
Administrative and Diplomatic Management (Administration; International Relations; Management Systems)
Economics and Financial Management (Economics; Finance; Management Systems)
Magisterial and Judicial Studies (Justice Administration)

Centres
Lifelong Education and Executive Retraining (Management)

ECOLE NATIONALE DE POLICE (ENP)
BP 855, Abidjan 08
Tel: +225(22) 44-02-82
Fax: +225(22) 44-62-43

Directeur: Edja Oi Edja (1998-) Tel: +225(22) 44-77-59

Founded: 1967
Police Studies

ECOLE NATIONALE DES BEAUX-ARTS (ENBA)
BP 49, Abidjan 08
Tel: +225(22) 44-16-25
EMail: padec@ci.refer.org

Directeur: Kouakou Jacques Bandama

Founded: 1991

Departments
Communication (Advertising and Publicity; Cinema and Television; Communication Studies; Graphic Arts; Journalism; Marketing; Photography; Publishing and Book Trade) *Head*: Noel Konan Brou
Environment (Building Technologies; Design; Furniture Design) *Head*: Kacou Amon

Fine Arts (Ceramic Art; Engraving; Fine Arts; Painting and Drawing; Sculpture) *Head*: Kouamé Kouakou
Textile (Art History; Fashion Design; Textile Design; Weaving) *Head*: Francis Morand Koye

Centres
Pedagogy

ECOLE NATIONALE SUPÉRIEURE DE STATISTIQUE ET D'ECONOMIE APPLIQUÉE (ENSEA)
BP 3, Abidjan 08
Tel: +225(22) 44-08-40
Fax: +225(22) 44-39-88
EMail: ensea@ensea.ed.ci
Website: http://www.ensea.refer.ci/

Directeur: Koffi N'guessan (1994-)

Founded: 1961

Programmes
Statistics and Applied Economics (Economics; Statistics)

ECOLE NORMALE SUPÉRIEURE D'ABIDJAN (ENS)
BP 10, Abidjan 08
Tel: +225(22) 44-31-10
Fax: +225(22) 44-42-32
Website:
http://www.ci.refer.org/ivoir_ct/edu/sup/gec/ens/accueil.htm
Directeur: Goze Tape Tel: +225(22) 44-52-34

Founded: 1964

Departments
Arts and Humanities
Educational Sciences
History and Geography (Geography; History)
Languages (Modern Languages)
Science and Technology (Natural Sciences; Technology)
Teacher Training

Sections
Mathematics

Degrees and Diplomas: *Certificat d'Aptitude au Professorat de l'Enseignement secondaire*

INSTITUT NATIONAL DE FORMATION DES AGENTS DE LA SANTÉ
BP 720, Abidjan 18
Tel: +225(21) 24-29-00
Fax: +225(21) 24-28-87

Founded: 1992

Programmes
Midwifery
Nursing
Technical Studies (Technology)

Schools
Specialization

INSTITUT NATIONAL DE FORMATION DES AGENTS DE LA SANTÉ
BP V 20, Bouaké
Tel: +225(31) 63-10-26
Fax: +225(31) 63-10-28
Founded: 1988

Programmes
Nursing

INSTITUT NATIONAL DE FORMATION DES AGENTS DE LA SANTÉ
BP 426, Korhogo
Tel: +225(36) 86-11-85
Fax: +225(36) 86-08-58
Founded: 1993

Programmes
Midwifery
Nursing

INSTITUT NATIONAL DE FORMATION SOCIALE (INFS)
BP 2625, Abidjan 01
Tel: +225(22) 44-16-72
Fax: +225(22) 44-90-75
Founded: 1978

Schools
Pre-School Teacher Training (Preschool Education)
Social Work
Specialized Teacher Training (Teacher Training)

INSTITUT NATIONAL DE LA JEUNESSE ET DES SPORTS (INJS)
BP V 54, Abidjan
Tel: +225(21) 35-70-60
Fax: +225(21) 25-76-60
Directeur: Ernest Dagrou-Zahui Tel: +225(21) 26-88-45
Secrétaire général: Désiré Honoré

Founded: 1961

Lifelong Education
Sports
Youth Studies (Social Studies)

INSTITUT PÉDAGOGIQUE NATIONAL DE L'ENSEIGNEMENT TECHNIQUE ET PROFESSIONNEL (IPNETP)
BP 2098, Abidjan
Tel: +225(22) 44-67-69
Fax: +225(22) 44-90-22
Founded: 1976

Programmes
Technology Education; Vocational Education

INSTITUT DES SCIENCES ET TECHNIQUES DE LA COMMUNICATION (ISTC)
BP V 205 Boulevard de l'Université, Abidjan
Tel: +225(22) 44-88-38
Fax: +225(22) 44-84-33
EMail: istc@caftic-istc.ci
Website: http://www.caftic-istc.ci
Directeur: Sassongo Jacques Silue
Tel: +225(22) 44-88-58 +225(22) 44-86-66

Founded: 1992

Departments
Advertising and Marketing (Advertising and Publicity; Marketing)
Audiovisual Production (Multimedia)
Journalism
Multimedia
Science and Technology (Science Education; Technology)

PRIVATE INSTITUTIONS

ACADÉMIE RÉGIONALE DES SCIENCES ET TECHNIQUES DE LA MER (ARSTM)
BP V 158, Locodjro
Tel: +225(23) 46-08-09
Directeur général: Pascal Porquet
Directeur général adjoint: Osseini Anem

Founded: 1987

Schools
Navigation Studies (Nautical Science)

Egypt

INSTITUTION TYPES AND CREDENTIALS

Types of higher education institutions:

State University
Private University
State Higher Institute
Private Higher Institute
State Middle (Intermediate) Institute (Post-secondary)
Private Middle (Intermediate) Institute (Post-secondary)
State Academy
Private Academy
Military Academy
Open University

School leaving and higher education credentials:

Technical Education School Certificate
Thanaweya Am'ma
Primary-School Teacher's Certificate
Technician's Diploma
Diploma
Baccalaureos
High Diploma
Magistr
Diplôme d'Etudes professionnelles approfondies
Doktora

STRUCTURE OF EDUCATION SYSTEM

Pre-higher education:

Duration of compulsory education:

> Age of entry: 6
> Age of exit: 14

Structure of school system:

> *Primary*
> Type of school providing this education: Primary School

Length of programme in years: 6
Age level from: 6 to: 12
Certificate/diploma awarded: Primary School Certificate

Preparatory
Type of school providing this education: Preparatory School
Length of programme in years: 3
Age level from: 12 to: 15
Certificate/diploma awarded: Basic Education Completion Certificate

General Secondary
Type of school providing this education: General Secondary School
Length of programme in years: 3
Age level from: 15 to: 18
Certificate/diploma awarded: Thanaweya a' Amma (General Secondary Education Certificate (GSEC)

Technical Secondary
Type of school providing this education: Technical Secondary School (for technicians)
Length of programme in years: 3
Age level from: 15 to: 18
Certificate/diploma awarded: Technical Education Diploma

Technical
Type of school providing this education: Technical Secondary School (for high level technicians)
Length of programme in years: 5
Age level from: 15 to: 20
Certificate/diploma awarded: Advanced Technical Diploma

School education:

Compulsory education lasts for nine grades and is known as "basic education", split into two stages, primary school (Grades 1 -6) and preparatory school (Grades 7-9). It leads to the award of the Basic Education Completion Certificate. Following the nine-year basic education, pupils have the choice of entering a general secondary school (academic option) or a technical option including three- and five-year technical schools as well as experimental schools teaching languages, education and physical education. Only general secondary school graduates (academic option) may be admitted to university after obtaining their General Secondary Education Certificate (GSEC) or an Advanced Technical Diploma with scores above 75%. However, since 1991, some graduates from technical schools have been allowed to enter higher education.

Higher education:

Higher education is provided by universities and higher institutes of technical and professional training, both public and private. Responsibility for higher education lies mainly with the Ministry of Higher Education. Organization and administration, as well as academic programmes, are determined by laws, decrees and government regulations. The State universities are under the authority of the Supreme Council of Universities. Universities have full academic and administrative autonomy. They also carry out scientific research. The higher institutes of professional and technical training award qualifications equivalent to the first qualification conferred by the universities. Open college education was introduced at the universities of Cairo, Alexandria and Assiut in 1991. Private universities are entitled to implement their own criteria of admission and to set fees without intervention from the Ministry.

Main laws/decrees governing higher education:

Decree: Law 101/1992   Year: 1992
Concerns: Private Universities

Decree: Law 49/1972   Year: 1972
Concerns: Universities

Decree: Law 52/1970   Year: 1970
Concerns: Higher Institutes

Academic year:

Classes from: October *to:* June

Long vacation from: 1 July *to:* 30 September

Languages of instruction:

Arabic, English, French

Stages of studies:

Non-university level post-secondary studies (technical/vocational type):

Non-university level post-secondary education is offered by industrial, commercial and technical institutes providing two-year courses leading to a Diploma in Accountancy, Secretarial Work, Insurance, Computer or Health Sciences and Electronics. Holders of a Technical Education Diploma in commercial, industrial and agricultural fields may be admitted to these technical institutes. Holders of an Advanced Technical Diploma, whose score is 75% and above may be admitted to Higher Institutes of similar specializations. Studies last for four to five years.

University level studies:

University level first stage:
The first stage of higher education consists of four to six years of multidisciplinary study in basic subjects. They lead to the award of the Baccalaureos degree. In Medicine, studies last for six years, with one additional year of practical work.

University level second stage:
The second stage is more specialized and comprises two to five years of training in individual research work culminating in the submission of a thesis. The degree awarded is that of Magistr.

University level third stage:
The third stage leads to the Doktora (PhD) after at least two years' study following the Magistr (Master's Degree). Students must have obtained the mark "good" in the Master's Degree. It is awarded for advanced research work culminating in a thesis. In Medicine, a Doktora in Medical Sciences may be prepared concurrently with the professional Doctor of Medicine Degree.

University level fourth stage:
In certain rare cases, after the Doktora, a degree of Doctor of Science is awarded. It is reserved for researchers who have undertaken a substantial body of research work.

Teacher education:

Training of pre-primary and primary/basic school teachers
Primary school teachers must hold a qualification from a University Faculty of Education. There is also a distance learning programme to upgrade, through the medium of Arabic, primary school teachers who do not hold a degree.The course leads to a BEd in Primary Education.

Training of secondary school teachers
Secondary school teachers are trained in the Faculties of Education of the universities in four years and in higher teacher-training colleges. Both preparatory and general secondary teachers follow the same course which leads to the Bachelor Degree. Graduates who hold a four-year university degree can also teach at secondary level after following a one-year postgraduate course at the Faculty of Education where they are awarded the General Diploma. Teachers of technical education are trained at special faculties.

Training of higher education teachers
Higher education teachers are required to hold at least a Magistr in the field of higher education.

Non-traditional studies:

Distance higher education
The Egyptian University for Distance Learning is being established.

Lifelong higher education
In some ministries full- or part-time in-service training is organized periodically. Non-formal studies are offered by universities in the form of refresher courses and evening or correspondence courses.

NATIONAL BODIES

Responsible authorities:

Ministry of Higher Education
    Minister: Moufed Mahmoud Shehab
    Under-Secretary, Head of the Minister's Cabinet: Khalifa Helmi
    101, Kasr Al-Aini Street
    Cairo
    Tel: +20(2) 795-2155
    Fax: +20(2) 794-2556
    Telex: 92312 frcu un
    EMail: info@egy-mhe.gov.eg
    WWW: http://www.egy-mhe.gov.eg

    Role of governing body: Coordinates and supervises post-secondary education

Supreme Council of Universities
   President: Moufid Shehab
   Secretary-General: Abdul-Hai Ebeid
   Cairo University Buildings
   Giza
   Cairo
   Tel: +20(2) 573-2727 +20(2) 573-8583
   Fax: +20(2) 582-8722
   EMail: info@frcu.eun.eg
   WWW: http://www.frcu.eun.eg/

Role of governing body: Determines the overall policy of higher education and scientific research in the universities and determines the number of students admitted in each faculty.

ADMISSIONS TO HIGHER EDUCATION

Admission to non university higher education studies

Name of secondary school credential required: Technical Education School Certificate
Minimum score/requirement: 70%
For entry to: Technical institutes

Admission to university-level studies

Name of secondary school credential required: Thanaweya Am'ma
Minimum score/requirement: 70% or above
For entry to: Universities and higher specialized institutes

Alternatives to credentials: Secondary school students holders of an Advanced Technical Education may enter university Higher Institutes in their speciality if they have obtained scores of at least 75%.

Numerus clausus/restrictions: The Supreme Council of Universities at the Ministry of Higher Education determines the number of students to be admitted by the faculties of each university.

Foreign students admission

Admission requirements: Foreign students should have qualifications equivalent to the Thanaweya A'amma or a university degree.

Entry regulations: Foreign students must obtain a student visa.

Language requirements: Knowledge of Arabic is essential for regular university studies. English is the language of instruction at the American University in Cairo, some faculties of Helwan University and at the Faculty of Agriculture of the University of Alexandria. French is the language of instruction at Senghor University.

Application procedures:

Apply to national body for entry to: Universities

Apply to: Supreme Council of Universities
   Cairo University
   Giza
   Cairo
   Tel: +20(2) 573-8583
   Fax: +20(2) 582-8722
   Telex: 92312 frcu un
   EMail: info@frcu.eun.eg
   WWW: http://www.frcu.eun.eg/supreme.html

Recognition of studies and qualifications:

Studies pursued in foreign countries (bodies dealing with recognition of foreign credentials):
Ministry of Higher Education
   101 Kasr Al-Aini Street
   Cairo
   Tel: +20(2) 795-2155
   Fax: +20(2) 794-2556
   Telex: 92312 frcu un
   EMail: info@egy-mhe.gov.eg
   WWW: http://www.egy-mhe.gov.eg

Services provided and students dealt with: Provides information on the admission of foreign students to universities and higher institutes.

Supreme Council of Universities
   Secretary-General: Abdul-Hai Ebeid
   Cairo University
   Giza
   Cairo
   Tel: +20(2) 573-8583
   Fax: +20(2) 582-8722
   Telex: 92312 frcu un
   EMail: info@frcu.eun.eg
   WWW: http://www.frcu.eun.eg

Services provided and students dealt with: Provides information on admission to universities.

Multilateral agreements concerning recognition of foreign studies

Name(s) of agreement(s): Convention on the Recognition of Studies, Certificates, Diplomas and Degrees in Higher Education in the Arab and European States Bordering on the Mediterranean
Year of signature: 1976

Convention on the Recognition of Studies, Certificates, Diplomas, Degrees and Other Academic Qualifications in Higher Education in the African States
Year of signature: 1981

Convention on the Recognition of Studies, Diplomas and Degrees in Higher Education in the Arab States
Year of signature: 1978

References to further information on foreign student admissions and recognition of studies

Title: A guide for the use of foreign students
Publisher: Students' Welfare Department

STUDENT LIFE

Student expenses and financial aid

Bodies providing information on student financial aid:

Supreme Council of Universities
   Cairo University
   Giza
   Cairo
   Tel: +20(2) 573-8583
   Fax: +20(2) 582-8722
   Telex: 92312 frcu un
   EMail: info@frcu.eun.eg
   WWW: http://www.frcu.eun.eg

   Category of students: African, Asian and Arab nationals.

Publications on student services and financial aid:

   Title: Study Abroad 2004-2005, 32nd Edition
   Author: UNESCO
   Publisher: UNESCO Publishing
   Year of publication: 2003

INTERNATIONAL COOPERATION AND EXCHANGES

Principal national bodies responsible for dealing with international cooperation and exchanges in higher education:

Ministry of Higher Education
   101, Kasr Al-Aini Street
   Cairo
   Tel: +20(2) 794-2556
   Fax: +20(2) 796-3722
   Telex: 92312 frcu un
   EMail: info@egy-mhe.gov.eg
   WWW: http://www.egy-mhe.gov.eg

Participation of country in multilateral or bilateral higher education programmes

Name(s) of exchange programme(s): Agreement Concerning Scholarships For Studying German Language in Austria

Agreement Concerning Training of Language Teachers in Spain

GRADING SYSTEM

Usual grading system in secondary school

Full Description: 75-100: distinguished, excellent, very good; 65-74: good; 50-64: pass; 0-49: poor
Highest on scale: 75-100: distinguished
Pass/fail level: 50-64: pass
Lowest on scale: 0-49: poor

Main grading system used by higher education institutions

Full Description: 75-100: distinguished, excellent, very good; 65-74: good; 50-64: pass; 0-49: poor
Highest on scale: 75-100 Distinguished
Pass/fail level: 50-64 Pass (60 - 64 for medical sciences)
Lowest on scale: 0-49 Poor

NOTES ON HIGHER EDUCATION SYSTEM

Data for academic year: 2002-2003
Source: Ministry of Higher Education, Cairo, 2003

INSTITUTIONS OF HIGHER EDUCATION

UNIVERSITIES

PUBLIC INSTITUTIONS

*• AIN SHAMS UNIVERSITY
Abbassia, Cairo 11566
Tel: +20(2) 285-4063 +20(2) 482-0230
Fax: +20(2) 685-9251 +20(2) 684-7824
EMail: info@asunet.shams.edu.eg
Website: http://net.shams.edu.eg

President: Saleh Hashem Mostapha (2002-)
Tel: +20(2) 284-7818 Fax: +20(2) 282-6107 EMail:
shashem@asunet.shams.eun.eg

Secretary-General: Gamal Kamel Atwa
Tel: +20(2) 284-7823 Fax: +20(2) 284-7824

International Relations: Mohamed Awad Afify Tag Al-den,
Vice-President for Postgraduate Studies and Research

Faculties

Agriculture (Agricultural Economics; Agricultural Equipment; Agriculture; Agronomy; Animal Husbandry; Botany; Food Science; Genetics; Horticulture; Meat and Poultry; Microbiology; Plant Pathology; Soil Science) *Dean:* Hussein Mansour

Arts (Ancient Civilizations; Arabic; Arts and Humanities; English; French; Geography; Hebrew; History; Library Science; Literature; Mass Communication; Persian; Philosophy; Psychology; Sociology; Tourism; Turkish; Urdu) *Dean:* Mohamed Abd El Latef Haredy

Commerce (Accountancy; Business Administration; Business and Commerce; Economics; Insurance; Mathematics; Statistics) *Dean:* Eglal Abdel Monem Hafez

Computer and Information Science (Computer Engineering; Computer Science) *Dean:* Mohamed Saaed Abdelwahab

Dentistry (Dentistry; Oral Pathology; Orthodontics; Periodontics) *Dean:* Mokhtar Nagi Ibrahim

Education (Arabic; Biology; Chemistry; Curriculum; Educational Psychology; Educational Sciences; English; French; Geography; Geology; German; History; Islamic Studies; Mathematics; Pedagogy; Philosophy; Physics; Psychiatry and Mental Health; Sociology) *Dean:* Mohamed Amin El-Mofti

Engineering (Architecture; Automation and Control Engineering; Civil Engineering; Computer Engineering; Design; Electrical and Electronic Engineering; Engineering; Hydraulic Engineering; Irrigation; Mechanical Engineering; Power Engineering; Production Engineering; Structural Architecture; Systems Analysis; Town Planning) *Dean:* Mohamed A. Sheirah

Languages *(Al-Alsun)* (African Languages; Arabic; Chinese; Czech; English; French; German; Italian; Japanese; Modern Languages; Persian; Russian; Spanish; Turkish; Urdu) *Dean:* Mohamed Shebl Emam Gad

Law (Civil Law; Commercial Law; Criminal Law; History of Law; International Law; Islamic Law; Law; Political Science; Private Law; Public Law) *Dean:* Omar Helmy Fahmy

Medicine (Anaesthesiology; Anatomy; Biochemistry; Cardiology; Clinical Psychology; Community Health; Dermatology; Forensic Medicine and Dentistry; Gerontology; Gynaecology and Obstetrics; Histology; Immunology; Medicine; Microbiology; Occupational Health; Ophthalmology; Otorhinolaryngology; Paediatrics; Parasitology; Pathology; Pharmacology; Physiology; Psychiatry and Mental Health; Radiology; Surgery; Toxicology; Tropical Medicine) *Dean:* Fathi Mohmed Tash

Nursing

Pharmacy (Biochemistry; Immunology; Microbiology; Organic Chemistry; Pharmacology; Pharmacy; Toxicology) *Dean:* Mohmed M. Mostafa

Science (Biochemistry; Botany; Chemistry; Entomology; Geology; Geophysics; Mathematics; Microbiology; Natural Sciences; Physics; Zoology) *Dean:* Mohamed Hassan Saad El Sayed

Specific Education (Art Education; Educational Technology; Home Economics; Journalism; Music Education; Psychology; Radio and Television Broadcasting; Special Education) *Dean:* Magdy Faried Abdel Hamid

Women for Arts, Science and Education (Arabic; Biochemistry; Botany; Chemistry; Curriculum; Education; English; French; Geography; History; Home Economics; Literature; Mathematics; Nutrition; Pedagogy; Philosophy; Physics; Psychology; Social Sciences; Zoology) *Dean:* Hamdya Abd El Hamed Zayed

Institutes

Childhood Postgraduate Studies (Child Care and Development; Psychology; Sociology) *Dean:* Mostafa El Nshaar

Environmental Studies and Research (Environmental Studies) *Dean:* Abdel Azim M. El-Hammady

Centres

Genetic Engineering and Biotechnology (Biotechnology; Genetics)

University Education Development (Higher Education)

Vectors of Diseases (Epidemiology)

Research Centres

Childhood Studies (Child Care and Development)

Middle East (Middle Eastern Studies)

Papyrus Studies (Ancient Civilizations)

Public Service and Development (Business Administration; English; French; German; Oriental Languages; Radio and Television Broadcasting; Social and Community Services; Video)

Science Education Development (Science Education)

Scientific Computing (Computer Science)

Further Information: Also University Hospitals and specialized Hospital

History: Founded 1950, incorporating Abbassia School of Medicine. Formerly known as Ibrahim Pasha University and also as University of Heliopolis. Faculties of Commerce, Education, Agriculture, and Veterinary Medicine at Zagazig detached 1973 to form new University.

Governing Bodies: University Council, composed of the President, three Vice-Presidents, Deans of the Faculties, a representative of the Ministry of Higher Education, the Secretary-General and three other members

Academic Year: September to May

Admission Requirements: Secondary school certificate or equivalent

Main Language(s) of Instruction: Arabic

Degrees and Diplomas: *Diploma*: Education and Psychology; Home Economics; Law; *Baccalaureos*: Agriculture; Arts; Arts and Education; Civil Engineering; Commerce; Electrical Engineering; Law; Mechanical Engineering; Science; Science and Education, 4-5 yrs; *Magistr.* Agricultural Science; Agriculture; Arts; Arts in Commerce; Education; Engineering; Medicine; Psychology; Science, a further 2-3 yrs; *Doktora*: Architecture; Law; Letters; Medicine; Science, Agriculture, Education, Commerce

Student Residential Facilities: Yes

Libraries: Central Library, c. 90,000 vols; Faculty libraries, c. 3300 vols

Publications: Annals of the Faculty of Arts; Al-Ulum Al-Kanounia wal Iktisadia (journal); Economics and Business Review; Bulletin of the Faculty of Engineering; Annals of Agricultural Science

Press or Publishing House: Ain Shams University Press

Academic Staff *2001-2002:* Total: c. 6,400

Student Numbers *2001-2002:* Total: c. 144,000

*• AL-AZHAR UNIVERSITY

PO Box 11751, Meddina Nasr, Cairo
Tel: +20(2) 262-3274   +20(2) 262-3278
Fax: +20(2) 261-1404
Telex: 21945 skircw
EMail: info@alazhar.org
Website: http://www.alazhar.org

Rector: Ahmed Omar Hashem (1995-) Tel: +20(2) 262-3282

Faculties

Agriculture *(Assiut, Cairo)*
Arabic *(Assiut, Mansoura, Menoufia, Behara (Itai Al-Baroud), Sohag, Zagazig)*
Commerce *(for women)* (Business and Commerce)
Commerce *(Cairo, Tafehna Al-Ashraf)* (Business and Commerce)
Dentistry *(Cairo, Assiut)*
Education and Instruction *(Cairo, Tafehna Al-Ashraf)* (Educational Sciences; Pedagogy)
Engineering *(Cairo, Kena)*
Humanities *(for women)* (Arts and Humanities; Social Sciences)
Islamic and Arab Studies *(Aswan, Beni-Suel, Cairo, Damietta, Kafr-Al-Sheikh)* (Arabic; Islamic Studies; Islamic Theology)

Islamic and Arab Studies *(for women, Cairo, Alexandria, Mansoura, Sohag, Zagazig)* (Arabic; Islamic Studies)
Islamic Call (Islamic Theology)
Islamic Fundamentals *(Cairo, Zagazig)* (Islamic Studies)
Islamic Fundamentals and Call *(Assiut, Mansoura, Tanta, Shebin El-Kom)* (Islamic Studies)
Islamic Jurisprudence and Law *(Zagazig, Tanta, Cairo, Assiut, Damanhour, Tafehna Al-Ashraf)*
Languages and Translation (Modern Languages; Translation and Interpretation)
Medicine *(Assiut, Cairo, Damietta)*
Medicine *(for Women)*
Pharmacy *(Cairo, Assiut)*
Pharmacy *(For women, Tanta)*
Science *(for Women)* (Natural Sciences)

Colleges
Islamic Studies *(for Women)*

Centres
Heart Diseases and Surgery (Cardiology; Surgery)

Research Centres
Childhood Disabilities (Child Care and Development)
Islamic Commercial Studies *(Saleh Kamel)* (Business and Commerce; Islamic Law)
Population Studies *(The International Islamic Centre)* (Demography and Population)

History: Founded 1970 as a school and developed 1961.

Governing Bodies: University Council

Academic Year: October to June

Admission Requirements: Secondary certificate of Al-Azhar or equivalent

Main Language(s) of Instruction: Arabic

Degrees and Diplomas: *Baccalaureos*: 4-5 yrs; *Magistr.* 2-3 yrs; *Doktora*: 2-3 yrs following Magistr

Libraries: c. 80,000 vols

Academic Staff *2001-2002:* Total: c. 6,000

Student Numbers *2001-2002:* Total: c. 155,000

*• ALEXANDRIA UNIVERSITY

22 Al-Guish Avenue, El Chatby, Alexandria
Tel: +20(3) 591-1152
Fax: +20(3) 596-0720
EMail: alex@alex.eun.eg
Website: http://www.alexandriauniversity.org

President: Mohamed Abdellah (2001-)
Tel: +20(3) 596-1152 +20(3) 597-1678
Administrative Officer: Mohamed Roshdy Abdul-Ghany

Faculties

Agriculture *(Alexandria, Saba Pasha)* (Agriculture; Dairy; Entomology; Forestry; Genetics; Home Economics; Horticulture; Soil Science; Water Science; Wood Technology)
Arts (Arts and Humanities; Social Sciences)
Commerce (Business and Commerce)

Dentistry (Dentistry; Surgery)

Education (Arabic; Biology; Chemistry; Curriculum; Education; Foreign Languages Education; Mathematics; Modern Languages; Physics; Psychology; Social Sciences; Teacher Trainers Education)

Engineering (Architecture; Building Technologies; Chemical Engineering; Computer Engineering; Electrical Engineering; Engineering; Irrigation; Marine Engineering; Mathematics; Mechanical Engineering; Nuclear Engineering; Physics; Production Engineering; Sanitary Engineering; Textile Technology; Transport Engineering)

Fine Arts

Kindergarten (Preschool Education)

Law

Medicine (Dermatology; Gynaecology and Obstetrics; Health Sciences; Medicine; Neurological Therapy; Oncology; Ophthalmology; Paediatrics; Surgery; Tropical Medicine)

Nursing

Pharmacy

Physical Education

Physical Education *(For women)*

Science (Biochemistry; Botany; Chemistry; Environmental Studies; Geology; Marine Science and Oceanography; Mathematics; Natural Sciences; Physics; Zoology)

Specific Education (Education)

Tourism and Hotel Studies (Hotel Management; Tourism)

Veterinary Medicine *(Edfina)* (Veterinary Science)

Institutes

Medical Research (Medicine; Radiology)

Higher Institutes

Postgraduate Studies (Higher Education)

Public Health (Behavioural Sciences; Public Health; Statistics; Tropical Medicine)

History: Founded 1942 as State University, incorporating former branches of the Faculties of Arts, Law, and Engineering of Fouad I University (Cairo), and known as Farouk University until 1953. Faculty of Medicine and Colleges of Education at Tanta detached 1972 to form new University.

Governing Bodies: University Senate

Academic Year: October to June (October-February; March-June)

Admission Requirements: Secondary school certificate or equivalent

Main Language(s) of Instruction: Arabic, English

Degrees and Diplomas: *Baccalaureos*: Arts and Education; Science and Education, 4 yrs; Science in Anatomy; Science in Physiology, 5 yrs; *Magistr*: a further 1-3 yrs and thesis; *Doktora*: 2 yrs after Magistr and dissertation; Science, awarded after Doctorate for distinguished contributions to knowledge. Also postgraduate Diplomas

Student Residential Facilities: For c. 5 700 students

Special Facilities: Archaeology Museum. Forensic Medical Museum

Libraries: Central Library, c. 28,000 vols; also Faculty and Institute libraries, c. 40,000 vols

Publications: Bulletins

Academic Staff *2001-2002:* Total: c. 5,300

Student Numbers *2001-2002:* Total: c. 76,000

DAMANHOUR BRANCH
Damanhour

Vice-President: Ibrahim Abdel Salam Al Samra (1997-)

Faculties

Agriculture

Arts (Fine Arts)

Commerce (Business and Commerce)

Education

History: Founded 1988.

• ASSIUT UNIVERSITY
PO Box 71515, Assiut
Tel: +20(88) 324-040   +20(88) 314-527
Fax: +20(88) 312-564   +20(88) 322-562
Telex: 92863 asunv-un
EMail: assiut@frcu.eun.eg
Website: http://www.aun.eun.eg

President: Mohamed Raafat Mahmoud (1996-)
Tel: +20(88) 314-527 EMail: rmahmoud@aun.eun.eg

Secretary-General: Nabila Mahmoud Abd El Maged
Tel: +20(88) 322-000

International Relations: Ibrahim M.S. Taha
Tel: +20(88) 324-033 Fax: +20(88) 313-970
EMail: Taha.is@aun.eun.eg

Faculties

Agriculture *Dean*: Mohamed Atef Ahmed Sallam

Arts (Arabic; Archaeology; Arts and Humanities; English; French; Geography; History; Information Sciences; Library Science; Media Studies; Philosophy; Psychology; Sociology) *Dean*: Hassan Zein El-Abedin M.

Commerce (Business and Commerce) *Dean*: Abd El-Hadi Saleh Swify

Computer and Information Science (Computer Science) *Dean*: Hosni Mohamed Ibrahim

Education *Dean*: Abdel Tawab A. Abdel Tawab

Education *(New Valley) Dean*: Abd Allah E. Abd El-Gawad

Engineering (Architecture; Civil Engineering; Electrical Engineering; Engineering; Mechanical Engineering; Metallurgical Engineering; Mining Engineering) *Dean*: Mohamed A. Ashour

Law (Islamic Law; Law) *Dean*: Gaber Ali Mahran

Medicine *Dean*: Magdy A. El-Akkad

Nursing *Dean*: Sana Soliman Kroosh

Pharmacy *Dean*: Mohamed A. El-Shanawany

Physical Education *Dean*: Mahmoud A. Abd El-Karim

Science (Botany; Chemistry; Entomology; Geology; Mathematics; Natural Sciences; Physics; Zoology) *Dean*: Mohamed Ibrahim Abd El-Kader

Social Work *Dean*: Badria Shawki Abd El-Wahab

Special Education *Dean*: Yousif H. Shahin

Veterinary Medicine (Veterinary Science) *Dean*: Mohamed S. Yousif

Institutes

Cancer *(South Egypt)* (Medicine; Oncology) *Dean*: Mohamed Atef Abd El-Aziz

Sugar Technology Research (Food Technology) *Dean*: Mohamed Ragab Bayoumi

Centres

Future Studies (Futurology) *Director*: Mohamed Ibrahim Mansour

Further Information: Also University Teaching Hospital

History: Founded 1949 by decree, opened 1957. A State Institution enjoying administrative autonomy. Faculties of Agriculture, Arts and Education at Minya detached 1976 to form new University. Financed by the State. Branches in Sohag, Qena and Aswan merged 1995 to form South Valley University.

Governing Bodies: University Council, comprising the President as Chairman, four Vice-Presidents, the Deans, the Secretary-General, and 4 other members selected by the Council

Academic Year: September to May (September-December; January-May)

Admission Requirements: Secondary school certificate or equivalent

Fees: (Egyptian Pounds): Undergraduate, 100-150; Postgraduate, 200-250; foreign students (Pounds Sterling), Undergraduate, 1000-1500; Postgraduate 1500-2000

Main Language(s) of Instruction: Arabic, English

Degrees and Diplomas: *Baccalaureos*: Science; Agriculture; Commerce; Education; Physical Education; Nursing; Social Work; Special Education; Computer and Information Science, 4 yrs; Pharmacy; Veterinary Science, 5 yrs; Health Studies, 6 yrs; *Magistr*. All fields, a further 2-3 yrs and thesis; *Doktora*: a further 2-4 yrs by dissertation. Also Diplomas of Specialization, 2 yrs following *Baccalaureos*, 4-yr Licence in Arts; Law; Education

Student Services: Academic Counselling, Social Counselling, Sports Facilities, Language Programmes, Health Services, Canteen

Student Residential Facilities: For 13,000 students

Special Facilities: Geological Museum. Architectural Gallery

Libraries: Central Library and Faculty libraries, c. 450,000 vols, 600 periodicals

Publications: Faculty Bulletins; Assiut Bulletin for Environmental Research

Press or Publishing House: Assiut University Publishing and Distributing House

Academic Staff *2002-2003*	MEN	WOMEN	TOTAL
FULL-TIME	1,998	893	**2,891**
STAFF WITH DOCTORATE			
FULL-TIME	1,267	372	1,639
PART-TIME	–	–	10
TOTAL	–	–	**1,649**

Student Numbers *2002-2003*	MEN	WOMEN	TOTAL
All (Foreign Included)	36,961	25,753	**62,714**

*•CAIRO UNIVERSITY

PO Box 12613, Nahdet Misr Street, Giza, Cairo
Tel: +20(2) 572-9584
Fax: +20(2) 568-8884
Telex: (091) 94372 uncai un
EMail: mailmaster@main-scc.cairo.eun.eg
Website: http://www.cairo.eun.eg

President: Nageeb E. Gohar (1999-) Tel: +20(2) 572-7066
Fax: +20(2) 572-8131
EMail: president@main-scc.cairo.eun.eg

Administrative Officer: Fayza Mogahed

Faculties

Agriculture

Arabic and Islamic Studies *(Dar El-Ulum)* (Arabic; Comparative Literature; Grammar; History; Islamic Law; Islamic Studies; Linguistics; Literature; Oriental Studies; Philosophy)

Archaeology (Ancient Civilizations; Archaeology; Art History; Museum Studies; Restoration of Works of Art; Tourism)

Arts (Arabic; Arts and Humanities; English; French; Geography; German; Greek (Classical); History; Japanese; Latin; Library Science; Philosophy; Psychology; Sociology; Spanish)

Commerce (Accountancy; Banking; Business Administration; Business and Commerce; Health Administration; Hotel Management; Insurance; Marketing; Mathematics; Public Administration; Taxation)

Computer Science and Informatics (Computer Science; Information Sciences; Information Technology)

Dentistry (Dental Hygiene; Dentistry; Oral Pathology; Orthodontics; Surgery)

Economics and Political Science (Economics; Political Science; Public Administration; Statistics)

Engineering (Aeronautical and Aerospace Engineering; Architecture; Biomedical Engineering; Civil Engineering; Electrical Engineering; Engineering; Hydraulic Engineering; Irrigation; Mathematics; Mechanical Engineering; Metallurgical Engineering; Petroleum and Gas Engineering; Physics; Telecommunications Engineering)

Kindergarten (Preschool Education)

Law (Civil Law; Commercial Law; Criminal Law; Finance; History of Law; International Law; Islamic Law; Labour Law; Law; Public Law)

Mass Communication (Advertising and Publicity; Journalism; Mass Communication; Radio and Television Broadcasting)

Medicine (Anaesthesiology; Anatomy; Biochemistry; Cardiology; Dermatology; Forensic Medicine and Dentistry; Gynaecology and Obstetrics; Histology; Hygiene; Medicine; Neurology; Occupational Health; Ophthalmology; Orthopedics; Paediatrics; Parasitology; Pathology; Physiology; Psychiatry and Mental Health; Radiology; Surgery; Tropical Medicine; Urology; Venereology)

Nursing

Pharmacy (Analytical Chemistry; Biochemistry; Microbiology; Organic Chemistry; Pharmacology; Pharmacy)

Physiotherapy (Gynaecology and Obstetrics; Neurological Therapy; Orthopedics; Physical Therapy; Plastic Surgery)

Regional and Urban Planning (Regional Planning; Town Planning)

Science (Analytical Chemistry; Astronomy and Space Science; Botany; Chemistry; Computer Science; Entomology; Geology; Geophysics; Mathematics; Meteorology; Microbiology; Mineralogy; Natural Sciences; Physics; Statistics; Zoology)

Special Education

Veterinary Medicine (Anatomy; Animal Husbandry; Biochemistry; Fishery; Forensic Medicine and Dentistry; Histology; Microbiology; Nutrition; Parasitology; Pharmacology; Physiology; Toxicology; Veterinary Science)

Institutes

African Studies and Research (African Languages; African Studies; Anthropology; Economics; Geography; History; Natural Resources; Political Science)

Cancer *(National)* (Anaesthesiology; Biology; Oncology; Pathology; Radiology; Surgery)

Educational Studies and Research (Curriculum; Educational and Student Counselling; Educational Research; Educational Technology; Pedagogy; Preschool Education; Teacher Training)

Laser Science *(National)* (Laser Engineering)

Statistical Studies and Research (Statistics)

Centres

Development and Technology Planning (Development Studies; Technology)

Environmental Studies and Research (Environmental Studies)

Future Studies and Research (Futurology)

Further Information: Also Qars El Ainy Hospital; Tumour Hospital and Infants Hospital

History: Founded 1908 as National University, became State University 1925. Known as Fouad I University between 1940 and 1953.

Governing Bodies: University Council, composed of the President, Deputies, Heads of the Faculties and Institutes, and four members dealing with university affairs (appointed for two years)

Academic Year: September to June (September-January; January-June)

Admission Requirements: Secondary school certificate or equivalent. University degree for Institutes of Statistical Studies and African Studies

Main Language(s) of Instruction: Arabic, English, French

Degrees and Diplomas: *Diploma*: African Studies; Statistics, 2 yrs; *Baccalaureos*: Commerce; Journalism; Science in Economics; Science in Political Science; Science in Statistics, 4 yrs; Dental Surgery, 4 yrs following preparatory yr; Chemical Engineering; Civil Engineering; Electrical Engineering; Mechanical Engineering; Mining Engineering; Petroleum Engineering; Pharmaceutical Chemistry, 5 yrs; *Magistr*: Dental Surgery; Journalism; Surgery, a further 2 yrs; *Doktora*: Medical Science; Medicine; Pharmacy; Veterinary Medicine and Surgery, 2 yrs following Magistr; Dental Medicine, 2 yrs following Magistr

Student Services: Academic Counselling, Social Counselling, Employment Services, Foreign Student Adviser, Nursery Care, Cultural Centre, Sports Facilities, Handicapped Facilities, Health Services, Canteen

Student Residential Facilities: For c. 3150 men students, and c. 7650 women students

Special Facilities: Museum of Egyptology; Islamic Museum; Museum of Entomology. Collection of Papyrii and Ancient Coins

Libraries: Central Library, c. 950,000 vols. Fayoum Branch, c. 33,200 vols; Beni Sweif Branch, c. 37,000 vols

Publications: Egyptian Journal of Genetics and Psychology; The Egyptian Statistical Magazine; Medical Journal of Cairo University; Population and Family Planning Magazine; Publications of the Faculties; Computer Magazine

Press or Publishing House: Cairo University Press; Agriculture Faculty Press; Statistical Studies and Research Press; Law Faculty Press; Science Faculty Press

Academic Staff *2001-2002:* Total: c. 5,550

Student Numbers *2001-2002:* Total: **155,000**

AL-FAYOUM BRANCH
Al-Fayoum
Tel: +20(2) 572-8779

Vice-President: Abdul-Fattah El-Shershabi (2001-)

Faculties

Agriculture

Arabic and Islamic Studies *(Dar El-Ulum)* (Arabic; Islamic Studies)

Archaeology

Dar El-Ulum (Islamic Theology)

Education

Engineering

Medicine

Science (Natural Sciences)

Social Work (Social Welfare)

Special Education

Tourism (Hotel Management; Tourism)

History: Founded 1988.

BENI-SUEF BRANCH
Beni-Suef
Tel: +20(2) 573-5334

Vice-President: Mohamed Anas Gha'far (1998-)

Faculties

Arts (Arts and Humanities)

Commerce (Business and Commerce)

Education

Law

Medicine

Pharmacy

Science

Veterinary Medicine (Veterinary Science)

History: Founded 1981.

KHARTOUM BRANCH
Khartoum

Faculties

Arts (Arts and Humanities)
Commerce (Business and Commerce)
Law
Science (Natural Sciences)

History: Founded 1955.

* HELWAN UNIVERSITY CAIRO

Ein Helwan, Cairo 11790
Tel: +20(2) 557-1441
Fax: +20(2) 555-6008
Telex: 345-5461
EMail: helwan@helwan.edu.eg
Website: http://www.helwan.edu.eg

President: Amr Ezzat Salama (2002-) Tel: +20(2) 556-9061
Fax: +20(2) 556-5820 EMail: president@helwan.edu.eg

Secretary-General: Ekram Mohamed Abdel Hamed
Tel: +20(2) 555-6013 Fax: +20(2) 555-6013

International Relations: Ahmed Abdel-Krem Salama

Faculties

Applied Arts (Advertising and Publicity; Architectural Restoration; Ceramic Art; Cinema and Television; Design; Glass Art; Graphic Arts; Interior Design; Metal Techniques; Photography; Printing and Printmaking; Sculpture; Textile Design) *Dean*: Adel El Hefnawy

Art Education (Art Criticism; Art Education; Design; Handicrafts; Painting and Drawing) *Dean*: Abla Hanafy

Arts (Ancient Civilizations; Arabic; Arts and Humanities; English; French; Geography; German; Hebrew; History; Information Sciences; Italian; Library Science; Mass Communication; Modern Languages; Persian; Philosophy; Psychology; Sociology; Spanish; Theatre; Turkish) *Dean*: Zbeda Atta

Commerce and Business Administration (Accountancy; Business Administration; Business and Commerce; Insurance; International Business; Political Science; Statistics) *Dean*: Mostafa Ezz El Arab

Computer and Information Sciences (Computer Science; Information Sciences) *Dean*: Ebada Sarhan

Education (Curriculum; Education; Educational Psychology; Educational Technology; Pedagogy) *Dean*: Abdel Motlib El Koraty

Engineering (Computer Engineering; Electrical and Electronic Engineering; Engineering; Production Engineering; Telecommunications Engineering) *Dean*: Omar Hanafy

Engineering *(Mattaria)* (Architecture; Automation and Control Engineering; Civil Engineering; Engineering; Mechanical Engineering; Power Engineering) *Dean*: Mostafa El Demerdash

Fine Arts (Architecture; Fine Arts; Graphic Arts; Interior Design; Painting and Drawing; Sculpture) *Dean*: Mohamed Abdel Gwad

Home Economics (Food Science; Home Economics; Nutrition; Textile Technology) *Dean*: Abdel Rahman Attia

Law (Civil Law; Commercial Law; Criminal Law; History of Law; International Law; Law; Private Law; Public Law) *Dean*: Galal Ebraheem

Music Education (Music Education; Musical Instruments; Singing) *Dean*: Ameera Farag

Pharmacy (Analytical Chemistry; Biochemistry; Chemistry; Microbiology; Organic Chemistry; Pharmacology; Pharmacy) *Dean*: Ebraheem Mahmoud

Physical Education *(for Men)* (Health Sciences; Parks and Recreation; Physical Education; Physical Therapy; Sports Management) *Dean*: Sobhy Hasaneen

Physical Education *(for Women) Dean*: Aziza Salem

Science (Astronomy and Space Science; Botany; Chemistry; Geology; Natural Sciences; Physics; Zoology) *Dean*: Mohamed Osman

Social Work (Social and Community Services; Social Work) *Dean*: Rashad Abdel Latif

Tourism and Hotel Management (Hotel Management; Tourism) *Dean*: Ali Omar

Centres

Foreign Trade Studies and Research (International Business)
Scientific Computing (Computer Science)
Scientific Instrument Maintenance (Instrument Making)
Small Projects Support
Social Service (Social and Community Services)
Technology Development Studies and Research (Technology)
University Education Development (Pedagogy)
Youth Studies and Research (Child Care and Development)

Further Information: Also 46 self-sponsored Research Centres and Units

History: Founded 1975, incorporating previously existing Faculties and Institutes of Higher Education. A state Institution under the supervision of the Ministry of Higher Education and financed by the State.

Governing Bodies: University Council, comprising twenty-eight members

Academic Year: September to June

Admission Requirements: Secondary school certificate or equivalent

Main Language(s) of Instruction: Arabic, English

International Co-operation: With universities in China, Romania, Aden.

Degrees and Diplomas: *Diploma*: Education; Science, 1-2 yrs; *Baccalaureos*: Arts (B.A.), 4 yrs; Science (B.Sc.), 4-5 yrs; *Magistr*: Arts (M.A.); Science (M.Sc.), a further 2 yrs; *Doktora*: Arts; Science (PhD), 3 yrs following Magistr

Student Services: Academic Counselling, Social Counselling, Employment Services, Nursery Care, Cultural Centre, Sports Facilities, Language Programmes, Handicapped Facilities, Health Services, Canteen, Foreign Student Centre

Student Residential Facilities: Yes

Special Facilities: Art Gallery

Libraries: Central Library, 250,000 vols; Faculty libraries, 338,089 vols

Publications: Helwan University Journal

Press or Publishing House: University Press at the Faculty of Applied Arts

Academic Staff *2001:* Total: **3,854**

Staff with doctorate: Total: **1,080**

Student Numbers 2002	TOTAL
All (Foreign Included)	**96,206**
FOREIGN ONLY	535

*• MANSOURA UNIVERSITY

60, El Gomhoria Street, Mansoura, Dakahliya 35516
Tel: +20(50) 224-7055
Fax: +20(50) 224-7330
EMail: mua@mans.eun.eg;hamzaaa@mum.mans.eun.eg
Website: http://www.mans.eun.eg

President: Yehia Hussein Ebeid (2001-)
Tel: +20(50) 247-800 Fax: +20(50) 247-900
EMail: yehiaebeid@mans.edu.eg

Secretary-General: Amira Al-Sorongy Tel: +20(50) 247-330
Fax: +20(50) 247-330

International Relations: Yehia Hussein Ebeid
Tel: +20(50) 243-587 Fax: +20(50) 243-587

Faculties

Agriculture (Agricultural Economics; Agricultural Engineering; Agriculture; Agronomy; Animal Husbandry; Botany; Chemistry; Dairy; Floriculture; Food Science; Genetics; Microbiology; Plant Pathology; Soil Science; Vegetable Production; Zoology) *Dean:* Maher M. Ibrahim

Arts (Arabic; Archaeology; Arts and Humanities; Documentation Techniques; English Studies; French Studies; Geography; Greek; History; Journalism; Latin; Library Science; Oriental Languages; Philosophy; Psychology; Sociology) *Dean:* Mohamed Eisa Saber Al-Harery

Commerce (Accountancy; Business Administration; Business and Commerce; Economics; Insurance; Statistics) *Dean:* Ahmed Hamed Hagag

Computer and Information Science (Computer Science; Information Management; Information Sciences) *Dean:* Mostafa Mohamed El Arabaty

Dentistry (Dentistry; Oral Pathology; Orthodontics) *Dean:* Ali Abdel-Mageed Sawan

Education (Arabic; Chemistry; Curriculum; Education; Educational Psychology; Educational Technology; Geography; Geology; History; Islamic Studies; Modern Languages; Primary Education; Teacher Training) *Dean:* Talaat Hasan Abdel-Raheem

Education *(Damietta)* (Arabic; Biology; Curriculum; Education; Educational Psychology; Educational Technology; English; French; Geography; Geology; History; Islamic Studies; Modern Languages; Philosophy) *Dean:* Farouk Abdou Hassan Felia

Engineering (Architectural and Environmental Design; Automation and Control Engineering; Civil Engineering; Computer Engineering; Construction Engineering; Electrical and Electronic Engineering; Engineering; Hydraulic Engineering; Industrial Engineering; Irrigation; Mathematics; Mechanical Engineering; Physics; Power Engineering; Textile Technology) *Dean:* Hamdi Ahmed El-Mikati

Law (Civil Law; Commercial Law; Criminal Law; History of Law; International Law; Islamic Law; Law; Private Law; Public Law) *Dean:* Mahmoud Mohamed Hasan

Medicine (Anaesthesiology; Anatomy; Biochemistry; Cardiology; Community Health; Dermatology; Forensic Medicine and Dentistry; Gynaecology and Obstetrics; Histology; Medicine; Microbiology; Neurology; Ophthalmology; Orthodontics; Orthopedics; Paediatrics; Parasitology; Pathology; Pharmacology; Physical Therapy; Physiology; Psychiatry and Mental Health; Radiology; Surgery; Urology) *Dean:* Aly Abd El-Lattif Hegazy

Nursing (Community Health; Gerontology; Gynaecology and Obstetrics; Hygiene; Nursing) *Dean:* Olfat Ferag Mohamed Ali

Pharmacy (Analytical Chemistry; Microbiology; Pharmacy) *Dean:* Ali Abdel-Rahman Al-Eman

Physical Education (Health Sciences; Physical Education; Sports; Sports Management) *Dean:* Mohamed El-Said Khalil

Science (Botany; Chemistry; Geology; Mathematics; Natural Sciences; Physics; Zoology) *Dean:* Fathy Abd El-Kader Amer

Science *(Damietta)* (Botany; Chemistry; Environmental Studies; Geology; Mathematics; Physics; Science Education; Zoology) *Dean:* Salah Kamel El-Labany

Special Education

Special Education *(Damietta)*

Veterinary Science (Anatomy; Animal Husbandry; Biochemistry; Embryology and Reproduction Biology; Food Science; Forensic Medicine and Dentistry; Histology; Hygiene; Immunology; Nutrition; Parasitology; Pathology; Pharmacology; Physiology; Surgery; Veterinary Science; Virology) *Dean:* El Said El Sherbini El-Said

Centres

Urology and Nephrology (Nephrology; Surgery; Urology)

Further Information: Also 2 Teaching Hospitals and 3 Laboratories

History: Founded 1972 as East Delta University, incorporating Faculties previously attached to the University of Cairo. Acquired present title 1973. A State Institution under the authority of the Ministry of Higher Education.

Governing Bodies: Board; Boards of the Faculties

Academic Year: September to June (September-January; February-June)

Admission Requirements: Secondary school certificate or equivalent

Main Language(s) of Instruction: Arabic

Degrees and Diplomas: *Baccalaureos*: 4-6 yrs; *Magistr*: a further 2-3 yrs; *Doktora*: (PhD), a further 2-4 yrs

Student Services: Academic Counselling, Social Counselling, Employment Services, Nursery Care, Cultural Centre, Sports Facilities, Health Services, Canteen

Student Residential Facilities: For c. 6000 students

Special Facilities: Midwifery Museum; Anatomy Museum; Forensic Medicine Museum; Pharmacology Museum; Zoology Museum; Botany Museum

Libraries: Central Library; Faculty libraries, total, c. 425,000 vols

Publications: Scientific Journal; Periodicals of the Community and Environmental Council and the Cultural Affairs and Research Branch

Press or Publishing House: University Press

Academic Staff *2001-2002*: Full-Time: c. 1,930 Part-Time: c. 20 Total: c. 1,950

Staff with Doctorate: Total: c. 1,950

Student Numbers *2001-2002:* Total: c. 12,600

*• MINIA UNIVERSITY

PO Box 61519, El-Minia
Tel: +20(86) 321-443
Fax: +20(86) 342-601
EMail: rumenia@rusys.eg.net
Website: http://www.minia.edu.eg

President: Abdel-Monem A. El-Bassuoni
Tel: +20(86) 361-443

Vice-President, Graduate Studies and Research:
Mohammed Said M. Ali Tel: +20(86) 363-544

Faculties

Agriculture *Dean*: Atif Kishk Mohamed
Arabic and Islamic Studies *(Dar El-Uloom)* (Arabic; Islamic Studies) *Dean*: Muhey O. Mohasib
Arts (Arts and Humanities) *Dean*: Mohammad Naguib
Dentistry *Dean*: Hany H. Ameen
Education *Dean*: Atta Taha Zidan
Engineering (Architecture; Automation and Control Engineering; Chemical Engineering; Civil Engineering; Electrical Engineering; Energy Engineering; Engineering; Mechanical Engineering; Production Engineering) *Dean*: Mohamed Moness Bayoumi
Fine Arts (Architecture; Fine Arts; Graphic Arts; Interior Design; Painting and Drawing; Sculpture) *Dean*: Wafaa A. Musalam
Languages *(Al-Alsun)* (English; French; German; Spanish) *Dean*: Khaled Abu-Hattab
Medicine (Anatomy; Biochemistry; Community Health; Embryology and Reproduction Biology; Forensic Medicine and Dentistry; Gynaecology and Obstetrics; Histology; Medicine; Ophthalmology; Otorhinolaryngology; Paediatrics; Physiology; Surgery) *Dean*: Hany S. El-Tonsi
Nursing *Dean*: Iglal A. Shawky
Pharmacy (Analytical Chemistry; Anatomy; Botany; Histology; Organic Chemistry; Pharmacy; Physics; Physiology) *Dean*: Mohamed Khalifa
Physical Education (Physical Education; Sports) *Dean*: Bahaa Salama
Science (Biology; Chemistry; Computer Science; Geology; Mathematics; Natural Sciences; Physics) *Dean*: Mohamed Said Ali
Special Education *Dean*: A. El-Fergany
Tourism and Hotel Management (Hotel Management; Tourism) *Dean*: Abdel–Bary A Dawood

History: Founded 1976, incorporating Faculties of Agriculture, Education, Humanities, Science, and Engineering, previously forming part of the University of Assiut. A State Institution enjoying administrative autonomy. Financed by the Government.

Governing Bodies: University Council; Council for Undergraduate Studies; Council for Graduate Studies and Research

Academic Year: October to May (October-January; February-May)

Admission Requirements: Secondary school certificate or equivalent

Main Language(s) of Instruction: Arabic, English

Degrees and Diplomas: *Diploma*; *Baccalaureos*: Agriculture; Education; Physical Education; Science, 4 yrs; Engineering, 5 yrs; Surgery, 6 yrs; *Magistr*: Arts and Education, a further 2 yrs; *Doktora*: 2 yrs following Magistr, by thesis

Student Residential Facilities: For c. 3000 students

Special Facilities: Art Gallery

Libraries: Central Library, c. 7200 vols; libraries of the Faculties, c. 130,000 vols

Publications: Educational and Psychological Research Magazine; History and Future Magazine; Technical Scientific Magazine; Minia Medical Magazine; Physical Education Magazine; Journal of Agricultural Research; Bulletins

Press or Publishing House: University Press

Academic Staff *2001-2002:* Total: c. 770

Student Numbers *2001-2002:* Total: c. 16,200

*• MINUFIYA UNIVERSITY

PO Box 32511, Gamal Abdel Nasser Street, Shebin Al-Kom, Menoufia
Tel: +20(48) 222-170 +20(48) 224-216
Fax: +20(48) 226-454 +20(2) 575-2777
Telex: (091) 23832 muske un
EMail: menofia@menofia.edu.eg
Website: http://www.menofia.edu.eg

President: Abbas Aly El-Hefnawy (2002-)
Tel: +20(48) 225-298
EMail: abbas.elhefnawy@menofia.edu.eg

Secretary-General: Mostafa S. Khalil Tel: +20(48) 220-894
Fax: +20(48) 223-898

International Relations: Abbas Aly El-Hefnawy, President
EMail: menofia.president@menofia.edu.eg

Faculties

Agriculture (Agricultural Engineering; Agriculture; Agronomy; Animal Husbandry; Dairy; Food Technology; Genetics; Horticulture; Meat and Poultry; Soil Science) *Dean*: Osman Moustafa Asal
Arts (Arabic; Arts and Humanities; English; French; Geography; German; History; Library Science; Literature; Oriental Languages; Philosophy; Psychology; Sociology) *Dean*: Zenab A. Shaker
Commerce (Accountancy; Business Administration; Business and Commerce; Economics; Insurance; Statistics) *Dean*: Thabet A. Edrees
Computer Science and Information Technology (Computer Science; Information Technology) *Dean*: Fawzy A. Towrky
Education (Curriculum; Education; Educational Psychology; Pedagogy) *Dean*: Abd Elhadi Elsayed Abdu

Electronic Engineering *(Menouf)* (Automation and Control Engineering; Computer Engineering; Computer Science; Electronic Engineering; Telecommunications Engineering) *Dean*: Hossam Eldin Ahmed

Engineering (Civil Engineering; Electrical Engineering; Engineering; Mechanical Engineering; Power Engineering) *Dean*: Abd El Mohsen Mohamed Kenawee

Home Economics (Clothing and Sewing; Food Science; Home Economics; Nutrition; Textile Design) *Dean*: Mahmoud Saad Ali

Law (Civil Law; Commercial Law; Criminal Law; International Law; Islamic Law; Law; Public Law) *Dean*: Abd El Azeem Abd El Salam

Medicine (Anaesthesiology; Anatomy; Biochemistry; Cardiology; Forensic Medicine and Dentistry; Histology; Medicine; Microbiology; Oncology; Ophthalmology; Orthopedics; Otorhinolaryngology; Paediatrics; Parasitology; Pathology; Pharmacology; Physiology; Radiology; Surgery; Toxicology; Tropical Medicine; Urology) *Dean*: Mohamed Ibrahim Ahmed Ibrahim

Nursing (Health Administration; Nursing) *Dean*: Magda M. Mohammed

Physical Education *(Sadat City) Dean*: Mohammed G. Hamada

Science (Botany; Chemistry; Geology; Mathematics; Mathematics and Computer Science; Natural Sciences; Physics; Zoology) *Dean*: Anwar A. Hegazi

Special Education *(Ashmon) Dean*: Faroq Osman

Tourism and Hotels *(Sadat City)* (Hotel and Restaurant; Hotel Management; Tourism) *Dean*: Ahmed A. El-Sharkawy

Veterinary Medicine *(Sadat City)* (Veterinary Science) *Dean*: Ahmed H. Zakhal

Institutes

Biotechnology Engineering *(Sadat City)* (Biotechnology; Genetics; Molecular Biology) *Dean*: Khalil A. El-Halafawy

Desert Environment Research *(Sadat City)* (Arid Land Studies) *Dean*: Mohamed El-Shanawany

Liver Studies and Research *(Shebin)* (Hepatology) *Dean*: Salah Mahmoud Salah

History: Founded 1976. A State institution under the authority of the Ministry of Higher Education.

Governing Bodies: University Council

Academic Year: October to May

Admission Requirements: Secondary school certificate or equivalent

Fees: (Egyptian Pound): 85-100 per annum

Main Language(s) of Instruction: Arabic, English

Accrediting Agencies: Ministry of Higher Education, Supreme Council of Universities

Degrees and Diplomas: *Baccalaureos*: (BSc), 4-5 yrs; *Magistr.* (MSc), a further 2-3 yrs; *Doktora*: (PhD), 3-4 yrs following Magistr. Also Diploma, 1-2 yrs following Baccaloureos

Student Services: Academic Counselling, Social Counselling, Employment Services, Foreign Student Adviser, Nursery Care, Cultural Centre, Sports Facilities, Language Programmes, Handicapped Facilities, Health Services, Canteen, Foreign Student Centre

Student Residential Facilities: Yes

Libraries: Central Library, c. 31,500 vols; faculty libraries

Publications: University Guide (monthly); Minufiya Journal of Agricultural Research (quarterly); Minufiya Journal of Electronic Engineering Research; Minufiya Veterinary Journal (2 per annum); Journal of Psychological and Educational Research

Academic Staff 2002	MEN	WOMEN	TOTAL
FULL-TIME	1,894	819	**2,713**
STAFF WITH DOCTORATE			
FULL-TIME	1,154	279	**1,433**

Student Numbers 2002	TOTAL
All (Foreign Included)	**67,871**
FOREIGN ONLY	43

• SOUTH VALLEY UNIVERSITY
Kena
Tel: +20(96) 211-279
Fax: +20(96) 211-717
EMail: sci@svalleyu-jwnet.eun.eg
Website: http://www.svu.eun.eg

President: Abd El Mateen Moussa

Administrative Officer: Kamel Mahmoud Mousa

Faculties

Arts (Arts and Humanities)
Education
Fine Arts *(Louxor)*
Science (Mathematics and Computer Science; Natural Sciences)
Special Education
Veterinary Medicine

History: Founded 1994.

International Co-operation: UNESCO-Cousteau Ecotechnic Chair

ASWAN BRANCH
Aswan
Vice-President: Mohamed Hussein Amen (1996-)

Faculties

Arts (Arabic; English; History)
Education
Engineering
Science (Mathematics and Computer Science; Natural Sciences)
Social Work

History: Founded 1979.

SOHAG BRANCH
Sohag
Vice-President: Mahmoud Riad Moatamed (2001-)

Faculties

Agriculture
Arts (Arts and Humanities)
Commerce (Business and Commerce)

Education
Medicine
Science (Mathematics and Computer Science; Natural Sciences)

History: Founded 1979.

• SUEZ CANAL UNIVERSITY
4,5 Km, New Building, Ismailia
Tel: +20(64) 327-125
Fax: +20(64) 211-279
Cable: 63297 scu.fm.um
EMail: infor@suez.eun.eg
Website: http://www.suez.edu.eg
President: Farouk Mahmoud Abd El-Kader (2002-)

Faculties
Agriculture (Agriculture; Animal Husbandry; Crop Production; Dairy; Fishery; Food Science; Food Technology; Horticulture; Plant and Crop Protection; Soil Science; Water Science) Dean: Said Khamees El-Shamy
Commerce (Accountancy; Advertising and Publicity; Business Administration; Business and Commerce; Economics; Insurance; Marketing; Political Science; Public Relations; Statistics; Taxation) Dean: Sabry Abou-Zeid
Computer and Information Science (Computer Science; Information Sciences)
Dentistry
Education (Curriculum; Education; Educational Psychology; Home Economics; Pedagogy)
Engineering and Technology (Engineering; Technology)
Medicine (Anaesthesiology; Anatomy; Biochemistry; Cardiology; Community Health; Dermatology; Forensic Medicine and Dentistry; Genetics; Gynaecology and Obstetrics; Histology; Medicine; Microbiology; Neurology; Occupational Health; Ophthalmology; Osteopathy; Paediatrics; Pathology; Physiology; Psychiatry and Mental Health; Public Health; Radiology; Speech Therapy and Audiology; Surgery; Tropical Medicine; Urology) Dean: Adel Abd El-Kafy
Pharmacy (Analytical Chemistry; Biochemistry; Immunology; Microbiology; Organic Chemistry; Pharmacology; Pharmacy; Toxicology) Dean: Mostafa K. Mesbah
Science (Botany; Chemistry; Geology; Marine Science and Oceanography; Mathematics and Computer Science; Natural Sciences; Toxicology; Zoology)
Special Education
Tourism and Hotel Management (Hotel Management; Tourism) Dean: Ahmed Nour El-Din Elias
Veterinary Medicine (Biochemistry; Forensic Medicine and Dentistry; Histology; Microbiology; Parasitology; Pathology; Pharmacology; Physiology; Veterinary Science; Wildlife; Zoology)

Research Institutes
Biotechnology
Further Information: Also Teaching Hospital

History: Founded 1976. A State institution under the supervision of the Ministry of Higher Education.

Governing Bodies: University Council
Academic Year: September to June (September-January; February-June)
Admission Requirements: Secondary school certificate or equivalent
Main Language(s) of Instruction: Arabic
Degrees and Diplomas: Baccalaureos: Arts in Education; Science; Science in Agriculture; Science in Education, 4 yrs; Commerce; Engineering; Science in Veterinary Science, 5 yrs; Medicine and Surgery, 6 yrs; Magistr: a further 1-5 yrs; Doktora: (PhD); Agriculture; Commerce; Education; Engineering; Science; Veterinary Science. Also postgraduate Diplomas
Student Residential Facilities: Yes
Libraries: Central Library, c. 6500 vols; faculty libraries, c. 190,000
Publications: Scientific Bulletins (Human Sciences, Basic Sciences, Applied Sciences); Statistical Journal
Press or Publishing House: Suez Canal University Press
Academic Staff 2001-2002: Total: c. 700
Student Numbers 2001-2002: Total: c. 13,000

EL-ARISH BRANCH
El-Arish

Faculties
Education (Arabic; Botany; Chemistry; Curriculum; Education; Educational Psychology; English; Geology; Islamic Studies; Mathematics; Pedagogy; Physics; Social Studies; Zoology)
Environmental Agricultural Sciences (Agricultural Economics; Agriculture; Animal Husbandry; Aquaculture; Environmental Studies; Fishery; Plant and Crop Protection; Rural Planning; Soil Science; Water Science)
Degrees and Diplomas: Baccalaureos; Magistr; Doktora. Also Post-graduate Diploma

PORT-SAID BRANCH
Port-Said
President: M. El-Sayed Rahem (2002-)

Faculties
Commerce (Accountancy; Business Administration; Business and Commerce; Economics; Government; Insurance; Law; Management; Political Science; Statistics) Dean: Abdullah Sayed Abdul-Majid
Education (Arabic; Biology; Chemistry; Education; Educational Psychology; Geology; Islamic Studies; Literature; Mathematics; Modern Languages; Physics; Social Sciences) Dean: Fekry Ibrahim Khalaf
Nursing (Nursing; Paediatrics; Psychiatry and Mental Health; Public Health) Director: Moussa Abdel-Hamid Moussa
Physical Education (Health Education; Hygiene; Physical Education) Dean: Sayed Abdel Gawad El-Sayed

History: Founded 1989.

SUEZ BRANCH
Suez

Faculties

Education (Arabic; Biology; Chemistry; Curriculum; Education; Educational Psychology; English; French; Geology; Islamic Studies; Mathematics; Modern Languages; Pedagogy; Physics; Social Studies) *Dean*: Mahmoud Abbas Abdeen

Industrial Education (Architecture; Building Technologies; Chemical Engineering; Electrical Engineering; Electronic Engineering; Science Education; Textile Technology; Wood Technology)

Petroleum Engineering and Mining (Engineering; Geological Engineering; Mathematics; Metallurgical Engineering; Mining Engineering; Petroleum and Gas Engineering; Science Education)

Degrees and Diplomas: *Baccalaureos*; *Magistr*; *Doktora*

*• TANTA UNIVERSITY

PO Box 31512, El-Geish Street, Tanta, Al-Gharbia
Tel: +20(40) 337-7929
Fax: +20(40) 331-3308
Telex: 23605 un tha
EMail: tanta@frcu.eun.eg
Website: http://www.tanta.edu.eg

President: Fouad Khalifa Harras (2000-)
Tel: +20(40) 331-7928 Fax: +20(40) 330-2785
EMail: fharras@dec1.tanta.eun.eg

Secretary-General: Rawia Soliman Gad
Tel: +20(40) 331-7947 Fax: +20(40) 331-3308

International Relations: Mohamed Shafik Saied,
Vice-President Tel: +20(40) 330-5978 Fax: +20(40) 330-5978
EMail: mshafeek@dec1.tanta.eun.eg

Faculties

Agriculture (Agricultural Equipment; Agriculture; Agronomy; Animal Husbandry; Botany; Dairy; Economics; Food Science; Food Technology; Genetics; Horticulture; Soil Science) *Dean*: Mohamed El Fateh Raid

Arts (Arabic; Arts and Humanities; French; Geography; History; Philosophy; Psychology; Sociology) *Dean*: El Said Aboul Azam Dawood

Commerce (Accountancy; Business Administration; Business and Commerce; Economics; Finance; Insurance; Mathematics; Public Administration; Statistics; Taxation) *Dean*: El Saaid Mohamed Lebda

Dentistry *Dean*: Mohamed Saad Nasser

Education (Science Education)

Engineering (Architecture; Design; Electrical Engineering; Electronic Engineering; Engineering; Hydraulic Engineering; Irrigation; Mathematics; Mechanical Engineering; Physical Engineering; Production Engineering; Town Planning) *Dean*: Mohamed Abd Alla El Khazendar

Law *Dean*: Mostafa Ahmed Fouad

Medicine (Anaesthesiology; Gynaecology and Obstetrics; Medicine; Paediatrics) *Dean*: Osama Mohamed Abo Faarha

Nursing (Gynaecology and Obstetrics; Nursing; Paediatrics) *Dean*: Naeim Fatouh El Far

Pharmacy (Biochemistry; Microbiology; Pharmacy; Toxicology) *Dean*: Ibrahim El Khalil El Shamy

Physical Education

Science (Botany; Chemistry; Geology; Mathematics; Natural Sciences; Physics; Zoology) *Dean*: Mohamed Ezzat Abd El Monsif

Specific Education (Art Education; Educational Technology; Home Economics; Mass Communication; Music Education; Psychology) *Dean*: Abd El Hameed Mohamed Nowir

Further Information: Also Teaching Hospital and Study Abroad Programmes

History: Founded 1972, incorporating Faculties attached to the University of Alexandria. A State Institution under the supervision of the Ministry of Higher Education.

Governing Bodies: University Council, comprising seventeen members

Academic Year: October to June

Admission Requirements: Secondary school certificate or equivalent

Fees: None

Main Language(s) of Instruction: Arabic, English

International Co-operation: With universities in Hungary, USA, Turkey, Romania, Uzbekistan, Poland, United Kingdom, France, China, Morocco, Jordan, Syria, Saudi Arabia.

Degrees and Diplomas: *Diploma*: Commerce; Education; Law, 2 yrs; *Baccalaureos*: Agriculture; Arts; Arts in Education; Commerce; Law; Science; Science in Education, 4 yrs; Dentistry; Pharmacy, 5 yrs; Medicine and Surgery, 6 yrs; *Magistr*: a further 1-6 yrs; *Doktora*: Arts, Dentistry, Law, Medicine, Philosophy, Agriculture, Commerce, Pharmacy, Nursing, Education, a further 2 yrs; Science, Engineering, Specific Education, Physical Education, Veterinary Medicine, a further 2-3 yrs

Student Residential Facilities: Yes

Libraries: Faculty libraries: c. 135,000 vols in Arabic; c. 85,000 vols in other languages

Publications: Bulletin (monthly); Tanta University Mirror (quarterly); Commerce and Finance (biannually); Annual Report (annually)

Academic Staff *2001-2002*	MEN	WOMEN	TOTAL
FULL-TIME	2,178	1,118	**3,296**

Student Numbers *2001-2002*: Total: **106,472**

KAFR EL-SHEIKH BRANCH
Kefr Al-Sheikh
Tel: +20(47) 223-419
Fax: +20(47) 223-419

Vice-President: Hassan Ibrahim Eid Ali (2000-)

Faculties

Agriculture *Dean*: Shawky Mohamed Ibrahim Metali

Education (Education; Special Education) *Dean*: Radwan Mohamed El Baroody

Specific Education (Art Education; Educational Sciences; Educational Technology; Home Economics; Mass Communication; Music Education; Psychology) *Dean*: Ahmed Hafez Masaoud

Veterinary Medicine (Veterinary Science) *Dean*: Mahmoud Abd El Nabi Seifi

History: Founded 1979.

*• ZAGAZIG UNIVERSITY

Zagazig, Sharkeya
Tel: +20(55) 324-577
Fax: +20(55) 345-452
Telex: 92860 zu un
EMail: zag@frcu.eun.eg
Website: http://www.zagazigunv.edu.eg

President: Abdel Hameed Bahgat (2003-)
Tel: +20(55) 363-635 Fax: +20(55) 344-550

Secretary-General: Mohamed Sayed Morsi

International Relations: Ahmed Hashim Basyuny
Tel: +20(55) 322-918

Faculties

Agriculture (Agriculture; Agronomy; Animal Husbandry; Biochemistry; Fruit Production; Geophysics; Harvest Technology; Nutrition; Plant and Crop Protection) *Dean*: Hassan Ahmed Hassan Rabiea

Arts (Arabic; Arts and Humanities; English; French; Geography; History; Media Studies; Philosophy; Physiology; Sociology) *Dean*: Farouk Kamel Mohamed Ezz El-Deen

Commerce (Accountancy; Business Administration; Business and Commerce; Mathematics; Statistics) *Dean*: Mohamed Shawky Ahmed Shawky

Computer and Information Science (Computer Science; Information Sciences; Information Technology) *Dean*: Ismail Amro Ismail

Education (Curriculum; Education; Educational Psychology; International and Comparative Education; Pedagogy; Psychiatry and Mental Health) *Dean*: Ahmed El-Rafaey Ghoneim

Engineering (Civil Engineering; Computer Engineering; Construction Engineering; Electronic Engineering; Engineering; Industrial Engineering; Materials Engineering; Mathematics; Mechanical Engineering; Physical Engineering; Power Engineering; Production Engineering; Structural Architecture) *Dean*: Mohammed Kamal Mohammed Tolba Ewada

Law (Civil Law; Commercial Law; Criminal Law; History of Law; International Law; Islamic Law; Law) *Dean*: Nabil Helmy

Medicine (Anaesthesiology; Anatomy; Biochemistry; Cardiology; Community Health; Dermatology; Forensic Medicine and Dentistry; Gynaecology and Obstetrics; Histology; Medicine; Microbiology; Neurology; Ophthalmology; Orthopedics; Paediatrics; Parasitology; Pathology; Pharmacology; Physiology; Psychiatry and Mental Health; Radiology; Rheumatology; Surgery; Tropical Medicine; Urology) *Dean*: Abd El-Zahar El-Sayed Tantawy

Nursing (Gynaecology and Obstetrics; Health Education; Nursing; Surgery) *Dean*: Zeinab Hamed Swan

Pharmacy (Analytical Chemistry; Biochemistry; Organic Chemistry; Pharmacology; Pharmacy) *Dean*: Maher Mohamed Ali El-Domiaty

Physical Education *Dean*: Hamed Mahmoud El-Kanwaty

Physical Education *(for Women)* *Dean*: Nahid Ali Mohammed Ali

Science (Botany; Chemistry; Geology; Mathematics and Computer Science; Natural Sciences; Physics; Zoology) *Dean*: Bayoumy Awad Allah Tartour

Special Education (Art Education; Educational Sciences; Educational Technology; English; Home Economics; Music Education; Preschool Education; Special Education) *Dean*: Bahaa El Deen El Sayed Abdel Haleem El Nager

Veterinary Medicine (Biochemistry; Embryology and Reproduction Biology; Fishery; Food Science; Histology; Hygiene; Immunology; Limnology; Meat and Poultry; Pathology; Pharmacology; Veterinary Science; Virology) *Dean*: Labib Ismail Mohamed Hassan Mwafy

Higher Institutes

Ancient Near Eastern Studies (Middle Eastern Studies)

Asian Studies and Research (Asian Studies)

Production Efficiency (Agriculture; Civil Engineering; Economics; Industrial and Production Economics; Management) *Dean*: Abd El-Aziz Lofty Hassan Sharaf

History: Founded 1969 as a branch of Ain-Shams University. Acquired present status 1974.

Academic Year: October to May (October-January; January-May)

Admission Requirements: Secondary school certificate or equivalent

Fees: None

Main Language(s) of Instruction: Arabic, English, French

Degrees and Diplomas: *Diploma*; *Baccalaureos*: Arts (B.A.); Science (B.Sc.), 4-6 yrs; *Magistr*: Arts (M.A.); Science (M.Sc.), a further 2-4 yrs; *Doktora*: (PhD), 3 yrs following Magistr

Student Services: Social Counselling, Foreign Student Adviser, Nursery Care, Cultural Centre, Sports Facilities, Handicapped Facilities, Health Services, Canteen

Student Residential Facilities: Yes

Special Facilities: Tell Basta Museum (Arts)

Libraries: Central Library; libraries of the Faculties

Publications: Scientific Journals

Academic Staff *2001-2002:* Total: **3,929**

Student Numbers *2001-2002:* Total: **94,156**

BANHA BRANCH
Banha

Vice-President: Hossam El-Din Al-Attar (2001-)

Faculties

Agriculture *(Moshtohor)* *Dean*: Ibrahim Ibrahim Soliman El-Shawaf

Arts (Arts and Humanities) *Dean*: Mustafa Yasin El-Sayed Saadny

Commerce (Business and Commerce) *Dean*: Hamid Tolba Mohamed Abu Heiba

Education *Dean*: Ali Khalil Mostafa Abo El-Einin

Engineering *(Shoubra)* *Dean*: Mohamed Mohamed Mahmoud

Law *Dean*: Ahmed Abd El Hamid Ashoush

Medicine *Dean*: Abd El Shafi Mohmdady Tabey

Nursing *Dean*: Samia Mostafa Mohamed Rashed

Physical Education *(for Men)* *Dean*: Mahmoud Yehia Mohamed Saad

Science (Mathematics and Computer Science; Natural Sciences) *Dean*: Sabry Sadek El-Sairafy

Specific Education (Special Education) *Dean*: Ali Khalil Mostafa Abo El-Einin
Veterinary Science *(Moshtohor)* *Dean*: Mohamed Amro Hussein El-Shaib

History: Founded 1976.
Academic Staff *2001-2002:* Total: **2,063**
Student Numbers *2001-2002:* Total: **52,660**

PRIVATE INSTITUTIONS

*• THE AMERICAN UNIVERSITY IN CAIRO (AUC)

PO Box 2511, 113 Sharia Kasr El-Aini, Cairo 11511
Tel: +20(2) 794-2964 +1(212) 7308800 (New York Office)
Fax: +20(2) 795-7565 +1(212) 7301600 (New York Office)
EMail: webley@aucegypt.edu
Website: http://www.aucegypt.edu
President: David A. Arnold (2003-) Tel: +20(2) 797-5161
Fax: +20(2) 799-1830 EMail: president@aucegypt.edu

International Relations: John Swanson, Assistant Provost for International Programmes Tel: +20(2) 797-5193
Fax: +20(2) 795-7565 EMail: swanson@aucegypt.edu

Schools
Business, Economics and Communication (Accountancy; Business Administration; Business and Commerce; Communication Studies; Economics; Journalism; Management; Mass Communication)
Humanities and Social Sciences (Anthropology; Arts and Humanities; Comparative Law; Comparative Literature; Demography and Population; English; Film; History; International Relations; Islamic Studies; Middle Eastern Studies; Music; Performing Arts; Political Science; Psychology; Social Sciences; Sociology; Theatre; Visual Arts)
Science and Engineering (Analytical Chemistry; Biology; Chemistry; Engineering; Mathematics and Computer Science; Natural Sciences; Organic Chemistry; Physical Chemistry; Physics)

Institutes
Gender and Women's Studies (Gender Studies; Women's Studies)

Centres
Adult and Continuing Education
Desert Development (Arid Land Studies; Development Studies)
Social Research (Social Studies)

Further Information: Through the Centre of Adult and Continuing Education's Outreach Services programme in English, Computer Education, Arabic and Translation, and/or Business Studies are offered in: The United Arab Emirates (Abu Dhabi and Dubai), Saudi Arabia (Jeddah and Riyadh), and in other cities in Egypt (Alexandria, Damanhour, Ismailia, El Minia, Esna, Heliopolis, Hurgada, Kafr El Sheikh, Mansoura, Tabbin, and Tanta)

History: Founded 1919. A private non-profit Institution located on five campus/building sites in the heart and other parts of the Cairo metropolitan area. It operates as a private educational/cultural Institute within the framework of the 1962 Egyptian-American Cultural Co-operation Agreement and in accordance with a protocol with the Government of Egypt through which the University's degrees are recognized as those awarded by the Egyptian national universities. Accredited in the United States by the Commission on Higher Education through the Middle States Association of Colleges and Schools in Washington, D.C. and licensed to confer degrees by the Educational Institution Licensure Commission of the District of Columbia.

Governing Bodies: Board of Trustees, comprising primarily American educators and corporate administrators

Academic Year: September to July (September-January; February-June; June-July)

Admission Requirements: Secondary school certificate (Thanawiya 'Amma) or recognized equivalent

Main Language(s) of Instruction: English

Degrees and Diplomas: *Baccalaureos*: Arts in Anthropology; Arts in Business Administration; Arts in Economics; Arts in Egyptology; Arts in Journalism and Mass Communication; Arts in Middle Eastern History; Arts in Political Science; Arts in Psychology; Arts in Sociology; Arts in Theatre, 4 yrs; Science in Chemistry; Science in Computer Science; Science in Construction Engineering; Science in Mathematics; Science in Mechanical Engineering; Science in Physics, 4-5 yrs; *Magistr*: Arts in Economics; Arts in Mass Communication; Arts in Political Science; Arts in Sociology-Anthropology; Arts in Teaching Arabic as a Foreign Language, Teaching English as a Foreign Language; Science in Business Administration; Science in Engineering; Science in Public Administration, a further 2 yrs. Also graduate Diplomas

Student Residential Facilities: Yes

Libraries: Central Library, c. 225,500 vols; Cresswell Collection of Islamic Art and Architecture, c. 10,000 vols

Publications: Cairo Papers in Social Science; Middle East Management Review; AUC News (quarterly); ALIF: Journal of Comparative Poetry (annually)

Press or Publishing House: American University Press in Cairo

Academic Staff *2001-2002:* Total: c. 360
Student Numbers *2001-2002:* Total: c. 4,600

* ARAB ACADEMY FOR SCIENCE AND TECHNOLOGY AND MARITIME TRANSPORT (AASTMT)

PO Box 1029, Gamal Abdel Nasser Street, Miami, Alexandria
Tel: +20(3) 556-1497
Fax: +20(3) 550-6042
EMail: webmaster@aast.edu
Website: http://www.aast.edu
President: Gamal Eldin A. Mokhtar (1972-)
Tel: +20(3) 548-7785 Fax: +20(3) 548-7786
EMail: mokhtar@intouch.com

Colleges

Engineering and Technology (Architectural and Environmental Design; Automation and Control Engineering; Computer Engineering; Construction Engineering; Electrical Engineering; Electronic Engineering; Engineering; Industrial Engineering; Marine Engineering; Mechanical Engineering; Natural Sciences; Technology)

Management and Technology (Arts and Humanities; Business Administration; Hotel Management; Management; Modern Languages; Tourism)

Maritime Transport (Economics; Fishery; Management; Marine Engineering; Marine Science and Oceanography; Marine Transport; Meteorology; Nautical Science; Safety Engineering)

Institutes

Advanced Management (Management)
Port Training (Nautical Science)
Productivity and Total Quality (Production Engineering; Safety Engineering)
Sea Training (Nautical Science)

Centres

Maritime Research and Consultation

History: Founded 1972. A specialized University in Maritime Transport. Buildings, land, majority of national staff members and personnel provided by the Egyptian Government.

Governing Bodies: Board of Directors

Main Language(s) of Instruction: Arabic

Degrees and Diplomas: *Baccalaureos*: 4-5 yrs; *High Diploma*: 1 further yr; *Magistr*: Science in Computer Science from George Washington University: off campus degree); a further 2 yrs; *Doktora*: (PhD), a further 3 yrs

Student Services: Academic Counselling, Social Counselling, Employment Services, Foreign Student Adviser, Cultural Centre, Sports Facilities, Health Services, Canteen

Libraries: AASTMT Library, c. 36,000 vols, 350 periodicals

Publications: Journal of Arab Maritime Academy (biannually); MRCC Research Magazine (annually); MRCC Bulletin; Bulletin of Arab Maritime Academy

Academic Staff 2001-2002: Full-Time: c. 230 Part-Time: c. 260 Total: c. 490

Student Numbers 2001-2002: Total: c. 4,000

FRENCH UNIVERSITY OF EGYPT
Université française d'Egypte
BP 21 , Km 37 Cairo-Ismailia Highway, Shorouk City
Tel: +20(2) 687-52-52
Fax: +20(2) 687-53-53
EMail: info@ufe-eg.org
Website: http://www.ufe-eg.org

President: Tahany Omar (2002-)

Director of Registrations: Naira Boutros

Faculties

Applied Languages (Modern Languages) *Dean*: Sahar Moharram

Engineering (Automation and Control Engineering; Information Technology; Production Engineering; Telecommunications Engineering) *Doyen*: Mohamed-Nabil Sabry
Management and Information Technology (Information Management; Information Technology; Management) *Dean*: Kamal Abdel Rahman

Units
Lifelong Education and Distance Education

History: Founded 2002.

THE GERMAN UNIVERSITY IN CAIRO
New Cairo City
President: Mahmoud Hashem Abdul-Ghafar (2002-)

Faculties

Applied Science and Arts (Fine Arts; Natural Sciences)
Basic Science (Natural Sciences)
Engineering and Basic Materials Science (Engineering; Materials Engineering)
Humanities and Languages (Arts and Humanities; Modern Languages)
Information Engineering and Technology (Computer Engineering; Information Technology)
Management Technology (Management)
Mass Media Engineering and Technology (Mass Communication; Media Studies)
Pharmacy and Biotechnology (Biotechnology; Pharmacy)
Post-graduate Studies and Research

Centres

Languages and Translation (Modern Languages; Translation and Interpretation)
Lifelong Learning and Distance Education (Continuing Education)

History: Founded 2002.

MISR INTERNATIONAL UNIVERSITY
Ismalia Road, Km 28, Cairo
Tel: +20(2) 477-1560
Fax: +20(2) 477-1566
EMail: miu@miuegypt.com
Website: http://www.miuegypt.com

President: Mohamed Shebl El Komy

Faculties

Al Alsun (English) *Dean*: Hamdy Hassan
Business Administration and International Trade (Accountancy; Business Administration; Economics; Finance; International Business; Marketing)
Computer and Information Science (Computer Science; Information Technology; Software Engineering; Systems Analysis) *Dean*: Mostafa El Arabaty
Dentistry (Anatomy; Biochemistry; Botany; Chemistry; Dentistry; Microbiology; Pathology; Pharmacology; Physics; Physiology; Surgery; Zoology) *Dean*: Abdel Hamid Mahboub

Engineering (Architecture; Engineering) *Dean*: Salah Eddin Zaki

Mass Communication (Advertising and Publicity; Journalism; Mass Communication; Public Relations; Radio and Television Broadcasting) *Dean*: Hamdy Hassan

Pharmacy (Microbiology; Pharmacology; Pharmacy; Toxicology) *Dean*: Mohamed Younis Haggag

History: Founded 1996.

Governing Bodies: Board of Trustees; University Council

• MISR UNIVERSITY FOR SCIENCE AND TECHNOLOGY (MUST)
Al Motamayez District, 6th of October City, Giza
Tel: +20(11) 354-685
Fax: +20(11) 354-687
EMail: iu@soticom.eg
Website: http://www.must.edu

President: Ahmed Khodeir Tel: +20(11) 354-708
Fax: +20(11) 354-689

Registrar: Mahmoud Abd El Rahman Tel: +20(11) 354-703

International Relations: Mahmoud El-Diri

Colleges
Business Administration and Economics (Accountancy; Business Administration; Business and Commerce; Computer Science; Economic and Finance Policy; Information Sciences; Political Science) *Dean*: Mahmoud Hashem Zaki

Dentistry *Dean*: Adel Abdul-Hakim

Engineering (Computer Engineering; Construction Engineering; Electronic Engineering; Engineering; Industrial Engineering; Technology) *Dean*: Mahmoud Abo El-Nasr

Information Technology

Languages and Translation (Modern Languages; Translation and Interpretation) *Dean*: Abdel Aziz Hammouda

Mass Media and Communication (Mass Communication; Media Studies) *Dean*: Farouk Abu Zaid

Medicine *Dean*: Salah Eid

Pharmacy *Dean*: Mostafa Tawakkol

Physiotherapy (Physical Therapy; Physiology) *Dean*: Ebtisam Kattab

History: Founded 1996.

Degrees and Diplomas: *Baccalaureos*; *Magistr*, *Doktora*

MODERN SCIENCE AND ARTS UNIVERSITY (MSA)
14 Amer Street, Mesaha Square, Dokki, Giza
Tel: +20(2) 336-7845
Fax: +20(2) 760-3811
EMail: admissions@msa.eun.eg
Website: http://www.msa.eun.eg

President: Hassan Hamdy Tel: +20(2) 336-7844

Secretary-General: Omayma Ouf

Faculties
Computer Science (Computer Science; Software Engineering) *Dean*: Ismail H. Abdel Fattah

Engineering (Architectural and Environmental Design; Computer Engineering; Electrical and Electronic Engineering; Electrical Engineering; Electronic Engineering) *Dean*: Said Ashour

Management (Accountancy; Economics; International Business; Management; Marketing) *Dean*: Ahmed I. Ghoneim

Mass Communication (Advertising and Publicity; Journalism; Mass Communication; Public Relations; Radio and Television Broadcasting)

History: Founded 1996.

• OCTOBER 6 UNIVERSITY (O6U)
Giza-Governerate, Central Axis-Plot 1, 6th of October City, Giza
Tel: +20(8) 353-942   +20(8) 353-987
Fax: +20(8) 353-867   +20(8) 353-987
EMail: info@o6u.edu.eg
Website: http://www.o6u.edu.eg

President: Ahmad Atteya Saida

Secretary-General: Talat Kenawy Tel: +20(11) 351-279

International Relations: Nehal Salah

Faculties
Applied Arts (Advertising and Publicity; Cinema and Television; Fine Arts; Furniture Design; Interior Design; Photography; Printing and Printmaking; Publishing and Book Trade) *Dean*: Gamal Abood

Applied Medical Sciences (Laboratory Techniques; Medical Auxiliaries; Nursing; Radiology) *Dean*: Talaat Rihan

Computer Science

Dentistry *Dean*: Yehia Boughdady

Economics and Management (Accountancy; Business Administration; Economics; Management; Political Science) *Dean*: Gaber Abuel Enein

Education (Arabic; Biology; Computer Science; Education; English; French; German; Mathematics; Preschool Education; Primary Education) *Dean*: Mohammed Abdal Ghaffar

Engineering (Architecture; Building Technologies; Computer Engineering; Construction Engineering; Electrical Engineering; Engineering; Industrial Engineering; Mechanical Engineering; Political Science) *Dean*: Ali Talaat

Hotels and Tourism (Hotel Management; Tourism) *Dean*: Abdel Fattah Elsabahy

Languages and Translation (English; French; German; Modern Languages; Spanish; Translation and Interpretation) *Dean*: Baher Mohammed Al Gohary

Mass Communication (Journalism; Mass Communication; Media Studies; Radio and Television Broadcasting) *Dean*: Laila Abdel Megeed

Medicine (Anatomy; Biochemistry; Biology; Biophysics; English; Histology; Medicine; Physiology; Surgery) *Dean*: Bahaa-Eldin Mohamed Elserwi

Pharmacy *Dean*: Mustafa El Sayed El Sayed

Physiotherapy (Nutrition; Physical Therapy; Physiology; Psychology) *Dean*: Azza Adel Hady

Social Sciences (Library Science; Political Science; Psychology; Social Sciences; Theatre) *Dean*: Salah Houtar
Tourism and Hotel Management (Hotel Management; Tourism)
Further Information: University Hospital

History: Founded 1996.
Admission Requirements: High school certificate
International Co-operation: With universities in the United Kingdom, Sweden, Denmark, Spain, USA, France, China.
Degrees and Diplomas: *Diploma*; *Baccalaureos*: 4-6 yrs

SENGHOR UNIVERSITY ALEXANDRIA
Université Senghor/Université internationale de Langue française au Service du Développement africain
BP 21111-415, 1, Midan Ahmed Orabi, El Mancheya, Alexandria
Tel: +20(3) 484-3371 to 73
Fax: +20(3) 484-3374 20(3) 484-3479
EMail: rectorat@usenghor-francophonie.org
Website: http://www.usenghor-francophonie.org
Recteur: Fred Constant (2001-) Tel: +20(3) 484-3504
Secrétaire général: Harry Dowidar Tel: +20(3) 484-3458

Departments
Environmental Management *Director*: Rolando Marin
General Administration (Administration) *Director*: André Courtemanche
Heritage Management (Heritage Preservation) *Director*: Caroline Gaultier
Nutrition and Health Studies (Health Administration; Nutrition)

Centres
Law and Development *(René-Jean Dupuy)* (Development Studies; Law) *Director*: Ahmed El Kosheri

History: Founded 1990 following a meeting of Heads of State of Francophone Countries. A private postgraduate institution whose objective is to train and assist professionals and higher level teachers.
Governing Bodies: Haut Conseil de l' Université; Conseil d' Administration; Conseil Scientifique
Academic Year: September to May
Admission Requirements: University degree and professional experience
Main Language(s) of Instruction: French
Degrees and Diplomas: *Diplôme d'Etudes professionnelles approfondies*: 2 yrs
Student Services: Foreign Student Adviser, Sports Facilities, Health Services, Canteen
Libraries: Giovanni Agnelli Library, c. 12,580 vols
Publications: Patrimoine Culturel Francophone; Lettres d'Alexandrie; Actes des Conférences; Faits et Chiffres
Student Numbers *2001-2002:* Total: **50**

OTHER UNIVERSITY LEVEL INSTITUTIONS

PUBLIC INSTITUTIONS

* HIGHER INSTITUTE OF TECHNOLOGY-BENHA
New Benha, El-Kaludia, Benha City 13512
Tel: +20(13) 233-0297
Fax: +20(13) 233-0297
EMail: bhit-egypt@hotmail.com

Dean: El Sayed El Kasaby (2003-2004)
EMail: Prof.-Dr-Kasaby@hotmail.com
Vice-Dean for Postgraduates: Adel Alam El-Din Omar
Tel: +20(13) 233-0297 EMail: adelomar988@hotmail.com
Vice-Dean for Students: Mahmoud Fathy M. Hassan
Tel: +20(13) 233-0297 Fax: +20(13) 233-0297
EMail: MFMHassan@hotmail.com

Departments
Basic Sciences (Mathematics and Computer Science; Natural Sciences) *Head*: Hassan Nasr
Civil Engineering *Head*: El Sayed El Kasaby
Electrical Engineering *Head*: Salah Ramadan
Mechanical Engineering *Head*: Ahmed Soliman

History: Founded 1988, a public Institution.
Degrees and Diplomas: *Baccalaureos*: Civil Engineering Technology; Electrical Engineering Technology; Mechanical Engineering Technology, 2 yrs following High Diploma; *High Diploma*: Civil Engineering Technology; Electrical Engineering Technology; Mechanical Engineering Technology, 3 yrs; *Magistr*: Civil Engineering Technology; Electrical Engineering Technology; Mechanical Engineering Technology, a further 2 yrs. Also Postgraduate Diploma (2 yrs following Baccalaureos)
Libraries: c. 8100 vols
Academic Staff *2002-2003*: Full-Time: c. 115 Part-Time: c. 210 Total: c. 325
Staff with doctorate: Total: c. 150
Student Numbers *2002-2003:* Total: **2,462**

OTHER INSTITUTIONS

PUBLIC INSTITUTIONS

COLLEGE OF INDUSTRIAL EDUCATION
Shark-El-Nil , PO Box 65513, Beni-Suef
Tel: +20(82) 240-931
Director: Mohamed Naguib Ahmed Al-Sheikh (1999-)
International Relations: Ibrahim El Tayeb
Founded: 1992

Architecture
Automation and Electrical Engineering (Automation and Control Engineering; Electrical Engineering)
Civil Works (Civil Engineering)
Electrical and Electronic Engineering
Mechanics of Production (Mechanical Engineering; Production Engineering)
Mechanics of Sophisticated Instruments (Mechanical Engineering)

History: Founded 1992

COLLEGE OF INDUSTRIAL EDUCATION
Al-Sawah, Cairo
Tel: +20(2) 454-7544

Director: Fared Abdel-Aziz Tolba (1998-)
International Relations: Safy El-Ghandour

Founded: 1989
Electrical Engineering; Electronic Engineering; Heating and Refrigeration; Production Engineering
Automation and Tractors (Industrial Engineering)
Freezing and Air Conditioning Technology (Heating and Refrigeration)

History: Founded 1989

HIGHER INSTITUTE FOR POWER
Aswan

Head: Salama Abdel-Hadi Mohamed

Founded: 1989

Departments
Electric Power (Electrical Engineering; Power Engineering)
Mechanical Power (Mechanical Engineering; Power Engineering)

PRIVATE INSTITUTIONS

AKHBAR AL-YOUM ACADEMY FOR ENGINEERING, PRINTING AND PRESS TECHNOLOGY
Fourth Industrial Zone, Akhbar Al-Youm Building, 6th of October City
Tel: +20(11) 334-811

Director: Ahmad Zaki Badr (2000-)

Founded: 1999

Departments
Printing and Press Engineering (Printing and Printmaking)

154

AL-ALSUN HIGHER INSTITUTE OF TOURISM AND HOTEL MANAGEMENT
Block n° 96, Makram Ebeid Ex., 8th District, Nasr City
Tel: +20(2) 287-7522

Director: Nadia Refa'at Abdel-Rahman (2000-)

Founded: 1992
Hotel Management; Tourism

AL-GEZIRA HIGHER INSTITUTE FOR COMPUTER SCIENCE AND INFORMATION MANAGEMENT SYSTEMS
Al-Moqattem, Cairo

Director: Mohamed Hassan Fayeq

Programmes
Computer Science
Information Management Systems (Information Management)

AL-MA'AREF HIGHER INSTITUTE FOR LANGUAGE AND TRANSLATION
10, Nasouh Str., Al-Zaytoun
Tel: +20(2) 257-1324

Director: Mervat Mahmoud Ali (2000-)

Founded: 1994
Modern Languages; Translation and Interpretation

AL-MADINA HIGHER INSTITUTE FOR INTERNATIONAL LANGUAGES
Shoubra Ment

Director: Ahmad Kamal Mohamed Safwat

Programmes
International Languages (Modern Languages)

AL-UBOUR HIGHER INSTITUTE FOR ENGINEERING AND TECHNOLOGY
31 Km, Cairo-Ismaelia High Way
Tel: +20(2) 477-0037
Fax: +20(2) 241-3550

Director: Refa'at Rezq Baseli (2000-)

Founded: 1996
Engineering; Technology

AL-UBOUR HIGHER INSTITUTE FOR MANAGEMENT AND INFORMATION SYSTEMS
21, Belbais High Way, Sharquia
Tel: +20(2) 263-6882
Fax: +20(2) 403-0804

Director: Al-Sayed Abdel-Qader Zedan (1999-)

Founded: 1999
Computer Science; Information Management; Information Technology; Management Systems

ALEXANDRIA HIGHER INSTITUTE FOR TECHNOLOGY
Victor Emanuel Str., Sidi Gaber, Alexandria
Tel: +20(3) 425-4942

Director: Mahmoud Mohamed Shabana (1998-)

Founded: 1997
Technology

ARTS ACADEMY
Gamal El-Din Al-Afghani Str., Al-Haram Route, Giza
Tel: +20(2) 585-0727
Fax: +20(2) 561-1230

Director: Fawzy M. Fahmy

Founded: 1959, 1969

Higher Institutes
Arab Music (Music)
Art Criticism
Ballet (Dance)
Cinema (Cinema and Television)
Folklore
Theatre

Conservatories
Music

CAIRO HIGHER INSTITUTE FOR COMPUTER, INFORMATICS AND MANAGEMENT "AL-GOLF"
2, Samir Mokhtar Str., Nabil Al-Waqad Corner, Heliopolis
Tel: +20(2) 417-6550
Fax: +20(2) 417-6551

Director: Mohamed Abdul-Moneim Hashish (1995-)

Founded: 1995
Computer Science; Management; Management Systems

CAIRO HIGHER INSTITUTE FOR LANGUAGES, SIMULTANEOUS

INTERPRETATION AND ADMINISTRATIVE SCIENCES
5,54 Str., off Route 9, Moqattam, Cairo
Tel: +20(2) 508-1700
Fax: +20(2) 508-1613

Director: Mohamed Rehan Hussein (2002-)

Founded: 1995
Administration; Modern Languages; Translation and Interpretation

CAIRO HIGHER INSTITUTE FOR TOURISM AND HOTEL MANAGEMENT
5,54 Str., off Route 9, Moqattam, Cairo
Tel: +20(2) 508-1600
Fax: +20(2) 508-3303

Director: Mohamed Baher Omar (2002-)

Founded: 1995
Hotel Management; Tourism

DELTA HIGHER INSTITUTE FOR COMPUTERS
Mansoura

Director: Yehia Abdul-Aziz Mashrafi (2000-)

Founded: 2000
Computer Science

EGYPTIAN HIGHER INSTITUTE FOR TOURISM AND HOTEL MANAGEMENT
Final Station of Nozha Metro, behind Sheraton blocks, Cairo
Tel: +20(2) 266-5951
Fax: +20(2) 266-5950

Director: Ahmad Abdul-Razek Mohamed (2001-)

Founded: 1992
Hotel Management; Tourism

EGYPTIAN HIGHER INSTITUTE OF ALEXANDRIA ACADEMY FOR MANAGEMENT AND ACCOUNTANCY
Medan Al-Masaged, Alexandria
Tel: +20(3) 484-3384

Director: Adel Abdel-Hamid Ez (2000-)

Founded: 1996
Accountancy; Management

HIGHER INSTITUTE FOR ADMINISTRATIVE SCIENCES
Division 1/1, Central Route, 6th of October City
Tel: +20(11) 354-271

Head: Mohamed Sayed Hamzawi

Founded: 1994
Administration

HIGHER INSTITUTE FOR AGRICULTURAL COOPERATIVE STUDIES
Assiut
Tel: +20(88) 322-281

Director: Abdel-Razeq Abdel-Aleem (1999-)

Founded: 1968
Agriculture

HIGHER INSTITUTE FOR AGRICULTURAL COOPERATIVE STUDIES
Shobra Al-Keima, Cairo
Tel: +20(2) 444-4850
Fax: +20(2) 444-1400

Director: Hafez A. Shalabi (2002-)

Founded: 1965
Agriculture

HIGHER INSTITUTE FOR APPLIED ARTS
Distinguished District, 51B, Second Adjacency, 6th of October City
Tel: +20(11) 352-806

Director: Mahmoud Ahmad Abdel A'al (1998-)

Founded: 1994
Applied Arts (Graphic Arts; Handicrafts)

HIGHER INSTITUTE FOR ARCHITECTURE
Third District, Second Adjacency, 6th of October City
Tel: +20(11) 356-463
Fax: +20(11) 359-464

Director: Hassan Abdel-Maged Wahbi (2001-)

Founded: 1993
Architecture

HIGHER INSTITUTE FOR COMPUTER AND ADMINISTRATION
Corniche Al-Nile, behind Al-Nile Badrawi Hospital, Al-Maadi, Cairo
Tel: +20(2) 524-7982

Director: Abdel-Aziz Abbas Al-Sherbeni (2000-)

Founded: 1999
Administration; Computer Science; Management Systems

HIGHER INSTITUTE FOR COMPUTER AND BUSINESS ADMINISTRATION
High Way, Al-Zarqa City, Damietta
Tel: +20(57) 852-236

Director: Rashed Mokhtar (2002-)

Founded: 1999
Business Administration; Business Computing; Computer Science

HIGHER INSTITUTE FOR COMPUTER SCIENCE
King Maryot, Alexandria

Director: Kamal Sultan M. Salem (1999-)

Founded: 1997

Programmes
Computer Science

HIGHER INSTITUTE FOR COMPUTER SCIENCES AND INFORMATICS
Division 1/1, Central Road, 6th of October City
Tel: +20(11) 231-041

Director: Hussein Magdy Zain Al-Din (2001-)

Founded: 1994
Computer Science

HIGHER INSTITUTE FOR COMPUTER SCIENCES AND MANAGEMENT TECHNOLOGY
Street n° 304, New Maadi, Cairo
Tel: +20(2) 702-9850
Fax: +20(2) 702-3105

Head: Said Ibrahim Refa'y

Founded: 1993
Computer Science; Engineering Management; Management Systems

HIGHER INSTITUTE FOR COMPUTER SCIENCES AND MANAGEMENT TECHNOLOGY
Agricultural School Str., Sohag
Tel: +20(93) 605-714

Director: Ahmad Abdel A'al Al-Darder (1999-)

Founded: 1996
Computer Science; Management Systems

HIGHER INSTITUTE FOR COMPUTER STUDIES
31 Km Al-Kafouri, Cairo Alexandria High Way, King Maryout, Alexandria
Tel: +20(3) 448-3200
Director: Hussein Ahmad Al-Sheikh (1999-)

Founded: 1996
Computer Science

HIGHER INSTITUTE FOR COOPERATIVE AND ADMINISTRATIVE STUDIES
Al-Mounia, Sayeda Zainab, Cairo
Tel: +20(2) 795-5135
Fax: +20(2) 795-5686
Director: Kamel Hamdi Abou Al-Khair (1999-)

Founded: 1964
Administration; Public Administration; Social and Community Services

HIGHER INSTITUTE FOR DEVELOPED STUDIES
Al-Sherif Str., off Al-Haram Str., besides Al-Farouq School, Giza
Tel: +20(2) 386-0008
Fax: +20(2) 388-5405
Director: Lucy Hakem Abou-Saif (1997-)

Founded: 1995
Development Studies

HIGHER INSTITUTE FOR ECONOMICS AND THE ENVIRONMENT
Division 1/1, Central Road, 6th of October City
Tel: +20(11) 231-161
Director: Doreya Shafeq Basiouni (2002-)

Founded: 1994
Economics; Environmental Studies

HIGHER INSTITUTE FOR ENGINEERING
Corniche Al-Nile, behind Al-Nile Badrawi Hospital, Al-Maadi, Cairo
Tel: +20(2) 524-7982
Head: Ahmad Ahmad Al-Qadi

Founded: 1999
Engineering

HIGHER INSTITUTE FOR ENGINEERING
Adjacency n°13, 10th of Ramadan City
Tel: +20(15) 365-667
Director: Hazem Ali Basiouni (2000-)

Founded: 1995
Engineering

HIGHER INSTITUTE FOR ENGINEERING AND AVIATION TECHNOLOGY
Imbaba, Giza
Director: Ali M. Ibrahim Al-Guindi

Programmes
Aviation Technology (Aeronautical and Aerospace Engineering)
Engineering

HIGHER INSTITUTE FOR HOTEL MANAGEMENT "EGOTH"
Alexandria
Tel: +20(2) 390-1768
Director: Mena Omar Barakat (2001-)

Founded: 1999
Hotel Management

HIGHER INSTITUTE FOR HOTEL MANAGEMENT "EGOTH"
Luxor
Tel: +20(2) 391-2688
Director: Mohamed Samir Abdul-Fattah (2001-)

Founded: 1999
Hotel Management

HIGHER INSTITUTE FOR INDUSTRIAL ENGINEERING
Division 1/1, Central Route, 6th of October City
Tel: +20(11) 355-275
Head: Ali Mohamed Tal'at

Founded: 1994
Industrial Engineering

HIGHER INSTITUTE FOR LANGUAGES
Division 1/1, Central Route, 6th of October City
Tel: +20(11) 231-161
Fax: +20(2) 231-560
Director: Baher Mohamed Al-Gohary (2000-)

Founded: 1994
Modern Languages

HIGHER INSTITUTE FOR LANGUAGES
Behind Al-Sheraton Blocks, Heliopolis
Tel: +20(2) 266-4472
Director: Salama Mohamed Soliman (1999-)

Founded: 1993
Modern Languages

HIGHER INSTITUTE FOR LITERARY STUDIES
King Maryout, Alexandria
Tel: +20(2) 484-6155

Director: Farouq Othman Abaza (2000-)

Founded: 2000
Literary Studies (Arts and Humanities)

HIGHER INSTITUTE FOR MANAGEMENT AND COMPUTER
Port Said

Head: Zain Al-Albdeen Hassan Faris

Founded: 1995

Departments
Administration and Computer (Administration; Computer Science; Management)

HIGHER INSTITUTE FOR MANAGEMENT AND INFORMATION TECHNOLOGY
Sakkara, Giza
Tel: +20(2) 381-0318
Fax: +20(2) 381-0313

Director: Sedek Mohamed Afify (1996-)

Founded: 1995
Information Technology; Management; Management Systems

HIGHER INSTITUTE FOR MANAGEMENT AND TECHNOLOGY
Shobra Ment

Director: Amr Ghanayem (2000-)

Founded: 2000
Management; Management Systems; Technology

HIGHER INSTITUTE FOR MANAGEMENT SCIENCES AND FOREIGN TRADE
New Cairo City

Programmes
Foreign Trade (International Business)
Management (International Business; Management)

HIGHER INSTITUTE FOR MASS MEDIA AND COMMUNICATION ARTS
Division 1/1, Central Route, 6th of October City
Tel: +20(11) 355-281
Fax: +20(2) 266-4472

Director: Layla Mohamed Abdel-Maged (2000-)

Founded: 1994
Communication Arts; Mass Communication; Media Studies

158

HIGHER INSTITUTE FOR OPTICS TECHNOLOGY
Al-Sheraton blocks, Heliopolis
Tel: +20(2) 266-5950
Fax: +20(2) 267-2688

Director: Ahmad Abdel-Samea Al-Hamalawy (1995-)

Founded: 1993
Optical Technology

HIGHER INSTITUTE FOR SOCIAL WORK
73, Al-Resafa Street, Moharam Bek, Alexandria
Tel: +20(3) 494-8190
Fax: +20(3) 495-1560

Director: Ibrahim Abdul-Hadi Al-Melegi (2002-)

Founded: 1934
Social Work

HIGHER INSTITUTE FOR SOCIAL WORK
Aswan
Tel: +20(97) 314-995

Director: Gaber Sayed Ahmad (1997-)

Founded: 1974
Social Work

HIGHER INSTITUTE FOR SOCIAL WORK
8th District, Madinet Nasr, Cairo
Tel: +20(2) 272-7325
Fax: +20(2) 272-0556

Director: Ali Al-Din Al-Sayed Mohamed Soliman (1998-)

Founded: 1937
Social Work

HIGHER INSTITUTE FOR SOCIAL WORK
Damanhour
Tel: +20(45) 315-386
Fax: +20(45) 318-420

Director: Mohamed Nabil Salem (2001-)

Founded: 1980
Social Work

HIGHER INSTITUTE FOR SOCIAL WORK
Port-Said
Tel: +20(66) 324-365

Director: Abdul-Khalek M. Afify (1998-)

Founded: 1981
Social Work

HIGHER INSTITUTE FOR SOCIAL WORK
Division 1/1, Central Route, 6th of October City
Tel: +20(11) 355-276

Director: Hassan A. Hamam (2002-)

Founded: 1994
Social Work

HIGHER INSTITUTE FOR SOCIAL WORK
Al-Guish Street, King Fouad Palace, Kafr Al-Sheikh
Tel: +20(47) 227-835
Fax: +20(47) 223-184

Director: Mohamed Ahmad Abdel-Hadi (1998-)

Founded: 1971
Social Work

HIGHER INSTITUTE FOR SOCIAL WORK
Abdel-Salam Aref Str., Mansoura
Tel: +20(50) 367-077

Director: M. Abdill Razek Ghoneim (2001-)

Founded: 1995
Social Work

HIGHER INSTITUTE FOR SOCIAL WORK
Al-Almal Str., Al-Sadat City, New Banha
Tel: +20(13) 235-885
Fax: +20(13) 220-554

Director: Al-Sayed Metwali Al-Ashmawi (2000-)

Founded: 1993
Social Work

HIGHER INSTITUTE FOR SOCIAL WORK
Qena
Tel: +20(96) 334-908

Director: Gaber Sayed Ahmad (1997-)

Founded: 1997
Social Work

HIGHER INSTITUTE FOR SOCIAL WORK
Sohag
Tel: +20(93) 640-222

Director: Fawzy Al-Desouki Mohamed (1997-)

Founded: 1993
Social Work

HIGHER INSTITUTE FOR SPECIALIZED TECHNOLOGICAL STUDIES
32 Km. Cairo Ismaelia High Way, Ismaelia
Tel: +20(2) 477-2888
Fax: +20(2) 477-1900

Director: Hesham Hassan Makhlouf (1997-)

Founded: 1993
Technology

HIGHER INSTITUTE FOR SPECIFIC STUDIES
Nazlet Al-Seman, behind Seyag Hotel, Al-Haram, Giza
Tel: +20(2) 385-9104
Fax: +20(2) 384-5505

Director: Fouad Eskandar Niqola (1995-)

Founded: 1995

HIGHER INSTITUTE FOR TOURISM AND HOTEL MANAGEMENT
Sakkara Route, Al-Haram, Giza

Director: Abdel-Halim Abdel Fattah Ewais (2002-)

Founded: 2000
Hotel Management; Tourism

HIGHER INSTITUTE FOR TOURISM AND HOTEL MANAGEMENT
Hurghada
Tel: +20(2) 290-1017

Director: Ali Omar Abdullah (2002-)

Founded: 2000
Hotel Management; Tourism

HIGHER INSTITUTE FOR TOURISM AND HOTEL MANAGEMENT
Ra'as Sedr, South Sinai
Tel: +20(62) 400-871
Fax: +20(62) 770-752

Director: Nervana Mokhtar Harraz (1999-)

Hotel Management; Tourism

HIGHER INSTITUTE FOR TOURISM AND HOTEL MANAGEMENT
6th District, 6th of October City
Tel: +20(11) 330-342

Director: Hassan Abbas Al-Mansouri (1998-)

Hotel Management; Tourism

HIGHER INSTITUTE FOR TOURISM, HOTEL MANAGEMENT AND COMPUTER SCIENCE

2, Adel Mostafa Shawqi Str., Al-Seouf, Alexandria
Tel: +20(3) 502-1055

Director: Abdul-Fattah Ali Ghazal (2001-)

Founded: 1994
Computer Science; Hotel Management; Tourism

HIGHER INTERNATIONAL INSTITUTE FOR LANGUAGES AND SIMULTANEOUS INTERPRETATION

New Cairo City

Director: Mostafa Mohamed Al-Shakaa

Programmes
Languages (Modern Languages)
Simultaneous Interpretation

HIGHER TECHNOLOGICAL INSTITUTE

Al-Guish Str., King Fouad Palace , Kafr Al-Sheikh, 10th of Ramadan City
Tel: +20(15) 363-497
Fax: +20(15) 364-269

Director: Mostafa Mahmoud Thabet (1996-)

Founded: 1988
Technology

LABOUR UNIVERSITY

Al-Nasr Str., Abbas Al-Aquad, Nasr City, Cairo
Tel: +20(2) 275-4646

Head: Emad Al-Din Hassan

Labour and Industrial Relations

POST-GRADUATE HIGHER INSTITUTE FOR ISLAMIC STUDIES

26, Yolyo Str., Meet Oqba, Giza
Tel: +20(2) 346-8547

Director: Baghat Oteba

Founded: 1955
Islamic Studies

POST-GRADUATE HIGHER INSTITUTE FOR SOCIAL DEFENCE STUDIES

1, Al-Shahed Ra'af Zaki, Polak Al-Dakrour, Giza
Tel: +20(2) 330-5352

Director: Mohamed Shehata Ali

Founded: 1991
Social Defence Studies (Social and Community Services; Social Policy; Social Problems; Social Welfare)

RA'AS AL-BAR HIGHER INSTITUTE FOR SPECIFIC STUDIES AND COMPUTER SCIENCE

Ra'as Al-bar

Director: Ahmad Diaa M. Mousa

Programmes
Computer Science

SADAT ACADEMY FOR ADMINISTRATIVE SCIENCES

Corniche El-Nil, Maadi Entrance Road, Cairo
Tel: +20(2) 350-1033
Fax: +20(2) 777-175

Director: Amin Al-Dorghamy

Programmes
Administrative Sciences (Administration; Public Administration)
Bank Management (Banking)
Computer and Information Systems (Computer Networks; Information Technology)
Insurance

Note: Also 24 Technical Commercial Institutes, 21 Technical Industrial Institutes, and 11 other Intermediate Institutes offering 2-year Diplomas.

Eritrea

INSTITUTION TYPES AND CREDENTIALS

Types of higher education institutions:

University
Teacher Training Institute

School leaving and higher education credentials:

Eritrean Secondary Education Certificate Examination (ESECE)
Bachelor's Degree
Master's Degree

STRUCTURE OF EDUCATION SYSTEM

Pre-higher education:

Duration of compulsory education:

Age of entry: 7
Age of exit: 14

Structure of school system:

Elementary
Type of school providing this education: Elementary school
Length of programme in years: 5
Age level from: 7 to: 12

Junior Secondary
Type of school providing this education: Junior Secondary School
Length of programme in years: 2
Age level from: 12 to: 14

Senior Secondary
Type of school providing this education: Senior Secondary School
Length of programme in years: 4
Age level from: 14 to: 18
Certificate/diploma awarded: Eritrean Secondary Education Certificate Examination (ESECE)

Technical
Type of school providing this education: Technical School
Length of programme in years: 3

Age level from: 16 to: 19

Certificate/diploma awarded: Eritrean Secondary Education Certificate Examination (ESECE)

School education:

Elementary education lasts for five years followed by two years of junior secondary education. Together they form seven years of basic, compulsory education. Senior secondary education lasts for four years after completion of the basic education cycle. At the end of the course, pupils sit for the Eritrean Secondary Education Certificate Examination.

Students who leave school at the end of the basic cycle can enter basic-level technical training. Following completion of training, they may enter intermediate level technical schools after passing an entrance examination. The other route to entry into intermediate technical schools is direct, after completing Grade 10 at senior secondary school level and passing an entrance examination. Courses last for three years. They prepare skilled workers for industry, agriculture and other development areas.

Higher education:

Higher education is provided by the University of Asmara. It was founded in 1958 and was granted full university status in 1968. The University consists of Colleges of Science, Arts, Business and Economics, Education, Agriculture, Health Science, Engineering and Law. The governing bodies are the Board of Trustees and the Academic Senate.

Academic year:

Classes from: September *to:* June

Long vacation from: 1 July *to:* 31 August

Languages of instruction:

English

Stages of studies:

Non-university level post-secondary studies (technical/vocational type):

Students completing the full eleven-year cycle may enter diploma-level professional colleges, still in the process of being established.

University level studies:

University level first stage:

Courses for Bachelor's Degrees are generally obtained after four years of regular study for day students and seven years for extension students.

University level second stage: *Master's Degree*:

As from 2004, the University will offer Master's Degree programmes in English, Geography, Statistics and Demography, Plant and Soil Science, Economics and Management and Science.

Teacher education:

Training of pre-primary and primary/basic school teachers

Teacher Training Institutes (TTI) offer a training programme for primary-school teachers. It admits secondary school graduates who have sat for an entrance examination for a one-year course. At the end of this course, trainees are awarded the TTI Certificate. In-service courses are also offered during the long vacation, July and August, to upgrade unqualified primary school teachers and school directors. Unqualified elementary teachers can follow the Distance Education programme for Elementary Teachers in Eritrea.

Training of secondary school teachers
Junior and senior secondary school teachers follow a four-year degree programme at the University of Asmara. Directors of schools are trained in the College of Education. The third and final level of technical education institutions provide training in professional education fields.

NATIONAL BODIES

Responsible authorities:

Ministry of Education
    Minister: Osman Saleh
    Director, Administration: Haile Alazar
    PO Box 1056
    Asmara
    Tel: +291(1) 11-66-44   +291(1) 12-78-17
    Fax: +291(1) 11-83-51   +291(1) 12-19-13

ADMISSIONS TO HIGHER EDUCATION

Admission to university-level studies

Name of secondary school credential required: Eritrean Secondary Education Certificate Examination (ESECE)
Minimum score/requirement: Five subject passes

Other admission requirements: Advice by the University Placement Office

Foreign students admission

Admission requirements: Foreign students must hold the Eritrean Secondary School Leaving Certificate Examination or its equivalent.

Entry regulations: A visa is required.

Language requirements: Good knowledge of English is essential.

Application procedures:

Apply to individual institution for entry to: University

Apply to: Admissions Office, University of Asmara
    PO Box 1220
    Asmara
    Tel: +291(1) 16-19-26

Fax: +291(1) 16-22-36
EMail: samuelktt@asmara.uoa.edu.er
WWW: http://www.uoa.edu.er/

STUDENT LIFE

Main student services at national level

Registrar's Office, University of Asmara
PO Box 1220
Asmara
Tel: +291(1) 16-19-26
Fax: +291(1) 16-22-36
WWW: http://www.uoa.edu.er/

Student expenses and financial aid

Student costs:

Average living costs: 1,900 (US Dollar)
Foreign students tuition fees: Maximum: 1,660 (US Dollar)

INTERNATIONAL COOPERATION AND EXCHANGES

Principal national bodies responsible for dealing with international cooperation and exchanges in higher education:

Ministry of Education
Minister: Osman Saleh
Director, Administration: Haile Alazar
PO Box 1056
Asmara
Tel: +291(1) 12-78-17
Fax: +291(1) 12-19-13

GRADING SYSTEM

Usual grading system in secondary school

Full Description: At middle and secondary school 50% and above is the pass mark.

Main grading system used by higher education institutions

Full Description: Letter grades (A,B,C,D, or F) are used to indicate the academic achievement of a student in a course. The value of each grade is as follows: A: excellent (4); B: very good (3); C: good (2); D: unsatisfactory (1); F: failure (0)

Highest on scale: A
Lowest on scale: F

NOTES ON HIGHER EDUCATION SYSTEM

Data for academic year: 2002-2003
Source: University of Asmara, updated by the International Association of Universities (IAU) from IBE website, 2003 (www.ibe.unesco.org/International/Databanks/Wde/profilee.htm)

INSTITUTIONS OF HIGHER EDUCATION

UNIVERSITIES

PUBLIC INSTITUTIONS

*• UNIVERSITY OF ASMARA
PO Box 1220, Asmara
Tel: +291(1) 161-926
Fax: +291(1) 162-236
EMail: postmaster@uoa.edu.er
Website: http://www.uoa.edu.er/

President: Wolde-Ab Yisak (1993-) Tel: +291(1)161-935
EMail: woldeab@asmara.uoa.edu.er

Director of Academic Affairs: Jadesse Mehari
Tel: +291(1) 116-1141

Director, Administration and Strategic Planning: Tewelde
Zerom Tel: +291(1) 119-035 Fax: +291(1) 124-300

International Relations: Tewolde Zerom, Director of
Strategic Planning/Projects Tel: +291(1) 116-1932
EMail: tewelde@ipc.uoa.edu.er

Head Librarian: Assefaw Abraha
EMail: assefawa@asmara.uoa.edu.er

Colleges

Agriculture and Aquatic Sciences (Agriculture; Animal Hus-
bandry; Marine Biology; Soil Science) *Director*: Bissrat Ghebru
Arts (English; Journalism; Mass Communication; Philosophy)
Director: Peter R. Schmidt
Business and Economics (Accountancy; Business Adminis-
tration; Business and Commerce; Economics; Finance; Law;
Public Administration) *Dean*: Mehari Tewolde

Education (Education; Educational Administration; Educa-
tional Psychology) *Dean*: Belaynesh Araya
Engineering (Civil Engineering; Electrical Engineering; Engi-
neering; Mechanical Engineering) *Dean*: N.V. Rao
Health Sciences (Biomedicine; Community Health; Health Sci-
ences; Nursing; Pharmacy) *Director*: Asefaw Tekeste
Law
Science (Biology; Chemistry; Mathematics; Natural Sciences;
Physics) *Dean*: Ghebrebrhan Ogubazghi
Social Sciences (Anthropology; Archaeology; Demography
and Population; Geography (Human); History; Political Sci-
ence; Social Work; Sociology)

History: Founded 1958. Dismantled and relocated to Ethiopia
1990. Re-established 1991 as an Autonomous University by the
Provisional Government of Eritrea (PGE).

Governing Bodies: Board of Trustees; Academic Senate

Academic Year: September to June (September-January;
January-June)

Admission Requirements: Eritrean Secondary Examination
Certificate Examination (ESECE) or equivalent

Fees: (US Dollars): 1,660

Main Language(s) of Instruction: English

Degrees and Diplomas: *Bachelor's Degree*: Arts; Science, 4
yrs. As from 2004, the University will offer Master's Degree
programmes in English, Geography, Statistics and Demography, Plant and Soil Science, Economics and Management and
Science.

Libraries: c. 60,000 vols

Publications: Seismic Bulletin (2 per annum)

Academic Staff *2001:* Total: c. 225

Student Numbers *2001:* Total: c. 4,100

Ethiopia

INSTITUTION TYPES AND CREDENTIALS

Types of higher education institutions:

University
Institute
College
University College

School leaving and higher education credentials:

Ethiopian School Leaving Certificate Examination
Ethiopian Higher Education Entrance Examination
Diploma
Bachelor's Degree
Doctor
Master's Degree
Specialization Diploma
Doctorate (PhD)

STRUCTURE OF EDUCATION SYSTEM

Pre-higher education:

Duration of compulsory education:

Age of entry: 6
Age of exit: 14

Structure of school system:

Primary
Type of school providing this education: Primary School
Length of programme in years: 8
Age level from: 6 to: 14

First Cycle Secondary
Type of school providing this education: General Secondary School
Length of programme in years: 2
Age level from: 14 to: 16
Certificate/diploma awarded: Ethiopian School Leaving Certificate Examination (ESLCE)

Second Cycle Secondary
Type of school providing this education: Preparatory Secondary School
Length of programme in years: 2
Age level from: 16 to: 18
Certificate/diploma awarded: Ethiopian Higher Education Entrance Examination (EHEEE)

Technical
Type of school providing this education: Technical School and Junior College
Age level from: 16 to: 19

Vocational
Type of school providing this education: Vocational School and Junior College
Length of programme in years: 3
Age level from: 16 to: 19
Certificate/diploma awarded: Ethiopian General School Leaving Certificate

School education:

According to the new structure of the education system, primary education lasts for eight years (age group 6-14) and is divided into two cycles: basic education (Grades I-IV) and general education (Grades V-VIII). Junior secondary schools no longer exist, as Grades VII and VIII have become the two upper classes of the second cycle of primary education. Secondary education is organized into two cycles: the first (Grades IX and X) or general secondary education, and the second cycle (Grades XI and XII) or preparatory secondary education. Since the education reform, completion of Grade X leads to the Ethiopian School Leaving Certificate Examination (ESLCE). It used to be at the end of Grade XII. The second cycle prepares students for continuing their studies at the higher education level or selecting their own vocations. It offers a science option and a social science option. At the end, students take the Ethiopian Higher Education Entrance examination to enter higher education institutions.
Technical and vocational education and training is institutionally separate from the regular education system and runs in parallel with it.

Higher education:

Higher education is provided by universities, university colleges and specialized institutions. They are under the responsibility of the Ministry of Education. Junior colleges and colleges offering diploma programmes are also under regional governments and private providers.

Main laws/decrees governing higher education:

Decree: Council of Ministers Regulation   Year: 1999
Concerns: Universities of Debub and Bahir Dar

Decree: Council of Ministers Regulation N° 197/1994   Year: 1994
Concerns: Administration of Higher Education Institutions in the regions.

Decree: Council of Ministers Regulation No. 113/1993   Year: 1993
Concerns: Addis Ababa University

Decree: Proclamation No. 109 of 1977   Year: 1977
Concerns: Higher Education Institutions

Academic year:

Classes from: September *to:* July

Long vacation from: 8 July *to:* 11 September

Languages of instruction:

English

Stages of studies:

Non-university level post-secondary studies (technical/vocational type):

Higher vocational and technical education are offered by agricultural colleges, teacher training colleges, engineering and technological institutes, health and commercial institutions. Courses last between two and three years and lead to diplomas.

University level studies:

University level first stage: Bachelor's Degree:
The first stage of university level education leads to the Bachelor's Degree after four to five years' study. Examinations are organized at the end of each semester. In Medicine and Veterinary Medicine, the professional qualification of Doctor is conferred after six years' study.

University level second stage: Master's Degree; Specialization:
The second stage leads to a Master's Degree after a minimum of two years' further study. In Medicine and Veterinary Medicine the specialization degree is obtained after a minimum of three years' further study beyond the MD and DVM degrees.

University level third stage: Doctor of Philosophy:
The Doctor of Philosophy is conferred after some three years' study beyond the Master's degree.

Teacher education:

Training of pre-primary and primary/basic school teachers
First Cycle primary school teachers follow a one-year course after grade 12 in regional Primary Teacher Training Institutes (TTI). A diploma awarded by Teacher Training Colleges (TTC) is required to teach in the second cycle of primary education.

Training of secondary school teachers
Secondary school teachers must have at least a first degree. They are trained at the Faculties of Education of Addis Ababa University, Bahir Dar University, Alemaya University and Debub University (Dila), Jima University and Mekelle University which offer a three-year course leading to the degree of Bachelor of Education. Technical education teachers follow a three-year degree course at Nazreth Technical Teachers College.

Training of higher education teachers
Masters and PhD level teacher/staff training is undertaken at Addis Abeba University Graduate School. Many teachers are also trained abroad. Debub University and Alameya Universities are currently training students at Master's level. Other higher education institutions (Jimma, Mekelle) are planning to do that shortly.

Non-traditional studies:

Distance higher education

Distance learning in MBA is offered by Addis Ababa University. Diploma level training is offered by Addis Ababa Commercial College, Bahinder, Mekelle, Jima and Awasa.

Lifelong higher education

There are continuing education programmes in almost all institutions of higher education in Ethiopia. They mainly serve the needs of adult students and are offered after regular hours as evening programmes and during the summer season (Kiremt) on a tuition fee paying basis.

NATIONAL BODIES

Responsible authorities:

Higher Education Sector, Ministry of Education

    Minister of Education: Genet Zewde

    Vice-Minister for Higher Education: Teshome Yizengaw

    PO Box 1367

    Addis Ababa

    Tel: +251(1) 55-31-33 +251(1) 56-00-63

    Fax: +251(1) 55-08-77 +251(1) 56-55-65

    Telex: 21435

    EMail: heardmoe@telecom.net.et

Role of governing body: Coordinates tertiary level education in Ethiopia and assists higher education institutions.

ADMISSIONS TO HIGHER EDUCATION

Admission to non university higher education studies

Name of secondary school credential required: Ethiopian School Leaving Certificate Examination
Minimum score/requirement: Grade point average of 2.8/4, or 2 subjects with C grades and 3 with D grades.
For entry to: 2/3- year Technical/Vocational colleges

Admission to university-level studies

Name of secondary school credential required: Ethiopian Higher Education Entrance Examination
Minimum score/requirement: Passes in 4 subjects at C-level

Entrance exams required: This will be a requirement as of the 2003/04 academic year.

Other admission requirements: Special privileges for female students and students from disadvantaged/remote regions.

Foreign students admission

Definition of foreign student: A person enrolled at an institution of higher education in a country of which he/she is not permanently resident.

Quotas: The School of Information Studies for Africa (SISA) admits students from the Eastern and Southern African Region on a quota basis.

Admission requirements: Foreign students must provide the academic certificates required by the institution concerned. Foreign qualifications recognized as equivalent to the Ethiopian school-leaving certificate are: the General Certificate of Education of the University of London; the Cambridge Overseas Examination; the West African School Certificate and the Oxford Examination. The Higher Education Department may grant equivalence to other secondary school-leaving certificates in individual cases. All foreign students must cover their living expenses.

Entry regulations: Visas; financial guarantee. In addition, all foreign students, including ECOWAS citizens, are required to secure resident permits for the period of their stay.

Health requirements: Students must present a health certificate.

Language requirements: Students must be proficient in English at TOEFL level.

Application procedures:

Apply to individual institution for entry to: University/College

Apply to: Ministry of Education
 PO Box 1367
 Addis Ababa
 Tel: +251(1) 55-31-33; 251(1) 56-00-63
 Fax: +251(1) 56-55-65

Application closing dates:
 For university level studies: 1 July
 For advanced/doctoral studies: 1 July

Recognition of studies and qualifications:

Studies pursued in home country (System of recognition/accreditation): The University Senate awards credentials which are recognized by the country. The Ministry of Education is mandated to accredit private and public higher education institutions according to whether they fulfil the required standards.

Studies pursued in foreign countries (bodies dealing with recognition of foreign credentials):
Higher Education Sector, Ministry of Education
 Vice-Minister for Higher Education: Teshome Yizengaw
 PO Box 1367
 Addis Ababa
 Tel: +251(1) 55-31-33 +251(1) 56-00-63
 Fax: +251(1) 55-08-77 +251(1) 55-02-99
 Telex: 21435

Deals with credential recognition for entry to: University and Profession

Special provisions for recognition:

For access to non-university post-secondary studies: It applies to nationals.

For access to university level studies: It applies to nationals who wish to enter medical schools

References to further information on foreign student admissions and recognition of studies

Title: Higher Education in Ethiopia: Facts and Figures 2001/2002
Author: Ministry of Education

STUDENT LIFE

Student expenses and financial aid

Student costs:

Average living costs: 10,000 (Ethiopian Birr)
Home students tuition fees: Minimum: 1,200 (Ethiopian Birr)
Maximum: 3,000 (Ethiopian Birr)
Foreign students tuition fees: Maximum: 18,000 (Ethiopian Birr)

Bodies providing information on student financial aid:

Registrar Offices in universities and colleges

Deals with: Grants

Scholarship Panel, Higher Education Human Resources Department
PO Box 1367
Addis Ababa
Tel: +251(1) 55-31-33 +251(1) 56-55-32
Fax: +251(1) 55-08-77 +251(1) 56-55-65

Deals with: Grants

Publications on student services and financial aid:

Title: Facts and Figures 2001/2002
Author: Ministry of Education

Title: Institutional Information Booklets

INTERNATIONAL COOPERATION AND EXCHANGES

Principal national bodies responsible for dealing with international cooperation and exchanges in higher education:

Higher Education Sector, Ministry of Education
Vice-Minister for Higher Education: Teshome Yizengaw
PO Box 1367
Addis Ababa

Tel: +251(1) 55-31-33; +251(1) 56-00-63
Fax: +251(1) 55-08-77 +251(1) 56-55-65

Human Resources Department, Ministry of Education
Department Head: Yeromnesh Ayele
PO Box 1367
Addis Ababa
Tel: +251(1) 55-31-33; +251(1) 56-40-44
Fax: +251(1) 55-08-77; +251(1) 56-55-65

GRADING SYSTEM

Usual grading system in secondary school

Full Description: 100-0
Highest on scale: 100
Pass/fail level: 50
Lowest on scale: 1

Main grading system used by higher education institutions

Full Description: It is A-F. The highest on scale is "A" and the lowest is "F". The pass/fail level for undergraduates is "C", and for postgraduates is "B".
Highest on scale: "A"
Pass/fail level: "C" (for undergraduates), "B" (for postgraduates)
Lowest on scale: "F"

Other main grading systems

Marks are sometimes out of 100 with the lowest pass mark set at 60.

NOTES ON HIGHER EDUCATION SYSTEM

Education for both undergraduate and postgraduate level regular programmes is provided free of charge for Ethiopians. This includes free board and lodging in all institutions of higher education. According to the Government's new Education and Training Policy, priority for financial support will depend on the completion of general secondary education and related training. Hence, cost-sharing of higher education is to be implemented possibly as of 2003/2004. The form of cost-sharing will be a "graduate tax" scheme.

Data for academic year: 2002-2003
Source: Ministry of Education, Addis Ababa, 2003

INSTITUTIONS OF HIGHER EDUCATION

UNIVERSITIES

PUBLIC INSTITUTIONS

*• ADDIS ABABA UNIVERSITY (AAU)

PO Box 1176, Addis Ababa
Tel: +251(1) 55-08-44
Fax: +251(1) 55-06-55 +251(1) 55-09-72
Telex: 21205
EMail: kennedy.aau@telecom.net.et
Website: http://www.aau.edu.et

President: Endrias Eshete (2002-) Tel: +251(1) 55-74-78

Academic Vice-President: Gemechu Megerssa
Tel: + 251(1) 55 74 77

Faculties

Business and Economics (Accountancy; Economics; Management; Public Administration)
Education (Business Education; Curriculum; Education; Educational Psychology) *Dean:* Ato Birara Gebru
Law *Dean:* Getachew Abera
Medicine (Anaesthesiology; Anatomy; Biochemistry; Community Health; Gynaecology and Obstetrics; Medicine; Microbiology; Ophthalmology; Orthopedics; Paediatrics; Parasitology; Pathology; Pharmacology; Physiology; Psychiatry and Mental Health; Surgery) *Dean:* Abubeker Bedri
Science (Biology; Chemistry; Geology; Geophysics; Mathematics; Natural Sciences; Physics; Sanitary Engineering; Statistics) *Dean:* Afework Bekele
Technology (Architecture; Building Technologies; Chemical Engineering; Civil Engineering; Electrical Engineering; Mechanical Engineering; Technology) *Dean:* Abebe Dinku
Veterinary Medicine *(Debre Zeit)* (Anatomy; Biochemistry; Biology; Embryology and Reproduction Biology; Microbiology; Parasitology; Pathology; Pharmacology; Physiology; Veterinary Science) *Dean:* Getachew Abebe

Programmes

Distance Education

Schools

Geography; History; International Relations; Philosophy; Political Science; Social Sciences; Sociology *Dean:* Bekele Gutema
Information Studies (Information Sciences; Library Science) *Director:* Getachew Birru
Language Studies (Linguistics; Literature; Modern Languages; Native Language; Theatre)
Pharmacy

Research Institutes
Development Research (Development Studies)
Education
Education Research
Ethiopian Studies *Director:* Baye Yimam
Pathobiology (Pathology)

History: Founded 1961 as Haile Sellassie I University, incorporating University College of Addis Ababa, founded 1950; Imperial College of Engineering, 1953; Ethio-Swedish Institute of Building Technology, 1954; Imperial Ethiopian College of Agricultural and Mechanical Arts, 1951; Public Health College, 1954; and Theological College of the Holy Trinity, 1960. Acquired present title 1975.

Governing Bodies: Board of Governors

Academic Year: September to July (September-February; February-July). Also Summer programme (July-August)

Admission Requirements: Secondary school certificate, or foreign equivalent

Main Language(s) of Instruction: English

Degrees and Diplomas: *Diploma:* Building Technology; Veterinary Science, 2-3 yrs; *Bachelor's Degree:* Arts (BA); Science (BSc), 4-5 yrs; Engineering; Law, 5 yrs; *Doctor:* Medicine (MD); Veterinary Medecine (DVM), 6 yrs; *Master's Degree:* Arts (MA); Science (MSc), a further 2 yrs; *Specialization Diploma:* a further 2 yrs following MD; *Doctorate (PhD):* History, Languages, Chemistry, Biology, a further 3-4 yrs following MA/MSc

Student Services: Academic Counselling, Social Counselling, Foreign Student Adviser, Cultural Centre, Sports Facilities, Health Services, Canteen

Special Facilities: Archives Museum; Natural Museum. Geophysical Observatory. Cultural Centre. Herbarium. Audio-Visual Centre

Libraries: Total, c. 493,000 vols

Publications: Ethiopian Journal of Development Research; Journal of Ethiopian Studies; Ethiopian Journal of Education; Ethiopian Journal of Science (SINET) (biannually); Register of Current Research on Ethiopia and Horn of Africa

Press or Publishing House: Addis Ababa University Press

Academic Staff *2000-2001:* Total: **802**

Student Numbers *2000-2001:* Total: **11,200**

Evening Students, 9,374

Note: Evening students are not included in total

ALEMAYA UNIVERSITY (AU)

PO Box 138, Dire Dawa, Harar, Alemaya
Tel: +251(5) 11-13-99
Fax: +251(5) 11-40-08
EMail: alemaya.univ@telecom.net.et
Website: http://www.telecom.net.et/~alemayau

President: Desta Hamito Tel: +251(5) 11-23-64
EMail: alemaya.univ@telecom.net.et
Academic Vice-President: Belay Kassa
Tel: +251(5) 11-23-74
Head Librarian: Ato Yared Mammo
EMail: y_mammo@hotmail.com

Faculties

Education (Biology; Chemistry; Education; English; Geography; History; Mathematics; Physics) *Dean*: Tadesse Zerihun
Health Sciences (Health Sciences; Laboratory Techniques; Public Health) *Dean*: Melake Damena

Colleges

Agriculture (Agricultural Economics; Agricultural Engineering; Agriculture; Animal Husbandry; Botany) *Dean*: Heluf Kidan

Schools

Graduate Studies (Agricultural Economics; Agronomy; Animal Husbandry; Harvest Technology; Horticulture; Plant and Crop Protection; Soil Science; Water Science) *Dean*: Fekadu Lemessa

Further Information: Also international Research Centres

History: Founded 1954 as College of Agriculture. A State institution. Acquired present status 1985.

Governing Bodies: University Board; Senate

Academic Year: September to July (September-February; February-July)

Admission Requirements: Secondary school certificate or equivalent

Main Language(s) of Instruction: English

Degrees and Diplomas: *Diploma*: 2 yrs; *Bachelor's Degree*: Science (BSc), 4-5 yrs; *Master's Degree*: Science (MSc), a further 2-3 yrs

Student Services: Academic Counselling, Social Counselling, Nursery Care, Cultural Centre, Sports Facilities, Health Services

Student Residential Facilities: For c. 1700 students

Special Facilities: Arboretum. Greenhouse

Libraries: 45,759 vols, 103 periodical subscriptions

Publications: Annual Research Reports (annually); Newsletter; The Alemayan

Academic Staff *2001-2002:* Total: c. 210

Student Numbers *2001-2002:* Total: c. 5,000

International Relations: Tesfaye Dagnew
Tel: +251(8) 20-59-25 Fax: +251(8) 20-20-27
EMail: bdtc@ytelecom.net.et
Head Librarian: Yeshimebrat Mersha Tel: +251(8) 20-59-28
EMail: bdtc@telecom.net.et

Faculties

Business and Economics (Accountancy; Business and Commerce; Economics; Law; Management; Marketing; Secretarial Studies) *Dean*: Mesfin Teshager
Education (Biology; Chemistry; Education; English; Geography; History; Mathematics; Pedagogy; Physics) *Dean*: Tsetadirgachew Legese
Engineering (Chemical Engineering; Civil Engineering; Electrical Engineering; Engineering; Industrial Engineering; Mechanical Engineering; Textile Technology) *Dean*: Nigussie Mulugeta

History: Founded 1972, acquired present status and title 2000.

Governing Bodies: Board for Higher Education

Academic Year: September to June

Admission Requirements: Ethiopian school leaving certificate (ESLCE) or equivalent

Fees: None for national students

Main Language(s) of Instruction: English

International Co-operation: With universities in United Kingdom and India.

Degrees and Diplomas: *Bachelor's Degree*: Accountancy, Economics (BA); Education (BEd), 4 yrs; Engineering (BSc); Law (LLB), 5 yrs

Student Services: Cultural Centre, Sports Facilities, Health Services, Canteen

Student Residential Facilities: Yes

Libraries: Central Library with computer facilities; Engineering Faculty Library

Publications: News Letter (quarterly); Bulletin, Research articles on Education, Engineering, Linguistics (biannually)

Academic Staff *2001-2002*	MEN	WOMEN	TOTAL
FULL-TIME	192	3	195
PART-TIME	14	–	14
TOTAL	**206**	**3**	**209**

Staff with doctorate: Total: **14**

Student Numbers *2001-2002*	MEN	WOMEN	TOTAL
All (Foreign Included)	3,400	600	**4,000**

Evening Students, 4,000 **Distance Students,** 1,000

BAHIR DAR UNIVERSITY (BDU)

PO Box 79, Bahir Dar, Amhara
Tel: +251(8) 20-01-43
Fax: +251(8) 20-20-25
EMail: bdtc@telecom.net.et
Website: http://www.telecom.net.et/~bdu

President: Shimelis Haile (2000-) Tel: +251(8) 20-01-37
EMail: Shimelis8@yahoo.com
Academic Vice-President: Gizachew Adugna
Tel: +251(8) 20-07-60 EMail: tinsaef@yahoo.com

DEBUB/SOUTHERN UNIVERSITY (DU)

PO Box 5, Awassa
Tel: +251(6) 20-03-13 +251(6) 20-02-21
Fax: +251(6) 20-54-21
EMail: aca@telecom.net.et

President: Zinabu G. Mariam (2000-) Tel: +251(6) 20-46-26
Fax: +251 (6) 20-54-21 EMail: aca.dean@telecom.net.et
Academic Vice President: T. Teshome
Tel: +251(6) 20-46-27

International Relations: Feleke Debela
Tel: +251(6) 20-47-40

Head Librarian: Mohammed Dabullo Tel: +251(6) 20-25-02
EMail: aca@telecom.net.et

Faculties

Agriculture (Agriculture; Agronomy; Animal Husbandry; Engineering; Food Science) *Dean*: Ferdu Azerefegne
Education *Dean*: Bogale Teferi
Forestry *Dean*: Abdu Abdulkadir
Health Sciences (Health Sciences; Medical Technology; Nursing) *Dean*: Tadesse Anteneh
Natural Sciences (Biology; Chemistry; Mathematics; Natural Sciences; Physics) *Dean*: Alay Hagos
Social Sciences (Accountancy; Economics; Linguistics; Management; Modern Languages; Social Sciences) *Dean*: Abdisa Zerai

Colleges

Agriculture *(Awassa)*
Forestry *(Wondo Genet)*
Teacher Education and Health Sciences *(Dilla)* (Biology; Chemistry; Education; English; Geography; Health Education; Health Sciences; History; Hygiene; Laboratory Techniques; Mathematics; Native Language; Nursing; Physics; Teacher Training) *Dean*: Menna Olango

History: Founded 1976. Acquired present status 2000.

Academic Year: September to June

Admission Requirements: Secondary school leaving certificate

Fees: (US Dollars): 100 per credit hour for foreign students

Main Language(s) of Instruction: English

Accrediting Agencies: Ministry of Education

Degrees and Diplomas: *Diploma*: 2 yrs; *Bachelor's Degree*: Science; Education; Arts, 4 yrs; Agricultural Engineering (BSc), 5 yrs

Student Services: Academic Counselling, Social Counselling, Sports Facilities, Health Services

Student Residential Facilities: Yes (for all regular students)

Libraries: Central Library (Email and Photocopy services)

Academic Staff 2001-2002	MEN	WOMEN	TOTAL
FULL-TIME	330	25	**355**

Staff with doctorate: Total: **25**

Student Numbers 2001-2002	MEN	WOMEN	TOTAL
All (Foreign Included)	4,378	956	**5,334**

Evening Students, 1,280 Distance Students, 177

JIMMA UNIVERSITY (JU)

PO Box 378, Jimma, Tigray Region
Tel: +251(7) 11-13-40 +251(7) 11-14-58
Fax: +251(7) 11-14-50
EMail: jihs@telecom.net.et
Website: http://www.telecom.net.et/~junv.edu

President: Damtew W/ Mariam (2000-)
Tel: +251(7) 11-14-57

Vice-President for Administration and Development: Kora Tushune Tel: +251(7) 11-09-51

International Relations: Chali Jira Tel: +251(7) 11-22-02

Head of Library and Documentary Services: Mr Getachew Bayisa

Faculties

Business (Business Administration; Management) *Dean*: Shimels Zewde
Education *Dean*: Zelalem Teshome
Medical Sciences (Laboratory Techniques; Medicine; Pharmacy) *Dean*: Minas W/Tsadik
Public Health *Dean*: Kifle W/Michael
Technology (Civil Engineering; Electrical Engineering; Mechanical Engineering; Technology) *Dean*: Addis Hailu

Colleges

Agriculture *Dean*: Kaba Urgessa

History: Founded 1983, acquired present status and title 1999. Jimma University is a national pioneer of community-oriented higher education.

Governing Bodies: Board of Appointees; University Senate

Academic Year: September to June

Admission Requirements: Secondary school leaving certificate

Fees: None

Main Language(s) of Instruction: English

International Co-operation: Member of network of community-oriented Educational Institutions of Health Sciences

Degrees and Diplomas: *Bachelor's Degree*: Environmental Health (BSc); Nursing (BSc); Public Health (BSc); Science (BSc), 3 yrs following successful completion of 2 yrs' studies; Accountancy (BA); Biology (BSc); Business Management (BA); Chemistry (BSc); English (BA); Horticulture (BSc); Mathematics (BSc); Physics (BSc), 4 yrs; Civil Engineering (BSc); Electrical Engineering (BSc); Mechanical Engineering (BSc); Medical Laboratory Technology (BSc); Pharmacy (BSc), 5 yrs; *Doctor*: Medicine (MD), 7 yrs. Also Diplomas in most fields

Student Services: Academic Counselling, Cultural Centre, Sports Facilities, Health Services, Canteen

Student Residential Facilities: Yes

Special Facilities: Computer Centre; Audio-Visual Service

Libraries: University Library

Publications: Innovation, Newsletter (quarterly); Ethiopian Journal of Health Science (2 per annum)

Academic Staff 2001-2002: Total: **370**

Student Numbers 2001-2002	MEN	WOMEN	TOTAL
All (Foreign Included)	3,074	1,199	**4,273**

Evening Students, 1,030

• MEKELLE UNIVERSITY (MU)

PO Box 231, Mekelle, Tigray Region
Tel: +251(4) 40-08-12 +251(4) 40-08-20
Fax: +251(4) 40-07-93
EMail: mekelle.university@telecom.net.et

President: Haile Mitiku (1999-) Tel: +251(4) 40-92-28
Fax: +251(4) 40-76-10
Administrator/Vice-President: Gebrehawaria Gebregziabher
Tel: + 251(4) 40-75-00 Fax: +251(4) 40-93-04

Agriculture; Business and Commerce; Engineering

OTHER INSTITUTIONS

PUBLIC INSTITUTIONS

ADDIS ABABA COMMERCIAL COLLEGE (AACC)
PO Box 3131, Addis Ababa
Tel: +251(1) 51-80-20
Fax: +251(1) 51-57-86
EMail: aacomcollege@telecom.net.et
Dean: Fesseha Afewase (2003-)
Vice-Dean for Administration: Woldermanned Wolambo

Business and Commerce

AMBO COLLEGE OF AGRICULTURE (ACA)
PO Box 19, Ambo, Oromya Region
Tel: +251(1) 36-00-96
Fax: +251(1) 36-15-14
EMail: aca.ethiopia@telecom.net.et
Agriculture

ARBA MINCH WATER TECHNOLOGY INSTITUTE (AMTI)
PO Box 21, Arba Minch
Tel: +251(6) 81-00-97
Fax: +251(6) 81-02-79
Dean: Sileshi Bekele (2002-)

Founded: 1986
Business and Commerce; Engineering; Natural Sciences; Technology; Water Science

History: Founded 1986

ETHIOPIAN CIVIL SERVICE COLLEGE (ECSC)
PO Box 5648, Addis Ababa
Tel: +251(1) 60-17-62
Fax: +251(1) 60-17-64
EMail: ethcscol@excite.com
President: Haile Michael Aberra (1996-)
Tel: +251(1) 60-17-59 EMail: hailem@excite.com

Associate Vice-President for Business and Development: Solomon Fisseha EMail: solomonfis@hotmail.com
International Relations: Negussie Negash
Tel: +251(1) 60-17-10

Founded: 1995

Schools
Business and Economics (Accountancy; Business Adminis-tration; Economics) *Director:* Meshesha Shewarega
Legal Studies (Law) *Director:* Assefa Fisseha

Institutes
Urban Development Studies (Town Planning; Urban Studies) *Director:* Assefa Woldem

History: Founded 1995

Governing Bodies: Board; Senate

Academic Year: September to August

Admission Requirements: Ethiopian School Leaving Certifi-cate and pass in entrance examination

Fees: Cost sharing scheme adopted, students pay 25% of net salary to the college

Main Language(s) of Instruction: English

Accrediting Agencies: Ministry of Education

Degrees and Diplomas: *Bachelor's Degree:* Accountancy (BAcc); Development Administration (BDA); Economics (BEc), 3 yrs; Law (LLB); Urban Planning (BSc), 4 yrs. Also Advanced Diploma in Urban Engineering, 3 yrs

Student Services: Academic Counselling, Social Counselling, Sports Facilities, Language Programmes, Health Services, Canteen

Student Residential Facilities: Yes

Special Facilities: Interactive video conferencing centre

Libraries: Three libraries in three campuses

Publications: Interaction (quarterly); Ethiopian Law Review (biannually); ECSC Newsletter

Academic Staff *2001-2002:* Full-Time: c. 140 Part-Time: c. 15 Total: c. 155

Staff with doctorate: Total: c. 15

Student Numbers *2001-2002:* Total: c. 1,640

Evening Students, c. 300 **Distance Students,** c. 180

GONDER COLLEGE OF MEDICAL SCIENCES (GCMS)
PO Box 196, Gonder, Amhare
Tel: +251(8) 11-01-74
Fax: +251(8) 11-14-79
EMail: gcms@eth.healthnet.org
Dean: Yared Wondinkun (2003-) Tel: +251(8) 11-02-43

Health Sciences; Medicine; Social Sciences

KOTEBE COLLEGE OF TEACHER EDUCATION (KCTE)
PO Box 31248, Addis Ababa
Tel: +251(1) 60-09-21
Fax: +251(1) 60-09-22
EMail: ccte@telecom.net.et

Dean: Bikale Siyoum (2003-) Tel: 251(1) 60-12-77

International Relations: Endalew Amenu

Founded: 1969, 1989

Departments

Teacher Education (Biology; Chemistry; English; Geography; Health Education; History; Mathematics Education; Native Language Education; Physical Education; Physics; Primary Education; Teacher Training) *Head*: Zerhihun Kebede

History: Founded 1969 as Teacher Training College. Acquired present status and title 1989.

Governing Bodies: Administrative Board

Academic Year: September to July. Also Summer sesssion, July- September

Admission Requirements: Secondary school leaving certificate or equivalent

Main Language(s) of Instruction: English

Accrediting Agencies: Ministry of Education

Degrees and Diplomas: *Diploma*: Education, 2 yrs; *Bachelor's Degree*: Education (BEd), 4 yrs. Also Certificate, 1 yr

Note: Also Defence University College, Oromya

Student Services: Academic Counselling, Social Counselling, Sports Facilities, Language Programmes, Handicapped Facilities, Health Services, Canteen

Student Residential Facilities: Yes

Special Facilities: Computer Centre. Language Laboratory

Libraries: Main Library with Braille section

Publications: KCTE Newsletter (annually); JOLS, Journal of Language Studies

Academic Staff *2001-2002:* Total: c. 90

Staff with doctorate: Total: c. 5

Student Numbers *2001-2002:* Total: c. 5,400

NAZARETH TECHNICAL TEACHERS COLLEGE (NTTC)
PO Box 1888, Nazareth, Oromyia Region
Tel: +251(2) 11-04-00
Fax: +251(2) 11-04-80
EMail: makoto.manabe@telecom.net.et

Dean: Solomon Shiferan (2002-)

Business
Teacher Training
Technology

Gabon

INSTITUTION TYPES AND CREDENTIALS

Types of higher education institutions:

Université (University)
Institut (Institute)
Ecole (School)

School leaving and higher education credentials:

Baccalauréat
Capacité en Droit
Brevet de Technicien supérieur
Diplôme d'Etat de Sage-Femme
Diplôme de Technicien supérieur
Diplôme universitaire d'Etudes économiques (DUEE)
Diplôme universitaire d'Etudes juridiques (DUEJ)
Diplôme universitaire d'Etudes littéraires (DUEL)
Diplôme universitaire d'Etudes scientifiques (DUES)
Certificat d'Aptitude au Professorat des Collèges d'Enseignement technique
Licence
Certificat d'Aptitude au Professorat de l'Enseignement secondaire
Certificat d'Aptitude pédagogique des Lycées techniques
Diplôme d'Ingénieur
Diplôme d'Administrateur civil
Diplôme d'Administration de l'Economie et des Finances
Maîtrise
Doctorat

STRUCTURE OF EDUCATION SYSTEM

Pre-higher education:

Structure of school system:

Primary
Type of school providing this education: Ecole primaire
Length of programme in years: 5
Age level from: 6 to: 11
Certificate/diploma awarded: Certificat d'Etudes primaires élémentaires (CEPE), Concours d'Entrée

First Cycle Secondary
Type of school providing this education: Premier Cycle secondaire
Length of programme in years: 4
Age level from: 11 to: 15
Certificate/diploma awarded: Brevet d'Etudes du premier Cycle (BEPC)

Technical Secondary
Type of school providing this education: Enseignement secondaire technique
Length of programme in years: 3
Age level from: 15 to: 18
Certificate/diploma awarded: Brevet de Technicien

Second Cycle Secondary
Type of school providing this education: Deuxième Cycle secondaire
Length of programme in years: 3
Age level from: 15 to: 18
Certificate/diploma awarded: Baccalauréat

Technical
Type of school providing this education: Enseignement secondaire technique
Length of programme in years: 4
Age level from: 15 to: 19
Certificate/diploma awarded: Baccalauréat technique

School education:

Primary education lasts for six years and leads to the Certificat d'Etudes primaires élémentaires (CEPE). For access to secondary schools, students have to pass an entrance examination. Secondary-school education covers seven years, divided into a lower (premier) cycle lasting for four years and an upper (deuxième) cycle lasting for three years. On conclusion of the lower cycle, pupils obtain the Brevet d'Etudes du Premier Cycle (BEPC). During the upper cycle, pupils may specialize in Mathematics, Natural Sciences or Humanities, Economics and Science and Technology. On completion of this cycle, pupils take the examinations for the Baccalauréat. Pupils who do not qualify for the Baccalauréat are awarded the Certificat de Fin d'Etudes secondaires and a record of attendance and performance in the final year. On completion of the lower cycle pupils may opt to take a 'short' or a 'long' course of technical secondary education. The former leads to the Brevet de Technicien and the latter to the Baccalauréat technique.

Higher education:

Higher education is provided by three universities: Omar Bongo University, the Université des Sciences de la Santé at Libreville, and the University of Science and Technology of Masuku (USTM at Franceville), as well as by various independent institutions. These are all public and receive little or no subsidies from the private sector. The Universities benefit from a certain degree of autonomy. They are headed by Rectors who are solely responsible for the University. Higher education is financed exclusively by public funds.

Academic year:

Classes from: October *to:* June

Long vacation from: 1 July *to:* 30 September

Languages of instruction:

French

Stages of studies:

University level studies:

University level first stage: Premier Cycle:
The entrance requirement for degree studies is the Baccalauréat. The first phase leads, after two years' study to the Diplôme universitaire d'Etudes littéraires (DUEL) in Arts and Humanities, Diplôme universitaire d'Etudes scientifiques (DUES) in scientific subjects, Diplôme universitaire d'Etudes juridiques (DUEJ) in Law, and the Diplôme universitaire d'Etudes économiques (DUEE) in Economics. Most of these qualifications now come under the overall title of Diplôme d'Etudes universitaires générales (DEUG). Students who wish to study Law but do not hold the Baccalauréat may undertake a two-year course leading to the Capacité en Droit.

University level second stage: Deuxième Cycle:
The second stage leads, after a further year of study in Arts and Sciences, Economics and Law, to the Licence. A further year of study leads to the Maîtrise in Arts and Humanities, Law, Economics, Management, Social Communication Techniques, Economics and Finance, Juridical Sciences and General Administration. The Ecole nationale de la Magistrature trains Magistrates in four years after the Baccalauréat and in two years for holders of the Licence in Law. The titles of Ingénieur, Ingénieur informaticien, and Géographe-Aménagiste are awarded on completion of five years' study.

University level third stage: Troisième Cycle:
The Ecole nationale d'Administration (advanced cycle) offers two-year training to holders of a Maîtrise following a competitive examination. Candidates are then awarded the Diplôme d'Administrateur civil (General Administration, Diplomacy, Factory Inspectorate). The Doctorat d'Etat in Medicine is awarded after six years' study. It leads to three post-doctoral specializations: Paediatrics, Surgery, and Gynaecology. A Doctorate is awarded in scientific subjects by the Université des Sciences et Techniques de Masuku.

Teacher education:

Training of pre-primary and primary/basic school teachers
Primary-school teachers are trained in teacher-training colleges after lower secondary education. This four-year course leads to the Certificat d'Aptitude pédagogique.

Training of secondary school teachers
Secondary-school teachers are trained in three years after the Baccalauréat for lower-level secondary education and five years for upper-level secondary education at the Ecole normale supérieure. These courses lead to the award of the Certificat d'Aptitude pédagogique des Collèges d'Enseignement général (CAPCEG) and the Certificat d'Aptitude au Professorat de l'Enseignement secondaire (CAPES) respectively. Technical education teachers are trained in five years'

advanced-level technical secondary education at the Ecole normale supérieure d'Enseignement technique. They are awarded the Certificat d'Aptitude pédagogique des lycées techniques.

Training of higher education teachers
According to the provisions of the Conseil Africain et Malgache pour l'Enseignement supérieur (CAMES), higher education teachers must hold a university degree equivalent to the French Diplôme d'Etudes approfondies (DEA). They generally hold a Doctorat or an Agrégation.

NATIONAL BODIES

Responsible authorities:

Ministry of Higher Education and Scientific Research (Ministère de l'Enseignement supérieur et de la Recherche scientifique)
    Minister: Vincent Moulengui Boukossou
    Secretary-General: Maurice Bouma
    International Relations: Yolande Ozouaki
    BP 2217
    Libreville
Estuaire
    Tel: +241 76-07-64
    Fax: +241 76-43-45

ADMISSIONS TO HIGHER EDUCATION

Admission to university-level studies

Name of secondary school credential required: Baccalauréat
For entry to: University

Alternatives to credentials: Capacité en Droit (for studies in law)

Foreign students admission

Admission requirements: For access to university-level studies, foreign students must hold a secondary school leaving Certificate (Baccalauréat) or its equivalent and/or obtain the approval of the teachers' Commission of the department where they wish to be admitted. For access to postgraduate study and research, they must hold a Maîtrise or its equivalent.

Entry regulations: Foreign students must hold a visa and have financial guarantees. There is no rigid quota system.

Language requirements: Students must have a good command of French.

Application procedures:

Apply to individual institution for entry to: University

Recognition of studies and qualifications:

Studies pursued in foreign countries (bodies dealing with recognition of foreign credentials):
Université Omar Bongo
    BP 13131
    Boulevard Léon M'ba
    Libreville
    Tel: +241 73-20-45
    Fax: +241 73-45-30
    Telex: ung 5336
    WWW: http://www.uob.ga.refer.org

Multilateral agreements concerning recognition of foreign studies

Name(s) of agreement(s): Convention on the Recognition of Studies, Certificates, Diplomas, Degrees and Other Academic Qualifications in Higher Education in the African States
Year of signature: 1981

STUDENT LIFE

Student expenses and financial aid

Bodies providing information on student financial aid:

Commission nationale des Bourses et Stages
    PO Box 165
    Libreville
    Deals with: Grants

INTERNATIONAL COOPERATION AND EXCHANGES

Principal national bodies responsible for dealing with international cooperation and exchanges in higher education:

Ministère des Affaires Etrangères, de la Coopération et des Affaires francophones
    Minister: Jean Ping
    Libreville
    Tel: +241 73-94-65 +241 73-94-69

Ministry of Higher Education and Scientific Research (Ministère de l'Enseignement supérieur et de la Recherche scientifique)
    Director (Higher Education and University Cooperation): Yolande Ozouaki
    B.P. 2217
    Libreville
Estuaire
    Tel: +241 76-07-64
    Fax: +241 76-43-45

GRADING SYSTEM

Usual grading system in secondary school

Full Description: Marking is on a scale of 0-20 (maximum) per subject, with no official minimum pass mark (though in practice 9 is the minimum pass mark). Overall grades of Baccalauréat are classified: très bien, bien, assez bien, passable.
Highest on scale: 20
Pass/fail level: 9
Lowest on scale: 0

Main grading system used by higher education institutions

Full Description: The Licence is graded as: très bien (very good), bien (good), assez bien (fair), passable (pass)

NOTES ON HIGHER EDUCATION SYSTEM

Data for academic year: 2002-2003
Source: International Association of Universities (IAU), 2003

INSTITUTIONS OF HIGHER EDUCATION

UNIVERSITIES

OMAR BONGO UNIVERSITY

Université Omar Bongo
BP 13131, Boulevard Léon M'ba, Libreville
Tel: +241 73-20-45   +241 72-69-10
Fax: +241 73-45-30   +241 73-04-17
Telex: 5336 go
EMail: uob@internetgabon.com

Recteur: Jean-Emile Mbot

Secrétaire général: Guy Rossatanga-Rignault

International Relations: Jérôme Ndzoungou, Vice-Recteur, Administration et Coopération interuniversitaire

Faculties

Arts and Humanities (Anthropology; Archaeology; Arts and Humanities; English; Geography; History; Latin American Studies; Modern Languages; Philosophy; Psychology; Social Sciences; Sociology; Spanish)
Law and Economics (Economics; Law)

History: Founded 1970 incorporating institutions which were previously part of the Fondation de l'Enseignement supérieur en Afrique Centrale. Renamed 1978. A State institution enjoying financial autonomy with some aid from France. Acquired present status 2002.

Academic Year: October to June (October-December; January-Easter; Easter-June)

Admission Requirements: Secondary school certificate (baccalauréat) or equivalent or entrance examination

Main Language(s) of Instruction: French

Degrees and Diplomas: *Diplôme universitaire d'Etudes économiques (DUEE):* 2 yrs; *Diplôme universitaire d'Etudes juridiques (DUEJ):* 2 yrs; *Diplôme universitaire d'Etudes littéraires (DUEL):* 2 yrs; *Diplôme universitaire d'Etudes scientifiques (DUES):* 2 yrs; *Certificat d'Aptitude au Professorat des Collèges d'Enseignement technique:* (CAPCET); *Licence:* Law; Letters, 3 yrs; Economics, 4 yrs; *Certificat d'Aptitude pédagogique des Lycées techniques:* (CAPLT); *Diplôme d'Ingénieur:* Engineering; *Maîtrise:* Letters, 1 yr following Licence; *Doctorat:* Medicine

Libraries: Central Library, c. 12,000 vols; libraries of the faculties and schools

Academic Staff *2001-2002:* Total: c. 300

Student Numbers *2001-2002:* Total: c. 4,800

UNIVERSITY OF HEALTH SCIENCES

Université des Sciences de la Santé
BP 18231, Owendo, Libreville
Tel: +241 70-20-28
Fax: +241 70-28-19
EMail: rectorat@uss-univ.com
Website: http://www.uss-univ.com

Recteur: André Moussavou-Mouyama

Programmes
Health Sciences

History: Founded 2002.

• UNIVERSITY OF SCIENCES AND TECHNIQUES OF MASUKU

Université des Sciences et Techniques de Masuku
BP 901, Franceville
Tel: +241 67-77-25 +241 67-74-49
Fax: +241 67-75-20 +241 67-74-49
Telex: 6723 go
Website: http://oceantys.com/ustm/

Recteur: Jacques Lebibi (1992-) EMail: jlebibi@hotmail.com

Secrétaire général: Anselme Punga Tel: +241-67-77-35

International Relations: Jacques Lebibi

Faculties
Science (Biology; Chemistry; Computer Science; Geology; Mathematics; Modern Languages; Natural Sciences; Physics)

Schools
Polytechnic (Agricultural Engineering; Automation and Control Engineering; Biotechnology; Civil Engineering; Electrical Engineering; Engineering; Industrial Engineering; Industrial Maintenance; Mechanical Engineering; Technology)

History: Founded 1986, incorporating faculty and school of Université Omar Bongo.

Degrees and Diplomas: *Diplôme de Technicien supérieur:* Agricultural Engineering; Civil Engineering; Electrical Engineering; Industrial Engineering; *Diplôme universitaire d'Etudes scientifiques (DUES):* 2 yrs; *Diplôme d'Ingénieur:* Engineering; *Maîtrise:* Science

Academic Staff *2001:* Total: c. 110

Student Numbers *2001:* Total: c. 550

OTHER INSTITUTIONS

CENTRE INTERNATIONAL DE RECHERCHES MÉDICALES DE FRANCEVILLE
BP 769, Franceville
Tel: +241 67-70-92
Fax: +241 67-72-95

Directeur général: Philippe Blot

Founded: 1979

Departments
Medicine

ECOLE NATIONALE D'ADMINISTRATION
BP 86, Libreville
Tel: +241 74-56-37

Directeur: M.P. Moundounga-Kabila

Founded: 1962

Departments
Administration
Diplomacy (International Relations)
School Administration (Educational Administration)
University Administration (Educational Administration)

ECOLE NATIONALE DES EAUX ET FORÊTS
BP 7052, Libreville
Tel: +241 74-33-42
Fax: +241 76-61-83
Website: http://www.gabon-forests.org
Founded: 1953, 1975

Departments
Basic Sciences (Natural Sciences)
Fauna and Hunting
Fishing and Aquaculture (Aquaculture; Fishery)
Forest and Environmental Management (Environmental Management; Forest Management)
Forest Exploitation and Wood Technology (Forestry; Wood Technology)

History: Founded 1953. Acquired present status 1975.

ECOLE NATIONALE DE MAGISTRATURE
BP 46, Libreville
Tel: +241 72-00-06
Founded: 1971

Departments
Administrative Law

Civil Law
Commercial Law
Justice (Justice Administration)
Law
Magistracy (Justice Administration)
Penal Law (Criminal Law)

ECOLE NATIONALE SUPÉRIEURE DE SECRÉTARIAT (ENSS)
BP 17014, Libreville
Tel: +241 76-18-22
Computer Science; Law; Modern Languages; Secretarial Studies

ECOLE NORMALE SUPÉRIEURE
BP 17009, Libreville
Tel: +241 76-31-59
Fax: +241 73-20-73
Telex: uob 5336 go

Founded: 1972
Teacher Training

ECOLE NORMALE SUPÉRIEURE DE L'ENSEIGNEMENT TECHNIQUE
BP 3989, Libreville
Tel: +241 73-29-88
Fax: +241 73-20-73
Telex: uob 5336 go
Automotive Engineering; Civil Engineering; Mechanical Engineering; Metallurgical Engineering; Wood Technology; Technology Education (Automotive Engineering; Civil Engineering; Mechanical Engineering; Metallurgical Engineering; Technology Education; Wood Technology)

INSTITUT AFRICAIN D'INFORMATIQUE (IAI)
BP 2263, Libreville
Tel: +241 72-00-05
Fax: +241 72-00-11

Directeur général: Fabien Mballa

Departments
Computer Science

INSTITUT NATIONAL DES SCIENCES DE GESTION
BP 190, Libreville
Tel: +241 73-28-45
Fax: +241 73-20-73
Founded: 1973
Accountancy; Business and Commerce; Finance; Marketing

Gambia (The)

INSTITUTION TYPES AND CREDENTIALS

Types of higher education institutions:

University
Institute
College

School leaving and higher education credentials:

West African Examinations Council Senior Secondary School Leaving Certificate
Gambia Basic Teachers' Certificate
Gambia Higher Teachers' Certificate
Gambia Primary Teachers' Certificate
Bachelor of Arts
Bachelor of Science
Bachelor of Medicine

STRUCTURE OF EDUCATION SYSTEM

Pre-higher education:

Structure of school system:

Basic First Stage
Type of school providing this education: Lower basic school
Length of programme in years: 6
Age level from: 7 to: 13

Basic Second Stage
Type of school providing this education: Upper basic school
Length of programme in years: 3
Age level from: 13 to: 16

Senior Secondary
Type of school providing this education: Senior Secondary School
Length of programme in years: 3
Age level from: 16 to: 19
Certificate/diploma awarded: West African Examinations Council Senior Secondary School
Certificate

School education:

Until 2002, primary education lasted for six years and led to the Primary School Leaving Certificate (phased out). Secondary education was divided into junior secondary schools which offered a three-year course leading to the Junior School Leaving Certificate, and Senior Secondary schools which offered a three-year course.

Since 2002, the new basic education programme lasts nine years, divided into two cycles: lower basic (Grades I–VI) and upper basic (Grades VII–IX). Senior secondary education (Grades X–XII) is for pupils between the ages of 16 and 18 years. Secondary schools offer a variety of subjects (science, arts, commerce, vocational and technical). Given the diverse number of subjects available at this level, schools are tracked to offer at most three groups of subjects. At the end of Grade XII, pupils sit for the West African Secondary School-leaving Certificate Examinations (WASSCE) conducted by the sub-regional examinations body for West Africa, i.e. the West African Examinations Council.

Higher education:

Higher education in the Gambia is provided by the University of The Gambia, created in 1999, which comprises four faculties and Gambia College which includes four schools: Agriculture, Education, Nursing and Midwifery, and Public Health.

Main laws/decrees governing higher education:

Decree: Education Act   Year: 1992
Concerns: Education services in the Gambia

Academic year:

Classes from: December *to:* August
Long vacation from: 1 September *to:* 30 November

Languages of instruction:

English

Stages of studies:

Non-university level post-secondary studies (technical/vocational type):

Higher technical and vocational education is offered at the Gambia Technical Training Institute which offers courses leading to the examinations of the City and Guilds of London Institute and the Royal Society of Arts. Gambia College offers courses in Agriculture, Teacher Training, Nursing and Midwifery, Public Health, Catering, Management Development and vocational training. Studies lead to Certificates and Diplomas.

University level studies:

University level first stage: Bachelor's Degree:
The first stage of university education leads to a Bachelor's Degree after four years of study in Humanities and Social Studies, Economics and Management Science and Nursing and Public Health and six years in Medicine and Surgery.

Teacher education:

Training of pre-primary and primary/basic school teachers

Basic school teachers are trained at the Gambia College School of Education which offers a two-year course leading to the Gambia Primary Teachers' Certificate. A three-year in-service course leading to the award of the Gambia Basic Teachers' Certificate is now offered to unqualified teachers. Admission is based on completion of basic education.

Training of secondary school teachers

Secondary school teachers are trained at the Gambia College School of Education in a two-year course leading to the Gambia Higher Teachers' Certificate. Students enter with the West African Examinations Council School Certificate.

NATIONAL BODIES

Responsible authorities:

Department of State for Education
    Secretary of State: Ann Therese Ndong-Jatta
    Bedford Place Building
    Banjul
    Tel: +220 22 7236 +220 22 7646
    Fax: +220 22 8140   +220 22 7034
    WWW: http://www.edugambia.gm

ADMISSIONS TO HIGHER EDUCATION

Admission to non university higher education studies

Name of secondary school credential required: West African Examinations Council Senior Secondary School Leaving Certificate

Admission to university-level studies

Name of secondary school credential required: West African Examinations Council Senior Secondary School Leaving Certificate
Minimum score/requirement: Five credits

Alternatives to credentials: Mature students

Foreign students admission

Admission requirements: Foreign students wishing to enrol at Gambia College should have qualifications equivalent to 3 passes at ordinary level GCE including English, successful completion of an entrance examination and of upgrading courses for service officers. For the University, West African Senior School Certificate with five credits or General Certificate of Education with five credits.

Entry regulations: A visa is required for non-Commonwealth citizens as well as study or residential permits for all non-Gambians.

Language requirements: Proficiency in English is required.

STUDENT LIFE

Student expenses and financial aid

Student costs:

Home students tuition fees: Minimum: 14,000 (Dalasis)
Maximum: 18,000 (Dalasis)
Foreign students tuition fees: Minimum: 2,500 (US Dollar)
Maximum: 3,000 (US Dollar)

GRADING SYSTEM

Usual grading system in secondary school

Full Description: For the West African Examinations Council Senior Secondary School Certificate: 1-9.
Highest on scale: 1
Pass/fail level: 7-8
Lowest on scale: 9

NOTES ON HIGHER EDUCATION SYSTEM

Data for academic year: 2002-2003
Source: International Association of Universities (IAU), updated from IBE website, 2003
(www.ibe.unesco.org/International/Databanks/Wde/profilee.htm)

INSTITUTIONS OF HIGHER EDUCATION

UNIVERSITIES

UNIVERSITY OF THE GAMBIA

PO Box 3530, Administration Building, Kanifing, Serrekunda, Greater Banjul
Tel: +220 372-213
Fax: +220 395-064
EMail: unigambia@qanet.gm
Website: http://www.unigambia.gm/

Vice-Chancellor: Donald Ekong Tel: +220 395-062
EMail: dekong@unigambia.gm

Registrar: Emmanuel Akpan EMail: ejakpan@unigambia.gm

Faculties

Economics and Management Sciences (Economics; Finance; Human Resources; Information Technology; Management; Marketing) *Co-ordinator:* Sulayman Fye

Humanities and Social Sciences (Arts and Humanities; English; French; Geography; History; Social Sciences) *Co-ordinator:* Boro Suso

Medicine and Allied Health Sciences (Medicine; Nursing; Public Health; Surgery)

Science and Agriculture (Agriculture; Biology; Chemistry; Environmental Studies; Mathematics; Physics; Statistics) *Dean:* Felixtina Josnyn

History: Founded 1999. Established by an Act of the National Assembly. Introduction of a 2-year Higher National Diploma (HND) programme in Construction Management in the Gambia Technical Training Institute, GTTI, under a franchise from South Bank University, London. With assistance from the Ministry of Health of Cuba, the pre-medical programme began September 1999.

Governing Bodies: University Council; Senate

Academic Year: December to August (December-April; May-August)

Admission Requirements: West African Senior School Certificate with five credits; General Certificate of Education with five credits

Fees: (Dalasis): Other than Science, c. 14,000; Science, c. 16,000; Medicine, c. 18,000.

Main Language(s) of Instruction: English

Degrees and Diplomas: *Bachelor of Arts*: Development Studies, History, French, Geography, English (BA), 4; *Bachelor of Science*: Environment Science, Agriculture, Biology, Chemistry, Physics, Mathematics/Statistics (BsC), 4; *Bachelor of Medicine*: Nursing, Public Health (BsC), 4; Medicine, Surgery (MB/CHB), 6

Student Services: Academic Counselling, Social Counselling, Sports Facilities, Health Services

Special Facilities: Computer Laboratory

Libraries: Technical Training Institute Library

Academic Staff *2000*	MEN	WOMEN	TOTAL
FULL-TIME	28	7	35
PART-TIME	7	1	8
TOTAL	**35**	**8**	**43**
STAFF WITH DOCTORATE			
FULL-TIME	12	4	16
PART-TIME	–	–	2
TOTAL	**–**	**–**	**18**
Student Numbers *2000*	MEN	WOMEN	TOTAL
All (Foreign Included)	267	66	**333**
FOREIGN ONLY	3	2	5

OTHER INSTITUTIONS

GAMBIA COLLEGE

Brikama
Tel: +220 714

President: N.S.Z. Njie
Registrar: N.S. Manneh

Founded: 1978

Schools
Agriculture
Education
Nursing and Midwifery
Public Health

History: Founded 1978.

Ghana

INSTITUTION TYPES AND CREDENTIALS

Types of higher education institutions:

University
Polytechnic
Specialized Institution

School leaving and higher education credentials:

Senior Secondary Certificate Examination
WAEC General Certificate of Education Ordinary Level
WAEC General Certificate of Education Advanced Level
Certificate
Diploma
National Diploma
Bachelor's Degree
Bachelor of Dental Surgery
Bachelor of Medicine and Surgery
Graduate Diploma
Master's Degree
Master of Philosophy
Doctorate

STRUCTURE OF EDUCATION SYSTEM

Pre-higher education:

Duration of compulsory education:

Age of entry: 6
Age of exit: 15

Structure of school system:

Primary
Type of school providing this education: Primary School
Length of programme in years: 6
Age level from: 6 to: 12

Junior Secondary
Type of school providing this education: Junior Secondary School

Length of programme in years: 3
Age level from: 12 to: 15
Certificate/diploma awarded: Basic Education Certificate Examination (BECE)

Senior Secondary
Type of school providing this education: Senior Secondary School
Length of programme in years: 3
Age level from: 15 to: 18
Certificate/diploma awarded: Senior Secondary School Certificate (SSCE)

Technical
Type of school providing this education: Technical/Vocational School
Length of programme in years: 3
Age level from: 15 to: 18

School education:

The new educational system consists of six years' primary school (compulsory) followed by three years' junior secondary and three years' senior secondary education at the end of which pupils sit for the Senior Secondary Certificate Examination (SSCE). The six years of primary education and the three years of junior secondary school form nine years of basic education. .

Higher education:

The system of higher education includes universities and university colleges; polytechnics; professional institutes and pre-service training institutes. All public higher education institutions are under the National Council for Tertiary Education which forms an advisory and coordinating body at the national level. The Council is under the Minister of Education. Each higher institution has its own Council and its Academic Board or their equivalents. The polytechnics, which are currently offering Higher National Diploma (HND) programmes, are now in the process of being upgraded to offer university-level courses. A new University of Development Studies has been opened in the North and the University College of Education, Winneba, has become University of Education, Winneba. Teacher training colleges are to be upgraded to tertiary institution status.

Main laws/decrees governing higher education:

Decree: White Paper on Reforms to the Tertiary Education System   Year: 1991
Concerns: Expansion of tertiary education

Decree: PNDC Law 42   Year: 1983
Concerns: Modifies Education Act of 1961

Decree: NLC Decree 401   Year: 1969
Concerns: Universities and equivalents

Decree: Act 87, the Education Act Parts IV and V   Year: 1961
Concerns: Higher Education

Academic year:

Classes from: September *to:* June

Long vacation from: 22 May *to:* 21 August

Languages of instruction:

English

Stages of studies:

Non-university level post-secondary studies (technical/vocational type):

Higher technical/vocational education is provided by polytechnics and post-secondary pre-service training institutions, under sector Ministries. These include: Health Training Institutes, Nursing Training Colleges, Agricultural Colleges, Schools of Forestry and Teacher Training Colleges. Courses generally last for three years and lead to the award of a certificate/diploma. Polytechnics offer courses of varying length, depending on the discipline, leading to the award of Ordinary Diploma (DBS for non-tertiary programmes and Higher National Diploma (HND) for tertiary programmes). Courses offered are Business Studies, Engineering and Applied Arts, Science and Technology.

University level studies:

University level first stage: *First Degree*:

The Universities in Ghana - University of Ghana, Kwame Nkrumah University of Science and Technology, University of Cape Coast, University for Development Studies and University of Education - offer degree courses of four years' duration for Senior Secondary school candidates and three years for GCE 'A' level candidates. Some universities also offer two-year diploma programmes.

University level second stage: *Second Degree*:

These degrees are open to graduates with the Bachelor's Degree of approved universities. Graduate Diploma courses are of two semesters' full-time or four semesters' part-time study. Primary Master's and Master of Philosophy courses last for one to two years. At least two semesters must be spent studying in the University. Candidates are awarded the Graduate Diploma, Master's or Master of Philosophy Degree. The one-year course involves course work and a dissertation. For the MPhil Degree, two years of study, including a year of course work, are required, followed by research work leading to a thesis. It is possible to transfer to MPhil and PhD courses from the one-year Master's.

University level third stage: *Doctorate*:

The Doctorate Degree is open to graduates of approved universities with Master's or Master of Philosophy Degrees. Candidates must spend the first two years at the university. If the candidate has taken the Master's degree in the same university, this period is one year. Thereafter, subject to approval by the Board of Graduate Studies, candidates may pursue their studies outside the university. Doctorate courses (PhD) are completed entirely by research (i.e. presentation and defence of a thesis) and require a minimum of three years' study. Candidates are awarded the Doctorate Degree at the end of their studies. The DPhil is also entirely by research and is awarded on consideration of published works of academic merit, the standard being no less than that of a PhD. Only graduates from universities with 10 years standing are eligible. The Doctor of Medicine (MD degree) covers the medical specialities only. Conditions for the award of the MD are the same as for the D.Phil.

The degrees of LLD, DCL, DLitt and DSc may only be conferred honoris causa.

Teacher education:

Training of pre-primary and primary/basic school teachers

Primary school teacher training is the responsibility of the post-secondary teacher training colleges. Training lasts for three years after the Senior Secondary Certificate Examination at the end of which candidates are awarded the Post-Secondary Teacher's Certificate A. The curriculum of the teacher training colleges was revised to reflect changes in the content and method of basic education.

Training of secondary school teachers

The University of Education, Winneba, offers one-year courses leading to the award of the Certificate in Education for non-professional teachers in technical and vocational subjects; three-year courses for holders of the Certificate A, Specialist Certificate and two level subjects leading to the award of a Diploma; and two-year degree courses for holders of a Certificate or Diploma in educational subjects.

Training of higher education teachers

Higher education teachers are trained in two to three years at the universities where they obtain a Master's or a Doctor's degree.

Non-traditional studies:

Distance higher education

The recently created Ghana National Tertiary Level Distance Education Programme opens up access to higher education; provides an alternative, off-campus channel for tertiary education for qualified people; provides a complementary avenue to higher forms of education provided by the traditional, residential universities; provides an opportunity to those who have the requisite qualifications but have been prevented from having access to tertiary education by various circumstances; and makes the acquisition of a degree more flexible, especially for older adults (such as graduates who want to shift to new areas of studies and lifelong learners). Universities in Ghana offer some of their courses to students outside their walls. Such off-campus students study the same courses and take the same examinations as those in on-campus programmes and are awarded the same degrees when they pass their final examinations. The programme adopts a multi-media approach but the main medium for teaching is self-instructional printed materials sent to students for study. Study centres will be opened in all regional capitals where students can go for tutorials and counselling. Student assessment is continuous and based on assignments and final examinations.

NATIONAL BODIES

Responsible authorities:

Ministry of Education, Youth and Sports
  Minister: Christopher Ameyaw-Akumfi
  Minister of State in charge of Tertiary Education: Elizabeth Ohene
  Minister of State in charge of Basic, Secondary and Girl Child Education: Christine Churcher
  Minister of State in Charge of Youth and Sports: Rashid Bawa

PO Box M.45

Accra

Tel: +233(21) 662-772

Fax: +233(21) 662-718

WWW: http://www.ghana.edu.gh

Role of governing body: Authority responsible for policy formulation, the administration and financing of education at the national level.

National Council on Tertiary Education (NCTE)

Executive Secretary: Paul Effah

Administrative Secretary: Paul Dzandu

International Relations: Paul Effah

PO Box MB 28

First Roman Ridge Road

Bungalow no. C27

Accra

Tel: +233(21) 770-197 +233(21) 770-198 +233(21) 770-173

Fax: +233(21) 770-194

EMail: ncte@edu.ug.gh

WWW: http://www.ghana.edu.gh/present/moeAgencies.html

Role of governing body: State agency dealing with higher education.

Committee of Vice-Chancellors and Principals of the Universities of Ghana

Chairman: J.B.K. Kaburise

Secretary: S.W. Opoku-Agyakwa

PO Box 25

Legon

Accra

Tel: +233(21) 501-967 +233(21) 512-415

Fax: +233(21) 502-701 +233(21) 512-409

Telex: 2556 UGL GH

EMail: cvcpgh@ug.edu.gh

Role of governing body: 1. Acts as consultative and advisory body to provide common perspectives in matters of common interest of the public universities in Ghana; 2. Promotes the needs, interest and aims of public universities in Ghana; 3. Advocates and provides Staff Development and Training programmes; 4. Representation on relevant national bodies/committees.

National Accreditation Board (NAB)

Executive Secretary: Nikoi Kotey

Deputy Executive Secretary: Francis Y.O. Amoah

International Relations: Francis Y.O. Amoah

PO Box M28

Accra

Tel: +233(21) 25-40-95
Fax: +233(21) 25-40-97
EMail: nab@ghana.com
WWW: http://www.ghana.edu.gh/present/moeAgencies.html

Role of governing body: State agency responsible for the accreditation of tertiary institutions and programmes

National Board for Profession and Technician Examinations
Head: Ben Antwi-Boasiako
Administrative Secretary: Charles Badoo
PO Box 50109
Accra
Tel: +223(21) 672-461
Fax: +223(21) 672-463

Role of governing body: State agency responsible for quality assurance of programmes ran in non-university tertiary institutions

ADMISSIONS TO HIGHER EDUCATION

Admission to non university higher education studies

Name of secondary school credential required: Senior Secondary Certificate Examination

Admission to university-level studies

Name of secondary school credential required: Senior Secondary Certificate Examination
Minimum score/requirement: Minimum aggregate of 24 at the SSCE with credit passes in core English, core Mathematics, core Science and any three electives

Name of secondary school credential required: WAEC General Certificate of Education Advanced Level
Minimum score/requirement: 2 or 3 "A" levels, plus 5 "O" levels with credit passes in English and Mathematics

Foreign students admission

Definition of foreign student: Any student who is not a Ghanaian.

Admission requirements: Foreign students should have good CGE "O" level passes (or their equivalent) in English language and four other subjects plus three "A" level passes (required subjects vary according to degree course).

Entry regulations: Foreign students with the exception of ECOWAS citizens need visas to enter Ghana. All foreign students, including ECOWAS citizens, are required to secure resident permits for the period of their study. Foreign students are required to pay their fees in convertible currency to be drawn on a American or British bank.

Health requirements: Health certificate required.

Language requirements: Good knowledge of English required for all regular university courses. English-language proficiency courses are offered as well as general orientation programmes for all freshmen.

Application procedures:

Apply to individual institution for entry to: Universities, Polytechnics, and other Institutions of Higher Education.

Application closing dates:

For non-university level (technical/vocational type) studies: 30 April
For university level studies: 30 April
For advanced/doctoral studies: 30 April

Recognition of studies and qualifications:

Studies pursued in home country (System of recognition/accreditation): Once the higher institutions from which the credentials are awarded are recognized by the country, the credentials are also recognized. Transfer and recognition of studies and degrees exist between the institutions of a similar type, i.e. university with university, polytechnic with polytechnic.
The National Accreditation Board (NAB) reviews programmes in Business Management, Engineering, Religious Studies, Computer Science and Economics
(http://www.ghana.edu.gh/present/moeAgencies.html)
Other information sources on recognition of foreign studies: The Academic Section of the Universities

Special provisions for recognition:

For access to non-university post-secondary studies: Credentials should be sent to the Executive Secretary, National Accreditation Board P.O.Box M28, Accra. These should be in the form of certificates.

For access to university level studies: Foreign credentials in the form of certificates should be sent to the Academic Registrar of the University. This applies to both nationals with foreign credentials and foreigners.

For access to advanced studies and research: Foreign credentials in the form of certificates, transcripts and Referee's report of two or three people should be sent to the office of the Dean of Graduate Studies of the University. This applies to both nationals and foreigners.

For the exercise of a profession: Access to the professions is subject to the recognition of credentials by the professional associations and to passing professional qualifying examinations. Foreign credentials should be sent to the Board or Institute of the individual professions. In addition, candidates should pass the professional examination conducted by the professional body.

References to further information on foreign student admissions and recognition of studies

Title: University Calendars

STUDENT LIFE

Health/social provisions

Social security for home students: No

Special student travel fares:

By air: Yes
Available to foreign students: Yes

Student expenses and financial aid

Student costs:

Foreign students tuition fees: Minimum: 11,000,000 (Cedi)
Maximum: 18,000,000 (Cedi)

Bodies providing information on student financial aid:

Association of African Universities
PO Box 5744
Accra North
Tel: +233(21) 774-495
Fax: +233(21) 774-821
WWW: http://www.aau.org

The Scholarship Secretariat
PO Box M75
Accra
Tel: +233(21) 665-461

Deals with: Grants
Category of students: All students.

Publications on student services and financial aid:

Title: Study Abroad 2004-2005, 32nd Edition
Author: UNESCO
Publisher: UNESCO Publishing
Year of publication: 2003

GRADING SYSTEM

Usual grading system in secondary school

Full Description: A-F; A excellent; B very good; C good; D credit; E pass; F fail
Highest on scale: A
Pass/fail level: E
Lowest on scale: F

Main grading system used by higher education institutions

Full Description: 4-0, A-F: 4.00(80-100)=A+; 4.00(70-79)=A; 3.75=A-; 3.50=B+; 3.00=B; 2.50=B-; 2.00=C+; 1.50=C; 1.00=D; 0=F.

Highest on scale: A+

Pass/fail level: D

Lowest on scale: F

Other main grading systems

Honours Degrees: First Class; Second Class, Upper Division; Second Class, Lower Division, Pass

NOTES ON HIGHER EDUCATION SYSTEM

Data for academic year: 2003

Source: National Council on Tertiary Education (NCTE), 2003

INSTITUTIONS OF HIGHER EDUCATION

UNIVERSITIES

ASHESI UNIVERSITY
No 87, 3rd Noria Extension, North Labone, Accra
Tel: +233(21) 777-902
Fax: +233(21) 784-768
EMail: admissions@ashesi.edu.gh
Website: http://www.ashesi.org

President: Patrick G. Awuah

Executive Vice-President: Kofi Bonner

International Relations: David Leonard

Courses
Business Administration (Accountancy; Business Administration; Finance; Marketing)
Computer Science (Computer Networks; Computer Science; Data Processing; Software Engineering)
Liberal Arts Core (Communication Studies; Design; Economics; History; Leadership; Mathematics; Philosophy; Statistics)

History: Founded 2002.
Governing Bodies: Board of Trustees
Degrees and Diplomas: *Bachelor's Degree*: 4 yrs
Libraries: Yes

• CENTRAL UNIVERSITY COLLEGE (CUC)
PO Box DS 2310, Dansoman, Accra
Tel: +233(21) 311-040
Fax: +233(21) 311-042
Website: http://www.centraluniversity.org

Vice-Chancellor: E. Kingsley Larbi

Registrar: Johnson Edward Kanda
EMail: registrar@centraluniversity.org

Head Librarian: Samual Agyenkwa

Schools
Business Management and Administration (Accountancy; Administration; Agricultural Business; Business Administration; English; Finance; French; Human Resources; Information Technology; Management; Marketing; Modern Languages; Secretarial Studies; Social Studies) *Dean (Acting)*: K.B. Appiah-Mensah
Graduate (New Testament; Religious Studies; Theology)
Theology and Missions (Bible; Theology) *Dean*: R.A. Andersen-Mensah

Centres
Pentecostal Studies (Religion)

History: Founded 1988. Acquired present status 1997.

Degrees and Diplomas: *Diploma*; *Bachelor's Degree*; *Master's Degree*; *Master of Philosophy*

*• 'KWAME NKRUMAH' UNIVERSITY OF SCIENCE AND TECHNOLOGY, KUMASI (KNUST)
University Post Office, Kumasi
Tel: +233(51) 60334
Fax: +233(51) 60137
Telex: 2555 ust gh
Cable: kumasitech, kumasi
EMail: ul@knust.edu.gh
Website: http://www.knust.edu.gh

Vice-Chancellor: Kwesi Andam (2002-2006)
EMail: vc@knust.edu.gh

Registrar and Secretary: Sophia Quashie-Sam
Tel: +233(51) 60331 Fax: +233(51) 60331

International Relations: G. Andy Mensah-Agboh, Senior Assistant Registrar Tel: +233(51) 60021
EMail: ust.uro@ighmail.com

Head Librarian: Helena Asamoah-Hassan

Faculties
Agriculture (Agricultural Economics; Animal Husbandry; Crop Production; Farm Management; Horticulture) *Dean*: Daniel B. Okai
Environmental and Development Studies (Architecture; Building Technologies; Development Studies; Environmental Studies; Town Planning) *Dean*: E. Badu
Law
Pharmacy *Dean*: J.K. Kwakye
Science (Biochemistry; Biological and Life Sciences; Chemistry; Computer Science; Mathematics; Natural Sciences; Physics) *Dean*: Aboagye Menyeh
Social Sciences (African Studies; Economics; Industrial Management; Modern Languages; Social Sciences) *Dean*: S.K. Okleme

Colleges
Art (Art Education; Ceramic Art; Design; Fine Arts; Industrial Design; Painting and Drawing; Sculpture; Textile Design) *Dean*: Ato Delaquis
Western *(Tarkwa)* (Mining Engineering) *Provost*: D. Mireku-Gyimah

Schools
Engineering (Agricultural Engineering; Chemical Engineering; Civil Engineering; Electrical and Electronic Engineering; Engineering; Materials Engineering; Mechanical Engineering) *Dean*: E.A. Jackson
Graduate Studies

Medical Sciences (Health Sciences; Medicine) *Director*: Tsiri Agbenyega

Institutes

Land Management and Development *(ILMAD)* (Natural Resources; Rural Planning) *Director*: S.O. Asiama

Mining and Mineral Engineering *(IMME)* (Geological Engineering; Metallurgical Engineering; Mining Engineering) *Director*: E.N. Tsidzi

Renewable Natural Resources *(IRNR)* (Agronomy; Fishery; Forestry; Natural Resources; Wildlife; Wood Technology) *Director*: William Oduro

Technical Education *(ITE)* (Technology Education) *Director*: P.P. Adolinama

Centres

Technology Consultancy *(TCC)* (Technology Education) *Director*: Peter Donkor

Bureaux

Integrated Rural Development *(BIRD)* (Rural Planning) *Director*: Nana Edusah

History: Founded 1951 as Kumasi College of Technology, acquired present status and title 1961.

Governing Bodies: University Council

Academic Year: September to June (September-January; March-June)

Admission Requirements: General Certificate of Education (GCE), Ordinary ('O') level, with 5 credits, including English, and General Certificate of Education Advanced ('A') level, with 2 passes. Senior Secondary School Certificate (SSCE) with passes in core English and Mathematics and three elective subjects relevant to chosen programme with a total aggregate of 24

Fees: (Cedi): Foreign students, undergraduate, 14 m.-26 m. per annum; postgraduate, 16 m.-28 m.

Main Language(s) of Instruction: English

Degrees and Diplomas: *Diploma*: 2 yrs; *Bachelor's Degree*: 4 yrs; *Master's Degree*: a further 2 yrs; *Doctorate*: a further 3 yrs following Master

Student Services: Academic Counselling, Nursery Care, Cultural Centre, Sports Facilities, Health Services, Canteen

Special Facilities: Botanical Garden

Libraries: Central Library, 270,562 vols; 750 periodicals. Special collections

Publications: Journal of the University of Science and Technology (3 per annum); University Calendar; Newsletter; Recorder (biannually); Annual Report (annually)

Press or Publishing House: University Printing Press. Design Press (College of Art)

Academic Staff 2002	MEN	WOMEN	TOTAL
FULL-TIME	452	37	**489**

Student Numbers 2002	MEN	WOMEN	TOTAL
All (Foreign Included)	9,671	3,460	**13,131**
FOREIGN ONLY	152	79	231

• UNIVERSITY OF CAPE COAST (UCC)
University Post Office, Cape Coast
Tel: +233(42) 32440 +233(42) 32480
Fax: +233(42) 32484
Telex: 2552 ucc gh
Cable: University, Cape Coast
EMail: ucclib@libr.ug.edu.gh;kakitaz@yahoo.com
Website: http://www.ucc.edu.gh/

Vice-Chancellor: Emmanuel Adow Obeng (2001-)
Tel: +233(42) 32378 +233(42) 32050 Fax: +233(42) 32485
EMail: eaobeng@ucc.edu.gh;vc_ucc@yahoo.com

Registrar: Kofi Ohene Tel: +233(42) 32139
Fax: +233(42) 32484 EMail: kohene@ucc.edu.gh

Pro-Vice-Chancellor: Kobina Yankson Tel: +233(42) 32489
EMail: kyankson@ucc.edu.gh

International Relations: Kwadwo Opoku-Agyemang, Director (Acting) Tel: +233(42) 33807 Fax: +233(42) 33304
EMail: kopokuagyemang@hotmail.com;uccoip@ghana.com

Faculties

Arts (African Languages; Arts and Humanities; Classical Languages; English; French; History; Modern Languages; Music; Native Language; Religious Studies) *Dean*: D.D. Kuupole

Education (Education; Educational Sciences; Health Sciences; Parks and Recreation; Physical Education; Primary Education; Science Education; Social Sciences; Technology Education; Vocational Education) *Dean (Acting)*: J.A. Opare

Graduate Studies (Higher Education) *Dean*: Jane Opoku-Agyemang

Science (Botany; Chemistry; Laboratory Techniques; Mathematics; Natural Sciences; Physics; Statistics; Zoology) *Dean*: V.P.Y. Gadzekpo

Social Sciences (Business Administration; Development Studies; Economics; Family Studies; Geography; Social Sciences; Sociology; Tourism) *Dean*: K. Awusabo-Asare

Units

Consultancy (Agriculture; Educational Research; Industrial Management; Natural Sciences; Tourism) *Director (Acting)*: A.B. Abane

Laboratory Technician Course (Instrument Making; Laboratory Techniques) *Co-ordinator*: John Blay Jr.

Schools

Agriculture (Agricultural Economics; Agriculture; Animal Husbandry; Crop Production; Soil Science) *Dean*: P.K. Turkson

Institutes

Education *Director*: K. Acheampong

Educational Planning and Administration *(IEPA)* (Educational Administration; Educational Research) *Director*: A.L. Dare

Centres

African Virtual University *(AVU)* (Computer Education) *Coordinator*: V.P.Y Gadzekpo

Computer (Computer Science) *Co-ordinator*: Daniel Obuobi

Development Studies *(CDS)* (Development Studies; Economics; Environmental Studies; Rural Planning; Social Studies; Town Planning) *Director*: S.B. Kendie

Distance Education (CDE) Director (Acting): A.K Koomson

Laser and Fibre Optics (LAFOC) (Laser Engineering; Optics) Co-ordinator: P.K Buah-Bassuah

Research on Improving Quality of Primary Education in Ghana (CRIQPEG) (Educational Research; Primary Education) Co-ordinator: J.M. Dzinyela

History: Founded 1962 as University College of Cape Coast, acquired present status and title 1971.

Governing Bodies: University Council

Academic Year: October to July (October-February; March-July)

Admission Requirements: General Certificate of Education/advanced level or recognized foreign equivalent, or senior secondary school certificate and entrance examination

Fees: (US Dollars): Foreign Students, 600-1500 per semester

Main Language(s) of Instruction: English

International Co-operation: With universities in USA; United Kingdom; Sweden; Nigeria; Italy; South Africa; Netherlands

Degrees and Diplomas: Bachelor's Degree: Agriculture (BSc); Arts (BA); Education (BEd); Science (BSc); Social Sciences, 4 yrs; Graduate Diploma: Education (PGDE), 2-3 yrs; Master's Degree: Arts (MA); Science (MSc), 1 yr; Education (MEd), 1-2 yrs; Philosophy (MSc), 2 yrs; Doctorate: Social Sciences (PhD), 2 yrs; Science (PhD), 3 yrs. Also Post Diploma (2-3 yrs following Bachelor's Degree) in Agriculture, Arts, Education, Science and Social Sciences

Student Services: Academic Counselling, Social Counselling, Employment Services, Nursery Care, Cultural Centre, Sports Facilities, Language Programmes, Handicapped Facilities, Health Services, Canteen

Student Residential Facilities: For 11,545 students

Special Facilities: Botanical Garden. Technology Village (UCC Farm)

Libraries: Main Library, 212,000 vols

Publications: University this Week (weekly); University Bulletin; University Gazette (monthly); University Calendar (Triannually)

Press or Publishing House: University Printing Press

Academic Staff 2001-2002	MEN	WOMEN	TOTAL
FULL-TIME	256	29	285
PART-TIME	–	–	59
TOTAL	–	–	**344**
STAFF WITH DOCTORATE			
FULL-TIME	106	10	**116**

Student Numbers 2001-2002	MEN	WOMEN	TOTAL
All (Foreign Included)	8,030	3,515	**11,545**
FOREIGN ONLY	10	18	28

• UNIVERSITY OF EDUCATION
PO Box 25, Winneba
Tel: +233(432) 22-261 +233(432) 22-269
Fax: +233(432) 22-268
EMail: ucewlib@lib.ug.edu.gh

Vice-Chancellor: Jophus Anamuah-Mensah (1998-)
Tel: +233(432) 22361 Fax: +233(432) 22361
EMail: pucew@africaonline.com.gh

Registrar: Justice Nii Aryeetey Tel: +233(432) 22269

International Relations: Justice Nii Aryeetey

Divisions

Applied Arts and Technology (Agricultural Education; Home Economics; Technology Education) Dean: J.K.N. Sackey

General Cultural and Social Studies (Art Education; Cultural Studies; Music Education; Social Studies) Dean: S.M. Quartey

Languages (African Languages; English; French; Modern Languages) Dean: L. Koranteng

Science (Natural Sciences; Science Education) Dean: H.A. Brown-Acquaye

Specialized Professional Studies in Education (Business Education; Education; Special Education) Dean: J.K. Aboagye

Institutes

Educational Development and Extension (Distance and continuing education) Director: S.K.E. Mensah

Centres

Basic Education Co-ordinator: R. Eshun

Educational Policy Studies (Educational Sciences)

Educational Resources Co-ordinator: R.K. Biney

School and Community Science and Technology Studies (SACOST) (Educational Sciences; Educational Technology; Social and Community Services)

Further Information: Also campuses in Kumasi and Mampong

History: Founded 1992, merging seven diploma-awarding colleges.

Academic Year: October to July (October-February; March-July)

Admission Requirements: General Certificate of Education (GCE) with 5 Ordinary ('O') levels at grade 6; Teachers' Certificate ('A'); at least 2 yrs' teaching experience, and entrance examination

Fees: (Cedi): Tuition, 100,000 per annum; foreign students, (US Dollars): 3,928

Main Language(s) of Instruction: English

Degrees and Diplomas: Certificate: Education, 1 yr; Diploma: 3 yrs; Bachelor's Degree: Education (BEd), a further 2 yrs

Student Services: Social Counselling, Sports Facilities, Handicapped Facilities, Health Services, Canteen

Libraries: Osagyefo Library and Kumasi Centre Library, 65,011 vols; 567 periodicals

Publications: Journal of Special Education; Ghana Educational Media and Technology Association (GEMTA) Journal

Academic Staff 2001-2002: Total: c. 205

Student Numbers 2001-2002: Total: c. 2,600

• UNIVERSITY FOR DEVELOPMENT STUDIES (UDS)

PO Box 1350, Tamale
Tel: +233(71) 22078 +233(71) 26633
Fax: +233(71) 22080 +233(71) 23957

Vice-Chancellor: John B.K. Kaburise (2002-)
Tel: +233(71) 22369 EMail: saaditt@africaonline.com.gh

Registrar: Felix Akuffo Tel: +233(71) 23371

International Relations: George Debrie, Assistant Registrar
Fax: +233(71) 23957

Faculties

Agriculture *(Nyankpala)* (Agriculture; Agronomy; Animal Husbandry; Environmental Studies; Horticulture; Irrigation; Natural Resources; Rural Planning) *Dean:* Thomas Bayorbor

Applied Sciences *(Navrongo)* (Biochemistry; Biological and Life Sciences; Botany; Chemistry; Computer Science; Mathematics; Physical Engineering) *Dean:* Walter Kpikpi

Integrated Development Studies *(Wa)* (Development Studies; Economics; History; Management; Social Studies) *Dean:* Daniel Bagah

Medicine and Health Sciences (Community Health; Health Sciences; Medicine; Nutrition) *Dean (Acting):* Rowland Otchewemah

Programmes

Allied Health Sciences (Health Sciences; Nursing) *Head:* Robert Kuganab-Lem

Centres

Inter-disciplinary Research *Director (Acting):* Ismail Bin Yahya

Further Information: Also Branches in Nyankpala, Kintampo, Tamale, Wa, Navrongo/Bolgatanga

History: Founded 1992. First students admitted September 1993.

Governing Bodies: University Council

Academic Year: December to November (December-April; May-August; September-November)

Admission Requirements: General Certificate of Education (GCE). Ordinary ('O') level with 5 credits, including English and Mathematics, and General Certificate of Education, Advanced ('A') level with 3 passes, pass in a general paper, and entrance examination

Fees: (Cedi): Tuition, 8 m.-16 m. per annum

Main Language(s) of Instruction: English

International Co-operation: With universities in Canada.

Accrediting Agencies: National Accreditation Board

Degrees and Diplomas: *Diploma:* Nursing, 2 yrs; *Bachelor's Degree:* Applied Sciences (BSc); Arts (BA); Nutrition, 4 yrs; Medicine (MB ChB), 7 yrs

Student Services: Academic Counselling, Social Counselling, Sports Facilities, Health Services, Canteen

Student Residential Facilities: Yes

Libraries: Total, 21,000 vols

Publications: UDS Newsletter (quarterly)

Academic Staff *2002-2003*	MEN	WOMEN	TOTAL
FULL-TIME	91	5	**96**

Staff with doctorate: Total: **19**

Student Numbers *2002-2003*	MEN	WOMEN	TOTAL
All (Foreign Included)	1,339	508	**1,847**

*• UNIVERSITY OF GHANA (UG)

PO Box 25, Legon, Accra
Tel: +233(21) 501-967
Fax: +233(21) 502-701
EMail: vcoffice@ug.edu.gh
Website: http://www.ug.edu.gh

Vice-Chancellor: Kwadwo Asenso-Okyere (2002-)
EMail: kasenso@ug.edu.gh

Registrar: A.T Konu Tel: +233(21) 500-390
EMail: atkonu@yahoo.com

International Relations: Chris Gordon
Tel: +233(21) 507-147 Fax: +233(21) 500-389
EMail: inep@ug.edu.gh

Faculties

Agriculture (Agricultural Business; Agricultural Economics; Agricultural Equipment; Agriculture; Animal Husbandry; Crop Production; Soil Science) *Dean:* Anna Barnes

Arts (Arts and Humanities; Classical Languages; Dance; English; Linguistics; Modern Languages; Music; Philosophy; Theatre) *Dean:* K. Yankah

Law (Constitutional Law; Environmental Studies; Family Studies; Human Rights; International Business; International Law; Law) *Dean:* A. Kuenyehia

Science (Biochemistry; Botany; Chemistry; Computer Science; Environmental Studies; Fishery; Food Science; Geography; Geology; Marine Science and Oceanography; Mathematics; Natural Resources; Natural Sciences; Nursing; Nutrition; Physics; Psychology; Statistics; Zoology) *Dean:* W.A. Asomaning

Social Studies (Archaeology; Computer Science; Economics; Geography; History; Information Sciences; Mathematics; Nursing; Political Science; Psychology; Social Work; Sociology; Statistics) *Dean:* J.R.A. Ayee

Colleges

Health Sciences (Dentistry; Health Sciences; Medicine; Public Health) *Provost:* A.S. Ayettey

Programmes

Environmental Sciences (Environmental Studies) *Co-ordinator:* Chris Gordon

Schools

Administration (Accountancy; Administration; Health Administration; Management; Public Administration) *Director:* Kofi O. Nti

Allied Health Sciences (Health Sciences; Laboratory Techniques; Physical Therapy; Radiology) *Dean:* E.K. Wiredu

Communication Studies (Advertising and Publicity; Communication Studies; Public Relations; Social Psychology) *Director:* K. Ansu-Kyeremeh

Dentistry (Dental Hygiene; Dental Technology; Dentistry; Social and Preventive Medicine; Surgery) *Dean:* Nii Oto Nartey

Medicine (Dentistry; Medicine; Radiology; Surgery) *Director*: C.N.B. Tagoe
Performing Arts (Dance; Music; Performing Arts; Theatre) *Director*: Martin Owusu
Public Health *Director*: Isabella A. Quakyi

Centres

African Music and Dance *(International Centre, ICAMD)* (African Studies; Dance; Music) *Director (Acting)*: Asante Darkwa
African Wetlands *(CAWS)* (African Studies; Environmental Studies) *Director*: Chris Gordon
Languages (Modern Languages) *Director*: K. Andoh-Kumi
Music and Dance *(International)* (Dance; Music) *Director*: J.N. Nketiah
Rehabilitation Medicine and Therapy (Rehabilitation and Therapy)
Tropical Clinical Pharmacology and Therapeutics (Pharmacology; Physical Therapy) *Director*: F. Ofei

Further Information: Also United Nations University Institute for Natural Resources in Africa (UNU/INRA); Volta Basin Research Project; agricultural research stations (Nungua, Kade, Kpong). English proficiency course for foreign students

History: Founded 1948 as University College of Gold Coast, became University College of Ghana 1957, and acquired present status and title 1961.

Governing Bodies: University Council

Academic Year: August to June (August-September; May-June)

Admission Requirements: General Certificate of Education (GCE) with 5 credits including English, Mathematics, Arts and Science or West Africa School Certificate (WASC) Ordinary ('O') level and three passes at Advanced ('A') level, with a minimum grade D for one. Senior Secondary School Certificate with passes in core English, Mathematics and any 3 elective subjects, with aggregate score of 24 in the WAEC entrance examination

Fees: (US Dollars): Foreign students, 2,475-3,500 per semester

Main Language(s) of Instruction: English

International Co-operation: With universities in USA; Russian Federation; Japan; Netherlands; Canada; Norway; Belgium; United Kingdom; France; Hong Kong; Germany; Benin; Australia; South Africa; Swaziland. Also participates in the Commonwealth Universities Abroad Consortium (CUSAC), the Council for International Education Exchange (CIEE), the International Students Exchange Programme (ISEP), and the Fulbright Programme

Degrees and Diplomas: *Diploma*: 4-6 semesters; *Bachelor's Degree*: Administration (BSc); Agriculture (BSc); Arts (BA); Dental Surgery (BOS); Fine Arts (BFA); Home Science (BSc); Law (LLB); Medical Sciences (BSc); Medicine and Surgery (MBchB); Music (BMus); Natural Sciences (BSc); Nursing (BSc), 6-12 semesters; *Master's Degree*: Administration; African Studies; Agriculture; Entomology (Mphil); Linguistics; Population Studies; Theatre; Environmental Studies (Mphil), 1-2 years; Arts (Mphil); Business Administration (MBA); Law (LLM); Public Administration (MPA), a further 1-2 yrs; Philosophy (PhD), a further 2-4 yrs; *Doctorate*: (PhD), 3-7 yrs

Student Services: Academic Counselling, Social Counselling, Foreign Student Adviser, Cultural Centre, Sports Facilities, Language Programmes, Handicapped Facilities, Health Services, Canteen, Foreign Student Centre

Student Residential Facilities: Yes

Special Facilities: Botanical Garden. Seismological Observatory. Drama Studio

Libraries: Balme Library, 366,191 vols

Publications: University Newsletter; University of Ghana Reporter (monthly); Vice-Chancellor's Annual Report to Congregation (annually); Campus Update (fortnightly)

Press or Publishing House: School of Communication Studies Printing Press; Institute of Adult Education Printing Press; Institute of African Studies Printing Press; Balme Library Tec

Academic Staff *2003*: Total: **735**

Staff with doctorate: Total: **354**

Student Numbers 2001-2002	MEN	WOMEN	TOTAL
All (Foreign Included)	11,496	6,020	**17,516**
FOREIGN ONLY	–	–	270

INSTITUTE OF ADULT EDUCATION
PO Box 31, Legon, Accra
Tel: +233(21) 501-789
Fax: +233(21) 500-391
EMail: iae@ug.edu.gh

Director: Kobina Asiedu (1998-)
EMail: iae.ad@libr.ug.edu.gh

History: Founded 1948.

INSTITUTE OF AFRICAN STUDIES
PO Box 73, Legon, Accra
Tel: +233(21) 500-512
Fax: +233(21) 502-397
EMail: iasgen@ug.edu.com.gh

Director: Takyiwah Manu

African Studies

History: Founded 1961.

INSTITUTE OF STATISTICAL, SOCIAL AND ECONOMIC RESEARCH
PO Box 74, Legon, Accra
Tel: +233(21) 501-182
Fax: +233(21) 500-937
EMail: isser.@ug.edu.gh;sadaocgh@ghana.com
Website: http://www.isser.org

Director: Ernest Aryeetey EMail: sadaocgh@ghana.com

Economics; Social Policy; Statistics

History: Founded 1962.

NOGUCHI MEMORIAL INSTITUTE FOR MEDICAL
RESEARCH
PO Box 25, Legon, Accra
Tel: +233(21) 500-374
Fax: +233(21) 502-182
EMail: director@noguchi.mimcom.net

Director: David Ofori-Adjei (1998-)
EMail: dofori-adjei@noguchi.mimcom.net

Biomedicine; Medicine

History: Founded 1979.

REGIONAL INSTITUTE FOR POPULATION STUDIES
PO Box 96, Legon, Accra
Tel: +233(21) 500-274
Fax: +233(21) 500-273
Telex: 2164 rips gh

Director: S.O. Kwankye EMail: kwankyesk@hotmail.com

Demography and Population

History: Founded 1972.

OTHER UNIVERSITY LEVEL INSTITUTIONS

• GHANA INSTITUTE OF MANAGEMENT AND PUBLIC ADMINISTRATION
PO Box AH 50, Achimota, Accra
Tel: +233(21) 401-681   +233(21) 401-682 +233(21) 401-338
Fax: +233(21) 405-805
Telex: 2551 gimpa gh
EMail: gimpa@excite.com
Website: http://www.gimpa.edu.gh/

Note: There are also several polytechnics at non-university level.

Director-General/Rector: Stephen Adei (1999-)
Tel: +233(21) 405-801 EMail: directorgeneral@gimpa.edu.gh

Director of Administration and Finance: E.A. Cooper
Tel: +233(21) 400-457 Fax: +233(21) 400-457

International Relations: Mercy Bampo Addo
Tel: +233(21) 402-381

Divisions
Consultancy Services (Management)

Human Resources and Private Sector Development (Human Resources; Management; Private Administration)

Public Management and Strategic Studies (Management; Public Administration)

Colleges
Tutorial College

Schools
Multimedia Studies (Multimedia)

Centres
Distance Learning *(DLC)*

Graduate Schools
Management

History: Founded 1961

Degrees and Diplomas: *Master's Degree*

Guinea

INSTITUTION TYPES AND CREDENTIALS

Types of higher education institutions:

Université (University)
Institut supérieur (Higher Institute)

School leaving and higher education credentials:

Baccalauréat 2ème Partie
Diplôme de Technicien supérieur
Diplôme d'Etudes universitaires générales (DEUG)
Licence
Diplôme d'Ingénieur
Maîtrise
Diplôme d'Etudes supérieures (DES)
Diplôme d'Etudes Approfondies (DEA)
Diplôme d'Etat de Docteur

STRUCTURE OF EDUCATION SYSTEM

Pre-higher education:

Duration of compulsory education:

Age of entry: 7
Age of exit: 13

Structure of school system:

Primary
Type of school providing this education: Primary School
Length of programme in years: 6
Age level from: 7 to: 13
Certificate/diploma awarded: Certificat d'Etudes primaires élémentaires (CEPE)

First Cycle Secondary
Type of school providing this education: Collège
Length of programme in years: 4
Age level from: 13 to: 17
Certificate/diploma awarded: Brevet d'Etudes du premier Cycle (BEPC)

Second Cycle Secondary
Type of school providing this education: Lycée
Length of programme in years: 3
Age level from: 17 to: 20
Certificate/diploma awarded: Baccalauréat première Partie (after Grade 12); Baccalauréat deuxième Partie (after Grade 13)

Vocational Secondary
Type of school providing this education: Ecole professionnelle
Length of programme in years: 3
Age level from: 17 to: 20
Certificate/diploma awarded: Brevet d'Etudes professionnelles (BEP)

School education:

Primary education lasts for six years leading to the Certificat d'Etudes primaires élémentaires (CEPE). There is an entrance examination to access secondary education. First cycle secondary education lasts for four years and is taken at a Collège. It leads to the Brevet d'Etudes du premier Cycle (BEPC). The second cycle lasts for three years and takes place in a Lycée. It leads to the Baccalauréeat 1ère partie (première) and the Baccalauréat 2ème partie the following year (terminale). Students specialize in Experimental Sciences, Mathematics or Social Sciences. Students must pass an entrance examination (concours d'entrée) to enter university. Technical and vocational education lasts for three years in type B vocational schools and leads to the Brevet d'Etudes professionnelles.

Higher education:

Higher education is provided by two universities and three higher institutes. Higher education institutions are under the responsibility of the Ministère de l'Enseignement supérieur et de la Recherche scientifique.

Main laws/decrees governing higher education:

Decree: Loi d'Orientation de l'Education nationale L/97/022/AN   Year: 1997
Concerns: Education system

Academic year:

Classes from: October *to:* June
Long vacation from: 1 July *to:* 15 September

Languages of instruction:

French

Stages of studies:

Non-university level post-secondary studies (technical/vocational type):

National professional schools (A type) train middle-level personnel who have completed Grade 13 and passed an entrance examination. Training lasts for three years and leads to the Brevet de Technicien supérieur.

University level studies:

University level first stage: DEUG, Licence:
A Diplôme d'Etudes universitaires générales (DEUG) is awarded after two years in Arts and Humanities. The Licence is awarded after three years.

University level second stage: Maîtrise, DES:
A further year beyond the Licence or two years beyond the DEUG leads to the Maîtrise/Diplôme d'Etudes supérieures (DES) and to a Diplôme d'Ingénieur in various fields. A Diplôme de Docteur en Médecine and Docteur en Pharmacie are conferred after six and five years of study respectively.

University level third stage: DEA:
This is the third cycle of higher education. Entry to the course is based on the Maîtrise and it lasts for at least one year. Students must complete a research project.

Teacher education:

Training of pre-primary and primary/basic school teachers
Primary teacher training colleges (Ecoles normales d'Instituteurs, ENI) offer three-year courses leading to the Certificat d'Aptitude à l'Enseignement élémentaire to those who have reached Baccalauréat level and have passed a competitive examination.

Training of secondary school teachers
Secondary school college teachers must hold the DEUG and are trained in service. Lycée teachers and ENI teachers must hold a Maîtrise before embarking on a one-year course at the Institut supérieur des Sciences de l'Education. Vocational secondary school teachers are trained in two years at the Ecole normale de l'Enseignement technique. Admission is through an entrance examination and the course leads to the Certificat d'Aptitude à l'Enseignement professionnel (CAEP). Technical education teachers are trained in one year after passing an entrance examination also at the Ecole normale de l'Enseignement technique where they obtain the Certificat d'Aptitude à l'Enseignement technique (CAET).

Training of higher education teachers
Higher education teachers must hold a Diplôme d'Etudes approfondies or a Doctorat.

Non-traditional studies:

Distance higher education
Distance education consists in radio courses produced by the Service national de Télé-enseignement.

Lifelong higher education
Decentralized lifelong education has been developed with the creation of regional and prefectoral centres to upgrade the knowledge of school teachers. Courses last between three and nine months.

NATIONAL BODIES

Responsible authorities:

Ministry of Higher Education and Scientific Research (Ministère de l'Enseignement supérieur et de la Recherche scientifique)

Ministre: Eugène Camara
Directeur national de l'Enseignement supérieur: Ibrahima Moriah Conté
PO Box 2201
Conakry
Tel: +224 44-19-50   +224 44-37-02
Fax: +224 41-31-45

ADMISSIONS TO HIGHER EDUCATION

Admission to university-level studies

Name of secondary school credential required: Baccalauréat 2ème Partie
For entry to: Universities

Entrance exams required: Concours d'Entrée for universities

Recognition of studies and qualifications:

Studies pursued in foreign countries (bodies dealing with recognition of foreign credentials):
Direction de l'Enseignement supérieur, Ministère de l'Enseignement supérieur et de la Recherche scientifique
PO Box 964
Conakry
Tel: +224 44-19-50   +224 44-37-02
Fax: +224 41-31-45

Multilateral agreements concerning recognition of foreign studies

Name(s) of agreement(s): Convention on the Recognition of Studies, Certificates, Diplomas, Degrees and Other Academic Qualifications in Higher Education in the African States
Year of signature: 1981

GRADING SYSTEM

Usual grading system in secondary school

Full Description: 0-20: 16-20 très bien; 14-15 bien; 12-13 assez bien; 10-11 passable; 0-10 fail
Highest on scale: 20
Pass/fail level: 11-10
Lowest on scale: 0

Main grading system used by higher education institutions

Full Description: 0-20: 16-20 très bien; 14-15 bien; 12-13 assez bien; 10-11 passable; 0-10 fail
Highest on scale: 20
Pass/fail level: 11-10
Lowest on scale: 0

NOTES ON HIGHER EDUCATION SYSTEM

Data for academic year: 2002-2003

Source: International Association of Universities (IAU), updated from IBE website, 2003 (www.ibe.unesco.org/International/Databanks/Wde/profilee.htm)

INSTITUTIONS OF HIGHER EDUCATION

UNIVERSITIES

PUBLIC INSTITUTIONS

JULIUS NYERERE UNIVERSITY OF KANKAN
Université Julius Nyerere de Kankan
BP 209, Kankan
Tel: +224 71-20-93
Recteur: Seydoubu Camara **EMail:** seycam@sotelgui.net.gn
Secrétaire général: Dominique Koly **Tel:** +224 71-20-94
International Relations: Martin Koïvogui
EMail: seycam@sotelgui.net.gn

Faculties
Natural Sciences (Mathematics and Computer Science; Natural Sciences) *Dean*: Bakary Kamano
Social Sciences *Dean*: Amadou Baïlo Barry

History: Founded 1963 as school, became Institut polytechnique 1967 and acquired present status and title 1984. A State institution under the supervision of the Ministry of Education.

Academic Year: October to June (October-December; January-March; April-June)

Admission Requirements: Secondary School Certificate (baccalauréat) and competitive entrance examination

Main Language(s) of Instruction: French

Degrees and Diplomas: *Diplôme d'Etudes supérieures (DES)*: 5 yrs

Student Residential Facilities: Yes

Academic Staff 2001-2002	MEN	WOMEN	TOTAL
FULL-TIME	82	1	**83**

Staff with doctorate: Total: **18**

Student Numbers 2001-2002	MEN	WOMEN	TOTAL
All (Foreign Included)	2,001	236	**2,237**
FOREIGN ONLY	15	3	18

UNIVERSITY OF CONAKRY
Université de Conakry
BP 1147, Conakry
Tel: +224 46-46-89
Fax: +224 46-48-08
EMail: uganc@mirinet.net.gn
Recteur: Ousmane Sylla (2003-)

Faculties
Law, Economics and Management (Economics; Law; Management)

Letters and Humanities (Arts and Humanities; English; French; Geography; History; Philosophy; Sociology; Spanish)
Medicine and Pharmacy (Biochemistry; Dentistry; Medicine; Paediatrics; Pharmacy; Public Health)
Science (Biochemistry; Biology; Chemistry; Energy Engineering; Mathematics; Microbiology; Natural Sciences; Physics; Physiology; Zoology)

Institutes
Polytechnic (Chemical Engineering; Civil Engineering; Electrical Engineering; Engineering; Food Technology; Technology; Telecommunications Engineering; Telecommunications Services)

Centres
Applied Technology (Technology)
Computer Science
English Studies *(CELA)* (English)
Environmental Studies and Research (Environmental Studies)
French Studies *(CELF)*

Further Information: Also 2 University Hospitals

History: Founded 1962 as Institut Polytechnique, became University 1984. Acquired present status 1989. A State institution under the supervision of the Ministry of Education.

Governing Bodies: Conseil d'Administration; Conseil de l'Université

Academic Year: September to June (September-January; February-June)

Admission Requirements: Secondary school certificate (baccalauréat) and competitive entrance examination

Main Language(s) of Instruction: French

Degrees and Diplomas: *Diplôme de Technicien supérieur*: Computer Science (DTSI), 3 1/2 yrs; *Diplôme d'Etudes universitaires générales (DEUG)*: Human Sciences; *Licence*: 3 yrs; *Diplôme d'Ingénieur*: Engineering, 5 yrs; *Maîtrise*: 4 yrs; *Diplôme d'Etudes Approfondies (DEA)*: Business Administration; Economics; Law; Management; *Diplôme d'Etat de Docteur*: Pharmacy, 5 yrs; Medicine, 6 yrs

Student Residential Facilities: Yes

Special Facilities: Zoo. Meteorology Station. Radiotelescope. Audiovisual Centre

Libraries: Central Library, c. 23,000 vols; libraries of the faculties and departments, c. 11,730

Publications: Bulletin de la Recherche (monthly); Guinée Médicale (quarterly); Annales de l'Université (annually)

Press or Publishing House: Service des Editions Universitaires

Academic Staff 2001-2002: Full-Time: c. 340 Part-Time: c. 110 Total: c. 450

Student Numbers 2001-2002: Total: c. 4,700

OTHER INSTITUTIONS

PUBLIC INSTITUTIONS

HIGHER INSTITUTE OF AGRICULTURE AND VETERINARY MEDICINE
Institut supérieur agronomique et vétérinaire Valéry Giscard d'Estaing
BP 131, Faranah
Tel: +224 81-02-15
Telex: 22331/mdec/ge
Founded: 1978, 1991

Departments
Agriculture
Rural Engineering (Agricultural Engineering)
Stockraising and Veterinary Medicine (Cattle Breeding; Veterinary Science)
Water and Forestry (Forestry; Water Science)

History: Founded 1978, acquired present status and title 1991.

HIGHER INSTITUTE OF EDUCATIONAL SCIENCES OF MANÉAH
Institut supérieur des Sciences de l'Education de Manéah
BP 795, Conakry
Founded: 1991

Departments
Continuing Education and Research (Educational Research; Literacy Education) *Head*: Adrian Koffa Kamano
Educational Administration *Head*: Dian Gongoré Djallo
Educational Sciences *Director*: Amadou Tidjiani Diallo
Teacher Training (Secondary Education; Teacher Training) *Head*: Lansana Camara
Teacher Training Education (Staff Development; Teacher Trainers Education; Teacher Training) *Head*: Amadou Camara

History: Founded 1991 by the transformation of the "Ecole Normale Supérieure ".

Governing Bodies: Conseil d' Administration; Conseil de l' Institut

Academic Year: October to July

Admission Requirements: University degree (Maîtrise) and entrance examination. Professional experience may also be required in some sections

Main Language(s) of Instruction: French

Degrees and Diplomas: Certificate in Teacher Training

Student Services: Sports Facilities, Health Services, Canteen

Student Residential Facilities: For 300 students

Libraries: Main Library, c. 3,500 vols

Publications: Faisceau, Educational Sciences (biannually)

Academic Staff *2000*	MEN	WOMEN	TOTAL
FULL-TIME	40	4	44
PART-TIME	8	–	8
TOTAL	**48**	**4**	**52**

Staff with doctorate: Total: **16**

Student Numbers *2000*	MEN	WOMEN	TOTAL
All (Foreign Included)	399	23	**422**

Distance Students, 635

HIGHER INSTITUTE OF MINING AND GEOLOGY OF BOKÉ
Institut supérieur des Mines et Géologie de Boké
Boké
Founded: 1991

Departments
Geology
Mining Engineering
Technical and Basic Sciences (Natural Sciences; Technology)

History: Founded 1991

Kenya

INSTITUTION TYPES AND CREDENTIALS

Types of higher education institutions:
University
College
Institute
Teachers College
Polytechnic

School leaving and higher education credentials:
Kenya Certificate of Secondary Education
Diploma
Bachelor's Degree
Bachelor of Arts
Bachelor of Education
Bachelor of Medicine/Bachelor of Surgery
Bachelor of Science
Bachelor of Technology
Bachelor of Veterinary Medicine
Postgraduate Diploma
Master's Degree
Master of Philosophy
Doctor's Degree

STRUCTURE OF EDUCATION SYSTEM

Pre-higher education:

Duration of compulsory education:

Age of entry: 6
Age of exit: 14

Structure of school system:

Primary
Type of school providing this education: Primary School
Length of programme in years: 8

214

Age level from: 6 to: 14
Certificate/diploma awarded: Kenya Certificate of Primary Education (KCPE)

Secondary
Type of school providing this education: Secondary School
Length of programme in years: 4
Age level from: 14 to: 18
Certificate/diploma awarded: Kenya Certificate of Secondary Education (KCSE)

School education:

A new system of education, known as the 8-4-4 system, was introduced in 1985. Under this system, eight years of primary schooling (leading to the Kenya Certificate of Primary Education) are followed by four years of secondary schooling (leading to the Kenya Certificate of Secondary Education (KCSE)) and four years of first degree studies at university. This scheme replaces one which was based on the English pattern culminating in A levels and a three-year first degree course. The introduction of the 8-4-4 education system has led to tremendous changes in the secondary school curriculum. This is in line with the need for a broad-based curriculum that prepares students for self-reliance, vocational training and further education. In 1990, the first KCSE students entered university to begin four years of study for a general degree. The KCSE is administered by the Kenya National Examinations Council.

Higher education:

Higher education is offered in public universities that have been established by Acts of Parliament (some of them with constituent colleges), private institutions with a charter (fully accredited), private universities with a letter of Interim Authority, and private institutions without a charter. Universities are autonomous. All administrative functions are independently managed through University Councils. Though autonomous, universities receive funding from the Ministry of Education. Alongside these universities, there are several private institutions, without a charter, offering degree courses in Kenya. All of them, except the United States International University, are theologically-oriented. These universities are advised by the Commission for Higher Education to diversify their curricula to meet the needs of Kenyan society. They raise funds from their own sources and do not receive any grants from the State. Apart from the universities, there are a number of post-secondary institutions offering training at diploma and certificate levels. In the field of teacher training, these include diploma colleges for the training of non-graduate secondary school teachers, and teacher training colleges for primary school teachers. For technical education they include national polytechnics, Institutes of technology and technical training institutes. In addition to these, a number of government ministries also offer three years' professional training at diploma level for their middle-level manpower requirements.

Main laws/decrees governing higher education:

Decree: The Universities (Establishment of Universities)   Year: 1989
Concerns: Standards and Procedures of Accreditation

Decree: Universities Act   Year: 1985
Concerns: Coordination and Accreditation of Universities

Academic year:

Classes from: October *to:* July

Long vacation from: 1 August *to:* 30 September

Languages of instruction:

English

Stages of studies:

Non-university level post-secondary studies (technical/vocational type):

Institutes of technology have been set up through local and provincial initiatives and they provide training for school leavers with the Kenyan Certificate of Secondary Education, equipping them for employment in medium and large-scale industry. The Government, through the Ministry of Technical Training and Technology, provides some financial assistance as well as soliciting aid from willing donors to establish such institutions. Courses last between two and four years and cover subjects such as Construction, Engineering, Business Studies, Textiles, Agriculture, etc. Technical training institutes offer training at both Craft and Diploma level. The national polytechnics offer Certificate, Diploma and Higher Diploma courses.

University level studies:

University level first stage: *Bachelor's Degree*:
At the University of Nairobi, Bachelor's Degrees with Honours (there are no Ordinary degrees) are generally obtained four years after entering with KCSE, including those in Law and Engineering; Veterinary Medicine takes five years, and Architecture and Medicine six years. At Kenyatta University, most students read for a Bachelor of Education (BEd).

University level second stage: *Master's Degree*:
At the University of Nairobi, Master's Degrees in Architecture, Humanities, Law, Commerce, Science, Engineering, Medicine and Education take between one and three years' further study after the Bachelor's Degree. Kenyatta University offers a two-year Master's Degree.

University level third stage: *Doctorate*:
Holders of a Master's Degree need a minimum of two years' research to obtain a PhD. Kenyatta University offers a one-year Postgraduate Diploma in Education.

Teacher education:

Training of pre-primary and primary/basic school teachers
There are twenty primary teachers' colleges. All students admitted to teacher training colleges must hold the Kenyan Certificate of Secondary Education and have completed four years of secondary education. The teacher training course lasts two years, at the end of which students are awarded a P1, P2 or P3 Certificate, depending on their success in centrally set examinations.

Training of secondary school teachers
Training of secondary school teachers is carried out at two levels. In universities, graduate teachers are trained in four years for the Bachelor of Education Degree (BEd). Graduates holding a BA, BSc or BCom take a one-year post-graduate diploma course in education. Teachers are also trained at

two diploma colleges. The three-year course leads to a Diploma in Education. Kenyatta University is a major teacher training institution. It has begun an in-service Postgraduate Diploma programme.

Training of higher education teachers
There is no formal training for higher education teachers who wish to teach in universities. Candidates must hold a first class or upper second class Honours Degree, followed by a Master's Degree.

Non-traditional studies:

Distance higher education
The University of Nairobi offers an external degree programme for the Bachelor of Education in Arts-based subjects.

Higher education training in industry
A number of government Ministries offer three years' professional training at Diploma level for their middle-level manpower requirements.

Other forms of non-formal higher education
The University of Nairobi offers external study via six centres located throughout Kenya. Non-degree external study offerings include Community Education, Continuing Education, Cultural programmes, Information and Public Relations programmes, and Leadership and Management training. Instruction and examinations are administered by the University of Nairobi and Kenyatta University and the degree is awarded by the University of Nairobi.

NATIONAL BODIES

Responsible authorities:

Ministry of Education
    Minister: George Saitoti
    Permanent Secretary: Karega Mutahi
    PO Box 30040
    Nairobi
    Tel: +254(2) 334-411
    Fax: +254(2) 214-287

Commission for Higher Education
    Commission Secretary: Justin Irina
    Deputy Commission Secretary: Wilson Kipng'eno
    PO Box 54999
    Nairobi
    Tel: +254(2) 228-753
    Fax: +254(2) 222-218
    Cable: comhigh
    EMail: che@kenyaweb.com

Role of governing body: Planning, budgeting and financing of public universities; accreditation of private universities; coordination of education and training in middle level colleges for the purpose of admission to universities; standardization, equation and recognition of qualifications; advices and recommendations to the Government on matters relating to university education

ADMISSIONS TO HIGHER EDUCATION

Admission to non university higher education studies

Name of secondary school credential required: Kenya Certificate of Secondary Education
Minimum score/requirement: D+
For entry to: non-university post-secondary programmes

Other admission requirements: Apprenticeship programmes are organized by industries for their employees. Progression depends on passing government trade tests at various levels.

Admission to university-level studies

Name of secondary school credential required: Kenya Certificate of Secondary Education
Minimum score/requirement: C+ in at least ten subjects
For entry to: University

Alternatives to credentials: Under the Mature Age Scheme, candidates over 25 who do not meet entry requirements may take an entrance examination. Graduates of post-secondary institutions may be admitted to universities.

Foreign students admission

Quotas: Admission depends on availability of places and ability to pay.

Admission requirements: Foreign students should have qualifications equivalent to the Cambridge High School Certificate, GCE or East African Certificate of Education at 'A' level; special one-year courses are arranged under the Mature Age Scheme to allow students over 25 not meeting university requirements to take the entrance examination.

Entry regulations: Visas are required from countries that require visas for Kenyans.

Language requirements: Good knowledge of English is essential.

Application procedures:

Apply to individual institution for entry to: Parallel programmes

Apply to national body for entry to: Universities (for entry to regular programmes)

Apply to: Joint Admissions Board
PO Box 30197
Nairobi

Recognition of studies and qualifications:

Studies pursued in home country (System of recognition/accreditation): Recognition is by a Committee of the Commission for Higher Education. Experts in relevant disciplines are invited to the Committee

Studies pursued in foreign countries (bodies dealing with recognition of foreign credentials):
Recognition & Equation of Qualifications & Inspection, Commission for Higher Education
    Senior Assistant Commission Secretary: George Njine
    Assistant Commission Secretary: Margaret Kobia
    PO Box 54999
    Nairobi
    Tel: +254 (2) 228-753
    Fax: +254 (2) 222-218
    Cable: comhigh
    EMail: che@kenyaweb.com
    Deals with credential recognition for entry to: University
    Services provided and students dealt with: Evaluation of qualifications for purposes of employment
and higher education

Special provisions for recognition:

For access to non-university post-secondary studies: Secondary school attended must be recognized in
own country.

For access to university level studies: University attended must be recognized in own country

For access to advanced studies and research: University attended must be recognized in own country

For the exercise of a profession: University attended must be recognized in own country

References to further information on foreign student admissions and recognition of studies

Title: University calendars, catalogues or student's guides

STUDENT LIFE

Student expenses and financial aid

Student costs:
    Home students tuition fees: Minimum: 40,000 (Kenyan Shilling)
    Maximum: 450,000 (Kenyan Shilling)
    Foreign students tuition fees: Maximum: 450,000 (Kenyan Shilling)

Bodies providing information on student financial aid:
African Network of Scientific and Technological Institutions (ANSTI)
    PO Box 30592
    Nairobi
    Category of students: Graduates from ANSTI States who are proficient in French and English
Higher Education Loans Board
    PO Box 69489
    Nairobi

Deals with: Loans

Publications on student services and financial aid:

Title: Study Abroad 2004-2005, 32nd Edition
Author: UNESCO
Publisher: UNESCO Publishing
Year of publication: 2003

INTERNATIONAL COOPERATION AND EXCHANGES

Principal national bodies responsible for dealing with international cooperation and exchanges in higher education:

Commission for Higher Education
Commission Secretary: Justin Irina
PO Box 54999
Nairobi
Tel: +254 (2) 228-753
Fax: +254 (2) 222-218
Cable: comhigh
EMail: che@kenyaweb.com

Ministry of Education
PO Box 30040
Nairobi
Tel: +254(2) 334-411
Fax: +254(2) 214-287
Telex: Education

GRADING SYSTEM

Usual grading system in secondary school

Full Description: In the Kenyan Certificate of Secondary Education candidates are graded on a twelve-point scale as follows: A, A- (distinction/very good); B+,B,B- (credit/good); C+,C,C- (average); D+,D,D- (fair); E (poor).
Highest on scale: A
Lowest on scale: E

Main grading system used by higher education institutions

Full Description: A=70%-100% (First Class Honours), B=60%-69% (Second Class Honours (upper division)), C=50%-69% (Second Class Honours (lower division)), D=40%-49% (Pass), E=0%-39% (Fail).
Highest on scale: A
Pass/fail level: D (for Medicine & Veterinary Medicine : C)
Lowest on scale: E

Other main grading systems

For national polytechnics, institutes of technology: Distinction 70%; Credit 50%-69%; Pass 40%-49%; Fail Below 40%

NOTES ON HIGHER EDUCATION SYSTEM

A major development in the universities' financing has been the introduction of cost-sharing, under which all Kenya nationals are entitled to an annual maximum loan of Kes 42,000, repayable when the student starts working, after a grace period.

A recent development is the introduction of parallel programmes in universities with flexible time tables and where students pay full fees without Government grants.

Data for academic year: 2002-2003
Source: Commission for Higher Education, Nairobi, 2003

INSTITUTIONS OF HIGHER EDUCATION

UNIVERSITIES AND UNIVERSITY LEVEL INSTITUTIONS

PUBLIC INSTITUTIONS

• EGERTON UNIVERSITY (EU)
PO Box 536, Njoro
Tel: +254(37) 622-82 +254(37) 622-78
Fax: +254(37) 625-27
Telex: (037) 61620 nakuru
Cable: university njoro
EMail: info@egerton.ac.ke
Website: http://www.egerton.or.ke

Vice-Chancellor: Ezra Maritim (2000-) Tel: +254(37) 624-54
EMail: vc@egerton.ac.ke

Registrar (Academic): Nephat J. Kathuri
Tel: +254(37) 623-32 Fax: +254(37) 622-13
EMail: registrar@egerton.ac.ke

International Relations: Ronald Chepkilot, Public Relations Officer Tel: +254(37) 624-64

Faculties
Agriculture (Agriculture; Agronomy; Animal Husbandry; Botany; Horticulture; Natural Resources) *Dean*: Erasius Njoka
Arts and Social Sciences (Anthropology; Arts and Humanities; Geography; History; Linguistics; Literature; Modern Languages; Philosophy; Religious Studies; Social Sciences; Sociology) *Dean*: Thuo Kuria
Education and Human Resources (Agricultural Education; Curriculum; Pedagogy; Psychology) *Dean*: Simiyu Barasa
Engineering and Technology (Agricultural Engineering; Automation and Control Engineering; Engineering; Environmental Studies; Industrial Engineering; Technology; Water Science) *Dean*: Polycampus Kimani
Environmental Studies and Natural Resources (Environmental Studies; Geography; Natural Resources) *Dean*: Abdulah Aboud
Science (Botany; Chemistry; Computer Science; Mathematics; Natural Sciences; Physics; Zoology) *Dean*: Daniel Muchiri

Divisions
Finance and Administration (Administration; Finance) *Director*: James Tuitoek
Research *Director*: Richard Mwangi

Schools
Continuing Education *Director*: Francis Wegulo

Further Information: Also Laikipia, Kisii, Nakuru Town Campuses

History: Founded 1939 as Egerton Agricultural College, became a University College of University of Nairobi 1986, and acquired present status and title 1987.
Governing Bodies: University Council
Academic Year: September to May
Admission Requirements: Kenya Certificate of Secondary Education (KCSE) or equivalent
Main Language(s) of Instruction: English
International Co-operation: With universities in China, United Kingdom, Austria, South Africa, India, USA, the Netherlands, Australia, Tanzania, Egypt.
Degrees and Diplomas: *Diploma*: 4 yrs; *Bachelor of Arts*: (BA), 4 yrs; *Bachelor of Science*: (BSc), 4 yrs; *Master's Degree*: a further 2 yrs; *Doctor's Degree*
Student Services: Academic Counselling, Social Counselling, Employment Services, Nursery Care, Sports Facilities, Language Programmes, Health Services, Canteen
Student Residential Facilities: For over 90% of the students
Libraries: c. 150,000 vols
Publications: Egerton Journal; Egerton News (annually)
Press or Publishing House: Education Media Centre (EMC)
Academic Staff *2001-2002:* Total: c. 600

Student Numbers *2001-2002*	MEN	WOMEN	TOTAL
All (Foreign Included)	5,400	2,600	**8,000**
FOREIGN ONLY	5	2	7

Evening Students, 250 **Distance Students,** 300

• INTERNATIONAL CENTRE OF INSECT PHYSIOLOGY AND ECOLOGY (ICIPE)
PO Box 30772, Nairobi
Tel: +254(20) 802-501 +254(20) 861-680
Fax: +254(20) 803-360
EMail: icipe@icipe.org
Website: http://www.icipe.org

Director: Hans Herren (1994-)

Director for Administration: Tina Kuklenski

International Relations: Mudiumbula T. Futa

Research Departments
Behavioural and Chemical Ecology *(BCE)* (Chemistry; Ecology)
Population Ecology and Ecosystems Science *(PEES)* (Ecology; Environmental Studies)

Research Units
Animal Breeding & Quarantine
Biostatistics
Biosystematics
Entomopathology
Information Services

Information Technology
Laboratory Management (Laboratory Techniques)
Molecular Biology and Biochemistry (Biochemistry; Molecular Biology)
Social Sciences

History: Founded 1970 as a Company. Acquired present status and title in mid-80' s. Campuses in Nairobi, Kenya West Coast, Ethiopia.

Governing Bodies: Council; ARPIS Academic Board

Fees: (US Dollars): c. 1000 per annum. Scholarships provided for ARPIS students

Main Language(s) of Instruction: English

International Co-operation: With 30 African universities.

Student Residential Facilities: For c. 100 students

Special Facilities: Biosystematics Unit

Libraries: Information Resource Centre

Publications: Insect Science and its Applications

Press or Publishing House: ICIPE Science Press

*• JOMO KENYATTA UNIVERSITY OF AGRICULTURE AND TECHNOLOGY (JKUAT)

PO Box 62000, Nairobi, 00200
Tel: +254(20) 1515-2711
Fax: +254(20) 1515-2164
Cable: thika
EMail: info@jkuat.ac.ke
Website: http://www.jkuat.ac.ke

Vice-Chancellor: Nick G. Wanjohi (2003-)
Tel: +254(20) 1515-2165 EMail: jku-vc@nbnet.co.ke

Deputy-Vice-Chancellor (Academic Affairs): Henry M. Thairu Tel: +254(20) 1515-2053 EMail: dvcaca@nbnet.co.ke

International Relations: Michael Ngonyo
Tel: +254(20) 1515-2181

Faculties
Agriculture (Agriculture; Crop Production; Engineering; Food Science; Horticulture) *Dean:* Florence Lenga
Engineering (Architecture; Civil Engineering; Electrical and Electronic Engineering; Engineering; Mechanical Engineering) *Dean:* Paul Kioni
Science (Botany; Chemistry; Mathematics; Natural Sciences; Physics; Statistics; Zoology) *Dean:* Mabel Imbuga

Programmes
Continuing Education *Director:* John Ochora

Schools
Architecture and Building Sciences (Architecture; Building Technologies) *Director:* P.G. Ngunjiri

Institutes
Alternative Medicine and Infectious Diseases (Tropical Medicine) *Director:* Japheth Magambo
Computer Science and Information Technology (Computer Science; Information Technology) *Director:* Leonard Mengo

Energy and Environmental Technology (Energy Engineering; Environmental Engineering) *Director:* Isaac Inoti
Human Resources Development (Human Resources) *Director:* L. A. Oyugi

Centres
Biotechnology *Director:* Esther Kahangi

Further Information: Also Student (Monbusho) Programme in Japan

History: Founded 1981, became Constituent College of Kenyatta University 1988. Acquired present status 1994.

Governing Bodies: University Council; University Management Board; University Senate

Academic Year: March to March (March-July; August-December; January-March)

Admission Requirements: Kenya Certificate of Secondary Education (KSCE)

Fees: (K. Shillings): 280,000-415,000 per annum

Main Language(s) of Instruction: English

Degrees and Diplomas: *Diploma:* 3 yrs; *Bachelor's Degree:* Architecture (BScArch), 6 yrs; *Bachelor of Science:* (BSc), 4 yrs; Engineering (BScE), 5 yrs

Student Services: Academic Counselling, Social Counselling, Employment Services, Nursery Care, Cultural Centre, Sports Facilities, Health Services, Canteen

Student Residential Facilities: For 2500 students

Special Facilities: Botanical Garden

Libraries: Jomo Kenyatta University Library

Publications: Agritech Update (monthly); Agritechnews (quarterly); Journal of Architecture (biannually); Journal of Agriculture, Science and Technology; Journal of Civil Engineering (annually)

Academic Staff *2001-2002:* Total: c. 310

Staff with doctorate: Total: c. 60

Student Numbers *2001-2002:* All (Foreign Included): Men: c. 1,955 Women: c. 315 Total: c. 2,270

• KENYATTA UNIVERSITY (KU)

PO Box 43844, Nairobi
Tel: +254(20) 810-901 +254(20) 810-912
Fax: +254(20) 810-759
Telex: 25483 kenun ke
Cable: kenuco
EMail: info@ku.ac.ke
Website: http://www.ku.ac.ke

Vice-Chancellor: Everett Standa (2003-)
Tel: +254(20) 811-231 +254(20) 812-677
Fax: +254(20) 811-575 EMail: kuvc@nbnet.co.ke

Deputy-Vice-Chancellor (Academic): Julius Ongong'a
Tel: +254(20) 811-380

Faculties
Arts (Arts and Humanities) *Dean:* I. Nbaabu
Commerce (Business and Commerce) *Dean:* J.N. Chege
Education *Dean:* P.K. Mutunga

223

Environmental Studies *Dean*: K Kerich
Home Economics *Dean*: O. Nugenda
Science (Computer Science; Mathematics; Natural Sciences) *Dean*: S.W. Waudo

Board of Studies
Postgraduate *Director*: S.W. Waudo

Centres
Computer (Computer Science) *Director*: H.K. Rono

Bureaux
Educational Research *Director*: R. Karega

History: Founded 1965 as Kenyatta University College, acquired present status and title 1985.

Governing Bodies: Council; Senate

Academic Year: September to June

Admission Requirements: Kenya Certificate of Secondary Education (KCSE)

Fees: (K. Shillings): c. 16,000 per semester; foreign students, c. 216,000 per semester; summer term, c. 8000

Main Language(s) of Instruction: English

Degrees and Diplomas: *Bachelor's Degree*: 3-4 yrs; *Postgraduate Diploma*: Education, 1 yr; *Master's Degree*: a further 2 yrs; *Doctor's Degree*: (PhD), a further 3-4 yrs

Student Services: Academic Counselling, Social Counselling, Employment Services, Nursery Care, Cultural Centre, Sports Facilities, Handicapped Facilities, Health Services, Canteen

Student Residential Facilities: For c. 6000 students

Libraries: Digital Library, 2000 journals

Publications: Calendar; Annual Report; Directory of Research (annually)

Academic Staff 2000	TOTAL
FULL-TIME	420
PART-TIME	175
TOTAL	**595**
STAFF WITH DOCTORATE	
FULL-TIME	165
PART-TIME	30
TOTAL	**195**

Student Numbers 2000	TOTAL
All (Foreign Included)	**9,500**
FOREIGN ONLY	10

Distance Students, 150

• MASENO UNIVERSITY (MSU)
PO Box Private Bag, Maseno
Tel: +254(35) 510-08 +254(35) 510-11
Fax: +254(35) 511-53

Vice-Chancellor: Frederick Onyango (2001-)
Tel: +254(35) 516-22 Fax: +254(35) 512-21
EMail: vc-maseno@swiftkisumu.com

Administrative Officer: John Agak

International Relations: Patrick O. Ayiecho, Coordinator

Head Librarian: Gad Ojuando Tel: +254(35) 516-20
Fax: +254(35) 516-22 EMail: vc-maseno@swiftkisumu.com

Faculties
Arts and Social Sciences (Arts and Humanities; Economics; Geography; History; Literature; Modern Languages; Music; Religion) *Dean*: Ezekiel Kasiera
Education (Education; Psychology; Special Education) *Dean*: Lucas Othuon
Science (Botany; Chemistry; Computer Science; Environmental Studies; Horticulture; Mathematics; Natural Sciences; Physics; Zoology) *Dean*: Joseph Akeyo

Schools
Family Consumer Science and Technology (Consumer Studies; Family Studies; Hotel Management; Technology) *Director*: Mary K. Walingo
Public Health and Community Development (Biomedicine; Community Health) *Director*: Philip Aduma

Institutes
Research and Postgraduate Studies *Director*: B.A. Ogot
Undergraduate Studies *Director*: Monica Ayieko

Further Information: Also Sandwich Courses, M.Phil

History: Founded 1990 as a Constituent College of Moi University. Acquired present status 2001.

Governing Bodies: Senate

Academic Year: September-May (September-December; January-May)

Admission Requirements: Kenya Certificate of Secondary Education (KCSE), level B

Main Language(s) of Instruction: English

International Co-operation: With universities in Germany, USA, South Africa, Sweden.

Degrees and Diplomas: *Bachelor of Arts*: Interior Design (B.A.), 4 yrs; *Bachelor of Education*: Arts; Home Science and Technology; Science; Music; French (B.Ed.), 4 yrs; *Bachelor of Science*: Biomedical Science and Technology; Textile Design and Merchandising; Hotel and Institutional Management; Home Science and Technology; Computer Science and Engineering; Environmental Studies; Applied Statistics (B.Sc.), 4 yrs; *Master's Degree*: Horticulture; Botany; Cell Biology; Economics and Planning of Education; English; History; Literature; Zoology; Health Promotion and Internal Health (M.Sc.); Plant Pathology; Molecular Epidemiology and Biotechnology; Educational Administration; Mathematics; Community Nutrition; Hospitality (M.Sc.), A further 2 yrs; *Doctor's Degree*: Social and Cultural Studies; Biological Sciences; Physics; Mathematics; Agricultural Sciences; Environmental Sciences (Ph.D)

Student Services: Academic Counselling, Social Counselling, Employment Services, Cultural Centre, Sports Facilities, Health Services, Canteen

Student Residential Facilities: Yes

Libraries: University Library

Publications: Equator News (4 per annum); Maseno Journal of Education, Arts and Science (2 per annum)

Press or Publishing House: Maseno University Desktop Publishing Unit

Academic Staff 2001-2002: Total: c. 180

Student Numbers 2001-2002: Total: c. 1,830

• MOI UNIVERSITY (MU)

PO Box 3900, Eldoret, Rift Valley
Tel: +254(32) 143-001
Fax: +254(32) 143-047
Telex: 254 321 35047
Cable: moi varsity, eldoret
EMail: vcmu@mu.ac.ke
Website: http://www.mu.ac.ke

Vice-Chancellor: David Some (2002-) Tel: +254(32) 143-363

Chief Administrative Officer: J.K. Sang
Tel: +254(32) 143-184 Fax: +254(32) 143-288
EMail: jksang@irmmoi.com;cado@mu.ac.ke

International Relations: B.M. Khaemba
Tel: +254(32) 143-069 EMail: ipo@irmmoi.com;ipo@mu.ac.ke

Faculties

Agriculture *(Chepkoilel Campus) Dean*: Mark Adhiambo
Education *(Kesses Campus, Cheipkoilel Campus) Dean*: B.W. Kerre
Forest Resources and Wildlife Management *(Chepkoilel Campus)* (Forest Products; Forestry; Wildlife) *Dean*: B.C.C. Wangila
Health Sciences *Dean*: B.O. Khwa Otsyula
Information Sciences *(Kesses Campus) Dean*: C. Odini
Law *(Kesses Campus) Dean*: F.X. Njenga
Science *(Chepkoilel Campus)* (Computer Science; Mathematics; Natural Sciences) *Dean*: Peter K. Torongey
Social, Cultural and Development Studies *(Kesses Campus)* (Cultural Studies; Development Studies; Social Studies) *Dean*: J.J. Akonga
Technology *(Kesses Campus) Dean*: H.L. Kaane

Programmes

International Relations *(Kesses Campus) Head*: Battan. M. Khaemba
Research *(Chepkoilel Campus) Head*: Samuel Gudu
University-Industry Cooperation *(Chepkoilel Campus) Head*: Paul K. Ndalut

Schools

Business and Management *(Kesses Campus)* (Business Administration; Business and Commerce; Management) *Dean*: H.K. Maritim
Environmental Studies *(Kesses Campus) Dean*: W.K. Yabann

Institutes

Human Resources Development *(Kesses Campus)* (Human Resources) *Director*: P.K. Chepkuto
Public Health (Paramedical Sciences; Public Health) *Dean*: A.K. Chemtai

Centres

Refugees Studies *(Kesses Campus)* (Demography and Population) *Coordinator*: John J. Okumu

History: Founded 1984.

Governing Bodies: Council; Senate

Academic Year: October to July (October-December; January-March; March-July). Undergraduates, September to May (September-January; February-May)

Admission Requirements: Kenya Certificate of Secondary Education (KCSE)

Fees: (K. Shillings): 108,960 per annum

Main Language(s) of Instruction: English

International Co-operation: With Universities in USA, United Kingdom, Germany, Netherlands, South Africa, China.

Degrees and Diplomas: *Bachelor's Degree*: Medicine, 6 yrs; *Bachelor of Arts*: (BA), 4 yrs; *Bachelor of Science*: (BSc), 4 yrs; *Bachelor of Technology*: (BTech), 5 yrs; *Master of Philosophy*: (MPhil), 2 yrs; *Doctor's Degree*: Philosophy (PhD), 3-6 yrs

Student Services: Academic Counselling, Social Counselling, Nursery Care, Cultural Centre, Sports Facilities, Language Programmes, Handicapped Facilities, Health Services, Canteen, Foreign Student Centre

Student Residential Facilities: Yes

Libraries: Margaret Thatcher Library, c. 100,000 vols

Academic Staff 2001-2002	MEN	WOMEN	TOTAL
FULL-TIME	547	108	655
PART-TIME	74	10	84
TOTAL	**621**	**118**	**739**
STAFF WITH DOCTORATE			
FULL-TIME	167	13	180
PART-TIME	11	1	12
TOTAL	**178**	**14**	**192**

Student Numbers 2001-2002	MEN	WOMEN	TOTAL
All (Foreign Included)	4,224	1,808	**6,032**
FOREIGN ONLY	11	2	13

Evening Students, 1,256

*• UNIVERSITY OF NAIROBI

PO Box 30197, University Way, Nairobi
Tel: +254(20) 334-244 +254(20) 332-986
Fax: +254(20) 336-885
Telex: 22095 varsity ke
Cable: varsity, nairobi
Website: http://www.uonbi.ac.ke

Vice-Chancellor: Crispus M. Kiamba (2002-)
Tel: +254(20) 216-030 Fax: +254(20) 212-604
EMail: vc@uonbi.ac.ke

Deputy-Vice-Chancellor (Administration and Finance):
G.A.O. Magoha Tel: +254(20) 336-109
Fax: +254(20) 226-329 EMail: dvcaf@ies.uonbi.ac.ke

International Relations: Kenneth Mavuti, Director
EMail: kmavuti@ics.uonbi.ac.ke

Faculties

Agriculture *(Upper Kabete) Dean*: J.K. Imungi
Architecture, Design and Development (Architecture; Design; Development Studies) *Dean*: P.M. Syagga
Arts (Arts and Humanities) *Dean*: M. Yambo
Commerce (Business and Commerce) *Dean*: J.K. Kenduiwo
Dentistry *Dean*: J.T. Kaimenyi
Education *(Kikuyu) Dean*: G.N. Kimani
Engineering *Dean (Acting)*: D.K. Macoco

225

Law *(Parklands) Dean*: E.M. Nderitu
Medicine *Dean*: J.O. Ndinya-Acholla
Pharmacy *Dean*: A.N. Guantai
Science (Mathematics; Natural Sciences) *Dean*: R.K. Mibey
Social Sciences *Dean*: M. Okoth-Okombo
Veterinary Medicine *(Upper Kabete)* (Veterinary Science) *Dean*: M.M. Kagiko

Schools
Journalism *Director*: L. Odhiambo

Institutes
African Studies *Director*: I.K. Nyamongo
Computer Science *Director*: K.W. Getao
Development Studies *(IDS) Director*: D. McCormick
Diplomacy and International Studies *(IDIS)* (International Relations; International Studies) *Director*: Joshua Olewe-Nyunya
Dryland Research, Development and Utilization *(Upper Kabete)* (Arid Land Studies) *Director*: J.P. Mbuvi
Nuclear Science (Nuclear Engineering) *Director*: D.M. Maina
Population Studies and Research *(PSRI)* (Demography and Population) *Director*: A.B.C. Ocholla Alayo

History: Founded 1956 as Royal Technical College of East Africa, became University College Nairobi 1963 and acquired present status and title 1970. Also branches in Chiromo, Lower Kabete, Upper Kabete, Kikuyu and Parklands.

Governing Bodies: University Senate; University Council; College Academic Boards; College Management Boards; University Management Board

Academic Year: September to June

Admission Requirements: School Certificate or General Certificate of Education (GCE), prior to Higher School Certificate (HSC) or GCE Advanced ('A') level examinations

Fees: (K. Shillings): 80,000-450,000 per annum

Main Language(s) of Instruction: English

Degrees and Diplomas: *Bachelor's Degree*: 4-5 yrs; *Postgraduate Diploma*: Mass Communication; *Master's Degree*: a further 1-3 yrs; *Doctor's Degree*: (PhD), at least 2 yrs

Student Services: Academic Counselling, Social Counselling, Employment Services, Foreign Student Adviser, Cultural Centre, Sports Facilities, Handicapped Facilities, Health Services, Canteen

Student Residential Facilities: Yes

Special Facilities: Biological Garden

Libraries: c. 350,000 vols

Publications: Calendar (1 per annum)

Press or Publishing House: Nairobi University Press

Academic Staff *2001-2002*: Full-Time: c. 435 Part-Time: c. 20 Total: c. 455

Student Numbers *2001-2001*: All (Foreign Included): Men: c. 8,000 Women: c. 3,110 Total: c. 11,110
Foreign Only: Men: c. 10 Women: c. 5 Total: c. 15

Distance Students, c. 1,000

PRIVATE INSTITUTIONS

AFRICA NAZARENE UNIVERSITY (ANU)
PO Box 53067 Ongata Rongal area of Kajiado District, Nairobi
Tel: +254(30) 324-190
Fax: +254(30) 324-352
EMail: registrar@anu.ac.ke
Website: http://www.africanazarene.org

Vice-Chancellor: Leah Marangu (1997-)
Dean of Students: Peter Kangori

Departments
Commerce (Accountancy; Banking; Business and Commerce; Finance; Management; Marketing)
Computer Science
Theology (Religion; Theology)

History: Founded 1993. Acquired present status 2002.

Degrees and Diplomas: *Bachelor's Degree*; *Master's Degree*

* THE CATHOLIC UNIVERSITY OF EASTERN AFRICA (CUEA)
PO Box 62157, City Square, Nairobi, 00200
Tel: +254(20) 891-601 +254(20) 891-606
Fax: +254(20) 891-261
EMail: admin@cuea.edu
Website: http://www.cuea.edu

Vice-Chancellor: John C. Maviiri (2002-)
Tel: +254(20) 890-095 Fax: +254(20) 891-261
EMail: rector@cuea.edu

Deputy Vice-Chancellor (Administration): Francis Muchoki
Tel: +254(20) 891-601 Fax: +254(20) 891-261
EMail: admin@cuea.edu

International Relations: John C. Maviiri, Rector

Faculties
Arts and Social Sciences (Accountancy; Anthropology; Arts and Humanities; Business Administration; Business and Commerce; Computer Science; Economics; Education; Finance; History; Marketing; Mathematics; Philosophy; Political Science; Religious Studies; Social Sciences; Social Work; Sociology) *Dean*: Selline A Oketch Mbewa
Commerce (Business and Commerce) *Dean*: Atheru Kalenywa
Science (Computer Science; Mathematics) *Dean*: Anthony G K Thuo
Theology (Bible; Canon Law; Pastoral Studies; Theology) *Dean (Acting)*: Dieudonné Ngona

History: Founded 1984 as the Catholic Higher Institute of Eastern Africa. Acquired present status and title 1992.

Governing Bodies: University Council; Senate; Management Boards

Academic Year: August to April (August-December; January-April)

Admission Requirements: Kenya Certificate of Secondary Education (KCSE); Kenya Advanced Certificate of Education or equivalent

Fees: (K. Shillings): 130,000 per annum; postgraduate, 152,000

Main Language(s) of Instruction: English

Accrediting Agencies: Commission for Higher Education

Degrees and Diplomas: *Bachelor's Degree*: Business and Commerce (BCom); Religious Studies, 3-4 yrs; *Bachelor of Arts*: Social Sciences; Geography; History; Philosophy; Theology (BA), 3-4 yrs; *Bachelor of Education*: Education (BEd), 3-4 yrs; *Bachelor of Science*: Mathematics; Computer Science (BSc), 3-4 yrs; *Postgraduate Diploma*: Education; Project Planning and Management (PGDE/DPM), 1 yr following Bachelor; *Master's Degree*: Master of Education, Education (MED); Master of Arts, Philosophy; Religious Studies (MA); Theology, a further 2 yrs; *Doctor's Degree*: Philosophy; Theology; Religious Studies (PhD), a further 3 yrs

Student Services: Academic Counselling, Social Counselling, Employment Services, Cultural Centre, Sports Facilities, Language Programmes, Health Services, Canteen

Student Residential Facilities: For c. 160 students

Libraries: Total, 53,130 vols; 11,568 periodicals

Publications: African Christian Studies; C.U.E.A., Eastern Africa Journal of Humanities and Sciences (4 per annum)

Press or Publishing House: Catholic University of Eastern Africa Publications

Academic Staff 2002-2003	MEN	WOMEN	TOTAL
FULL-TIME	83	19	102
PART-TIME	76	14	90
TOTAL	**159**	**33**	**192**
STAFF WITH DOCTORATE			
FULL-TIME	25	2	27
PART-TIME	20	3	23
TOTAL	**45**	**5**	**50**

Student Numbers *2002-2003*: Total: **1,908**

• DAYSTAR UNIVERSITY
PO Box 44400, Nairobi
Tel: +254(20) 732-002 to 004
Fax: +254(20) 728-338
Telex: 22615 worgon
EMail: daystar@maf.or.ke
Website: http://www.daystar.ac.ke/

Vice-Chancellor: Stephen E. Talitwala (1979-)
Tel: +254(20) 720-650 EMail: tibaga@insight.com

Deputy Vice-Chancellor for Academic Affairs: Samuel K. Katia

International Relations: Rosemary Ngige
Tel: +254(20) 717-309

Faculties
Arts (Arts and Humanities; Bible; English; Literature; Mass Communication; Modern Languages; Theology) *Dean*: Faith Nguru
Science and Technology (Computer Science; Electronic Engineering; Technology) *Dean*: Jon Masso

Social Sciences (Accountancy; Business and Commerce; Development Studies; Economics; Education; Information Management; Marketing; Psychology; Social Sciences; Sociology) *Dean*: David Mbiti

Institutes
Christian Ministries and Training *(ICMT)* (Christian Religious Studies; Communication Studies; Development Studies; Management; Missionary Studies; Music; Pastoral Studies) *Director*: Samson Obwa

History: Founded 1984, previously Daystar University College. Acquired present status and title 1994. Also 2 branches in Athi River and Nairobi.

Governing Bodies: Daystar Company and Daystar University Council

Academic Year: August to May

Admission Requirements: Kenya Certificate of Secondary Education grade C+, or equivalent

Fees: (K. Shillings): Tuition, Diploma, c.110,000; undergraduate, c.135,000 ; graduate, c.150,000 per annum

Main Language(s) of Instruction: English

Accrediting Agencies: Commission for Higher Education

Degrees and Diplomas: *Bachelor's Degree*: Accountancy, Business Administration and Management, Economics and Marketing, 4 yrs; *Bachelor of Arts*: Bible and Religious Studies, Communication, Community Development, English and Psychology, 4 yrs; *Bachelor of Education*: Accountancy, Bible and Religious Studies, Business Administration and Management, Economics, English, Marketing, 4 yrs; *Postgraduate Diploma*: Communication Arts, Christian Ministries in Counselling, Christian Ministries in Missions, Christian Music Communication, Management and Development, 2 yrs. Also Minors in most of the undergraduate courses in addition to Music, Mathematics, Peace and Reconciliation

Student Services: Academic Counselling, Social Counselling, Employment Services, Foreign Student Adviser, Sports Facilities, Language Programmes, Health Services, Canteen

Student Residential Facilities: For c. 800 students

Libraries: Main Library, 10,000 vols

Publications: Pespectives, An interdisciplinary Academic Journal (2 per annum)

Academic Staff 2000	MEN	WOMEN	TOTAL
FULL-TIME	62	47	109
PART-TIME	49	22	71
TOTAL	**111**	**69**	**180**
STAFF WITH DOCTORATE			
FULL-TIME	20	6	26
PART-TIME	4	2	6
TOTAL	**24**	**8**	**32**

Student Numbers 2000	MEN	WOMEN	TOTAL
All (Foreign Included)	814	1,139	**1,953**
FOREIGN ONLY	102	122	224

Evening Students, 126

SCOTT THEOLOGICAL COLLEGE (STC)

PO Box 49, Muchakos
Tel: +254(145) 210-86
Fax: +254(145) 213-36
EMail: scott-theol_college@aimint.org

Principal: Jacob Kibor (1999-) EMail: scott-tc@maf.org

Deputy Principal for Academic Affairs: Paul Kisau
Tel: +254(145) 206-33

International Relations: Kioko Mwangangi

Head Librarian: Daniel Rutto Tel: +254(145) 210-86
EMail: scott-tc@maf.org

Programmes
Theology

Departments
Biblical and Theological Studies (Bible; Theology)
Church Ministry and Missions (Missionary Studies; Pastoral Studies) *Head*: Esther Kibor

Institutes
Church Renewal (Christian Religious Studies) *Director*: Richard Gehman

History: Founded 1962, acquired present status and title 1997.

Governing Bodies: Governing Council; Academic Council (Senate); Management Board

Academic Year: September to July

Admission Requirements: Kenya Certificate of Secondary Education (KCSE), C+ or above

Main Language(s) of Instruction: English

Accrediting Agencies: Accreditation Council for Theological Education in Africa (ACETEA); Commission for Higher Education (CHE)

Degrees and Diplomas: *Bachelor's Degree*: Theology (BTh), 4 yrs

Student Services: Academic Counselling, Social Counselling, Foreign Student Adviser, Sports Facilities

Publications: African Journal of Evangelical Theology, Academic Journal (biannually)

Academic Staff 2001-2002	MEN	WOMEN	TOTAL
FULL-TIME	10	3	13
PART-TIME	4	1	5
TOTAL	**14**	**4**	**18**

Student Numbers 2001-2002	MEN	WOMEN	TOTAL
All (Foreign Included)	84	18	**102**
FOREIGN ONLY	10	2	12

UNIVERSITY OF EASTERN AFRICA BARATON

PO Box 2500, Eldoret
Tel: +254(32) 626-25
Fax: +254(32) 622-63
EMail: ueab@tt.gn.apc.org

Vice-Chancellor: Mutuku J. Mutinga (1995-)
Tel: +254(32) 624-70 EMail: 1016632423@compuserve.com

Registrar: Gibson S. Moyo

International Relations: Mutuku J. Mutinga
Tel: +254(32) 624-72 Fax: +254(32) 624-70
EMail: 1016632423@compuserve.com

Schools
Business (Business and Commerce; Home Economics) *Dean*: Habtalem Kenea

Education (Curriculum; Education) *Dean*: Danford Musvosvi

Humanities and Social Sciences (Arts and Humanities; Geography; History; Literature; Modern Languages; Religious Studies; Social Sciences; Theology) *Dean*: Wa-Githumo Mwangi

Science and Technology (Agriculture; Biological and Life Sciences; Mathematics; Natural Sciences; Physics; Technology) *Dean*: Asaph Maradufu

History: Founded 1980. Chartered by the Government 1991. A private institution.

Governing Bodies: University Council

Academic Year: September to September (September-December; January-March; April-June; July-September)

Admission Requirements: Kenya Certificate of Secondary Education (KCSE), with C+ average grade in 8 subjects

Main Language(s) of Instruction: English

Degrees and Diplomas: *Bachelor's Degree*: Business Administration (BBA), 4 yrs; *Bachelor of Arts*: Guidance and Counselling; (BA), 4 yrs; *Bachelor of Science*: (BSc), 4 yrs; *Bachelor of Technology*: (BTech), 4 yrs; *Master's Degree*: Education, 2 yrs

Student Services: Academic Counselling, Social Counselling, Employment Services, Foreign Student Adviser, Sports Facilities, Language Programmes, Health Services, Canteen

Student Residential Facilities: Yes

Libraries: Central Library, c. 45,000 vols

Academic Staff *2001-2002:* Total: c. 60

Student Numbers *2001-2002*: All (Foreign Included): c. 1,100
Foreign Only: c. 170

• UNITED STATES INTERNATIONAL UNIVERSITY (USIU)

PO Box 14634, Nairobi
Tel: +254(20) 3606-000
Fax: +254(20) 3606-100
EMail: admit@usiu.ac.ke
Website: http://www.usiu.ac.ke

Vice-Chancellor: Frieda Brown Fax: +254(20) 862-017
EMail: fbrown@usiu.ac.ke

Administration Manager: Samuel Waweru
EMail: swaweru@usiu.ac.ke

International Relations: Catherine Wambui
EMail: cawambui@usiu.ac.ke

Schools

Arts and Science (Arts and Humanities; International Relations; Journalism; Natural Sciences; Psychology) *Dean*: Mathew Buyu

Business Administration (Business Administration; Hotel and Restaurant; Information Technology; Management; Tourism) *Dean*: Meoli Kashorda

History: Founded 1969.

Governing Bodies: Board of Governors, Management Council, Faculty Senate

Admission Requirements: Kenya Certificate of Secondary Education (KCSE), C+ and above.TOEFL score of 550 and above or Cambridge Certificate of Proficiency for foreign students. Bachelor's Degree for Graduate

Fees: (US Dollars): 1113 per quarter for undergraduates; 968 for graduates

Main Language(s) of Instruction: English

Accrediting Agencies: Commission for Higher Education

Degrees and Diplomas: *Bachelor of Arts*: Counselling Psychology; International Relations; Journalism, 4 yrs; *Bachelor of Science*: Business Administration; Hotel and Restaurant Management; Information Systems and Technology; International Business Administration; Tourism Management, 4 yrs; *Master's Degree*: Business Administration; Counselling Psychology; International Business Administration; International Relations; Management and Organizational Development, a further 2 yrs

Student Services: Academic Counselling, Social Counselling, Employment Services, Foreign Student Adviser, Sports Facilities, Language Programmes, Health Services, Canteen

Student Residential Facilities: Yes

Special Facilities: Computerized teaching labs

Publications: USIU Gazette (quarterly)

Academic Staff *2001-2002*	MEN	WOMEN	TOTAL
FULL-TIME	149	81	**230**
STAFF WITH DOCTORATE			
FULL-TIME	16	6	22
PART-TIME	12	2	14
TOTAL	**28**	**8**	**36**

Student Numbers *2001-2002*	MEN	WOMEN	TOTAL
All (Foreign Included)	1,125	1,219	**2,344**
FOREIGN ONLY	59	66	125

Part-time Students, 408

Lesotho

INSTITUTION TYPES AND CREDENTIALS

Types of higher education institutions:

University
Institute
Polytechnic

School leaving and higher education credentials:

Cambridge Overseas School Certificate
Diploma in Primary Education
Primary Teachers' Certificate
Secondary Teachers' Certificate
Diploma
Bachelor's Degree
Postgraduate Certificate in Education
Master's Degree
Doctorate

STRUCTURE OF EDUCATION SYSTEM

Pre-higher education:

Structure of school system:

Primary
Type of school providing this education: Primary School
Length of programme in years: 7
Age level from: 6 to: 13
Certificate/diploma awarded: Primary School Leaving Examination

Junior Secondary
Type of school providing this education: Junior Secondary School
Length of programme in years: 3
Age level from: 13 to: 16
Certificate/diploma awarded: Junior Certificate Examination

Senior Secondary
Type of school providing this education: High School
Length of programme in years: 2

Age level from: 16 to: 18
Certificate/diploma awarded: Cambridge Overseas School Certificate/GCE "O" levels

School education:

After seven years of primary school which lead to the Primary School Leaving Examination, pupils enter a junior secondary school which offers three years of secondary schooling leading to the Junior Certificate Examination (minimum requirement for admission to craft courses), followed by a two-year course in a senior secondary school leading to the Cambridge Overseas School Certificate. Various home economics and craft schools offer courses for primary school leavers. Two trade schools offer two- or three-year diploma and certificate courses for holders of the Junior Certificate.

Higher education:

Higher education is provided by the National University of Lesotho and its affiliated institutions. It is a public, autonomous institution sponsored primarily by the government. The government has prime responsibility for the development of higher education which is accomplished through legislation. It also controls most of the budget of the University. The objectives of higher education are communicated through national development plans. The University also draws up its own development plan in consultation with the government. The Council is the supreme governing body of the University whose President - Chancellor is the Head of State. Administrative, academic and non-academic staff are represented on the Council and most members are either elected or nominated. There are several foreign members and one university graduate. The Senate is in charge of all academic matters and is composed of academic and senior administrative staff. Both the Council and the Senate have a number of Committees and Boards. All teaching staff have representation in the Senate. Other bodies responsible for academic affairs are the Academic Planning Committee, faculty boards (or advisory boards in the case of institutes), departments and course development committees.

Main laws/decrees governing higher education:

Decree: Education Act   Year: 1971
Concerns: Education system

Academic year:

Classes from: August *to:* May
Long vacation from: 15 May *to:* 15 August

Languages of instruction:

English

Stages of studies:

Non-university level post-secondary studies (technical/vocational type):

Higher technical and vocational education are mainly provided by the Lesotho Agricultural College which offers a three-year Diploma course to holders of the Cambridge Overseas School Certificate; schools of Nursing and a Polytechnic which offers two-year Diploma courses in Civil, Electrical and Mechanical Engineering, Business Studies and Secretarial Studies.

University level studies:

University level first stage: *Diploma, Bachelor's Degree*:

A Diploma is conferred in Theology and Agriculture after two years' study. The Bachelor's Degree is conferred after four years in Arts and Humanities, Science, Commerce and Education, divided into two two-year cycles. In Law, the Bachelor of Law Degree is conferred after obtaining the Bachelor of Arts Degree and a minimum of two years' full-time study.

University level second stage: *Master's Degree*:

The Master's Degree is conferred in Arts (MA) and Science (MSc) after two years' study beyond the Bachelor's Degree. The Master of Education Degree (MEd) is awarded to holders of a Bachelor's Degree in a teaching subject on submission of a thesis and after one year's full-time study and one-and-a-half years' research work or after two years' part-time study and one or two years' research work.

University level third stage: *Doctorate*:

The Doctorate is conferred in Agriculture, Education and the Humanities after a minimum of two years' study beyond the Master's Degree and three years from the Bachelor's Degree. Candidates must submit a thesis and sit for an oral examination.

Teacher education:

Training of pre-primary and primary/basic school teachers

Primary school teachers are trained in three years at the National Teacher Training College (NTTC). The entrance requirement is the Junior Certificate of Secondary Education although, in practice, the Cambridge Overseas School Certificate is required. Studies lead to the Primary Teachers' Certificate (PTC) and to the Diploma in Primary Education.

Training of secondary school teachers

The Secondary Teachers' Certificate for non-specialist teachers of the junior secondary classes is awarded after three years to holders of the Cambridge Overseas School Certificate. The Bachelor of Education Degree, obtained after four years at the University, qualifies teachers for higher secondary classes. Experienced teachers who hold the Primary Teachers' Certificate may obtain the degree after two years. The Secondary Technical Teachers Certificate (STCC) was introduced in 1980 and the Diploma in Technology Education can be obtained by holders of the STCC. The Postgraduate Certificate in Education is a one-year Graduate Certificate.

Training of higher education teachers

The minimum qualifications required to teach in the College are a bachelor's degree in or with education, plus teaching experience of at least three years. Many lecturers, however, now hold a master's degree. It is also envisaged that some of the lecturers should begin to enrol for doctoral studies as a way of improving standards in general.

Non-traditional studies:

Distance higher education

Distance education is provided by the Lesotho Distance Teaching Centre and the Institute of Extra-Mural Studies of the University of Lesotho. The Institute offers short-term courses and off-campus Business studies and Adult Education programmes at certificate and diploma level. The

Lesotho Distance Teaching Centre offers Correspondence courses at the Junior Certificate and COSC levels, Radio programmes, Literacy programmes and plays an important part in the Lesotho In-service Education for Teachers programme which is run in cooperation with the National Teacher Training Centre. It is intended to upgrade the academic and pedagogical skills of primary school teachers and head teachers.

NATIONAL BODIES

Responsible authorities:

Ministry of Education
　　Minister: Archibald Lesao Lehohla
　　Principal Secretary: Chabana Moshapane
　　International Relations: Kekeletso Tsekoa
　　PO Box 47
　　Maseru 100
　　Tel: +266 312-849 +266 315-932
　　Fax: +266 310-297
　　EMail: unescom.sg@education.gov.ls
　　WWW: http://www.lesotho.gov.ls/mneducate.htm

ADMISSIONS TO HIGHER EDUCATION

Admission to non university higher education studies

Name of secondary school credential required: Cambridge Overseas School Certificate

Admission to university-level studies

Name of secondary school credential required: Cambridge Overseas School Certificate
Minimum score/requirement: 1st or 2nd division with credit in English and Mathematics (for science)

Alternatives to credentials: Holders of the General Certificate of Education ('O' level) with at least four passes including English may also gain entrance to the university under certain conditions.

Foreign students admission

Admission requirements: Foreign students must hold qualifications equivalent to those required for entry to the university.

Application procedures:

Apply to individual institution for entry to: University

Apply to: University Admissions Secretariat
　　Roma 180
　　Tel: +266 340-601
　　Fax: +266 340-000

EMail: info@nul.ls
WWW: http://www.nul.ls

Application closing dates:

For university level studies: 1 April
For advanced/doctoral studies: 1 April

Multilateral agreements concerning recognition of foreign studies

Name(s) of agreement(s): Convention on the Recognition of Studies, Certificates, Diplomas, Degrees and Other Qualifications in Higher Education in the African States
Year of signature: 1981

STUDENT LIFE

Student expenses and financial aid

Student costs:

Home students tuition fees: Minimum: 2,000 (Maloti)
Maximum: 3,400 (Maloti)
Foreign students tuition fees: Minimum: 2,000 (Maloti)
Maximum: 10,500 (Maloti)

GRADING SYSTEM

Usual grading system in secondary school

Full Description: Cambridge Overseas School Certificate is graded: 1-9.
Highest on scale: 1
Pass/fail level: 7-8
Lowest on scale: 9

Main grading system used by higher education institutions

Full Description: A-F
Highest on scale: A
Pass/fail level: D
Lowest on scale: F

NOTES ON HIGHER EDUCATION SYSTEM

Data for academic year: 2002-2003
Source: International Association of Universities (IAU), updated from IBE website, 2003
(www.ibe.unesco.org/International/Databanks/Wde/profilee.htm)

INSTITUTIONS OF HIGHER EDUCATION

UNIVERSITIES

PUBLIC INSTITUTIONS

*• NATIONAL UNIVERSITY OF LESOTHO (NUL)
PO 180, Roma, Maseru District
Tel: +266 340-601
Fax: +266 340-000
EMail: info@nul.ls
Website: http://www.nul.ls

Vice-Chancellor: Tefetso Henry Mothibe (2001-2005)
Tel: +266 340-269 Fax: +266 340-702
EMail: th.mothibe@nul.ls;vc@nul.ls

Registrar: Anne Masefinela Mphuthing
EMail: registrar@nul.ls

International Relations: Khoeli Pholosi, Information and Public Relations EMail: kepholosi@nul.ls

Head Librarian: Mampala M. Lebotsa

Faculties

Agriculture *(Maseru)* (Agricultural Economics; Agriculture; Animal Husbandry; Ecology; Natural Resources; Rural Planning) *Dean*: Patrick M. Sutton

Education (Education; Humanities and Social Science Education; Science Education) *Dean*: Matora Ntimo-Makara

Health Sciences *(Roma Campus)* (Health Sciences; Midwifery; Nursing; Nutrition; Pharmacy) *Dean*: Philip O. Odonkor

Humanities *(Roma Campus)* (African Languages; Development Studies; English; French; History; Literature; Philosophy; Theology) *Dean*: M.I. Mokitimi

Law (Private Law; Public Law) *Dean*: W. Kulundu-Bitonye

Postgraduate Studies *Dean*: T.A. Balogun

Science *(Roma Campus)* (Biology; Chemistry; Computer Science; Electronic Engineering; Geography; Mathematics and Computer Science; Physics) *Dean*: K. K. Gopinathan

Social Sciences (Accountancy; Anthropology; Business Administration; Demography and Population; Economics; Geography; Human Resources; Marketing; Political Science; Public Administration; Regional Planning; Social Work; Sociology; Statistics; Urban Studies) *Dean*: M.M. Shale

Institutes

Education *(Roma Campus)* (Documentation Techniques; Education; Educational Research; Information Technology; Teacher Training) *Director*: S.T. Mutlomelo

Extramural Studies (Adult Education; Business Administration; Continuing Education; Management; Media Studies)

Labour Studies *(Maseru)* (Labour and Industrial Relations; Labour Law) *Director*: Sehoai Santho

Southern African Studies (African Studies) *Director*: G. Prasad

History: Founded 1945 as Pius XII College, became University of Basuto land, Bechuana land Protectorate and Swaziland 1964; part of the trinational University of Botswana, Lesotho and Swaziland 1966. Acquired present status 1975.

Governing Bodies: Council; Senate

Academic Year: August to May (August-December; January-May)

Admission Requirements: Cambridge Overseas School Certificate or equivalent, with credit in English

Fees: (Loti): 2000-3400; foreign students, 2000-10,500

Main Language(s) of Instruction: English

Degrees and Diplomas: *Bachelor's Degree*: Arts (BA); Commerce (BCom); Education (BEd); Education (BAEd); Law; Science (BSc); Science in Agriculture (BScAgric); Science with Education (BScEd), 1-4 yrs; *Master's Degree*: Arts (MA); Education (MEd); Laws (LLM); Science (MSc); Social Work (MSW), a further 1-2 yrs; *Doctorate*: (PhD), a further 2-3 yrs

Student Services: Social Counselling, Employment Services, Nursery Care, Sports Facilities, Handicapped Facilities, Health Services, Canteen

Student Residential Facilities: Yes

Special Facilities: Botanical Garden

Libraries: Thomas Mofolo Library, c. 150,000 vols, Roma Campus; IEMS Centre, Maseru, c. 3000 vols

Publications: Review of Southern African Studies; Lesotho Law Journal (biannually); Lesotho Social Science Review (annually); NUL Journal of Research (occasionally); Academic Calendar; NUL Student Law Review

Press or Publishing House: NUL Publishing House

Academic Staff *2001-2002:* Total: c. 350

Student Numbers *2001-2002:* All (Foreign Included): Men: c. 1,000 Women: c. 125 Total: c. 1,125
Foreign Only: Total: c. 135

OTHER INSTITUTIONS

PUBLIC INSTITUTIONS

LESOTHO AGRICULTURAL COLLEGE
Private Bag A4, Maseru 100
Tel: +266 322-484
Fax: +266 400-022
Founded: 1955
Departments
Agriculture Mechanization

Agronomy
Animal Science (Animal Husbandry)
Forestry and Resources Management (Forestry; Natural Resources)
Home Economics
Socio-economics and Quantitative Studies (Economics; Social Studies)

Further Information: Also Campus in Leribe

History: Founded 1955.

Academic Year: August to May

Main Language(s) of Instruction: English

Degrees and Diplomas: *Diploma*: 3 yrs

Liberia

INSTITUTION TYPES AND CREDENTIALS

Types of higher education institutions:

University
University College
Junior College

School leaving and higher education credentials:

West African Examination Council (WAEC) Certificate
Associate Degree
Bachelor's Degree
Master's Degree
Doctorate

STRUCTURE OF EDUCATION SYSTEM

Pre-higher education:

Duration of compulsory education:

Age of entry: 6
Age of exit: 16

Structure of school system:

Primary
Type of school providing this education: Elementary School
Length of programme in years: 6
Age level from: 6 to: 12
Certificate/diploma awarded: School Leaving Certificate Examination (planned)

Junior Secondary
Type of school providing this education: Junior High School
Length of programme in years: 3
Age level from: 12 to: 15
Certificate/diploma awarded: Examination by the West African Examination Council (WAEC)

Senior Secondary
Type of school providing this education: Senior High School
Length of programme in years: 3

Age level from: 15 to: 18
Certificate/diploma awarded: West African Examination Council (WAEC) Certificate

School education:

Elementary education lasts for six years. Secondary education consists of two three-year cycles: three years of Junior secondary (Grades VII-IX) and three years of Senior secondary education (Grades X-XII). At the end of Grade IX, students sit for an examination administered by the West African Examination Council (WAEC). Successful students are eligible to enter Senior High School. Upper secondary education culminates in the WAEC Certificate Examination, which is the basis for access to higher education institutions. An entrance examination is required for access to higher education.

Higher education:

Higher education is provided by universities, colleges of education, business and polytechnics as well as institutions that offer professional courses such as bookkeeping and accounting, architecture, law, medicine, and mass communication. Universities train high-level manpower in various fields. The University of Liberia is given the responsibility for research. The civil war has seriously damaged the University. Over 90% of its facilities were looted or destroyed. Many faculty members fled to other countries, and student enrolment dropped. The Cuttington University College has now reopened. Each tertiary education institution is under the Ministry of Education, the National Commission on Higher Education and the Board of Trustees but sets its own standards.

Academic year:

Classes from: March *to:* December

Long vacation from: 1 January *to:* 28 February

Languages of instruction:

English

Stages of studies:

Non-university level post-secondary studies (technical/vocational type):

Non-university level post-secondary education consists of two-year courses offered by junior colleges leading to the award of an Associate Degree. Other colleges also offer middle-level technical training and Liberal Arts education.

University level studies:

University level first stage: Bachelor's Degree:
The first stage lasts for four years and leads to the award of the Bachelor's Degree. The curricular structure generally provides for the first two years to include basic and general courses, such as English, introductory Physical and Social Sciences, Physical Education and general Mathematics. This is followed by courses in the student's area of specialization. Entry to legal studies requires at least two years' previous higher education; the degree of Bachelor of Laws is awarded after three years of specialization.

University level second stage: *Master's Degree*:
A second stage leads to the Master of Science Degree, awarded by the University of Liberia after two years' graduate study. In Medicine, the Doctorate is conferred after seven years of study.

Teacher education:

Training of pre-primary and primary/basic school teachers
Primary-school teachers are trained at upper secondary level at a Teacher Training Institute. Courses last for three years and lead to a Primary Teacher's Certificate/Grade C Teaching Certificate.

Training of secondary school teachers
A Grade B Teaching Certificate is required to teach in Junior High Schools. Upper Secondary-school teachers are graduates. They are trained at the Teachers' College of the University of Liberia and the Department of Education at Cuttington University College where courses last for four years and lead to a Bachelor's Degree in Education. They may also follow a two-year course leading to a Grade A Teaching Certificate if they already hold a degree in another subject.

Training of higher education teachers
A Master's Degree is required to teach in Colleges of Education, together with a teaching qualification. University teachers must hold a Doctorate.

NATIONAL BODIES

Responsible authorities:

Ministry of Education
 Minister: Evelyn D.S. Kandakai
 Deputy Minister of Education for Administration: Marcus G. Dahn
 International Relations: Peter N. Ben
 PO Box 10-9012
 E.G.V. King Plaza, Broad Street, 4th Floor, Room 413
 Monrovia
 Tel: +231 226-406
 Fax: +231 226-144
 EMail: lnatcomunesco1951@yahoo.com

National Commission on Higher Education
 Ministry of Education
 PO Box 10-9012
 Broad Street, 4th Floor, Room 413
 Monrovia
 Tel: +231 226-406
 Fax: +231 226-144
 EMail: lnatcomunesco1951@yahoo.com

 Role of governing body: Supervises tertiary-level institutions.

ADMISSIONS TO HIGHER EDUCATION

Admission to university-level studies

Name of secondary school credential required: West African Examination Council (WAEC) Certificate

Entrance exams required: Entrance examination.

GRADING SYSTEM

Usual grading system in secondary school

Full Description: Marking is on a percentage scale, the pass mark being 70%.
Highest on scale: 100%
Pass/fail level: 70%
Lowest on scale: 0%

Main grading system used by higher education institutions

Full Description: A=90-100; B=80-89; C=70-79; D=60-69; F=fail
Highest on scale: A
Pass/fail level: D
Lowest on scale: F

NOTES ON HIGHER EDUCATION SYSTEM

Data for academic year: 2002-2003
Source: Liberian National Commission for Unesco, Monrovia and IBE website
(www.ibe.unesco.org/International/Databanks/Wde/profilee.htm), 2003

INSTITUTIONS OF HIGHER EDUCATION

UNIVERSITIES

PUBLIC INSTITUTIONS

• UNIVERSITY OF LIBERIA
PO Box 9020, Capital Hill, Monrovia
Tel: +231(22) 4670
Fax: +231(22) 6418

President: Ben Roberts

Colleges
Agriculture and Forestry (Agriculture; Forestry)
Business and Public Administration (Business and Commerce; Public Administration)
Medicine *(A.M. Douglas)* (Medicine; Pharmacy; Public Health)
Science and Technology (Natural Sciences; Technology)
Social Sciences and Humanities (Arts and Humanities; Political Science; Social Sciences)
Teacher Training *(William V. S. Tubman)* (Education)

Schools
Law *(Louis Arthur-Grimes)*

Departments
Lifelong Education

Institutes
African Studies and Research (African Studies)

History: Founded 1851 as Liberia College, opened 1862. Became university 1951. The institution is responsible to the Ministry of Education and is financed by the State.

Governing Bodies: Faculty Senate; University Council

Academic Year: March to December (March-July; August-December)

Admission Requirements: Secondary school certificate and entrance examination

Fees: (Liberian Dollars): 2800 per annum; 700 per credit

Main Language(s) of Instruction: English

Degrees and Diplomas: *Bachelor's Degree*: Laws (LL.B.), 3 yrs, (4 yrs evening course); Arts (B.A.); Science (B.Sc.), 4 yrs; *Doctorate*: Medicine, 7 yrs

Student Residential Facilities: For c. 420 students

Libraries: c. 108,000 vols

Publications: Liberia Law Journal (biannually); Varsity Pilot; Science Magazine; Journal

Academic Staff *2000-2001:* Total: c. 260

Student Numbers *2000-2001:* Total: c. 3,400

PRIVATE INSTITUTIONS

AFRICAN METHODIST EPISCOPAL UNIVERSITY (AMEU)
PO Box 3340, Camp Johnson Road, Monrovia, Montserrado County
Tel: +231(22) 7964

Head: Louise C. York (1995-) **Tel:** +377 4751-6114
Vice-President for Academic Affairs: Siahe Benson Barh
Tel: +377 4751-5703 **EMail:** barhsay@yahoo.com

Colleges
Biyant Theological Seminary (Religious Education; Theology) *Dean*: E. Topo Johnson
Business and Public Administration (Accountancy; Business and Commerce; Economics; Management; Public Administration) *Dean*: Anselme B. Sao
Liberal Arts and Social Sciences (Arts and Humanities; Social Sciences) *Dean*: Dunalo B. G'dings

History: Founded 1995.

Governing Bodies: Board of Trustees, comprising 21 members

Academic Year: September to July

Admission Requirements: Secondary school certificate, present WAEC certificate and entrance examination

Fees: (Liberian Dollars): Tuition, 187,5 per credit; other fees, 1,8m. per annum. Foreign Students, US $5 per credit and US $76,5 per annum

Main Language(s) of Instruction: English

Accrediting Agencies: Commission of Higher Education and University of Liberia

Degrees and Diplomas: *Bachelor's Degree*: English; Sociology; Political Science; Economics; Theology; Religious Education; Business Administration, 4 yrs

Student Services: Academic Counselling, Social Counselling, Sports Facilities, Language Programmes, Health Services

Special Facilities: Science Laboratory

Publications: Periodic Handbills, Information on current academic events of the university (bimonthly)

Academic Staff 2001-2002	MEN	WOMEN	TOTAL
FULL-TIME	50	3	53
PART-TIME	–	–	7
TOTAL	–	–	**60**
STAFF WITH DOCTORATE			
FULL-TIME	8	1	**9**

Student Numbers 2001-2002	MEN	WOMEN	TOTAL
All (Foreign Included)	727	354	**1,081**
FOREIGN ONLY	18	5	23

Part-time Students, 4

OTHER INSTITUTIONS

PRIVATE INSTITUTIONS

• CUTTINGTON UNIVERSITY COLLEGE (CUC)
PO Box 10-0277, Suacoco, Bond County, Monrovia, 10
Tel: +231(22) 7413
Fax: +231(22) 6059
Website: http://www.cuttington.org
Founded: 1889, 1976

Departments
Education
Humanities (Arts and Humanities)
Nursing *Head*: Cecilia Morris
Science (Biology; Chemistry; Mathematics; Natural Sciences) *Head*: Frankie Cassell
Social Sciences (Accountancy; Business Administration; Business and Commerce; Economics; History; Political Science; Public Administration; Social Sciences) *Head*: John Gornuyer

Institutes
Rural Development (Agriculture; Rural Studies) *Head*: David Kenkpen

History: Founded 1889 as Hoffman Institute. Renamed Cuttington College and Divinity School 1897. Closed 1929 to 1949. Acquired present title 1976. Administered by the Protestant Episcopal Church. Was closed for 9 years and re-opened in 1998.

Governing Bodies: Board of Trustees, of which the Episcopal Bishop is President, and including the Minister of Education

Academic Year: September to July (September-February; March-July)

Admission Requirements: Secondary school certificate or recognized equivalent, and entrance examination

Main Language(s) of Instruction: English

Accrediting Agencies: Commission for Higher Education in Liberia; Association of Episcopal Colleges, USA; Association of African Universities

Degrees and Diplomas: *Bachelor's Degree*: Arts (BA); Science (BSc), 4 yrs. Also Honoris Causa Doctorate

Student Services: Academic Counselling, Social Counselling, Foreign Student Adviser, Sports Facilities, Health Services, Canteen

Student Residential Facilities: Yes

Special Facilities: Africana Collection

Libraries: William V.S. Tubman Library, c.100,000 vols

Publications: Cuttington Research Journal (biannually)

Academic Staff *2001-2002:* Total: c. 65

Student Numbers *2001-2002:* Total: c. 500

Note: Also United Methodist University and African Methodist Episcopal Zion University College.

Libya

INSTITUTION TYPES AND CREDENTIALS

Types of higher education institutions:

University
Higher Institute
Research Centre

School leaving and higher education credentials:

Secondary Education Certificate
Higher Technical Diploma
Bachelor's Degree
Higher Diploma
Master's Degree
Doctorate

STRUCTURE OF EDUCATION SYSTEM

Pre-higher education:

Duration of compulsory education:

Age of entry: 6
Age of exit: 15

Structure of school system:

Basic
Type of school providing this education: Basic School
Length of programme in years: 9
Age level from: 6 to: 15
Certificate/diploma awarded: Basic Education Certificate

Secondary
Type of school providing this education: Intermediate School
Length of programme in years: 4
Age level from: 15 to: 19
Certificate/diploma awarded: Secondary Education Certificate

Vocational Secondary
Length of programme in years: 3

Age level from: 15 to: 18
Certificate/diploma awarded: Intermediate Training Diploma

School education:

Basic education lasts for nine years divided into three cycles and leading to the Basic Education Certificate. It is followed by four years of "intermediate" (secondary) education. Intermediate level education lasts from three to four years and comprises a number of secondary school types: general secondary schools (Science and Arts sections); specialized secondary schools (in Economics, Biology, Arts and Media, Social Sciences and Engineering), teacher training institutes, vocational training centres and sector specialized secondary schools and institutes. Secondary studies last for four years in technical education, three years in general secondary and vocational training schools, and five years in teacher training institutions. Studies lead to the Secondary Education Certificate and to the Intermediate Training Diploma in vocational training centres.

Higher education:

Higher education is offered in Universities, both general and specialized, and higher technical and vocational institutes. These include Teacher Training higher vocational institutes; higher institutes for Technical, Industrial and Agricultural Sciences. Several higher institutes for Teacher Training were founded in 1997. New scientific institutions called Scientific Research Centres have been created in such fields as Health and Pharmacy, Education, the Environment and Basic Sciences. They are both educational and research institutions. The National Authority for Scientific Research is responsible for higher education and research and the University People's Committee, chaired by a Secretary, manages university education. Each Faculty also has a People's Committee, chaired by the Dean and with heads of departments as members. Each university manages its administration and its budget. It is to be noted that the General People's Committee for Education and Vocational Training was dissolved in 2000 and that all responsiblities moved to the municipalities.

Main laws/decrees governing higher education:

Decree: Law 186   Year: 1995
Concerns: Committee for Universities

Decree: Law no. 1 concerning Higher Education   Year: 1992

Academic year:

Classes from: September *to:* June

Languages of instruction:

Arabic, English

Stages of studies:

Non-university level post-secondary studies (technical/vocational type):

Higher vocational and technical education is provided by higher institutes which offer courses of three to five years' duration in such fields as Electricity, Mechanical Engineering, Finance, Computer Studies, Industrial Technology, Social Work, Medical Technology and Civil Aviation. At the end of their studies, graduate technicians are assigned to work in development projects. The qualification awarded after three years is the Higher Technician Diploma; otherwise, after four or five years, the Bachelor's degree is awarded.

University level studies:

University level first stage: Bachelor's Degree:
The Bachelor's Degree is conferred after four to five years' university study (five years in Architecture and Engineering) in universities and higher institutes.

University level second stage: Master's Degree:
A Higher Diploma is conferred after two years' study following the Bachelor's Degree. A Master's Degree (MA or MSc) is conferred after two years' study following the Bachelor's Degree. These programmes are mainly concentrated in the large Universities, such as Garyounis and El-Fateh.

University level third stage: Doctorate:
A Doctorate may be awarded after a further two years of research in such fields as Arabic, Islamic studies and Humanities. The award of this degree is conditional upon the submission of a thesis. Many students are still sent abroad.

Teacher education:

Training of pre-primary and primary/basic school teachers
Basic education teachers are trained in four years in State Higher Teacher Training Institutes after seconday school education. Several centres for in-service training were opened in 1995-96. A training centre was opened to train teachers for intermediate levels.

Training of secondary school teachers
Secondary school teachers are trained in four years at higher education level (Faculty of Education). Teachers at intermediate training centres are graduates of the higher technical institutes.

Training of higher education teachers
MA holders can become assistant lecturers. They can be promoted to lecturer status after three years of teaching. They are promoted to assistant professor status after having taught for four years and submitted three theses evaluated by a scientific committee of three teaching staff members. PhD holders are appointed as lecturers and promoted to assistant professor status after four years of teaching. They are then promoted to joint professor status after four further years of teaching and submission of published scientific theses evaluated by a scientific committee of three teaching staff members. Teachers are promoted to the status of Professor after being a joint Professor and having taught for five years and presented three published theses evaluated as above.

Non-traditional studies:

Distance higher education
Distance education is provided by the Open University, created in 1987. Its main centre is in Tripoli but it has opened branches in Benghazi, Sebha, Ejdabia, Derna, Misurata and El-Kufra. The number of credits needed for graduation is between 120 and 150 credit hours as per the school year system. Curricula and teaching programmes are conveyed via written and audiovisual material (learning package).

Other forms of non-formal higher education
Non-formal studies consist of short postsecondary courses for training paramedical personnel, inspectors of hygiene, etc.

NATIONAL BODIES

Responsible authorities:

National Academy for Scientific Research (NASR)
>   Director-General: Matoug Mohamed Matoug
>   PO Box 12312
>   Tripoli
>   Tel: +218(21) 462-4350
>   Fax: +218(21) 462-3353
>   EMail: nasr@nasrlibya.net
>   WWW: http://www.nasrlibya.net
>   *Role of governing body:* Develop educational content

ADMISSIONS TO HIGHER EDUCATION

Admission to non university higher education studies

Name of secondary school credential required: Secondary Education Certificate

Alternatives to credentials: Intermediate Training Diploma

Admission to university-level studies

Name of secondary school credential required: Secondary Education Certificate
Minimum score/requirement: A minimum of 65% , 75% for Medicine and Engineering
For entry to: Universities

Foreign students admission

Admission requirements: All foreign students should hold the Libyan Secondary Education Certificate or its equivalent, issued in the same or previous year of application. Grade averages required are the following: in scientific fields: medicine 90%, science 80%, engineering and veterinary science 85%, agriculture 80%, economy 80%; in liberal arts: law, art and information 85%, languages 80%, education 80%, social sciences, physical education and sports 75%. The original certificate should be submitted. A coordinating committee undertakes the placement of students admitted to the respective faculties in accordance with their total grades and percentage. Students have to pay the tuition fees fixed by the universities.

Language requirements: Language proficiency is required. The language of instruction for undergraduate studies is Arabic for Humanities and Arabic and English for courses in the Science faculties.

Recognition of studies and qualifications:

Studies pursued in home country (System of recognition/accreditation): Convention on the Recognition of Studies, Diplomas and Degrees in Higher Education in the Arab States, 1978.

Multilateral agreements concerning recognition of foreign studies

Name(s) of agreement(s): Convention on the Recognition of Studies, Diplomas and Degrees in Higher Education in the Arab States
Year of signature: 1978

STUDENT LIFE

Student expenses and financial aid

Student costs:

Home students tuition fees: Minimum: 0 (Libyan Dinar)

GRADING SYSTEM

Usual grading system in secondary school

Full Description: Each subject has minimum and maximum marks appearing on the Certificate (260 for literary subjects with pass at 130; 330 for science subjects with pass at 165)

Main grading system used by higher education institutions

Full Description: 0-100%
Highest on scale: 100%
Pass/fail level: 50%
Lowest on scale: 0%

NOTES ON HIGHER EDUCATION SYSTEM

Data for academic year: 2002-2003
Source: International Association of Universities (IAU), updated from IBE website, 2003
(www.ibe.unesco.org/International/Databanks/Wde/profilee.htm)

INSTITUTIONS OF HIGHER EDUCATION

UNIVERSITIES

• AL-ARAB MEDICAL UNIVERSITY
PO Box 18251, Benghazi
Tel: +218(61) 225-007
Fax: +218(61) 222-195

President: Amer Kahil (1999-)

Head Librarian: Mohammed El Said

Faculties
Dentistry (Dentistry; Surgery)
Medicine (Gynaecology and Obstetrics; Medicine; Ophthalmology; Paediatrics; Surgery)
Pharmacy

Institutes
Medical Technology

Further Information: Also 8 Teaching Hospitals; 2 Medical Centres

History: Founded 1984.

Academic Year: September to May

Admission Requirements: Secondary school certificate or equivalent

Main Language(s) of Instruction: Arabic, English

Degrees and Diplomas: *Bachelor's Degree*: Dental Surgery; Medicine and Surgery, 5-7 yrs; *Higher Diploma*: Community Medicine; Dermatology; Laboratory Medicine; Paediatrics, 1-2 yrs following Bachelor; *Master's Degree*: Anaesthesia; Anatomy; Biochemistry; Dermatology; Histology; Laboratory Medicine; Pathology; Pharmacology; Physiology; Public Health, a further 2-3 yrs; *Doctorate*: a further 2-3 yrs

Student Services: Academic Counselling, Foreign Student Adviser, Cultural Centre, Sports Facilities, Health Services, Canteen

Special Facilities: Anatomy Museum

Libraries: Central Library, c. 30,500 vols

Publications: Garyounis Medical Journal (biannually)

Academic Staff *2001-2002:* Total: c. 300

Student Numbers *2001-2002:* Total: c. 2,000

AL-ASMARIA UNIVERSITY
Zlitin

Faculties
Arabic
Shari'a (Islamic Law)

History: Founded 1997.

• AL-FATEH UNIVERSITY
PO Box 3601381, Tripoli, Sedi El-Masri
Tel: +218(22) 605-441
Fax: +218(22) 605-460
Telex: 20629

Faculties
Agriculture
Arts and Media Studies (Fine Arts; Media Studies)
Economics and Political Science (Economics; Political Science)
Education
Engineering
Languages (Modern Languages)
Science (Mathematics; Natural Sciences; Physics)
Social Sciences

History: Founded 1957 as University of Libya, reorganized as two separate universities in Tripoli and Benghazi, 1973. Under the jurisdiction of the Ministry of Education and financed by the government.

Academic Year: September to June (September-January; February-June)

Admission Requirements: Secondary school certificate or equivalent

Fees: None

Main Language(s) of Instruction: Arabic, English

Degrees and Diplomas: *Bachelor's Degree*: 4-5 yrs; *Master's Degree*: Science (MSc), a further 2 yrs

Libraries: c. 10,000 vols

Academic Staff *2001-2002:* Total: c. 2,000

Student Numbers *2001-2002:* Total: c. 35,000

AL-FATEH UNIVERSITY FOR MEDICAL SCIENCES
PO Box 13040, Tripoli

Faculties
Dentistry
Medical Technology *(Misurata)*
Medicine
Pharmacy

History: Founded 1986.

Academic Year: September to June

Degrees and Diplomas: *Bachelor's Degree*: 3-4 yrs; *Master's Degree*

AL-TAHADI UNIVERSITY
PO Box 674, Sirt
Tel: +218(54) 60636
Fax: +218(54) 62152
EMail: tahdi51@hotmail.com

Faculties
Agriculture
Arts (Fine Arts)
Economics and Political Science (Economics; Political Science)
Engineering
Mechanical and Electrical Engineering *(Hoon)* (Electrical Engineering; Mechanical Engineering)
Medicine
Science *(Misurata)* (Mathematics and Computer Science; Natural Sciences)

History: Founded 1989.

Academic Year: September to July

BRIGHT STAR UNIVERSITY OF TECHNOLOGY
PO Box 858, Mersa-El-Brega
Tel: +218(64) 23012 +218(61) 240-851
Fax: +218(21) 600-185

Chancellor: Ali Saleh Elfazzani

Head Librarian: Ibrahim Mohamed Amir

Departments
Chemical Engineering
Electrical and Electronic Engineering (Computer Science; Electrical and Electronic Engineering)
Materials Engineering
Mechanical Engineering
Petroleum Engineering (Petroleum and Gas Engineering)

History: Founded 1981.

Academic Year: October to June

Main Language(s) of Instruction: Arabic, English

Academic Staff *2001-2002:* Total: c. 80

Student Numbers *2001-2002:* Total: c. 1,200

DERNA UNIVERSITY
Derna

Faculties
Accountancy and Economics (Accountancy; Economics)
Electrical and Mechanical Engineering (Electrical Engineering; Mechanical Engineering)
Fine Arts and Architecture (Architecture; Fine Arts)
Law
Medical Technology
Social Sciences

History: Founded 1995.

Academic Year: September to July

Main Language(s) of Instruction: Arabic, English

NASIR UNIVERSITY
PO Box 48222, Tripoli
Tel: +218(325) 660-080
Fax: +218(325) 660-048

Faculties
Arts (Fine Arts)
Economics and Political Science (Economics; Political Science)
Education and Science (Education; Natural Sciences)
Engineering
Law
Science (Natural Sciences)

History: Founded 1986.

OMAR-AL-MUKHTAR UNIVERSITY
PO Box 991, Al-Bayda
Tel: +218(84) 6310-719
Fax: +218(84) 632-233
EMail: info@omulibya.org
Website: http://www.omulibya.org

President: Abdalla A. M. Zaied Tel: +218(84) 631-541
Fax: +218(84) 631-549 EMail: zaied@omulibya.org

Faculties
Agriculture
Engineering
Literature and Education (Education; Literature)
Science (Natural Sciences)
Veterinary Medicine (Veterinary Science)

History: Founded 1985.

Academic Year: September to July

THE OPEN UNIVERSITY
PO Box 13375, Tripoli
Tel: +218(21) 462-5507
Fax: +218(21) 462-5527

President: Ibrahim Abu-Farwa Fax: +218(21) 462-5507

Vice-President: Emhamed El-Harma
Tel: +218(21) 462-5501

Departments
Accountancy
Administration
Arabic
Economics
Education and Psychology (Education; Psychology)
Geography
History
Islamic Studies
Law

Political Science
Sociology and Social Work (Social Work; Sociology)

History: Founded 1987.

Academic Year: September to July

Admission Requirements: Secondary school certificate

Fees: (Libyan Dinar) 100 per annum + 10 per subject

Main Language(s) of Instruction: Arabic

Degrees and Diplomas: *Bachelor's Degree*: Law, Geography, History, Islamic Studies, Arabic, Sociology, Education, Economics, Administration, Accountancy, Political Science (BA, BSc), 4 yrs. Curricula and teaching programmes, both theoretical and applied, are via written and audiovisual material.

Student Services: Academic Counselling, Handicapped Facilities

Academic Staff 2001-2002	MEN	WOMEN	TOTAL
FULL-TIME	20	2	22
PART-TIME	25	–	25
TOTAL	**45**	**2**	**47**
STAFF WITH DOCTORATE			
FULL-TIME	17	2	19
PART-TIME	20	–	20
TOTAL	**37**	**2**	**39**

Student Numbers 2001-2002: Total: **16,027**

• SEBHA UNIVERSITY
PO Box 18758, Sebha
Tel: +218(71) 21575
Fax: +218(71) 29201
EMail: alfahary@yahoo.com

Chancellor: Abu Bakr Abdullah Otman

Assistant Director, Cultural Cooperation Office:
Mohammed Lawan Tel: +218(71) 26012
Fax: +218(71) 29201 EMail: lawan52@yahoo.com

Head Librarian: Zidan Al-Breiky

Faculties
Agriculture
Economics and Accountancy *(Merzig)* (Accountancy; Economics)
Education *(Obari)*
Engineering and Technology *(Brak)* (Engineering; Technology)
Law
Medicine
Physical Education *(For men, Ghat)*
Science (Mathematics and Computer Science; Natural Sciences)

History: Founded 1983, incorporating the Faculty of Education of the University of Al-Fateh.

Academic Year: October to August.

Admission Requirements: Secondary school certificate

Main Language(s) of Instruction: Arabic, English

Degrees and Diplomas: *Bachelor's Degree*: 3-4 yrs; *Master's Degree*; *Doctorate*: (PhD)

Student Residential Facilities: Yes

Libraries: Central Library, c. 110,000 vols

Academic Staff 2001-2002: Total: c. 280

Student Numbers 2001-2002: Total: c. 3,000

• SEVENTH OF APRIL UNIVERSITY
PO Box 16418, Al-Zawia
Tel: +218(23) 26882
EMail: 7april_univ@mail.lttnet.net

Faculties
Economics and Accountancy (Accountancy; Economics)
Education
Engineering
Physical Education *(For women)*
Science (Natural Sciences)

History: Founded 1988.

Academic Year: September to July

Main Language(s) of Instruction: Arabic, English

• UNIVERSITY OF GARYOUNIS
PO Box 1308, Benghazi
Tel: +218(61) 20148   +218(61) 25007
Fax: +218(61) 20051
Telex: (0901) 40175
EMail: info@garyounis.edu
Website: http://www.garyounis.edu

Faculties
Arts and Education (Arabic; Education; Educational Administration; English; French; Geography; History; Information Sciences; Library Science; Media Studies; Philosophy; Psychology; Sociology)
Economics (Accountancy; Business Administration; Economics; Political Science; Statistics)
Engineering (Civil Engineering; Electrical Engineering; Engineering; Industrial Engineering; Mechanical Engineering; Town Planning)
Law (Administrative Law; Commercial Law; Criminal Law; International Law; Islamic Law; Law; Private Law)
Medicine and Dentistry (Anaesthesiology; Anatomy; Biochemistry; Community Health; Dentistry; Dermatology; Forensic Medicine and Dentistry; Gynaecology and Obstetrics; Histology; Laboratory Techniques; Medicine; Microbiology; Ophthalmology; Paediatrics; Parasitology; Pathology; Pharmacology; Physiology; Psychiatry and Mental Health; Radiology; Surgery)
Science (Astronomy and Space Science; Botany; Chemistry; Geology; Mathematics; Mathematics and Computer Science; Physics; Statistics; Zoology)

Research Centres
Social and Economic Sciences (Economics; Social Sciences)

History: Founded 1955 as University of Libya, reorganized as two separate Universities in Benghazi and Tripoli, 1974.

Acquired present name 1976. Under the jurisdiction of the Ministry of Education and financed by the government.

Governing Bodies: University Council

Academic Year: October to June (October-January; February-June)

Admission Requirements: Secondary school certificate or equivalent

Fees: None

Main Language(s) of Instruction: Arabic, English

Degrees and Diplomas: *Bachelor's Degree*: 4 yrs; *Higher Diploma*; *Master's Degree*; *Doctorate*

Student Residential Facilities: Yes

Libraries: c. 295,000 vols

Publications: Arts; Faculty Journals; Law; Economics (annually)

Academic Staff *2001-2002:* Total: c. 600

Student Numbers *2001-2002:* Total: c. 15,000

Evening Students, c. 4,050

UNIVERSITY OF MORAGAB
PO Box 40414-40397, Ain Zara
Tel: 218(31) 629-365
Fax: 218(31) 629-366

Faculties
Economics *(Zlaitin)*
Education and Science (Education; Science Education)
Education and Science *(Tarhuna)* (Education; Science Education)
Engineering
Law *(Tarhuna)*
Literature and Education *(Zlaitin)* (Education; Literature)

History: Founded 1987 as Nasser University.

OTHER INSTITUTIONS

• FACULTY OF ISLAMIC CALL (FIC)
PO Box 71771, Tariq Assawani, Tripoli
Tel: +218(21) 480-0167 +218(21) 480-1473
Fax: +218(21) 480-0059
EMail: mu_dyab@yahoo.com

Programmes
Arabic; Islamic Studies

Further Information: Branches at Damascus, Syria, Beirut, Lebanon and N'Djamena, Chad

HIGHER INSTITUTE OF CIVIL AVIATION
Sebha

Programmes
Civil Aviation (Air Transport)

HIGHER INSTITUTE OF COMPUTER TECHNOLOGY
PO Box 6289, G.S.P.L.A.J, Tripoli
Tel: +218(21) 480-0413
Fax: +218(21) 480-0199
Founded: 1990

Divisions
Training (Business Computing; Computer Education) *Head*: Kes Housen

Departments
Computer Engineering (Computer Engineering; Software Engineering)
Software Engineering (Computer Engineering; Data Processing; Maintenance Technology; Software Engineering) *Head*: Moftah Algorni

Admission Requirements: High school certificate

Fees: None

Main Language(s) of Instruction: Arabic, English

Student Services: Academic Counselling, Social Counselling, Employment Services, Sports Facilities, Canteen

Libraries: Central Library, fullly computerized with internet facilities

Academic Staff *2001-2002*: Full-Time: c. 30 Part-Time: c. 85 Total: c. 115

Staff with Doctorate: Total: c. 30

Student Numbers *2001-2002*: All (Foreign Included): c. 1,850 Foreign Only: c. 50

HIGHER INSTITUTE OF ELECTRICITY
Benghazi

Programmes
Electricity (Electrical Engineering)

HIGHER INSTITUTE OF ELECTRONICS
PO Box 8645, Beni Walid/Souk Jin
Founded: 1976

Programmes
Electronics (Electronic Engineering)

HIGHER INSTITUTE OF FINANCE AND ADMINISTRATION
Benghazi
Administration; Finance

HIGHER INSTITUTE OF FINANCE AND ADMINISTRATION
Gadames

Administration; Finance

HIGHER INSTITUTE OF FINANCE AND ADMINISTRATION
Tripoli

Programmes
Administration; Finance

HIGHER INSTITUTE FOR GENERAL VOCATIONS
Derna

HIGHER INSTITUTE FOR GENERAL VOCATIONS
El-Bayda

HIGHER INSTITUTE FOR GENERAL VOCATIONS
Garyan

HIGHER INSTITUTE FOR GENERAL VOCATIONS
Misurata

HIGHER INSTITUTE FOR GENERAL VOCATIONS
Nalut

HIGHER INSTITUTE FOR GENERAL VOCATIONS
Sebha

HIGHER INSTITUTE FOR GENERAL VOCATIONS
Surman

HIGHER INSTITUTE OF INDUSTRIAL TECHNOLOGY
Misurata
Industrial Technology (Industrial Engineering)

HIGHER INSTITUTE OF INDUSTRIAL TECHNOLOGY
Tripoli

Programmes
Industrial Engineering

HIGHER INSTITUTE OF MECHANICAL AND ELECTRICAL ENGINEERING
PO Box 61160, Hon
Tel: +218 2154
Telex: 30254

Founded: 1976
Mechanical and Electrical Engineering (Electrical Engineering; Mechanical Engineering)

HIGHER INSTITUTE FOR MECHANICAL VOCATIONS
Benghazi
Mechanics (Mechanical Engineering)

HIGHER INSTITUTE FOR MECHANICAL VOCATIONS
Tripoli
Mechanics (Mechanical Engineering)

HIGHER INSTITUTE OF MEDICAL TECHNOLOGY
Tripoli

Programmes
Medical Technology

HIGHER INSTITUTE OF SOCIAL WORK
Benghazi

Programmes
Social Work

HIGHER INSTITUTE OF TECHNOLOGY
PO Box 68, Brack
Tel: +218 45300
Founded: 1976

Departments
Environmental Sciences (Environmental Studies)
Food (Food Science)
General Sciences (Natural Sciences)
Medical Technology

INDUSTRIAL SAFETY TRAINING INSTITUTE
Tripoli

Programmes
Industrial Safety (Safety Engineering)

Madagascar

INSTITUTION TYPES AND CREDENTIALS

Types of higher education institutions:

Université (University)
Ecole normale (Teacher Training College)
Institut supérieur technique (Higher Technical Institute)

School leaving and higher education credentials:

Baccalauréat de l'Enseignement secondaire
Baccalauréat de l'Enseignement technique
Diplôme universitaire de Technicien supérieur (DUTS)
Diplôme d'Etudes universitaires générales (DEUG)
Diplôme d'Etudes universitaires littéraires (DEUL)
Diplôme d'Etudes universitaires scientifiques (DEUS)
Diplôme d'Etudes universitaires technologiques (DUET)
Certificat d'Aptitude pédagogique (CAPEN)
Licence
Diplôme d'Ingénieur
Docteur en Chirurgie dentaire
Maîtrise
Diplôme d'Etudes supérieures spécialisées (DESS)
Doctorat en Médecine
Diplôme d'Etudes approfondies (DEA)
Diplôme d'Etudes supérieures (DES)
Doctorat de troisième Cycle
Doctorat Ingénieur
Doctorat d'Etat

STRUCTURE OF EDUCATION SYSTEM

Pre-higher education:

Duration of compulsory education:

Age of entry: 6
Age of exit: 11

Structure of school system:

Primary
Type of school providing this education: Ecole primaire
Length of programme in years: 5
Age level from: 6 to: 11
Certificate/diploma awarded: Certificat d'Etudes primaires élémentaires (CEPE)

First Cycle Secondary
Type of school providing this education: Collège d'Enseignement général or technique
Length of programme in years: 4
Age level from: 11 to: 15
Certificate/diploma awarded: Brevet d'Etudes du premier Cycle (BEPC)

Technical Secondary
Type of school providing this education: Lycée d'Enseignement technique
Length of programme in years: 3
Age level from: 15 to: 18
Certificate/diploma awarded: Baccalauréat de l'Enseignement technique

Second Cycle Secondary
Type of school providing this education: Lycée d'Enseignement général
Length of programme in years: 3
Age level from: 15 to: 18
Certificate/diploma awarded: Baccalauréat de l'Enseignement secondaire

School education:

Primary education is compulsory and lasts for five years, leading to the Certificat d'Etudes primaires élémentaires (CEPE). Secondary education then covers seven years divided into a four-year first cycle and a three-year second cycle. On completion of the first cycle of secondary education in a general or technical Collège, pupils obtain the Brevet d'Etudes du premier Cycle (BEPC). On completion of the second cycle, pupils obtain the Baccalauréat de l'Enseignement secondaire. Pupils not wishing to proceed to university may take only the four-year lower cycle programme. Technical secondary education lasts for three years, also divided into two cycles. At the end of the three-year upper cycle they obtain the Baccalauréat de l'Enseignement technique.

Higher education:

Higher education is mainly provided by universities, higher technical institutes and teacher training colleges. The universities are autonomous institutions. Each university is headed by a Rector and administered by a Conseil d'Administration. In January 1999, a National Evaluation Agency (Agence nationale d'Evaluation (Agenate)) was created to evaluate the public and private institutions of higher education. Higher education is administered by the Ministère de l'Enseignement supérieur et de la Recherche scientifique with the help of the Conférence des Présidents ou des Recteurs d'Institutions d'Enseignement supérieur publiques et privées (COPRIES).

Main laws/decrees governing higher education:

Decree: Décret n°95-681   Year: 1995
Concerns: Organization of private higher education

Decree: Directive 92-030   Year: 1992
Concerns: Foundation of universities

Academic year:

Classes from: October *to:* July

August September

Languages of instruction:

French, Malagasy

Stages of studies:

Non-university level post-secondary studies (technical/vocational type):

Higher technical studies lead, after three years of post-secondary education, to the Brevet de Technicien supérieur.

University level studies:

University level first stage: *Premier Cycle*:
The first stage of higher education comprises a two-year broad-based multidisciplinary course common to all students wishing to study Letters, Science, Law, Economics, Management and Sociology. Students have to obtain a minimum number of credit units at the end of each year and then obtain the Diplôme universitaire d'Etudes littéraires (DUEL) in Humanities, the Diplôme universitaire d'Etudes scientifiques (DUES) in Science, the Diplôme universitaire d'Etudes technologiques or the Diplôme universitaire de Technicien supérieur en Informatique and the Diplôme de Fin d'Etudes du premier Cycle en Droit, Economie et Sociologie. It is foreseen that the first two years of the first cycle of studies will be extended to three years, including in Medicine.

University level second stage: *Deuxième Cycle*:
A year of specialization leads to the Licence. The Maîtrise is conferred after one year's further study beyond the Licence. If students successfully present a short thesis they are awarded the Maîtrise d'Enseignement. The Diplôme d'Ingénieur is conferred after five years' study. The title of Docteur en Chirurgie dentaire is conferred at the end of five years' study. Studies in Medicine last for seven years (plus one year of hospital practice) and lead to the Doctorat de Médecine.

University level third stage: *Troisième Cycle*:
A Diplôme d'Etudes approfondies is conferred one year after the Maîtrise. A Diplôme d'Etudes supérieures (DES) may be conferred after two years' study following upon the Maîtrise. Presentation of a thesis then leads to the Doctorat de troisième Cycle after a minimum of one year's further study beyond the Diplôme d'Etudes approfondies and research work. A Certificat d'Etudes spécialisées (CES) is to be introduced in Medicine and post-university studies in Humanities, Social Sciences and Technical Sciences will be reinforced. A Doctorat Ingénieur is offered to engineers four years after graduating.

University level fourth stage:
A Doctorat d'Etat is now being offered by the University of Antananarivo.

Teacher education:

Training of pre-primary and primary/basic school teachers
Primary school teachers are trained in Ecoles normales d'Instituteurs in courses lasting for two years and five months. Candidates must hold the Brevet d'Etudes du Premier Cycle (BEPC), but this requirement will be upgraded to the Baccalauréat.

Training of secondary school teachers
Collège secondary school teachers usually hold the Baccalauréat and have three years of higher education training. For the second cycle of secondary education (lycées), training takes place at one of the Ecoles normales supérieures within the universities. Access is via a competitive examination and training lasts for five years. Technical education teachers are trained in the Ecole normale supérieure de l'Enseignement technique or in one of the Institut supérieur de Technologie (IST).

Non-traditional studies:

Distance higher education
Distance education courses are provided in Law and Management by the Centre national de Télé-Enseignement (CNTEMAD).

NATIONAL BODIES

Responsible authorities:

Ministry of Higher Education and Scientific Research (Ministère de l'Enseignement supérieur et de la Recherche scientifique)
    Minister: Hajanirina Razafinjatovo
    Secrétaire général: Adolphe Rakotomanga
    International Relations: Jean-Claude Andriamaharo
    PO Box 4163
    Antananarivo 101
    Tel: +261(20) 22-271-85 +261(20) 22-211-09
    Fax: +261(20) 22-238-97
    EMail: spensup@syfed.refer.mg
    WWW: http://www.refer.mg/madag_ct/edu/minesup

    Role of governing body: Oversee national higher education policy.

Universities Communication Centre (Maison de la Communication des Universités)
    Directeur général: Michel Norbert Rejela
    Directeur administratif et financier: John Guy Patrice
    International Relations: Lantoniaina Ralaimidona
    BP 7559
    Antananarivo 101

Tel: +261(20) 22-693-48
Fax: +261(20) 22-692-84

ADMISSIONS TO HIGHER EDUCATION

Admission to non university higher education studies

Name of secondary school credential required: Baccalauréat de l'Enseignement technique

Admission to university-level studies

Name of secondary school credential required: Baccalauréat de l'Enseignement technique
Minimum score/requirement: 10/20

Name of secondary school credential required: Baccalauréat de l'Enseignement secondaire
Minimum score/requirement: 10/20

Entrance exams required: entrance examination

Foreign students admission

Admission requirements: Foreign students must hold the Baccalauréat or an equivalent qualification.

Entry regulations: They must hold a visa and be officially presented by the competent authorities of their country.

Language requirements: Good knowledge of French.

Recognition of studies and qualifications:

Studies pursued in foreign countries (bodies dealing with recognition of foreign credentials):
Ministry of Higher Education and Scientific Research (Ministère de l'Enseignement supérieur et de la Recherche scientifique)
PO Box 4163
Antananarivo 101
Tel: +261(2022) 27185 +261(2022) 21109
Fax: +261(2022) 23897
Telex: 22539 mrstd
EMail: spensup@syfed.refer.mg
WWW: http://www.refer.mg/madag_ct/edu/minesup

References to further information on foreign student admissions and recognition of studies

Title: Livret de l'étudiant
Publisher: Université d'Antananarivo

Title: Présentation de l'Université de Madagascar et renseignements pratiques
Publisher: Université de Madagascar

STUDENT LIFE

Main student services at national level

Centre régional des Oeuvres universitaires
Université d'Antananarivo, Campus universitaire Ambohitsaina, PO Box 354
Antananarivo 101
Tel: +261(20) 22-241-14   +261(20) 22-211-03
Fax: +261(20) 22-256-87
WWW: http://www.univ-antananarivo.mg

Student expenses and financial aid

Student costs:

Average living costs: 600,000 (Malagasy Franc)
Home students tuition fees: Minimum: 50,000 (Malagasy Franc)
Maximum: 200,000 (Malagasy Franc)

Bodies providing information on student financial aid:

Service de l'Orientation, de l'Information, des Bourses et des Etudiants
Université d'Antananarivo, PO Box 566
Ambohitsaina
Antananarivo 101
Tel: +261(20) 22- 241-14
Fax: +261(20) 22-256-87
WWW: http://www.univ-antananarivo.mg

GRADING SYSTEM

Usual grading system in secondary school

Full Description: 0-20
Highest on scale: 20
Pass/fail level: 10
Lowest on scale: 0

Main grading system used by higher education institutions

Full Description: 0-20
Highest on scale: 20
Pass/fail level: 10
Lowest on scale: 0

Other main grading systems

For thesis: passable: 10-12; assez bien: 12-14; bien 14-16; très bien: 16-18; très honorable: 18 or more.

NOTES ON HIGHER EDUCATION SYSTEM

Data for academic year: 2002-2003

Source: Ministère de l'Enseignement supérieur, Antananarivo, updated by the International Association of Universities (IAU) from IBE website, 2003 (www.ibe.unesco.org/International/Databanks/Wde/profilee.htm)

INSTITUTIONS OF HIGHER EDUCATION

UNIVERSITIES AND UNIVERSITY LEVEL INSTITUTIONS

PUBLIC INSTITUTIONS

*• UNIVERSITY OF ANTANANARIVO
Université d'Antananarivo
BP 566, Ambohitsaina, Antananarivo 101
Tel: +261(20-22) 24114   +261(20-22) 21103
Fax: +261(20-22) 25687
Telex: 22304 recumt mg
EMail: recunivtana@simicro.mg
Website: http://www.univ-antananarivo.mg

Recteur: Pascal Rakotobe (2002-) Tel: +261(20-22) 32639
Fax: +261(20-22) 27926
EMail: presidence@univ-antananarivo.mg

Administrative Officer: Roger Andrianasy

International Relations: Liliane Ramarosoa, Vice-Président
Tel: +261(20-22) 29917
EMail: lramarosoa@univ-antananarivo.mg

Faculties
Arts and Humanities (Arts and Humanities; English; French; Geography; German; History; Literature; Modern Languages; Philosophy) *Dean:* G. Rabearimanana
Law, Economics, Administration and Sociology *(DEGS)* (Administration; Economics; Law; Sociology) *Dean:* Rado Rakotoarison
Medicine (Gynaecology and Obstetrics; Medicine; Paediatrics; Surgery) *Dean:* Pascal Rakotobe
Science (Chemistry; Mathematics; Natural Sciences; Physics) *Dean:* M. Rafazy-Andriamampianima

Schools
Agronomy (Agricultural Engineering; Agricultural Management; Agriculture; Agronomy; Animal Husbandry; Food Technology; Forestry; Water Management) *Director:* Daniel Razakanindriana

History: Founded 1955 as Institut des hautes Etudes tracing origins to School of Medicine (1896) and School of Law (1941). Became Université de Madagascar 1960. Reorganized 1973 with six main divisions, and 1976 as a decentralized institution with six Regional Centres. Acquired present status as independent university 1988.

Governing Bodies: Administration Council

Academic Year: October to July (October-February; March-July)

Admission Requirements: Secondary school certificate (baccalauréat) or equivalent, and entrance examination

Main Language(s) of Instruction: French, Malagasy

International Co-operation: With Institutions in Algeria, Belgium, Canada, France, Germany, Italy, La Réunion, Netherlands, South Africa, Switzerland, United Kingdom and USA

Degrees and Diplomas: *Diplôme d'Etudes universitaires littéraires (DEUL):* 2 yrs; *Diplôme d'Etudes universitaires scientifiques (DEUS):* 2 yrs; *Diplôme d'Etudes universitaires technologiques (DUET):* 2 yrs; *Licence:* 1 further yr; *Diplôme d'Ingénieur:* 4 yrs; *Maîtrise:* 1yr following Licence; *Doctorat en Médecine:* 7 yrs; *Diplôme d'Etudes approfondies (DEA):* 1yr following Maîtrise; *Diplôme d'Etudes supérieures (DES):* 2 yrs following Maîtrise; *Doctorat de troisième Cycle; Doctorat d'Etat.* Also teaching qualifications

Student Residential Facilities: Yes

Special Facilities: Museum of Art and Archaeology. Institute of Civilizations

Libraries: c. 120,000 vols

Publications: Revue de Géographie; Terre Malgache, Sciences Agronomiques; Omaly Sy Anio (Hier et Aujourd'hui)

Academic Staff *2001-2002:* Total: c. 635

Student Numbers *2001-2002:* Total: c. 14,100

GEOPHYSICAL INSTITUTE AND OBSERVATORY OF ANTANANARIVO
INSTITUT ET OBSERVATOIRE GEOPHYSIQUE D'ANTANANARIVO
BP 3843 Ambohidempona, Campus Universitaire,
Antananarivo 101
Tel: +261(20-22) 25353
Fax: +261(20-22) 25353
EMail: ioga@syfed.refer.mg

Directeur: Jean-Bruno Ratsimbazafy

Departments
Geophysics

History: Founded 1989.

HIGHER PEDAGOGICAL SCHOOL
ECOLE NORMALE SUPÉRIEURE
BP 881, Antananarivo 101
Fax: +261(20-22) 35584
EMail: ens@syfed.refer.mg;ens@dts.mg

Directeur: William R. Ratrema

Departments
Education
Teacher Training

History: Founded 1980. acquired present status 1994.
Academic Staff *2001-2002:* Total: c. 75
Student Numbers *2001-2002:* Total: c. 650

HIGHER POLYTECHNIC
ECOLE SUPÉRIEURE POLYTECHNIQUE
BP 1500, Vontovorona, Antananarivo 101
Tel: +261(20-22) 29490
Fax: +261(20-22) 27696

Directeur: Benjamin Randrianoelina

International Relations: Nicole Ravelomanantsoa

Departments

Building Technology and Civil Engineering (Building Technologies; Civil Engineering)
Chemical Engineering
Electrical Engineering
Electronic Engineering
Geology
Hydraulic Engineering
Materials Engineering and Metallurgical Engineering (Materials Engineering; Metallurgical Engineering)
Mechanical Engineering
Meteorology
Mining Engineering
Surveying and Mapping
Telecommunications Engineering
Town Planning and Urban Studies (Town Planning; Urban Studies)

History: Founded 1975. Acquired present status 1994.

INSTITUTE OF CIVILIZATIONS, MUSEUM OF ART AND
ARCHAEOLOGY
INSTITUT DES CIVILISATIONS, MUSÉE D'ART ET
D'ARCHÉOLOGIE
BP 564, 17 rue Docteur Villette, Isoraka, Antananarivo 101
EMail: icmaa@dts.mg

Directeur: Jean-Aimé Rakotoarisoa

Anthropology; Archaeology; Arts and Humanities; Cultural Studies; Ethnology; Folklore; Geography; History; Musicology; Prehistory

History: Founded 1964.

INSTITUTE OF ENERGY STUDIES
INSTITUT POUR LA MAÎTRISE DE L'ENERGIE
BP 566, Ambohitsaina, Antananarivo 101
Tel: +261(20-22) 30953
Fax: +261(20-22) 22316
EMail: enertech@dts.mg

Directeur: Edmond Razafindrakoto

Energy Engineering; Thermal Engineering

History: Founded 1977.

NATIONAL CENTRE OF ENGLISH TEACHING
CENTRE NATIONAL D'ENSEIGNEMENT DE LA LANGUE
ANGLAISE
BP 109, Antananarivo 101
Tel: +261(20-22) 26028
Fax: +261(20-22) 66462

Directeur: M. Rasoloheritsimba

Centres
English Teaching (Foreign Languages Education)

History: Founded 1985.

RADIO-ISOTOPES LABORATORY
LABORATOIRE DE RADIO-ISOTOPES
BP 3383, Antananarivo 101
Tel: +261(20-22) 40488
EMail: lrililia@dts.mg

Directeur: Jean-Rubis Andriantsoa

Nuclear Medicine and Biology (LRI) (Biology; Medical Technology)

History: Founded 1956.

• UNIVERSITY OF ANTSIRANANA
Université Nord Madagascar (UNA)
BP 0, Antsiranana 201
Tel: +261(20-82) 29409   +261(20-82) 21137   +261(20-82) 21483
Fax: +261(20-82) 29409
EMail: unm@dts.mg
Website:
http://www.refer.mg/madag_ct/madag_ct/edu/minesup/antsiran/antsiran

Présidente: Cécile Marie Ange Manorohanta-Dominique (2002-) EMail: rec.unm@dts.mg;cmanoroh@dts.mg

Directeur Administratif: Aly Ahmad Tel: +261(20-82) 22095

International Relations: Alex Totomarovario
EMail: atotomar@syfed.refer.mg

Faculties
Arts and Humanities (Arts and Humanities; Modern Languages) *Dean:* Jean de Dieu Kalobotra
Science (Chemistry; Natural Sciences; Physics) *Director:* Hiviel Tsiresena Riziky

History: Founded 1975 as Regional Centre of the Université de Madagascar. Acquired present status as independent university 1992.

Governing Bodies: Board of Governors

Academic Year: November to July

Admission Requirements: Secondary school certificate (baccalauréat) or equivalent, and entrance examination

Main Language(s) of Instruction: French

Degrees and Diplomas: *Diplôme d'Etudes universitaires littéraires (DEUL):* Language Studies, 2 yrs; *Diplôme d'Etudes universitaires scientifiques (DEUS):* Physics/Chemistry, 2 yrs;

Diplôme d'Etudes universitaires technologiques (DUET): 2 yrs; *Certificat d'Aptitude pédagogique (CAPEN)*: Teacher Training, 5 yrs; *Licence*: 3 yrs; *Diplôme d'Ingénieur*: 5 yrs; *Maîtrise*: 4 yrs; *Diplôme d'Etudes approfondies (DEA)*: Technology, a further 2 yrs; *Doctorat Ingénieur*: Engineering, 4 yrs. Also teaching qualifications

Student Services: Academic Counselling, Cultural Centre, Sports Facilities, Health Services

Student Residential Facilities: For c. 1000 students

Libraries: Bibliothèque universitaire, 13,000 vols

Academic Staff 2001-2002	MEN	WOMEN	TOTAL
FULL-TIME	55	8	63
PART-TIME	–	–	29
TOTAL	–	–	92
STAFF WITH DOCTORATE			
FULL-TIME	34	3	37
PART-TIME	–	–	13
TOTAL	–	–	50

Student Numbers 2001-2002	MEN	WOMEN	TOTAL
All (Foreign Included)	608	200	808
FOREIGN ONLY	–	–	31

HIGHER POLYTECHNIC
ECOLE SUPÉRIEURE POLYTECHNIQUE
BP 0, Antsiranana 201
Tel: +261(20-82) 21137, Ext. 49
EMail: antenais@syfed.refer.mg

Directeur: Chrysostôme Raminosoa (2002-2005)

Departments
Electrical Engineering
Electronic Engineering
Hydraulic Engineering
Mechanical Engineering

History: Founded 1977. Acquired present status 1994.

TEACHER TRAINING COLLEGE FOR TECHNICAL STUDIES
ECOLE NORMALE SUPÉRIEURE POUR L'ENSEIGNEMENT TECHNIQUE
BP, Antsiranana 201
Tel: +261(20-82) 21137, Ext. 50
Fax: +261(20-82) 29409

Directeur: Tsirobaka Rabe (2002-2005)

Departments
Electrical Engineering (Electrical Engineering; Technology Education)
Mathematics and Computer Science (Mathematics and Computer Science; Mathematics Education)
Mechanical Engineering

History: Founded 1991. Acquired present status 1994.

*• UNIVERSITY OF FIANARANTSOA

Université de Fianarantsoa (UF)
BP 1264, Fianarantsoa 301
Tel: +261(20-75) 50802
Fax: +261(20-75) 50619
EMail: ufianara@syfed.refer.mg
Website:
http://www.refer.mg/madag_ct/madag_ct/edu/minesup/fianaran/fianaran

Recteur: Marie Dieu Donné Michel Razafindrandriatsimaniry (2002-) Tel: +261(20-75) 51091

Directeur administratif: Dominique Razafimanampy
Tel: +261(20-75) 51092

International Relations: Alphonsine Rasoanirina

Faculties
Law *Dean*: Patrice Goussot
Science (Chemistry; Mathematics and Computer Science; Natural Sciences; Physics; Social Sciences) *Dean*: Tsilavo Mandresy Razafindrazaka

History: Founded 1977 as Regional Centre of the Université de Madagascar. Acquired present status as independent University 1988.

Academic Year: October to June

Admission Requirements: Secondary school certificate (baccalauréat) or equivalent, and entrance examination

Fees: (Malagasy francs-MGF) 1st Cycle, 50,000-90,000; 2nd Cycle, 60,000-90,000; 3rd Cycle, 100,000-200,000

Main Language(s) of Instruction: French, Malagasy

International Co-operation: With universities in France, United States, Indian Ocean

Degrees and Diplomas: *Diplôme universitaire de Technicien supérieur (DUTS)*: Environmental Sciences; Computer Sciences; *Diplôme d'Etudes universitaires générales (DEUG)*: 2 yrs; *Diplôme d'Etudes universitaires scientifiques (DEUS)*: Mathematics; Physics and Chemistry; Mathematics and Computing for Social Sciences, 2 yrs; *Certificat d'Aptitude pédagogique (CAPEN)*: Pedagogy; *Licence*: Mathematics; Physics and Chemistry; Mathematics and Computing for Social Sciences, 3 yrs; *Diplôme d'Ingénieur*: 4 yrs; *Maîtrise*: Mathematics; Physics and Chemistry; Mathematics and Computing for Social Sciences, 4 yrs; *Diplôme d'Etudes supérieures spécialisées (DESS)*: Training for Adult Education, 5 yrs; *Diplôme d'Etudes approfondies (DEA)*: Law; Physics; Environmental Sciences, 5 yrs; *Diplôme d'Etudes supérieures (DES)*: Law (DEJSC), 5 yrs

Student Services: Cultural Centre, Sports Facilities, Language Programmes, Health Services

Academic Staff *2001-2002*: Full-Time: c. 70 Part-Time: c. 95 Total: c. 165

Staff with doctorate: Full-Time: c. 25 Part-Time: c. 35 Total: c. 60

Student Numbers 2001-2002	MEN	WOMEN	TOTAL
All (Foreign Included)	1,100	760	1,860

HIGHER PEDAGOGICAL SCHOOL
ECOLE NORMALE SUPÉRIEURE
BP 1264, Fianarantsoa 301
Tel: +261(20-75) 50812
Fax: +261(20-75) 50619
EMail: ufianara@syfed.refer.mg

Directeur: Roger Ratovonjanahary

Departments
Mathematics
Physics

INSTITUTE OF ENVIRONMENTAL TECHNIQUES AND SCIENCES
INSTITUT DES SCIENCES ET TECHNIQUES DE L' ENVIRONNEMENT
BP 1264, Fianarantsoa 301
Tel: +261(20-75) 50812
Fax: +261(20-75) 50619

Directeur: Pascal Ratalata

Environmental Studies

NATIONAL SCHOOL OF COMPUTER SCIENCE
ECOLE NATIONALE D'INFORMATIQUE
BP 1487, Tanambao, Fianarantsoa 301
Tel: +261(20-75) 50801
Fax: +261(20-75) 50619
EMail: eni@syfed.refer.mg

Directeur: Josvah Paul Razafimandimby

Computer Science

History: Founded 1980. Acquired present status 1983.

* UNIVERSITY OF MAHAJANGA
Université de Mahajanga
BP 652, Immeuble Kakal, 5 rue Georges V, Mahajanga 401
Tel: +261(20-62) 22724
Fax: +261(20-62) 23312
EMail: recifmaj@dts.mg
Website:
http://www.refer.mg/madag_ct/madag_ct/edu/minesup/mahajang/mahajang

Recteur: Andrianaivo Ralison (2003-)
Tel: +261(20-62) 23312

Directeur Administratif: Jeanette Razafindralinina

Faculties
Medicine
Science (Biochemistry; Biology; Botany; Chemistry; Earth Sciences; Environmental Studies; Natural Sciences)

History: Founded 1977 as Regional Centre of the Université de Madagascar. Acquired present status as independent University 1992.

Academic Year: November to July

Admission Requirements: Secondary school certificate (baccalauréat) or equivalent, and entrance examination

Main Language(s) of Instruction: French, Malagasy

Degrees and Diplomas: *Diplôme d'Etudes universitaires littéraires (DEUL)*: 2 yrs; *Diplôme d'Etudes universitaires scientifiques (DEUS)*: 2 yrs; *Diplôme d'Etudes universitaires technologiques (DUET)*: 2 yrs; *Licence*: 1 further yr; *Diplôme d'Ingénieur*: 4 yrs; *Maîtrise*: 1 further yr; *Doctorat en Médecine*: 7 yrs; *Diplôme d'Etudes approfondies (DEA)*: 1 further yr; *Diplôme d'Etudes supérieures (DES)*: a further 2 yrs; *Doctorat de troisième Cycle*. Also teaching qualifications

Student Numbers: Total: c. 1,300

INSTITUTE OF TROPICAL DENTISTRY
INSTITUT D'ODONTO-STOMATOLOGIE TROPICALE
BP 453, Mahajanga 401
Tel: +261(20-62) 22834
EMail: cdrom@dts.mg

Directrice: Noëline Razanamihaja

Institutes
Tropical Dentistry (Dentistry; Stomatology)

*• UNIVERSITY OF TOAMASINA
Université de Toamasina
BP 591, Barikadimy, Toamasina 501
Tel: +261(20-53) 32244
Fax: +261(20-53) 33566
EMail: univtoam@dts.mg
Website: http://www.univ-toamasina.mg/

Président: Roger Rajaonarivelo (2003-)
Tel: +261(20-53) 32454

Directeur administratif: Rachelle Bienvenue Radifison

Faculties
Arts and Humanities *Director:* Jacques Randrianatoandro
Economics and Management (Economics; Management) *Director:* Raymond Kasave

Higher Schools
National Customs (Cultural Studies)

Centres
Applied Modern Language Studies (Modern Languages) *Director:* Germain F. Davidson
Computer-Aided Management (Management) *Director:* Paul Henri Alex
Entrepreneurship Training (Management) *Director:* Ernest Marinasy
Environment and Integrated Development (Development Studies; Environmental Studies; French; Geography; History; Philosophy)
Foreign Languages (Modern Languages) *Director:* Germain Franck Davidson

History: Founded 1977 as Regional Centre of the Université de Madagascar. Acquired present status as independent University 1992.

Governing Bodies: Board of Trustees

Academic Year: October to June

Admission Requirements: Secondary school certificate (baccalauréat) or equivalent, and entrance examination

Fees: (Malagasy Francs-MGF): 25,000-30,000 per annum

Main Language(s) of Instruction: French, Malagasy

Degrees and Diplomas: *Diplôme d'Etudes universitaires générales (DEUG):* 2 yrs; *Diplôme d'Etudes universitaires littéraires (DEUL):* 2 yrs; *Licence:* 1 further yr; *Diplôme d'Ingénieur.* 4 yrs; *Maîtrise:* 1 yr following Licence; *Diplôme d'Etudes approfondies (DEA):* 1 further yr; *Diplôme d'Etudes supérieures (DES):* a further 2 yrs

Special Facilities: Archaeological and Cultural Museum

Libraries: Management Library, 5000 vols; Letters, 4600 vols

Academic Staff *2001-2002:* Total: **54**

Student Numbers *2001-2002:* Total: c. 3,400

UNIVERSITY OF TOLIARA
Université de Toliara
BP 185, Maninday, Toliara 601
Tel: +261(20-94) 41773
EMail: rectul@syfed.refer.mg;rectul@dts.mg
Website:
http://www.refer.mg/madag_ct/madag_ct/edu/minesup/toliara/toliara

Recteur: M. Theodoret (2003-)

Directeur administratif et financier: Dimby Vaovolo

International Relations: Jean Riel

Faculties
Arts and Humanities (Arts and Humanities; French; Geography; History; Literature; Philosophy) *Dean:* Marc Joseph Razafindrakoto
Science (Biology; Chemistry; Earth Sciences; Natural Sciences; Physics) *Dean:* Hery Anteniaia Razifimandimby

History: Founded 1977 as Regional Centre of the Université de Madagascar. Acquired present status as independent University 1988.

Academic Year: November to July

Admission Requirements: Secondary school certificate (baccalauréat) or equivalent, and entrance examination

Main Language(s) of Instruction: French, Malagasy

Degrees and Diplomas: *Diplôme d'Etudes universitaires littéraires (DEUL):* 2 yrs; *Diplôme d'Etudes universitaires scientifiques (DEUS):* 2 yrs; *Diplôme d'Etudes universitaires technologiques (DUET):* 2 yrs; *Licence:* 1 further yr; *Diplôme d'Ingénieur.* 4 yrs; *Maîtrise:* 1 further yr; *Diplôme d'Etudes approfondies (DEA):* 1 further yr; *Diplôme d'Etudes supérieures (DES):* a further 2 yrs; *Doctorat de troisième Cycle.* Also teaching qualifications

Libraries: Calvin Tiesbo Library, 8000 vols

DOCUMENTATION AND RESEARCH CENTRE FOR ART AND ORAL TRADITIONS OF MADAGASCAR
CENTRE DE DOCUMENTATION ET DE RECHERCHE SUR L'ART ET LES TRADITIONS ORALES À MADAGASCAR
BP 185, Toliara 601
Tel: +261(20-9) 41033
Fax: +261(20-9) 41802

Directeur: M. Tsiazonera

Centres
Arts and Oral Traditions (Ethnology; Fine Arts)

History: Founded 1985.

HIGHER PEDAGOGICAL SCHOOL
ECOLE NORMALE SUPÉRIEURE
BP 185, Maninday, Toliara 601
Tel: +261(20-94) 41773
Fax: +261(20-94) 41802

Directeur: Jean Rakotoarivelo

Departments
Philosophy

INSTITUTE OF MARINE SCIENCE
INSTITUT D'HALIEUTIQUE ET DES SCIENCES MARINES
BP 141, Toliara 601
Tel: +261(20-94) 41612
Fax: +261(20-94) 41612
EMail: ihsm@syfed.syfed.refer.mg

Directeur: Man Wai Rabenievanana

Departments
Aquaculture
Fishery
Safety Engineering

History: Founded 1986.

NATIONAL INSTITUTE OF NUCLEAR SCIENCES AND TECHNIQUES
Institut national des Sciences et Techniques nucléaires (Madagascar-INSTN)
BP 4279, Antananarivo 101
Tel: +261(20-22) 61181
Fax: +261(20-22) 35583
EMail: instn@dts.mg
Website: http://www.refer.mg/madag_ct/edu/minesup/organe

Directeur général: Raoelina Andriambololona
Tel: +261(20-22) 61180

Directeur administratif et financier: Chrysante Solofoarisina

International Relations: Joël Rajaobelison

Departments
Energy Engineering *Head:* Bienvenu Ramanana

Maintenance and Nuclear Instrumentation (Maintenance Technology; Nuclear Engineering) *Head*: Hery Andrianiaina
Nuclear Analysis and Techniques (Nuclear Engineering) *Head*: Naivo Rabesiranana
Radiation Protection and Dosimetry (Safety Engineering) *Head*: Francis Ratovonjanahary
Theoretical Physics (Physics) *Head*: Roland Raboanary
XRF Techniques and Environment (Environmental Engineering) *Head*: Lucienne Randriamanivo

History: Founded 1976 as Laboratory for Nuclear and Applied Physics (L.P.N.P.A.). Acquired present status and title 1992. A public autonomous institution.

Governing Bodies: Board of Governors

Academic Year: October to September

Admission Requirements: Baccalauréat scientifique for two-year cycle leading to technician in radiation protection; Maîtrise ès Sciences for post-graduate study

Fees: (Malagasy Francs-MGF): 50,000

Main Language(s) of Instruction: French, English

Accrediting Agencies: International Atomic Energy Agency

Degrees and Diplomas: *Diplôme d'Etudes approfondies (DEA)*: Nuclear Physics, 2 yrs; *Doctorat de troisième Cycle*: Nuclear Physics, 3-5 yrs; *Doctorat d'Etat*: Nuclear Physics, 4-7 yrs. Also Diplôme de Technicien Supérieur (DTS) in Radiation Protection

Student Services: Academic Counselling, Employment Services, Foreign Student Adviser, Sports Facilities, Language Programmes

Libraries: Raoelina Andriambololona Library

Publications: Raoelina Andriambololona Interdisciplinary Seminar; Journal des Sciences et Techniques Nucléaires

Press or Publishing House: Publishing Unit

Academic Staff *2001-2002*	TOTAL
FULL-TIME	10
PART-TIME	35
TOTAL	**45**
STAFF WITH DOCTORATE	
FULL-TIME	7
PART-TIME	5
TOTAL	**12**

Student Numbers *2001-2002:* Total: c. 35

Dean: Germain Rajoelison EMail: ucm@dts.mg
General Secretary: Laurent Razafindrazaka

Faculties
Social Sciences (Economics; Law; Management; Political Science)

Schools
Management *(ESSVA)* (Communication Studies; Management; Tourism) *Director*: Donat Andiramparany

Departments
Philosophy *Head*: Simon Zafisoratra
Theology *Head*: Charles Ratongavao

History: Founded 1960, acquired present status and title 1997.

Admission Requirements: Secondary school certificate (Baccalauréat) and entrance examination.

Fees: (Malagasy francs-MGF): Undergraduate, 875,000 per annum; graduate, 1.05m.

Main Language(s) of Instruction: French

International Co-operation: With universities in France, USA

Degrees and Diplomas: *Diplôme d'Etudes universitaires générales (DEUG)*: Social Sciences, 2 yrs; *Maîtrise*: Social Sciences, 4 yrs

Student Services: Academic Counselling, Sports Facilities, Health Services, Canteen

Student Residential Facilities: No

Libraries: Yes

Publications: Aspect du Christianisme à Madagascar, Theological review (quarterly); Collection - ISTA - ICM Antananarivo, Publishes studies in anthropology, social sciences, theology (biannually)

Academic Staff *2002-2003*	MEN	WOMEN	TOTAL
FULL-TIME	18	35	53
PART-TIME	141	86	227
TOTAL	**159**	**121**	**280**
STAFF WITH DOCTORATE			
FULL-TIME	7	2	9
PART-TIME	13	–	13
TOTAL	**20**	**2**	**22**
Student Numbers *2002-2003*	MEN	WOMEN	TOTAL
All (Foreign Included)	390	659	**1,049**

PRIVATE INSTITUTIONS

CATHOLIC INSTITUTE OF MADAGASCAR
Institut Catholique de Madagascar (ICM)
BP 6059, Ambatoroka, Antananarivo 101
Tel: +261(20-22) 34009
Fax: +261(20-22) 34013
EMail: ucm@dts.mg
Website: http://takelaka.dts.mg/ucm/

ST FRANÇOIS D'ASSISE SCHOOL OF NURSING
ECOLE D'INFIRMIERS(ÈRES) ST FRANÇOIS D'ASSISE
BP 7002, Antananarivo 101

Directeur: Angelina De Nobrega Baptista

Departments
Nursing (Nursing; Pharmacology; Psychology)

History: Founded 1993.

SOCIAL SERVICE SCHOOL
ECOLE DE SERVICE SOCIAL
BP 7570, 133 Avenue Lénine, Antanimena, Antananarivo 101

Departments

Social Sciences (Social and Community Services; Social Sciences)

OTHER INSTITUTIONS

PUBLIC INSTITUTIONS

HIGHER INSTITUTE OF TECHNOLOGY, ANTANANARIVO

Institut Supérieur de Technologie (IST)
BP 8122, Ampasapito, Antananarivo 101
Tel: +261(20-22) 41423
Fax: +261(20-22) 40543

Directeur général: Josoa Ramamonjisoa

Directeur administratif et financier: Antoine Razafindramanana

Founded: 1989, 2001

Departments

Civil Engineering
Industrial Engineering
Tertiary Studies

History: Founded 1989. Acquired present status 2001.

HIGHER INSTITUTE OF TECHNOLOGY, ANTSIRANANA

Institut supérieur de Technologie (IST)
BP 453, Antsiranana 201
Tel: +261(20-82) 22431
Fax: +261(20-82) 29425
Website: http://www.refer.mg/madag-ct/edu/diego/ist.htm

Directeur général: Fortunat Ramahatandrina
Directeur Administratif et financier: Ederaly
International Relations: Dominique Rakoto

Founded: 1989, 2001

Departments

Maintainance Technology (Maintenance Technology)
Tertiary Studies

History: Founded 1989. Acquired present status 2001.

266

NATIONAL DISTANCE LEARNING CENTRE OF MADAGASCAR

Centre national de Télé-Enseignement de Madagascar (CNTEMAD)
BP 78, Antananarivo 101
Tel: +261(20-22) 60057
Fax: +261(20-22) 36090
EMail: cntemad@syfed.refer.mg

Directeur: Norbert Ralison Tel: +261(20-22) 60386

Directeur des Affaires Générales: Jacques Roland Rakotondrasanjy Tel: +261(20-22) 64563

Founded: 1992

Centres

Law and Administration (Administration; Law)

History: Founded 1992

NATIONAL INSTITUTE OF ACCOUNTANCY AND BUSINESS ADMINISTRATION, ANTANANARIVO

Institut national des Sciences comptables et de l'Administration d'Entreprises, Antananarivo
BP 946, Antananarivo 101
Tel: +261(20-22) 28444
Fax: +261(20-22) 30895

Directeur général: Victor Harison

Directeur Administration et Finances: François Marie M. Rakotoarimanana

Departments

Accountancy
Business Administration

NATIONAL SCHOOL OF ADMINISTRATION

Ecole nationale d'Administration
BP 1163, Antananarivo
Tel: +261(20-22) 42091
Fax: +261(20-22) 31815

Directeur: Falitiana Randriamiariso

Departments

Administration

PRIVATE INSTITUTIONS

HIGHER CHRISTIAN STUDIES IN MANAGEMENT AND APPLIED MATHEMATICS

Hautes Etudes Chrétiennes du Management et de Mathématiques appliquées (HECMMA)
BP 7686 Ancien Bâtiment Ennet Ltd Alarobia, Antananarivo 101
Tel: +261(20-22) 29863
EMail: rasoloar@dts.mg
Website:
http://www.refer.mg/edu/minesup/prive/hecmma/heaccue.htm
Founded: 1997

Departments
Economics and Political Science (Economics; Political Science)
Engineering
Management and Applied Mathematics in Economics (Applied Mathematics; Economics; Management)

HIGHER INSTITUTE OF BUSINESS, COMMUNICATION AND MANAGEMENT

Institut supérieur de la Communication, des Affaires et du Management (ISCAM)
BP 8224, Ankadifotsy, Antananarivo 101
Tel: +261(20-22) 22488
Fax: +261(20-22) 25543
EMail: iscam@bow.dts.mg
Website:
http://www.refer.mg/madag_ct/edu/minesup/prive/iscam/iscam.htm

Directeur général: Douglas Rambelo

Founded: 1992, 1994

Programmes
Business Administration
International Commerce (Business and Commerce; International Business)
Sales Techniques
Tourism

Malawi

INSTITUTION TYPES AND CREDENTIALS

Types of higher education institutions:

University
College
Polytechnic

School leaving and higher education credentials:

Malawi School Certificate of Education
Teacher's Certificate
Diploma
Bachelor's Degree
Master's Degree
Doctor's Degree

STRUCTURE OF EDUCATION SYSTEM

Pre-higher education:

Duration of compulsory education:

Age of entry: 5
Age of exit: 13

Structure of school system:

Primary
Type of school providing this education: Primary School
Length of programme in years: 8
Age level from: 5 to: 13
Certificate/diploma awarded: Primary School Leaving Certificate Examination (PSLCE)

Junior Secondary
Type of school providing this education: Secondary School
Length of programme in years: 2
Age level from: 13 to: 15
Certificate/diploma awarded: Junior Certificate Examination (JCE)

Senior Secondary
Type of school providing this education: Secondary School
Length of programme in years: 2

Age level from: 15 to: 17
Certificate/diploma awarded: Malawi School Certificate of Education (MSCE)

School education:

Primary education lasts for eight years, organized into three cycles (Infant, Junior and Senior). It leads to the Primary School Leaving Certificate which is mostly used to access secondary education. Secondary education lasts for four years, divided into two stages of two years' duration. At the end of the second year, pupils take the Junior Certificate Examination. Successful students may enter form III. At the end of form IV, pupils take the Malawi School Certificate of Education.

Higher education:

Higher education is provided by the University of Malawi and its constituent colleges. The University is governed by a Council, most of whose members are appointed by the Government. The Senate, composed of academics, is responsible for academic matters. It is mainly supported by government grants and miscellaneous income. The Government has opened the Mzuzu University to train secondary school teachers.

Academic year:

Classes from: September *to:* July

Languages of instruction:

English

Stages of studies:

Non-university level post-secondary studies (technical/vocational type):

Technical and training colleges offer courses in such fields as Forestry, Marine Science, Social Welfare and Hotel Management, as well as in various trades. These courses lead to certificates awarded after studies lasting between six months and four years.

University level studies:

University level first stage: Bachelor's Degree:
The Bachelor's Degree is generally conferred after five to six years' study. A professional qualification is awarded as a Diploma after three years' study.

University level second stage: Master's Degree:
A Master's degree or a professional qualification is conferred after one to two years' study beyond the Bachelor's Degree.

University level third stage: Doctor's Degree:
The Doctor's Degree is conferred after three to five years' study beyond the Master's Degree. Candidates must submit a thesis and spend at least six months in residence.

Teacher education:

Training of pre-primary and primary/basic school teachers
Primary school teachers are trained in primary teacher training colleges. Teachers obtain the T2 (senior primary) or T3 (junior primary) Teachers Certificate after one year's study. T2 colleges admit

students with the Malawi School Certificate of Education (MSCE) and T3 colleges admit students with the Junior Certificate Examination (JCE). The Malawi Institute of Education provides introduction courses to give school-leavers the basic skills to act as "assistant" or "pupil teachers".

Training of secondary school teachers
Secondary school teachers are trained at Chancellor College which offers a four-year educational programme and at a college of education for secondary school teachers at Domasi in Zomba. The fifth year consists of professional studies and teaching practice. The course leads to a Bachelor of Education degree. Technical teachers are trained jointly at the Polytechnic and Chancellor College. The Government has opened the Mzuzu University which now trains secondary school teachers.

NATIONAL BODIES

Responsible authorities:

Ministry of Education, Science and Technology
  Minister: George Mtafu
  Principal Secretary: Z.D. Chikhosi
  Private Bag 328
  Lilongwe 3
  Tel: +265 784-800
  Fax: +265 782-873

  Role of governing body: Government Ministry

ADMISSIONS TO HIGHER EDUCATION

Admission to university-level studies

Name of secondary school credential required: Malawi School Certificate of Education
Minimum score/requirement: Excellent results in subjects the candidate wishes to study.

Entrance exams required: Entrance examination to the University

Foreign students admission

Admission requirements: Foreign students should hold qualifications equivalent to the Malawi School Certificate of Education with two of the six credits in English and Mathematics.

Entry regulations: Foreign students must be in possession of a visa. Confirmation of admission to the university must be obtained prior to departure as well as an entry permit from the Chief Immigration Officer, Box. 331, Blantyre.

Language requirements: Good knowledge of English for regular university courses.

Application procedures:

Apply to individual institution for entry to: University

Apply to: The Registrar, University of Malawi
    PO Box 278
    Zomba
    Tel: +265 526-622
    Fax: +265 524-760
    EMail: university.office@unima.mw
    WWW: http://www.unima.mw

STUDENT LIFE

Student expenses and financial aid

Student costs:

    Home students tuition fees: Minimum: 40,000 (Malawi Kwacha)
    Maximum: 92,000 (Malawi Kwacha)
    Foreign students tuition fees: Minimum: 3,000 (US Dollar)

GRADING SYSTEM

Usual grading system in secondary school

Full Description: The Malawi Certificate of Education is graded 1-9.
Highest on scale: 1
Pass/fail level: 7,8
Lowest on scale: 9

Main grading system used by higher education institutions

Full Description: 0-100%
Highest on scale: 100%
Pass/fail level: 50-59%
Lowest on scale: 0%

NOTES ON HIGHER EDUCATION SYSTEM

Data for academic year: 2002-2003
Source: University of Malawi, Zomba, updated by the International Association of Universities (IAU) from IBE website, 2003 (www.ibe.unesco.org/International/Databanks/Wde/profilee.htm)

INSTITUTIONS OF HIGHER EDUCATION

UNIVERSITIES

PUBLIC INSTITUTIONS

MZUZU UNIVERSITY
Private Bag 1, Luwinga, Mzuzu 2
Tel: +265 333-575
Fax: +265 333-497
EMail: mzuni@sdnp.org.mw
Website: http://www.mzuzu.leland-mw.org

Vice-Chancellor: Peter Mwanza (2000-)
EMail: gola@sdnp.org.mw

Registrar: Reginald M. Mushani Fax: +265 333-568
EMail: rmushani@sdnp.org.mw

International Relations: Reginald M. Mushani

Faculties
Education (Continuing Education; Humanities and Social Science Education; Literature; Mathematics; Modern Languages; Natural Sciences; Science Education; Teacher Training) *Dean*: Mzoma R. Ngulube
Environmental Sciences (Environmental Engineering; Forestry) *Dean*: Mzoma R. Ngulube

History: Founded 1997.

Governing Bodies: Council

Academic Year: January to October (January-June; June-October)

Admission Requirements: Malawi Certificate of Education or equivalent

Fees: (Kwacha): Undergraduate, 43,200 per annum; foreign students, 92,500

Main Language(s) of Instruction: English

Degrees and Diplomas: *Bachelor's Degree*: Science (Forestry); Science (Health Science Education), 2 yrs; Arts (Education); Science (Education), 4 yrs; *Master's Degree*; *Doctor's Degree*

Academic Staff 2001-2002	MEN	WOMEN	TOTAL
FULL-TIME	34	5	39
PART-TIME	10	1	11
TOTAL	**44**	**6**	**50**
STAFF WITH DOCTORATE			
FULL-TIME	5	1	6
PART-TIME	4	1	5
TOTAL	**9**	**2**	**11**

Student Numbers 2001-2002	MEN	WOMEN	TOTAL
All (Foreign Included)	271	74	**345**

*• UNIVERSITY OF MALAWI (UNIMA)
PO Box 278, Zomba
Tel: +265 526-622
Fax: +265 524-297
EMail: university.office@unima.mw
Website: http://www.unima.mw/

Vice-Chancellor: David Rubadiri (2000-2004)
Tel: +265 524-305 Fax: +265 524-297 +265 524-760
EMail: vc@sdnp.org.mw

Registrar: Ben W. Malunga Tel: +265 524-754

International Relations: Nita Chivwara Tel: +265 526-561
Fax: +265 524-760

Faculties
Agriculture *(Lilongwe) Dean*: D. Kanyama-Phiri
Applied Studies *(Blantyre) Dean*: C.R. Mtogolo
Commerce *(Blantyre)* (Business and Commerce) *Dean*: B.J.B. Chiodezka
Education *(Chanco) Dean*: F.G.W. Msiska
Education *Dean*: O.J. Kathamalo
Engineering *(Blantyre) Dean*: V.H. Chipofya
Humanities (Arts and Humanities) *Dean*: H.F. Chidammodzi
Law *Dean*: G. Kamchedzera
Medicine *(Blantyre) Dean*: O.O. Komolafe
Nursing *(Lilongwe) Dean*: S.I. Kachingwe
Science (Natural Sciences) *Dean*: M. Palamuleni
Social Sciences *Dean*: P. Kishindo

Units
Agricultural Policy Research (Agronomy)
Gender Studies

Centres
Educational Research and Training (Educational Research) *Director*: J.P.G. Chimombo
Language Studies (Linguistics) *Director*: Alfred Mtenje
Management *(Blantyre) Director*: J. Kamwachale-Khomba
Social Research (Social Studies) *Director*: S.W. Khaila

History: Founded 1964, integrating all the country's facilities for further and higher education.

Governing Bodies: University Council

Academic Year: September to June (September-December; January-March; April-June)

Admission Requirements: Malawi Certificate of Education or equivalent

Fees: (Kwacha): 1500 per annum

Main Language(s) of Instruction: English

Degrees and Diplomas: *Bachelor's Degree*: Education (BEd(Hons)); Science (BSc(Hons)), 1 further yr; 5-6 yrs; *Master's Degree*: Arts (MA); Education (MEd); Law (LLM(Hons)); Science (MSc); Science in Agriculture (MSc (Agri)), a further 1-2 yrs; Business (MBA); Economics (MA(eco)); Environmental

Science (MSc(Env)), a further 2-3yrs; *Doctor's Degree*: Theology (PhD(Theo)), a further 3-5 yrs; Agriculture (PhD(Agri)), a further 3-5yrs

Student Services: Academic Counselling, Social Counselling, Employment Services, Nursery Care, Cultural Centre, Sports Facilities, Health Services, Canteen

Student Residential Facilities: Yes

Special Facilities: Art and Design exhibitions

Libraries: Total, 338,121 vols; 1074 periodicals

Publications: Journal of Religious Education; Journal of Humanities; UNIMA Newsletter; Report on Animal Research Conferences; Advancement of Science in Malawi and Luso; Journal of Social Science; Calendar; Physical Scientist; Bunda College Research Bulletin

Press or Publishing House: Montfort Press

Academic Staff *2002-2003:* Total: c. 480

Student Numbers *2002-2003:* Total: **4,600**

BUNDA COLLEGE OF AGRICULTURE
PO Box 219, Lilongwe
Tel: +265 277-222
Fax: +265 277-364
EMail: bcaprincipal@sdnp.org.mw
Website: http://chirunga.sdnp.org.mw/bunda/intro.htm

Principal: G.Y. Kanyama-Phiri (2000-) Tel: +265 277-324
Fax: +265 277-324 EMail: bcaprincipal@sdnp.org.mw

Registrar: F.T. Zalira Msonthi

Head Librarian: Geoffrey F. Salanje

Departments
Agricultural Engineering (Agricultural Engineering; Agriculture) *Head*: H.F. Mbeza
Animal Science (Animal Husbandry) *Head*: J.P. Mtimuni
Aquaculture and Fisheries (Aquaculture; Fishery) *Head*: Jeromey Likongwe
Crop Science (Crop Production) *Head*: Greenwell Nyirenda
Forestry and Horticulture (Forestry; Horticulture) *Head*: M.B. Kwapata
Home Economics and Human Nutrition (Home Economics; Nutrition) *Head*: Beatrice Mtimuni
Language and Development Communication (Communication Studies; Modern Languages) *Head*: Sam Samu
Rural Development (Rural Studies) *Head*: C. Masangano

History: Founded 1964

CHANCELLOR COLLEGE
PO Box 280, Zomba
Tel: +265 524-222
Fax: +265 522-046
EMail: ccadmin@chanco.unima.mw
Website: http://www.chanco.unima.mw

Principal: Francis Moto (2000-) Tel: +265 525-083
EMail: fmoto@chirunga.sdnp.org.mw

Registrar: M. Chimoyo

Head Librarian: A. Msiska
EMail: amsiska@canco.unima.mw

Faculties
Education *Dean*: G.W. Msiska
Humanities (Arts and Humanities) *Dean*: E. Kayambazinthu
Law *Dean*: Garton Kamchedzera
Science (Natural Sciences) *Dean*: J. Namangale
Social Sciences *Dean*: L. B. Dzimbiri

Centres
Language Studies (Communication Studies; Modern Languages) *Director*: Alfred Mtenje
Social Research (Social Studies) *Director*: D. Chilowa

History: Founded 1964

COLLEGE OF MEDICINE
Private Bag 360, Chichiri, Blantyre 3
Tel: +265 677 245
Fax: +265 674-700
EMail: registrar@medcol.mw
Website: http://www.medcol.mw

Principal: Robin Broadhead (1995-) Tel: +265 674-473
EMail: Principal@medcol.mw

Registrar: Chifundo Trigu EMail: Registrar@medcol.mw

Colleges
Basic Sciences (Anatomy; Biochemistry; Natural Sciences; Pharmacology; Physiology) *Director*: B. Msamati
Clinical Medicine (Gynaecology and Obstetrics; Medicine; Paediatrics; Surgery) *Director*: O.O. Komolafe
Medicine

History: Founded 1991.

Academic Year: January to November

Admission Requirements: 'A' level passes in Biology, Chemistry, Mathematics or Physics

Fees: (Kwacha): 46,000

Main Language(s) of Instruction: English

Degrees and Diplomas: *Master's Degree:* 5 yrs

Student Services: Academic Counselling, Social Counselling, Sports Facilities

Student Residential Facilities: Yes

Libraries: Sharing facilities with The Polytechnic

Academic Staff *2000*	MEN	WOMEN	TOTAL
FULL-TIME	60	8	**68**

Staff with doctorate: Total: **45**

Student Numbers *2000*	MEN	WOMEN	TOTAL
All (Foreign Included)	70	30	**100**

KAMUZU COLLEGE OF NURSING
Private Bag 1, Lilongwe
Tel: +265 721-622
Fax: +265 752-327
Cable: Nursing Lilongwe
EMail: kcnll@sdnp.org.mw

Principal: Christina N. Chihana

Registrar: M.M. Chimoyo

Departments
Nursing *Director*: S.I. Kachingwe

History: Founded 1964.

Main Language(s) of Instruction: English

THE POLYTECHNIC
Private Bag 303, Chichiri, Blantyre 3
Tel: +265 670-411
Fax: +265 670- 578

Principal: Henry Chibwana (1996-) Tel: +265 671-637
EMail: hchibwana@sdnp.org.mw

Registrar: John Kandzanja

Faculties
Applied Sciences (Environmental Engineering; Environmental Studies; Health Sciences; Mathematics and Computer Science) *Dean*: C.M. Chawanje
Commerce (Accountancy; Business Administration; Commercial Law; Management) *Dean*: B. Njobvu
Education and Media Studies (Education; Journalism; Media Studies) *Dean*: G. Manganda
Engineering (Architecture; Civil Engineering; Electrical Engineering; Engineering; Mechanical Engineering) *Dean*: T. Ben
Postgraduate *Dean*: F. Gomile Chidyaonga

History: Founded 1964

Academic Year: February to December

Admission Requirements: A minimum of 'O' levels with at least 6 credits including English or the equivalent from a recognized institution

Fees: (Kwacha): Government sponsored students (local), 50,000; economic fees (local) 20,000; foreign students, US$7213. All admissions must be forwarded to the Registrar, University Office, Box 278, Zonta, Malawi

Main Language(s) of Instruction: English

International Co-operation: With University of Strathclyde (exchange of technical staff)

Degrees and Diplomas: *Bachelor's Degree*: Accountancy (BAc); Arts; Business Administration (BBA); Science, 4 yrs; Engineering, Architecture, 5 yrs. 10 Diplomas in Technology and Business, 3-4 yrs

Student Services: Academic Counselling, Social Counselling, Sports Facilities, Language Programmes, Health Services, Canteen

Student Residential Facilities: Yes

Special Facilities: Audio Visual unit

Libraries: Central Library

Press or Publishing House: The Nation Publication

Student Numbers *2000:* Total: **1,500**

Mali

INSTITUTION TYPES AND CREDENTIALS

Types of higher education institutions:
Université (University)
Ecole normale supérieure (Teacher Training College)
Ecole nationale (National School)
Institut supérieur (Higher Institute)

School leaving and higher education credentials:
Baccalauréat
Baccalauréat technique
Diplôme d'Etudes universitaires générales (DEUG)
Diplôme universitaire de Technicien supérieur
Diplôme
Diplôme d'Ingénieur
Licence
Diplôme de Pharmacien
Maîtrise
Doctorat en Médecine
Certificat d'Etudes spécialisées
Diplôme d'Etudes approfondies
Doctorat

STRUCTURE OF EDUCATION SYSTEM

Pre-higher education:

Duration of compulsory education:

Age of entry: 7
Age of exit: 13

Structure of school system:

Basic First Stage
Type of school providing this education: Enseignement fondamental (Premier Cycle)
Length of programme in years: 6
Age level from: 7 to: 13

Certificate/diploma awarded: Certificat de Fin d'Etudes du premier Cycle de l'Enseignement fondamental (CFEPCEF)

Basic Second Stage
Type of school providing this education: Enseignement fondamental (Deuxième Cycle)
Length of programme in years: 3
Age level from: 13 to: 16
Certificate/diploma awarded: Diplôme d'Etudes fondamentales (DEF)

General Secondary
Type of school providing this education: Lycée
Length of programme in years: 3
Age level from: 16 to: 19
Certificate/diploma awarded: Baccalauréat

Technical Secondary
Length of programme in years: 2
Age level from: 16 to: 18
Certificate/diploma awarded: Certificat d'Aptitude professionnelle (CAP)

Technical Secondary
Type of school providing this education: Lycée technique
Length of programme in years: 3
Age level from: 16 to: 19
Certificate/diploma awarded: Baccalauréat technique

Vocational Secondary
Length of programme in years: 4
Age level from: 16 to: 20
Certificate/diploma awarded: Brevet de Technicien (BT)

School education:

Basic education (enseignement fondamental) lasts for nine years, divided into two cycles, the first of six years, leading to the Certificat d'Etudes du premier Cycle de l'Enseignement fondamental, and the second of three years leading to the Diplôme d'Etudes fondamentales (DEF). Secondary education lasts for three years and is divided into two streams: one general leading to the Baccalauréat and one technical divided into elementary technical (two years leading to the Certificat d'Aptitude professionnelle) and vocational technical (four years leading to the Brevet de Technicien). Technical Lycées prepare for the Baccalauréat technique in three years.

Higher education:

Higher education is provided by the Université du Mali which was created by incorporating some existing higher education centres and the creation of four faculties; Medicine, Pharmacy and Dentistry; Technical Sciences; Juridical and Economic Sciences; Languages, Arts and Humanities; and schools of Administration, Engineering and Teacher Training, and higher Institutes. The Institut supérieur de Formation et de Recherche appliquée (ISFRA) of the University, offers post-graduate training.

Main laws/decrees governing higher education:

Decree: A law stipulating the creation of a decentralized and vocationalized university   Year: 1986
Concerns: University

Academic year:

Classes from: October *to:* June

Long vacation from: 1 July *to:* 30 September

Languages of instruction:

French

Stages of studies:

Non-university level post-secondary studies (technical/vocational type):

The Institut Polytechnique rural de Katibougou offers two-year programmes in Stockraising, Forestry, Veterinary Medicine and Animal Husbandry leading to the award of the Diplôme de Technicien Supérieur. A further three years' study lead to the Diplôme d'Ingénieur. The Ecole des Hautes Etudes pratiques offers two-year courses in Business Studies, Bilingual Secretarial Studies and Accountancy leading to the award of the Diplôme de Technicien supérieur.

University level studies:

University level first stage:
The Institut de Sciences politiques offers a Diplôme d'Etudes universitaires générales after two years. Otherwise, the duration of studies varies from four years in Engineering, Management and Teacher Training (Diplôme d'Ingénieur, Diplôme de l'Ecole nationale d'Administration, Diplôme de l'Institut supérieur pour la Formation et la Recherche appliquée (ISFRA)) to five and six years in Pharmacy and Medicine (Diplôme de Pharmacien, Diplôme de Docteur en Médecine).

University level second stage:
The Institut de Sciences politiques offers a Maîtrise after four years of study. The Institut supérieur pour la Formation et la Recherche appliquée offers a Diplôme d'Etudes approfondies after two years.

University level third stage:
A Doctorat is offered after a further three years and a thesis.

Teacher education:

Training of pre-primary and primary/basic school teachers
Teacher training for teachers of the first cycle of Enseignement fondamental takes place at the regional Instituts pédagogiques d'Enseignement général (IPEG). Teachers of the second cycle of Enseignement fondamental are trained in the Ecole normale secondaire. Candidates to both types of teacher training schools must hold the Baccalauréat and follow a two-year course.

Training of secondary school teachers
Higher secondary school teachers are trained in four years after the Baccalauréat (and an entrance examination) in the Ecole normale supérieure where they obtain a Diplôme de l'Ecole normale Supérieure.

277

NATIONAL BODIES

Responsible authorities:

Ministry of National Education (Ministère de l'Education nationale)
  Minister: Mamadou Lamine Traore
  Secretary-General: Kénékouo dit Barthélemy Togo
  International Relations: Bonaventure Maïga
  BP 71
  Place de la Liberté
  Bamako
  Tel: +223 222-21-25 +223 222-21-25
  Fax: +223 222-77-67
  Role of governing body: Manages and administers higher education

ADMISSIONS TO HIGHER EDUCATION

Admission to non university higher education studies

Name of secondary school credential required: Baccalauréat technique

Entrance exams required: Competitive entrance examination for the Institut Polytechnique rural de Katibougou

Admission to university-level studies

Name of secondary school credential required: Baccalauréat

Name of secondary school credential required: Baccalauréat technique

STUDENT LIFE

Student expenses and financial aid

Student costs:

  Home students tuition fees: Minimum: 5,000 (CFA Franc)
  Maximum: 150,000 (CFA Franc)
  Foreign students tuition fees: Minimum: 250,000 (CFA Franc)
  Maximum: 300,000 (CFA Franc)

INTERNATIONAL COOPERATION AND EXCHANGES

Principal national bodies responsible for dealing with international cooperation and exchanges in higher education:

Ministry of National Education (Ministère de l'Education nationale)
    Conseiller Technique/MEN: Mamadou Keita
    Directeur National Enseignement supérieur: Koïba Tangara
    International Relations: Doulaye Konate
    BP 71
    Bamako
    Tel: +223 222-21-25 223 222-24-50
    Fax: +223 222-77-67

GRADING SYSTEM

Usual grading system in secondary school
Full Description: Baccalauréat and school education are graded on a scale of 0-20 (maximum), with 10 as the minimum pass mark. 16-20 très bien; 14-15 bien; 12-13 assez bien; 10-11 passable; 8-9 médiocre; 6-7 faible; 3-5 très faible; 0-2 nul
Highest on scale: 16-20, très bien
Pass/fail level: 10-11, passable
Lowest on scale: 0-2, nul

Main grading system used by higher education institutions
Full Description: Higher education is graded on a scale of 0 to 20.
Highest on scale: 16-20
Pass/fail level: 12
Lowest on scale: 0-2

Other main grading systems
At the Ecole d'Ingénieurs the grading system is 0-5, with 3 as the minimum pass mark.

NOTES ON HIGHER EDUCATION SYSTEM

Data for academic year: 2002-2003
Source: International Association of Universities (IAU), updated from IBE website, 2003 (www.ibe.unesco.org/International/Databanks/Wde/profilee.htm))

INSTITUTIONS OF HIGHER EDUCATION

UNIVERSITIES

• UNIVERSITY OF MALI
Université du Mali
BP 2528, Rue Baba Diarra Porte 113, Bamako
Tel: +223 222-19-33
Fax: +223 222-19-32

Recteur: Doulaye Konaté (2002-)
Secrétaire général: Mansa Makan Diabate
International Relations: Dauda Diallo

Faculties
Law and Economics (Economics; Law) *Dean*: Antoine Fernand Camara
Letters, Languages, Arts and Humanities (Arts and Humanities; Modern Languages) *Dean*: Drissa Diakite
Medicine, Pharmacy and Dentistry (Medicine; Pharmacy) *Dean*: Moussa Traoré
Science and Technology (Natural Sciences; Technology) *Dean*: Abdoul Karim Sanogo

Schools
Administration
Engineering *Director*: Moussa Kante
Teacher Training *(ENS) Director*: Bouba Diarra

Institutes
Agricultural Training and Applied Research (Agriculture) *Director*: Fafré Samake
Management *Director*: Siby Ginette Bellegarde
Training and Applied Research *(ISFRA) Director*: N'Golo Diarra

History: Founded 1993.

Governing Bodies: University Council

Academic Year: October to July

Admission Requirements: Secondary school certificate (baccalauréat) or equivalent

Fees: (Franc CFA): 5000-150,000 per annum; foreign students, 250,000-300,000

Main Language(s) of Instruction: French

Degrees and Diplomas: *Diplôme universitaire de Technicien supérieur*: 2 yrs; *Diplôme*: Administration; Economy; Foreign Languages Education; Humanities and Social Science Education; Law; Management; Science Education, 4 yrs; *Diplôme d'Ingénieur*: Applied Sciences, 5 yrs; *Licence*; *Diplôme de Pharmacien*: Pharmacy, 5 yrs; *Maîtrise*: 4 yrs; *Certificat d'Etudes spécialisées*: Dermatology; Ophthalmology; Public Health; Surgery; *Diplôme d'Etudes approfondies*: 1-2 further yrs following Maîtrise; *Doctorat*: a further 2-4 yrs

Academic Staff *2001-2002*	TOTAL
FULL-TIME	540
PART-TIME	400
TOTAL	**940**

Student Numbers *2001-2002:* Total: **19,800**

Note: Including c. 480 foreign students.

OTHER UNIVERSITY LEVEL INSTITUTIONS

INSTITUTE OF POLITICAL SCIENCE, INTERNATIONAL RELATIONS AND COMMUNICATION
Institut des Sciences Politiques, des Relations internationales et de la Communication
BP 763, Bamako
Tel: +223 220-19-26 +223 220-15-52

Directeur général: Abdouramane Gakou

Departments
Communication Studies and Journalism (Communication Studies; Journalism)
Economics (Economics; Management; Statistics)
International Relations
Law (International Law; Law; Private Law; Public Law)
Political Science

History: Founded 1999.

Degrees and Diplomas: *Diplôme d'Etudes universitaires générales (DEUG)*; *Licence*; *Maîtrise*

Academic Staff *2002-2003*	TOTAL
FULL-TIME	15
PART-TIME	35
TOTAL	**50**

Student Numbers *2002-2003:* Total: **324**

Mauritania

INSTITUTION TYPES AND CREDENTIALS

Types of higher education institutions:

Université (University)
Institut (Institute)
Centre supérieur (Higher Centre)
Ecole normale supérieure (Teacher Training College)

School leaving and higher education credentials:

Baccalauréat
Diplôme de Fin d'Etudes normales
Diplôme d'Etudes universitaires générales (DEUG)
Diplôme de Technicien supérieur
Certificat d'Aptitude de Professeur de l'Enseignement secondaire
Diplôme d'Ingénieur
Maîtrise

STRUCTURE OF EDUCATION SYSTEM

Pre-higher education:

Duration of compulsory education:

Age of entry: 6
Age of exit: 16

Structure of school system:

Basic
Type of school providing this education: Ecole fondamentale
Length of programme in years: 6
Age level from: 6 to: 12
Certificate/diploma awarded: Certificat d'Etudes fondamentales (CEF)

First Cycle Secondary
Type of school providing this education: Collège
Length of programme in years: 3
Age level from: 12 to: 15
Certificate/diploma awarded: Brevet d'Etudes du Premier Cycle (BEPC)

Technical Secondary
Length of programme in years: 3
Age level from: 15 to: 18
Certificate/diploma awarded: Brevet d'Enseignement professionnel (BEP)

Second Cycle Secondary
Type of school providing this education: Lycée
Length of programme in years: 3
Age level from: 15 to: 18
Certificate/diploma awarded: Baccalauréat

Technical
Length of programme in years: 2
Age level from: 18 to: 20
Certificate/diploma awarded: Brevet de Technicien (BT)

School education:

Basic education is compulsory and lasts for six years. It leads to the Certificat d'Etudes fondamentales. Secondary education lasts for six years, divided into three years' first cycle secondary (Collège) and three years' second cycle secondary (Lycée) education. There is a special entrance examination for access to secondary education (Concours d'Entrée en Première Année secondaire et technique). The lower cycle leads to the Brevet d'Etudes du premier Cycle. The second cycle culminates in the Baccalauréat in one of the following specializations: Arts/Literature; Mathematics, Physics and Chemistry; Natural Sciences or Koran and Arabic. It gives access to higher education. Technical secondary education also lasts three years and includes two streams: one leading to the Brevet d'Enseignement professionnel (BEP) for those holding the BEPC; and one leading to the Brevet de Technicien (BT) after two years' study. Candidates for the latter must have reached the last year of the second cycle secondary (Terminale).

Higher education:

Higher education is mainly provided by the University of Nouakchott, which comprises faculties of Letters and Humanities, Law and Economics and Science and Technology and other institutions of higher education, such as the Ecole normale supérieure, the Centre supérieur d'Enseignement technique, the Institut supérieur d'Etudes et de Recherches islamiques and the Ecole nationale d'Administration. The University is a public institution managed by an Administrative Board, a Management Committee and a Rector.

Main laws/decrees governing higher education:

Decree: Décret no 95-035   Year: 1995
Concerns: Ecoles normales d'instituteurs

Decree: Décret 86-212   Year: 1986
Concerns: Status of higher education

Decree: Loi 70-243   Year: 1970
Concerns: Higher Education

Academic year:

Classes from: October *to:* June

Languages of instruction:

Arabic, French

Stages of studies:

Non-university level post-secondary studies (technical/vocational type):

Higher technical education is mainly offered at the Centre supérieur d'Enseignement technique which comprises departments of Mechanical and Electrical Engineering.

University level studies:

University level first stage: *Diplôme d'Etudes universitaires générales*:
The first stage of higher education leads to the Diplôme d'Etudes universitaires générales (DEUG) after two years' university study. The Ecole nationale d'Administration confers a Diplôme after five years' study.

University level second stage: *Maîtrise*:
The Maîtrise is conferred after two years' study beyond the Diplôme d'Etudes universitaires générales. Postgraduate and doctoral degrees are completed abroad.

Teacher education:

Training of pre-primary and primary/basic school teachers
Priamary school teachers are trained in two years after the Baccalauréat in one of the Ecoles normales d' Instituteurs (ENI). Holders of the BEPC can follow a one-year course to become assistant teacher. There is an entrance examination for both courses and they lead to a Certificat d'Aptitude pédagogique.

Training of secondary school teachers
To teach in a Collège, teachers must have followed a one-year course at the Ecole normale supérieure and have obtained the Certificat d'Aptitude aux fonctions de Professeur du premier Cycle (CAPPC). To teach in a Lycée, teachers must have followed a course at the Ecole normale supérieure and have obtained the Certificat d'Aptitude au Professorat de l'Enseignement secondaire (CAPES). Courses last for two years for Instituteurs with three years' experience who hold a DEUG and one year for those who hold a Maitrise. Technical secondary schools teachers are recruited on the basis of a direct competitive examination and follow a one-year trainership.

Training of higher education teachers
Higher education teachers must hold a Licence or a Maîtrise and a third cycle Degree. They must sit for a competitive examination.

NATIONAL BODIES

Responsible authorities:

Ministry of National Education (Ministère de l'Education nationale)
    Minister: Aboubekrine Ould Ahmed
    BP 227
    Nouakchott
    Tel: +222 25-11-25
    Fax: +222 25-12-22

ADMISSIONS TO HIGHER EDUCATION

Admission to university-level studies

Name of secondary school credential required: Baccalauréat

Alternatives to credentials: Entrance examination.

Numerus clausus/restrictions: For lack of space, access to the university is reserved to new Baccalauréat holders.

GRADING SYSTEM

Usual grading system in secondary school

Full Description: 0-20
Highest on scale: 20
Pass/fail level: 10-11
Lowest on scale: 0

Main grading system used by higher education institutions

Full Description: 0-20
Highest on scale: 20
Pass/fail level: 10-11
Lowest on scale: 0

NOTES ON HIGHER EDUCATION SYSTEM

Data for academic year: 2002-2003
Source: International Association of Universities (IAU), updated from IBE website, 2003
(www.ibe.unesco.org/International/Databanks/Wde/profilee.htm)

INSTITUTIONS OF HIGHER EDUCATION

UNIVERSITIES

• UNIVERSITY OF NOUAKCHOTT
Université de Nouakchott
BP 5026, Nouakchott
Tel: +222(2) 513-82
Fax: +222(2) 539-97
EMail: webmaster@univ-nkc.mr
Website: http://www.univ-nkc.mr
Recteur: Mohamed El Hacen Ould Lebatt
Secrétaire Général: M. Ould Jiddu **EMail:** jid@univ-nkc.mr

Faculties
Arts and Humanities (Arabic; Arts and Humanities; English; Geography; History; Linguistics; Native Language; Philosophy; Translation and Interpretation) *Dean*: Diallo Ibrahima
Law and Economics (Economics; Law; Management; Private Law; Public Law)
Science and Technology (Biology; Chemistry; Computer Science; Geology; Management; Mathematics; Natural Sciences; Physics; Technology; Technology Education) *Dean*: Ahmedou Ould Haouba

History: Founded 1981.
Governing Bodies: Assemblée de l'Université
Main Language(s) of Instruction: French
Degrees and Diplomas: *Diplôme d'Etudes universitaires générales (DEUG)*: Arabic; Chemistry; Economics; English; Geography; History; Law; Modern Languages; Natural Sciences; Philosophy; Physics; Science, 2 yrs; *Diplôme de Technicien supérieur*: Fishery, 2 yrs; *Diplôme d'Ingénieur*: Fishery; *Maîtrise*: Arabic; Biology; Chemistry; Economics; English; Geography; Geology; History; Law; Modern Languages; Philosophy, 2 yrs after DEUG
Academic Staff *2001-2002:* Total: c. 70
Student Numbers *2001-2002:* Total: c. 9,100

OTHER INSTITUTIONS

CENTRE SUPÉRIEUR D'ENSEIGNEMENT TECHNIQUE
BP 986, Nouakchott
Tel: +222(2) 530-17
Fax: +222(2) 544-29
Telex: 5719
Founded: 1982

Departments
Electrical Engineering
Mechanical Engineering

Main Language(s) of Instruction: Arabic, French

ECOLE NATIONALE D'ADMINISTRATION (ENA)
BP 252, Nouakchott
Tel: +222(2) 532-22
Fax: +222(2) 575-17
Founded: 1969
Programmes
Administration

ECOLE NATIONALE DE L'ENSEIGNEMENT MARITIME ET DES PÊCHES
Nouakchott
Programmes
Fishery; Marine Science and Oceanography

ECOLE NORMALE SUPÉRIEURE
BP 990, Nouakchott
Tel: +222(2) 531-84
Fax: +222(2) 531-72
Founded: 1970, 1987
Programmes
Education

History: Founded 1970, acquired present status and title 1987.

INSTITUT BEN ABASS
Nouakchott
Programmes
Cultural Studies

INSTITUT SUPÉRIEUR DES ETUDES ET RECHERCHES ISLAMIQUES (ISERI)
BP 635, Nouakchott
Founded: 1979
Programmes
Islamic Studies

INSTITUT SUPÉRIEUR SCIENTIFIQUE
BP 5026, Nouakchott
Tel: +222(2) 511-68
Fax: +222(2) 539-97
Telex: 598 mtn nktt
Founded: 1986
Biology; Chemistry; Computer Science; English; Geology; Mathematics; Modern Languages; Physics

Mauritius

INSTITUTION TYPES AND CREDENTIALS

Types of higher education institutions:

University
Institute
College

School leaving and higher education credentials:

General Certificate of Education Ordinary Level
School Certificate
General Certificate of Education Advanced Level
Higher School Certificate
Bachelor's Degree
Diploma
Master's Degree
Master of Philosophy
Doctor of Philosophy

STRUCTURE OF EDUCATION SYSTEM

Pre-higher education:

Duration of compulsory education:

Age of entry: 5
Age of exit: 12

Structure of school system:

Primary
Type of school providing this education: Primary School
Length of programme in years: 6
Age level from: 5 to: 12
Certificate/diploma awarded: Certificate of Primary Education

Lower Secondary
Type of school providing this education: Lower Secondary School
Length of programme in years: 5
Age level from: 12 to: 17
Certificate/diploma awarded: General Certificate of Education O-Level/School Certificate

Upper Secondary
Type of school providing this education: Upper Secondary School
Length of programme in years: 2
Age level from: 17 to: 19
Certificate/diploma awarded: General Certificate of Education A-Level/Higher School Certificate

School education:

Primary education lasts for six years and culminates in the Certificate of Primary Education. Secondary education covers seven years: Forms I to V leading to the examinations for the School Certificate, followed by two years leading to the examination for the General Certificate of Education Advanced ('A') level or Higher School Certificate. Technical secondary education is provided by a College, Lycées Polytechniques, Institutes and Industrial Trade Training Centres.

Higher education:

The higher education system consists of two universities, the University of Mauritius (UoM) and the University of Technology, Mauritius (UTM), a teacher training college, the Mauritius Institute of Education (MIE), the Mahatma Gandhi Institute (MGI) which specializes in the promotion of Indian culture, the Mauritius College of the Air (MCA), as well as polytechnics, all operating in the public sector.

Furthermore, there are over 30 private organizations operating in the country which deliver tertiary-level programmes. Most of these institutions are relatively small and are affiliated to an international institution in delivering tertiary-level courses using a mixed mode system, encompassing both distance learning and face-to-face tutorials.

Main laws/decrees governing higher education:

Decree: Education Act   Year: 1996
Concerns: Education at all levels

Academic year:

Classes from: July *to:* May

Languages of instruction:

English, French

Stages of studies:

Non-university level post-secondary studies (technical/vocational type):

The polytechnics offer a two-year diploma course in Technology, Information Systems or Business Administration, and a three-year course leading to the Diplôme Universitaire Supérieur de Technologie (DUST). Several institutions also offer tertiary level programmes (at the Higher National Diploma level) in the public sector, such as the Mauritius Institute of Health and the Industrial and Vocational Training Board.

University level studies:

University level first stage:
At the basic level, diploma programmes are offered upon specific requests from Government or other

bodies mainly for in-service training of their staff. These diploma programmes are normally of two years' duration on a part-time basis.

University level second stage:
This stage consists in three- to four- year Bachelor (with Honours) degree programmes on a full-time basis.

University level third stage:
The third level relates to Master's programmes offered either in the form of taught (e.g. MSc, MBA, etc.) or research (I.e. Mphil) programmes. The taught Master's degrees are normally two-year degrees run on a part-time basis. The Mphil lasts for a maximum of three years full-time or four years part-time.

University level fourth stage:
This stage normally relates to Doctor in Philosophy (PhD) programmes that are undertaken through research. PhD students are required to complete their research/studies within a maximum of five years' full-time or seven years' part-time studies.

Teacher education:

Training of pre-primary and primary/basic school teachers
Teacher training is provided by the Mauritius Institute of Education. A two-year full-time or three-year part-time course leads to a Teacher's Diploma. A two-year course leads to a Teacher's Certificate. Trainee teachers have to earn a minimum of 48 credits out of 50 and obtain a grade point average of at least 2.0.

Training of secondary school teachers
Secondary school teachers must hold a university degree or a non-graduate professional qualification for teaching. The Mauritius Institute of Education (MIE) runs a one-year full-time/two-year part-time postgraduate certificate in education and a two-year part-time certificate in educational administration. The Bachelor of Education Single Honours is a three-year, part-time post A-level and post-teachers' diploma (three-year part-time training course) run jointly by the Mauritius Institute of Education and the University of Mauritius.

Non-traditional studies:

Distance higher education
The University of Mauritius, the Mauritius College of the Air and the Mauritius Institute of Education each have a Centre for Distance Learning.

NATIONAL BODIES

Responsible authorities:
Ministry of Education and Scientific Research
    Minister: Steven Obeegadoo
    Permanent Secretary: Soopramanien Kandasamy Pather
    Principal Assistant Secretary: Rajeshwara Duva-Pentiah

International Relations: Hiranand Boolchand Dansinghani
International Relations: Rajeshwara Duva-Pentiah
3rd Floor, IVTB House
Pont Fer
Phoenix
Tel: +230(698) 0464
Fax: +230(698) 2550
EMail: meduhrd@bow.intnet.mu
WWW: http://ministry-education.gov.mu

Tertiary Education Commission
Chairman: Donald Ah-Chuen
Executive Director: Raj Sunkur Lutchmeah
International Relations: Deochund Sookhoo
Réduit
Tel: +230(467) 6632
Fax: +230(467) 6579
EMail: sookhoo@intnet.mu
WWW: http://tec.intnet.mu

Role of governing body: Promote and develop the tertiary education system to attain world standards

ADMISSIONS TO HIGHER EDUCATION

Admission to non university higher education studies

Name of secondary school credential required: School Certificate

Name of secondary school credential required: General Certificate of Education Ordinary Level
Minimum score/requirement: Passes in five subjects including English.

Admission to university-level studies

Name of secondary school credential required: Higher School Certificate
Minimum score/requirement: A pass in English Language or a pass in English Language and Credits in five other subjects or Credit in English Language and four other subjects
For entry to: Undergraduate degrees

Name of secondary school credential required: General Certificate of Education Advanced Level
Minimum score/requirement: Passes in three subjects at Advanced Level or at least two passes at Advanced level
For entry to: Undergraduate degrees

Alternatives to credentials: The French Baccalauréat; The IGCSE and the International Baccalaureate awarded by the International Baccalaureate Organisation, Switzerland; Qualifications awarded by other universities and institutions which have been approved by the governing body as satisfying the minimum requirements for admission; or Relevant subjects/combinations of related subjects included in any qualifications as may be approved by the governing body as being equivalent or comparable to an 'O' level or 'A' level may be accepted in lieu of equivalence

Foreign students admission

Definition of foreign student: Non-nationals of the Republic of Mauritius

Quotas: none

Admission requirements: For higher degrees students must hold a Bachelor Degree (at least 2nd class Honours) or a first degree; for degree courses they must hold GCE 'O' level passes in five subjects, two of which must be at A level; for diploma courses they must hold five GCE 'O' level passes including English and Mathematics; for certificate courses they must generally hold a Cambridge SC with passes in five subjects, including English language.

Entry regulations: Foreign students must hold a visa (http://passport.gov.mu) and a residence permit and present financial guarantees.

Health requirements: As established by the Ministry of Health and Quality of Life (http://health.gov.mu).

Language requirements: Students must have a good command of English.

Application procedures:

Apply to individual institution for entry to: Undergraduate and postgraduate programmes at publicly founded institutions

Recognition of studies and qualifications:

Studies pursued in home country (System of recognition/accreditation): The Mauritius Qualifications Authority which has just been created will be responsible for accreditation of institutions and programmes

Studies pursued in foreign countries (bodies dealing with recognition of foreign credentials):
National Accreditation and Equivalence Council, Ministry of Education and Scientific Research
> 3rd Floor, IVTB House
> Pont Fer
> Phoenix
> Tel: +230(698) 0464 +230(698) 3566
> Fax: +230(698) 2550
> EMail: meduhrd@bow.intnet.mu

References to further information on foreign student admissions and recognition of studies

Title: University Calendar
Publisher: University of Mauritius

290

STUDENT LIFE

Main student services at national level

Youth Guidance Unit
    Ministry of Employment
    Reduit

Student expenses and financial aid

Student costs:

Home students tuition fees: Minimum: 0 (Mauritius Rupee)
Maximum: 4,850 (Mauritius Rupee)
Foreign students tuition fees: Minimum: 50,000 (Mauritius Rupee)
Maximum: 60,000 (Mauritius Rupee)

Publications on student services and financial aid:

Title: Study Abroad 2004-2005, 32nd Edition
Author: UNESCO
Publisher: UNESCO Publishing
Year of publication: 2003

GRADING SYSTEM

Usual grading system in secondary school

Full Description: Overseas School Certificate and CGE Examinations:
A-E with U as Fail
Highest on scale: A very good
Pass/fail level: C or D
Lowest on scale: U

Main grading system used by higher education institutions

Full Description: Bachelor degree: class I; class II division i; class II division ii; class III or pass.

NOTES ON HIGHER EDUCATION SYSTEM

Data for academic year: 2002-2003
Source: Ministry of Education and Scientific Research, 2003

INSTITUTIONS OF HIGHER EDUCATION

UNIVERSITIES

*• UNIVERSITY OF MAURITIUS
Réduit, Moka
Tel: +230(454) 1041
Fax: +230(454) 9642
Telex: 4621 unim iw
Cable: university mauritius
Website: http://www.uom.ac.mu

Head: Goolam Mohamedbhai (1995-) Tel: +230(465) 6985
Fax: +230(465) 1337 EMail: mobhai@uom.ac.mu

Administrative Officer: Sassista D. Goordyal
Tel: +230(464) 7409 Fax: +230(465) 1336
EMail: sgdyal@uom.ac.mu

International Relations: Indurlall Fagoonee
Fax: +230(466) 7900 EMail: goofa@uom.ac.mu

Faculties
Agriculture (Agricultural Engineering; Agricultural Management; Agriculture; Crop Production; Food Science; Horticulture) *Dean:* Das R. Vencatasmay
Engineering (Chemical Engineering; Civil Engineering; Computer Science; Electrical and Electronic Engineering; Engineering; Food Technology; Industrial Engineering; Mechanical Engineering; Production Engineering; Textile Technology) *Dean:* Harry Coomar Shumsher Rughooputh
Law and Management (Accountancy; Business Administration; Business and Commerce; Finance; Human Resources; International Business; Law; Management; Marketing; Public Administration; Tourism) *Dean:* Dharambeer Gokhool
Science (Chemistry; Health Sciences; Mathematics; Medical Technology; Natural Sciences; Physics) *Dean:* Soonil Rughooputh
Social Studies and Humanities (Arts and Humanities; Communication Studies; Economics; English; French; Hindi; History; Library Science; Media Studies; Social Studies; Social Work; Statistics) *Dean:* Sham Nath

Centres
Distance Learning *(J. Baguant)* (Curriculum; Distance Education; Information Technology) *Director:* Azad Parahoo
Information Technology and Systems *(Providing IT services to the University)* (Information Management; Information Technology; Systems Analysis) *Officer in Charge:* Arvind Rosunee
Innovative Learning Technology (Information Technology) *Director:* Alain Senteni
Medical Research and Studies *(SSR)* (Anatomy; Epidemiology; Genetics; Haematology; Medicine; Molecular Biology; Pathology) *Director (Acting):* Meera Manraj

History: Founded 1965.
Governing Bodies: Council; Senate
Academic Year: July to May (July-November; January-May)

Admission Requirements: General Certificate of Education (GCE) with pass at Ordinary 'O' level or equivalent in English Language, and either passes in 4 other subjects with at least 2 passes at 'A' level or passes in 3 other subjects at 'A' level

Fees: (Mauritius Rupees): None for Mauritian school leavers. Other Mauritian students, 3850-4850. Foreign students, 50,000-60,000

Main Language(s) of Instruction: English

International Co-operation: With universities in Brunei; United Kingdom; France; Canada

Degrees and Diplomas: *Bachelor's Degree*: 3-4 yrs; *Diploma*: 2-3 yrs; *Master's Degree*: 2-3 yrs; *Master of Philosophy*: (MPhil), 2-3 yrs; *Doctor of Philosophy*: (PhD), 3-5 yrs. Also Certificates, 1-2 yrs

Student Services: Employment Services, Cultural Centre, Sports Facilities

Special Facilities: 21 acre University Farm. Crop Museum

Libraries: 125,000 vols including bound vols and periodicals

Publications: Newsletter (3 per annum); Calendar; Annual Report (annually); Journal

Academic Staff 2001-2002	MEN	WOMEN	TOTAL
FULL-TIME	133	67	200
PART-TIME	100	33	133
TOTAL	**233**	**100**	**333**
STAFF WITH DOCTORATE			
FULL-TIME	34	13	47
PART-TIME	24	7	31
TOTAL	**58**	**20**	**78**

Student Numbers 2001-2002	TOTAL
All (Foreign Included)	**5,048**
FOREIGN ONLY	37

UNIVERSITY OF TECHNOLOGY, MAURITIUS (UTM)
La Tour Koenig, Pointe-aux-Sables
Tel: +230(234) 7624 +230(234) 7632
Fax: +230(234) 1660
Website: http://ncb.intnet.mu/utm/

Director-General: Peter Coupe
EMail: director@utm.intnet.mu

Registrar: Teeluck Bhuwanee Fax: +230(234) 6727
EMail: registrar@utm.intnet.mu

International Relations: Galib Fakim

Schools
Business Informatics and Software Development (Business Computing; Software Engineering) *Head:* Devarajen Venethethan

Public Sector Policy and Management (Management; Public Administration) *Head*: Soodhir Kumar Joypaul

Sustainable Development Science (Tourism) *Head*: Soodhir Kumar Joypaul

History: Founded 2000.

Governing Bodies: Board of Governors; Academic Council

Academic Year: August to June

Admission Requirements: 5 'O' level (pass) including English + 2 'A' level/'O' level in English (pass) + 3 'A' level/ French baccalauréat/IGCSE + International Baccalauréat

Fees: (Mauritius rupees) 20,000-35,000 per annum

Main Language(s) of Instruction: English

International Co-operation: With universities in India; United Kingdom

Degrees and Diplomas: *Bachelor's Degree*: Information Technology (BSc (Hons)), 3 yrs full-time; 41/2 yrs part-time; Public Management (BPAM), 31/2 yrs full-time; 5 yrs part-time; *Master's Degree*: Public Sector Management (MPM), 2 yrs

Student Services: Academic Counselling, Sports Facilities, Canteen

Student Residential Facilities: Yes

Libraries: yes

Academic Staff 2001-2002	MEN	WOMEN	TOTAL
FULL-TIME	9	3	12
PART-TIME	18	4	22
TOTAL	**27**	**7**	**34**
STAFF WITH DOCTORATE			
FULL-TIME			1
PART-TIME			2
TOTAL			**3**

Student Numbers 2001-2002	MEN	WOMEN	TOTAL
All (Foreign Included)	212	156	**368**

Part-time Students, 259

OTHER INSTITUTIONS

HIGHER INSTITUTE OF TECHNOLOGY

Institut Supérieur de Technologie
Rue de la Concorde, Camp Levieux, Rose-Hill
Tel: +230(466) 0118
Fax: +230(466) 3774
EMail: istrh@intnet.mu

Directrice: Yassodha Benoît

Technology

LYCÉE POLYTECHNIQUE SIR GUY FORGET
Rue François Mitterrand, Central Flacq
Tel: +230(413) 2959
Fax: +230(413) 2938
EMail: lpsgf@intnet.mu

Head: Lutchman Sakurdeep Tel: +230(413) 2420
EMail: sakurdeep@yahoo.com

Founded: 1982

Departments
Automobile Mechanics (Automotive Engineering)
Building Construction (Building Technologies; Construction Engineering)
Electrotechnics and Electronics (Electronic Engineering)
Maintenance and Production Mechanics (Maintenance Technology; Production Engineering)

MAHATMA GANDHI INSTITUTE (MGI)
Moka
Tel: +230(403) 2000
Fax: +230(433) 2235
EMail: centrems@intnet.mu
Website: http://www.mgi.intnet.mu

Director: Soorya Nursumloo Gayan Tel: +230(433) 2166
Fax: +230(433) 2160

Founded: 1970

Schools
Fine Arts (Fine Arts; Painting and Drawing; Sculpture) *Head (Acting)*: Mala Ramyead
Indian Music and Dance (Dance; Fine Arts; Music; Musical Instruments; Singing) *Head*: Indurduth Deerpaul
Indian Studies (Curriculum; Hindi; Indic Languages; Literature; Philosophical Schools; Philosophy; Teacher Trainers Education; Urdu) *Head*: Cassam Heerah
Mauritian, African and Asian Studies (African Studies; Arts and Humanities; Asian Studies; Comparative Literature; Continuing Education; Cultural Studies; Development Studies; Economic History; Ethnology; Geography (Human); Indigenous Studies; International Relations; Island Studies; Social Problems; Social Psychology; Social Sciences; Translation and Interpretation) *Associate Professor*: Sooryankanti Nirsimloo-Gayan

Departments
Folklore and Oral Traditions (Cultural Studies; Folklore) *Head*: Suchita Ramdin

Governing Bodies: Ministry of Education and Scientific Research

Main Language(s) of Instruction: English, French

Degrees and Diplomas: *Bachelor's Degree*: Fine Arts (BA Hons); Fine Arts with Education (BA Hons); Hindi (BA Hons); Hindi (BA Joint Hons); Hindi with Education (BA Hons); Indian

Philosophy with Education (BA Hons); Marathi with Education (BA Hons); Performing Arts with Education (BA Hons); Tamil with Education (BA Hons); Telugu with Education (BA Hons); Urdu with Education (BA Hons); *Diploma*: Fine Arts; Indian Philosophy with Sanskrit; Vocational Hindustani, 2 yrs

Student Services: Cultural Centre, Language Programmes

Student Residential Facilities: Guest House

Special Facilities: Museum. Art Gallery

Libraries: Central Library

Publications: Vasant, Creative Writings (Hindi); Rimjhim, Children's Creative Writings (Hindi) (quarterly); Journal of Mauritian Studies, Mauritian Studies (English, French) (biannually)

Academic Staff *2001-2002:* Total: c. 200

Student Numbers *2001-2002*: All (Foreign Included): c. 900 Foreign Only: c. 15

MAURITIUS COLLEGE OF THE AIR (MCA)
Réduit
Tel: +230(403) 8200
Fax: +230(464) 8854

Director: Meenakshi Seetulsingh (1986-)
Tel: +230(464) 6662 Fax: +230(465) 9440
EMail: meena@bow.intnet.mu

Administrative Secretary: Leela Devi Ramburuth
Tel: +230(465) 9480 EMail: leelaram@bow.intnet.mu

Founded: 1985

Divisions
Distance Education (Business and Commerce; Preschool Education; Teacher Trainers Education; Tourism) *Senior Lecturer*: Issawar Jheengut
Media (Media Studies; Printing and Printmaking) *Director*: Shakuntala Hawoldar

Centres
National Resources for Audio and Video Programmes *Head*: Christine Ah Fat

History: Founded 1985.

Main Language(s) of Instruction: English, French

Degrees and Diplomas: *Bachelor's Degree*: Commerce; Computer Applications; Tourism Studies, 36 months. Also Certificates (12-15 months); Diplomas (12-24 months)

Student Services: Academic Counselling

Libraries: Central Library

MAURITIUS INSTITUTE OF EDUCATION (MIE)
Réduit
Tel: +230(454) 1031
Fax: +230(466) 8242
EMail: sthand@intnet.mu
Website: http://www.mie.intnet.mu

Director (Acting): Sheela Thancanammootoo

Founded: 1974

Departments
Agricultural Education
Business Education
Curriculum Studies (Curriculum)
Design and Technology (Design; Technology)
Educational Administration and Management (Educational Administration)
Educational Studies (Education)
English
French
Home Economics
Mathematics and Computer Education (Computer Education; Mathematics Education)
Media and Communication Studies (Media Studies)
Movement and Physical Education (Physical Education)
Science Education
Social Studies
Visual Arts

History: Founded 1974.

SWAMI DAYANAND INSTITUTE OF MANAGEMENT
Round About Beau Plan SE, Pamplemousses
Tel: +230(243) 0045
Fax: +230(243) 5154
EMail: sdim@intnet.mu

Head: Krishna Saurty EMail: ksaurty@intnet.mu

Management

Note: Also three regional institutions, the University of the Indian Ocean, the Institut de la Francophonie pour l'Entrepreunariat and the Sir Seewoosagur Ramgoolam Medical College operating locally with their students coming from various regions of the Indian Ocean.

Morocco

INSTITUTION TYPES AND CREDENTIALS

Types of higher education institutions:

Université (University)
Ecole normale supérieure (Higher Teacher-Training College)
Grande Ecole (Higher College)
Etablissement de Formation des Cadres (Training Institution for Executives)

School leaving and higher education credentials:

Baccalauréat
Capacité en Droit
Diplôme universitaire de Technologie (DUT)
Certificat universitaire
Diplôme d'Etudes universitaires générales (DEUG)
Diplôme de Technicien supérieur
Diplôme d'Architecte (DENA)
Diplôme d'Ingénieur d'Etat
Diplôme/Diplôme supérieur
Licence
Maîtrise
Certificat d'Aptitude à l'Enseignement du second Degré
Diplôme d'Etudes supérieures spécialisées (DESS)
Diplôme de Professeur de deuxième Cycle
Diplôme d'Etudes supérieures (DES)
Certificat d'Etudes spécialisées (CES)
Diplôme d'Etudes supérieures approfondies (DESA)
Diplôme de Professeur agrégé
Doctorat

STRUCTURE OF EDUCATION SYSTEM

Pre-higher education:

Duration of compulsory education:

Age of entry: 6
Age of exit: 15

Structure of school system:

Basic First Stage
Type of school providing this education: Ecole primaire
Length of programme in years: 6
Age level from: 6 to: 12

Basic Second Stage
Type of school providing this education: Collège
Length of programme in years: 3
Age level from: 12 to: 15

General Secondary
Type of school providing this education: Lycée
Length of programme in years: 3
Age level from: 15 to: 18
Certificate/diploma awarded: Baccalauréat

Technical Secondary
Type of school providing this education: Technical Secondary School
Length of programme in years: 3
Age level from: 15 to: 18
Certificate/diploma awarded: Baccalauréat Technique

Technical
Type of school providing this education: Technical institutions
Length of programme in years: 2
Age level from: 18 to: 20
Certificate/diploma awarded: Brevet de Technicien supérieur

School education:

Basic (fondamental) education is compulsory and lasts for nine years. It is divided into two cycles of six and three years respectively. After basic education, students enter either general secondary education or technical education and study for three years. General secondary education offers three options: letters, sciences or mathematics leading to the Baccalauréat. Technical education leads to the Baccalauréat technique. Some technical schools offer two years' training after the Baccalauréat leading to the Brevet de Technicien supérieur (BTS).

Access to vocational education at basic education level (crafts and agriculture) is open to pupils in Forms 7 or 8 following a competitive examination. Pupils in Form 9 or in the first 2 years of secondary education may also opt for vocational training after passing a competitive examination. They are awarded a Certificat de Qualification professionnelle at the end. Pupils opting for vocational education in the third year of secondary education are awarded a Diplôme de Technicien whereas pupils who hold the Baccalauréat obtain a Diplôme de Technicien spécialisé.

Higher education:

Higher education is provided by universities, Grandes Ecoles, institutes, teacher-training schools and centres under the supervision of the Ministère de l'Enseignement supérieur. Some Grandes Ecoles and

Institutes are under specific ministries. A characteristic feature of training is the existence, besides the traditional system of higher education, of institutions of higher education (Etablissements de Formation des Cadres) which provide specialized training for high-level personnel in Science/Technology; Law/Economics/Administration/Social Sciences and Teacher Training under the direct control of ministerial departments. There are also eight Grandes Ecoles d'Ingénieurs (engineering schools). University councils rule on important questions related to university life. Universities are public institutions with budgetary autonomy. Le Conseil national de l'Enseignement supérieur establishes higher education policy. The Mission de Coordination de l'Enseignement privé accredits newly created private establishments.

Main laws/decrees governing higher education:

Decree: Projet de loi n° 01-00   Year: 2000
Concerns: Higher education

Decree: N° 2-96-796   Year: 1997
Concerns: Organization of the Doctorate, DESA and DESS and Accreditation of institutions

Decree: Décret ministériel n° 1446-87   Year: 1987
Concerns: Reform of the Baccalauréat

Decree: Dahir portant loi n°1-75-102   Year: 1975
Concerns: Organization of Universities

Academic year:

Classes from: September *to:* July

Languages of instruction:

Arabic, French

Stages of studies:

Non-university level post-secondary studies (technical/vocational type):

Postsecondary technical institutes offer two to four-year programmes in Law, Economics, Administration, Social Sciences and Engineering. Some offer a Brevet de Technicien supérieur (BTS) after two years' training. Most private technical institutions offer programmes in Computer Science and Business and Management. Private institutions confer Engineering degrees. Secondary schools offer two years of post-Baccalauréat preparatory training for the Grandes Ecoles, after which students may pass the competitive entrance examination of the school(s) they have opted for.

University level studies:

University level first stage: 1er Cycle:
The first stage at university lasts for two years and is devoted to broadly-based studies; it leads to a Certificat universitaire d'Etudes littéraires (CUEL) in Arts and Humanities and a Certificat universitaire d'Etudes scientifiques (CUES) in Science and Economics. At the Facultés des Sciences et Techniques a Diplôme d'Etudes universitaires générales (DEUG) in Applied Sciences and a Diplôme d'Etudes universitaires de Technologie (DEUT) are conferred after two years' study. Two years in Classes Préparatoires aux Grandes Ecoles (CPGE) are required to enter a Grande Ecole.

University level second stage: *2ème Cycle*:

The second stage is a phase of in-depth training lasting two years and leading to the Licence. A further two years' study beyond the DEUG and the DEUT lead to the Maîtrise. The Diplôme d'Ingénieur d'Etat is conferred after a total of five years' study (including two years in Classes Préparatoires aux Grandes Ecoles (CPGE)) by the Grandes Ecoles d'Ingénieurs in Engineering and Agriculture. A Diplôme supérieur is conferred in Business after four years' study and a Diplôme d'Architecte after six years. The Doctorat in Medicine is conferred after seven years, the Doctorat in Pharmacy after six years and the Doctorat in Dentistry after five years.

University level third stage: *3ème Cycle*:

The third stage leads to the Dipôme d'Etudes supérieures approfondies (DESA) which is conferred after two years' further study beyond the Licence. A Diplôme d'Etudes supérieures (DES) (Takhsis) in Arts, Science, Law and Economics is usually awarded at the end of one to three years' study beyond the Licence. It includes theoretical courses, individual research work and the submission of a dissertation. The Diplôme d'Etudes supérieures spécialisées (DESS) requires two years' study.

University level fourth stage: *Doctorat*:

The Doctorat is obtained by holders of a DES or DESA in Arts, Science, Law, Economics and Education after three to five years' study and defence of a thesis.

Teacher education:

Training of pre-primary and primary/basic school teachers

Teachers of the first cycle of basic education are trained in Centres de Formation des Instituteurs (CFI). Teachers of the second cycle are trained in Centres pédagogiques régionaux (CPR) where two-year training programmes are offered to Baccalauréat holders. They must sit for an entrance examination. Holders of a Certificat universitaire or a DEUG may follow a one-year pedagogical course. The title of Professeur du 2ème Cycle fondamental is conferred.

Training of secondary school teachers

Teachers of general secondary education are trained at Ecoles normales supérieures (ENS). If they hold a DEUG or another 1st cycle qualification, they follow a two-year course. Holders of a Licence may follow a one-year course at an ENS or a faculty of education and obtain a Diplôme de Professeur du 2ème Cycle or a Certificat d'Aptitude à l'Enseignement du second Degré after passing a competitive examination. A Professeur du 2ème Cycle or a Licence holder may also pass a competitive examination to study for the Agregation (two years of study) at one of the Ecoles normales supérieures.

Technical secondary school teachers are trained at the Ecole normale supérieure technique (ENSET).

Training of higher education teachers

Higher education teachers must hold a post-graduate degree.

NATIONAL BODIES

Responsible authorities:

Ministry of Higher Education, Executive Training & Scientific Research (Ministère de l'Enseignement supérieur, Formation des Cadres & Recherche scientifique)

Minister: Khalid Alioua
Secrétaire générale: Abdessattar Amrani
International Relations: Mustapha Haddou
 BP 4500, Ilassan
35 Ave. Ibn Sina, Agdal
1000   Rabat
Tel: +212(37) 70-61-92 +212(37) 70-64-92
Fax: +212(37) 70-61-88
EMail: des@dfc.gov.ma
WWW: http://www.enssup.gov.ma

Conference of Moroccan University Presidents (Conférence des Présidents des Universités marocaines)
President: Ahmed Jebli
Secrétaire Général: Rachid Hilal
International Relations: Rachida Saigh-Bousta
BP 511
Présidence de l'Université Cadi Ayyad
Avenue Prince My Abdellah
Marrakech
Tel: +212(4) 43-48-13
Fax: +212(4) 43-44-94
EMail: presidence@ucam.ac.ma
WWW: http://www.ucam.ac.ma

ADMISSIONS TO HIGHER EDUCATION

Admission to non university higher education studies

Name of secondary school credential required: Baccalauréat

Alternatives to credentials: Baccalauréat technique

Admission to university-level studies

Name of secondary school credential required: Baccalauréat

Other admission requirements: There is an entrance examination for the Faculties of Medicine, Pharmacy, Dentistry, higher schools of Technology, the School for Translation and Interpreting and the Grandes Ecoles d'Ingénieurs.

Foreign students admission

Entry regulations: Foreign students must hold the Baccalauréat or an equivalent qualification. Within the framework of agreements or conventions concluded with other countries, foreign applicants may be admitted to the Ecoles normales supérieures on the basis of their academic record, provided they hold a Licence entitling them to practise as a teacher.

Language requirements: Good knowledge of Arabic or French

Recognition of studies and qualifications:

Studies pursued in foreign countries (bodies dealing with recognition of foreign credentials):
Division de la Règlementation et des Equivalences de Diplômes, Ministère de l'Education nationale et de la Jeunesse

  24 rue du Sénégal-Océan
  Rabat
  Tel: +212(37) 77-18-22 +212(37) 68-72-27
  Fax: +212(37) 77-20-34 +212(37) 68-72-28
  Telex: 31016 meps-mes
  WWW: http://www.men.gov.ma

Multilateral agreements concerning recognition of foreign studies

Name(s) of agreement(s): Convention on the Recognition of Studies, Certificates, Diplomas and Degrees in Higher Education in the Arab and European States Bordering on the Mediterranean
Year of signature: 1976

Convention on the Recognition of Studies, Diplomas and Degrees in Higher Education in the Arab States
Year of signature: 1978

References to further information on foreign student admissions and recognition of studies

Title: Directory of Higher Education Institutions http://www.dfc.gov.ma
Author: Ministère de l'Enseignement supérieur,Formation des Cadres & Recherche scientif.

STUDENT LIFE

Main student services at national level

Direction de la Recherche scientifique et de la Coopération universitaire
  Service des Etudiants étrangers
  Rabat
  Tel: +212(37) 73-72-22

Student expenses and financial aid

Student costs:

  Home students tuition fees: Minimum: 0 (Moroccan Dirham)
  Maximum: 24,000 (Moroccan Dirham)
  Foreign students tuition fees: Minimum: 4,700 (US Dollar)

Publications on student services and financial aid:

  Title: Study Abroad 2004-2005
  Author: UNESCO

Publisher: UNESCO Publishing
Year of publication: 2003

GRADING SYSTEM

Usual grading system in secondary school

Full Description: 16-20 très bien; 14-15 bien; 12-13 assez bien; 10-11 passable; 0-9 insuffisant.
Highest on scale: 20
Pass/fail level: 10
Lowest on scale: 0

Main grading system used by higher education institutions

Full Description: 16.0-20.0 Très bien; 14.0-15.9 Bien; 12.0-13.9 Assez bien; 10.0-11.9 Passable
Highest on scale: 20
Pass/fail level: 10
Lowest on scale: 0

NOTES ON HIGHER EDUCATION SYSTEM

Data for academic year: 2002-2003
Source: International Association of Universities (IAU), updated from IBE website, 2003
(www.ibe.unesco.org/International/Databanks/Wde/profilee.htm)

INSTITUTIONS OF HIGHER EDUCATION

UNIVERSITIES

PUBLIC INSTITUTIONS

IBNOU ZOHR UNIVERSITY-AGADIR
Université Ibnou Zohr-Agadir
BP 32/S, Agadir
Tel: +212(48) 22-70-17 +212(48) 22-71-25
Fax: +212(48) 22-72-60
EMail: ibnzohr@marocnet.net.ma

Recteur: Ahmed Jebli (1997-) Tel: +212(8) 22-74-69
EMail: jebli@esta.ac.ma

Secrétaire général: Abderrahmane Rida
Tel: +212(8) 23-32-25 EMail: rida@esta.ac.ma

International Relations: Abderrahmane Rida

Faculties
Arts and Humanities *Dean*: Lahcen Benhalima
Science (Mathematics and Computer Science; Natural Sciences) *Dean*: Mohamed Amine Serghini

Schools
Commerce and Management *(National, ENCG)* (Business and Commerce; Management) *Director*: Mohamed Marzak
Technology *(Advanced Studies)*

History: Founded 1989.

Governing Bodies: Ministère de l'Enseignement supérieur, de la Formation des Cadres et de la Recherche scientifique

Academic Year: September to July (September-December; January-March; April-July)

Admission Requirements: Secondary school certificate (baccalauréat)

Fees: None

Main Language(s) of Instruction: Arabic, French

Degrees and Diplomas: *Diplôme universitaire de Technologie (DUT)*: 2 yrs; *Certificat universitaire*: Arab Language and Literature (CUEL); Biology-Geology (CUES); English Language and Literature (CUEL); French Language and Literature (CUEL); History-Geography (CUEL); Islamic Studies (CUEL); Mathematics-Physics (CUES); Physics-Chemistry (CUES); Spanish Language and Literature (CUEL), 2 yrs; *Diplôme/Diplôme supérieur*: Business and Management, 4 yrs; *Licence*: 4 yrs; *Diplôme d'Etudes supérieures (DES)*: a further 3-4 yrs; *Diplôme d'Etudes supérieures approfondies (DESA)*: a further 2 yrs following Licence; *Doctorat*

Student Services: Academic Counselling, Social Counselling, Nursery Care, Cultural Centre, Sports Facilities, Language Programmes, Handicapped Facilities, Health Services

Student Residential Facilities: Yes

Special Facilities: Theatre. Exhibition Centre. Movie studio

Libraries: Yes

Academic Staff *2001-2002*	MEN	WOMEN	TOTAL
FULL-TIME	376	90	**466**
STAFF WITH DOCTORATE			
FULL-TIME	58	9	**67**

Student Numbers *2001-2002*	MEN	WOMEN	TOTAL
All (Foreign Included)	9,300	5,998	**15,298**
FOREIGN ONLY	86	21	107

HASSAN II UNIVERSITY AÏN CHOCK OF CASABLANCA
Université Hassan II Aïn Chock de Casablanca
19, rue Tarik Bnou Ziad, Casablanca
Tel: +212(22) 27-37-37
Fax: +212(22) 27-61-50
Website: http://www.rectorat-uh2c.ac.ma

Recteur: Mohammed Barkaoui (2002-) Tel: +212(2) 26-26-72
EMail: president@rectorat-uh2c.ac.ma

Secrétaire général: Noreddine Siraj
EMail: siraj@rectorat-uh2c.ac.ma

Faculties
Dentistry (Dental Technology; Dentistry) *Dean*: Latifa Tricha
Law, Economics, Social Studies and Political Science (Economics; Law; Political Science; Social Studies) *Dean*: El Bachir Kouhlani
Letters, Arts and Humanities *(Aïn Chock)* (Arabic; Arts and Humanities; English; French; Geography; German; History; Islamic Studies; Spanish) *Dean*: Ahmed Bouchareb
Medicine and Pharmacy (Anaesthesiology; Anatomy; Biology; Cardiology; Dermatology; Epidemiology; Gastroenterology; Gynaecology and Obstetrics; Haematology; Medical Technology; Medicine; Nephrology; Neurology; Neurosciences; Oncology; Ophthalmology; Orthopedics; Otorhinolaryngology; Paediatrics; Pharmacy; Pneumology; Psychiatry and Mental Health; Rheumatology; Surgery; Urology) *Dean*: Ahmed Farouki
Science *(Aïn Chock)* (Biology; Chemistry; Computer Science; Electrical Engineering; Engineering; Environmental Management; Geology; Mathematics; Mechanical Engineering; Natural Sciences; Physics) *Dean*: Driss El Khyari

Higher Schools
Electrical and Mechanical Engineering (Electrical Engineering; Mechanical Engineering) *Director*: Touriya Berradia
Technology (Electrical Engineering; Engineering Management; Mechanical Engineering; Technology) *Dean*: Abdelillah Afifi

History: Founded 1975.

Academic Year: September to July

Admission Requirements: Secondary school certificate (baccalauréat) and entrance examination

Fees: None

Main Language(s) of Instruction: Arabic, French

International Co-operation: With universities in Belgium, Canada, Egypt, Spain, France, Iraq, Italy, Mali, Senegal, Switzerland, Tunisia, USA

Degrees and Diplomas: *Diplôme universitaire de Technologie (DUT)*: Electrical Engineering; Mechanical Engineering; Materials Engineering; Management, 2 yrs; *Certificat universitaire*: Arab Language and Literature; French Language and Literature; Spanish Language and Literature; German Language and Literature; English Language and Literature; History and Geography; Islamic Studies (CUEL); Law; Mathematics and Physics; Physics and Chemistry; Biology and Geology (CUES), 2 yrs; *Diplôme d'Ingénieur d'Etat*: Electrical Engineering; Mechanical Engineering, 5 yrs; *Licence*: History and Geography; Physics; Electrical Engineering; Mechanical Engineering; Chemistry; Computer Science; Biology; Engineering; Environment Management; Private Law; Public Law; Economics; Management; Commerce; Insurance; Business Law; Arabic Language and Literature; French Language and Literature; Spanish Language and Literature; German Language and Literature; English Language and Literature, 4 yrs; *Diplôme d'Etudes supérieures spécialisées (DESS)*: Economics; Public Law; Private Law; Engineering; Physics, 2 yrs following Licence; *Diplôme d'Etudes supérieures approfondies (DESA)*: Engineering; Public Law; Geography; Islamic Studies; Biology; Physics; Chemistry; Environment Sciences; Medicine, a further 2 yrs; *Doctorat*: Economics; Literature; Geography; Medicine, 3 yrs; Public Law; Private Law; Engineering; Geology; Physics; Mathematics; Chemistry, 4 yrs; Dentistry, 5 yrs

Student Services: Academic Counselling, Cultural Centre, Sports Facilities, Handicapped Facilities, Canteen, Foreign Student Centre

Student Residential Facilities: Yes

Libraries: Central Library, libraries of the Faculties and Schools, total, c. 150,320 vols

Publications: Le Bulletin de l 'Université; Les Cahiers de Recherche de l'Université Hassan II - Aïn Chock; Annales de la Faculté de Lettres Aïn Chok; Revue marocaine de Droit et de l'Economie de Développement; Revue Tribune

Academic Staff *2001-2002*	MEN	WOMEN	TOTAL
FULL-TIME	792	363	**1,155**

Student Numbers *2001-2002*	MEN	WOMEN	TOTAL
All (Foreign Included)	13,086	24,565	**37,651**
FOREIGN ONLY	–	–	420

UNIVERSITY CHOUAÏB DOUKKALI EL JADIDA
Université Chouaïb Doukkali El Jadida
BP 299, 2, avenue Mohamed ben Larbi Alaoui, Koudiate ben Driss, 24000 El Jadida
Tel: +212(23) 34-44-47, Ext. 48
Fax: +212(23) 34-44-49
Website: http://www.ucd.ac.ma

Recteur: Mohamed Kouam

Faculties
Arts and Humanities (Arabic; Arts and Humanities; Communication Studies; English; French; Geography; History; Islamic Studies; Literature)
Science (Biology; Chemistry; Geology; Mathematics; Natural Sciences; Physics)

History: Founded 1989, following the decentralization of higher education.

Governing Bodies: Rectorat

Academic Year: September to July

Admission Requirements: Secondary school certificate (baccalauréat)

Fees: None

Main Language(s) of Instruction: Arabic, French, English

Degrees and Diplomas: *Certificat universitaire*: Arab Language and Literature; Biology; Chemistry; English Language and Literature; French Language and Literature; Geography; Geology; History; Islamic Studies; Mathematics; Physics, 2 yrs; *Diplôme d'Etudes universitaires générales (DEUG)*: Applied Biology and Agro-Food Science; Applied Chemistry and Environment; Applied Geology; Applied Mathematics and Computer Science; Electrical and Mechanical Engineering, 2 yrs; *Licence*: Letters; Science, 4 yrs; *Maîtrise*: a further 2 yrs following Licence; *Diplôme d'Etudes supérieures (DES)*: 2-3 yrs following DEUG; *Doctorat*: Arab Language and Literature; English Language and Literature; French Language and Literature; Geography; History; Islamic Studies; Science and Technology

Student Services: Cultural Centre, Sports Facilities, Health Services

Student Residential Facilities: For c. 10,000 students

Libraries: Faculty Libraries, total, 14,460 vols

Publications: Magazine de la Faculté des Lettres parallèles; Revue de la Faculté des Lettres

Academic Staff *2001-2002:* Total: c. 440
Staff with doctorate: Total: c. 25

Student Numbers *2001-2002:* Total: c. 8,100

• UNIVERSITY QUARAOUIYINE FEZ
Université Quaraouiyine Fès
BP 2509, Fès
Tel: +212(55) 64-10-06
Fax: +212(55) 64-10-13
Telex: 31016

Recteur (par intérim): Ali Squalli Houssaini

Secrétaire général: Mohamed Bennani Zoubir

International Relations: Mohamed El Badri
Tel: +212(55) 64-10-16

Faculties

Arabic Language and Literature *(Marrakech)* (Arabic; Literature)

Islamic Law

Islamic Law *(Agadir)*

Theology and Philosophy *(Tétouan)* (Philosophy; Theology)

Centres

Islamic Studies and Research (Islamic Studies)

History: Founded 859, reorganized 1788-89 by Mohammed III. Became State institution 1947.

Academic Year: November to June (November-December; January-March; April-June)

Admission Requirements: Secondary school certificate (baccalauréat) or equivalent

Fees: None

Main Language(s) of Instruction: Arabic

Degrees and Diplomas: *Licence*: Arab Language and Literature; Islamic Law; Theology and Philosophy, 4 yrs; *Diplôme d'Etudes supérieures (DES)*: a further 2 yrs; *Doctorat*: 4 yrs

Student Residential Facilities: Yes

Libraries: Central Library; faculty libraries

Publications: Revues (quarterly); Bulletin Universitaire

Academic Staff *2001-2002:* Total: c. 120

Student Numbers *2001-2002:* Total: c. 5,595

UNIVERSITY SIDI MOHAMMED BEN ABDELLAH-FEZ

Université Sidi Mohammed Ben Abdellah-Fès
BP 2626, Boulevard des Almohades, Fès
Tel: +212(55) 62-55-85
Fax: +212(55) 62-36-41
EMail: recusmba@iam.net.ma
Website:
http://www.enssup.gov.ma/etablissements/univsmbafes.htm

Président: Mohammed El Kably (1998-)
Tel: +212(5) 65-04-52

Secrétaire général: Mohamed Ferhane
Tel: +212(5) 65-07-80 Fax: +212(5) 62-24-01

International Relations: Hassan Chergui
Tel: +212(5) 62-55-86

Faculties

Arts and Humanities *(Dhar El Mehraz)* (Arts and Humanities; Geography; History; Islamic Studies; Literature; Modern Languages; Philosophy; Psychology; Sociology) *Dean*: Mohammed Chad

Arts and Humanities *(Saïs)* (Arts and Humanities; Geography; History; Islamic Studies; Literature; Modern Languages) *Dean*: Mohammed Mezzine

Law, Economics and Social Sciences (Economics; Law; Social Sciences) *Dean*: Abdelkader Kadiri

Medicine and Pharmacy (Medicine; Pharmacology; Pharmacy) *Dean*: Abdelaziz Maouni

Science *(Dhar El Mehraz)* (Biological and Life Sciences; Chemistry; Geology; Mathematics; Natural Sciences; Physics) *Dean*: Mohammed Kadiri

Science and Techniques *(Saïs)* (Biology; Chemistry; Geology; Mathematics; Natural Sciences; Physics; Technology) *Dean*: Driss Bouami

Schools

Advanced Technology *(Saïs)* (Electrical Engineering; Engineering Management; Industrial Engineering; Management; Mechanical Engineering; Production Engineering) *Director*: Taoufik Ouazzani

History: Founded 1975.

Governing Bodies: Conseil

Academic Year: September to June (September-February; February-June)

Admission Requirements: Secondary school certificate (baccalauréat) or equivalent

Fees: None

Main Language(s) of Instruction: Arabic, French

Degrees and Diplomas: *Diplôme universitaire de Technologie (DUT)*: Chemical Engineering; Electrical Engineering; Industrial Maintenance; Management Technology; Mechanical Engineering, 2 yrs; *Certificat universitaire*: Biology and Geology; Economics; Law; Mathematics and Physics; Physics and Chemistry, 2 yrs; *Licence*: Arab Language and Literature; Biology; Chemistry; Economics; English Language and Literature; French Language and Literature; Geography; Geology; German Language and Literature; History; Islamic Studies; Mathematics; Philosophy; Physics; Private Law; Public Law; Spanish Language and Literature, 4 yrs; *Maîtrise*: a further 2 yrs; *Diplôme d'Etudes supérieures (DES)*: a further 2 yrs; *Doctorat*: Science, a further 2-4 yrs

Student Services: Social Counselling, Employment Services, Cultural Centre, Sports Facilities, Health Services, Canteen

Student Residential Facilities: For c. 5000 students

Libraries: c. 170,000 vols

Academic Staff *2001-2002:* Total: c. 1,010
Staff with doctorate: Total: c. 940

Student Numbers *2001-2002:* Total: c. 32,000

AL AKHAWAYN UNIVERSITY IFRANE

Université Al-Akhawayn Ifrane
BP 104, Hassan II Avenue, 53000 Ifrane
Tel: +212(55) 86-20-00
Fax: +212(55) 56-71-50
EMail: info@alakhawayn.ma
Website: http://www.alakhawayn.ma

Président: Rachid Benmokhtar Benabdellah (2002-)
Tel: +212(5) 86-20-01 Fax: +212(5) 56-71-42
EMail: president@alakhawayn.ma

Schools

Business Administration (Business Administration; Finance; International Business; Management; Marketing)

Humanities and Social Sciences (Arts and Humanities; Communication Studies; Media Studies; Social Sciences)

Science and Engineering (Biological and Life Sciences; Computer Science; Engineering; Environmental Studies; Natural Sciences)

Institutes

Economic Analysis and Prospective Studies (Economics)

Centres

Environmental Studies and Regional Development (Environmental Studies; Regional Planning)

Executive Education (Leadership)

Women Empowerment *(Hillary Rodham Clinton)* (Women's Studies)

Further Information: Also Arabic courses for foreign students

History: Founded 1995 as an English-language institution based on the American higher education model.

Governing Bodies: Board of Trustees

Academic Year: September to May (September-December; January-May). Also optional Summer Session (June-July)

Admission Requirements: Secondary school certificate (baccalauréat) with excellent academic credentials and an interview

Fees: (US Dollars): Foreign students, c. 4700

Main Language(s) of Instruction: English

Degrees and Diplomas: *Licence*: 4 yrs; *Maîtrise*: a further 2 yrs

Student Services: Academic Counselling, Social Counselling, Nursery Care, Cultural Centre, Sports Facilities, Health Services, Canteen, Foreign Student Centre

Student Residential Facilities: For c. 1000 students

Libraries: University Library, c. 30,000 vols

Publications: AUI News; AUI Horizons

Academic Staff *2001-2002*: Full-Time: c. 60 Part-Time: c. 10 Total: c. 70

Student Numbers *2001-2002*: All (Foreign Included): c. 800 Foreign Only: c. 20

UNIVERSITY IBN TOFAIL KENITRA

Université Ibn Tofail Kénitra

BP 242, 104, rue Ahmed Boughaba, Bir rami Est, 14000 Kenitra
Tel: +212(37) 37-28-09
Fax: +212(37) 37-40-52
EMail: ruitk@iam.net.ma
Website: http://www.univ-ibntofail.ma

Recteur: Mohamed Essouari (2002-)

Secrétaire général: Abdallah El Maliki

International Relations: Souad Guelzim

Faculties

Arts and Humanities (Arabic; Arts and Humanities; English; French; Geography; History; Islamic Studies; Literature) *Dean*: Abdelfettah Ben Kaddour

Science (Biology; Chemistry; Geology; Mathematics; Natural Sciences; Physics) *Dean*: Ali Boukhari

History: Founded 1989.

Academic Year: September to July

Admission Requirements: Secondary school certificate (baccalauréat)

Fees: None

Main Language(s) of Instruction: Arabic, French

International Co-operation: With universities in France; United States; Canada; Belgium; Tunisia; Sweden; Germany; Spain; Egypt. Also participates in FICU

Degrees and Diplomas: *Certificat universitaire*: Islamic Studies; Arab Language and Literature; Biology and Geology; English Language and Literature; French Language and Literature; History and Geography; Letters; Mathematics and Physics; Physics and Chemistry, 2 yrs; *Licence*: Biology; Chemistry; Geology; Letters; Mathematics; Physics, 4 yrs; *Diplôme d'Etudes supérieures spécialisées (DESS)*: Biology; Chemistry; Physics, 2 yrs; *Diplôme d'Etudes supérieures approfondies (DESA)*: Biology; Chemistry; Letters; Mathematics; Physics, 2 yrs; *Doctorat*: Biology; Chemistry; Geology; Letters; Mathematics; Physics, 4 yrs

Student Services: Sports Facilities, Health Services

Student Residential Facilities: Yes

Libraries: Faculty of Arts and Humanities 36,000 vols; Faculty of Science 6007 vols.

Academic Staff *2001-2002*	MEN	WOMEN	TOTAL
FULL-TIME	278	127	**405**
STAFF WITH DOCTORATE			
FULL-TIME	276	124	**400**
Student Numbers *2001-2002*	MEN	WOMEN	TOTAL
All (Foreign Included)	8,403	3,375	**11,778**
FOREIGN ONLY	–	–	62

UNIVERSITY CADI AYYAD MARRAKECH

Université Cadi Ayyad Marrakech

BP 511, Avenue Prince Abdellah, Marrakech
Tel: +212(44) 43-48-13
Fax: +212(44) 43-44-94
Telex: 74869
EMail: rectorat@ucam.ac.ma
Website: http://www.ucam.ac.ma

Recteur: Ahmed Jebli (2002-)

International Relations: Abdeljalil El Goraï
EMail: elgorai@ucam.ac.ma

Faculties

Arts and Humanities *(Beni-Mellal) Dean*: Ahmed Alaoui

Arts and Humanities *(FLSH)* (Arabic; Arts and Humanities; English; French; Geography; History; Islamic Studies) *Dean*: Abdeljalil Hanouche

Law, Economics, and Social Sciences *(FSJES)* (Economics; Law; Social Sciences) *Dean*: Ahmed Trachen

Medicine and Pharmacy (Medicine; Pharmacy) *Dean*: Badie Ezzaman Mehadji

Science *(Semlalia, FSSM)* (Biology; Chemistry; Computer Science; Geology; Mathematics; Natural Sciences; Physics) *Dean*: Mohamed Arsalane

Science and Technology (Biology; Chemistry; Geology; Mathematics; Natural Sciences; Physics; Technology) *Dean*: Mohamed Arsalane

Science and Technology *(Beni Mellal)* (Biology; Chemistry; Geology; Mathematics; Natural Sciences; Physics; Technology) *Dean*: Mohamed Ankrim

Higher Schools

Applied Sciences (Computer Engineering; Electrical Engineering; Telecommunications Engineering) *Director*: Mustapha El Adnani

Technology *(Safi)* (Industrial Maintenance; Management Systems; Production Engineering; Technology) *Director*: Ahmed Souissi

History: Founded 1978.

Academic Year: September to June (September-December; January-April; May-June)

Admission Requirements: Secondary school certificate (baccalauréat) or equivalent

Fees: None

Main Language(s) of Instruction: French

International Co-operation: With universities in Spain; Italy; France; Tunisia; Belgium; USA; Germany

Degrees and Diplomas: *Capacité en Droit*: Law, 2 yrs; *Diplôme universitaire de Technologie (DUT)*: Analysis Technology and Quality Control; Industrial Maintenance; Management Technology, 2 yrs; *Certificat universitaire*: Arabic; Bioscience and Earth Sciences; Economics; English; French; History and Geography; Islamic Studies; Law; Mathematics and Physics; Physics and Chemistry, 2 yrs; *Licence*: Agricultural Management; Applied Management; Applied Mathematics; Arab Literature; Biology; Chemistry; Computer Science; Computer Science and Management; Economics; English Literature; French Literature; Geography; Geology; History; Islamic Studies; Local and Regional Planning; Mathematics; Optics; Physics; Private Law; Public Law; Tourism, 4 yrs; *Maîtrise*: Science and Technology, 2 yrs following Licence; *Diplôme d'Etudes supérieures (DES)*: Arab Literature; Biology; Chemistry; French Literature; Geology; Mathematics, 2 yrs following Licence; *Doctorat*: Science

Student Services: Sports Facilities, Health Services, Canteen

Academic Staff *2001-2002:* Total: **1,234**

Student Numbers *2001-2002:* Total: **32,698**

UNIVERSITY MOULAY ISMAIL MEKNÈS
Université Moulay Ismail Meknès
1, Place Andalous BP298, Meknès
Tel: +212(5) 52-63-78
Fax: +212(5) 52-73-14
Website:
http://www.enssup.gov.ma/etablissements/univmisMeknes.htm

Président: Mohamed Bennani (1997-)
Tel: +212(55) 46-73-20 EMail: rectorat@extra.net.ma
Secrétaire général: Mejdoul El Houssine
International Relations: Nezha El Mernissi

Faculties

Arts and Humanities (Arabic; Arts and Humanities; English; French; Geography; History; Islamic Studies; Literature; Modern Languages) *Dean*: Mohamed Errafass
Law, Economics & Social Studies (Economics; Law; Social Studies) *Dean*: Abdelkader Hassani
Science (Biology; Chemistry; Mathematics and Computer Science; Natural Sciences; Physics) *Dean*: Mohamed Zaher Benabdellah
Science and Technology *(Errachidia)* (Natural Sciences; Technology) *Dean*: Abdelmajid Zayed

Higher Schools

Industrial Engineering *(ENSAM, Meknès)* (Electrical and Electronic Engineering; Industrial Engineering) *Directeur*: Mohamed Bouidida
Technology *Directeur*: Fouad Benyaîch

History: Founded 1982, acquired present status 1989.

Governing Bodies: Ministère de l'Enseignement Supérieur de la Formation des Cadres et de la Recherche Scientifique (MESFCRS)

Academic Year: September to July (September-December; January-March; April-July)

Admission Requirements: Secondary school certificate (baccalauréat)

Main Language(s) of Instruction: Arabic, French, English

International Co-operation: With universities in France, Belgium, Spain, Germany

Degrees and Diplomas: *Diplôme universitaire de Technologie (DUT)*: Business Management; Secretarial Studies, 2 yrs; *Certificat universitaire*: Arabic Language and Literature (DEUG); Biology and Geology (DEUG); Chemistry (DEUG); Economics (DEUG); English Language and Literature (DEUG); French Language and Literature (DEUG); History and Geography (DEUG); Islamic Studies (DEUG); Law (DEUG); Mathematics (DEUG); Physics (DEUG), 2 yrs; *Diplôme d'Etudes universitaires générales (DEUG)*: Biology; Bioscience and Earth Sciences; Geology; Physics and Chemistry, 2 yrs; *Diplôme d'Ingénieur d'Etat*: Electrical Engineering; Mechanical Engineering; Occupational Arts, 5 yrs; *Licence*: Biology; Chemistry; Economics; Geology; Literature; Mathematics; Physics; Private Law; Public Law, 4 yrs; *Maîtrise*: Biology; Chemistry; Geology; Mechanics, Geophysics (es Sciences Spécialisées) (MSS/MST); Physics; Science and Technology (es Sciences

Spécialisées) (MSS/MST); Social Sciences, a further 2 yrs; *Diplôme d'Etudes supérieures spécialisées (DESS)*: Biology; Community Law and Management; Public Law, a further 2 yrs; *Diplôme d'Etudes supérieures approfondies (DESA)*: Literature; Mathematics, a further 2 yrs; *Doctorat*: Biology; Chemistry; Mathematics; Physics, 2 yrs following DESA

Student Services: Academic Counselling, Social Counselling, Employment Services, Cultural Centre, Sports Facilities, Language Programmes, Handicapped Facilities, Health Services, Canteen, Foreign Student Centre

Student Residential Facilities: Yes

Libraries: Each Institute has its own Library

Publications: Minbar Al Mamiaa; Maknasat, Revue de la Faculté des Lettres (annually)

Academic Staff *2001-2002*	MEN	WOMEN	TOTAL
FULL-TIME	568	123	**691**

Student Numbers *2001-2002*	MEN	WOMEN	TOTAL
All (Foreign Included)	14,558	9,536	**24,094**
FOREIGN ONLY	122	14	136

HASSAN II UNIVERSITY MOHAMMEDIA

Université Hassan II Mohammedia
BP 150, 279 Cité Yassmina, Mohammedia
Tel: +212(23) 31-46-35
Fax: +212(23) 31-46-34
Website: http://www.uh2m.ac.ma

Rectrice: Rahma Bourqia (2002-)

Faculties

Arts and Humanities (Arabic; Arts and Humanities; English; French; Geography; History; Islamic Studies) *Dean*: Jawad Essakat

Arts and Humanities *(Ben M'Sik)* (Arabic; Arts and Humanities; English; French; Geography; History; Islamic Studies)

Law (Economics; Law; Social Studies)

Science *(Ben M'Sik)* (Natural Sciences)

Science and Technology (Biological and Life Sciences; Chemistry; Communication Studies; Electrical Engineering; Environmental Studies; Natural Sciences; Physics; Technology) *Dean*: Mohamed Rafik

History: Founded 1992.

Main Language(s) of Instruction: Arabic, French, English

Degrees and Diplomas: *Licence*: 4 yrs; *Doctorat*

Libraries: c. 100,000 vols

Publications: Bahuth; Basamat; Aqlam al-Jamia

Academic Staff *2001-2002*: Full-Time: c. 550 Part-Time: c. 30 Total: c. 580

Student Numbers *2001-2002*: Total: c. 14,100

*• MOHAMMED I UNIVERSITY OUJDA

Jami'at Muhammad Al-Awwal Oujda
BP 724, 60000 Oujda
Tel: +212(56) 50-06-12 +212(56) 50-06-14
Fax: +212(56) 50-06-09
EMail: rectorat@univ-oujda.ac.ma
Website: http://www.univ-oujda.ac.ma

Recteur: Mohamed El-Farissi (2003-) Tel: +212(56) 50-06-13
EMail: recteur@univ-oujda.ac.ma

Secrétaire général: Abderrahman Houtch
EMail: houtch@univ-oujda.ac.ma

International Relations: Youssef Smiri
EMail: smiri@univ-oujda.ac.ma

Faculties

Arts and Humanities (Arts and Humanities; English; French; Geography; History; Islamic Studies) *Dean*: Mohammed Laamiri

Law, Economics and Social Sciences (Economics; Law; Political Science; Social Sciences) *Dean*: Larbi M'Rabet

Science (Natural Sciences) *Dean*: Benaïssa Nciri

Schools

Applied Sciences *(National)* (Natural Sciences)

Higher Schools

Technology (Accountancy; Business Administration; Computer Science; Electrical Engineering; Electronic Engineering; Engineering; Technology) *Director*: Mohamed Barboucha

Centres

Migration Studies (Demography and Population)

History: Founded 1978.

Governing Bodies: Conseil

Academic Year: October to June

Admission Requirements: Secondary school certificate (baccalauréat) or equivalent

Fees: None

Main Language(s) of Instruction: Arabic, French

International Co-operation: With universities in France, Belgium, Italy, Spain, Netherlands, Germany, United Kingdom, Iraq, Algeria, Tunisia and Romania

Degrees and Diplomas: *Diplôme universitaire de Technologie (DUT)*: Electrical Engineering; Management, 2 yrs; *Certificat universitaire*: Arab Language and Literature; Biology and Geology; Economics; English Language and Literature; French Language and Literature; History and Geography; Islamic Studies; Law; Mathematics and Physics; Physics and Chemistry, 2 yrs; *Licence*: Arab Language and Literature; Biology; Chemistry; Economics; English Language and Literature; French Language and Literature; Geography; Geology; History; Islamic Studies; Mathematics; Physics; Private Law; Public Law, 4 yrs; *Diplôme d'Etudes supérieures (DES)*: Arab Language and Literature; Biology; Chemistry; Economics; French Language and Literature; Geography; Geology; History; Islamic Studies; Law; Mathematics, 1-2 yrs; *Doctorat*: Arab Language and Literature; Biology; Chemistry; Economics; English Language and

Literature; French Language and Literature; Geography; Geology; History; Islamic Studies; Law; Mathematics; Physics

Student Residential Facilities: Yes

Libraries: Faculty libraries, total, c. 128,612 vols

Publications: Moroccan Journal of International Relations; University Info; Journal of Juridical, Economic and Social Studies; Journal of Administrative Studies (1 per annum)

Academic Staff *2001-2002:* Total: c. 590

Student Numbers *2001-2002*: All (Foreign Included): c. 20,000 Foreign Only: c. 315

*• MOHAMMED V UNIVERSITY-AGDAL RABAT

Jamiât Mohammed Al-Khâmiss Rabat

BP 554, 3, rue Michlifen, Agdal, Rabat-Chellah
Tel: +212(37) 67-13-18
Fax: +212(37) 67-14-01
Telex: recuniv 32603
EMail: presidence@um5a.ac.ma
Website: http://www.um5a.ac.ma

Président: Hafid Boutaleb Joutei (2001-)
Tel: +212(37) 67-33-45 EMail: presidence@um5a.ac.ma

Secrétaire général: Mohammed Maniar
Tel: +212(37) 67-43-90

Faculties

Arts and Humanities *(Agdal)* (Arts and Humanities; English; French; Geography; German; History; Islamic Studies; Philosophy; Psychology; Sociology; Spanish) *Dean:* Saïd Bensaïd Alaoui

Law, Economics and Social Sciences (Economic and Finance Policy; Economics; Human Resources; International Relations; Law; Management; Political Science; Private Law; Public Law; Social Sciences) *Dean:* Abdelghani El Kadmiri

Science (Biology; Chemistry; Computer Science; Earth Sciences; Mathematics; Natural Sciences; Physics) *Dean:* Hajjoub Msougar

Schools

Engineering *(Mohammedia)* (Chemistry; Civil Engineering; Computer Science; Electrical Engineering; Engineering; Industrial Engineering; Mechanical Engineering; Mineralogy; Physics) *Director:* Mohammed Ali Taoud

Technology *(Salé)* (Environmental Studies; Industrial Maintenance; Management; Technology; Town Planning) *Director:* Saïd Naji

Institutes

Scientific Research (Botany; Geography; Natural Sciences; Physics; Surveying and Mapping; Zoology) *Director:* Driss Najid

Studies and Research on Arabization (Middle Eastern Studies; North African Studies) *Director:* Abdelkader Fassi-Fihri

History: Founded 1957 incorporating former Institutes of Letters (1912), Law (1920), and Science (1940) of the Mohammed V University. Reorganized 1975 and 1993. A state institution.

Governing Bodies: Conseil de l'Université

Academic Year: September to June (September-December; January-March; April-June)

Admission Requirements: Secondary school certificate (baccalauréat) or equivalent. Entrance examination for Engineering

Fees: None

Main Language(s) of Instruction: Arabic, French

International Co-operation: With universities in Belgium, Canada, France, Germany, Iraq, Tunisia, Mauritania, USA, Russia, Syria, Italy, Spain.

Degrees and Diplomas: *Diplôme universitaire de Technologie (DUT):* Engineering; Technology, 2 yrs; *Certificat universitaire:* Science (CUES), 2 yrs; *Diplôme d'Etudes universitaires générales (DEUG):* Economics; Law; Arts and Humanities, 2 yrs; *Diplôme d'Ingénieur d'Etat:* Engineering, 5 yrs; *Licence:* Economics; Arts and Humanities; Private Law; Public Law; Science, 4 yrs; *Diplôme d'Etudes supérieures spécialisées (DESS):* Engineering; Arts and Humanities; Science, a further 2 yrs; *Diplôme d'Etudes supérieures approfondies (DESA):* Economics; Engineering; Law; Arts and Humanities; Science, a further 2 yrs; *Doctorat:* Economics; Engineering; Arts and Humanities; Private Law; Public Law; Science. Also Diplôme de Spécialité de 3e cycle en Science.

Student Services: Academic Counselling, Sports Facilities, Language Programmes, Health Services, Canteen, Foreign Student Centre

Student Residential Facilities: Yes

Special Facilities: Scientific Research Institute Museum

Libraries: Rectorate, c. 28,000 vols; Faculty libraries, 427,168 vols, 40,998 periodicals

Publications: Annales du Centre des Etudes stratégiques de Rabat; Revue de la Faculté des Lettres et des Sciences humaines; Hespéris Tamuda; Bulletin de l'Institut scientifique; La Recherche scientifique; Bulletins du Département de Physique du globe; Signes du Présent; Revue juridique, politique, économique du Maroc; Journal marocain d'Automatisation, d'Informatique et de Traitement de Signal; Revue Attadriss; Travaux de l'Institut scientifique

Academic Staff *2001-2002:* Total: c. 1,200

Student Numbers *2001-2002*: All (Foreign Included): c. 26,000 Foreign Only: c. 440

• MOHAMMED V SOUISSI UNIVERSITY RABAT

Jâmiât Mohammed El-Khâmiss Souissi Rabat

BP 8007, N.U., Agdal-Rabat
Tel: +212(37) 68-11-60
Fax: +212(37) 68-11-63
EMail: um5souissi@ac.ma

Recteur: Mohammed Tahar Alaoui

Secrétaire général: Mohammed Belfquih

International Relations: Rachid Agaddou

Faculties

Law, Economics and Social Sciences *(Sale)* (Economics; Law; Social Sciences) *Dean*: Mohammed Benallal

Law, Economics and Social Sciences *(Souissi)* (Economics; Law; Social Sciences) *Dean*: Moulay Rachid Abderrazzak

Medicine and Pharmacy (Medicine; Pharmacy) *Dean*: Najia Hejaj

Schools

Computer Science and Systems Analysis *(National)* (Computer Science; Systems Analysis) *Director*: Adelhak Mouradi

Dentistry *Head*: Bouchaib Jidal

Educational Sciences *Head*: Mohammed Zgor

Institutes

African Studies *Director*: Fatima Errahala

Scientific Research (History; Literature; Social Sciences) *Director*: Abdelkébir Khatibi

Studies and Research on Arabization (Linguistics; Middle Eastern Studies; North African Studies) *Director*: Abdelkader Fassi-Fihri

History: Founded 1992 incorporating faculties which were originally part of the Mohammed V University after division of this institution into two universities: Mohammed V Souissi and Mohammed V Agdal.

Governing Bodies: Conseil de l'Université

Fees: None

Main Language(s) of Instruction: Arabic, French

International Co-operation: With universities in Italy, Belgium, Germany, Egypt, Senegal.

Accrediting Agencies: Association of African Universities (AAU); Agence Universitaire de la Francophonie (AUF); Federation of the Universities of the Islamic World (FUIW)

Degrees and Diplomas: *Diplôme d'Ingénieur d'Etat*: Computer Science, Systems Analysis, 3 yrs; *Diplôme d'Etudes supérieures spécialisées (DESS)*: 2 yrs following Licence; *Diplôme d'Etudes supérieures approfondies (DESA)*: 2 yrs following Licence; *Doctorat*: (PhD), 4-5 yrs; Pharmacy, 5 yrs; Medicine, 7 yrs. Also Medical Speciality Diploma (4-5 yrs)

Student Services: Academic Counselling, Social Counselling, Foreign Student Adviser, Cultural Centre, Sports Facilities, Language Programmes, Health Services, Canteen, Foreign Student Centre

Student Residential Facilities: Yes

Libraries: Faculty libraries

Publications: Linguistic Research, Studies and Research on Arabization (monthly); Bulletin d' Information, Scientific Research Institute (2 per annum); Al Maghrin Al Ifriqi, African Studies Institute (annually); Al Ifrane

Academic Staff *2001-2002*	MEN	WOMEN	TOTAL
FULL-TIME	723	341	**1,064**

Student Numbers *2001-2002*	MEN	WOMEN	TOTAL
All (Foreign Included)	11,009	10,036	**21,045**
FOREIGN ONLY	445	173	618

HASSAN I UNIVERSITY SETTAT

Université Hassan 1er

BP 539, 50 rue Ibn Al Haithem, 26000 Settat
Tel: +212(23) 72-12-75
Fax: +212(23) 72-12-74
EMail: essaid@onpt.net.ma
Website: http://www.uh1.ac.ma

Recteur: Mohamed Rahj (2002-)

Faculties

Law, Economics and Social Sciences (Economics; Law; Social Sciences)

Science and Technology (Biological and Life Sciences; Chemistry; Computer Science; Earth Sciences; Electronic Engineering; Mathematics; Mechanical Engineering; Physics; Technology)

Schools

Commerce and Management *(National)* (Accountancy; Business Administration; Business and Commerce; Economics; Law; Management)

Main Language(s) of Instruction: French and Arabic

International Co-operation: With universities in France; Spain, Belgium

Degrees and Diplomas: *Licence*: Law; Economics, 4 yrs; *Maîtrise*: Quality Analysis and Control; Mathematics Applied to Engineering; Biomedical Technology; Computer Science; Water Science and Techniques; Mechanical Engineering; Microbiology (MST; MSS), 4 yrs. Also 4-year Diplôme de l'Ecole Nationale de Commerce et de Gestion

Student Services: Academic Counselling, Sports Facilities, Health Services

Student Residential Facilities: Yes

Academic Staff *2001-2002*	MEN	WOMEN	TOTAL
FULL-TIME	143	61	**204**

Student Numbers *2001-2002*	MEN	WOMEN	TOTAL
All (Foreign Included)	3,502	3,177	**6,679**
FOREIGN ONLY	119	31	150

UNIVERSITY ABDELMALEK ESSAÂDI TÉTOUAN

Université Abdelmalek Essaâdi Tétouan

Route de l'Aéroport, Tétouan
Tel: +212(39) 99-51-34
Fax: +212(39) 97-91-51
Website: http://www.uae.ac.ma

Recteur: Mustapha Bennouna (2002-)
EMail: president@uae.ac.ma

Secrétaire général: Larbi Kabbab

International Relations: Ahmed El Moussaoui
EMail: elmoussaoui@uae.ac.ma

Faculties

Arts and Humanities

Law *(Tangiers)*

Law, Economics and Social Sciences *(Tangiers)* (Economics; Law; Social Sciences)
Science (Biology; Chemistry; Geology; Mathematics; Natural Sciences; Physics)
Science and Technology *(Tangiers)* (Natural Sciences; Technology)

Schools
Commerce and Management *(National,Tangiers)* (Business Administration; Business and Commerce; Management)
Translation *(King Fahd, Tangiers)* (Arabic; English; French; Spanish; Translation and Interpretation)

History: Founded 1989.
Academic Year: September to July (September-December; January-March; April-July)
Admission Requirements: Secondary school certificate (baccalauréat)
Fees: None
Main Language(s) of Instruction: Arabic, French
Degrees and Diplomas: *Licence*: 4 yrs; *Diplôme d'Etudes supérieures spécialisées (DESS)*; *Diplôme d'Etudes supérieures approfondies (DESA)*: 2 yrs; *Doctorat*: 3-4 yrs
Libraries: Libraries of the Faculties and Schools
Publications: Tourjouman, Journal of the School of Translation
Academic Staff *2001-2002:* Total: **632**
Student Numbers *2001-2002:* Total: c. 17,150

OTHER UNIVERSITY LEVEL INSTITUTIONS

PUBLIC INSTITUTIONS

NATIONAL INSTITUTE OF ARCHAEOLOGY AND CULTURAL HERITAGE SCIENCES
Institut national des Sciences de l'Archéologie et du Patrimoine
Avenue Kennedy, Route des Zaers, 10 000 Rabat-Souissi
Tel: +212(37) 75-09-61
Fax: +212(37) 75-08-84
EMail: archeo@iam.net.ma
Directeur: Joudia Hassar-Benslimane (1986-)
Directeur adjoint: Aomar Akerraz
International Relations: Abdelfettah El Rhazoui, Secrétaire général

Departments
Anthropology (Anthropology; Ethnology; Social Sciences) *Head*: Naïma Chikhaoui
Archaeology and Cultural Heritage (Archaeology; Heritage Preservation; Museum Studies) *Head*: M. Abdelaziz El Khayari
Heritage Studies (Fine Arts; Heritage Preservation; Restoration of Works of Art) *Head*: Elarbi Erbati

Islamic Studies and Archaeology (Archaeology; Art History; Ceramic Art; Islamic Studies) *Head*: Saehir Mabrouk
Prehistory (Ancient Civilizations; Ceramic Art; Geology; Prehistory) *Head*: Fahti Ammani

History: Founded 1986
Admission Requirements: Secondary school certificate (baccalauréat)
Fees: None
Main Language(s) of Instruction: Arabic, French
International Co-operation: With universities in France; Germany; Spain; Italy; United Kingdom; Belgium
Degrees and Diplomas: *Diplôme d'Etudes supérieures (DES)*: Archaeology and Cultural Heritage, 1st and 2nd cycles, 2 yrs each; *Diplôme d'Etudes supérieures approfondies (DESA)*: Archaeology and Cultural Heritage, 3rd cycle, 5 yrs
Student Services: Health Services, Foreign Student Centre
Special Facilities: Museum
Libraries: Central Library
Publications: Bulletin d'Archéologie Marocaine (1 per annum)
Press or Publishing House: Nouvelles d'Archéologie et du Patrimoine

Academic Staff *2001-2002*	MEN	WOMEN	TOTAL
FULL-TIME	41	19	**60**

Student Numbers *2001-2002*	MEN	WOMEN	TOTAL
All (Foreign Included)	29	21	**50**
FOREIGN ONLY	2	1	3

NATIONAL SCHOOL OF ARCHITECTURE
Ecole nationale d' Architecture (ENA)
BP 6372, Chariaa Allal El Fassi, Rabat
Tel: +212(37) 77-52-29
Fax: +212(37) 77-52-76
EMail: ena@maghrebnet.net.ma
Directeur: Abderrahmane Chorfi Tel: +212(37) 77-52-41
Fax: +212(37) 77-52-76

Architecture
Regional Town Planning and Housing (House Arts and Environment; Regional Planning; Town Planning)

History: Founded 1980.
Admission Requirements: Secondary school certificate (baccalauréat) and entrance examination
Main Language(s) of Instruction: French
International Co-operation: With institutions in France, Italy, Spain
Accrediting Agencies: Ministère de l' Aménagement du Territoire, de l' Urbanisme et de l' Habitat
Degrees and Diplomas: *Diplôme d'Architecte (DENA)*: Architecture, 6 yrs
Student Services: Sports Facilities, Language Programmes
Student Residential Facilities: None
Libraries: Documentation Centre

Academic Staff *2001-2002*

	TOTAL
FULL-TIME	45
PART-TIME	15
TOTAL	**60**

Student Numbers *2001-2002*: All (Foreign Included): c. 400
Foreign Only: c. 30

PRIVATE INSTITUTIONS

HIGHER SCHOOL OF FOOD INDUSTRY

Ecole supérieure de l'Agro-Alimentaire (Sup Agro)
22, rue le Catelet, Belvedère, Casablanca
Tel: +212(22) 24-54-05
Fax: +212(22) 24-53-99
EMail: supagro@casanet.net.ma
Website: http://www.casanet.net.ma/users/supagro

Directeur Pédagogique: Abdelrhafour Tantaoui Elaraki

Directeur Exécutif: Hicham Arsaoui

International Relations: Hicham Arsaoui

Schools
Food Industry (Food Technology) *Director*: Abdelrhafour Tantaoui Elaraki

History: Founded 1997

Governing Bodies: Administrative Board

Academic Year: October to July

Admission Requirements: Secondary school certificate (baccalauréat)

Fees: (Moroccan Dirhams): Registration, 3,000 per annum; tuition, 24,900 per annum

Main Language(s) of Instruction: French

Degrees and Diplomas: *Diplôme universitaire de Technologie (DUT)*: Contrôle Qualité des Aliments, 2 yrs; *Maîtrise*: Technologie Alimentaire, 4 yrs; *Diplôme d'Etudes supérieures spécialisées (DESS)*: Qualité (DESS), 5 yrs

Student Services: Social Counselling, Language Programmes, Canteen

Libraries: Central Library

Academic Staff *2000-2001*

	MEN	WOMEN	TOTAL
FULL-TIME	5	5	10
PART-TIME	70	10	80
TOTAL	**75**	**15**	**90**

Student Numbers *2000-2001*: All (Foreign Included): Men: c. 40 Women: c. 30 Total: c. 70
Foreign Only: Men: c. 3 Women: c. 7 Total: c. 10

HIGHER SCHOOL OF MANAGEMENT, COMMERCE AND COMPUTER SCIENCE

Ecole supérieure de Management, du Commerce et d'Informatique (Sup' Management)
28, place du 11 Janvier et rue Patrice Lumumba, Ville Nouvelle, Fès
Tel: +212(55) 65-34-31 +212(55) 94-08-25
Fax: +212(55) 65-27-32
EMail: supmgt@iam.net.ma
Website: http://www.supmanagement.org.ma

Président: Abdesselam Erkik (1985-) Tel: 212(61) 21-64-72

Sécretaire Générale: Laila El Alaoui El Mdaghri

International Relations: Rachida Erkik

Departments
Computer Science (Computer Engineering; Computer Science; Information Sciences) *Head*: Mohamed El Hajjami
Financial Management (Accountancy; Finance) *Head*: Ahmed Maghni
International Commerce and Marketing (Business and Commerce; Insurance; International Business; Marketing; Transport Management) *Head*: Siham Sahbani
Management (Accountancy; Administration; Communication Studies; Human Resources; International Law; International Relations; Management; Private Law) *Head*: Abdellah Lakhouil

History: Founded 1995.

Governing Bodies: Conseil d' Administration

Academic Year: October to June

Admission Requirements: Secondary school certificate (baccalauréat), bac + 4 for advanced cycle

Fees: (Moroccan Dirhams): 20,300-22,800 per annum

Main Language(s) of Instruction: French, English, German, Spanish, Arabic

Degrees and Diplomas: *Maîtrise*: Computer Engineering, Finance Management, Management and Commerce, 4 yrs; *Diplôme d'Etudes supérieures spécialisées (DESS)*: Commercial Engineering, Financial Engineering, Computer Engineering, Quality Engineering, 6 yrs. Certificats de formation continue (CFC). Certificats de Cycles Spéciaux (CCS)

Student Services: Academic Counselling, Social Counselling, Employment Services, Foreign Student Adviser, Sports Facilities, Language Programmes, Foreign Student Centre

Student Residential Facilities: Yes

Libraries: Central Library and computer facilities

Publications: Flash Managers, Cultural Studies, Management, Economics and Leisure (3 per annum)

Academic Staff *2001-2002*

	MEN	WOMEN	TOTAL
FULL-TIME	35	25	60
PART-TIME	25	14	39
TOTAL	**60**	**39**	**99**
STAFF WITH DOCTORATE			
FULL-TIME	7	4	11
PART-TIME	22	10	32
TOTAL	**29**	**14**	**43**

Student Numbers *2001-2002*

	MEN	WOMEN	TOTAL
All (Foreign Included)	163	108	**271**
FOREIGN ONLY	97	38	135

Part-time Students, 7 Evening Students, 450

OTHER INSTITUTIONS

PUBLIC INSTITUTIONS

CENTRE DE FORMATION DES TECHNICIENS DE L'AÉRONAUTIQUE CIVILE ET DE LA MÉTÉOROLOGIE
BP 8088, Km. 7 Route d'El Jadida, Casablanca-Oasis
Tel: +212(2) 23-06-55
Fax: +212(2) 23-06-52

Directeur: Amal Kabbaj

Programmes
Aeronautics (Aeronautical and Aerospace Engineering)
Meteorology
Telecommunications (Telecommunications Engineering)

COMPLEXE HORTICOLE
BP 18/S, Agadir
Tel: +212(48) 24-10-06
Fax: +212(48) 24-22-43

Directeur: Brahim Hafidi

Horticulture

ECOLE HASSANIA DES TRAVAUX PUBLICS ET DES COMMUNICATIONS (EHTP)
BP 8108, Km. 7, Route d'El Jadida, Casablanca
Tel: +212(22) 23-07-10
Fax: +212(22) 23-07-17
Website: http://www.ehtp.ac.ma

Directeur: Abdeslam Messaoudi
Secretary-General: Abdelouahed Boudlal
International Relations: Mohamed Saoudi

Founded: 1971

Departments
Civil Engineering and Transport (Civil Engineering; Transport and Communications) *Head*: Ali Azizi
Hydraulics (Hydraulic Engineering) *Head*: Brahim Lekhlif
Industrial Engineering and Telecommunications (Industrial Engineering; Telecommunications Engineering) *Head*: Ahmed El Bahraoui
Management
Mathematics and Computer Science (Computer Science; Mathematics) *Head*: Malika Addou

ECOLE NATIONALE D'ADMINISTRATION DE RABAT (ENA)
1, avenue de la Victoire, Rabat
Tel: +212(37) 72-44-00
Fax: +212(37) 73-09-29
Website: http://www.ena.ac.ma

Directeur: Mostafa Taimi

Founded: 1948

Programmes
Administration

ECOLE NATIONALE D'AGRICULTURE DE MEKNÈS
BPS/40, Meknès
Tel: +212(55) 30-02-39
Fax: +212(55) 30-02-38
Telex: 421 54
EMail: ena@enameknes.ac.ma
Website: http://www.enameknes.ac.ma

Directeur: Abdelhafid Debbarh

Founded: 1942

Programmes
Agricultural Pedagogy (Agriculture; Pedagogy)
Agriculture
Animal Production (Animal Husbandry)
Fruit Production Techniques (Fruit Production)
Plant Protection (Plant and Crop Protection)
Rural Economics (Agricultural Economics)
Vegetable Production

ECOLE NATIONALE DE COMMERCE ET DE GESTION (ENCG)
BP 1255, Ancienne route de l'aéroport, Tanger princip., Tanger
Tel: +212(39) 31-34-87 +212(39) 31-34-89
Fax: +212(39) 31-34-93
Website: http://www.encgt.ma

Directeur: Abdelbaqui Agrar

Programmes
Advertising and Communication (Advertising and Publicity; Communication Studies)
Business Computing
Finance and Accountancy (Accountancy; Finance)
International Trade (Business and Commerce; International Business)
Marketing

ECOLE NATIONALE FORESTIÈRE D'INGÉNIEURS (ENFI)

BP 511, Tabriquet, Salé
Tel: +212(37) 78-97-04
Fax: +212(37) 78-71-49

Directeur: Mohamed Sabir (2003-)

Founded: 1968

Programmes
Forestry

ECOLE NATIONALE DE L'INDUSTRIE MINÉRALE (ENIM)

BP 753, Avenue Hadj Ahmed, Cherkaoui, Agdal, Rabat
Tel: +212(7) 68-02-30
Fax: +212(7) 77-10-55
EMail: info@enim.ac.ma
Website: http://www.enim.ac.ma

Directeur: Omar Debbaj

Secretary-General: Abdellah Adnani

Founded: 1972

Departments
Computer Science
Earth Sciences (Earth Sciences; Geological Engineering)
Materials Engineering
Mining (Mineralogy; Mining Engineering)
Process Engineering (Energy Engineering; Production Engineering)

ECOLE NORMALE SUPÉRIEURE, CASABLANCA (ENS)

Route d'El Jadida, Casablanca
Tel: +212(22) 23-22-77
Fax: +212(22) 98-53-26

Directeur: Lahcen Oubahamou

Programmes
Mathematics; Physics
Education

ECOLE NORMALE SUPÉRIEURE, FÈS (ENS)

BP 5206, Kariat Ben Souda Ahouaz-Oued Fès, Fès
Tel: +212(55) 65-50-83
Fax: +212(55) 65-50-69

Directeur: Abdenbi Rejouani

Programmes
Mathematics; Physics
Translation (Translation and Interpretation)

ECOLE NORMALE SUPÉRIEURE, MARRAKECH (ENS)

BP S41, Douar El Askar, Route d'Essaouira, Marrakech
Tel: +212(44) 34-01-25 +212(44) 34-22-58
Fax: +212(44) 34-22-87

Directeur: Mohamed Fliou

Programmes
Computer Science; Mathematics; Physics

ECOLE NORMALE SUPÉRIEURE, MEKNÈS (ENS)

BP 3104, Toulal, Meknès
Tel: +212(55) 53-38-85
Fax: +212(55) 53-38-83

Directeur: Mbarek Hanoun (2000-)

Directeur-Adjoint: Hammani Akefli

Founded: 1983

Departments
Arabic (Arabic; Teacher Training) *Head*: Hassan Youssif
French (French; Teacher Training) *Head*: Mohammed Faragi
Philosophy (Philosophy; Teacher Training) *Head*: Mohammed Kechkech
Translation (Translation and Interpretation) *Head*: Nour Eddine Denkir

Institutes
Teacher Training (Education; Teacher Training) *Director*: Mbarek Hanoun

History: Founded 1983.

Governing Bodies: Ministry of Education

Fees: None

Main Language(s) of Instruction: Arabic, French

Student Services: Academic Counselling, Employment Services, Nursery Care, Sports Facilities, Language Programmes, Health Services, Canteen

Student Residential Facilities: Yes

Special Facilities: Local audio-visual equipments

Libraries: Local and National Libraries

Academic Staff *2001-2002:* Total: c. 20

ECOLE NORMALE SUPÉRIEURE, RABAT (ENS)

BP 5118, Av. Oued Akrach, Takaddoum, Rabat
Tel: +212(37) 75-00-25 +212(37) 75-22-61
Fax: +212(37) 75-00-47

Directeur: Abdeltif Mogine

Programmes
Computer Science; English; Geography; History; Physics

ECOLE NORMALE SUPÉRIEURE, TÉTOUAN (ENS)
BP 209, Martil, Tétouan
Tel: +212(39) 97-91-75 +212(39) 97-90-48
Fax: +212(39) 97-91-80

Directeur: Arid Eljalali

Programmes
Arabic; Education; French

ECOLE DE PERFECTIONNEMENT DES CADRES DU MINISTÈRE DE L'INTÉRIEUR
BP 124, Kenitra
Tel: +212(37) 37-13-66

Founded: 1964

Programmes
Executives Training (Leadership)

ECOLE DES SCIENCES DE L' INFORMATION (ESI)
Avenue Maa Al Aïnaïne, Haut Agdal, Rabat
Tel: +212(37) 77-49-04 +212(37) 77-49-07
Fax: +212(37) 77-02-32
EMail: esi@cnd.mpep.gov.ma
Website: http://www.esi.ac.ma

Directeur: Mohamed Benjelloun Tel: +212(37) 68-12-90
EMail: mbenjelloun@cnd.mpep.gov.ma
Directeur Adjoint: Abdelmoula El Hamdouchi
Tel: +212(37) 68-12-91 Fax: +212(37) 68-12-91
International Relations: Nazha Hachad
Tel: +212(37) 77-49-13 EMail: n-hachad@yahoo.com

Founded: 1974
Information Sciences

History: Founded 1974 to meet the needs of the country for professionnals by ensuring their training in the areas of Documentation Techniques, Information Sciences, Science and Librarianship.
Admission Requirements: Secondary school certificate (baccalauréat)
Fees: None
Main Language(s) of Instruction: French
Accrediting Agencies: Ministry of Economic Prevision and Planning; Ministry of Higher Education, Professional Training and Research
Degrees and Diplomas: *Maîtrise*: Information Sciences, 4 yrs. Also Specialist Diploma, 2 yrs
Student Services: Employment Services, Sports Facilities, Language Programmes, Canteen
Student Residential Facilities: Yes
Libraries: Central Library
Publications: Revue de la Science de l' information (biannually)

Academic Staff *2001-2002*: Full-Time: c. 25 Part-Time: c. 45 Total: c. 70
Staff with Doctorate: Total: c. 15
Student Numbers *2001-2002*: All (Foreign Included): c. 300
Foreign Only: c. 30

INSTITUT AGRONOMIQUE ET VÉTÉRINAIRE HASSAN II
BP 6202, Rabat
Tel: +212(37) 77-17-58
Fax: +212(37) 77-81-35
Website: http://www.iav.ac.ma

Directeur: Fouad Guessouss EMail: dg@iav.ac.ma
Secrétaire général: Mostafa Agbani EMail: sg@iav.ac.ma

Founded: 1966

Programmes
Veterinary Science
Agricultural and Food Industries (Agricultural Business; Food Technology)
Agronomy (Agriculture; Agronomy)
Horticulture (Fishery; Horticulture; Landscape Architecture; Natural Resources; Plant and Crop Protection)
Rural Equipment (Agricultural Equipment)
Topography (Surveying and Mapping)

INSTITUT DAR-AL-HADITH AL-HASSANIA
BP 7844, 2, rue du Dahomey, Rabat
Tel: +212(37) 72-25-87
Fax: +212(37) 72-62-01

Directeur: Ahmed El Khamlichi

Founded: 1964

Programmes
Islamic Studies (Islamic Studies; Koran)

INSTITUT DE FORMATION AUX CARRIÈRES DE SANTÉ, AGADIR (IFCS)
Hôpital Hassan II, Agadir
Tel: +212(48) 84-14-77
Fax: +212(48) 84-39-87

Founded: 1994

Programmes
Health Sciences
Midwifery
Nursing

INSTITUT DE FORMATION AUX CARRIÈRES DE SANTÉ, CASABLANCA
Rue Jenner, Casablanca
Tel: +212(22) 26-02-85

Head: Mohamed Achiri

Programmes
Health Sciences

INSTITUT DE FORMATION AUX CARRIÈRES DE SANTÉ, FÈS
Hôpital Ibnou El Khatib, Fès
Tel: +212(55) 62-29-76

Head: Thami Merrouni

Health Sciences

INSTITUT DE FORMATION AUX CARRIÈRES DE SANTÉ, MARRAKECH
Riad Si Aissa Moussine, Marrakech
Tel: +212(44) 44-21-95

Head: Said El Amiri

Programmes
Health Sciences

INSTITUT DE FORMATION AUX CARRIÈRES DE SANTÉ, MEKNÈS
Hôpital Mohamed V, Meknès
Tel: +212(55) 52-09-27
Fax: +212(55) 52-09-27

Head: Ahmed Oalla

Programmes
Health Sciences (Health Sciences; Midwifery; Nursing)

INSTITUT DE FORMATION AUX CARRIÈRES DE SANTÉ, OUJDA
Bd El Maghreb El Arabi, Oujda
Tel: +212(56) 68-49-73
Fax: +212(56) 68-49-73

Head: Benyounes Benhaala

Programmes
Health Sciences (Health Sciences; Midwifery; Nursing)

INSTITUT DE FORMATION AUX CARRIÈRES DE SANTÉ, RABAT
Av. Hassan II, Km. 4, Route de Casa, Rabat
Tel: +212(37) 69-19-38
Fax: +212(37)69-27-96
EMail: mboulgana@santé.gov.ma

Head: Mohamed Boulgana

Founded: 1993

Programmes
Health Sciences (Health Sciences; Midwifery; Nursing)

INSTITUT DE FORMATION AUX CARRIÈRES DE SANTÉ, TÉTOUAN
Hôpital Civil, Tétouan
Tel: +212(39) 97-10-92

Head: Mohamed Khbiez

Founded: 1975

Programmes
Health Sciences (Health Sciences; Midwifery; Nursing)

INSTITUT NATIONAL DE L'ACTION SOCIALE (INAS)
BP 1168, Rue Hariri, Tanger
Tel: +212(39) 94-09-71
Fax: +212(39) 94-07-96

Directeur: Mohammed Zanouny

Founded: 1983

Programmes
Economics and Management (Economics; Management)
Law
Social Sciences (Social Sciences; Social Work)

INSTITUT NATIONAL D'AMÉNAGEMENT ET D'URBANISME (INAU)
BP 6215, Avenue Allal El Fassi, Rabat
Tel: +212(37) 77-16-24
Fax: +212(37) 77-50-09
EMail: inau@maghrebnet.net.ma
Website: http://www.inau.ac.ma

Directeur: Abdellah Lehzam
Secrétaire général: Yahia Bechrouri

Founded: 1981

Programmes
Regional and Town Planning (Economics; Environmental Studies; Law; Regional Planning; Rural Planning; Town Planning)

Research Centres
Town and Regional Planning (Regional Planning; Town Planning)

INSTITUT NATIONAL D'ADMINISTRATION SANITAIRE (INAS)
College de Santé publique, KM 4,5 Route de Casa, Rabat
Tel: +212(37) 69-16-26
Fax: +212(37) 69-16-26
EMail: inas@mtds.com

Directeur: Fikri Benbrahim Tel: +212(37) 29-98-34

Founded: 1989

Programmes
Health Sciences (Health Administration; Health Sciences)

History: Founded 1989

INSTITUT NATIONAL DES BEAUX-ARTS (INBA)
BP 89, Av. Mohamed V BP 89, Tétouan
Tel: +212(39) 96-15-45
Fax: +212(39) 96-42-92
EMail: cultinba@iam.net.ma

Directeur: Abdelkrim Ouazzani

Founded: 1947, 1993

Departments
Design (Design; Industrial Design; Interior Design)
Fine Arts (Engraving; Fine Arts; Painting and Drawing; Sculpture)

INSTITUT NATIONAL D'ETUDES JUDICIAIRES (INEJ)
PO Box 1007, Boulevard Mehdi Ben Berka, Souissi, Rabat
Tel: +212(37) 75-19-92 +212(37) 75-39-16
Fax: +212(37) 75-25-13
Website: http://www.justice.gov.ma

Directeur: Abdelkébir Zeroual Fax: +212(37) 75-49-02

Assistant Directeur: Abdeslam Hassi-Rahou
Tel: +212(37) 75-25-46

Founded: 1969, 1970

Institutes
Legal Studies *(National)* (Law) *Director:* Abdelkebir Zeroual

History: Founded 1969, acquired present status and title 1970.
Admission Requirements: Secondary school certificate (baccalauréat) and competitive entrance examination
Fees: None
Main Language(s) of Instruction: Arabic
Accrediting Agencies: International Agency of Cooperation
Degrees and Diplomas: *Capacité en Droit:* Law, 2 yrs
Student Services: Nursery Care, Sports Facilities, Canteen
Student Residential Facilities: Yes
Libraries: Central Library
Publications: The Judicial Attaché
Academic Staff *2001-2002:* Total: c. 50
Staff with doctorate: Total: c. 10
Student Numbers *2001-2002:* All (Foreign Included): c. 170
Foreign Only: c. 10

316

INSTITUT NATIONAL DES POSTES ET TÉLÉCOMMUNICATIONS (INPT)
2 Avenue Allal El Fasse, Madinat Al Irfane, Rabat
Tel: +212(37) 77-30-79
Fax: +212(37) 77-30-44
EMail: riouch@inpt.ac.ma
Website: http://www.inpt.ac.ma

Directeur: Mohamed Abdelfattah Charif Chefchaouni
EMail: charifm@inpt.ac.ma
Secrétaire général: Abderrazak Sebbata
EMail: sebbata@inpt.ac.ma

Founded: 1971
Telecommunications Engineering

INSTITUT NATIONAL DES STATISTIQUES ET D'ECONOMIE APPLIQUÉE
BP 6217, Madinat El Irfane, Rabat
Tel: +212(7) 77-48-59
Fax: +212(7) 77-94-57
EMail: webmaster@insea.ac.ma
Website: http://www.insea.ac.ma

Directeur: Abdelaziz El Ghazali
Secrétaire général: Mohamed Saoud

Founded: 1961

Departments
Computer Science
Demography and Humanities (Arts and Humanities; Demography and Population)
Economics
Mathematics and Operational Research (Mathematics; Operations Research)
Statistics

INSTITUT ROYAL DE FORMATION DES CADRES DE LA JEUNESSE ET DES SPORTS
Belle-Vue, Avenue Ibn Sina, Agdal, Rabat
Tel: +212(37) 72674

Directeur: Mohammed Kaach

Founded: 1980
Executives Training (Leadership)

INSTITUT SUPÉRIEUR D'ART DRAMATIQUE ET D'ANIMATION CULTURELLE (ISADAC)
BP 1355, Charii Al Mansour Addahbi, Rabat
Tel: +212(37) 72-17-02
Fax: +212(37) 70-34-23

Directeur: Ahmed Massaia

Programmes
Cultural Studies; Theatre

INSTITUT SUPÉRIEUR DE COMMERCE ET D'ADMINISTRATION DES ENTREPRISES (ISCAE)

Km. 9.5 Route de Nousser, BP 8114, Casa Oasis, Casablanca
Tel: +212(22) 33-54-82
Fax: +212(22) 33-54-96
EMail: iscac@iscac.ac.ma

Directeur: Rachid M'Rabet

Founded: 1971

Programmes
Accountancy
Business Administration (Business Administration; Business and Commerce)
Finance
International Commerce (Business and Commerce)

INSTITUT SUPÉRIEUR DES ETUDES MARITIMES

Km 7, Route d'El Jadida, Casablanca
Tel: +212(22) 23-07-40
Fax: +212(22) 23-15-68

Directeur: Miloud Loukili

Founded: 1957

Programmes
Marine Science and Oceanography

INSTITUT SUPÉRIEUR DE L'INFORMATION ET DE LA COMMUNICATION (ISIC)

BP 6205, Madinat Al Irfane, Rabat
Tel: +212(37) 77-33-40
Fax: +212(37) 77-27-89
Website: http://www.isic.ac.ma

Directeur: Latifa Akharbach

Founded: 1969

Departments
Journalism
Audio-Visual Studies
Communication Studies

INSTITUT SUPÉRIEUR INTERNATIONAL DU TOURISME

BP 651, Baie de Tanger, Tanger
Tel: +212(39) 94-59-04
Fax: +212(39) 94-59-05

Directrice: Souad Hassoun

Founded: 1972
Tourism

PRIVATE INSTITUTIONS

ECOLE D' ADMINISTRATION ET DE DIRECTION DES AFFAIRES (EAD)

2, avenue Moulay Youssef, Rabat
Tel: +212(37) 70-19-23
EMail: ead@mail.sis.net.ma

Directeur: Ahne Berrezel (1984-) Tel: +212(37) 70-19-23
Study Director: Abdelah Chriai Tel: +212(37) 70-81-36
International Relations: M. Jamila

Founded: 1984

Institutes
Business, Finance and Management (Business Administration; Finance; Management) *Director:* Ahmed Berrezel

History: Founded 1984.

Academic Year: September to June

Admission Requirements: Secondary school certificate (baccalauréat)

Main Language(s) of Instruction: French, English

Degrees and Diplomas: *Maîtrise:* Finance, 4 yrs; *Diplôme d'Etudes supérieures spécialisées (DESS)*; *Diplôme d'Etudes supérieures (DES)*: Management; Commerce, 4 yrs

Student Services: Academic Counselling, Employment Services, Foreign Student Adviser, Nursery Care, Cultural Centre, Sports Facilities, Language Programmes, Canteen, Foreign Student Centre

Student Residential Facilities: Yes

Libraries: Central Library

Publications: Le Matin; La Vie Economique; L'Opinion

Academic Staff *2001-2002:* Total: c. 50

Student Numbers *2001-2002*: All (Foreign Included): Men: c. 120 Women: c. 80 Total: c. 200
Foreign Only: Men: c. 20 Women: c. 30 Total: c. 50

Evening Students, c. 60

ECOLE DES HAUTES ETUDES DE BIOTECHNOLOGIE

26 Avenue Mers Sultan, Casablanca
Tel: +212(2) 27-66-36
Fax: +212(2) 22-74-180
EMail: eheb@iam.net.ma

Founded: 1996

Departments
Biotechnology

History: Founded 1996.

ECOLE DES HAUTES ETUDES DE COMMERCE, CASABLANCA
Angle rue de Strasbourg et boulevard de la Résistance, Casablanca
Tel: +212(22) 44-00-40
Fax: +212(22) 44-00-57

Directeur: A. Sekkaki

Founded: 1992

Programmes
Business and Commerce

ECOLE DES HAUTES ETUDES DE COMMERCE, FÈS
1, rue Jaber Al Ansari et boulevard Hamza, Bnou Abdel Moutalib, Fès
Tel: +212(55) 64-33-28
Fax: +212(55) 64-04-56
EMail: hec@fesnet.net.ma

Directrice: Ilham Skalli

Founded: 1988
Business and Commerce

ECOLE DES HAUTES ETUDES DE COMMERCE, RABAT
67, rue Jaafar Assadiq, Agdal, Rabat
Tel: +212(37) 67-12-76
Fax: +212(37) 67-12-77

Directeur: Khalil El Kouhen

Founded: 1993
Business and Commerce

ECOLE DES HAUTES ETUDES COMMERCIALES ET INFORMATIQUES, AGADIR (HECI)
Avenue Hassan II, Immeuble Inbiaat, Stade Hassania, Agadir
Tel: +212(48) 84-71-74
Fax: +212(48) 82-11-03

Directeur: Driss Benserighe

Business and Commerce; Computer Science

ECOLE DES HAUTES ETUDES COMMERCIALES ET INFORMATIQUES, CASABLANCA (HECI)
27, rue Tata, Casablanca
Tel: +212(22) 26-25-68
Fax: +212(22) 20-22-10

Directeur: Fayçal Ghissassi

Founded: 1986

Programmes
Computer Science
Business Administration

ECOLE DES HAUTES ETUDES COMMERCIALES ET INFORMATIQUES, FÈS (HECI)
Avenue Allal Ben Aboulevardellah, rue No. 134, Fès
Tel: +212(55) 93-12-03
Fax: +212(55) 93-12-03

Founded: 1992
Business and Commerce; Computer Science

ECOLE DES HAUTES ETUDES COMMERCIALES ET INFORMATIQUES, KENITRA (HECI)
535, boulevard Mohammed V, Kénitra
Tel: +212(37) 37-93-25
Business and Commerce; Computer Science

ECOLE DES HAUTES ETUDES COMMERCIALES ET INFORMATIQUES, MEKNÈS (HECI)
9, rue de Chinon, Es-Saada, Meknès
Tel: +212(55) 53-84-43
Fax: +212(55) 55-01-34

Founded: 1992
Business and Commerce; Computer Science

ECOLE DES HAUTES ETUDES COMMERCIALES ET INFORMATIQUES, MOHAMMADIA (HECI)
Bd Yacoub Al Mansour, Lot. Al Wafaa Mohammadia, Mohammadia
Tel: +212(23) 30-49-10
Business and Commerce; Computer Science

ECOLE DES HAUTES ETUDES COMMERCIALES ET INFORMATIQUES, RABAT (HECI)
89, rue Sebou, Agdal, Rabat
Tel: +212(37) 77-07-05
Fax: +212(37) 77-11-62

Directeur: Moulay Hachem Kacimi

Founded: 1991
Business and Commerce; Computer Science

ECOLE DES HAUTES ETUDES COMMERCIALES ET INFORMATIQUES, TANGER (HECI)

Place des Nations, avenue Mohammed V, Résidence Molk Allah, 1er Etage, Tanger
Tel: +212(39) 94-06-91

Directeur: Mohamed Fikri

Founded: 1993
Business and Commerce; Computer Science

ECOLE DES HAUTES ETUDES ÉCONOMIQUES ET COMMERCIALES (EHEEC)

Avenue Allal El Fassi, Rue Abou Oubaida Daoudiate, Marrakech
Tel: +212(44) 31-44-10
Fax: +212(44) 31-44-20
Website: http://ecoleheec.ac.ma

Directeur: Adnan Toughrai

Programmes
Business Administration (Business Administration; Economics; Law)

ECOLE DES HAUTES ETUDES EN GESTION, INFORMATIQUE ET COMMUNICATION DE CASABLANCA (EDHEC)

201, boulevard de Bordeaux, Casablanca
Tel: +212(22) 49-14-98
Fax: +212(22) 49-25-53
Website: http://www.edhec.ac.ma

Directeur Général: Nasser Hefiri

Founded: 1995

Programmes
Computer Science
Management
Systems and Networks (Computer Networks; Systems Analysis)

ECOLE MAROCAINE DES SCIENCES DE L'INGÉNIEUR EN INFORMATIQUE DE GESTION ET EN INFORMATIQUE INDUSTRIELLE, CASABLANCA (EMSI)

154, rue Al Bakri, Casablanca
Tel: +212(22) 54-31-70
Fax: +212(22) 54-31-66
EMail: info@emsi.ac.ma
Website: http://www.emsi.ac.ma

Founded: 1986

Programmes
Computer Engineering and Networks (Computer Engineering; Computer Networks)
Industrial Engineering and Telecommunications
Industrial Engineering and Telecommunications (Industrial Engineering; Telecommunications Engineering)

ECOLE MAROCAINE DES SCIENCES DE L'INGÉNIEUR EN INFORMATIQUE DE GESTION ET EN INFORMATIQUE INDUSTRIELLE, RABAT

49, rue Patrice Lumumba Place Pietri, Rabat
Tel: +212(37) 76-40-50
Fax: +212(37) 76-40-51

Founded: 1996

Programmes
Computer Engineering; Management

ECOLE POLYFINANCE

309, boulevard Ziraoui, Casablanca
Tel: +212(22) 47-63-63
Fax: +212(22) 47-63-65
Website: http://www.polyfinance.ac.ma

Founded: 1996
Finance

ECOLE POLYVALENTE SUPÉRIEURE D'INFORMATIQUE ET DU GÉNIE ÉLECTRIQUE (EPSIEL)

4, avenue Allal Ben Abdellah, Imm Abou, 30000 Fès
Tel: +212(55) 65-40-37
Fax: +212(55) 62-52-68
EMail: epsiel@fesnet.net.ma

Head: Abdelilah Benani

Founded: 1993

Programmes
Computer Science; Electrical Engineering

ECOLE SUPÉRIEURE D'ARCHITECTURE D'INTÉRIEUR (ESAI)

3, rue Amir Sidi Mohammed Souissi, Rabat
Tel: +212(37) 75-58-20
Fax: +212(37) 75-58-20

Interior Design

ECOLE SUPÉRIEURE DE COMMERCE (ESC)

BP 595, Boulevard Prince Moulay Abdellah, Gueliz, 40000
Marrakech
Tel: +212(44) 43-33-93
Fax: +212(44) 43-60-67
EMail: supdeco@esc.marrakech.ac.ma
Website: http://www.supdeco-marrakech.com

President: Bennis Ahmed (1986-)

Founded: 1987

Programmes

Environment: Economics and Law (Economics; Law)
Finance
Information Management
Languages and Culture (Cultural Studies; English; French;
Modern Languages; Spanish)
Management and Marketing (Management; Marketing)

History: Founded 1987.

Admission Requirements: Secondary school certificate
(baccalauréat), entrance examination and interview

Main Language(s) of Instruction: French

Degrees and Diplomas: *Maîtrise*: Management, 4 yrs

Student Services: Academic Counselling, Social Counselling,
Employment Services, Foreign Student Adviser, Nursery Care,
Cultural Centre, Sports Facilities, Language Programmes,
Health Services, Canteen, Foreign Student Centre

Student Residential Facilities: Yes

Libraries: Central Library, c. 3000 vols

Academic Staff *2001-2002:* Total: c. 50

Staff with doctorate: Total: c. 30

Student Numbers *2001-2002*: All (Foreign Included): c. 330
Foreign Only: c. 70

ECOLE SUPÉRIEURE DE COMMERCE ET DES AFFAIRES (ESCA)

55, rue Jaber Ben Hayan, boulevard d'Anfa, Casablanca
Tel: +212(22) 20-91-20

Founded: 1992

Programmes

Business and Commerce

ECOLE SUPÉRIEURE DE COMMUNICATION (ESC)

73, rue Pierre Parent, Casablanca
Tel: +212(22) 31-09-09
Fax: +212(22) 31-09-39

Programmes

Communication Studies

ECOLE SUPÉRIEURE DE COMMUNICATION ET DE PUBLICITÉ (COM SUP)

18, rue Bachir Al Ibrahimi, Quartier Belair, Casablanca
Tel: +212(2) 47 30 67
Fax: +212(2) 48 07 79
EMail: comsup@marocnet.net.ma

Programmes

Advertising and Publicity; Communication Studies
Marketing

ECOLE SUPÉRIEURE DE L'ECONOMIE SCIENTIFIQUE ET DE GESTION (ESES)

34, rue Mediouna, Hay Aviation, Rabat
Tel: +212(37) 75-04-94
Fax: +212(37) 75-04-95

Directeur pédagogique: Younies Naciri

Founded: 1989
Business and Commerce; Management

ECOLE SUPÉRIEURE DE GESTION D'ENTREPRISE

Avenue de la Résistance, Angle Puissesseau, Casablanca
Tel: +212(22) 30-81-50

ECOLE SUPÉRIEURE DE GESTION MAROC (ESG)

32 rue El Bakri, Casablanca
Tel: +212(22) 44-40-01
Fax: +212(22) 44-39-42
Website: http://www.esg.ma

Président délégué: Jacques Knafo

Founded: 1985

Programmes

Management
Commerce (Business and Commerce)

ECOLE SUPÉRIEURE DE GESTION ET DE COMMERCE (EGICO)

2, rue Chouaib Doukkali, angle boulevard Ibn Toumart,
Quartier les Orangers, Rabat
Tel: +212(37) 73-25-64
Fax: +212(37) 73-25-70

Directeur: Khalid Tarik

Founded: 1995
Business Administration; Management

ECOLE SUPÉRIEURE D'INFORMATIQUE APPLIQUÉE (ESIA)

Avenue de la Résistance, Casablanca
Tel: +212(22) 30-64-24

Directeur: Mohamed Ziani

Founded: 1993

Programmes
Computer Science

ECOLE SUPÉRIEURE D'INFORMATIQUE APPLIQUÉE À LA GESTION (ESIAG)

Villa Thérèse 1, Quartier Saadia, Gueliz, Marrakech
Tel: +212(44) 43-39-82
Fax: +212(44) 43-72-95

Directeur: Mohammed Kabbaj

Founded: 1987
Computer Science; Management

ECOLE SUPÉRIEURE D'INFORMATIQUE ET DE MANAGEMENT DES AFFAIRES (ESIMA)

Place Hansali, Imm. Mounia, El Jadida
Tel: +212(23) 34-04-04
Fax: +212(23) 34-06-61

Business Administration
Computer Science

ECOLE SUPÉRIEURE INTERNATIONALE DE GESTION, CASABLANCA (ESIG)

Route de Nouasser, Sidi Maârouf, Casablanca
Tel: +212(22) 33-59-69
Fax: +212(22) 33-56-72
EMail: esigcasa@wanadoo.net.ma

Directeur: Azzedine Bennani

Founded: 1985

Programmes
Management

ECOLE SUPÉRIEURE INTERNATIONALE DE GESTION, FÈS (ESIG)

Km 3, route d'Immouzer, Fès
Tel: +212(5) 60 11 39
Fax: +212(5) 60-34-91
EMail: groupe.esig.fes@casanet.net.ma
Founded: 1985

Programmes
Management
Finance and Business (Business Administration; Finance)
Marketing

ECOLE SUPÉRIEURE INTERNATIONALE DE GESTION, MARRAKECH (ESIG)

Boulevard Mansour Eddahbi, angle rue Mohammed Baqual, Marrakech
Tel: +212(44) 44-71-43
Fax: +212(44) 44-71-45
EMail: esig@aim.net.ma

Founded: 1993

Programmes
Management (Accountancy; Finance; International Business; Management; Marketing)

ECOLE SUPÉRIEURE INTERNATIONALE DE GESTION, RABAT (ESIG)

32, rue Moulay Ali Cherif, Rabat
Tel: +212(37) 76-94-57
Fax: +212(37) 76-28-09
EMail: esigraba@elan.net.ma

Directeur: Mohamed Kabbaj Tel: +212(37) 76-94-58

International Relations: Merieme Drissi

Founded: 1991
Accountancy; Administration; Finance; Information Management; International Business; Management; Marketing

History: Founded 1991

Academic Year: October to June

Admission Requirements: Secondary school certificate (baccalauréat), and entrance examination

Main Language(s) of Instruction: French

Degrees and Diplomas: *Maîtrise:* Administration; Computer Science, 4 yrs

Student Services: Academic Counselling, Social Counselling, Employment Services, Foreign Student Adviser, Cultural Centre, Sports Facilities, Language Programmes, Health Services, Canteen, Foreign Student Centre

Student Residential Facilities: Yes

Libraries: Central Library

Publications: Revue de l' Ecole (quarterly)

Academic Staff *2001-2002:* Full-Time: c. 20 Part-Time: c. 50 Total: c. 70

Student Numbers *2001-2002:* Total: c. 190

ECOLE SUPÉRIEURE DE MANAGEMENT (ESM)

Bd. de la Résistance, Casablanca
Tel: +212(2) 30-63-32

Founded: 1994

Programmes
Management

ECOLE SUPÉRIEURE DE MANAGEMENT APPLIQUÉ (ESMA)
1 Avenue Moulay Abdellah, Marrakech
Tel: +212(44) 30-02-23

Directeur: Mohammed Berrada Elazizi

Founded: 1997

Programmes
Management

ECOLE SUPÉRIEURE DE MANAGEMENT DE LA QUALITÉ (ESIMAQ)
56, rue Ibnou Hamdis, Casablanca
Tel: +212(22) 36-92-27
Fax: +212(22) 94-00-37

Directeur: Mohamed Afif

Programmes
Industrial Management

ECOLE SUPÉRIEURE D'OPTIQUE ET DE LUNETTERIE (ESOL)
5, rue Bizerte Hay Zouhour 2, route d'Immouzer, Fès V.N.
Tel: +212(55) 60-11-87
Fax: +212(55) 60-76-42
EMail: direction@esol.ac.ma
Website: http://www.esol.ac.ma

Directeur: Farouk Blidi

Founded: 1996

Programmes
Optical Technology

ECOLE SUPÉRIEURE DE PROTHÈSE (ESP)
5, rue du Lieutenant Berger, Casablanca
Tel: +212(22) 40-52-88
Fax: +212(22) 40-33-63

Directeur: Nabil Daoudi

Founded: 1993

Programmes
Dental Technology
Prosthetics (Medical Technology)

ECOLE SUPÉRIEURE DE SECRÉTARIAT, INFORMATIQUE ET COMPTABILITÉ, FÈS (ESSIC)
Angle Avenue Abdelkrim Al Khattabi et Houssein Khadar, Fès
Tel: +212(55) 51-41-65

Directeur: Abdelaziz Badaoui

Accountancy; Computer Science; Secretarial Studies

322

ECOLE SUPÉRIEURE DE SECRÉTARIAT, INFORMATIQUE ET COMPTABILITÉ, KENITRA (ESSIC)
40, Avenue Hassan II, Kenitra
Tel: +212(37) 68-19-41
EMail: essic@france.mail.com

Founded: 1999
Accountancy; Computer Science; Secretarial Studies

History: Founded 1999

ECOLE SUPÉRIEURE DE SECRÉTARIAT, D' INFORMATIQUE ET DE COMPTABILITÉ, MEKNÈS (ESSICM)
132, avenue des FAR, 50000 Meknès
Tel: +212(55) 51-41-64
Fax: +212(55) 51-41-63
EMail: essic@caramail.com

President: Fuad Benchekroune

Directeur: Abdelaziz Badaoui

Founded: 1990

Higher Schools
Secretarial Studies, Computer Science and Accountancy
(Accountancy; Computer Science; Finance; Management; Secretarial Studies)
Systems Analysis

History: Founded 1990

Admission Requirements: Secondary school certificate (baccalauréat)

Main Language(s) of Instruction: French, English

Degrees and Diplomas: *Maîtrise*: Finance; Management; Informatics, 4 yrs

Student Services: Foreign Student Adviser, Nursery Care, Cultural Centre, Sports Facilities, Language Programmes, Foreign Student Centre

Student Residential Facilities: Yes (free of charge)

Libraries: Central Library; Photographic library

Publications: Le Guide, Studies in Morocco

Academic Staff *2001-2002*: Full-Time: c. 10 Part-Time: c. 20 Total: c. 30

Staff with doctorate: Total: c. 5

Student Numbers *2001-2002:* Total: c. 100

ECOLE SUPÉRIEURE DE SECRÉTARIAT, D'INFORMATIQUE ET DE COMPTABILITÉ, RABAT (ESSIC)
80, rue de Sebou, Agdal, Rabat
Tel: +212(37) 68-19-41
Fax: +212(37) 51-41-63

Directeur: Mohammed Toma

Accountancy; Computer Science; Secretarial Studies

ECOLE TECHNIQUE DES RÉSEAUX ET SYSTÈMES (ETRS)
46, avenue Mohammed V (2ème et 3ème Etages), Settat
Tel: +212(23) 40-27-05
Fax: +212(23) 40-27-67

Directeur: Abdelaly Guissj

Networks and Systems Technology (Computer Networks; Telecommunications Engineering)

HIGH TECHNOLOGY SCHOOL IN MOROCCO (HIGH-TECH)
10 bis, rue El Yamana, Rabat
Tel: +212(37) 76-93-97
Fax: +212(37) 20-12-50
Website: http://www.hightech.edu

Président: Zouhair Benfaida

Founded: 1986

Programmes
Commerce and Finance (Business and Commerce; Finance)
Computer Engineering
Management

INSTITUT D'ADMINISTRATION DES ENTREPRISES (IAE)
422, Bir Rami, Est, Kénitra
Tel: +212(37) 37-74-06
Fax: +212(37) 37-74-23
Website: http://www.iae.8m.com

Programmes
Business Administration

INSTITUT DE FORMATION AUX FONCTIONS SOCIALES ET ÉDUCATIVES SPÉCIALISÉES (IFFSES)
Rue 9 Avril, Maârif, Casablanca
Tel: +212(22) 21-57-00
Fax: +212(22) 25-57-11

Programmes
Social Work
Special Education

INSTITUT DES HAUTES ETUDES BANCAIRES ET FINANCIÈRES, CASABLANCA (HBF)
4, rue Van Zeeland angle 113 Bd Abdelmoumen Quartier des Hôpitaux, Casablanca
Tel: +212(22) 47-65-54
Fax: +212(22) 47-65-97

Directeur: Tayeb Rhafes

Banking; Finance

INSTITUT DES HAUTES ETUDES BANCAIRES ET FINANCIÈRES, OUJDA
Rue Al Khalil, Quartier El Qods, Oujda
Tel: +212(56) 74-60-60

Directeur: Moulay Abdelhamid Smaili

Banking; Finance

INSTITUT DES HAUTES ETUDES ÉCONOMIQUES ET SOCIALES (IHEES)
3 rue Taieb Abdelkrim, Casablanca
Tel: +212(22) 30-01-95
Fax: +212(22) 30-28-90
EMail: ihees@mail.cfc.net.ma

Directeur: Abdelhamid Lazrak

Founded: 1985

Programmes
Business Administration (Business Administration; Economics; Social Studies)

INSTITUT DES HAUTES ETUDES DE MANAGEMENT, CASABLANCA (HEM)
52, avenue de Nador, Polo, Casablanca
Tel: +212(22) 52-52-52
Fax: +212(22) 21-55-30
EMail: hem@hem.ac.ma
Website: http://www.hem.ac.ma

Président: Abdelali Benamour

Academic Affairs Director: Hassan Sayarh
EMail: hassan.sayarh@hem.ac.ma

Administrative Officer: Mouloud Sadat
EMail: m.sadat@hem.ac.ma

Founded: 1988

Schools
Business (Business Administration; Finance; Information Management; Management; Marketing)

History: Founded 1988. HEM has set as its major goal the promotion of ethics and the pursuit of scholarly work of high quality. A private Institution.

Governing Bodies: Board of Directors

Academic Year: September to June

Admission Requirements: Secondary school certificate (baccalauréat), and entrance examination

Main Language(s) of Instruction: French

Accrediting Agencies: Ministry of Higher Education, Professional Training and Research

Degrees and Diplomas: *Maîtrise*: Management, 4 yrs; *Diplôme d'Etudes supérieures spécialisées (DESS)*: Finance; Marketing (MBA/DESS), 2 yrs. Also Diploma in Management, 1 yr

Student Services: Academic Counselling, Social Counselling, Employment Services, Foreign Student Adviser, Nursery Care, Cultural Centre, Sports Facilities, Language Programmes, Canteen

Student Residential Facilities: Yes

Special Facilities: Conference Hall. Computer Centre. Workshops (Painting, Theatre, Dance, Music)

Libraries: Central Library, c. 1000 vols

Publications: Penser l' Entreprise, Revue Marocaine de Management (biannually)

Academic Staff *2001-2002*: Full-Time: c. 20 Part-Time: c. 90 Total: c. 110

Student Numbers *2001-2002:* Total: c. 600

INSTITUT DES HAUTES ETUDES DE MANAGEMENT, RABAT (HEM)
8, rue Hamza, Agdal, Rabat
Tel: +212(37) 67-36-47
Fax: +212(37) 67-42-56
EMail: hem@maghrebnet.net.ma

Président: Abdellatif Homy

Founded: 1994

Schools
Management

INSTITUT MAROCAIN D'ETUDES SUPÉRIEURES (IMES)
181, boulevard Derfoufi, Oujda
Tel: +212(56) 68-78-12

Directeur: Hassan Jaali

Founded: 1986

Programmes
Accountancy
Business Computing
Finance
Management

INSTITUT MAROCAIN DE MANAGEMENT (IMM)
Rue Chouia Angle Bd Mohammed V -, Casablanca
Tel: +212(22) 20-22-88
Fax: +212(22) 20-26-39
Website: http://www.imm.ac.ma

Directeur: Mustapha Benchehla

Founded: 1990

Programmes
Management
Business Administration
Commerce (Business and Commerce)

INSTITUT SUPÉRIEUR EN ADMINISTRATION ET MANAGEMENT (ISHAM)
Palais de la Foire, route Sidi Allal, Al Bahraoui, Kénitra
Tel: +212(73) 37-10-80
Fax: +212(73) 37-15-44
Administration; Management

INSTITUT SUPÉRIEUR DES ARTS ET MÉTIERS (ISAM)
Iman Center, angle rue My Abderrahmane et rue de la place, Casablanca, Casablanca
Tel: +212(2) 44-90-39

Directeur: Mohamed Jaouad Marrakchi

Founded: 1990

Programmes
Accountancy
Finance
Marketing and Commerce (Business and Commerce; Marketing)
Production (Production Engineering)
Quality

INSTITUT SUPÉRIEUR DE BIOLOGIE ET DE BIOCHIMIE, CASABLANCA (ISBB)
34, boulevard Mohammed V, Casablanca
Tel: +212(22) 26-26-01
Fax: +212(22) 20-22-12
EMail: export@mbox.azure.net

Directeur: Ahmed Essadki

Founded: 1991
Biochemistry; Biology

INSTITUT SUPÉRIEUR DE BIOLOGIE ET DE BIOCHIMIE, MARRAKECH (ISBB)
100 Quartier Semlalia, Marrakech
Tel: +212(44) 44-87-34

Directrice: Saida Chahbouni

Founded: 1994

Programmes
Biochemistry
Biology

INSTITUT SUPÉRIEUR DE BIOLOGIE ET DE BIOCHIMIE, TÉTOUAN (ISBB)
Route de Martil, Tétouan
Tel: +212(39) 68-83-46

Directeur: Nard Bennas

Founded: 1996

Programmes
Biochemistry
Biology

INSTITUT SUPÉRIEUR DU COMMERCE INTERNATIONAL (CNCD)
13, rue Lavoisier, Casablanca
Tel: +212(22) 82-62-33
Fax: +212(22) 28-89-42
EMail: cncd@casanet.net.ma

Directeur: Mohamed Aoune

Founded: 1992

Programmes
International Business
International Management (Management)

INSTITUT SUPÉRIEUR DE COMPTABILITÉ, AUDIT ET FINANCE (ISCAF)
21, rue de l'Olympe, Quartier des Hopitaux, Casablanca
Tel: +212(22) 80-20-40
Fax: +212(22) 80-20-40
Website: http://147.210.86.79

Directeur: Mohamed Douch

Founded: 1996

Programmes
Accountancy
Business Administration
Commerce (Business and Commerce)
Finance

INSTITUT SUPÉRIEUR D'ELECTRONIQUE ET DES RÉSEAUX DE TÉLÉCOMMUNICATION (ISERT)
30, rue Kamel Mohammed, Casablanca
Tel: +212(22) 45-08-45
Fax: +212(22) 45-08-47
EMail: isert@open.net.ma

Directeur: Boujemaâ Charoub

Founded: 1996
Telecommunications Engineering

INSTITUT SUPÉRIEUR DES ETUDES INFORMATIQUES (IN. SUP. INFO)
3, rue Ibrahim Ibnou El Adham, Maarif, Casablanca
Tel: +212(22) 98-25-25
Fax: +212(22) 99-39-39

Directeur: Soûad Bhanimi

Founded: 1994
Computer Science

INSTITUT SUPÉRIEUR DE FORMATION AUX TECHNIQUES DE GESTION (ISFOTEG)
47, boulevard Pasteur, Tanger
Tel: +212(39) 93-71-01
Fax: +212(39) 93-17-71
EMail: isfoteg@marocnet.net.ma
Founded: 1988

Programmes
Management
Finance and Banking (Banking; Finance)
Industrial and Commercial Management (Business and Commerce; Industrial Management)

INSTITUT SUPÉRIEUR DE FORMATION EN TECHNOLOGIE ALIMENTAIRE (ISFORT)
94, rue Allal Ben Aboulevardellah, 2000 Casablanca
Tel: +212(22) 44-88-28
Fax: +212(22) 44-88-26
EMail: isfortdirection@isfort.ac.ma
Website: http://www.isfort.ac.ma

Directeur: Mounir Diouri

Founded: 1995

Programmes
Food Technology
Bio-Pharmaceutical Sciences (Biomedicine; Pharmacy)
Chemical Processes (Chemical Engineering)

INSTITUT SUPÉRIEUR DU GÉNIE APPLIQUÉ, CASABLANCA (IGA)
Place du Prince Sidi Med, 20300 Casablanca
Tel: +212(2) 40-40-37
Fax: +212(2) 40-40-38
EMail: iga@iga.ma
Website: http://www.iga.ma

Programmes
Business Administration
Computer Engineering
Electronic Engineering

INSTITUT SUPÉRIEUR DU GÉNIE APPLIQUÉ, RABAT (IGA)
27, rue Oqba, Rabat
Tel: +212(37) 77-14-68
Fax: +212(37) 77-14-72

Directeur: Naoufal Bennouna

Founded: 1996

Programmes
Accountancy; Business and Commerce; Electronic Engineering; Marketing
Computer Engineering

INSTITUT SUPÉRIEUR DU GÉNIE ÉLECTRIQUE, CASABLANCA (ISGE)
Place de la Gare Voyageurs, Casablanca
Tel: +212(2) 24-06-42

Founded: 1985

Programmes
Electrical Engineering
Computer Engineering

INSTITUT SUPÉRIEUR DU GÉNIE ÉLECTRIQUE, RABAT (ISGE)
27, rue Oqba, Agdal, Rabat

Programmes
Computer Engineering
Electrical Engineering

INSTITUT SUPÉRIEUR DE GESTION (ISG)
23, rue Houssein Benali, Anfa, Casablanca
Tel: +212(22) 27-71-22
Fax: +212(22) 27-71-22

Directeur: Driss Skalli

Founded: 1985
Management

INSTITUT SUPÉRIEUR DE GESTION ET DE COMMERCE (ISGC)
23, rue Hafid Ibrahim, Quartier Gauthier, Casablanca
Tel: +212(22) 26-63-12
Fax: +212(22) 47-46-43

Directeur: Azzedine Chraibi

Founded: 1989

Programmes
Accountancy
Commerce (Business and Commerce)
Computer Science
Management

INSTITUT SUPÉRIEUR DE GESTION ET DU DROIT DES ENTREPRISES
24, rue Badi El Kobra, Meknès
Tel: +212(55) 40-32-29
Business Administration
Law (Medicine)

INSTITUT SUPÉRIEUR D'INFORMATIQUE APPLIQUÉE ET DE MANAGEMENT (ISIAM)
BP 805, Boulevard Hassan 1er, Agadir
Tel: +212(8) 22-32-10
Fax: +212(8) 22-33-68
EMail: isiam@iam.net.ma
Website: http://www.isiam.org.ma

Directeur: Aziz Bouslikhane

Founded: 1989

Programmes
Computer Science
Management (Management; Marketing)

INSTITUT SUPÉRIEUR D'INFORMATIQUE ET DE MANAGEMENT (ISIM)
RP 39, Imm Good-Year - N° 206 - à Côté. Masjid Passo, Nador
Tel: +212(56) 60-22-00
Fax: +212(56) 33-34-03

Directeur: Bensalem El Hanafi

Founded: 1995

Programmes
Computer Science; Management

INSTITUT SUPÉRIEUR D'OPTIQUE 'IBN AL HAITAM' (ISOPIH)
176 Zone Industrielle, BP 6060, Tétouan
Tel: +212(39) 68-88-52
Fax: +212(39) 68-88-54

Directeur: Adil Khayat

Founded: 1996

Programmes
Optics

INSTITUTE FOR LANGUAGE AND COMMUNICATION STUDIES (ILCS)
29, rue Oukaimeden, Agdal, 10100 Rabat
Tel: +212(37) 67-59-68
Fax: +212(37) 67-59-65
EMail: ilcs@acdim.net.ma
Website: http://www.ilcs.ac.ma

Directrice: Amal Daoudi

Founded: 1996

Programmes
Language and Communication Studies (Advertising and Publicity; Arts and Humanities; Business Administration; Communication Studies; English; French; Human Resources; Management; Marketing; Mass Communication; Modern

Languages; Public Relations; Translation and Interpretation)
Head: Abderrafi Benhallam

History: Founded 1996 to train operational individuals in the fields of Business Communication and Languages.

Governing Bodies: Board of Advisers

Academic Year: October to June (October-January; February-June)

Admission Requirements: Secondary school certificate (baccalauréat)

Main Language(s) of Instruction: English, French

Accrediting Agencies: Ministry of Higher Education, Professional Training and Research

Degrees and Diplomas: *Maîtrise*: 4 yrs

Student Services: Academic Counselling, Employment Services, Foreign Student Adviser, Language Programmes, Canteen

Student Residential Facilities: None

Special Facilities: Multimedia Laboratory

Libraries: Central Library

Staff with doctorate: Part-Time: c. 10

Student Numbers *2001-2002*: All (Foreign Included): c. 50 Foreign Only: c. 10

INTERNATIONAL INSTITUTE FOR HIGHER EDUCATION (IIHE)
Avenue Imam Malik, Km 4,200 Souissi, Rabat
Tel: +212(37) 75-19-20
Fax: +212(37) 65-97-70
EMail: info@iihe.ac.ma
Website: http://www.iihe.ac.ma

Directeur: Dina Tidjani

Founded: 1988

Programmes
Computer Science (Computer Networks; Computer Science; Telecommunications Engineering)
Finance
Management
Marketing

INTERNATIONAL SCHOOL OF BUSINESS ADMINISTRATION (ISBA)
24, boulevard Mohammed V, Casablanca
Tel: +212(22) 26-30-53
Fax: +212(22) 26-29-98
EMail: isba@mail.cbi.net.ma

Directeur: Mammar El Mansari

Founded: 1994

Programmes
Business Administration

Mozambique

INSTITUTION TYPES AND CREDENTIALS

Types of higher education institutions:

Universidade (University)
Instituto Superior (Higher Institute)

School leaving and higher education credentials:

Certificado de Habilitações Literárias
Bacharelato
Licenciatura
Mestrado

STRUCTURE OF EDUCATION SYSTEM

Pre-higher education:

Duration of compulsory education:

   Age of entry: 6
   Age of exit: 13

Structure of school system:

   Primary
   Type of school providing this education: Primary School
   Length of programme in years: 7
   Age level from: 6 to: 13
   Certificate/diploma awarded: Carta de Ensino Primário de Segundo Grau

   First Cycle Secondary
   Type of school providing this education: Secondary School (ESG1)
   Length of programme in years: 3
   Age level from: 13 to: 16
   Certificate/diploma awarded: National Examination

   Technical Secondary
   Type of school providing this education: Technical Secondary School
   Length of programme in years: 3
   Age level from: 13 to: 16

   Second Cycle Secondary
   Type of school providing this education: Secondary School (ESG2)

Length of programme in years: 2
Age level from: 16 to: 18
Certificate/diploma awarded: Certificado de Habilitações Literárias (Secondary School Leaving Certificate)

Technical
Length of programme in years: 2
Age level from: 16 to: 18
Certificate/diploma awarded: Technician Diploma

School education:

Primary education lasts for seven years, subdivided into two levels: the first (EP1), of five years, and the second (EP2), of two years, leading to the Carta de Ensino Primário de Segundo Grau. Secondary education is offered in secondary, technical and agricultural schools. Ten per cent of students from primary education go on to this level. Under the National Education System, the best graduates of primary education follow five years of general secondary education, divided into the first cycle, lasting three years (ESG1) and the second, lasting two years (ESG2). Students take a national exam between the first and the second cycle. In the final year of secondary education students study Mathematics, Physics, Chemistry, Biology, Portuguese, Geography, History, Physical Education and English. The course leads to the Certificado de Habilitações Literárias (Secondary School Leaving Certificate). An entrance examination is necessary to enter university. Technical and professional education takes place in technical schools and institutes. Basic technical education (equivalent to the first cycle of general secondary) trains skilled workers; mid-level technical education (equivalent to the second cycle of general secondary) trains technicians.

Higher education:

Higher education is provided by public and private universities and higher institutes. Since 2000, higher education is the responsibility of the Ministry of Higher Education, Science and Technology (MESCT) which developed the "Stragegic Plan of Higher Education in Mozambique 2000-2010". Higher education is financed by the State but universities have a high degree of autonomy (in administration and finances) and coordinate their actions with the Conselho do Ensino Superior. Their internal governing body is the Conselho Universitário composed of the Rector and the deans of the faculties.

Main laws/decrees governing higher education:

Decree: Law no. 5/2003   Year: 2003
Concerns: New Law on Higher Education

Decree: Law no. 1/93   Year: 1993
Concerns: Law on Higher Education

Decree: Decree no. 11/90   Year: 1990
Concerns: Private education

Academic year:

Classes from: August *to:* June

Languages of instruction:

Portuguese

Stages of studies:

University level studies:

University level first stage: Bacharelato:
The first stage of higher education leads to the Bacharelato after two to three years' study in most subjects.

University level second stage: Licenciatura:
The second stage leads to the Licenciatura after two years' study following upon the Bacharelato. Only students having obtained the grades "good" or "very good" in the Bacharelato may proceed to this level. Licentiate degrees are offered in Agriculture, Veterinary Science, Engineering, Architecture, and Medical Sciences. Some programmes are direct-entry, lasting five years and do not require a Bacharelato stage. In Veterinary Medicine the degree is conferred after five years' study and in Medicine, seven years.

University level third stage: Mestrado:
Mestrado degrees have been implemented. Studies last at least two years after the Bacharelato.

University level fourth stage:
A doctoral degree lasting three to five years after the Mestrado is planned in the new law.

Teacher education:

Training of pre-primary and primary/basic school teachers
At present, the initial training of primary school teachers is done in primary school teacher training colleges where admission is based on seven years of schooling for the CFPP (EP1 teachers) and ten years of schooling for the IMP (EP2 teachers). The government advocates that primary school teachers will be trained at primary teacher training institutes for two years after having completed grade 10. They earn the Ensino de Professores para o Ensino Primário. In coordination with the Pedagogical University, courses leading to a Bachelor's Degree or Licenciatura in primary education are being implemented.

Training of secondary school teachers
Under the current scheme, secondary teachers are trained in at least two disciplines at the Universidade Eduardo Mondlane, the Universidade Pedagógica, the Maputo Institute Medio Pedagógico, or the Instituto Pedagógico Industrial. Secondary teacher training programmes require four years of study and include a teaching practice component. Upon completion of study, graduates earn the Ensino de Professores para o Ensino Secundária Geral.

Training of higher education teachers
Higher education teachers must hold at least a Licenciatura. Many hold a Master's Degree or a PhD. University teacher training is also available.

NATIONAL BODIES

Responsible authorities:

Ministry of Higher Education, Science and Technology (Ministério do Ensino Superior, Ciência e Tecnologia (MESCT))

Minister: Lidia Brito

Head of Minister Office: Óscar Basílio

International Relations: Danilo Parbato

Av. Patrice Lumumba, 770

Maputo

Tel: +258(1) 499-491

Fax: +258(1) 490-446

EMail: mesct@mesct.gov.mz

WWW: http://www.mesct.gov.mz

Role of governing body: Supervise the system of higher education, develop general policies and guidelines and propose new legislation; monitor the quality of higher education and coordinate accredidation mechanisms.

ADMISSIONS TO HIGHER EDUCATION

Admission to university-level studies

Name of secondary school credential required: Certificado de Habilitações Literárias
For entry to: Universities

Alternatives to credentials: Completion of middle level technical courses may also qualify a student for undergraduate entry.

Entrance exams required: Access to universities is based on the Secondary-School Leaving Certificate and an entrance examination.

STUDENT LIFE

Student expenses and financial aid

Student costs:

Foreign students tuition fees: Maximum: 2,500 (US Dollar)

GRADING SYSTEM

Usual grading system in secondary school

Full Description: 0-20
Highest on scale: 20

Pass/fail level: 10
Lowest on scale: 0

Main grading system used by higher education institutions

Full Description: Bacharelato: pass, good, very good; Licenciatura: marked on a scale of 1-20, 13 is considered satisfactory.

NOTES ON HIGHER EDUCATION SYSTEM

The academic year is divided into two semesters and varies: February-June and July-December for some institutions; and August-December and January-June for others.

Data for academic year: 2002-2003
Source: International Association of Universities (IAU), updated from EAIE Conference Paper "Development of Higher Education in Mozambique", 2002 and IBE website, 2003 (www.ibe.unesco.org/International/Databanks/Wde/profilee.htm)

INSTITUTIONS OF HIGHER EDUCATION

UNIVERSITIES AND UNIVERSITY LEVEL INSTITUTIONS

PUBLIC INSTITUTIONS

*• EDUARDO MONDLANE UNIVERSITY

Universidade Eduardo Mondlane (UEM)
Caixa postal 257, Praça 25 de Junho, Maputo
Tel: +258(1) 425-976   +258(1) 424-429
Fax: +258(1) 426-426   +258(1) 428-411
Telex: 6718 uem mo
EMail: aalberto@rei.uem.mz
Website: http://www.uem.mz

Reitor: Brazão Mazula (1995-) Tel: +258(1) 427-851
EMail: bmazula@rei.uem.mz

Vice-Reitor: Venâncio Massingue

International Relations: Zita Bauque Usta

Faculties
Agronomy and Forest Engineering (Agronomy; Forestry) *Dean:* Inácio Maposse
Architecture and Physical Planning (Architecture and Planning) *Dean:* José Forjáz
Arts and Humanities (Arts and Humanities; Geography; History; Linguistics; Translation and Interpretation) *Dean:* Armindo Ngunga
Economics *Dean:* Fernando Lichucha
Education (Adult Education; Curriculum; Education; Educational Psychology) *Dean:* Mouzinho Mário
Engineering (Chemical Engineering; Civil Engineering; Electrical Engineering; Engineering; Hydraulic Engineering; Mechanical Engineering) *Dean:* Gabriel Amós
Law *Dean:* Taibo Mocobora
Medicine *Dean:* João Schwalbach
Science (Biology; Chemistry; Computer Science; Geology; Natural Sciences; Physics) *Dean:* Francisco Viera
Veterinary Science *Dean:* Luis Bernardo Gil das Neves

Units
Social Sciences *Director:* Obede Suarte Baloi

Centres
African Studies *Director:* Teresa Cruz e Silva
Electronics and Instrumentation (Electronic Engineering; Instrument Making) *Director:* Venâcio Matusse
Engineering Studies *(UP)* (Engineering) *Director:* J. Diniz
Habitat Studies and Development *(CEDH)* (Town Planning) *Director:* Júlio Carrilho

Industrial Studies, Safety and Environment (Environmental Engineering; Industrial Engineering; Safety Engineering) *Director:* G. Amós
Population Studies *(CEP)* (Demography and Population) *Director:* Manuel de Araújo

History: Founded 1962 as Estudios Gerais Universitários, became Universidade de Lourenço Marques 1968, acquired present title 1976. A State institution responsible to the Ministry of Higher Education.

Governing Bodies: Conselho Universitário

Academic Year: August to June (August-December; February-June)

Admission Requirements: Secondary school certificate or equivalent, and entrance examination

Fees: (Metical): Home students: c.21m per annum plus c.10m enrolment fee. International students: c.70m per annum plus c.100m enrolment fee

Main Language(s) of Instruction: Portuguese

Degrees and Diplomas: *Bacharelato*: Law, 2 yrs; Agriculture; Biology; Chemistry; Economics; Engineering; Geography; Geology; History; Letters; Mathematics; Physics, 3 yrs; *Licenciatura*: 2 yrs following Bacharelato; Veterinary Medicine, 5 yrs; Medicine, 7 yrs; *Mestrado*

Student Services: Sports Facilities, Health Services, Canteen

Student Residential Facilities: For c.1000 students

Special Facilities: Natural History Museum.

Libraries: c. 85,000 vols; faculty libraries; special collections: World Bank publications, Mozambican fiction

Publications: Estudos Moçambicanos (biannually); Boletim informativo (annually)

Press or Publishing House: UEM Press

Academic Staff *2000-2001:* Total: **782**

Student Numbers *2000-2001*	MEN	WOMEN	TOTAL
All (Foreign Included)	5,430	1,877	**7,307**
FOREIGN ONLY	–	–	82

HIGHER INSTITUTE FOR INTERNATIONAL RELATIONS

Instituto Superior de Relações Internacionais (ISRI)
Rua Damião de Góis 100, Sommerchild, Maputo
Tel: +258(1) 491-233
Fax: +258(1) 493-213
EMail: ceei@zebra.uxm.mz
Website: http://www.isri.imoz.com

Reitor: Jamisse Wilson Taimo

Administrador: Simão Sacatúcua Tel: +258(1) 491-800
Fax: +258(1) 491-506

International Relations: Valter Fainda Tel: +258(1) 491-109
Fax: +258(1) 491-179

Departments
Economics *Head*: Ricardo M'Tumbuida
International Relations *Head*: Valter Fainda
Languages (Modern Languages) *Head*: Juvêncio Cumbane
Law *Head*: Espirito Santo Monjane
Pedagogy *Head*: David Cumbana
Social Sciences *Head*: Berno Kuchenje

Centres
Strategic and International Studies (Cultural Studies; Development Studies; Economics; International Studies; Peace and Disarmament; Political Science; Social Policy) *Director*: Belmiro Rodolfo

History: Founded 1986 to train diplomats and those concerned with international relations, acquired present status 1997.

Academic Year: August to June (August-December; January-June)

Admission Requirements: Secondary school certificate and entrance examination

Main Language(s) of Instruction: Portuguese

Degrees and Diplomas: *Licenciatura*: International Relations; Public Administration, 5 yrs

Student Services: Academic Counselling, Handicapped Facilities, Canteen

Student Residential Facilities: Yes

Libraries: c. 5000 vols

Academic Staff 2002-2003	MEN	WOMEN	TOTAL
FULL-TIME	24	4	28
PART-TIME	19	5	24
TOTAL	**43**	**9**	**52**

Student Numbers 2002-2003	MEN	WOMEN	TOTAL
All (Foreign Included)	119	30	**149**

• HIGHER INSTITUTE OF SCIENCE AND TECHNOLOGY
Instituto Superior de Ciências e Tecnologia de Moçambique (ISCTEM)
Rua 1394, Zona da Facim 322, Maputo
Tel: +258(1) 312-014   +258(1) 497-658
Fax: +258(1) 312-993   +258(1) 497-648
EMail: isctem@isctem.com
Website: http://www.isctem.com

Reitor: A. Saraiva de Sousa Tel: +258(1) 312-015

Higher Schools
Computer Science (Mathematics and Computer Science)
Economics and Management (Economics; Management)
Health Sciences
Law

History: Founded 1996.

334

Governing Bodies: Conselho Directivo

Main Language(s) of Instruction: Portuguese

Degrees and Diplomas: *Bacharelato*: Computer Engineering; Management; *Licenciatura*: Dentistry; Computer Engineering; Management; Accountancy; Law; *Mestrado*: Information Systems

• PEDAGOGICAL UNIVERSITY
Universidade Pedagógica
Com. Augusto Cardoso 135, Maputo
Tel: +258(1) 420-860
Fax: +258(1) 422-113
EMail: grupsede@zebra.uem.mz

Reitor: Carlos Machili (1989-)

Director of Administration: Freia Caiado

Faculties
Languages (English; French; Modern Languages; Portuguese)
Natural Sciences and Mathematics (Biology; Chemistry; Mathematics; Natural Sciences; Physics)
Pedagogy (Educational Sciences; Pedagogy; Psychology; Special Education)
Physical Education and Sports (Physical Education; Sports)
Social Sciences (Anthropology; Geography; History; Philosophy; Social Sciences)

Departments
Chemistry *(Beira)*
Geography *(Beira)*
Mathematics *(Beira)*
Physics *(Beira)*

History: Founded 1986.

Academic Year: August to June (August-December; January-June)

Admission Requirements: Secondary school certificate or equivalent, and entrance examination

Main Language(s) of Instruction: Portuguese

Degrees and Diplomas: *Bacharelato*: 3 yrs; *Licenciatura*: 5 yrs

Student Services: Sports Facilities, Health Services, Canteen

Special Facilities: Natural History Museum

Academic Staff *2001-2002:* Total: c. 215

Student Numbers *2001-2002:* Total: c. 1,400

PRIVATE INSTITUTIONS

• HIGHER POLYTECHNIC AND UNIVERSITY INSTITUTE
Instituto Superior Politécnico e Universitário (ISPU)
Avenida Paulo Samuel Kankhomba, 1170, Maputo
Tel: +258(1) 314-226
Fax: +258(1) 314-340
EMail: ispu@ispu.ac.mz
Website: http://www.ispu.ac.mz

Reitor: Lourenço Rosário Tel: +258(1) 314-229
EMail: lrosario@ispu.ac.mz

Chefe de Gabinete: Ana Vilela

International Relations: Rosânia Silva, Director
Tel: +258(1) 305-950 Fax: +258(1) 305-950
EMail: rosania@ispu.ac.mz

Schools
Business and Commerce (Business and Commerce; Management) *Director*: Joaquim Carvalho
Social Science and Law (Communication Studies; Law; Psychology; Social Sciences) *Director*: Maria Augusta Coutinho

Departments
Business Management and Technology (Business and Commerce; Management) *Head*: Joaquim Carvalho
Communication (Communication Studies; Marketing) *Head*: Alves Marcelino
Informatic Systems Management (Business Computing; Management) *Head*: Assane Miquidade
Legal Services (Law) *Head*: Teodósio MBanze
Psychology *Head*: Fernando Ribeiro

History: Founded 1995.
Academic Year: August to June
Admission Requirements: High school certificate and entrance examination
Fees: (US$): Admission Fee 225; Tuition 2400 per annum
Main Language(s) of Instruction: Portuguese
International Co-operation: With universities in Portugal and Brazil.
Degrees and Diplomas: *Licenciatura*: Accountancy (CA); Civil Engineering (EC); Informatic Systems Management (IG); Law (CJ); Management (AGE); Psychology (PS); Social Communications (CC); Tourism (TR), 5 yrs
Student Services: Cultural Centre, Sports Facilities, Canteen, Foreign Student Centre
Libraries: 3 Libraries
Publications: Infoispu (2 per annum)
Student Numbers *2001-2002:* Total: **2,293**

MOZAMBIQUE CATHOLIC UNIVERSITY
Universidade Católica de Moçambique (UCM)
Rua Marquês de Soveral, 960, Beira
Tel: +258(3) 312-835
Fax: +258(3) 311-520
EMail: ucm.beira@teledata.mz
Website: http://www.ucm.ac.mz

Reitor: Filipe José Couto Tel: +258(3) 313-077
Fax: +258(3) 311-520 EMail: fjcouto@teledata.mz
Vice-Reitor: Francisco Ponsi Tel: +258(3) 311-493
Fax: +258(3) 311-520
International Relations: Francisco Ponsi

Faculties
Agriculture *(Cuamba)*
Economics and Management (Economics; Management)
Education *(Nampula)* (Educational Sciences)
Law *(Nampula)*
Medicine
Tourism and Informatics (Computer Science; Tourism)

History: Founded 1996.
Main Language(s) of Instruction: Portuguese
Degrees and Diplomas: *Bacharelato*: Economics; Management; Law; Education; Agriculture, 3 yrs; *Licenciatura*; *Mestrado*: Economics; Management, 2 yrs following Bacharelato

Academic Staff *2001-2002*			TOTAL
FULL-TIME			60
PART-TIME			71
TOTAL			**131**

Student Numbers *2001-2002*	MEN	WOMEN	TOTAL
All (Foreign Included)	944	740	**1,684**

335

Namibia

INSTITUTION TYPES AND CREDENTIALS

Types of higher education institutions:

University
Polytechnic
College of Education
Vocational Training Centre

School leaving and higher education credentials:

International General Certificate of Secondary Education
Certificate
National Diploma
Baccalaureus Juris
Bachelor's Degree
Diploma
Master's Degree
Doctorate

STRUCTURE OF EDUCATION SYSTEM

Pre-higher education:

Structure of school system:

Primary
Type of school providing this education: Primary School
Length of programme in years: 7
Age level from: 5 to: 12

Junior Secondary
Type of school providing this education: Junior Secondary School
Length of programme in years: 3
Age level from: 12 to: 15
Certificate/diploma awarded: Namibian Junior Secondary Certificate

Senior Secondary
Type of school providing this education: Senior Secondary School
Length of programme in years: 2

Age level from: 15 to: 17

Certificate/diploma awarded: International General Certificate of Secondary Education (IGCSE)

School education:

Primary education lasts for seven years divided into lower primary (four years) and upper primary (three years). Junior secondary education lasts for three years and leads to the Namibian Junior Secondary Certificate. Admission to senior secondary education is based on the six best subjects in the Junior Secondary Certificate. Senior secondary education lasts for two years and leads to the International General Certificate of Secondary Education (IGCSE) which gives access to higher education. Vocational training centres offer technical subjects at the junior secondary level: options include Bricklaying and Plastering, Electricity, Motor Mechanics, Metalwork and Welding and Woodwork, etc...

Higher education:

Higher education is mainly provided by the University of Namibia, the Polytechnic of Namibia and Colleges of Education.

Academic year:

Classes from: February *to:* November

Languages of instruction:

English

Stages of studies:

Non-university level post-secondary studies (technical/vocational type):

Vocational Institutions offer Diploma courses that last for three to four years. Studies at the Polytechnic of Namibia lead to Certificates and Diplomas in Accounting, Information Systems, Law, Management and Natural Resources Management.

University level studies:

University level first stage: *Diploma, Certificate, Bachelor's Degree*:

Diplomas are conferred after three years' study in Humanities, Science, Education, Commerce, Economics, Administration, Nursing and Law. In Social Work, studies last for four years. Honours Degrees are conferred after one year's full-time or two years' part-time study in such fields as Nursing, Diagnostic Radiography and Education. Certificates are awarded after studies lasting between two and three years. The Bachelor's Degree is conferred after one year's full-time or two years' part-time study.

University level second stage: *Master's Degree*:

The Master's Degree is conferred after one year's full-time and two years' part-time study following upon the Bachelor's Degree by research in an approved topic or thesis and an oral or written examination or a mini thesis and a comprehensive written examination.

University level third stage: *Doctorate*:

A PhD is conferred after a minimum of two years' full-time or four years' part-time study in Administration, Political Studies, Adult Education, Humanities and Nursing. Students must present a dissertation and sit for an examination based on the dissertation.

Teacher education:

Training of pre-primary and primary/basic school teachers
Primary school teachers are trained at each of the four Colleges of Education at Windhoek, Ongwediva, Rundu and Caprivi. They are awarded the Basic Education Teacher Diploma (BETD) after three years of study. The minimum requirement for the BETD is a grade 12 with IGCSE passes or the equivalent.

Training of secondary school teachers
Junior secondary school teachers receive the same training as primary school teachers and take the Basic Education Teacher Diploma. The BETD is a unified general preparation for all basic education teachers (primary and junior secondary), combining a common core foundation for all, with opportunities for specialization in relation to phases of schooling and subject areas. Senior secondary school teachers are trained at the Faculty of Education of the University of Namibia.

Non-traditional studies:

Distance higher education
The College of Distance Education offers courses for those in full-time employment. There are also outreach centres and satellite campuses.

NATIONAL BODIES

Responsible authorities:
Ministry of Higher Education, Training and Employment Creation
   Minister: Nahas Angula
   Permanent Secretary: Vitalis Ankama
   Private Bag 13391
   Windhoek
9000
   Tel: +264(61) 270-6111
   Fax: +264(61) 253-672
   WWW: http://www.op.gov.na/Decade_peace/h_edu.htm

ADMISSIONS TO HIGHER EDUCATION

Admission to university-level studies

Name of secondary school credential required: International General Certificate of Secondary Education
Minimum score/requirement: 5 subjects passed in not more than the 3rd examination sitting and with a minimum of 25 points in the university scale.
For entry to: University

Entrance exams required: Entrance Examination or interview

Other admission requirements: English IGCSE compulsory

Foreign students admission

Admission requirements: Foreign students must hold qualifications required of Namibian students. Applications should be made to the university registrar before 30 September in Health Sciences and 31 October for all other courses.

Language requirements: Students whose language of education is not English may be required to pass an approved test in English.

Application procedures:

Apply to individual institution for entry to: University

Application closing dates:

> *For university level studies:* 31 October

Recognition of studies and qualifications:

Studies pursued in home country (System of recognition/accreditation): The Namibia Qualification Authority (NQA) establishes and maintains a comprehensive national qualification framework with evaluation of qualifications, accreditation of institutions, standards setting etc...

Studies pursued in foreign countries (bodies dealing with recognition of foreign credentials): Namibia Qualifications Authority (NQA)

> Head, Standards Setting: Frank E. Gertze
> Private Bag 13391
> Windhoek 9000
> Tel: +264(61) 27-10-83
> Fax: +264(61) 22-43-25
> EMail: fegertze@mhevtst.gov.na

STUDENT LIFE

National student associations and unions

Namibia National Student Organisation (NANSO)
> PO Box 22013
> Windhoek
> Tel: +264(61) 213-091

Student expenses and financial aid

Student costs:

> Home students tuition fees: Minimum: 3,250 (Namibian Dollar)
> Maximum: 12,500 (Namibian Dollar)

Bodies providing information on student financial aid:

NSFAS
> PO Box 13391
> Windhoek

Deals with: Loans

GRADING SYSTEM

Usual grading system in secondary school

Full Description: A, B, C, D, E, F and G.
Highest on scale: A
Pass/fail level: G

Main grading system used by higher education institutions

Full Description: A-E or 4.00-0.0
Highest on scale: A Distinction
Pass/fail level: D Satisfactory
Lowest on scale: E Fail

NOTES ON HIGHER EDUCATION SYSTEM

Data for academic year: 2003-2004
Source: Ministry of Higher Education, Training and Employment Creation, 2003

INSTITUTIONS OF HIGHER EDUCATION

UNIVERSITIES

PUBLIC INSTITUTIONS

*• UNIVERSITY OF NAMIBIA

Private Bag 13303, 340 Mandume Ndemufayo Avenue,
Pioneerspark, Windhoek
Tel: +264(61) 206-3111
Fax: +264(61) 206-3866
Telex: (50) 908 7271
EMail: postmaster@grumpy.cs.unam.na
Website: http://www.unam.na

Vice-Chancellor: Peter H. Katjavivi (1992-)
Tel: +264(61) 206-3937 +264(61) 206-3933
Fax: +264(61) 206-3320 EMail: pkatjavivi@unam.na

Registrar: Z.J.N. Kazapua Tel: +264(61) 206-3082
EMail: zkazapua@unam.na

International Relations: Itah Kandjii-Murangi, Director
Tel: +264(61) 206-3068 Fax: +264(61) 206-3820
EMail: ikandjii@unam.na

Faculties

Agriculture and Natural Resources (Agricultural Economics;
Agriculture; Animal Husbandry; Crop Production; Food Science; Food Technology; Natural Resources) *Dean:* Osmund D.
Mwandemele

Economics and Management Sciences (Economics; Management; Public Administration) *Dean:* André du Pisani

Education (Adult Education; Curriculum; Education; Educational Administration; Educational Psychology; Physical Education; Science Education; Special Education) *Dean:* P.K.
Wainana

Humanities and Social Sciences (African Languages; Arts
and Humanities; Christian Religious Studies; English; Environmental Studies; Geography; German; History; Performing Arts;
Romance Languages; Social Sciences; Social Work; Sociology; Theology; Visual Arts) *Dean:* A.G. Behrens

Law (Commercial Law; Human Rights; Justice Administration;
Law; Public Law) *Dean:* M.O. Hinz

Medical and Health Sciences (Health Sciences; Medicine;
Nursing; Radiology) *Dean:* A. van Dyk

Science (Biology; Chemistry; Engineering; Geology; Mathematics; Natural Sciences; Physics; Statistics) *Dean:* G.E.
Kiangi

Centres
External Studies

Language (Modern Languages) *Director:* R.K. Ndjoze-Ojo

Multidisciplinary Research *Director:* H.M. Ashekele

History: Founded 1992 to provide a University responsive to
the needs, culture and values of Namibia through highest quality education and research for students who may benefit from
them, regardless of race, colour, gender, ethnic origin, religion,
creed, social and economic status or physical condition.

Governing Bodies: University Council; Senate

Academic Year: January to November

Admission Requirements: International General Certificate of
Secondary Education, with 5 subjects passed normally in not
more than 3 examination sittings, and with a minimum of 25
points on the UNAM evaluation scale. English IGCSE (English
as First, or Second, Language) compulsory. Entrance
examination and/or interview

Fees: (Namibian Dollars): Registration, c. 140; First year, c.
3700-5400 per annum

Main Language(s) of Instruction: English

Accrediting Agencies: Ministry of Education

Degrees and Diplomas: *National Diploma:* Radiography (Diagnostic), 3 yrs; *Baccalaureus Juris:* Law, 3 yrs; *Bachelor's Degree:* Laws (LLB), 2 yrs; Accountancy; Administration; Adult
Education; Business Administration; Economics; Education;
Science (BSc); Science (Population and Development), 4-6 yrs;
Science (Engineering), 5 yrs; Agriculture and Natural Resources; Arts (BA); Arts (Library Science and Archiving); Arts
(Media Studies); Arts (Social Work); Arts (Theology and Religion); Arts (Tourism), 6 yrs; *Diploma:* Comprehensive Nursing
and Midwifery Science, 4 yrs; Adult Education, 4-6 yrs; *Master's
Degree:* 1 yr following Bachelor; *Doctorate:* 2-3 yrs following
Master. Also undergraduate and postgraduate Certificates and
Diplomas.

Student Residential Facilities: Yes (4 hostels)

Libraries: Central Library, 86,137 vols; 40,000 UNIN books
and documents; 498 periodical subscriptions

Academic Staff *2000:* Total: **443**

Student Numbers *2000*	MEN	WOMEN	TOTAL
All (Foreign Included)	1,711	2,491	**4,202**
FOREIGN ONLY	–	–	488

Distance Students, 1,736

OTHER INSTITUTIONS

PUBLIC INSTITUTIONS

CAPRIVI COLLEGE OF EDUCATION
Private Bag 1069, Katima Mulilo
Tel: +264(66) 253-422
Fax: +264(66) 253-934
Rector: J. Nyambe (2000-) Tel: +264(66) 252-053

Education
Governing Bodies: College Council
Academic Year: January to December
Admission Requirements: Certificate, grade 12 or equivalent
Main Language(s) of Instruction: English
Degrees and Diplomas: *Bachelor's Degree*: Teacher Education, 3 yrs
Student Services: Academic Counselling, Sports Facilities, Language Programmes, Health Services, Canteen
Student Residential Facilities: For 280 students
Libraries: Central Library

ONGWEDIVA COLLEGE OF EDUCATION
Private Bag X5507, Oshakati
Tel: +264(65) 230-001
Fax: +264(65) 230-006
Rector: F. Uahengo
Vice-Rector: I. Shipena

Education

POLYTECHNIC OF NAMIBIA
13 Storch Street, Private Bag 13388, Windhoek
Tel: +264(61) 207-9111
Fax: +264(61) 207-2100
Telex: (50) 908-727
EMail: polytech@polytechnic.edu.na
Website: http://www.polytechnic.edu.na
Rector: Tjiama Tjivikua (1995-) Tel: +264(61) 207-2000
Fax: +264(61) 207-2053 EMail: tjivikua@polytechnic.edu.na
Registrar: Corneels Jafta Tel: +264(61) 207-2008
Fax: +264(61) 207-2113 EMail: cjafta@polytechnic.edu.na

Founded: 1985, 1995

Schools
Business and Management (Accountancy; Business Administration; Human Resources; Management; Marketing) *Director*: Kofi Boamah
Communication, Legal and Secretarial Studies (Communication Studies; Law; Police Studies; Secretarial Studies) *Director*: Tara Elyssa

Engineering and Information Technology (Business Computing; Civil Engineering; Electrical Engineering; Electronic Engineering; Engineering; Information Technology)
Natural Resources and Tourism (Ecology; Hotel and Restaurant; Natural Resources; Rural Studies; Tourism) *Director*: Willen Jankowitz

History: Founded 1985 as Academy of Tertiary Education, the first Black college of higher learning in Namibia. Reorganized 1994, incorporating the Technikon Namibia and College for Out-of-School Training. Acquired present status 1994.
Governing Bodies: Council
Academic Year: February to November (February-June; July-November)
Admission Requirements: Senior certificate
Main Language(s) of Instruction: English
Accrediting Agencies: Certification Council for Technical Education
Degrees and Diplomas: *Bachelor's Degree*: (BTech), 4 yrs
Student Services: Academic Counselling, Social Counselling, Employment Services, Cultural Centre, Sports Facilities, Health Services, Canteen
Student Residential Facilities: For 470 students
Libraries: Central Library
Publications: Poly Quil (quarterly)
Academic Staff *2001-2002*: Full-Time: c. 150 Part-Time: c. 80 Total: c. 230
Staff with Doctorate: Total: c. 15
Student Numbers *2001-2002*: All (Foreign Included): c. 3,600 Foreign Only: c. 60
Part-time Students, c. 1,730 **Evening Students,** c. 960 **Distance Students,** c. 910

RUNDU COLLEGE OF EDUCATION
PO Box 88, Rundu
Tel: +264(66) 255-699
Fax: +264(66) 255-564
Rector: S. Mbambo

Education

WINDHOEK COLLEGE OF EDUCATION
Private Bag 13317, Andrew Kloppers Road, Khomasdal, Windhoek
Tel: +264(61) 270-3111
Fax: +264(61) 212-169
Website: http://www.wce.edu.na
Rector: M. Mbudje Tel: +264(61) 270-3201
Vice-Rector: E. Kirchner Tel: +264(61) 270-3253

Education

Niger

INSTITUTION TYPES AND CREDENTIALS

Types of higher education institutions:

Université (University)
Grande Ecole (Higher School)
Centre régional (Regional Centre)

School leaving and higher education credentials:

Baccalauréat
Diplôme de Technicien supérieur
Diplôme d'Aptitude pédagogique au Professorat des Colleges d'Enseignement Général
Diplôme d'Etudes universitaires générales (DEUG)
Diplôme universitaire d'Etudes économiques générales (DUEEG)
Diplôme universitaire d'Etudes juridiques générales (DUEJG)
Diplôme universitaire d'Etudes littéraires (DUEL)
Diplôme universitaire d'Etudes scientifiques (DUES)
Diplôme d'Ingénieur des Techniques agricoles
Licence
Diplôme d'Agronomie approfondie/d'Ingénieur Agronome
Maîtrise
Docteur en Médecine
Diplôme d'Etudes approfondies (DEA)
Diplôme d'Etudes supérieures spécialisées (DESS)
Doctorat de 3e Cycle
Doctorat d'Etat

STRUCTURE OF EDUCATION SYSTEM

Pre-higher education:

Duration of compulsory education:

  Age of entry: 6
  Age of exit: 12

Structure of school system:

  Primary
  Type of school providing this education: Ecole primaire (new cycle de base I)

Length of programme in years: 6

Age level from: 6 to: 12

Certificate/diploma awarded: Certificat de fin d'Etudes du premier Degré (CFEPD)

First Cycle Secondary

Type of school providing this education: Collège d'Enseignement général (new cycle de base II)

Length of programme in years: 4

Age level from: 12 to: 16

Certificate/diploma awarded: Brevet d'Etudes du premier Cycle (BEPC) or Diplôme de Fin d'Etudes de Base (DFEB)

Second Cycle Secondary

Type of school providing this education: Lycée

Length of programme in years: 3

Age level from: 16 to: 19

Certificate/diploma awarded: Baccalauréat

School education:

Primary education lasts for six years and leads to the Certificat de fin d'Etudes du premier Degré (CFEPD). However, according to the new law, basic education now includes Basic Cycle I (six years) and Basic Cycle II (four years). Secondary school education is subdivided into two cycles: the first cycle, or Basic Cycle II, lasting four years and leading to the Brevet d'Etudes du premier Cycle (BEPC) or the new Diplôme de Fin d'Etudes de Base (DFEB) and the second cycle lasting three years and culminating in the Baccalauréat. The Baccalauréat gives access to university education.

Higher education:

Postsecondary-level education, for the most part, takes place at the Université Abdou Moumouni, Niamey, and the Islamic University. The Université Abdou Moumouni is a State institution under the jurisdiction of the Ministère des Enseignements secondaire et supérieur, de la Recherche et de la Technologie. Its Council defines the guidelines for teaching, curricula and study systems and the organization of examinations and votes the budget. There are also specialized institutions of higher education such as the Ecole normale supérieure or the Ecole nationale d'Administration which come under the responsibility of the corresponding ministries, as well as several Grandes Ecoles régionales, such as the Ecole des Mines et de la Géologie (EMIG) which are sub-regional or continental institutions.

Main laws/decrees governing higher education:

Decree: Loi d'Orientation du Système éducatif   Year: 1998

Concerns: Organization of the educational system

Decree: N° 95-20/PRN   Year: 1995

Concerns: Reorganization of the Ministry of Education and creation of the Ministry of Higher Education and Research

Academic year:

Classes from: October *to:* June

Long vacation from: 1 July *to:* 30 September

Languages of instruction:

French

Stages of studies:

Non-university level post-secondary studies (technical/vocational type):

Technical education remains separate from the universities and is usually provided at the postsecondary level by institutes or centres falling under the responsibility of the relevant Ministry. The Centre régional d'Application en Agrométéorologie (AGRHYMET) offers a Diplôme de Technicien supérieur after two years' study; the Ecole nationale de la Santé publique and the Ecole des Mines et de la Géologie after three years' study after the Baccalauréat and an entrance examination.

University level studies:

University level first stage: Premier Cycle:

The first cycle is a two-year period of general university studies. It leads to the Diplôme universitaire d'Etudes littéraires (DUEL) in Arts and Humanities; to the Diplôme universitaire d'Etudes scientifiques (DUES) in Science; to the Diplôme universitaire d'Etudes économiques générales (DUEEG) in Economics and to the Diplôme universitaire d'Etudes générales (DEUG).

University level second stage: Deuxième Cycle:

The second cycle lasts for a further two years, the first leading to the Licence, and the second to the Maîtrise. In Engineering, the Diplôme d'Ingénieur des Techniques agricoles is conferred after two years' post-first cycle studies. Longer studies in Agriculture lead to the Diplôme d'Ingénieur agronome/Diplôme d'Agronomie approfondie. The title of Docteur en Médecine is conferred after six to seven years' study.

University level third stage: Troisième Cycle:

The third cycle is open to holders of the Maîtrise. The Diplôme d'Etudes supérieures spécialisées (DESS) is conferred after one year's specialized study following upon the Maîtrise in a particular field, combined with a special training session. The Diplôme d'Etudes approfondies (DEA) is conferred after one and sometimes two years beyond the Maîtrise. The Doctorat de 3ème Cycle is conferred after a minimum of two and a maximum of three years' study, with the first year spent working on the DEA. The Doctorat d'Etat is the most advanced third cycle degree. It is mainly awarded in Science. The course normally lasts for five years. Candidates must carry out original research. They must hold the DEA or the DESS and defend their thesis in front of a jury.

Teacher education:

Training of pre-primary and primary/basic school teachers

Primary school teachers are trained at Ecoles normales. They must hold the BEPC or the Baccalauréat and sit for an entrance examination. After three years' study they obtain the Diplôme de Fin d'Etudes normales (DFEN). Instituteurs adjoints are trained in two years after which they obtain the Certificat de Fin d'Etudes normales (CFEN).

Training of secondary school teachers

Teachers for first cycle secondary schools are trained at the Ecole normale supérieure. A one-year programme after the DEUG and an entrance examination lead to a professional diploma, the Diplôme d'Aptitude professionnelle au Professorat des Collèges d'Enseignement général (DAP/CEG). Teachers of Lycées are trained in one year after the Maîtrise (and the passing of an entrance exam) and obtain the Certificat d'Aptitude professionnelle à l'Enseignement secondaire (CAPES). The Ecole normale supérieure also trains inspectors and advisers for primary and secondary levels.

NATIONAL BODIES

Responsible authorities:

Ministry of Higher and Secondary Education, Research and Technology (Ministère des Enseignements secondaire et supérieur , de la Recherche et de la Technologie)
Ministre: Habi Mahamadou Salissou
Directrice de l'Enseignement supérieur: Aissata Niandou
PO Box 628
10896	Niamey
Tel: +227 72-26-20
Fax: +227 72-40-40 +227 72-42-21
EMail: mesrt@intnet-ne

ADMISSIONS TO HIGHER EDUCATION

Admission to non university higher education studies

Name of secondary school credential required: Baccalauréat
For entry to: All institutions

Alternatives to credentials: Baccalauréat de Technicien

Entrance exams required: Competitive entrance examination for access to BTS in most schools.

Admission to university-level studies

Name of secondary school credential required: Baccalauréat
For entry to: University

Entrance exams required: Entrance Examination

Foreign students admission

Admission requirements: Foreign students should hold a Baccalauréat or an equivalent qualification. They also have to sit for a special entrance examination.

Language requirements: Good knowledge of French or English is required.

Recognition of studies and qualifications:

Studies pursued in home country (System of recognition/accreditation): Standards are set by the Ministry of Higher and Secondary Education, Research and Technology

Studies pursued in foreign countries (bodies dealing with recognition of foreign credentials):
Ministry of Higher and Secondary Education, Research and Technology (Ministère des Enseignements secondaire et supérieur , de la Recherche et de la Technologie)

Directrice de l'Enseignement supérieur: Aissata Niandou
PO Box 628
10896   Niamey
Tel: +227 72-26-20 +227 72-42-50
Fax: +227 72-40-40 +227 72-42-21
EMail: mesrt@intnet-ne

Multilateral agreements concerning recognition of foreign studies

Name(s) of agreement(s): Convention on the Recognition of Studies, Certificates, Diplomas, Degrees and Other Academic Qualifications in Higher Education in the African States
Year of signature: 1981

STUDENT LIFE

Student expenses and financial aid

Student costs:

Home students tuition fees: Minimum: 0 (CFA Franc-O)

Bodies providing information on student financial aid:

Université Abdou Moumouni
B.P. 237
10896   Niamey
Tel: +227 73 27 13
Fax: +227 73 38 62
Telex: UNINIM(975) 5258 NI

Deals with: Grants
Category of students: Students from all countries holding a Secondary School Leaving Certificate and with a good knowledge of French and English. Applications have to go through their Government or through international organizations.

GRADING SYSTEM

Usual grading system in secondary school

Full Description: 16-20=Très bien; 14-15=Bien; 12-13=Assez Bien; 10-11=Passable; 0-9=Ajourné.
Highest on scale: 20
Pass/fail level: 10
Lowest on scale: 0

Main grading system used by higher education institutions

Full Description: 16-20=Très bien; 14-15=Bien; 12-13=Assez bien; 10-11=Passable.
Highest on scale: 20
Pass/fail level: 10
Lowest on scale: 0

NOTES ON HIGHER EDUCATION SYSTEM

Data for academic year: 2002-2003
Source: Université de Niamey, Service des Equivalences de Diplômes, updated by the International Association of Universities (IAU) from IBE website, 2003 (www.ibe.unesco.org/International/Databanks/Wde/profilee.htm)

INSTITUTIONS OF HIGHER EDUCATION

UNIVERSITIES

ISLAMIC UNIVERSITY OF NIGER
Université Islamique du Niger
11507 Niamey, Say
Tel: +227 72-39-03
Fax: +227 73-37-96
Vice-Chancellor: Abdelali Oudrhiri (1994-)

Faculties
Arabic Language and Islamic Studies (Arabic; Islamic Studies)

History: Founded 1987 by the Islamic Conference Organization.

Academic Year: October to June (October-February; March-June)

Admission Requirements: High school leaving certificate or equivalent

Fees: None

Main Language(s) of Instruction: Arabic (French, English optional)

Degrees and Diplomas: *Licence*: Arabic; Shari'a, 4 yrs

Academic Staff *2001-2002:* Total: c. 20

Student Numbers *2001-2002:* Total: c. 350

• UNIVERSITY ABDOU MOUMOUNI
Université Abdou Moumouni
BP 237, 10896 Niamey
Tel: +227 73-27-13 +227 73-27-14
Fax: +227 73-38-62
Telex: UNINIM(975) 5258 NI
EMail: resadep@ilimi.uam.ne
Website: http://www.ird.ne/resadep
Recteur: Bouli Ali Diallo Fax: +227 73-39-43
Secrétaire général: Maïga Djibo
International Relations: Boukari Dodo

Faculties
Agronomy

Arts and Humanities (Arts and Humanities; English; Geography; History; Philosophy; Psychology; Sociology)

Economics and Law (Economics; Law)

Health Sciences

Pedagogy (Pedagogy; Teacher Training)

Science (Agronomy; Biology; Chemistry; Geology; Mathematics; Natural Sciences; Physics)

Schools
Teacher Training *(ENS)*

Research Institutes
Humanities (Arts and Humanities; Social Sciences)
Mathematics Education

History: Founded 1971 as Centre d'Enseignement supérieur. Became university 1973. Under the jurisdiction of the Ministry of Secondary and Higher Education, Research and Technology.

Governing Bodies: Conseil, composed of the Rector, Deans and Directors of the faculties and institutes, representatives of the academic staff and student body, and government representatives

Academic Year: October to June (October-December; January-March; April-June)

Admission Requirements: Secondary school certificate (baccalauréat) or special entrance examination

Main Language(s) of Instruction: French

Degrees and Diplomas: *Diplôme d'Etudes universitaires générales (DEUG)*: Law and Economics, 2 yrs; *Diplôme universitaire d'Etudes économiques générales (DUEEG)*: Economics, 2 yrs; *Diplôme universitaire d'Etudes juridiques générales (DUEJG)*: Law, 2 yrs; *Diplôme universitaire d'Etudes littéraires (DUEL)*: English; Geography; History; Letters; Linguistics; Philosophy; Psychology; Sociology, 2 yrs; *Diplôme universitaire d'Etudes scientifiques (DUES)*: Agronomy; Biology and Geology; Chemistry and Biology; Mathematics and Physics; Physics and Chemistry, 2 yrs; *Diplôme d'Ingénieur des Techniques agricoles*: Agricultural Engineering; *Licence*: Economics; Law; Letters, 1 yr following DUEL; Chemistry; Mathematics; Natural sciences; Physics, 1 yr following DUES; *Diplôme d'Agronomie approfondie/d'Ingénieur Agronome*: 5 yrs; *Maîtrise*: Agronomy; Chemistry; Mathematics; Natural Sciences; Physics, 1 yr following Licence; *Docteur en Médecine*: Medicine; *Diplôme d'Etudes approfondies (DEA)*: Science; *Doctorat de 3e Cycle*: Letters; Science; *Doctorat d'Etat*: Science. Also diplomas in school counselling and teaching (lower level)

Student Residential Facilities: Yes

Libraries: c. 62,000 vols

Academic Staff *2001-2002:* Total: c. 260

Student Numbers *2001-2002:* Total: c. 3,700

OTHER INSTITUTIONS

AGRHYMET REGIONAL CENTRE
Centre Régional Agrhymet (CRA/ARC)
BP 11011, Niamey
Tel: +227 73-31-16
Fax: +227 73-22-35
EMail: admin@sahel.agrhymet.ne
Website: http://www.agrhymet.ne

Director-General: Alhassane Adama Diallo
EMail: adiallo@sahel.agrhymet.ne
Administrative Officer: Sankung Bangally Sagnia

Founded: 1974

Units
Hydrology and Crop Protection (Agricultural Equipment; Meteorology; Plant and Crop Protection; Water Science) *Head*: B. Sagnia Sankung

History: Founded 1974 as specialized institute of the Permanent Interstate Committee for drought control in the Sahel (CILSS). Offers training and information in the fields of food security and sustainable natural resources management.

Governing Bodies: Technical and Management Committee; Scientific and Pedagogic Committee

Academic Year: October to June

Admission Requirements: Secondary school certificate (baccalaureat, Science option) or equivalent for the higher diploma; and higher diploma or equivalent for the "Ingénieur" diploma

Main Language(s) of Instruction: French

Accrediting Agencies: Conseil Africain et Malgache pour l' Enseignement Supérieur (CAMES)

Degrees and Diplomas: *Diplôme de Technicien supérieur*: Agrometeorology; Hydrology; Instrument Maintenance; Crop Protection, 2 yrs; *Diplôme d'Ingénieur des Techniques agricoles*: Agrometeorology; Hydrology, 3 yrs following 1st Cycle

Student Services: Academic Counselling, Cultural Centre, Sports Facilities, Language Programmes, Health Services

Student Residential Facilities: 110-Room Residence Halls

Special Facilities: Specialized Laboratories (Entomology, Phytopathology, Phytopharmacy, Electronics, Hydrology, Geographic Information Systems and Remote Sensing)

Libraries: Central Library, 28,000 references completely computerized and connected to Internet

Publications: Agrhymet Info, Information Bulletin on the Agrhymet Regional Centre (quarterly); Bulletin du Programme Majeur Formation, Liaison Bulletin specially designed for former students (2 per annum); Year book, Annuaire des Diplômes (once every 3 years)

Academic Staff *2001-2002*: Full-Time: c. 15 Part-Time: c. 20 Total: c. 35

Staff with Doctorate: Total: c. 10

Student Numbers *2001-2002:* Total: c. 80

Note: In addition to long-term students, the Centre trains more than 200 trainees annually through short-term programmes

ÉCOLE AFRICAINE ET MALGACHE DE L'AVIATION CIVILE (EAMAC)
BP 746, Niamey
Tel: +227 72-36-61

Programmes
Air Transport

ÉCOLE DES MINES ET DE LA GÉOLOGIE (EMIG)
BP 732, Niamey
Tel: +227 73-37-97
Fax: +227 73-51-37

Departments
Civil and Environmental Engineering (Civil Engineering; Environmental Engineering)
Electricity (Electrical Engineering)
General Studies
Management Studies (Management)
Mechanics
Mining and Geology (Geology; Mining Engineering)

ÉCOLE NATIONALE D'ADMINISTRATION (ENA)
BP 542, Rue Martin Luther King Jr, Niamey
Tel: +227 72-28-53

Founded: 1963

Programmes
Administration

ÉCOLE NATIONALE DE LA SANTÉ PUBLIQUE (ENSP)
BP 290, Niamey
Tel: +227 72-30-01

Programmes
Public Health

Nigeria

INSTITUTION TYPES AND CREDENTIALS

Types of higher education institutions:

Federal University
State University
University of Technology
University of Agriculture
Polytechnic
College

School leaving and higher education credentials:

Senior School Certificate
West African GCE "O" Level
West African GCE "A" Level
National Diploma
Bachelor's Degree
Higher National Diploma
Bachelor Honours Degree
Doctor of Veterinary Medicine
Postgraduate Diploma
Master's Degree
Master of Philosophy
Doctor of Philosophy

STRUCTURE OF EDUCATION SYSTEM

Pre-higher education:

Duration of compulsory education:

   Age of entry: 6
   Age of exit: 15

Structure of school system:

   Primary
   Type of school providing this education: Primary School
   Length of programme in years: 6
   Age level from: 6 to: 12

Junior Secondary
Type of school providing this education: Junior School
Length of programme in years: 3
Age level from: 12 to: 15
Certificate/diploma awarded: Junior School Certificate (JSSC)

Senior Secondary
Type of school providing this education: Senior Secondary School
Length of programme in years: 3
Age level from: 15 to: 18
Certificate/diploma awarded: Senior School Certificate (SSSC)

Technical
Type of school providing this education: Technical Secondary School
Length of programme in years: 6
Age level from: 12 to: 18
Certificate/diploma awarded: Senior School Certificate (SSSC)

School education:

Primary education lasts for six years. Entrance to secondary education is based on an examination. Secondary education is divided into junior and senior secondary, and technical and vocational education. The Junior School Certificate is awarded after three years of junior school. The Senior School Certificate is awarded after three years of senior secondary education. It replaced the West African GCE "O" level in 1989. Pupils who complete junior secondary school are streamed into senior secondary school, technical college, out of school vocation training centre or an apprenticeship. Technical secondary education is offered in secondary commercial schools which offer six-year courses including academic subjects and specialization. At the end of the course, students may take the examinations for the Senior School Certificate. Vocational education produces low level manpower and is offered in technical colleges or business and engineering skills training centres. Technical colleges are the only alternative to senior secondary schools as a route to further formal education and training after junior secondary education. To enter university, students have to pass the University Matriculation examination (UME).

Higher education:

Higher education is provided by universities, polytechnics, institutions of technology, colleges of education (which form part of the universities and polytechnical colleges or are affiliated to these) and professional institutions. Universities can be established either by federal or state governments. Each university is administered by a Council and a Senate. Within the universities, the institutes and colleges are more or less autonomous.

Main laws/decrees governing higher education:

Decree: Decree n.9, Education Amendment Decree   Year: 1993

Academic year:

Classes from: October *to:* July

Long vacation from: 15 July *to:* 30 September

Languages of instruction:

English

Stages of studies:

Non-university level post-secondary studies (technical/vocational type):

Higher technical education is offered in technical colleges, polytechnics and colleges of education. They offer two-stage National Diplomas and Higher National Diplomas of two years' duration. The colleges also offer various Certificates in technology which may be obtained after one, two or three years. Students are expected to have at least one year industrial attachment after obtaining the National Diploma to proceed to the Higher National Diploma course. The Colleges of Education in this sector train technical teachers.

University level studies:

University level first stage: *Bachelor's Degree*:

First degree courses in Arts, Social Sciences and Pure Sciences are usually of four years' duration (three years for students holding good GCE "A" levels), whilst professional degrees tend to last for five years. Degree courses in Medicine and Dentistry last for six years. The Bachelor's Degree may be awarded as an Honours degree: students take either a single subject Honours degree course or combined Honours.

University level second stage: *Master's Degree*:

Master's Degree courses usually last for one year after the Bachelor's Degree but, increasingly, where the qualification depends on research, it becomes a two-year course.

University level third stage: *Doctorate*:

The Doctorate Degree is usually conferred two to three years after the Master's Degree. Some first generation universities require students to complete a Master of Philosophy degree before being admitted to the PhD programme.

Teacher education:

Training of pre-primary and primary/basic school teachers

Four years' post primary study at a grade 2 teacher training college leads to a Grade 2 Certificate/Higher Elementary Teacher's Certificate. Holders of the former Grade 3 Certificate may take an upgrading course to become grade 2 teachers. As from 1998, the Nigerian Certificate in Education conferred by colleges of education is required for teaching in primary schools.

Training of secondary school teachers

Holders of the Nigerian Certificate of Education may teach in junior secondary schools and technical colleges. Senior secondary school teachers are trained at the universities. They must hold the BEd or a Bachelor's plus a Postgraduate Diploma in Education. Most students study for three years at an advanced teachers' college for the Nigerian Certificate of Education, which also gives access to university. As from 1998, no teacher with a qualification below this level will be able to teach in any school.

Non-traditional studies:

Distance higher education

Distance education is offered in Open Studies Centres of certain universities.

Lifelong higher education

Extension services are provided mainly in the area of Agriculture. In Education, vacation courses have become a very popular path for teachers wishing to obtain a Bachelor's or a Master's degree.

NATIONAL BODIES

Responsible authorities:

Federal Ministry of Education
    Minister: Babalola Borishade
    Permanent Secretary: Godfrey B. Preware mni
    International Relations: Samuel A.B. Atolagbe
    Federal Secretariat, PMB 146, Shehu Shagari Way-Maitama
    Abuja
    Tel: +234(9) 52-32-800
    Fax: +234(9) 53-37-839

Role of governing body: Ministerial responsibility for Education at Secondary and Tertiary levels in Universities, Polytechnics, Colleges of Education and Federal Government Colleges.

National Universities Commission
    Executive Secretary: Peter Okebukola
    Aja Nwachukwu House, Plot 430 Aguiyi-Ironsi St., Maitama District PMB 237 Garki GPO
    Abuja
    Tel: +234(9) 41-33-176-81
    Fax: +234(9) 41-33-250
    EMail: es@nuc.edu.ng
    WWW: http://www.nuc.edu.ng

Role of governing body: Allocates funds to Federal universities; examines the curriculum so that it corresponds to professional requirements; develops university education.

Committee of Vice-Chancellors of Nigerian Federal Universities
    Chairman: Abhulimen R. Anao
    Secretary-General: Gabriel M. Umezurike
    PMB 12002
    3, Idowu Taylor Street, Victoria Island
    Lagos
12022
    Tel: +234(1) 26-12-425

Role of governing body: Acts as coordinating body and offers advice to government and universities governing councils on matters of general concern.

ADMISSIONS TO HIGHER EDUCATION

Admission to non university higher education studies

Name of secondary school credential required: Senior School Certificate

Numerus clausus/restrictions: For most fields of study as determined by the National Board for Technical Education and as conditioned by the availability of instructional facilities in different programmes in each institution.

Admission to university-level studies

Name of secondary school credential required: West African GCE "O" Level
Minimum score/requirement: Credit passes in 5 subjects including English Language, Mathematics and Science.
For entry to: Bachelor's Degree

Name of secondary school credential required: Senior School Certificate
For entry to: Bachelor's degree

Name of secondary school credential required: West African GCE "A" Level
Minimum score/requirement: good grades allow for direct entry to universities
For entry to: Bachelor's degree

Alternatives to credentials: National Certificate of Education passes at Credit or Merit levels or Ordinary National Diploma at upper credit level.

Entrance exams required: Universities Matriculation Examination (UME) for all first Degrees. Good GCE 'A' level results give direct access to universities.

Numerus clausus/restrictions: For most fields as determined by the National Universities Commission and conditioned by availability of instructional facilities available in different programmes at the level of institution.

Other admission requirements: None

Foreign students admission

Definition of foreign student: Student who is not a citizen of Nigeria, where citizenship is defined in terms of being born in Nigeria after 1960, or both parents being Nigerian, and not being a citizen of another country.

Admission requirements: Foreign students should have qualifications equivalent to the General Certificate of Education in at least 5 subjects, after 6 years of secondary school. At postgraduate level, foreign students must have an appropriate first degree with upper second class honours. Those with a lower grade have to take admission exams.

Entry regulations: Resident permits required of ECOWAS Nationals. Visas and resident permits required of Nationals of other countries.

Health requirements: Certificate of medical fitness at Medical Centre of Institution

Application procedures:

Apply to individual institution for entry to: Post-Graduate Studies.

Apply to national body for entry to: First Degree Programmes.

Apply to: Joint Admissions and Matriculation Board (JAMB)
    PMB 12748
    11/13 Ojoro Road, IKOYI
    Lagos
    Telex: 28708 JAMB NG

Application closing dates:

   For non-university level (technical/vocational type) studies: 31 March
   For university level studies: 31 March
   For advanced/doctoral studies: 31 March

Recognition of studies and qualifications:

Studies pursued in home country (System of recognition/accreditation): Accreditation of Higher
Vocational / Technical programmes in Polytechnics and Colleges of Education is performed by the
National Board of Technical Education (NBTE). The Quality Assurance and Research Development
Agency (QAADAN) reviews higher education institutions programmes (PO Box 997, 75 Adisa Bashua
Street off Adelabu Street Surelere, Lagos; Tel.: +234(1) 583-0108; +234(1) 8030-67652)

Studies pursued in foreign countries (bodies dealing with recognition of foreign credentials):
National Standing Committee for the Evaluation of Foreign Qualifications, Federal Ministry of Education
    Director, E.S.S.: S.A.B. Atolagbe
    Deputy Director (E&A): S.O. Okunola
    International Relations: Marie Uko
    Educational Support Services Department
    Evaluation and Accreditation Division
    Federal Secretariat Phase III
    Shehu Shagari Way
    Abuja
    Tel: +234(9) 31-41-215
    Fax: +234(9) 31-41-215

Services provided and students dealt with: Deals with the broad principles and sets the criteria for the
evaluation of foreign certificates and diplomas; receives and considers representations from
aggrieved persons on the day-to-day evaluation carried out by the Evaluation and Accreditation
Division of the Federal Ministry of Education.

Other information sources on recognition of foreign studies: Universities, the Nigerian Law School, etc.
where each department often decides on the status of foreign credentials submitted by applicants.

Special provisions for recognition:

For the exercise of a profession: Access to Medicine, Pharmacy, Accountancy, Law and related professions is regulated by professional associations/societies. The associations/societies are supported by statutes and moderate qualifying examinations.

Multilateral agreements concerning recognition of foreign studies

Name(s) of agreement(s): Convention on the Recognition of Studies, Certificates, Diplomas, Degrees and Other Academic Qualifications in Higher Education in the African States
Year of signature: 1981

References to further information on foreign student admissions and recognition of studies

Title: Universities calendars

STUDENT LIFE

National student associations and unions

National Association of Nigerian Students
    Federal University of Technology
    PO Box 1526
    Oweri
Imo State
    Tel: +234(83) 233-974
    EMail: root@futo.edu.ng

Health/social provisions

Social security for home students: No

Social security for foreign students: No

Foreign student social security provisions: None

Special student travel fares:

By road: No
By rail: No
By air: No
Available to foreign students: No

Student expenses and financial aid

Student costs:

    Home students tuition fees: Minimum: 2,000 (Naira)
    Maximum: 8,000 (Naira)
    Foreign students tuition fees: Minimum: 6,000 (Naira)
    Maximum: 35,000 (Naira)

Bodies providing information on student financial aid:

Scholarships Division, Federal Ministry of Education
 Federal Secretariat, PMB 146, Shehu Shagari Way-Maitama
 Abuja
 Tel: +234(9) 52-32-800
 Fax: +234(9) 53-37-839

 Deals with: Grants
 Category of students: Commonwealth students.

Publications on student services and financial aid:

 Title: Nigerian Awards-Commonwealth Scholarships
 Publisher: Federal Ministry of Education, Scholarships Division

 Title: Study Abroad 2004-2005, 32nd Edition
 Author: UNESCO
 Publisher: UNESCO Publishing
 Year of publication: 2003

GRADING SYSTEM

Usual grading system in secondary school

Full Description: For the West African Senior School Certificate: 1-9
Highest on scale: A 1
Pass/fail level: P 8
Lowest on scale: F 9

Main grading system used by higher education institutions

Full Description: For the Ordinary National Diploma (OND):GPA 3.50+ (Distinction; 3.00-3.49 (Upper Credit); 2.50-2.99 (Lower Credit); 2.00-2.49 (Pass)
Highest on scale: 3.50+(Distinction)
Pass/fail level: 2.00-2.49(Pass)
Lowest on scale: 2.00

Other main grading systems

For the Bachelor' degree: 1st class (70-100), 2nd class upper division (60-69), 2nd class lower division (50-59), 3rd class pass (40-49).

NOTES ON HIGHER EDUCATION SYSTEM

Data for academic year: 2002-2003
Source: Federal Ministry of Education and National Universities Commission, Abuja, 2003

INSTITUTIONS OF HIGHER EDUCATION

UNIVERSITIES AND TECHNICAL UNIVERSITIES

PUBLIC INSTITUTIONS

• ABIA STATE UNIVERSITY (ABSU)

PMB 2000, Uturu, Abia State
Tel: +234(82) 440-291 to 93
Fax: +234(82) 440-294

Vice-Chancellor: Ogwo E. Ogwo (2000-)
EMail: vc@absu.edu.ng
Registrar: Madubuike Okoronkwo

Colleges

Agriculture and Veterinary Medicine (Agricultural Economics; Agriculture; Animal Husbandry; Food Science; Food Technology; Soil Science; Veterinary Science) *Dean:* L.C. Nwaigbo
Biological and Physical Sciences (Biochemistry; Biological and Life Sciences; Botany; Industrial Chemistry; Mathematics; Microbiology; Physics; Statistics; Zoology) *Dean:* Michael Oleka
Business Administration (Accountancy; Banking; Business Administration; Economics; Finance; Management; Marketing) *Dean:* Igwe Aja-Nwachuku
Education (Accountancy; Biology; Economics; English; Ethnology; French; Geography; Government; History; Mathematics; Religion; Social Studies) *Dean:* Michael Maduabum
Engineering and Environmental Studies (Architecture; Construction Engineering; Engineering; Environmental Studies; Geography; Real Estate; Regional Planning; Urban Studies) *Dean:* Innocent Mbadiwe
Humanities and Social Sciences (Arts and Humanities; English; French; Government; History; Library Science; Linguistics; Literature; Public Administration; Social Sciences; Sociology) *Dean:* Afam Ebeogu
Legal Studies (Civil Law; Commercial Law; Constitutional Law; International Law; Law; Private Law; Public Law) *Dean:* Ernest Ojukwu
Medicine and Health Sciences (Health Sciences; Medicine; Optometry) *Provost:* Frank Akpuaka
Postgraduate Studies (Architecture; Arts and Humanities; Biological and Life Sciences; Business Administration; Education; Environmental Studies; Law; Social Sciences) *Dean:* Geoffrey Nwaka

Institutes

Distance Education (Accountancy; Economics; Finance; Government; Marketing; Mass Communication; Public Administration) *Director:* Chinyere Nwahunanya
Pre-Science (Biology; Chemistry; Economics; English; Government; History; Literature; Mathematics; Physics; Religion)

Centres

Igbo Studies (Archaeology; Cultural Studies; Dance; Environmental Studies; Ethnology; Geography; Government; History; Law; Political Science; Religion; Social Studies; Theatre) *Director:* A.E. Afigbo

History: Founded 1981. The University operates a collegiate system with related disciplines clustered into Schools and Schools grouped into Colleges. Interdisciplinary in structure and mission, each school is flexible in function.
Governing Bodies: Council; Senate
Academic Year: October to July (October-March; April-July)
Admission Requirements: Universities Matriculation Examination (UME) following secondary school education
Main Language(s) of Instruction: English
Degrees and Diplomas: *Bachelor's Degree:* Arts (BA); Education (BEd); Science (BSc), 4 yrs; *Postgraduate Diploma:* 1 yr; *Master's Degree:* Arts (MA); Business Administration (MBA); Education (MEd); Laws (LLM); Library Studies (MLS); Public Administration (MPA); Science (MSc), a further 1-3 yrs; *Doctor of Philosophy:* Education (PhD), 2-3 yrs
Student Residential Facilities: Yes
Libraries: 27,000 vols, 35 periodical subscriptions
Academic Staff *2000:* Total: c. 340
Student Numbers *2000:* Total: c. 7,050

• ABUBAKAR TAFAWA BALEWA UNIVERSITY (ATBU)

PMB 0248, Bauchi, Bauchi State
Tel: +234(77) 542-464   +234(77) 543-500
Fax: +234(77) 542-065
Cable: Televarsity Bauchi
EMail: vc@atbunet.org;info@atbunet.org
Website: http://www.atbunet.org

Vice-Chancellor: Abubakar Sani Sambo (1995-)
Tel: +234(77) 542-065 EMail: sambo@atbu.edu.ng
Registrar: Ibrahim Musa Tel: +234(77) 542-092

Units

Industrial Training Coordination *Head:* T.O. Oseni
Management Information Systems (Management Systems) *Coordinator:* S. Ali

Programmes

Accountancy *Coordinator:* J. Yusuf
Agricultural Economics and Extension (Agricultural Economics) *Coordinator:* R.M. Sani
Agricultural Engineering *Coordinator:* H.I. Ahmed
Animal Husbandry *Coordinator:* R.I.S. Butswat
Architecture *Coordinator:* A.A. Isa

Banking and Finance (Banking; Finance) *Coordinator*: A. Dutse

Biological Sciences (Biological and Life Sciences) *Coordinator*: S.L. Kela

Building (Building Technologies) *Coordinator*: D.A. Mu'azu

Business Management (Business Administration) *Coordinator*: I.S. Dangs

Chemical Engineering *Coordinator*: A.U. Elinwa

Chemistry *Coordinator*: O.J. Abayeh

Civil Engineering *Coordinator*: J.A. Egwurube

Crop Production *Coordinator*: B.M. Auwalu

Electrical and Electronic Engineering *Coordinator*: M.S. Islam

Environmental Management Technology (Environmental Management) *Coordinator*: D.B. Ibrahim

Estate Management (Real Estate) *Coordinator*: S.A. Samaila

General Studies (Continuing Education) *Coordinator*: O.C. Ogidi

Geology *Coordinator*: N.K. Samaila

Industrial Design *Coordinator*: Y.O. Sadiq

Land Surveying (Surveying and Mapping) *Coordinator*: Y.L. Sumi

Mathematics *Coordinator*: M.S. Sesay

Mechanical and Production Engineering (Mechanical Engineering; Production Engineering) *Coordinator*: M.H. Muhammad

Petroleum Engineering (Petroleum and Gas Engineering) *Coordinator*: A.A. Asere

Physics *Coordinator*: M.F. Haque

Quantity Surveying (Mathematics) *Coordinator*: S.A. Sumaila

Science Education *Coordinator*: O.I. Oloyede

Urban and Regional Planning (Regional Planning; Town Planning) *Coordinator*: I.A. Harir

Schools

Agriculture and Agricultural Technology (Agricultural Equipment; Agriculture) *Dean*: S.T. Mbap

Engineering *Dean*: A.A. Asere

Environmental Technology (Environmental Engineering) *Dean*: S. Suleiman

Management Technology (Management; Management Systems) *Dean*: S. Kushwaha

Postgraduate Studies *Dean*: A.Q. Ibrahim

Science and Science Education (Natural Sciences; Science Education) *Dean*: E.J.A. Edemenang

Centres

Computer Science *Director*: S. Ali

Distance Learning *Director*: D.S. Matawal

Energy Research (Energy Engineering) *Director*: M.I. Onogu

Industrial Studies (Industrial Management) *Director*: J.S. Jatau

Research *(FEPA)* *Director*: M.O. Agho

History: Founded 1980 as the Federal University of Technology, Bauchi. Acquired present status 1988.

Governing Bodies: University Council

Academic Year: October to August (October-April; April-August)

Admission Requirements: Senior Secondary Certificate of Education (SSCE) or General Certificate of Education (GCE) 'O' levels with at least 5 credits

Main Language(s) of Instruction: English

Degrees and Diplomas: *Bachelor's Degree*: Technology (BTech), 5 yrs; *Master's Degree*: Science (MSc), a further 1-2 yrs; Engineering (MEng), a further 2 yrs; *Doctor of Philosophy*: (PhD), 2-3 yrs

Student Services: Academic Counselling, Social Counselling, Employment Services, Nursery Care, Sports Facilities, Health Services

Student Residential Facilities: For c. 1500 students

Libraries: University Library, 45,000 vols

Publications: University Bulletin (monthly); ATBU Annual Report (annually)

Press or Publishing House: ATBU Printing Press

Academic Staff *2002:* Total: c. 235

Student Numbers *2002*: All (Foreign Included): Men: c. 4,855 Women: c. 1,040 Total: c. 5,895
Foreign Only: Total: c. 45

• ADEKUNLE AJASIN UNIVERSITY (UNAD)
PMB 5363, Ado-Ekiti, Ekiti State
Tel: +234(30) 250-026   +234(30) 250-851
Fax: +234(30) 250-188
Cable: ondovarsity ado-ekiti
Website: http://www.unad.edu.ng

Vice-Chancellor: Akindele Babatunde Oyebode (2002-)
Tel: +234(30) 250-997 EMail: aoyebode@aol.com

Registrar: M.O. Ogunniyi Tel: +234(30) 250-650

International Relations: I.O. Orubuloye
Tel: +234(30) 250-906 EMail: cepher@sknnet.com

University Librarian (Acting): G.O. Ogunleye
Tel: +234(30) 251-520

Faculties

Agriculture (Agriculture; Forestry) J.A. Ogunwale

Arts (Arts and Humanities; History; Modern Languages; Philosophy; Religious Studies) *Dean (Acting)*: T.F. Jemiriye

Education *Dean (Acting)*: S.O. Bandele

Engineering (Civil Engineering; Electrical Engineering; Engineering; Mechanical Engineering; Physical Engineering) *Dean (Acting)*: S.B. Adeyemo

Law *Dean (Acting)*: G.D. Oke

Management (Accountancy; Banking; Business Administration; Finance; Management) *Dean*: C.S. Ola

Science (Botany; Chemistry; Geography; Microbiology; Natural Sciences; Zoology) *Dean*: O. Olaofe

Social Sciences (Accountancy; Economics; Psychology; Social Sciences; Sociology) *Dean*: D.C. Uguru-Okorie

Colleges

Medicine (Medicine; Surgery) *Dean*: D.O.O. Oyebola

Schools

Postgraduate *Dean*: O.A. Akande

History: Founded 1982 as Obafemi Awolowo University, renamed Ondo State University 1985, and University of Ado-Ekiti 1999. Acquired present status 1985.

Governing Bodies: Council, Senate, Faculty Boards

Academic Year: October to July (October-March; April-July)

Admission Requirements: Senior School Certificate (SSC) or General Certificate of Education (GCE) 'O' levels, with credits in 5 relevant subjects, obtained at no more than 2 sittings; and University Matriculation Examination (UME). Some courses have additional requirements. International applicants: equivalent qualifications and UME

Fees: (US Dollars): Home students, 35-52 (Humanities); 44-59

Main Language(s) of Instruction: English

Accrediting Agencies: National Universities Commission

Degrees and Diplomas: *Bachelor's Degree*: (BA, BEd, BSc), 4 yrs; *Master's Degree*: (MA, MEd, MSc), 1 further yr; *Doctor of Philosophy*: (PhD), a minimum of 2 yrs

Student Services: Academic Counselling, Social Counselling, Sports Facilities, Health Services

Student Residential Facilities: Yes

Libraries: 150,000 vols

Publications: Newsletter (quarterly); Annual Report (annually); Calendar; Handbook

Academic Staff *2001-2002:* Total: **291**

Student Numbers *2001-2002*	MEN	WOMEN	TOTAL
All (Foreign Included)	9,040	5,298	**14,338**

• AHMADU BELLO UNIVERSITY (ABU)
PMB 1045, Zaria
Tel: +234(69) 550-581
Fax: +234(69) 550-022
Telex: 75244 con ng
Cable: unibello, zaria
EMail: vc@abu.edu.ng

Vice-Chancellor: Abdullahi Mahadi (1998-)
Tel: +234(69) 550-691 Fax: abuvc@yahoo.com

Registrar: Alhaji Mairiga Mani Tel: +234(69) 551-294
EMail: registrar@abu.edu.ng

International Relations: Nasir Bello Tel: +234(69) 550-951
EMail: nasirbee@yahoo.co.uk

Faculties
Administration *Dean*: Ibrahim Abdulsalami
Agriculture (Agriculture; Animal Husbandry; Economics; Rural Studies) *Dean*: T.K. Atala
Arts (Arts and Humanities; English; French; History) *Dean*: Yakubu Nasidi
Education (Education; Health Education; Information Sciences; Library Science; Physical Education) *Dean*: Muhammded Ben-Yunusa
Engineering (Agricultural Engineering; Chemical Engineering; Civil Engineering; Electrical Engineering; Engineering; Surveying and Mapping) *Dean*: C.O. Okwofu

Environmental Design (Architectural and Environmental Design; Architecture; Fine Arts; Industrial Design; Regional Planning; Town Planning) *Dean*: Bashir Olurukoba
Law *Dean*: Aminu M. Gurin
Medicine (Gynaecology and Obstetrics; Medicine; Midwifery; Paediatrics; Psychiatry and Mental Health) *Dean*: H.A. Aikhionbare
Pharmaceutical Sciences (Pharmacy) *Dean*: Haruna Kaita
Science (Biochemistry; Biological and Life Sciences; Chemistry; Geology; Mathematics; Microbiology; Natural Sciences; Physics; Textile Technology) *Dean*: I.H. Nock
Social Sciences *Dean*: Stephen A. Nkom
Veterinary Medicine (Veterinary Science) *Dean*: David Ogwu

Schools
Postgraduate *Dean*: S.B. Ojo

Institutes
Administration *Director*: Sheikh Abdallah
Agricultural Research (Agriculture) *Director*: Stephen Misari
Animal Production Research (Animal Husbandry; Cattle Breeding) *Director*: L.O. Eduvie
Education (Distance Education; Education) *Director*: Y.A. Jatto
Health Studies (Health Sciences)

Centres
Agricultural Extension and Research Liaison Services (Agriculture) *Director*: Salihu Sintalima Abubakar
Energy Research and Training (Energy Engineering) *Director*: I.M. Umar
Islamic Law *Director*: Ibrahim Na'Iya Sada

Further Information: Also Teaching Hospitals and Veterinary Teaching Hospital

History: Founded 1962, acquired present status and title 1975.

Governing Bodies: Council; Senate

Academic Year: October to July

Admission Requirements: Direct entry for holders of the Higher School Certificate (General Certificate of Education, Advanced ('A') level). Evidence of minimum standard in English

Main Language(s) of Instruction: English

International Co-operation: With universities in United States; United Kingdom; India; Canada; Italy; Israel

Accrediting Agencies: National University Commission (NUC)

Degrees and Diplomas: *Bachelor's Degree*: Arts (BA); Education (BEd); Library Science (BLS); Science (BSc), 4 yrs; Law (LLB); Medicine and Surgery (MB BS); Pharmacy (BPharm), 5 yrs; *Doctor of Veterinary Medicine*: Veterinary Science (DVM), 5 yrs; *Master's Degree*: (MA/MSc), 1-2 yrs following Bachelor; *Doctor of Philosophy*: (PhD), 3-5 yrs

Student Services: Academic Counselling, Social Counselling, Foreign Student Adviser, Sports Facilities, Language Programmes, Health Services, Canteen, Foreign Student Centre

Student Residential Facilities: Yes

Special Facilities: Museums. Art Gallery. Biological Garden. Drama Village

Libraries: Kashim Ibrahim Library, c. 313,000 vols; President Kennedy Library and Departmental libraries, c. 84,000 vols

Publications: University Annual Report (annually); Calendar; History of Ahmadu Bello University at 25; Student Hand Book; Research Report; Prospectus; University Calendar

Press or Publishing House: Ahmadu Bello University Press Ltd

Academic Staff *2001-2002*: Full-Time: c. 730 Part-Time: c. 15 Total: c. 745

Student Numbers *2001-2002*

	MEN	WOMEN	TOTAL
All (Foreign Included)	17,000	11,000	**28,000**

• AMBROSE ALLI UNIVERSITY
PMB 14, Ekpoma
Tel: +234(55) 984-48 +234(55) 984-46
Telex: 98448
Cable: edo varsity, ekpoma
EMail: root@edosu.edu.ng

Vice-Chancellor: Dennis Edokpaigbe Agbonlahor
EMail: deagbonlahor@yahoo.com

Registrar: G.T. Olawole

Faculties

Agriculture (Agricultural Economics; Agriculture; Agronomy; Botany) *Dean*: P.O. Onolemhemhen

Arts (Architecture; English; Fine Arts; Modern Languages; Philosophy; Theatre) *Dean*: C.A. Dime

Education *(Abraka)* (Education; Vocational Education) *Dean*: A. Momodu

Engineering and Technology (Civil Engineering; Electrical and Electronic Engineering; Engineering; Mechanical Engineering; Technology) *Dean*: A.K. Yesufu

Environmental Sciences (Environmental Studies)

Law (Commercial Law; International Law; Law; Public Law) *Dean*: A. Emiola

Medicine *(Ekpoma)* (Anatomy; Medicine) *Dean*: C.P. Aloamaka

Natural Sciences (Microbiology; Natural Sciences; Pharmacology) *Dean*: I.O. Eguavoen

Social Sciences (Business Administration; Economics; Regional Planning; Sociology)

Further Information: Abraka campus

History: Founded 1981 as Bendel State University. Formerly known as Edo State University.

Governing Bodies: Council; Senate

Academic Year: October to June

Admission Requirements: Universities Matriculation Examination (UME) following secondary school education, or direct entry for holders of the Higher School Certificate (General Certificate of Education, Advanced ('A') level)

Main Language(s) of Instruction: English

Degrees and Diplomas: *Bachelor's Degree*: 3-4 yrs; *Master's Degree*: a further 2 yrs

Libraries: Central Library, 14,000 items; Abraka campus library, 80,000 vols

Publications: Faculty Journals; Calendar; Gazette

Press or Publishing House: University Press

Academic Staff *2001-2002:* Total: c. 500

Student Numbers *2001-2002:* Total: c. 15,000

• BAYERO UNIVERSITY, KANO (BUK)
PMB 3011, Kano, Kano State
Tel: +234(64) 666-021 +234(64) 666-023
Fax: +234(64) 665-904 +234(64) 661-480
Telex: 77189 unibayro ng
Website: http://www.kanoonline.com/buk/fd/index.htm

Vice-Chancellor: Musa Abdullahi (1999-2004)
EMail: vc@buk.edu.ng;bukvc@yahoo.com

Registrar: Faruk M. Yanganau EMail: registrar@buk.edu.ng

Faculties
Agriculture

Arts and Islamic Studies (Arabic; English; French; History; Islamic Studies; Mass Communication) *Dean*: Abubakar Rasheed

Education (Adult Education; Education; Health Education; Library Science; Physical Education; Special Education) *Dean*: Mansur Malumfashi

Law (Commercial Law; Islamic Law; Law; Private Law; Public Law) *Dean*: Haruna Balarabe Alhaji

Medicine (Anaesthesiology; Anatomy; Biochemistry; Community Health; Gynaecology and Obstetrics; Haematology; Medicine; Microbiology; Paediatrics; Parasitology; Pathology; Pharmacology; Physiology; Psychiatry and Mental Health; Surgery) *Dean*: Abdulhamid I. Dutse

Science (Biological and Life Sciences; Chemistry; Mathematics; Natural Sciences; Physics) *Dean*: Wahab L.O. Jimo

Social and Management Sciences (Accountancy; Business Administration; Economics; Geography; Management; Political Science; Public Law; Social Sciences; Sociology) *Dean*: Bala A. Kofar-Mata

Technology (Civil Engineering; Electrical Engineering; Mechanical Engineering; Technology) *Dean*: Abubakar B. Aliyu

Units
General Studies *Director*: Mustapha C. Duze

Centres
Democratic Research and Training (Political Science) *Director*: Attahiru Jega

Study of Nigerian Languages (African Languages; Native Language) *Director (Acting)*: Bello Sa'id

Further Information: Also Aminu Kano Teaching Hospital

History: Founded 1960 as Ahmadu Bello College, renamed Abdullahi Bayero College 1962. Acquired present status 1975 and title 1977.

Governing Bodies: Universities Governing Council

Academic Year: October to July (October-February; March-July)

Admission Requirements: Universities Matriculation Examination (UME) following secondary school education, or direct entry for holders of the Higher School Certificate (General Certificate of Education, Advanced ('A') level)

Fees: None for Nigerian students

Main Language(s) of Instruction: English

Accrediting Agencies: National Universities Commission; Nigerian Medical and Dental Council, COREN

Degrees and Diplomas: *Bachelor's Degree*: Arts (BA); Education; Science (BSc); Social Studies (B.Sc), 4 yrs; Engineering (BEng); Law (LLB); Medicine and Surgery (MBBS), 5 yrs; *Master's Degree*: (MA, MSc), a further 1-2 yrs; *Doctor of Philosophy*: (PhD), 2-5 yrs. Also undergraduate and postgraduate Diplomas.

Student Services: Academic Counselling, Social Counselling, Employment Services, Nursery Care, Sports Facilities, Health Services, Canteen

Student Residential Facilities: Yes

Libraries: Central Library, c. 200,000 vols; 2000 periodicals

Publications: Calendar; Prospectus (biennially)

Academic Staff 2000-2001	MEN	WOMEN	TOTAL
FULL-TIME	433	56	489
PART-TIME	20	2	22
TOTAL	**453**	**58**	**511**

Student Numbers 2000-2001	MEN	WOMEN	TOTAL
All (Foreign Included)	18,486	6,819	**25,305**
FOREIGN ONLY	16	16	32

Part-time Students, 1,274

BENUE STATE UNIVERSITY (BENSU)
PMB 102119, Makurdi, Benue State
Tel: +234(44) 533-811
Fax: +234(44) 531-260
Cable: unibenue
EMail: root@bensu.edu.ng

Vice-Chancellor: David I. Ker (2000-2005)
EMail: davidiker@hotmail.com

Registrar: W.I. Mozeh

Faculties
Arts (Arts and Humanities) *Dean*: Charity Angya
Education *Dean*: Nancy Agbe
Law *Dean*: Paul Belabo
Management Science (Management) *Dean*: Clement Ajekwe
Science (Natural Sciences) *Dean*: Solomon Abaa
Social Sciences *Dean*: Josiah Shindi

History: Founded 1992.

Governing Bodies: University Council

Academic Year: September to August

Admission Requirements: General Certificate of Education (Ordinary level) with minimum of 5 credits

Main Language(s) of Instruction: English

International Co-operation: With universities in United Kingdom.

Accrediting Agencies: National Universities Commission

Degrees and Diplomas: *Bachelor's Degree*: 4-5 yrs; *Master's Degree*; *Doctor of Philosophy*: (PhD)

Student Services: Academic Counselling, Nursery Care, Sports Facilities, Health Services

Student Residential Facilities: Yes

Publications: Students' Handbook

Student Numbers *2001-2002:* Total: c. 15,000

DELTA STATE UNIVERSITY (DELSU)
PMB 1, Abraka, Delta State 33106
Tel: +234(54) 66-027
Cable: delta versity
EMail: root@desu.edu.ng

Vice-Chancellor: Uvie Igun (1998-)
EMail: aruoturejr@yahoo.com

Registrar: Joseph Ubogu EMail: registrarng@yahoo.com

Faculties
Agriculture *(Asaba)* (Agricultural Economics; Agronomy; Forestry; Wildlife; Zoology) *Dean*: S.I. Omeje
Arts and Humanities (English; Fine Arts; French; History; Linguistics; Literature; Mass Communication; Music; Native Language; Theatre) *Dean*: Simon Umukoro
Basic Medical Sciences (Health Sciences) *Dean*: Towuawse Emudianughe
Education (Agricultural Education; Business Education; Education; Health Education; Home Economics; Library Science; Mathematics Education; Music Education; Physical Education; Primary Education; Religious Education; Science Education; Technology Education) *Dean*: Orona Oroka
Law (International Law; Private Law; Public Law) *Dean*: M.O.U. Gasiokwu
Management Sciences (Accountancy; Banking; Finance; Management; Marketing) *Dean*: Peter Eruotor
Natural Sciences (Biochemistry; Botany; Chemistry; Geology; Mathematics; Microbiology; Physics; Zoology) *Dean*: Robert Ikomi
Social Sciences (Accountancy; Business Administration; Economics; Finance; Geography (Human); Information Sciences; Library Science; Political Science; Regional Planning; Sociology) *Dean*: Gabriel Yomere

Further Information: Also Asaba and Oleg Campuses

History: Founded 1992.

Governing Bodies: Council

Fees: (Naira): 10,044 per annum

Main Language(s) of Instruction: English

Accrediting Agencies: National Universities Commission

Degrees and Diplomas: *Bachelor's Degree*: Arts (B.A.); Arts (Education) (B.A.(Ed.)); Science (B.Sc.); Sciences (Education) (B.Sc.(Ed.)), 4 yrs; Agriculture (B.Agric); Law (L.L.B.), 5 yrs; Medicine, Surgery (M.B.B.S.), 6 yrs; *Postgraduate Diploma*: Agriculture (P.G.D.E.); Communication Management (P.G.D.C.M.); Education (P.G.D.E.), 1 yr; *Master's Degree*: Banking and Finance (M.B.F.); Business Administration (M.B.A.); Energy and Petroleum Economics (M.E.P.E.);

Industrial and Labour Relations (M.I.L.R.); Public Administration (M.P.A.), 1 1/2 yrs; Arts (M.A.); Communication Management (M.C.M.); Education (M.Ed.); Fine Arts (M.F.A.); Science (M.Sc.), 1 yr; *Doctor of Philosophy*: (Ph.D.), 3 yrs

Student Services: Academic Counselling, Social Counselling, Nursery Care, Sports Facilities, Language Programmes, Handicapped Facilities, Health Services

Student Residential Facilities: Yes

Publications: University Inaugural Lecture Series; Convocation Lecture Series

Academic Staff 2001-2002	MEN	WOMEN	TOTAL
FULL-TIME	370	74	444
PART-TIME	22	6	28
TOTAL	**392**	**80**	**472**
STAFF WITH DOCTORATE			
FULL-TIME	127	14	141
PART-TIME	–	–	1
TOTAL	**–**	**–**	**142**

Student Numbers 2001-2002	MEN	WOMEN	TOTAL
All (Foreign Included)	5,835	5,687	**11,522**

Part-time Students, 1,752

*• ENUGU STATE UNIVERSITY OF SCIENCE AND TECHNOLOGY (ESUST)

PMB 01660, Independence Layout, Enugu, Enugu State
Tel: +234(42) 451-319
Fax: +234(42) 455-705
Telex: 51440 esutech ng
Cable: unitech, enugu

Vice-Chancellor: Samuel Chukwu (2000-)
Tel: +234(42) 451-244 Fax: +234(42) 455-765
EMail: esut@compuserve.com

Registrar: B.N. Uzoigwe

Faculties

Agricultural Sciences (Agricultural Economics; Agriculture; Soil Science) *Dean*: B.N. Marire
Applied Natural Sciences *(Nsukka)* (Biochemistry; Biology; Geological Engineering; Microbiology; Mining Engineering; Physical Engineering; Statistics) *Dean*: A.C. Okonkwo
Basic Medical Sciences (Anatomy; Biochemistry; Medicine; Pathology; Physiology) *Dean*: S.E. Asogwa
Clinical Medicine (Medicine)
Education *Dean*: O.O. Onowor
Law *Dean*: Obi S. Ogene
Management
Social Sciences (Anthropology; Social Sciences; Sociology) *Dean*: D.N. Nwatu

Divisions

General Studies

Colleges

Health Sciences *(Nsukka)* (Biochemistry; Community Health; Health Sciences; Pharmacology; Physiology; Rehabilitation and Therapy)

Programmes

Pre-Science

Schools

Engineering (Agricultural Engineering; Chemical Engineering; Civil Engineering; Electrical and Electronic Engineering; Engineering; Materials Engineering; Mechanical Engineering) *Dean*: G.N. Onoh
Environmental Sciences (Environmental Studies) *Dean*: A.N. Agu
Postgraduate Studies *Dean*: R.C.. Okafor

Institutes

Education

Centres

Biotechnology and Pest Management (Biotechnology; Pest Management)
Industrial Development (Industrial Management) *Director*: Boniface A. Okorie

History: Founded 1991, following creation of new States in Nigeria, and incorporating the Enugu and Abakaliki campuses of the former Anambra State University of Technology, founded 1980.

Governing Bodies: Council

Academic Year: September to August (September-March; April-August)

Admission Requirements: Universities Matriculation Examination (UME) following secondary school education, or direct entry for holders of the Higher School Certificate (General Certificate of Education, Advanced Level); or pre-science internal examination (science examination only).

Fees: (US Dollars): Foreign students, c. 5000

Main Language(s) of Instruction: English

Degrees and Diplomas: *Bachelor's Degree*: 4 yrs; *Master's Degree*: a further 1-1 1/2 yrs; *Doctor of Philosophy*: (PhD)

Student Services: Sports Facilities, Health Services, Canteen

Libraries: 35,000 vols; 1200 periodicals

Academic Staff 2000: Total: c. 410

Student Numbers 2000: Total: c. 9,700

• FEDERAL UNIVERSITY OF TECHNOLOGY AKURE (FUTA)

PMB 704, Akure, Ondo State
Tel: +234(34) 243-490
Fax: +234(34) 230-450
Telex: +32492 futatel-ng
Cable: Fedunitech, Akure
EMail: root@futa.edu.ng

Vice-Chancellor: P.O. Adeniyi (2002-)
Tel: +234(34) 243-060 EMail: vce@futa.edu.ng

Registrar: Eunice F. Oyebade Tel: +234(34) 240-450
Fax: +234(34) 241-190

Schools

Agriculture and Agricultural Technology (Agricultural Economics; Agricultural Engineering; Animal Husbandry; Crop Production; Fishery; Wildlife; Wood Technology) *Dean*: Joseph A. Fuwape

Engineering and Engineering Technology (Agricultural Engineering; Civil Engineering; Electrical and Electronic Engineering; Materials Engineering; Mechanical Engineering; Mining Engineering) *Dean*: Cyril O. Adegoke

Environmental Technology (Architecture; Design; Environmental Engineering; Industrial Design; Real Estate; Regional Planning; Surveying and Mapping; Town Planning) *Dean*: David O. Olarenwaju

Mines and Earth Sciences (Geology; Geophysics; Meteorology; Mining Engineering) *Dean*: John Ojo

Postgraduate Studies *Dean*: Valentine Aletor

Science (Biochemistry; Biology; Chemistry; Computer Science; Meteorology; Natural Sciences; Physics) *Dean*: Fatusa Adetuyi

History: Founded 1981

Governing Bodies: Council, comprising 17 members; Senate

Academic Year: October to June

Admission Requirements: Minimum 5 credits at GCE (General Certificate of Education), Ordinary ('O') level in relevant subjects including Mathematics and English Language. Admission is through Universities Matriculation Examinations conducted by Joint Admissions and Matriculation Board (JAMB).

Fees: (Naira): Foreign students c.10,000

Main Language(s) of Instruction: English

Accrediting Agencies: National Universities Commission (NUC) and the various professional bodies

Degrees and Diplomas: *Bachelor's Degree*: Agricultural Technology, Food Science, Forestry, Fisheries (BAgricTech); Engineering, Civil Engineering, Electrical and Electronic Engineering, Mechanical Engineering, Agricultural Engineering (BEng); Technology, Biochemistry, Chemistry, Computer Science, Microbiology (BTech), 5 yrs; Architecture, Industrial Design, Town and Regional Planning, Estate Management (BArch), 6 yrs; *Master's Degree*: a further 1-2 yrs; *Doctor of Philosophy*: (PhD), a further 2-3 yrs

Student Services: Academic Counselling, Social Counselling, Employment Services, Foreign Student Adviser, Nursery Care, Cultural Centre, Sports Facilities, Language Programmes, Handicapped Facilities, Health Services, Canteen, Foreign Student Centre

Student Residential Facilities: It is the policy of the University to accommodate all foreign students

Special Facilities: Meteorological Observatory

Libraries: c. 55,000 vols; 237 periodicals. Special collection: UN Food and Agricultural Organization's depositary library.

Publications: Bulletin (monthly); Calendar; Handbook

Academic Staff 2002-2003	TOTAL
FULL-TIME	375
PART-TIME	144
TOTAL	**519**
STAFF WITH DOCTORATE	
FULL-TIME	156
PART-TIME	85
TOTAL	**241**

Student Numbers 2002-2003	TOTAL
All (Foreign Included)	**5,002**
FOREIGN ONLY	53

Part-time Students, 909

• FEDERAL UNIVERSITY OF TECHNOLOGY MINNA (FUTM)

PMB 65, Minna, Niger State
Tel: +234(66) 222-422   +234(66) 222-397
Fax: +234(66) 224-482
Cable: futech minna
EMail: futmx@skannet.com

Vice-Chancellor: H.T. Saab (2003-) Tel: +234(66) 222-887
Fax: +234(66) 625-426

Registrar: Alhaji U.A. Sadiq Fax: +234(66) 224-305

Schools

Agriculture and Agricultural Technology (Agricultural Equipment; Agriculture; Cattle Breeding; Fishery; Soil Science) *Director*: S.L. Lamai

Engineering and Engineering Technology (Agricultural Engineering; Chemical Engineering; Civil Engineering; Electrical Engineering; Electronic Engineering; Mechanical Engineering) *Director*: R.H. Khan

Environmental Technology (Architecture; Building Technologies; Environmental Engineering; Real Estate; Regional Planning; Surveying and Mapping; Town Planning) *Director*: Olajide Solanke

Postgraduate *Director*: J.O. Adeniyi

Science and Science Education (Biological and Life Sciences; Chemistry; Geography; Geology; Industrial Engineering; Mathematics and Computer Science; Natural Sciences; Physics; Science Education) *Director*: K.R. Adeboye

History: Founded 1981, acquired present status and title 1983.

Governing Bodies: Council; Senate

Admission Requirements: Universities Matriculation Examination (UME) following secondary school education

Fees: (Naira): Nationals, c. 4,000-18,000; foreign students, 18,000-28,000; postgraduates, 12,000-21,000

Main Language(s) of Instruction: English

Accrediting Agencies: National Universities Commission

Degrees and Diplomas: *Bachelor's Degree*: 5 yrs; *Master's Degree*: a further 2 yrs; *Doctor of Philosophy*: (PhD), 3 yrs

Student Residential Facilities: Yes

Libraries: c. 20,000 vols

Publications: News Bulletin (weekly); Federal University of Technology; Minna at a Glance (1985)

Academic Staff 2000-2001: Total: c. 270

Student Numbers 2000-2001: Total: c. 5,000

• FEDERAL UNIVERSITY OF TECHNOLOGY OWERRI (FUTO)

PMB 1526, Owerri, Imo State
Tel: +234(83) 230-974   +234(83) 230-564
Fax: +234(83) 233-228
Cable: fedunitech, owerri
EMail: root@futo.edu.ng

Vice-Chancellor: Jude Ejike Njoku Tel: +234(83) 232-430
EMail: vc@futo.edu.ng
Registrar: M.O. Okoye

Units
General Studies .

Schools
Agriculture and Agricultural Technology (Agricultural Equipment; Agriculture) *Dean*: M.I. Nwufo
Engineering and Engineering Technology (Engineering; Technology) *Dean*: J.I. Ejimanya
Management Technology (Management Systems) *Dean*: L.C. Asiegbu
Postgraduate *Dean*: B.A. Nwachukwu
Science (Natural Sciences) *Dean*: U.B.C.O. Ejike

Departments
Agricultural Economics and Extension (Agricultural Economics)
Agricultural Engineering
Animal Science and Technology (Animal Husbandry)
Biological Sciences (Biological and Life Sciences)
Chemical Engineering (Chemical Engineering; Petroleum and Gas Engineering)
Chemistry
Civil Engineering
Crop and Soil Science Technology (Crop Production; Soil Science)
Electrical and Electronic Engineering
Food Science and Technology (Food Science; Food Technology) *Head*: O.S. Eke
Geology *Head*: K.M. Ibe
Materials and Metallurgical Engineering (Materials Engineering; Metallurgical Engineering)
Mathematics and Computer Science
Mechanical Engineering
Physics
Polymer and Textile Engineering (Polymer and Plastics Technology; Textile Technology)
Project Management Technology
Transport Management Technology (Transport Engineering; Transport Management)

Institutes
Erosion Studies (Soil Science) *Director*: S.E. Ananaba

Centres
Computer Science
Industrial Studies (Industrial Management) *Head*: O.0. Onyemaobi

History: Founded 1981.
Governing Bodies: Governing Council; Senate; Convocation
Academic Year: October to July (October-February; March-July)
Admission Requirements: At least 5 credits in General Certificate of Education (GCE), or Senior School Certificate (SSC), in relevant subjects
Fees: (Naira): Tuition, none

Main Language(s) of Instruction: English
Degrees and Diplomas: *Bachelor's Degree*: Agricultural Technology (BAgricTech); Engineering (BEng); Technology (BTech), 5 yrs; *Postgraduate Diploma*: 1 yr; *Master's Degree*: Business Administration (MBA); Engineering (MEng); Science (MSc), a further 1-2 yrs; *Doctor of Philosophy*: (PhD), 2-3 yrs
Student Services: Academic Counselling, Social Counselling, Employment Services, Sports Facilities, Health Services, Foreign Student Centre
Student Residential Facilities: For c. 1950 students
Special Facilities: Comskiptec
Libraries: c. 50,000 vols
Publications: Newsletter (monthly); FUTNOTES, FUTO Library (annually); Calendar
Press or Publishing House: FUTO Press
Academic Staff *2001-2002:* Total: c. 240
Student Numbers *2001-2002:* Total: c. 4,500

• FEDERAL UNIVERSITY OF TECHNOLOGY YOLA (FUTY)
PMB 2076, Yola, Adamawa State
Tel: +234(75) 624-532
Fax: +234(75) 624-416
Cable: futy yola
EMail: vc@futy.edu.ng

Vice-Chancellor: Salihu Mustafa (1995-)
Tel: +234(75) 624-416 Fax: +234(75) 625-176
EMail: vc@futy.edu.ng
Registrar: M. Aminu

Schools
Agriculture and Agricultural Technology (Agricultural Economics; Agricultural Engineering; Agriculture; Animal Husbandry; Forest Management; Forestry) *Dean*: L. Singh
Engineering and Engineering Technology (Agricultural Engineering; Civil Engineering; Electrical Engineering; Electronic Engineering; Mechanical Engineering; Technology) *Dean*: E. Smekhounov
Environmental Sciences (Architecture; Building Technologies; Environmental Studies; Geography; Industrial Design; Surveying and Mapping) *Dean*: A.L. Tukur
Management and Information Technology (Information Technology; Management) *Dean*: Kavin Nwogu
Postgraduate Studies
Pure and Applied Sciences (Biochemistry; Biological and Life Sciences; Chemistry; Computer Science; Geology; Mathematics; Mathematics and Computer Science; Microbiology; Natural Sciences; Operations Research; Physics; Statistics) *Dean*: Gregory Wajiga
Technology and Science Education (Science Education; Technology Education) *Dean*: J.M. Ndagana

Centres
Computer and Biotechnology *(CEMIT)* (Biotechnology; Computer Science; Maintenance Technology; Technology Education)

History: Founded 1981, acquired present title and status 1988.

Governing Bodies: Council; Senate

Academic Year: October to August (October-February; April-August)

Admission Requirements: Universities Matriculation Examination (UME) following secondary school education, or direct entry for holders of the Higher School Certificate (General Certificate of Education, Advanced ('A') level)

Main Language(s) of Instruction: English

Accrediting Agencies: National Universities Commission (NUC)

Degrees and Diplomas: *Bachelor's Degree*: 4-6 yrs; *Master's Degree*: (BTech), a further 2 yrs; *Doctor of Philosophy*: (PhD), 3 yrs

Student Services: Academic Counselling, Social Counselling, Employment Services, Sports Facilities, Health Services, Canteen

Student Residential Facilities: Yes

Libraries: 20,000 vols

Publications: Information Brochure, University prospectus; Journal of Technology (annually); FUTY News (Occasional)

Academic Staff *2001-2002*: Total: c. 500

Student Numbers *2001-2002*: Total: c. 7,000

IMO STATE UNIVERSITY (IMSU)
PMB 2000, Owerri, Imo State
Tel: +234(83) 231-433
Fax: +234(83) 232-716
Cable: imsu

Vice-Chancellor: A.C. Anwuka EMail: vc@imosu.edu.ng

Registrar: C.G. Ukaga

Faculties
Education
Humanities and Social Sciences (Arts and Humanities; Social Sciences)

Colleges
Agriculture
Business Administration
Engineering and Environmental Sciences
Legal Studies (Law)
Medical and Health Sciences (Health Sciences; Medicine)
Science (Mathematics and Computer Science; Natural Sciences)

History: Founded 1981.

KANO UNIVERSITY OF TECHNOLOGY, WUDIL (KUT)
PMB 3244, Kano, Kano State
Tel: +234(64) 241-149
Fax: +234(64) 241-175

Vice-Chancellor: Shawki A.A. Seoud

Registrar: A.U. Abdurahim

History: Founded 2001. Formerly Bagauda University of Science and Technology.

LADOKE AKINTOLA UNIVERSITY OF TECHNOLOGY (LAUTECH)
PMB 4000, Ogbomoso, Oyo State
Tel: +234(38) 720-285
Fax: +234(38) 720-750

Vice-Chancellor (Acting): Akinola M. Salau

Registrar: J.A. Oladokun

Faculties
Agriculture
Engineering and Technology (Engineering; Technology)
Environmental Sciences (Environmental Studies)
Medical Sciences (Health Sciences; Medicine)
Pure and Applied Sciences (Applied Chemistry; Applied Mathematics; Applied Physics; Engineering; Mathematics and Computer Science; Natural Sciences)

History: Founded 1990 as Oyo State University of Technology, acquired present title 1991.

LAGOS STATE UNIVERSITY (LASU)
PMB 1087, Badagry Expressway, Ojo, Apapa, Lagos State
Tel: +234(1) 588-4048
Fax: +234(1) 588-4048

Vice-Chancellor: Abisogun O. Leigh

International Relations: Kunle Lawal

Faculties
Arts (Arts and Humanities) *Dean*: M.O. Opeloye
Education *Dean*: A. Onifade
Engineering (Engineering; Environmental Studies; Technology) *Dean*: S.O. Ajose
Law *Dean*: O.A. Yerokun
Management Sciences (Business Administration; Management)
Science (Natural Sciences) *Dean*: M..A. Anatekhai
Social Sciences

Colleges
Medicine

Institutes
Education (*Epe Campue*)

Centres
Educational Technology *Head*: A.O. Shodehinde
Environmental Sciences and Education (Environmental Studies) *Head*: A.M. Olagunju

History: Founded 1983, acquired present status and title 1984.

Governing Bodies: Council; Senate

Academic Year: June to December

Admission Requirements: Universities Matriculation Examination (UME) following secondary school education, or direct entry for holders of the Higher School Certificate (General Certificate of Education, Advanced ('A') Level)

Main Language(s) of Instruction: English

Degrees and Diplomas: *Bachelor's Degree*: 3-5 yrs; *Postgraduate Diploma*; *Master's Degree*: Business Administration (MBA); Educational Management (MEdM); Public Administration (MPA); Science (MSc); Town Planning (MTP); Urban and Regional Planning (MURP), a further 1-2 yrs; *Master of Philosophy*: Philosophy (MPhil), a further 1-2 yrs; *Doctor of Philosophy*: (PhD), 2-3 yrs

Student Services: Academic Counselling, Nursery Care, Cultural Centre, Sports Facilities, Health Services, Canteen, Foreign Student Centre

Special Facilities: Fish Pond; Fish Hatchery

Libraries: 52,000 vols, 70 periodical subscriptions. Special collection: railway archives

Publications: Lasu Bulletin (monthly); Academic Calendar

Press or Publishing House: Lasu Press

Academic Staff *2001-2002:* Total: c. 330

Student Numbers *2001-2002:* Total: c. 13,000

• 'MICHAEL OKPARA' UNIVERSITY OF AGRICULTURE UMUDIKE (MOUAU)

PMB 7267, Umuahia, Abia State
Tel: +234(82) 440-555
Fax: +234(82) 440-555
EMail: onwudike@fuau.edu.ng

Vice-Chancellor: Ogbonnaya C. Onwudike (2000-)
EMail: vc@fuau.edu.ng

Registrar (Acting): Juliana Uche

Colleges

Agricultural Economics, Rural Sociology and Extension (Agricultural Economics; Development Studies; Rural Planning) *Dean:* Christian Onyenweaku

Animal Science and Animal Health (Animal Husbandry; Veterinary Science) *Dean (Acting):* Gbola Ojewola

Biological and Physical Sciences (Biological and Life Sciences) *Dean (Acting):* O.U. Ezereonye

Crop and Soil Science (Crop Production; Soil Science) *Dean:* C.I. Umechuruba

Food Processing and Storage Technology (Food Technology) *Dean (Acting):* M.O. Iwe

Natural Resources and Environmental Management (Environmental Management; Natural Resources) *Dean (Acting):* Roy Mbakwe

Schools

General and Remedial Studies *Director (Acting):* N. Oke
Postgraduate Studies *Director:* Sylvester Ibe

History: Founded 1993.

Governing Bodies: Governing Council

Academic Year: January-October

368

Admission Requirements: Universities Matriculation Examination (UME) following secondary school education, or direct entry.

Main Language(s) of Instruction: English

Accrediting Agencies: National Universities Commission

Degrees and Diplomas: *Bachelor's Degree*: Agriculture; Food Science and Technology; Forestry and Environmental Management; Home Economics (BSc); *Master's Degree*: (MSc); *Doctor of Philosophy*: (PhD)

Student Services: Academic Counselling, Social Counselling, Sports Facilities, Language Programmes, Health Services, Canteen

Student Residential Facilities: Yes

Libraries: 8500 vols, 460 periodical subscriptions

Publications: Journal of Sustainable Agriculture and the Environment (biannually)

Academic Staff *2001-2002*	MEN	WOMEN	TOTAL
FULL-TIME	120	37	157
PART-TIME	34	4	38
TOTAL	**154**	**41**	**195**
STAFF WITH DOCTORATE			
FULL-TIME	58	11	69
PART-TIME	28	3	31
TOTAL	**86**	**14**	**100**

Student Numbers *2001-2002*	MEN	WOMEN	TOTAL
All (Foreign Included)	1,078	835	**1,913**
FOREIGN ONLY	8	1	9

Part-time Students, 293

NNAMDI AZIKIWE UNIVERSITY

PMB 5025, Awka, Anambra State
Tel: +234(48) 550-018
Fax: +234(48) 550-018

Vice-Chancellor: Ilochi Okafor (1998-)
EMail: omenyinj@hotmail.com

Faculties

Arts (African Languages; Arts and Humanities; English; European Languages; Fine Arts; History; Linguistics; Music; Philosophy; Religious Studies; Theatre)

Education (Education; Health Education; Physical Education; Vocational Education)

Engineering and Technology (Civil Engineering; Computer Engineering; Electrical Engineering; Electronic Engineering; Engineering; Materials Engineering; Metallurgical Engineering)

Environmental Sciences (Architecture; Building Technologies; Environmental Studies; Surveying and Mapping)

Law

Management Sciences (Accountancy; Banking; Business Administration; Finance; Management; Marketing)

Medicine (Anatomy; Gynaecology and Obstetrics; Medicine; Paediatrics; Pathology; Pharmacology; Physiology; Surgery)

Natural Sciences (Biology; Botany; Chemistry; Computer Science; Entomology; Geology; Mathematics; Mathematics and

Computer Science; Microbiology; Natural Sciences; Parasitology; Physics; Statistics; Zoology)

Social Sciences (Economics; Mass Communication; Political Science; Psychology; Social Sciences; Sociology)

Further Information: Also Teaching Hospital, Nnewi

History: Founded 1980 as Anambra State University of Technology.

Governing Bodies: Council

Academic Year: November to August (November-March; April-August)

Admission Requirements: Five credits in West African School Certificate (WASC), Senior Secondary Certificate Examination (SSCE) or General Certificate of Education (GCE) 'O' level, with minimum grade C and including English language. For direct entry, candidates must possess a higher qualification from an accredited university or polytechnic

Fees: (Naira): Tuition, undergraduate, 5000-9400 per annum

Main Language(s) of Instruction: English

Degrees and Diplomas: *Bachelor's Degree*: Arts, Science, Education, 4 yrs; Engineering, Law, 5 yrs; Medicine, Surgery, 6 yrs; *Postgraduate Diploma*: 11/2 yrs; *Master's Degree*: a further 11/2-2 yrs; *Doctor of Philosophy*: (PhD), minimum 3 yrs

Student Services: Academic Counselling, Sports Facilities, Health Services, Canteen

Libraries: Main Library, c. 70,000 vols; 73 periodicals

Academic Staff *2002-2003*	TOTAL
FULL-TIME	552
PART-TIME	20
TOTAL	**572**

Student Numbers *2002-2003*: Total: **21,214**

• OBAFEMI AWOLOWO UNIVERSITY (OAU)

Ile-Ife, Osun State
Tel: +234(36) 230-290 to 299
Fax: +234(36) 233-971
Telex: 34261 oau ife nigeria
Cable: ifevarsity ile-ife, nigeria
EMail: oauife@oauife.edu.ng
Website: http://www.oauife.edu.ng

Vice-Chancellor: Roger O. Makanjuola (2001-)
Tel: +234(36) 230-661 Fax: +234(36) 232-401
EMail: rogerm@oauife.edu.ng

Registrar: B.O. Iluyomade

International Relations: G.O. Babalola

Faculties

Administration (Accountancy; Administration; Business Administration; Government; International Relations; Management; Public Administration) *Dean*: 0. Ojo

Agriculture (Agricultural Economics; Agriculture; Animal Husbandry; Plant and Crop Protection; Rural Studies; Soil Science) *Dean*: R. Adeyemo

Arts (African Languages; Archaeology; Arts and Humanities) *Dean*: O. Omosini

Basic Medical Sciences (Anaesthesiology; Anatomy; Cell Biology; Child Care and Development; Community Health; Dental Technology; Dermatology; Epidemiology; Forensic Medicine and Dentistry; Gynaecology and Obstetrics; Haematology; Health Sciences; Immunology; Medicine; Microbiology; Nursing; Nutrition; Orthopedics; Paediatrics; Parasitology; Physiology; Psychiatry and Mental Health; Radiology; Rehabilitation and Therapy; Surgery; Venereology) *Dean*: M.A. Durosinmi

Clinical Sciences (Dentistry; Paediatrics; Psychiatry and Mental Health; Radiology) *Dean*: M.O. Balogun

Education *Dean*: O.J. Ehindero

Environmental Design and Management (Architectural and Environmental Design) *Dean*: C.A. Ajayi

Law *Dean*: M.O. Adediran

Pharmacy *Dean*: A. Lamikanra

Science (Chemistry; Computer Science; Natural Sciences) *Dean*: C.O. Imoru

Social Sciences *Dean*: J.A. Fabayo

Technology (Agricultural Engineering; Chemical Engineering; Civil Engineering; Electrical and Electronic Engineering; Materials Engineering; Mechanical Engineering; Metallurgical Engineering; Technology)

Institutes

Agricultural Research and Training (Agriculture; Animal Husbandry; Crop Production; Farm Management; Soil Management; Water Management)

Cultural Studies *Head*: G.O. Olamola

Ecology and Environmental Studies (Ecology; Environmental Studies)

Education

Centres

Energy Research and Development (Energy Engineering)

Gender Studies

Industrial Research and Development (Industrial Engineering) *Director*: Josephine O. Abiodun

Space Research (Aeronautical and Aerospace Engineering)

Technology Management *(National)* (Technology)

History: Founded 1961 as University of Ife, acquired present title 1987.

Governing Bodies: Council; Senate

Academic Year: January to December (January-June; July-December)

Admission Requirements: Universities Matriculation Examination (UME), or five credits passes in relevant subjects at Senior Secondary Certificate (SSC) level, or at School Certificate/General Certificate of Education 'O' level in no more than two sittings.

Fees: (US Dollars): Foreign students, 1000-2000 per annum

Main Language(s) of Instruction: English

Degrees and Diplomas: *Bachelor's Degree*: 3 yrs; *Master's Degree*: a further 1 1/2-2 yrs; *Doctor of Philosophy*: (PhD), a further 2 yrs

Student Residential Facilities: Yes

Libraries: 400,919 vols; 7003 periodicals; Africana collection; audio-visual materials; government documents

Publications: Obafemi Awolowo University Law Reports (quarterly); Handbooks; Calendar; African Journal of Philosophy; Odu: a Journal of West African Studies; Postgraduate Handbook (biannually); Quarterly Journal of Administration

Press or Publishing House: University Press

Academic Staff *2001-2002:* Total: c. 1,300

Student Numbers *2001-2002:* Total: c. 21,800

Part-time Students, c. 1,800

• OLABISI ONABANJO UNIVERSITY (OOU)
PMB 2002, Ago-Iwoye, Ogun State
Tel: +234(37) 432-384   +234(37) 390-147
Cable: ogunvasity
Website: http://www.oou.i8.com

Vice-Chancellor: Afolabi Soyode
EMail: soyode@skannet.com;bolkem2003@yahoo.com

Registrar: Apostle S. Ajayi

Faculties
Arts (Arts and Humanities) *Dean (Acting)*: Sola O. Adebajo
Basic Medical Sciences (Health Sciences) *Dean*: Julius O. Olowookere
Clinical Sciences (Health Sciences) *Dean*: M.R.C. Oyegunle
Education *Dean*: Taiwo Ajayi
Law *Dean (Acting)*: Mojisola O. Ogungbe
Science (Natural Sciences) *Dean*: O.A. Sosanwo
Social and Management Sciences (Management; Social Sciences)

Colleges
Agricultural Sciences (Agriculture) *Provost*: B.O. Durojaiye
Health Sciences *(Obefami Alowolo) Provost*: Olalekan O. Adetoro

Schools
Postgraduate Studies *Dean*: Victor A. Awoderu

Further Information: Also Teaching Hospital

History: Founded 1982 as Ogun State University. One of the University's distinctive characteristics is the adoption of an innovative programme of compulsory credit-earning courses on modern agricultural and rural life, Nigerian life and culture for all students in their first 2 years of study.

Governing Bodies: Council

Academic Year: October to July (October-March; March-July)

Admission Requirements: Universities Matriculation Examination (UME) following secondary school education, or direct entry for holders of the Higher School Certificate (General Certificate of Education, Advanced 'A' Level)

Main Language(s) of Instruction: English

Degrees and Diplomas: *Bachelor's Degree:* 3-5 yrs; *Master's Degree:* 1 further yr; *Doctor of Philosophy:* (PhD)

Libraries: Main Library, c. 20,000 vols

Publications: Annual Report (annually); Handbook; University Calendar

Academic Staff *2001-2002:* Total: c. 300

Student Numbers *2001-2002:* Total: c. 5,800

• RIVERS STATE UNIVERSITY OF SCIENCE AND TECHNOLOGY (RSUST)
PMB 5080, Nkpolu Oroworukwo, Port Harcourt, Rivers State
Tel: +234(84) 335-823 +234(84) 235-808
Fax: +234(84) 230-720
Cable: riverstech port harcourt
EMail: rsust@alpha.linkserve.com;riversvarsity@yahoo.com
Website: http://www.rsust.edu.ng

Vice-Chancellor: Simeon Chituru Achinewhu
Tel: +234(84) 233-288
EMail: achinewhu@hotmail.com;achinewhu@yahoo.com

Registrar: M.Y. Oguru

Faculties
Agriculture (Agriculture; Animal Husbandry; Fishery; Food Technology; Forestry; Horticulture; Meat and Poultry; Soil Science; Viticulture; Water Science)
Engineering (Chemical Engineering; Civil Engineering; Computer Engineering; Construction Engineering; Electrical Engineering; Electronic Engineering; Engineering; Industrial Engineering; Marine Engineering; Materials Engineering; Metallurgical Engineering; Mining Engineering; Telecommunications Engineering; Transport Engineering)
Environmental Sciences (Environmental Studies)
Law
Management Sciences (Management)
Science (Mathematics; Natural Sciences)
Technical and Science Education (Science Education; Technology Education)

Schools
Postgraduate Studies

Institutes
Agricultural Research and Training *(Rivers State (RIART))* (Agriculture)
Education
Foundation Studies *(IFS)*
Geoscience and Space Technology *(IGST)* (Aeronautical and Aerospace Engineering; Geological Engineering)
Pollution Studies *(IPS)* (Environmental Studies)

Centres
Computer Science
Continuing Education
Niger Delta Studies (Regional Studies)
Special Projects

History: Founded as College of Science and Technology, acquired present status and title 1980.

Governing Bodies: Council; Senate

Academic Year: October to July (October-February; March-July)

Admission Requirements: Universities Matriculation Examination (UME) following secondary school education, or direct entry for holders of the Higher School Certificate (General Certificate of Education, Advanced ('A') Level)

Main Language(s) of Instruction: English

Degrees and Diplomas: *Bachelor's Degree*: 4 yrs; *Master's Degree*: a further 2 yrs; *Doctor of Philosophy*: (PhD), a further 2 yrs

Student Residential Facilities: Yes

Libraries: 125,900 vols, 220 periodical subscriptions

Publications: News Letter (monthly); Gazette (3 per annum); Calendar/Prospectus; Annual Report (annually)

Press or Publishing House: Rivers State University Press

Academic Staff *2001-2002:* Total: c. 450

Student Numbers *2001-2002:* Total: c. 10,000

• UNIVERSITY OF ABUJA (UNIABUJA)

PMB 117, Abuja, Federal Capital Territory
Tel: +234(9) 882-1379
Fax: +234(9) 882-1605
Cable: unibuja
EMail: vc@uniabuja.edu.ng

Vice-Chancellor: A.L. Gambo (1999-)
Registrar: Alhaji Yakubu Habi

Colleges

Arts and Education (Arts and Humanities; Education; History; Modern Languages; Theatre)
Law, Management and Social Sciences (Business Administration; Economics; Islamic Law; Law; Management; Social Sciences; Sociology)
Science and Agriculture (Agriculture; Chemistry; Mathematics; Physics)

Schools
Postgraduate Studies

Centres
Computer Science
Distance Learning and Lifelong Education

History: Founded 1988. A single-campus University with strong distance learning components.

Governing Bodies: Council; Senate

Academic Year: October to September

Admission Requirements: Senior School Certificate (SSC) with credits in 5 relevant subjects obtained at no more than 2 sittings, or General Certificate of Education (GCE) O level in 5 subjects, or equivalent qualification; and University Matriculation Examination (UME) in 3 relevant subjects and knowledge of English

Main Language(s) of Instruction: English

Degrees and Diplomas: *Bachelor's Degree*: 4 yrs; *Bachelor Honours Degree*: 4-5 yrs; *Master's Degree*: a further 1-2 yrs; *Doctor of Philosophy*: (PhD), a further 2-5 yrs

Special Facilities: Open Air Theatre

Publications: University of Abuja News Journal (quarterly); Abuja Journal of Education; Abuja Journal of Humanities (annually)

Academic Staff *2001-2002:* Total: c. 150

Student Numbers *2001-2002:* Total: c. 5,400

• UNIVERSITY OF AGRICULTURE, ABEOKUTA (UNAAB)

PMB 2240, Abeokuta, Ogun State
Tel: +234(39) 245-291   +234(39) 240-768
Fax: +234(39) 243-045   +234(39) 244-299
Telex: 24676 unaab ng
EMail: root@unaab.edu.ng
Website: http://www.unaab.edu.ng

Vice-Chancellor: Israel Folorunso Adu (2001-2006)
Tel: +234(39) 244-749
EMail: vcunaab@yahoo.com;vc@unaab.edu.ng

Registrar: Ademola Oyerinde EMail: vc@unaab.edu.ng

International Relations: Emi Alawode

Colleges

Agricultural Management, Rural Development, and Consumer Studies (Agricultural Economics; Agricultural Management; Consumer Studies; Farm Management; Food Science; Home Economics; Nutrition; Rural Planning)
Animal Husbandry and Livestock Production (Animal Husbandry; Cattle Breeding; Genetics)
Environmental Resources Management (Aquaculture; Environmental Studies; Fishery; Forestry; Meteorology; Toxicology; Water Management; Wildlife)
Natural Sciences and General Studies (Biology; Chemistry; Mathematics; Natural Sciences; Physics)
Plant Science and Crop Production (Botany; Crop Production)

Schools
Postgraduate *Director*: Omolayo J. Ariyo

Centres
Agricultural Media Resources and Extension (Agriculture) *Head*: Adepoju Aremu Adeoti
Research and Development (Development Studies) *Head*: Segun Toyosi O. Olagoke

History: Founded 1983 as Federal University of Technology, Abeokuta, merged with University of Lagos 1984, acquired present status 1988.

Governing Bodies: Council

Academic Year: October to July (October-February; March-July)

Admission Requirements: Universities Matriculation Examination (UME) following secondary school education, or direct entry for holders of the Higher School certificate (General Certificate of Education, Advanced ('A') level)

Fees: (Naira): Regular students, 895 per annum

Main Language(s) of Instruction: English

International Co-operation: Participates in the British Council-sponsored Academic Programme

Accrediting Agencies: Nigerian Universities Commission (NUC)

Degrees and Diplomas: *Bachelor's Degree*: Environment Management and Toxicology; Forestry; Wildlife Management; Science (BSc), 3-4 yrs; Agriculture (B. Agric.), 3-5 yrs

Student Services: Academic Counselling, Sports Facilities, Health Services, Canteen

Student Residential Facilities: For c. 30% of the students

Libraries: c. 38,242 vols

Publications: ASSET Journal; UNAAB Special Lecture Series; UNAAB Conference Proceedings Series; Student Handbook; UNAAB News

Academic Staff 2001-2002	MEN	WOMEN	TOTAL
FULL-TIME	196	68	264
PART-TIME	17	1	18
TOTAL	**213**	**69**	**282**
STAFF WITH DOCTORATE			
FULL-TIME	107	22	129
PART-TIME	16	1	17
TOTAL	**123**	**23**	**146**

Student Numbers 2001-2002	MEN	WOMEN	TOTAL
All (Foreign Included)	2,485	1,656	**4,141**
FOREIGN ONLY	55	6	61

Note: Also c. 560 students in Science Laboratory Technology Training Programme (SLTTP), pre-degrees

UNIVERSITY OF AGRICULTURE, MAKURDI (UNIAGRIC)

PMB 2373, Makurdi, Benue State
Tel: +234(44) 533-204 +234(44) 533-577
Fax: +234(44) 531-455
Telex: 85304

Vice-Chancellor: J.O.I. Ayatse Fax: +234(44) 531-455
EMail: vc@fuam.edu.ng

Registrar (Acting): Eraer Kureve

Faculties
Agricultural Economics and Extension (Agricultural Economics) *Dean*: C.P.O. Obinne
Agricultural Engineering and Engineering Technology (Agricultural Engineering; Technology) *Dean*: E.I. Kucha
Agronomy *Dean*: E.O. Ogunwolu
Animal Science (Animal Husbandry) *Dean*: N.G. Ehiobu
Food Technology *Dean*: Charles C. Ariahu
Science, Agriculture and Science Education (Agricultural Education; Natural Sciences; Science Education) *Dean*: O. Amali

Colleges
Forestry and Fisheries (Fishery; Forestry) *Dean*: Iorysa Verinumbe

Schools
Postgraduate *Dean*: M.C. Njike

Centres
Seed Technology (Crop Production) *Director*: B.A. Kalu

Research Centres
Co-operative Extension *Director*: D.K. Adedzwa
Food and Agricultural Strategy (Agriculture; Food Science; Food Technology)

History: Founded 1988.

Academic Year: March to September (March-June; June-September)

Admission Requirements: 5 credits in Senior Secondary School Certificate (SSSC) or West African School Certificate (WASC) or General Certificate of Education (GCE) ('O') level or equivalent, and English language. Entrance examination

Fees: (Naira): Postgraduate (foreign students): c. 7000

Main Language(s) of Instruction: English

Degrees and Diplomas: *Bachelor's Degree*: 4-5 yrs; *Master's Degree*: a further 1-4 yrs; *Doctor of Philosophy*: (PhD), 3-6 yrs

Libraries: c. 30,000 vols; 700 periodicals; Nigerian/Canadian soil science documents

Academic Staff *2001-2002:* Total: **225**

Student Numbers *2001-2002:* Total: c. 2,700

• UNIVERSITY OF BENIN (UNIBEN)

PMB 1154, Benin City, Edo State
Tel: +234(52) 600-443
Fax: +234(52) 600-273
Telex: 41365 uniben ng
Cable: uniben, benin
Website: http://www.uniben.edu

Vice-Chancellor: Abhulimen Richard Anao (1999-2004)
Tel: +234(52) 600-657 Fax: +234(52) 602-370
EMail: vc@uniben.edu

Registrar: Mary N. Idehen

Faculties
Agriculture (Agricultural Economics; Agriculture; Animal Husbandry; Botany; Crop Production; Fishery; Forestry; Soil Science) *Dean*: John O. Igene
Arts (Applied Chemistry; Arts and Humanities; Fine Arts; Graphic Arts) *Dean*: Aigbona I. Igbafe
Education (Curriculum; Education; Educational Administration; Health Education; Physical Education; Psychology; Vocational Education) *Dean*: David Awanbor
Engineering (Chemical Engineering; Civil Engineering; Electrical Engineering; Engineering; Mechanical Engineering) *Dean*: Thomas O. Audu
Law *Dean*: Patrick E. Oshio
Pharmacy (Chemistry; Microbiology; Pharmacology; Pharmacy; Toxicology) *Dean*: Augustine O. Okhamafe
Science (Biochemistry; Botany; Chemistry; Computer Science; Geology; Mathematics; Microbiology; Natural Sciences; Optometry; Physics; Zoology) *Dean*: John A. Okhunoya
Social Sciences (Accountancy; Anthropology; Business Administration; Economics; Geography; Political Science; Public Administration; Regional Planning; Social Sciences; Sociology; Statistics) *Dean*: Amorosu B. Agbadudu

Colleges

Medicine (Child Care and Development; Dentistry; Gynaecology and Obstetrics; Medicine; Ophthalmology; Psychiatry and Mental Health; Surgery) *Dean*: Friday E. Okonofua

Schools

Postgraduate Studies (Anaesthesiology; Arts and Humanities; Business Administration; Chemical Engineering; Computer Science; Education; Engineering; Finance; Fine Arts; Health Administration; History; International Relations; Law; Petroleum and Gas Engineering; Pharmacy; Philosophy; Public Administration; Science Education)

Institutes

Adult Education and Extramural Studies (Educational Research)

Child Health (Child Care and Development; Health Sciences) *Director*: Osawaru Oviawe

Education *Director*: A.O. Orubu

Public Administration and Extension Services (Public Administration) *Director (Acing)*: Samuel U. Akpovi

Centres

Educational Technology

Further Information: Also Teaching Hospital

History: Founded 1970 as the Institute of Technology Benin City, acquired present title 1972 and status 1975.

Governing Bodies: Council; Senate

Academic Year: October to June

Admission Requirements: Universities Matriculation Examination (UME) plus 5 General Certificate of Education (GCE) 'O' level passes, or 2 A level passes plus appropriate diploma/certificate

Main Language(s) of Instruction: English

Degrees and Diplomas: *Bachelor's Degree*: 3-5 yrs; *Master's Degree*: a further 1 1/2-2 yrs; *Doctor of Philosophy*: (PhD), at least 2 yrs following Master's Degree

Student Residential Facilities: Yes

Libraries: 204,329 vols; 145 periodical subscriptions; 3130 bound periodicals

Publications: University Newsletter (bimonthly); Faculty of Arts Journal (quarterly); University Report (biannually); Faculty of Education Journal (2 per annum); Calendar; Prospectus (annually); Physical Health Education and Recreational Journal; Nigerian Journal of Educational Research Association; Nigerian Bulletin of Contemporary Law; Bini Journal of Educational Studies

Academic Staff *2000-2001:* Total: **870**

Student Numbers *2000-2001*: All (Foreign Included): Men: c. 13,800 Women: c. 8,200 Total: c. 22,000

• UNIVERSITY OF CALABAR (UNICAL)

PMB 1115, Calabar, Cross River State
Tel: +234(87) 232-790
Fax: +234(87) 231-766
Telex: (0905) 6510 unical ng
Cable: unical, calabar
EMail: root@unical.anpa.net.ng

Vice-Chancellor: Ivara Ejemot Esu
EMail: vcunical@yahoo.com

Registrar: Effiom E. Effiom Tel: +234(87) 235-356

International Relations: Effiom E. Effiom, Registrar
Tel: +234(87) 235-356

Faculties

Agriculture (Agriculture; Animal Husbandry; Crop Production; Economics; Soil Science) *Dean*: A.I. Essien

Arts (Arts and Humanities; History; Linguistics; Modern Languages; Philosophy; Religion; Theatre) *Dean*: M.E. Noah

Education (Adult Education; Continuing Education; Curriculum; Education; Special Education; Vocational Education) *Dean*: S.E. Uche

Law (International Law; Law; Private Law; Public Law) *Dean*: N.O. Ita

Science (Biological and Life Sciences; Chemistry; Computer Science; Geology; Mathematics; Natural Sciences; Physics; Statistics) *Dean*: John O. Offem

Social Sciences (Accountancy; Banking; Business Administration; Economics; Finance; Management; Marketing; Political Science; Social Sciences; Sociology) *Dean*: John E. Ndebbio

Colleges

Medical Sciences (Anaesthesiology; Anatomy; Biochemistry; Community Health; Gynaecology and Obstetrics; Haematology; Health Sciences; Medicine; Microbiology; Ophthalmology; Paediatrics; Parasitology; Pathology; Pharmacology; Physiology; Psychiatry and Mental Health; Radiology; Surgery) *Provost*: Spencer E. Efem

Schools

Graduate Studies *Dean*: Ebong W. Mbipom

Institutes

Education (Distance Education; Education) *Director*: John U. Emeh

Oceanography (Marine Science and Oceanography) *Director*: Augustine I. Obiekezie

Public Policy and Administration (Rural Studies) *Director*: Okon E. Uya

History: Founded 1975. Also campus at Ogoja.

Governing Bodies: University Council; Senate; Committee of Deans

Academic Year: October to July (October-February; March-July)

Admission Requirements: Senior School Certificate (SSC) or its equivalent, with 5 passes at credit level, taken at no more than 2 sittings, and either University Matriculation Examination (UME) or (for direct entry) General Certificate of Education (GCE) 'A' level in 3 subjects or equivalent

Fees: (Naira): Tuition per annum: Undergraduate, 4440-5000 (Medicine, Science); 4090 (Non-science subjects). Postgraduate, 6000 (Arts), 4000 (part-time); 6000 (Science), 5000 (part-time); 8000 (MPA). Overseas students, undergraduate, 6000 (Arts, Law, Social Sciences); 8000 (Science); 12,000 (Medicine); postgraduate 24,800 (Arts, Science); 25,000 (MPA)

Main Language(s) of Instruction: English

Degrees and Diplomas: *Bachelor's Degree*: 4-5 yrs; *Master's Degree*: a further 1-2 yrs; *Doctor of Philosophy*: (PhD), 2-3 yrs following Master's Degree

Student Services: Academic Counselling, Social Counselling, Sports Facilities, Health Services, Canteen

Student Residential Facilities: for c. 3100 students

Special Facilities: Geography Observatory. Biological Garden. Theatre. Arts Gallery. Audiovisual Studio

Libraries: Total, 150,000 vols

Publications: News Bulletin (monthly); Introducing the University of Calabar; Calendar (annually)

Press or Publishing House: University of Calabar Press

Academic Staff 2001-2002	MEN	WOMEN	TOTAL
FULL-TIME	582	119	701
PART-TIME	5	1	6
TOTAL	**587**	**120**	**707**
STAFF WITH DOCTORATE			
FULL-TIME	219	42	**261**

Student Numbers 2001-2002	MEN	WOMEN	TOTAL
All (Foreign Included)	13,380	9,298	**22,678**
FOREIGN ONLY	17	7	24

Part-time Students, 12,437

*• UNIVERSITY OF IBADAN (UI)

Ibadan, Oyo State
Tel: +234(2) 810-1100-4   +234(2) 810-1188
Fax: +234(2) 810-2921
Telex: campus 31128 ng
Cable: university ibadan
EMail: registrar@kdl.ui.edu.ng
Website: http://www.ui.edu.ng

Vice-Chancellor: Ayobele Falase (2002-)
Tel: +234(2) 810-3168 Fax: +234(2) 810-3043

Registrar: Mojisola O. Ladipo Tel: +234(2) 810-4031
EMail: moji.ladipo@kdl.ui.edu.ng

International Relations: Duke Anoemuah, Principal Assistant Registrar Tel: +234(2) 810-3168

Faculties

Agriculture and Forestry (Agricultural Economics; Agricultural Engineering; Agriculture; Agronomy; Forestry) *Dean*: T. Ikotun
Arts (African Studies; Arabic; Arts and Humanities; Classical Languages; Communication Arts; English; History; Islamic Studies; Philosophy; Religious Studies; Theatre) *Dean*: A. Abeniran
Basic Medical Sciences (Medicine) *Dean*: Abeyombo Bolarinwa
Dentistry *Dean*: J.O. Lawoyin

Education (Adult Education; Education) *Dean*: Oluremi Ayobele-Bamsaiye
Law *Dean*: Abefolake Okediran
Pharmacy *Dean*: O.A. Itiola
Science (Archaeology; Botany; Chemistry; Computer Science; Crop Production; Geology; Mathematics; Microbiology; Natural Sciences; Physics; Statistics; Zoology) *Dean*: L.A. Hussain
Social Sciences (Economics; Geography (Human); Political Science; Psychology; Social Sciences; Sociology) *Dean*: A. Soyibo
Technology (Agricultural Engineering; Civil Engineering; Electrical Engineering; Engineering Management; Food Technology; Mechanical Engineering; Petroleum and Gas Engineering; Technology) *Dean*: B. Alabi
Veterinary Science (Animal Husbandry; Veterinary Science) *Dean*: B.O. Oke

Schools
Postgraduate *Dean*: I.A. Olayinka

Institutes
African Studies *Director*: Mosunmola Ominiyi-Obidike
Child Health (Health Sciences) *Director*: Foladale M. Akinkugbe
Education *Director*: S.O. Ayodele

Centres
Biomedical Communications (Biomedicine) *Head*: O.S. Ndekwu
Information Sciences *Director (Acting)*: I.S.Y. Ajiferuke

Further Information: Also Teaching Hospital

History: Founded as a college of the University of London 1948, acquired present status and title 1962.

Governing Bodies: University Council; University Senate

Academic Year: September to June

Admission Requirements: Universities Matriculation Examination (UME). Secondary School Certificate of Education (SSCE) with 5 credits, including English.

Fees: (Naira): Foreign students, undergraduate, 600-1000 per annum; postgraduate, 2500-35,000

Main Language(s) of Instruction: English

Degrees and Diplomas: *Bachelor's Degree*: 4-5 yrs; *Master's Degree*: a further 1-2 yrs; *Doctor of Philosophy*: (PhD), 3-4 yrs

Student Services: Academic Counselling, Social Counselling, Employment Services, Cultural Centre, Sports Facilities, Handicapped Facilities, Health Services, Foreign Student Centre

Student Residential Facilities: Yes

Libraries: Main Library, c. 560,000 vols; c. 6000 journals and other serials

Publications: African Notes (3 per annum); Annual Report; Student Handbook; Calendar (annually)

Press or Publishing House: University Press

Academic Staff 2001-2002: Total: **1,156**

Student Numbers 2001-2002: All (Foreign Included): Men: c. 13,840 Women: c. 7,485 Total: c. 21,325
Foreign Only: Total: c. 950

Evening Students, c. 1,200

*• UNIVERSITY OF ILORIN (UNILORIN)

PMB 1515, Ilorin, Kwara State
Tel: +234(31) 221-694
Fax: +234(31) 222-561
Telex: 33144 unilon ng
Cable: unilorin
EMail: vc@unilorin.edu.ng

Vice-Chancellor: Shamsudeen O.D. Amali (2003-2007)
Tel: +234(31) 221-911 EMail: vc@unilorin.edu.ng

Registrar: O.O. Oyeyemi Tel: +234(31) 221-937
EMail: registrar@unilorin.edu.ng

Head Librarian: M.I. Ajibero

Faculties

Agriculture (Agriculture; Cattle Breeding; Crop Production; Farm Management; Rural Planning) *Dean*: J.O. Atteh

Arts (Arabic; Arts and Humanities; Christian Religious Studies; English; French; History; Islamic Studies; Linguistics; Performing Arts; Social Sciences) *Dean*: R.D. Abubakre

Business and Social Sciences (Accountancy; Business Administration; Finance; Geography; Law; Political Science; Social Sciences; Sociology) *Dean*: I.O. Taiwo

Education (Education; Educational and Student Counselling; Health Education; Physical Education) *Dean*: E.A. Ogunsakin

Engineering and Technology (Agricultural Engineering; Civil Engineering; Electrical Engineering; Engineering; Mechanical Engineering; Technology) *Dean*: O.A. Adetifa

Law (International Law; Islamic Law; Law) *Dean (Acting)*: Z.O. Aje

Science (Biochemistry; Biological and Life Sciences; Botany; Chemistry; Geology; Mathematics; Microbiology; Mineralogy; Natural Sciences; Physics; Statistics; Zoology) *Dean*: T.O. Opoola

Divisions

General Studies *Director*: E.T. Jolayemi

Colleges

Medicine (Anatomy; Medicine; Physiology; Surgery) *Dean*: A.O. Soladoye

Schools

Postgraduate Studies *Dean*: J.A. Morakinyo

Institutes

Education *Director*: R.A. Lawal

Research Institutes

Sugar Technology (Food Technology) *Director*: J.O. Atteh

History: Founded 1975 as University College, acquired present status and title 1977. Under the jurisdiction of the Federal Government.

Governing Bodies: University Council

Academic Year: October to July (October-January; March-July)

Admission Requirements: Universities Matriculation Examination (UME) following secondary school education, or direct entry for holders of the Higher School Certificate (General Certificate of Education, Advanced ('A') level)

Fees: (Naira): c. 750-1200; postgraduate, c. 500-700; foreign students, US$ 2000-3000

Main Language(s) of Instruction: English

Accrediting Agencies: National Universities Commission (NUC); Nigeria Legal Council; Medical and Dental Council of Nigeria; Institute of Chartered Accountants of Nigeria; Nigeria Society of Engineers

Degrees and Diplomas: *Bachelor's Degree*: Arts in Education (BAEd); Science in Education (BSCEd), 3-4 yrs; Agriculture (BAgric), 4-5 yrs; Medicine and Surgery (MB BS), 5-6 yrs; *Bachelor Honours Degree*: Arts (BA(Hons)); Science (BSc(Hons)), 3-4 yrs; Engineering (Beng(Hons)), 4-5 yrs; *Master's Degree*: Arts (MA); Education (Med); Science (MSc), a further 1-2 yrs; *Doctor of Philosophy*: (PhD), 2-3 yrs

Student Services: Academic Counselling, Social Counselling, Employment Services, Sports Facilities, Language Programmes, Handicapped Facilities, Health Services, Canteen

Student Residential Facilities: For c. 3610 students

Special Facilities: Biological Garden

Libraries: University Library, 137,077 vols; 1675 periodical subscriptions

Publications: News Bulletin (weekly); University Calendar; Ilorin Lectures (annually)

Press or Publishing House: University Press

	MEN	WOMEN	TOTAL
Academic Staff *2002-2003*			
FULL-TIME	565	79	**644**
Student Numbers *2002-2003*	MEN	WOMEN	TOTAL
All (Foreign Included)	12,284	6,204	**18,488**

*• UNIVERSITY OF JOS (UNIJOS)

PMB 2084, Jos, Plateau State
Tel: +234(73) 610-936
Fax: +234(73) 610-514
Telex: 81136 unijos ng
Cable: unijos, nigeria 2019
EMail: unijos@aol.com
Website: http://128.255.135.155

Vice-Chancellor: Monday Y. Mangvwat (2001-)
Tel: +234(73) 453-724 +234(73) 612-513
Fax: +234(73) 611-928 EMail: vc@unijos.edu.ng

Registrar: Z.D. Galam

International Relations: Steve O. Otowo
Tel: +234(73) 453-724 EMail: otowos@unijos.edu.ng

Faculties

Arts (Arts and Humanities) *Dean*: S. Aje

Education *Dean*: C.T.O. Akinmade

Environmental Sciences (Environmental Studies) *Dean*: J.O. Kolawole

Law *Dean*: I.I. Gabriel

Medical Sciences (Health Sciences; Medicine) *Dean*: Abraham O. Malu

Natural Sciences (Botany; Geology; Natural Sciences; Zoology) *Dean*: C.O.E. Omwuliri

Pharmaceutical Sciences (Pharmacology; Pharmacy) *Dean*: T.A. Iranloye

Social Sciences (Economics; Political Science; Psychology; Social Sciences; Sociology) *Dean*: A. Nweze

Schools

Postgraduate Studies *Dean*: J.O.A. Onyeka

Institutes

Education *Director*: M.A. Adewole

Centres

Computer Science *Director*: E.G. Eseyin
Continuing Education *Director*: E.A. Abama
Development Studies *Director (Acting)*: Victor A.O. Adetula
General Studies *Director*: J.S. Illah

Further Information: Also Teaching Hospital

History: Founded 1971 as campus of University of Ibadan, acquired present status and title 1975.

Governing Bodies: Council; Senate

Academic Year: March to December (March-July; August-December)

Admission Requirements: Universities Matriculation Examination (UME) following secondary school education, or direct entry for holders of the Senior Secondary School Certificate (SSSC) or General Certificate of Education (GCE) with ('O') levels with at least 5 credits

Fees: (Naira): 1500-3000 per session; foreign students, 4000-8000

Main Language(s) of Instruction: English

International Co-operation: With universities in Canada, United Kingdom, Poland. Also cooperates with Japanese International Cooperation Agency

Accrediting Agencies: National Universities Commission

Degrees and Diplomas: *Bachelor's Degree*: Arts, Science, Law, 4-6 yrs; *Master's Degree*: Arts, Science, Law, a further 2 yrs; *Doctor of Philosophy*: (PhD), a further 2 yrs

Student Services: Academic Counselling, Social Counselling, Employment Services, Nursery Care, Sports Facilities, Handicapped Facilities, Health Services

Student Residential Facilities: Yes

Special Facilities: Anatomy Museum. Geography Observatory. House of Animal Pharmacology. Botanical Garden; Zoological Garden

Libraries: Total, 150,104 vols; 23,155 periodicals

Publications: News Flash (weekly); News Bulletin (monthly)

Press or Publishing House: University Press

Academic Staff *2001-2002*: Full-Time: c. 620

Student Numbers *2001-2002*: All (Foreign Included): Men: c. 6,930 Women: c. 4,120 Total: c. 11,050
Foreign Only: Men: c. 56 Women: c. 29 Total: c. 85

Part-time Students, c. 3,270

376

*• UNIVERSITY OF LAGOS (UNILAG)

Akoka, Yaba, Lagos, Lagos State
Tel: +234(1) 493-2660 +234(1) 582-0411
Fax: +234(1) 493-2667
Telex: 26983
Cable: university. lagos
EMail: admissions@unilag.edu
Website: http://www.unilag.edu

Vice-Chancellor: Oye Ibidapo-Obe (2002-2007)
Tel: +234(1) 493-2663 Fax: +234(1) 774-1872
EMail: vc@unilag.edu

Deputy Registrar: Biola Ladeinde Tel: +234(1) 493-2667
EMail: ibilad@yahoo.com

International Relations: Solomon Thomas
EMail: omotola@unilag.edu

Faculties

Arts (Arts and Humanities; English; Fine Arts; French; History; Linguistics; Philosophy; Russian)
Business Administration
Education (Adult Education; Art Education; Biology; Business and Commerce; Chemistry; Christian Religious Studies; Economics; Education; Educational Administration; Educational and Student Counselling; English; French; Geography; Health Education; History; Home Economics; Islamic Studies; Islamic Theology; Mathematics; Physical Education; Physics; Science Education; Technology Education)
Engineering (Chemical Engineering; Civil Engineering; Computer Engineering; Electrical and Electronic Engineering; Engineering; Marine Engineering; Materials Engineering; Mechanical Engineering; Metallurgical Engineering; Petroleum and Gas Engineering; Surveying and Mapping)
Environmental Sciences (Architectural and Environmental Design; Environmental Studies; Regional Planning; Town Planning)
Law
Science (Biochemistry; Botany; Cell Biology; Chemistry; Computer Science; Genetics; Marine Science and Oceanography; Mathematics; Microbiology; Physics; Zoology)
Social Sciences (Economics; Geography; Mass Communication; Political Science; Psychology; Social Sciences; Sociology)

Colleges

Medicine (Dental Technology; Medicine; Pharmacology; Pharmacy; Physical Therapy; Physiology; Surgery)

Schools
Postgraduate Studies

Institutes
Distance Learning

Centres
Educational Technology

Further Information: Also Teaching Hospital

History: Founded 1962.

Academic Year: October to July (October-February; March-July)

Admission Requirements: Universities Matriculation Examination (UME) following secondary school education, or direct entry for holders of the Higher School Certificate (General Certificate of Education, GCE, Advanced ('A') level)

Main Language(s) of Instruction: English

Degrees and Diplomas: *Bachelor's Degree*: Architecture (BArch); Arts (BA); Education (BEd); Environmental Science (BES); Pharmacy, 4 yrs; Science (BSc), 4-5 yrs; Dental Surgery (BDS); Medicine and Surgery (MB BS), 5 yrs; Laws, 5-7 yrs; *Master's Degree*: Arts in Translation; International Law and Diplomacy, a further 1-2 yrs; Banking and Finance (MBF); Business Administration (MBA); Public Administration (MPA), a further 3-5 sem; *Doctor of Philosophy*: (PhD), 2-3 yrs. Also undergraduate and postgraduate Diplomas

Student Services: Academic Counselling, Social Counselling, Employment Services, Nursery Care, Cultural Centre, Sports Facilities, Health Services, Canteen, Foreign Student Centre

Student Residential Facilities: Yes

Special Facilities: Biological Garden

Libraries: c. 270,000 vols

Publications: Calendar; Faculty prospectuses

Press or Publishing House: University of Lagos Press

Academic Staff *2001-2002:* Total: c. 900

Student Numbers *2001-2002:* Total: c. 35,000

• UNIVERSITY OF MAIDUGURI (UNIMAID)

PMB 1069, Bama Road, Maiduguri, Borno State
Tel: +234(76) 231-730
Fax: +234(76) 231-639
Telex: 82102 unimai ng
Cable: university maiduguri
EMail: unimaid@hotmail.com

Vice-Chancellor: J.B. Amin

Registrar: Umaru Ibrahim

Faculties

Agriculture (Agriculture; Crop Production; Food Science) *Dean*: A.O. Folorunso

Arts (Arts and Humanities; Fine Arts; History; Linguistics; Modern Languages) *Dean*: B.R. Badejo

Education *Dean*: P.F.C. Carew

Engineering (Civil Engineering; Electrical and Electronic Engineering; Engineering; Mechanical Engineering) *Dean*: M.A. Haque

Law *Dean*: Isa H. Chiroma

Science (Biological and Life Sciences; Chemistry; Geography; Mathematics; Natural Sciences) *Dean*: M.Y. Balla

Social and Management Sciences (Anthropology; Economics; Management; Political Science; Social Sciences; Sociology) *Dean*: H.D. Dlakwa

Veterinary Science *Dean*: T.I.O. Osiyemi

Colleges

Medical Sciences (Health Sciences; Medicine) *Dean*: M.I.A. Khalil

Schools

Postgraduate Studies *Dean*: Abdulhamid Abubakar

Centres

Arid Zone Studies (Arid Land Studies) *Director*: Pender O. Ugherughe

Trans-Saharan Studies (Arid Land Studies) *Director*: K. Tijani

Further Information: Also Teaching Hospital

History: Founded 1975.

Governing Bodies: Governing Council

Academic Year: October to June (October-February/March; March-June)

Admission Requirements: Either Senior School Leaving Certificate (SSLC) or General Certificate of Education (GCE) 'O' level with at least 5 credits in relevant subjects and good scores in the University Matriculation Examination; or GCE 'A' level with minimum C grade in at least 3 relevant subjects. Application is through Joint Admission and Matriculation Board (JAMB).

Main Language(s) of Instruction: English

Degrees and Diplomas: *Bachelor's Degree*: Engineering (BEng), 3-4 yrs; Medicine and Surgery (MB BS), 5 yrs; *Bachelor Honours Degree*: Arts (BAHons); Education (BEdHons); Library Science Studies (BLS(Hons)); Science (BSc(Hons)); Sharia (Islamic Law) (LLB(Hons)), 3-4 yrs; *Doctor of Veterinary Medicine*: Veterinary Medicine (DVM), 5 yrs; *Master's Degree*: Arts (MA); Education (MEd); Law (LLM); Library Science Studies (MLS); Performing Arts (MPA); Science (MSc), a further 1-2 yrs; *Master of Philosophy*: (MPhil), a minimum of 12 months' full-time study following Master's Degree; *Doctor of Philosophy*: (PhD), 2-5 yrs. Also Diplomas.

Student Services: Academic Counselling, Social Counselling, Nursery Care, Cultural Centre, Sports Facilities, Health Services, Foreign Student Centre

Student Residential Facilities: Yes

Libraries: Main Library, c. 116,500 vols

Publications: The Annals of Borno (Multidisciplinary Yearbook of Research) (annually); University Calendar

Press or Publishing House: University of Maiduguri Printing Press

Academic Staff *2001-2002:* Total: c. 650

Student Numbers *2001-2002:* Total: c. 10,000

*• UNIVERSITY OF NIGERIA (UNN)

Nsukka, Enugu State
Tel: +234(42) 771-500
Fax: +234(42) 770-644
EMail: misunn@aol.com
Website: http://www.unnedu.net

Vice-Chancellor: Ginigeme Mbanefoh (1997-2004)
Fax: +234(42) 770-644 EMail: ginimbanefoh@yahoo.com

Deputy Vice-Chancellor (Academic): A.U. Okorie
Tel: +234(42) 770-886

Deputy Registrar: Obi Nwala

International Relations: Rufus Ogbuji, Deputy Vice-Chancelor

Faculties

Agriculture Dean: J.S.C. Mbagwu

Arts (Archaeology; Arts and Humanities; Fine Arts; History; Modern Languages; Music; Performing Arts; Philosophy) Dean: Emeka P. Nwabueze

Biological Sciences (Biological and Life Sciences) Dean: I.C. Ononogbu

Business Administration Dean: Ike Nwosu

Education Dean: S.C.O.A. Ezeji

Engineering (Civil Engineering; Electrical and Electronic Engineering; Engineering; Mechanical Engineering) Dean: Anthony N. Nzeako

Environmental Studies Dean: L.C. Umeh

Pharmaceutical Sciences (Pharmacology; Pharmacy) Dean: G.B. Okide

Physical Sciences (Physics) Dean: Alphonsus C. Nwadinigwe

Social Sciences (Anthropology; Economics; Political Science; Psychology; Social Sciences; Sociology) Dean: R.N.C. Anaydike

Veterinary Science Dean: I.U. Asuzu

Schools

Postgraduate Studies Dean: Charles C. Okafor

Departments

Adult Education and Extramural Studies Head: Doris U. Egonu

Institutes

African Studies Director: Osmond O. Enekwe

Education Director: Eunice A.C. Okeke

Centres

Energy Research and Development (Energy Engineering) Director: Cajetan E. Okeke

Rural Development and Cooperatives (Rural Studies) Director: Eugene C. Okorji

Further Information: Also 2 Teaching Hospitals

History: Founded 1960. The former Nigerian College of Arts, Science and Technology, Enugu, was incorporated into the University 1961 and its buildings now form the Enugu campus of the University.

Governing Bodies: Governing Council, comprising 21 members; Senate

Academic Year: October to September

Admission Requirements: Universities Matriculation Examination (UME) following secondary school education, or direct entry for holders of the Higher School Certificate (General Certificate of Education, Advanced ('A') level)

Fees: (Naira): Tuition, undergraduate, free; postgraduate, 6,000-8,000 per annum; foreign students, African students, 8,000-16,000; students from Europe and North America, US$ 500-750

Main Language(s) of Instruction: English

Accrediting Agencies: National Universities Commission

Degrees and Diplomas: *Bachelor's Degree*: 3-6 yrs; *Master's Degree*: a further 1-3 yrs; *Doctor of Philosophy*: (Ph.D.), 2-5 yrs

Student Services: Academic Counselling, Nursery Care, Sports Facilities, Health Services, Canteen, Foreign Student Centre

Student Residential Facilities: for c. 11,230 students

Special Facilities: Zoological Garden

Libraries: Nnamdi Azikiwe Library, c. 700,500 vols

Publications: Annual Report (annually); Calendar (every three years); Undergraduate Prospectus

Press or Publishing House: University of Nigeria Press Ltd

Academic Staff 2002	MEN	WOMEN	TOTAL
FULL-TIME	855	196	**1,051**
STAFF WITH DOCTORATE			
FULL-TIME	810	152	**962**

Student Numbers 2002	MEN	WOMEN	TOTAL
All (Foreign Included)	16,248	13,234	**29,482**

*• UNIVERSITY OF PORT HARCOURT (UNIPORT)

PMB 5323, Choba, Port Harcourt, Rivers State
Tel: +234(84) 330-883   +234(84) 335-218
Fax: +234(84) 230-903
Telex: 61183 phuni ng
Cable: university pharcourt
EMail: uniport@phca.linkserve.com
Website: http://www.uniport.edu.ng

Vice-Chancellor: Nimi D. Briggs (2000-2005)
Tel: +234(84) 230-902 EMail: vc-uniport@phca.linkserve.com

Registrar: C.A. Tamuno Tel: +234(803) 3393-829

International Relations: Charles Uwadiae Oyegun, Dean, Student Affairs
Tel: +234(84) 230-890 Ext.2594 +234(803) 3420-259
EMail: deanstudents@uniport.edu.ng

Faculties

Education (Curriculum; Education; Educational Administration; Educational Psychology; Educational Technology) Dean: J.M. Kosemani

Engineering (Chemical Engineering; Civil Engineering; Electrical and Electronic Engineering; Engineering; Mechanical Engineering; Petroleum and Gas Engineering; Surveying and Mapping) Dean: I.L. Nwaogazie

Graduate Dean: E.N. Elechi

Humanities (Archaeology; Arts and Humanities; Fine Arts; History; Modern Languages; Theatre) Dean: S.I. Udoidem

Management Sciences (Business Administration; Management) Dean: D.O.N. Baridam

Science (Biochemistry; Botany; Chemistry; Geology; Natural Sciences; Physics; Zoology) Dean: E.S. Okoli

Social Sciences (Economics; Political Science; Social Sciences; Sociology) Dean: C.J.B. Ojo

Colleges

Health Sciences (Anaesthesiology; Anatomy; Gynaecology and Obstetrics; Haematology; Health Sciences; Medicine; Microbiology; Paediatrics; Pathology; Pharmacology; Physiology;

Psychiatry and Mental Health; Social and Preventive Medicine; Surgery) *Provost*: O.J. Odia

Institutes

Agricultural Research Development (Agriculture) *Director*: N.H. Igwiloh

Education (Education; Educational Psychology) *Director*: J.M. Kosemani

History: Founded 1975 as University College, acquired present status 1977.

Academic Year: October to July (October-February; April-July)

Admission Requirements: Universities Matriculation Examination (UME) following secondary school education

Fees: (Naira): 2700-6850

Main Language(s) of Instruction: English

Accrediting Agencies: National Universities Commission (NUC)

Degrees and Diplomas: *Bachelor's Degree*: (BA; BSc; BED), 2-6 yrs; *Higher National Diploma*: 3-4 yrs; *Postgraduate Diploma*: Education (PGDE), 1 yr following Bachelor's Degree; *Master's Degree*: (MA; MSc; MEd), a further 1-2 yrs; *Doctor of Philosophy*: (PhD), 3 yrs following Master's Degree. Also Diploma, and other Postgraduate diplomas (PGD)

Student Services: Academic Counselling, Social Counselling, Foreign Student Adviser, Nursery Care, Sports Facilities, Language Programmes, Health Services, Canteen

Student Residential Facilities: Yes

Libraries: Total, 77,622 vols

Publications: News Bulletin (monthly); Kiabara: A Journal of the Humanities (biannually); Students Handbook (1 per annum); Prospectus; Calendar; Diary

Press or Publishing House: University Press

Academic Staff *2001-2002:* Total: c. 540

Staff with doctorate: Total: c. 370

Student Numbers *2001-2002*	MEN	WOMEN	TOTAL
All (Foreign Included)	14,000	12,000	**26,000**
FOREIGN ONLY	10	3	13

Part-time Students, 6,000

• UNIVERSITY OF UYO (UNIUYO)

PMB 1017, Uyo, Akwa Ibom State
Tel: +234(85) 200-303   +234(85) 201-111
Fax: +234(85) 202-694
Cable: uniuyo
EMail: root@uniuyo.edu.ng

Vice-Chancellor: Akpan H. Ekpo (2000-)
Tel: +234(85) 202-693 EMail: vc@uniuyo.edu.ng

Registrar: Peter J. Efiong Tel: +234(85) 202-699

International Relations: Udo A. Etuk

Faculties

Agriculture (Agricultural Economics; Agriculture; Agronomy; Animal Husbandry; Fishery; Forestry) *Dean*: Bassey A. Nelon

Arts (Arts and Humanities; Communication Arts; English; History; Modern Languages; Music; Philosophy; Religious Studies; Theatre) *Dean*: Udo A. Etuk

Business Administration (Business Administration; Hotel Management; Tourism) *Dean*: Edet B. Akpakpan

Education (Curriculum; Education; Educational Administration; Educational and Student Counselling; Educational Technology; Health Education; Physical Education; Preschool Education; Science Education; Vocational Education) *Dean*: George S. Ibe-Bassey

Engineering (Agricultural Engineering; Chemical Engineering; Civil Engineering; Computer Engineering; Electrical Engineering; Electronic Engineering; Food Technology; Mechanical Engineering; Petroleum and Gas Engineering) *Dean*: Emme U. Nwa

Environmental Studies (Architecture; Building Technologies; Fine Arts; Real Estate; Regional Planning; Rural Planning; Surveying and Mapping; Town Planning)

Law *Dean*: Enefiok E. Essien

Natural and Applied Sciences (Biochemistry; Botany; Brewing; Chemistry; Computer Science; Mathematics; Microbiology; Natural Sciences; Physics; Statistics; Zoology) *Dean*: Nse M. Ekpo

Pharmacy (Pharmacology; Pharmacy) *Dean*: E.E. Essien

Social Sciences (Anthropology; Economics; Geography (Human); Political Science; Psychology; Public Administration; Social Sciences) *Dean*: Etop J. Usoro

Colleges

Health Sciences (Anatomy; Biochemistry; Health Sciences; Medicine; Physiology) *Provost*: Joseph J. Andy

Centres

Development Studies *Director*: Ignatius I. Ukpong

Further Information: Also Commercial Farm; Educational Technology Unit; Science laboratory Technology Training Unit

History: Founded 1983 as University of Cross River State. Acquired present status and title 1991.

Governing Bodies: Council; Senate

Academic Year: January to October (January-May; July-October)

Admission Requirements: Senior Secondary Certificate/West African School Certificate/General Certificate of Education (GCE), Ordinary ('O') level, or equivalent, with credit passes in at least 5 subjects, including English Language. Credit pass in Mathematics is required for Science-based and Social Science courses

Fees: None

Main Language(s) of Instruction: English

Degrees and Diplomas: *National Diploma*: Fine Arts; French; Public Administration; Theatre Arts; *Bachelor's Degree*: Arts (BA); Education (BEd); Science (BSc); Science Education (BScEd), 4 yrs; Agriculture (BAgr); Engineering (B.Eng); Forestry (BForestry); Law (LLB); Pharmacy (BPharm), 5 yrs; Architecture (B.Arch), 6 yrs; *Master's Degree*: a further 1-2 yrs; *Doctor of Philosophy*: (PhD), a further 3-4 yrs

Student Residential Facilities: Yes

Special Facilities: Geographical Observatory

Libraries: c. 44,150 vols

Academic Staff 2001-2002	MEN	WOMEN	TOTAL
FULL-TIME	603	113	716
PART-TIME	–	–	53
TOTAL	–	–	**769**
STAFF WITH DOCTORATE			
FULL-TIME	206	27	233
PART-TIME	–	–	53
TOTAL	–	–	**286**

Student Numbers 2001-2002	TOTAL
All (Foreign Included)	**16,707**
FOREIGN ONLY	90

• USMANU DANFODIYO UNIVERSITY, SOKOTO (UDU)

PMB 2346, Sokoto
Tel: +234(60) 233-221   +234(60) 234-039
Fax: +234(60) 236-688
Telex: 73134 udusok, nigeria
Cable: udusok, sokoto
EMail: registrar@udusok.edu.ng
Website: http://dns.udusok.edu.ng

Vice-Chancellor: Aminu Salihu Mikailu (1999-2004)
Tel: +234(60) 236-688 Fax: +234(60) 235-519
EMail: vc@udusok.edu.ng

Registrar: Abubakar Usman

Faculties

Agriculture (Agricultural Economics; Agricultural Engineering; Agriculture; Animal Husbandry; Crop Production; Fishery; Forestry; Soil Science)
Arts and Islamic Studies (Arabic; Arts and Humanities; History; Islamic Studies; Modern Languages) *Dean*: Mohammed Dangana
Education and Extension Services (Education; Primary Education) *Dean*: F.A. Kalgo
Law (Commercial Law; Islamic Law; Law; Private Law) *Dean*: M.I. Said
Management and Administration (Accountancy; Administration; Business Administration; Management; Public Administration) *Dean*: S.A. Diyo
Science (Biochemistry; Chemistry; Mathematics; Natural Sciences; Physics) *Dean*: Usman Abubakar
Social Sciences (Economics; Geography; Political Science; Social Sciences; Sociology)
Veterinary Science (Microbiology; Parasitology; Pathology; Pharmacology; Physiology; Surgery; Veterinary Science) *Dean*: A.I. Daneji

Colleges

Health Sciences (Anatomy; Community Health; Gynaecology and Obstetrics; Health Sciences; Medicine; Microbiology; Paediatrics; Pathology; Surgery) *Provost*: E.E.K. Opara

Centres

Energy Research *(Sokoto)* (Energy Engineering)
Islamic Studies

Bureaux

University Translation *(UNESCO)* (Translation and Interpretation)
Further Information: Also Teaching Hospital

History: Founded 1975 as University of Sokoto, acquired present title 1985.

Governing Bodies: Council; Senate

Academic Year: November to July (November-March; March-July)

Admission Requirements: Universities Matriculation Examination (UME) following secondary school education, or direct entry for holders of the Higher School Certificate (General Certificate of Education, Advanced ('A') level)

Fees: (Naira): Foreign students, postgraduate, c.5000-7000 per annum

Main Language(s) of Instruction: English, Hausa, Arabic

Degrees and Diplomas: *Bachelor's Degree*: 3 yrs; *Master's Degree*: a further 1-2 yrs; *Doctor of Philosophy*: (PhD), a further 3-5 yrs

Libraries: 233,000 vols; 3700 periodicals

Publications: Prospectus; Calendar

Press or Publishing House: University Press

Academic Staff *2001-2002:* Total: c. 310

Student Numbers *2001-2002:* Total: c. 7,500

PRIVATE INSTITUTIONS

• IGBINEDION UNIVERSITY, OKADA

PMB 006, Okada, 69, Airport Road, Benin City, Edo State
Tel: +234(52) 254-942
Fax: +234(52) 251-504
Website: http://www.igbinedion.com/iu

Vice-Chancellor: Anthony Uyekpen Osagie
Tel: +234(52) 602-097
EMail: au_osagie@hotmail.com;au_osagie@yahoo.com

Registrar: Sally Asagwara

Colleges

Arts and Social Sciences (Arts and Humanities; Social Sciences)
Business and Management (Business and Commerce; Management)
Health Sciences (Health Sciences; Medicine) Daramola
Law *Dean*: Joe Ojo
Natural and Applied Science (Natural Sciences)

History: Founded 1999.

Governing Bodies: University Senate, Council, Board of Regents

Academic Year: September to June

Admission Requirements: School certificate SSCE/GCE/NECO with Credit Passes in 5 subjects

Fees: (Naira): 300,000 per annum

Main Language(s) of Instruction: English

International Co-operation: Participates in ICAN, CIBN, NMDC, NUC programmes.

Degrees and Diplomas: *Bachelor's Degree*: Natural & Applied Sciences, Arts, Social Sciences, Business & Management (BSc), 4 yrs; Law (BL), 5 yrs; *Master's Degree*: Medicine (MB), 6 yrs

Student Services: Academic Counselling, Social Counselling, Sports Facilities, Health Services, Canteen

Student Residential Facilities: Yes

Special Facilities: Teaching Hospital

Libraries: c. 20,000 vols

Publications: Handbook, General Information & Prospectus; Brochure, Information for prospective students (1 per annum)

Academic Staff *2001-2002*	MEN	WOMEN	TOTAL
FULL-TIME	63	6	69
PART-TIME	–	–	9
TOTAL	–	–	**78**
STAFF WITH DOCTORATE			
FULL-TIME	21	3	24
PART-TIME	–	–	4
TOTAL	–	–	**28**
Student Numbers *2001-2002*	MEN	WOMEN	TOTAL
All (Foreign Included)	411	619	**1,030**

OTHER INSTITUTIONS

AKANU IBIAM FEDERAL POLYTECHNIC, UNMANA
PMB 1007, Afikpo, Abia State
Tel: +234(88) 521-574

Rector: Zak A. Obanu

Founded: 1981

Schools
Business (Business Administration)
Engineering
Science and General Studies (Mathematics and Computer Science; Natural Sciences)

BENUE STATE POLYTECHNIC, UGBOKOLO
PMB 2215, Otukpo, Benue State

Rector: Y.W. Awodi
Registrar: D.O. Ona

Founded: 1976

Schools
Art and Design (Design; Fine Arts)

Business and Administration (Administration; Business and Commerce)
Engineering
Technology

THE CATHOLIC INSTITUTE OF WEST AFRICA IN PORT HARCOURT
PO Box 499, Port Harcourt
Tel: +234(84) 612-690
Fax: +234(84) 612-690
EMail: registryciwa@infoweb.abs.net

Rector: James Shagba Moti
EMail: rectorciwa@infoweb.abs.net

Founded: 1981

Faculties
Theology (Canon Law; Theology)

Centres
Pastoral Communications and African Culture (African Studies; Pastoral Studies)

Degrees and Diplomas: *Bachelor's Degree*; *Master's Degree*; *Doctor of Philosophy*

FEDERAL POLYTECHNIC, ADO-EKITI
PMB 5351, Ado-Ekiti, Ekiti State
Tel: +234(30) 250-523

Rector: G.O.S. Adejinmi
Registrar: A.B. Omodele

Schools
Business Studies (Business and Commerce)
Engineering
Environmental Studies
Science and Computer Studies (Computer Science)

History: Founded 1977.

FEDERAL POLYTECHNIC, AUCHI
PMB 13, Auchi, Edo State
Tel: +234(57) 200-148

Founded: 1973

Schools
Applied Sciences and Technology (Applied Chemistry; Applied Mathematics; Applied Physics; Computer Science; Engineering; Technology)
Art and Design (Design; Fine Arts)
Business Studies (Business and Commerce)

Engineering
Environmental Studies

FEDERAL POLYTECHNIC, BAUCHI

PMB 0231, Bauchi, Bauchi State
Tel: +234(77) 543-630
Fax: +234(77) 540-465
Telex: 83273
Website: http://www.bauchipoly.edu.ng

Rector: M.L.I.S. Jahun (2000-) Tel: +234(77) 543-487
Fax: +234(77) 541-393 EMail: rector@bauchipoly.edu.ng

Registrar: Y.M. Maskano Tel: +234(77) 543-481
EMail: registrar@bauchipoly.edu.ng

Founded: 1979

Schools

Business Studies (Business Administration; Management) *Director:* R.C. Mamman

Engineering Technology (Engineering; Graphic Design; Industrial Design) *Director:* Samuel Sule

Environmental Studies *Director:* J.K. Tumba

General Studies (Teacher Training) *Director:* Ishaya Ludu

Technology (Engineering; Management; Technology) *Director:* I.S. Shinga

Governing Bodies: Governing Council

Academic Year: October to June (October-February; March-June)

Admission Requirements: Higher school certificate, with 4 passes including English and Mathematics

Main Language(s) of Instruction: English

Accrediting Agencies: National Board for Technical Education (NBTE)

Degrees and Diplomas: *National Diploma:* 2 yrs; *Higher National Diploma:* 2 yrs

Student Residential Facilities: Yes (limited)

Libraries: Central Library

Publications: Prospectus (biannually); Annual Report (annually)

Academic Staff *2001-2002:* Total: **220**

Staff with doctorate: Total: **5**

Student Numbers *2000:* Total: **2,910**

Part-time Students, 470

FEDERAL POLYTECHNIC, BIDA

PMB 55, Bida, Niger State
Tel: +234(66) 461-707

Rector: Umaru Sani-Ango

Registrar: S.F. Iko

Founded: 1977

Schools

Applied Arts and Science (Fine Arts; Natural Sciences)

Business and Management (Business and Commerce; Management)

Engineering

Environmental Studies

Preliminary Studies

FEDERAL POLYTECHNIC, IDAH

PMB 1037, Idah, Kogi State
Tel: +234(58) 800-128

Rector: Y.W. Awodi

Registrar: S.A. Ogunleye

Founded: 1977

Schools

Business Studies (Business and Commerce)

Engineering

General Studies

Metallurgy and Materials Technology (Materials Engineering; Metallurgical Engineering)

Technology

Departments

Accountancy

Business Administration

Civil Engineering

Continuing Education

Electrical Engineering

Food Technology

Foundry Technology (Industrial Engineering)

Hotel and Catering Management (Hotel and Restaurant)

Languages and Liberal Studies (Artificial Intelligence; Modern Languages)

Marketing

Mathematics and Statistics (Mathematics; Statistics)

Mechanical Engineering

Metallurgy (Metallurgical Engineering)

Science Technology (Technology)

Secretarial Studies

Social Sciences and Humanities (Arts and Humanities; Social Sciences)

Surveying (Surveying and Mapping)

FEDERAL POLYTECHNIC, ILARO

PMB 50, Ilaro, Ogun State
Tel: +234(39) 440-005
Rector: S.A. Olateru-Olagbegi
Registrar: R.O. Egbeyemi

Founded: 1979

Schools

Applied Sciences (Applied Chemistry; Applied Mathematics; Applied Physics; Computer Science; Engineering; Natural Sciences)
Business Studies (Business and Commerce)
Engineering

FEDERAL POLYTECHNIC, KAURA NAMODA

PMB 1012, Kaura Namoda, Sokoto State
Founded: 1983

Schools

Business Management (Management)
Engineering
Environmental Studies
General Studies
Science and Technology (Natural Sciences; Technology)

FEDERAL POLYTECHNIC, MUBI (FPM)

PMB 35, Mubi, Adamawa State
Tel: +234(75) 882-771
Rector: Aminu Muhammad Tel: +234(75) 882-771
Registrar: Bello Buba Tel: +234(75) 882-529
International Relations: Bakari Inuwa

Founded: 1979

Colleges

Technology (Business Administration; Engineering; Technology) *Rector*: Aminu Muhammad

History: Founded 1979.
Governing Bodies: Governing Council
Admission Requirements: Higher school certificate, with 4 passes in relevant subjects, including Mathematics and English
Main Language(s) of Instruction: English
Accrediting Agencies: National Board for Technical Education
Degrees and Diplomas: *National Diploma*: Engineering; Management (ND), 2 yrs; *Higher National Diploma*: Engineering; Management (HND), 2 yrs

Student Services: Academic Counselling, Social Counselling, Employment Services, Nursery Care, Sports Facilities, Health Services, Canteen
Academic Staff *2001-2002*: Full-Time: c. 190 Part-Time: c. 10 Total: c. 200
Student Numbers *2001-2002:* Total: c. 2,160

FEDERAL POLYTECHNIC, NEKEDE

PMB 1036, Owerri, Imo State
Tel: +234(83) 231-516
Rector: C.I. Osuoji
Registrar: G.T.U. Chiaha

Founded: 1978, 1993

Schools

Business and Public Administration (Business Administration; Public Administration)
Engineering and Technology (Engineering; Technology)
Environmental Design (Environmental Studies)
General Studies
Industrial Sciences (Industrial Engineering)

History: Founded 1978 as College of Technology, Owerri. Acquired present status and title 1993.
Governing Bodies: Federal Ministry of Education
Admission Requirements: General Certificate of Education; West African School Certificate with 4 passes
Main Language(s) of Instruction: English
Accrediting Agencies: National Board for Technical Education (NBTE)
Degrees and Diplomas: *National Diploma*: 2 yrs; *Higher National Diploma*: 2 yrs
Student Residential Facilities: For men and women students
Libraries: Central Library
Publications: Fedpno Bulletin, News and Information (quarterly)
Academic Staff *2001-2002:* Total: c. 150
Staff with doctorate: Total: c. 15
Student Numbers *2001-2002:* Total: c. 5,700
Evening Students, c. 680

FEDERAL POLYTECHNIC, OKO

PMB 21, Aguata, Anambra State
Tel: +234(48) 911-144
Rector: U.C. Nzewi
Registrar: O.C.A. Ofochebe

Founded: 1979
Accountancy; Architecture; Banking; Building Technologies; Business Administration; Environmental Studies;

Information Technology; Library Science; Marketing; Mass Communication; Secretarial Studies; Technology

History: Founded 1979.

HASSAN USMAN KATSINA POLYTECHNIC
PMB 2052, Katsina, Katsina State
Tel: +234(65) 32816

Colleges
Administration and Management (Administration; Business Administration; Management; Public Administration)
Legal and General Studies (Islamic Law; Law; Modern Languages; Private Law; Public Law)
Science and Technology (Agriculture; Applied Chemistry; Applied Mathematics; Applied Physics; Civil Engineering; Computer Science; Electrical Engineering; Engineering; Food Science; Hotel Management; Mathematics; Mechanical Engineering; Natural Sciences; Surveying and Mapping; Technology)

History: Founded 1983.

INSTITUTE OF MANAGEMENT AND TECHNOLOGY (IMT)
PMB 01079, Enugu, Enugu State
Tel: +234(42) 250-416

Rector: C.C. Njeze
Registrar: C.A. Attah

Schools
Business Studies (Business and Commerce)
Communication Arts
Continuing Education and Distance Learning
Engineering
Financial Studies (Finance)
General Studies
Science, Vocational and Technical Education (Science Education; Technology Education; Vocational Education)
Technology

History: Founded 1973.

KADUNA POLYTECHNIC
PMB 2021, Kaduna, Kaduna State
Tel: +234(62) 211-551
EMail: mis@kadpoly.edu.ng
Website: http://www.kadpoly.edu.ng

Rector (Acting): J.D.J. Dashe
Registrar: Alh. Garba I. Bakori

Founded: 1956, 1968

Colleges
Administrative and Business Studies (Administration; Business and Commerce)
Engineering
Environmental Studies
Science and Technology (Natural Sciences; Technology)

History: Founded 1956 as Kaduna Technical Institute. Acquired present status and title 1968.

KANO STATE POLYTECHNIC
PMB 3401, Kano, Kano State
Tel: +234(64) 625-658

Founded: 1976

Schools
Agriculture *(Audo Bako)*
Islamic Legal Studies *(Aminu)* (Islamic Law; Islamic Studies)
Management Studies (Management)
Social and Rural Development (Rural Studies; Social Studies)
Technology

KEBBI STATE POLYTECHNIC
PMB 1034, Birnin Kebbi, Kebbi State

Schools
Accounting and Finance (Accountancy; Finance)
Business and Public Administration (Business Administration; Public Administration)
Environmental Design (Environmental Studies)
Industrial Engineering
Natural Resources Engineering (Engineering; Natural Resources)
Science (Mathematics and Computer Science; Natural Sciences)
Surveying and Land Administration (Surveying and Mapping)
Vocational and Technical Education

History: Founded 1976.

KWARA STATE POLYTECHNIC
PMB 1375, Ilorin, Kwara State
Tel: +234(31) 221-441

Founded: 1972

Institutes
Administration
Basic and Applied Sciences (Applied Chemistry; Applied Mathematics; Applied Physics; Computer Science; Engineering; Natural Sciences)
Business and Vocational Studies (Business Administration)
Environmental Studies
General Studies
Technology

History: Founded 1972.

LAGOS STATE POLYTECHNIC
PMB 21606, Ikeja, Lagos State
Tel: +234(65) 523-528
Founded: 1977
Natural Sciences; Technology

OGUN STATE POLYTECHNIC
PMB 2210, Abeokuta, Ogun State
Tel: +234(39) 231-274
Founded: 1977

Departments
Accountancy
Architecture
Business Administration
Business Studies (Business and Commerce)
Civil Engineering
Continuing Education
Electrical and Electronic Engineering
Estate Management (Real Estate)
Financial Studies (Finance)
Food Science and Technology (Food Science; Food Technology)
Liberal Studies (Arts and Humanities)
Marketing
Mass Communication
Science Laboratory Technology (Laboratory Techniques)
Secretarial Studies
Town and Regional Planning (Regional Planning; Town Planning)

ONDO STATE POLYTECHNIC
PMB 1019, Owo, Ondo State
Founded: 1980

Colleges
Business Studies (Business and Commerce)
Engineering
Environmental Studies
Food Technology

PETROLEUM TRAINING INSTITUTE
PMB 20, Effurun, Delta State
Founded: 1972

Departments
Electrical and Electronic Engineering
General Studies
Industrial Continuing Education
Industrial Safety and Environmental Engineering (Environmental Engineering; Safety Engineering)
Mechanical Engineering
Petroleum Engineering and Geosciences (Earth Sciences; Geological Engineering; Petroleum and Gas Engineering)
Petroleum Processing Technology (Petroleum and Gas Engineering)
Welding and Underwater Operations (Hydraulic Engineering; Metal Techniques)

PLATEAU STATE POLYTECHNIC, BARKIN LADI
PMB 02023, Barakin Ladi, Buruku, Plateau State
Rector: Alexander A.T. Kebang
Registrar: Timothy A. Anjide

Founded: 1978

Schools
Administration and General Studies (Administration)
Engineering and Environmental Studies (Engineering; Environmental Studies)
Management Studies (Management)
Science and Technology (Mathematics and Computer Science; Natural Sciences; Technology)

POLYTECHNIC, CALABAR
PMB 1110, Calabar, Cross River State
Tel: +234(87) 222-303
Rector: R.E. Ekanem
Registrar: G.F.A. Onugba

Schools
Agriculture
Applied Sciences (Natural Sciences)
Business and Management (Business and Commerce; Management)
Communication Arts
Education
Engineering
Environmental Studies

Centres
Computer Science
Continuing Education

General and Preliminary Studies
Industrial Co-ordination and Public Relations (Industrial Management; Public Relations)

History: Founded 1973

POLYTECHNIC, IBADAN
PMB 22, U.I. Post Office, Ibadan, Oyo State
Tel: +234(22) 410-451
Telex: 31222 polyib ng

Rector: A.O. Alabi

Registrar: R.G. Olayiwola

Founded: 1960, 1970
Business and Commerce; Communication Studies; Engineering; Environmental Studies; Natural Sciences; Teacher Training

History: Founded 1960, acquired present status and title 1970.

Note: Also Federal and State Colleges of Education.

YABA COLLEGE OF TECHNOLOGY
PMB 2011, Yaba, Lagos State
Tel: +234(1) 800-160
Fax: +234(1) 860-211
Cable: tekinst
EMail: yabatech@anpa.net.ng
Website: http://www.yabatech.edu.ng

Rector: F.A. Odugbesan EMail: rector@yabatech.edu.ng

Registrar (Acting): F.F. Taiwo

Founded: 1947

Programmes
Technical Teachers Training (Teacher Training)

Schools
Applied Sciences (Applied Chemistry; Applied Mathematics; Applied Physics; Computer Science; Engineering)
Art, Design and Printing (Design; Fine Arts; Printing and Printmaking)
Engineering
Environmental Studies
Management and Business Studies (Business Administration; Management)

History: Founded 1947.

Rwanda

INSTITUTION TYPES AND CREDENTIALS

Types of higher education institutions:

Université (University)

Institut (Institute)

School leaving and higher education credentials:

Diplôme de Fin d'Etudes secondaires

Technicien supérieur

Baccalauréat

Diplôme

Bachelor's Degree

Diplôme d'Ingénieur

Maîtrise

Docteur en Médecine

STRUCTURE OF EDUCATION SYSTEM

Pre-higher education:

Duration of compulsory education:

　　Age of entry: 7
　　Age of exit: 13

Structure of school system:

　　Primary
　　Type of school providing this education: Primary School
　　Length of programme in years: 6
　　Age level from: 7 to: 13
　　Certificate/diploma awarded: Certificat national de sixième Année primaire (competitive examination)

　　First Cycle Secondary
　　Type of school providing this education: Tronc commun/Cycle d'Orientation
　　Length of programme in years: 3
　　Age level from: 13 to: 16
　　Certificate/diploma awarded: Certificat de Fin de Tronc commun

　　Second Cycle Secondary
　　Type of school providing this education: Sections moyennes générales

Length of programme in years: 3
Age level from: 16 to: 19
Certificate/diploma awarded: Diplôme de Fin d'Etudes secondaires

School education:

Primary education is compulsory and lasts for six years divided into two cycles, literacy (1-2) and general education (4-6). There is a competitive entrance examination at the end, the Certificat national de sixième Année primaire, to enter secondary school. Secondary education is divided into two three-year cycles. The first cycle is common to all pupils and leads to the Certificat de Fin de Tronc commun. The second cycle covers Modern or Classical Humanities. On successful completion of the second cycle, pupils are awarded the Diplôme de Fin d'Etudes secondaires. There is a variety of two-year technical secondary courses for pupils who have completed two to three years of academic secondary education, although pupils can also enter directly from primary school. Four-year technical courses are also offered.

Higher education:

Higher education is mainly provided by universities and specialized institutes, both public and private. Most institutions of higher education come under the jurisdiction of the Ministère de l'Education. The National University of Rwanda is an autonomous institution governed by a Council which is made up of a representative of the President of the Republic, the Minister of Education, the Rector and deans, the Secretary-General, the Treasurer and the Administrator. The Council proposes the creation of faculties, institutes, centres of research and university extension. It establishes the budget of the University and approves grants and donations. The Academic Senate coordinates academic activities. Members include the Vice-Rector, the deans of faculties, the heads of institutes, tenured professors and student representatives. The President of the Republic is Honorary President of the University. The Rector of the University is nominated by the President of the Republic for a three-year term which can be renewed, as are the Secretary-General and the Treasurer.

Main laws/decrees governing higher education:

Decree: Loi organique N° 1/1985 sur l'Education nationale   Year: 1985
Concerns: Organization of Education

Academic year:

Classes from: September *to:* June

Languages of instruction:

French, English

Stages of studies:

Non-university level post-secondary studies (technical/vocational type):

Higher technical and vocational studies are offered in universities and vocational institutions in Finance, Management, Computer Studies, Statistics, Economics and Secretarial Studies. Studies consist in short-term technical and professional education and lead to the title of Technicien supérieur after two years in Accountancy, Management, Computer Studies.

University level studies:

University level first stage: Premier Cycle:

The first stage of university-level studies lasts from two to three years (now three years) and leads to the Baccalauréat in Law, Science, Letters, Economics, Social Sciences, Human Biology, Management, Agriculture, Education, Nutrition, Public Health, Pharmacy and Engineering. Some institutions offer a Bachelor's Degree in four to five years.

University level second stage: Deuxième Cycle:

The second stage lasts between two and four years and leads to the Maîtrise or to the title of Ingénieur agronome or Ingénieur civil (five years). This second cycle lasts four years in Medicine, leading to the title of Docteur en Médecine, and three years in Pharmacy.

University level third stage: Troisième Cycle:

A third cycle leads to a Doctorate (with thesis) and to a Diplôme de Spécialisation in Medicine.

Teacher education:

Training of pre-primary and primary/basic school teachers

Primary school teachers are trained in secondary school teacher training institutions (Ecoles normales primaires) in a three-year post-tronc commun course (nine years of schooling). They obtain an A2 Diploma.

Training of secondary school teachers

Secondary school teachers must have a Baccalauréat to teach in the first cycle and a Maîtrise to teach in the second cycle. They may also follow refresher courses. Since 1999, secondary school teachers are also trained at the new Institut supérieur pédagogique (ISP) of Kigali. Training at ISP include two cycles: for admission to the first, students must hold a Diplôme de Fin d'Etudes secondaires. For the second cycle, they must hold a Baccalauréat in Pedagogy.

Training of higher education teachers

Higher education teachers are trained at the Université nationale du Rwanda. They must hold a Maitrîse or a Doctorat. They often go abroad to complete their training.

Non-traditional studies:

Lifelong higher education

Continuing education is mainly offered by the Extension Study Centre of the National University. It consists essentially in evening classes.

NATIONAL BODIES

Responsible authorities:

Ministry of Education, Science, Technology & Scientific Research (Ministère de l'Education, de la Science, de la Technologie et de la Recherche scientifique)
　　Secrétaire d'Etat: d'Arc Mujawamariya
　　International Relations: Casimir Rutayitera
　　PO Box 622

Kigali
Tel: +250 82-745
Fax: +250 82-162
EMail: info@mineduc.gov.rw
WWW: http://www.mineduc.gov.rw

ADMISSIONS TO HIGHER EDUCATION

Admission to non university higher education studies

Name of secondary school credential required: Diplôme de Fin d'Etudes secondaires

Admission to university-level studies

Name of secondary school credential required: Diplôme de Fin d'Etudes secondaires

Foreign students admission

Admission requirements: Foreign students must hold a secondary school leaving certificate or an equivalent qualification. They must pay registration fees that are higher than those paid by nationals.

Entry regulations: Students must have a valid passport, a visa, financial guarantees.

Health requirements: Students must have a health certificate

Language requirements: Students must be fluent in French but should also have some knowledge of English.

Application procedures:

Apply to individual institution for entry to: Universities

Apply to: Université nationale du Rwanda
PO Box 56
Butare
Tel: +250 530122
Fax: +250 530121
EMail: rectorat@nur.ac.rw
WWW: http://www.nur.ac.rw

Recognition of studies and qualifications:

Studies pursued in foreign countries (bodies dealing with recognition of foreign credentials): Ministry of Education, Science, Technology & Scientific Research (Ministère de l'Education, de la Science, de la Technologie et de la Recherche scientifique)
Secrétaire d'Etat: d'Arc Mujawamariya
International Relations: Casimir Rutayitera
PO Box 622
Kigali
Tel: +250 82-745
Fax: +250 82-162

EMail: info@mineduc.gov.rw
WWW: http://www.mineduc.gov.rw
Deals with credential recognition for entry to: University

Multilateral agreements concerning recognition of foreign studies

Name(s) of agreement(s): Convention on the Recognition of Studies,Certificates, Diplomas, Degrees and Other Academic Qualifications in Higher Education in the African States
Year of signature: 1981

References to further information on foreign student admissions and recognition of studies

Title: Annuaire de l'Université
Publisher: Université nationale du Rwanda

Title: Guide de l'Etudiant
Publisher: Université nationale du Rwanda

GRADING SYSTEM

Usual grading system in secondary school

Full Description: 50%-90%
Highest on scale: 90% plus grande distinction
Pass/fail level: 50% satisfaction

Main grading system used by higher education institutions

Full Description: 50%-90%
Highest on scale: 90% plus grande distinction
Pass/fail level: 50%-69% satisfaction

NOTES ON HIGHER EDUCATION SYSTEM

Data for academic year: 2002-2003
Source: International Association of Universities (IAU), updated from IBE website, 2003
(www.ibe.unesco.org/International/Databanks/Wde/profilee.htm)

INSTITUTIONS OF HIGHER EDUCATION

UNIVERSITIES AND UNIVERSITY LEVEL INSTITUTIONS

PUBLIC INSTITUTIONS

Academic Staff *2001-2002*   TOTAL
FULL-TIME   162
PART-TIME   39
TOTAL   **201**
Staff with doctorate: Total: **26**
Student Numbers *2001-2002*: Total: **3,292**

• KIGALI INSTITUTE OF SCIENCE, TECHNOLOGY AND MANAGEMENT
Institut des Sciences, de Technologie et de Gestion de Kigali (KIST)
BP 3900, Avenue de l'Armée, Kigali
Tel: +250 574-698
Fax: +250 571-924
EMail: info@kist.ac.rw
Website: http://www.kist.ac.rw

Recteur: Silas B. Lwakabamba (1997-) Tel: +250 574-696
Fax: +250 571-925 EMail: rector@kist.ac.rw

Vice-Recteur, Administration et Finance: George Katureebe EMail: gkatureebe@yahoo.com

International Relations: Pierre Karekezi K.
EMail: pierre@avu.org

Faculties
Management (Accountancy; Business Administration; Finance; Human Resources; Management; Marketing; Tourism)
Science (Chemistry; Mathematics; Mathematics and Computer Science; Natural Sciences; Physics; Statistics)
Technology (Civil Engineering; Computer Engineering; Electrical and Electronic Engineering; Environmental Engineering; Food Science; Food Technology; Hydraulic Engineering; Information Technology; Mechanical Engineering; Technology; Telecommunications Engineering)

Schools
Language Studies (African Languages; English; French; Modern Languages)

Centres
Continuing Education

History: Founded 1997.

Main Language(s) of Instruction: English and French

Degrees and Diplomas: *Diplôme*: Management; Automotive, Environmental, Information, Computer, Electronic and Food Technology; Civil, Computer, Electronic, Communications and Electromechanical Engineering; Food Science, 3 1/2 yrs; *Bachelor's Degree*: Business Administration; Commerce; Civil, Computer, Electrical, Electronic, Communications and Mechanical Engineering; Environmental, Information and Food Technology; Food Science (BA, BSc), 4 1/2-5 1/2 yrs

Libraries: Central Library, c. 8000 vols

• NATIONAL UNIVERSITY OF RWANDA
Université nationale du Rwanda (UNR)
BP 56, Butaré
Tel: +250 530-122 +250 530-160
Fax: +250 530-210
EMail: rectorat@nur.ac.rw;secvrac@nur.ac.rw
Website: http://www.nur.ac.rw

Recteur: Emile Rwamasirabo (1998-) Tel: +250 530-053
Fax: +250 530-121 EMail: rector@nur.ac.rw

Vice-Recteur Académique: Silas Mureramanzi
Tel: +250 530-160 Fax: +250 530-210
EMail: secvrac@nur.ac.rw

Vice-Recteur Administratif et Financier: Canisius Karuranga Tel: +250 530-177 Fax: +250 530-105
EMail: vraf@nur.ac.rw

Faculties
Agronomy (Agronomy; Animal Husbandry; Crop Production; Rural Studies; Soil Science) *Dean*: Canisius Kanangire
Arts and Humanities (African Studies; Arts and Humanities; English; French Studies; Geography; History; Literature) *Dean*: Deo Byanafashe
Economics, Social Sciences and Management (Accountancy; Anthropology; Banking; Business Administration; Development Studies; Economics; Finance; Human Resources; International Business; Management; Marketing; Political Science; Public Administration; Social Sciences; Social Work; Sociology; Tourism; Transport and Communications) *Dean*: Gérard Rutazibwa
Education (Arts and Humanities; Continuing Education; Education; Educational Sciences; Pedagogy; Psychology; Science Education) *Dean*: Jean Pierre Dusingizemungu
Law (Administration; Business and Commerce; Economics; Law) *Dean*: Louis Gatete
Medicine (Anaesthesiology; Anatomy; Biochemistry; Biology; Chemistry; Entomology; Epidemiology; Ethics; Gynaecology and Obstetrics; Immunology; Medical Technology; Medicine; Orthopedics; Paediatrics; Pharmacology; Philosophy; Physics; Physiology; Psychology; Surgery; Virology) *Dean*: Alexis Nyakayiro
Science and Technology (Biology; Chemistry; Civil Engineering; Computer Science; Electronic Engineering; Mathematics; Mechanical Engineering; Natural Sciences; Pharmacy; Physics; Technology) *Dean*: Safari Bonfils

Schools

Journalism and Communication *(EJC)* (Journalism; Mass Communication) *Director:* Jean Pierre Gatsinki

Modern Languages *(EPLM)* (English; French; Modern Languages) *Director:* Ildephonse Kereni

Public Health and Nutrition *(ESPN)* (Nutrition; Public Health) *Director:* Cyprien Munyanshongore

Centres

Arts and Drama (Cinema and Television; Dance; Music; Theatre)

Conflict Management (Peace and Disarmament)

Geographic Information Systems and Remote Sensing Regional Outreach (Geography; Surveying and Mapping)

Instructional Technology *(CIT)* (Educational Technology)

Mental Health *(UCMH)* (Psychiatry and Mental Health)

Research Centres

Human Sciences Contemporary Studies *(CERCOSH)* (Social Sciences)

History: Founded 1963 as a national institution and its initial organization and direction entrusted to the Dominican Order, Province of St. Dominic, Canada. Reorganized 1976 and Institut pédagogique national incorporated 1981.

Governing Bodies: Conseil universitaire, including a representative of the President of the Republic, the Minister of Education, the Rector, Vice-Rector and Deans; Sénat académique; Conseil de Faculté

Academic Year: May to February (May-September; October-February)

Admission Requirements: Secondary school certificate (Diplôme des Humanités complètes) or equivalent, or foreign equivalent

Main Language(s) of Instruction: French, English

Degrees and Diplomas: *Baccalauréat:* Agriculture; Economics; Education; Human Biology; Law; Letters; Management; Nutrition; Pharmacy; Public Health; Science; Social Sciences, 2 yrs; *Diplôme d'Ingénieur:* Engineering, 3 yrs; Agriculture, 5 yrs; *Maîtrise:* Economics; Education; Law; Letters; Management; Pharmacy; Science; Social Sciences, 4-5 yrs; *Docteur en Médecine:* Médecine, 6 yrs

Student Services: Social Counselling, Employment Services, Nursery Care, Cultural Centre, Handicapped Facilities, Health Services, Canteen

Student Residential Facilities: For c. 1620 students

Libraries: Central Library, c. 170,000 vols; Faculty of Medicine, c. 13,500

Academic Staff *2001-2002:* Full-Time: c. 165 Part-Time: c. 360 Total: c. 525

Student Numbers *2001-2002:* All (Foreign Included): c. 4,200 Foreign Only: c. 95

Evening Students, c. 2,600

PRIVATE INSTITUTIONS

ADVENTIST UNIVERSITY OF CENTRAL AFRICA

Université adventiste d'Afrique centrale (UAAC)
BP 2461, Kigali
Tel: +250 87147
Fax: +250 87147
EMail: auca@rwandatel1.rwanda1.com

Recteur: Jozsef Szilvasi (2001-)
EMail: szilvasij@hotmail.com

Administrateur: Samuel Gatoya-Habimana

International Relations: Jozsef Szilvasi, Recteur

Faculties

Business Administration (Administration; Business and Commerce; Computer Engineering) *Dean:* Abel Ngabo Sebahashyi

Education (Education; Modern Languages) *Dean:* Ephraim Kanyarukiga

Theology (Holy Writings; Religious Studies; Theology) *Dean:* Issacar Ntakirutimana

History: Founded 1978. Opened 1984.

Governing Bodies: Senate; Executive Committee

Academic Year: October to August

Admission Requirements: Secondary school certificate and entrance examination

Fees: (Rwanda Francs): c. 100,000 per semester

Main Language(s) of Instruction: French and English

Degrees and Diplomas: *Bachelor's Degree:* Business Administration; Education; Theology, 4 yrs

Student Services: Academic Counselling, Employment Services, Sports Facilities, Language Programmes, Canteen

Student Residential Facilities: None

Special Facilities: Computer Laboratory

Libraries: 20,000 vols

Publications: Student Yearbook (annually)

Academic Staff 2001-2002	MEN	WOMEN	TOTAL
FULL-TIME	17	3	20
PART-TIME	21	–	21
TOTAL	**38**	**3**	**41**

STAFF WITH DOCTORATE		
FULL-TIME		2
PART-TIME		3
TOTAL		**5**

Student Numbers 2001-2002	MEN	WOMEN	TOTAL
All (Foreign Included)	284	267	**551**
FOREIGN ONLY	2	–	2

KABGAYI CATHOLIC UNIVERSITY

Université catholique de Kabgayi (UCK)
Kabgayi, Gitarama
Tel: +250 563-155
EMail: uckabgayi@yahoo.fr

History: Founded 2002.

KIBONGO UNIVERSITY OF AGRICULTURE, TECHNOLOGY AND EDUCATION

Université d'Agriculture, de Technologie et d'Education de Kibungo (UNATEK)
BP 6, Kibongo
Tel: +250 566-693
EMail: musugwasi@yahoo.fr

Recteur: Sigfred Musangwa (2002-)
EMail: musangwasi@yahoo.fr

Agriculture; Education; Technology

History: Founded 2002.

KIGALI ADVENTIST UNIVERSITY

Université laïque adventiste de Kigali (UNILAK)
BP 592/6392, Kigali
Tel: +250 512-101
EMail: unilak@hotmail.com

KIGALI INDEPENDENT UNIVERSITY

Université libre de Kigali (ULK)
BP 2280, Kigali
Tel: +250 502-416 +250 502-417
Fax: +250 502-422
EMail: ulk@rwandatel1.rwanda1.com;info@ukl.ac.rw
Website: http://www.ulk.ac.rw

Recteur: Rwigamba Balinda (1996-)

Faculties
Economics and Management (Economics; Management)
Law
Social Sciences

History: Founded 1996. Acquired present status 1998.

394

OTHER INSTITUTIONS

PUBLIC INSTITUTIONS

BUSOGO INSTITUTE OF AGRICULTURE AND CATTLE BREEDING

Institut supérieur d'Agriculture et d'Élevage de Busogo (ISAE)
BP 210 Ruhengeri, Busogo, Ruhengeri
Tel: +250 516-045 +250 516-264
Fax: +250 516-265
EMail: isaedir@yahoo.fr
Founded: 1989
Agriculture; Cattle Breeding

History: Founded 1989

KIGALI HEALTH INSTITUTE

Institut supérieur de Santé de Kigali (KHI)
BP 3286, Kigali
Tel: +250 572-172 +250 571-788
Fax: +250 571-787
EMail: khi@africamail.com
Website: http://www.khi.ac.rw

Directrice: Thérèse Bishagara (1996-)
EMail: bishagara@yahoo.fr

Directeur Adjoint, Affaires Académiques: Jean-Marie Vianney Makuza EMail: makuzajmv@yahoo.fr

Directeur Adjoint, Affaires Administratives et Financières: Canisius Kayijaho EMail: kayijaho@yahoo.fr

Founded: 1996

Departments
Anaesthesiology
Dentistry
Laboratory Techniques
Mental Health (Psychiatry and Mental Health)
Nursing
Physiotherapy (Physical Therapy)
Radiology

KIGALI INSTITUTE OF EDUCATION

Institut supérieur pédagogique de Kigali (KIE)
BP 5039, Kigali
Tel: +250 86885
Fax: +250 86890
EMail: admin@kie.ac.rw
Website: http://www.kie.ac.rw

Recteur: Emmanuel Mudidi (2001-)

Vice-Recteur, Affaires académiques: Béatrice Mukabaranga EMail: b_mukabaranga@yahoo.com

Directeur, Affaires académiques: Augustin Ngabirame EMail: a_ngabirame@yahoo.fr

Founded: 1999

Faculties

Arts and Social Sciences (Arts and Humanities; Social Sciences)

Education

Science (Natural Sciences)

Programmes

Continuing Education

Distance Training

Great Lakes Documentation Network (African Studies)

Secretarial Studies

Note: In process of creation: Institut polytechnique de Byumba and Université internationale du Rwanda à Ruhengeri

SCHOOL OF FINANCE AND BANKING (SFP)
BP 1514, Kigali
Tel: +250 72513

Founded: 1986

Banking; Finance; Public Administration; Taxation

History: Founded 1986

PRIVATE INSTITUTIONS

GITWE INSTITUTE OF EDUCATION
Institut supérieur pédagogique de Gitwe (ISPG)
BP 1, Nyabisindu, Gitwe, Gitarama
Tel: +250 573-238

Directeur: Marc Habineza

Education

Senegal

INSTITUTION TYPES AND CREDENTIALS

Types of higher education institutions:

Université (University)
Grande Ecole (Higher School)
Ecole normale supérieure (Teacher Training College)
Ecole supérieure de Technologie (Technological College)
Institut (Institute)

School leaving and higher education credentials:

Baccalauréat
Baccalauréat technique
Capacité en Droit
Diplôme d'Etudes économiques générales (DEEG)
Diplôme d'Etudes juridiques générales (DEJG)
Diplôme d'Etudes universitaires générales (DEUG)
Diplôme universitaire d'Etudes littéraires (DUEL)
Diplôme universitaire d'Etudes scientifiques (DUES)
Diplôme universitaire de Technologie (DUT)
Certificat d'Aptitude à l'Enseignement dans les Collèges d'Enseignement moyen
Diplôme de Bibliothécaire/Archiviste/Documentaliste
Diplôme supérieur de Journalisme
Licence
Section des Normaliens-Instituteurs
Certificat d'Aptitude à l'Enseignement moyen
Certificat d'Aptitude à l'Enseignement moyen technique et professionnel
Certificat d'Aptitude aux fonctions de Professeur d'Education physique et sportive
Diplôme d'Ingénieur
Diplôme de Pharmacien
Maîtrise
Certificat d'Aptitude à l'Enseignement secondaire
Certificat d'Aptitude à l'Enseignement secondaire technique et professionnel
Certificat d'Aptitude aux fonctions de Psychologue-Conseiller
Certificat d'Etudes supérieures
Diplôme d'Etat de Docteur
Diplôme d'Etudes supérieures spécialisées (DESS)
Diplôme supérieur en Sciences de l'Information

Diplôme d'Etudes Approfondies (DEA)
Certificat d' Etudes spéciales (CES)
Doctorat d'Ingénieur
Doctorat de Troisième Cycle
Doctorat d'Etat

STRUCTURE OF EDUCATION SYSTEM

Pre-higher education:

Structure of school system:

Primary
Type of school providing this education: Ecole élémentaire
Length of programme in years: 6
Age level from: 6 to: 12
Certificate/diploma awarded: Certificat de Fin d'Etudes élémentaires (CFEE) and concours d'entrée en sixième

First Cycle Secondary
Type of school providing this education: Collège d'Enseignement moyen (CEM) or Lycée
Length of programme in years: 4
Age level from: 12 to: 16
Certificate/diploma awarded: Brevet de Fin d'Etudes moyennes (BFEM)

Technical Secondary
Type of school providing this education: Centre de Formation
Length of programme in years: 3
Age level from: 12 to: 16
Certificate/diploma awarded: Certificat d'Aptitude Professionnelle (CAP)

Second Cycle Secondary
Type of school providing this education: Lycée d'Enseignement général or Lycée Technique
Length of programme in years: 3
Age level from: 16 to: 19
Certificate/diploma awarded: Baccalauréat/Baccalauréat Technique

Vocational Secondary
Type of school providing this education: Technical/vocational Secondary School
Length of programme in years: 2
Age level from: 16 to: 18
Certificate/diploma awarded: Brevet de Technicien

School education:

Primary education lasts for six years, leading to the Certificat de Fin d'Etudes élémentaires (CFEE). Secondary schooling lasts for seven years, divided into four-year lower secondary and three-year upper secondary education. The lower cycle is offered by CEMs or Lycées, and leads to the Brevet de Fin d'Etudes moyennes (BFEM). The three-year upper cycle has four options (general, short and long technical and professionnal) and leads to the Baccalauréat, which may be taken in various sections depending on the specialization taken in the last two years.

Programmes offered by vocational schools range from three to four years in length at the first cycle of secondary education level. Three-year programmes are offered at Centres de Formation, leading to the Certificat d'Aptitude Professionnelle (CAP). Technicians' diplomas are also offered in other professional fields according to specialization. Technical education follows the completion of first-cycle secondary education and requires the BFEM. It either produces foremen and technicians or prepares candidates for post-secondary technical education. Students who have completed the two to three years required programmes obtain a Brevet de Technicien. Students may also continue through the fourth year of a technical lycée to obtain a Diplôme de Bachelier Technicien.

Higher education:

Access to higher education is based on the Baccalauréat or an equivalent qualification. Those who do not hold the Baccalauréat may enrol in universities if they have passed a special entrance examination or if they have received dispensation from a special committee. In addition, each institution lays down its own requirements. Higher education is provided by three universities (which are responsible to the Ministry of Education), and other higher colleges (e.g. Ecole normale supérieure) founded for the training of scientific, technical, teaching and administrative personnel. There are also research institutes and Grandes Ecoles - entry to which requires a special examination - which are similar to those in France and offer specialized courses.

Main laws/decrees governing higher education:

Decree: loi 91-22 d'Orientation de l'Education nationale   Year: 1991
Concerns: Organization of the educational system

Decree: Law   Year: 1971
Concerns: University

Decree: Law   Year: 1970
Concerns: University

Academic year:

Classes from: October *to:* July

Long vacation from: 1 August *to:* 1 October

Languages of instruction:

French

Stages of studies:

University level studies:

University level first stage: *Premier Cycle*:
The first stage or cycle of higher education offers multidisciplinary and basic studies. Two years' study in Humanities lead to the Diplôme universitaire d'Etudes littéraires (DUEL), in Science to the

Diplôme universitaire d'Etudes scientifiques (DUES), in Law and Economics to the Diplôme d'Etudes juridiques générales (DEJG) or économiques générales (DEEG). No qualification is awarded in Medicine and Pharmacy. Holders of the DUES may take the competitive entrance examination for the Grandes Ecoles of Engineering. Studies at the Ecole Nationale supérieure de Technologie (ENSUT) lead after two years to a Diplôme universitaire de Technologie (DUT). In Law, students may enter the university without the Baccalauréat for a two-year course leading to the qualification of Capacité en Droit. They may then enrol in the three-year Law degree course.

University level second stage: Deuxième Cycle:

The second stage (one further year of specialization) leads to the Licence. Students holding the Licence may undertake a one-year postgraduate course leading to the Maîtrise. In Law and Economics, studies lead to the Maîtrise in two years directly after the DEJG or DEEG. In Pharmacy, Dentistry and Veterinary Medicine, the first qualifications, obtained after five years or six years, are the Diplôme de Pharmacien, the Diplôme d'Etat de Docteur en Chirurgie Dentaire and the Doctorat d'Etat en Médecine vétérinaire respectively. In Medicine, the Diplôme d'Etat de Docteur en Médecine is obtained after seven years. In Engineering, a Dipôme d'Ingénieur is conferred.

University level third stage: Troisième Cycle:

At least one year's research following the Maîtrise leads to the Diplôme d'Etudes approfondies (DEA) and at least a further two years to the Doctorat de troisième Cycle. With either qualification students may undertake a minimum of two years' research and present a thesis in Law, Economics, Arts and Science, leading to the Doctorat d'Etat. This qualification is necessary to teach in higher education.

Teacher education:

Training of pre-primary and primary/basic school teachers

Training of elementary school teachers is offered by Ecoles de Formation des Instituteurs (EFI), which provide three-year programmes at the upper secondary level. Completion of the three-year programme leads to the Baccalauréat or the Certificat d'Aptitude Pédagogique (CAP).

A one-year instituteur adjoint programme leading to the Certificat Elémentaire d'Aptitude Pédagogique (CEAP) is available at the Centres régionaux de Formation pédagogique to holders of the BEFM.

Training of secondary school teachers

A two-year postsecondary programme at the Ecole Normale Supérieure (ENS), which is part of the Université Cheikh Anta Diop de Dakar, prepares teachers for the lower secondary schools, and a four-year post-secondary programme at the university, in collaboration with the ENS, prepares teachers for upper secondary school. Graduates of the ENS usually teach in CEMs, while those from the university generally teach in Lycées. The ENS provides four courses: history/geography, English, mathematics and physics/chemistry, and natural science, leading to the Certificat d'Aptitude pédagogiques (CAP). Licence holders follow a one-year course leading to a Certificat d'Aptitude à l'Enseignement moyen (CAEM) or to the Certificat d'Aptitude au Professorat de l'Enseignement secondaire (CAPES) ou technique (CAPET).

The Centre national de Formation des Instructeurs and the Ecole normale d'Enseignement technique masculin train vocational and technical instructors. Students at these centres obtain the Certificat d'Aptitude pédagogique (CAP).

The Ecole normale nationale d'Enseignement Technique féminin prepares female vocational and technical teachers. The school provides three programmes at the upper secondary level to train instituteurs adjoints in commercial home economics, and the Centre national de Formation de Monitrices rurales provides programmes to train rural home economics teachers. Both schools award the Certificat d'Aptitude pédagogique (CAP).

Training of higher education teachers
University teachers must hold a Doctorat d'Etat and be listed on a "liste d'aptitude". In Law, Economics and Medical fields, the Agrégation (delivered by the Conseil Africain et Malgache pour l'Enseignement supérieur (CAMES)) is necessary.

Non-traditional studies:

Lifelong higher education
Non-formal education is provided in the form of short courses in: Mechanics, Rural Engineering, Child Health Protection, Law and Economics.

NATIONAL BODIES

Responsible authorities:

Ministry of National Education (Ministère de l'Education nationale)
Minister: Moustapha Sourang
BP 4025
Rue Dr Calmette
Dakar
Tel: +221 821-0881
Fax: +221 821-4755
Telex: 3239 miensup sg
WWW: http://www.education.gouv.sn

ADMISSIONS TO HIGHER EDUCATION

Admission to university-level studies

Name of secondary school credential required: Baccalauréat

Name of secondary school credential required: Baccalauréat technique

Alternatives to credentials: Examen spécial d'entrée (Special entrance examination).

Numerus clausus/restrictions: Access is by merit (best marks in the Baccalauréat) depending on the number of places in the universities.

Foreign students admission

Admission requirements: Foreign students should hold the Baccalauréat or its equivalent. They must not be over 22 to enter Medicine and not over 23 for the other faculties.

Entry regulations: Students must be in possession of a visa. Applications by African candidates must be sponsored by their national governments. Students of the Sudano-Sahelian area are given priority. Applications from outside Africa are considered individually, although the university requirements may not be waived.

Language requirements: Students must have a good command of French. Courses are provided by the Institut français pour les étudiants étrangers, Université Cheikh Anta Diop, Dakar.

Recognition of studies and qualifications:

Studies pursued in foreign countries (bodies dealing with recognition of foreign credentials):
Rectorat, Université Cheikh Anta Diop (University of Dakar)
>B.P. 5005
>Dakar
>Tel: +221 825-7528
>Fax: +221 825-3724
>Telex: 51262 sg
>Cable: unidak.sg
>EMail: info@ucad.sn
>WWW: http://www.ucad.sn

Multilateral agreements concerning recognition of foreign studies

Name(s) of agreement(s): Convention on the Recognition of Studies, Certificates, Diplomas, Degrees and Other Academic Qualifications in Higher Education in the African States
Year of signature: 1981

References to further information on foreign student admissions and recognition of studies

Title: Guide de l'Etudiant
Publisher: Université Cheikh Anta Diop

STUDENT LIFE

Main student services at national level

Centre des Oeuvres universitaires de Dakar
>B.P. 2056
>Route de Ouakam
>Dakar
>Services available to foreign Students: Yes

Student expenses and financial aid

Student costs:
>Home students tuition fees: Minimum: 655,000 (CFA Franc)
>Maximum: 1,850,000 (CFA Franc)

Bodies providing information on student financial aid:

Direction des Bourses

  143 Avenue Lamine Gueye
  Building Maginot
  Dakar
  Tel: +221 821-3822

Publications on student services and financial aid:

  Title: Study Abroad 2004-2005, 32nd Edition
  Author: UNESCO
  Publisher: UNESCO Publishing
  Year of publication: 2003

INTERNATIONAL COOPERATION AND EXCHANGES

Principal national bodies responsible for dealing with international cooperation and exchanges in higher education:

Direction de l'Enseignement supérieur, Ministère de l'Education nationale

  BP 4025
  Rue Dr Calmette
  Dakar
  Tel: +221 821-0881
  Fax: +221 821-4755
  Telex: 3239 miensup sg
  WWW: http://www.education.gouv.sn

GRADING SYSTEM

Usual grading system in secondary school

Full Description: Marking is on a scale of 0-20 (maximum); 10 is the minimum pass mark (16-20: très bien/very good; 14-15: bien/good; 12-13: assez bien/quite good; 10-11: passable/average).
Highest on scale: 20
Pass/fail level: 10
Lowest on scale: 0

Main grading system used by higher education institutions

Full Description: Grades : 0-20 (16-20 : Très Bien; 14-15 : Bien; 12-13 : Assez Bien; 10-11 : Passable)
Highest on scale: 20
Pass/fail level: 10
Lowest on scale: 0

NOTES ON HIGHER EDUCATION SYSTEM

Data for academic year: 2002-2003

Source: International Association of Universities (IAU), updated from IBE website, 2003
(http://www.ibe.unesco.org/International/Databanks/Wde/profilee.htm)

INSTITUTIONS OF HIGHER EDUCATION

UNIVERSITIES

• GASTON BERGER UNIVERSITY OF SAINT-LOUIS

Université Gaston Berger de Saint-Louis (UGB)
BP 234, Saint-Louis
Tel: +221 961-1884
Fax: +221 961-1884
Telex: 75 128 UNIV. SI/SG
Website: http://www.ugb.sn

Recteur: Ndiawar Sarr (1999-) Tel: +221 961-2270
Fax: +221 961-5139 EMail: cabinet@ugb.sn;ndsarr@ugb.sn

Secrétaire général: Papa Sékou Sonko Tel: +221 961-2271

Units

Applied Science and Computer Science (Applied Mathematics; Computer Science; Physics) *Head*: Mary Teuw Niane
Arts and Humanities (Applied Linguistics; Arts and Humanities; English; French; Geography; Modern Languages; Sociology) *Head*: Gora Mbodj
Economics and Management (Agricultural Business; Economics; Management) *Head*: Adama Diaw
Law and Political Science (Law; Political Science) *Head*: Abdoullah Cissé

History: Founded 1990. Acquired present status 1996.

Governing Bodies: Assemblée

Academic Year: October to July

Admission Requirements: Secondary school certificate (baccalauréat)

Main Language(s) of Instruction: French

International Co-operation: With universities in Mauritania; Gabon; Mali; USA; Italy; France; Cameroon; Austria

Degrees and Diplomas: *Diplôme d'Etudes universitaires générales (DEUG)*: 2 yrs; *Licence*: 3 yrs; *Maîtrise*: 1 further yr; *Diplôme d'Etudes Approfondies (DEA)*: 5 yrs; *Doctorat de Troisième Cycle*; *Doctorat d'Etat*

Student Services: Academic Counselling, Social Counselling, Cultural Centre, Sports Facilities, Handicapped Facilities, Health Services, Canteen, Foreign Student Centre

Libraries: 18,500 vols

Publications: URED (Revue Scientifique)

Academic Staff 2001-2002	TOTAL
FULL-TIME	97
PART-TIME	140
TOTAL	**237**

Student Numbers 2001-2002: Total: **2,663**

• UNIVERSITY CHEIKH ANTA DIOP OF DAKAR

Université Cheikh Anta Diop de Dakar
BP 5005, Dakar-Fann
Tel: +221 825-7528
Fax: +221 825-3724
EMail: info@ucad.sn
Website: http://www.ucad.sn

Recteur: Abdou Salam Sall Tel: +221 825-7580
Fax: +221 825-2883 EMail: rectorat@ucad.sn

Secrétaire général: Abdoul Wahab Kâ Tel: +221 240-586

International Relations: Amadou Ly

Faculties

Arts and Humanities (Arabic; Arts and Humanities; English; Geography; German; History; Linguistics; Literature; Philosophy; Portuguese; Psychology; Social Sciences; Sociology; Spanish)
Economics and Management (Business Administration; Development Studies; Economics; Management)
Law and Political Science (Administrative Law; Constitutional Law; Finance; International Law; Law; Political Science) *Dean*: Moustapha Sourang
Medicine, Pharmacy and Odonto-Stomatology (Dentistry; Medicine; Pharmacy; Stomatology) *Dean*: René D. Ndoye
Science and Technology (Natural Sciences; Technology)

Schools

Librarians, Archivists and Documentalists *(EBAD)* (Archiving; Documentation Techniques; Information Sciences; Library Science)
Teacher Training *(Ecole normale supérieure (ENS))* *Directeur*: Valdiodio Ndiaye

Higher Schools

Polytechnic *(ESP (Also branch in Thiès))* (Artificial Intelligence; Automation and Control Engineering; Biochemistry; Biology; Biotechnology; Building Technologies; Chemical Engineering; Civil Engineering; Computer Science; Construction Engineering; Electrical Engineering; Engineering; Heating and Refrigeration; Management; Materials Engineering; Microbiology; Technology; Telecommunications Engineering) *Directeur*: Abib Ngom

Institutes

Applied Nuclear Technology *(ITNA)* (Nuclear Engineering)
Applied Tropical Medicine *(IMTA)* (Tropical Medicine)
French for Foreign Students *(IFE)* (French)
Health and Development *(ISD)* (Development Studies; Health Sciences)
Human Rights and Peace *(IDHP)* (Human Rights; Peace and Disarmament)
Social Paediatrics *(IPS)* (Paediatrics)

Higher Institutes
Popular Education and Sport *(INSEPS)* (Physical Education; Sports)

Centres
Applied Linguistics *(CLAD)* (Applied Linguistics; English; French)
Information Sciences and Techniques *(CESTI)* (Cinema and Television; Information Sciences; Journalism; Photography; Radio and Television Broadcasting)
Psychological Research *(CRPP)* (Psychiatry and Mental Health; Psychology)
Renewable Energies Research *(CERER)* (Natural Resources)

Research Institutes
Mathematics, Physics and Technology Teaching *(IREMPT)* (Mathematics Education; Physics; Science Education; Technology Education)

History: Founded 1918 as Ecole de Médecine, became Institut des hautes Etudes 1950 and University by decree 1957. A State institution.

Governing Bodies: Assemblée

Academic Year: October to July (October-February; March-July)

Admission Requirements: Secondary school certificate (baccalauréat) or recognized equivalent, and entrance examination

Main Language(s) of Instruction: French

International Co-operation: UNESCO Chair in Educational Sciences

Degrees and Diplomas: *Capacité en Droit*; *Diplôme d'Etudes économiques générales (DEEG)*: Economics, 2 yrs; *Diplôme d'Etudes juridiques générales (DEJG)*: Law, 2 yrs; *Diplôme universitaire d'Etudes littéraires (DUEL)*: Arts and Humanities, 2 yrs; *Diplôme universitaire d'Etudes scientifiques (DUES)*: 2 yrs; *Diplôme universitaire de Technologie (DUT)*: 2 yrs; *Certificat d'Aptitude à l'Enseignement dans les Collèges d'Enseignement moyen*; *Diplôme de Bibliothécaire/Archiviste/Documentaliste*: Library Science, 2 yrs; *Diplôme supérieur de Journalisme*: Journalism; *Licence*: Arts and Humanities; Science, 1 yr following DUES; *Certificat d'Aptitude à l'Enseignement moyen*; *Diplôme d'Ingénieur*: 3 yrs following DUT; *Diplôme de Pharmacien*: Pharmacy, 5 yrs; *Maîtrise*: Arts and Humanities; Science, 1 yr following Licence; Economics; Law, a further 2 yrs; *Certificat d'Aptitude à l'Enseignement secondaire*; *Certificat d'Etudes supérieures*: Economics; Law, 1 yr following Maîtrise; *Diplôme d'Etat de Docteur*: Dental Surgery, 5 yrs; *Diplôme d'Etudes supérieures spécialisées (DESS)*: Financial Management, 2 yrs following Maîtrise; *Diplôme supérieur en Sciences de l'Information*: Information Sciences; *Diplôme d'Etudes Approfondies (DEA)*: Arts and Humanities; Economics; Engineering; Law; Science, 2 yrs following Maîtrise; *Certificat d'Etudes spéciales (CES)*: 4 yrs following Doctor of Medicine; *Doctorat d'Etat*: Veterinary Medicine, 6 yrs; Medicine, 7 yrs; Pharmacy, 8-9 yrs. Also technical qualifications.

Student Residential Facilities: Yes

Special Facilities: Ethnology Museum; History Museum; Marine Museum

Libraries: c. 400,000 vols; faculty libraries

Publications: L'Enfant en Milieu tropical (monthly); Cancérologie tropicale (biannually); Annales africaines (Faculty of Law); Annales de la Faculté des Sciences; Bulletin et Mémoires de la Faculté de Médecine et Pharmacie (annually); Revue de Géographie d'Afrique Occidentale; Médecine d'Afrique noire; Bulletin de la Société médicale d'Afrique noire de Langue française; Notes africaines; Afrique médicale; Bulletin de l'Institut français d'Afrique noire; Psychopathologie africaine

Press or Publishing House: Presses Universitaires de Dakar

Academic Staff *2001-2002:* Total: c. 700

Student Numbers *2001-2002:* Total: c. 22,000

INSTITUTE OF BLACK AFRICAN STUDIES AND
RESEARCH
INSTITUT FONDAMENTAL D'AFRIQUE NOIRE CHEIKH
ANTA DIOP (IFAN/CAD)
BP 206, Dakar
Tel: +221 250-090
Fax: +221 244-918

Directeur: Djibril Sahib

Departments
African Literature and Civilization (African Studies; Anthropology; Islamic Studies; Linguistics)
Animal Biology (Biology; Marine Biology; Zoology)
Botany and Geology (Botany; Geology)
Humanities (Anthropology; Arts and Humanities; Geography; History; Prehistory; Social Sciences; Sociology)
Scientific Information (Information Sciences)

History: Founded 1936.

UNIVERSITY OF THE SAHEL
Université du Sahel (UNIS)
BP 5355 33, Mermoz, Dakar, 5355
Tel: +221 860-9975
Fax: +221 860-9975
EMail: unis@refer.sn
Website: http://www.cyg.sn/unis/

Président: El Hadji Issa Sall

Administrative Officer: Mounina Sy

International Relations: Assane Diouf

Programmes
Documentation Studies (Documentation Techniques)
History of Science (History; Natural Sciences)

Schools
Economics and Administration (Accountancy; Business Administration; Business and Commerce; Computer Science; Economics; Finance; Health Administration; Marketing) *Director*: Moustapha Thioune

Educational Sciences (Curriculum; Educational Sciences; Educational Testing and Evaluation; Literacy Education; Pedagogy) *Director*: Badara Sall

Law and Political Science (International Relations; Law; Political Science) *Director*: Marie-Pierre Sarr Traore

Letters and Civilizations (African Studies; American Studies; Arabic; Asian Studies; English; European Studies; French; Linguistics; Modern Languages; Philosophy) *Director*: Badara Sall

Science, Engineering and Technology (Agronomy; Architecture; Biology; Chemical Engineering; Chemistry; Civil Engineering; Computer Science; Electrical Engineering; Engineering; Environmental Studies; Forestry; Genetics; Geology; Mathematics; Mechanical Engineering; Physics; Rural Studies; Science Education; Technology; Telecommunications Engineering) *Director*: Khadir Diop

Social Sciences (Anthropology; Geography; History; Psychology; Social Sciences; Sociology) *Director*: Mouhamadou Dieye

History: Founded 1998.

Admission Requirements: Baccalauréat or equivalent

Fees: (CFA Francs): c. 655,000 per annum

Main Language(s) of Instruction: French

International Co-operation: With institutions in France, United States, Switzerland

Degrees and Diplomas: *Diplôme d'Etudes universitaires générales (DEUG)*: 2 yrs; *Licence*: 3 yrs; *Maîtrise*: 4 yrs; Engineering, 5 yrs; *Diplôme d'Etudes Approfondies (DEA)*: 6 yrs; *Doctorat d'Etat*: at least 9 yrs. Also DUT, DESS; DUP

Student Services: Academic Counselling, Social Counselling, Foreign Student Adviser, Sports Facilities, Language Programmes, Health Services, Canteen, Foreign Student Centre

Student Residential Facilities: Yes

Special Facilities: Museum

Libraries: Yes

Publications: Le Sahelien (monthly); Les Annales du Sahel (annually)

Press or Publishing House: Presses Universitaires du Sahel (PUNIS)

Academic Staff 2001-2002	MEN	WOMEN	TOTAL
FULL-TIME	12	6	18
PART-TIME	30	15	45
TOTAL	**42**	**21**	**63**
STAFF WITH DOCTORATE			
FULL-TIME	10	5	15
PART-TIME	25	10	35
TOTAL	**35**	**15**	**50**

Student Numbers 2001-2002	MEN	WOMEN	TOTAL
All (Foreign Included)	125	113	**238**
FOREIGN ONLY	50	42	92

OTHER UNIVERSITY LEVEL INSTITUTIONS

NATIONAL HIGHER SCHOOL OF AGRICULTURE
École nationale supérieure d' Agriculture (ENSA)
BP A 296, Thiès
Tel: +221 9511-257
Fax: +221 9511-551
EMail: ensath@telecomplus.sn
Website: http://www.Refer.sn/sngal_ct/édu/ensa/accueil.htm
Directeur: Papa Ibra Samb (2002-)
Directeur des Etudes: Abdoulaye Drame

Departments
Agronomy *Head*: Moussa Fall

Academic Year: January to November

Admission Requirements: Secondary school certificate (baccalauréat séries C, D, E)

Fees: (CFA Francs): 1,850,000 per annum

Main Language(s) of Instruction: French

Degrees and Diplomas: *Diplôme d'Ingénieur*: Agronomy, 5 yrs

Student Services: Academic Counselling, Social Counselling, Foreign Student Adviser, Cultural Centre, Sports Facilities, Language Programmes, Health Services, Canteen

Academic Staff 2001-2002	MEN	WOMEN	TOTAL
FULL-TIME	9	1	10
PART-TIME	54	2	56
TOTAL	**63**	**3**	**66**
STAFF WITH DOCTORATE			
FULL-TIME	7	–	7
PART-TIME	50	2	52
TOTAL	**57**	**2**	**59**

Student Numbers 2001-2002	MEN	WOMEN	TOTAL
All (Foreign Included)	109	18	**127**
FOREIGN ONLY	33	3	36

OTHER INSTITUTIONS

CENTRE AFRICAIN D'ÉTUDES SUPÉRIEURES EN GESTION
BP 3802, Boulevard Général de Gaulle, Dakar
Tel: +221 228-022
Fax: +221 213-215
Website: http://www.cesag.sn
Directeur: Patrice Kouame

Founded: 1978

Departments
Audit Procedures (Accountancy)
Business Management (Management)
Health Services Management (Health Administration)

History: Founded 1978

CENTRE DE FORMATION ET DE PERFECTIONNEMENT ADMINISTRATIF
Boulevard Dial Diop, Dakar
Tel: +221 250-058
Fax: +221 248-744

Founded: 1965

Programmes
Administration

CENTRE DE PERFECTIONNEMENT EN LANGUE ANGLAISE
35, rue Jules Ferry, Dakar
Tel: +221 210-359

Founded: 1973

Programmes
English

CONSERVATOIRE NATIONAL DE MUSIQUE, DE DANSE ET D'ARTS DRAMATIQUES
Dakar
Tel: +221 224-673

Programmes
Dance; Music; Theatre

ÉCOLE INTER-ÉTATS DES SCIENCES ET MÉDECINE VÉTÉRINAIRE (EISMV)
BP 5077 Fann, Dakar
Tel: +221 865-1008
Fax: +221 825-4283
EMail: mariamd@eismv.refer.sn
Website: http://www.refer.sn/eismv.htm
Directeur: François Adebayo Abiola (1994-)

Founded: 1971, 1976

Programmes
Veterinary Science (Anatomy; Biology; Embryology and Reproduction Biology; Ethnology; Food Technology; Genetics; Histology; Immunology; Microbiology; Parasitology; Pathology; Pharmacy; Physiology; Rural Planning; Toxicology; Veterinary Science; Zoology)

ÉCOLE NATIONALE D'ADMINISTRATION ET DE MAGISTRATURE
Rue Dial Diop, Dakar
Tel: +221 258-744
Fax: +221 258-744
EMail: enam@telecomplus.sn
Directeur: Abdoulaaye Camara

Founded: 1972

Administration
Magisterial Studies (Justice Administration)

ÉCOLE NATIONALE DES BEAUX ARTS
124/126, avenue A. Peytavin, Dakar
Founded: 1979

Programmes
Fine Arts

ÉCOLE NATIONALE DES CADRES RURAUX DE BAMBEY (ENCR)
BP 54, Bambey
Tel: +221 973-6195
Fax: +221 973-6061
EMail: encrbbey@cyg.sn

Founded: 1960

Departments
Animal Husbandry (Cattle Breeding) *Head:* Pap Sher Diop
Applications and Production (Crop Production) *Head:* Saliou Diouf
Counsel, Training, Development (Agricultural Economics; Development Studies; Rural Planning) *Head:* Diakho Makha
Forestry *Head:* Birahim Fall
Vegetal Production (Vegetable Production) *Head:* Ibrahima Mbodj

Governing Bodies: Ministère de l'Enseignement Supérieur et de la Recherche Scientifique

Academic Year: September to June

Admission Requirements: Secondary school certificate (baccalauréat toutes séries), or diplôme d'agent technique and 2 yrs experience

Main Language(s) of Instruction: French

Degrees and Diplomas: *Diplôme d'Ingénieur:* Agriculture (ITA); Stockbreeding; Water Science; Forestry (ITE), 3 yrs

Student Services: Employment Services, Sports Facilities, Language Programmes, Health Services

Student Residential Facilities: Yes

Libraries: Central Library; Library of the Centre National de Recherches Agricoles

Academic Staff *2001-2002:* Full-Time: c. 50 Part-Time: c. 20 Total: c. 70

Staff with doctorate: Total: c. 15

Student Numbers *2001-2002:* All (Foreign Included): c. 150 Foreign Only: c. 60

ÉCOLE NATIONALE DES DOUANES
Avenue Carde-Rue René Ndiayé, Dakar
Tel: +221 212-879

Founded: 1970

Programmes
Customs (Taxation)

ÉCOLE NATIONALE D'ÉCONOMIE APPLIQUÉE
Avenue Cheikh A. Diop, Dakar
Tel: +221 247-928

Founded: 1968

Programmes
Economics

ÉCOLE NATIONALE DE FORMATION MARITIME
Km 4, 5 Boulevard du Centenaire de la Commune de Dakar, Dakar
Tel: +221 213-823

Directeur: Alioune Abatalib Nguer

Programmes
Maritime Studies (Marine Science and Oceanography)

ÉCOLE NATIONALE D'HORTICULTURE CAMBÉRÈNE
Dakar
Tel: +221 357-821
Fax: +221 353-991

Programmes
Horticulture

ÉCOLE NATIONALE DE POLICE ET DE LA FORMATION PERMANENTE
BP 5025, Dakar-Fann
Tel: +221 252-818
Fax: +221 242-557

Founded: 1954

Programmes
Police Studies

ÉCOLE NATIONALE DES POSTES ET TÉLÉCOMMUNICATIONS
Rue Ousmane Socé Diop, Rufisque
Tel: +221 360-029

Programmes
Post and Telecommunications (Postal Services; Telecommunications Services)

ÉCOLE NORMALE SUPÉRIEURE D'ÉDUCATION ARTISTIQUE
124-126, avenue A. Peytavin, Dakar
Tel: +221 230-343
Fax: +221 221-638

Programmes
Communication (Communication Studies)
Environmental Studies
Plastic Arts (Painting and Drawing; Sculpture)

ÉCOLE SUPÉRIEURE MULTINATIONALE DES TÉLÉCOMMUNICATIONS (ESMT)
B.P. 10000, Dakar Liberté
Tel: +221 824-9806
Fax: +221 824-6890
Website: http://www.esmt.sn

Directeur: Idrissa Touré **Tel:** +221 869-0301
EMail: Idrissa.Toure@esmt.sn

Founded: 1981

Programmes
Telecommunications (Telecommunications Engineering)

INSTITUT SÉNÉGALAIS DE RECHERCHES AGRICOLES (ISRA)
BP 3120, Dakar
Tel: +221 821-1913
Fax: +221 822-3413
Website: http://www.isra.sn

Directeur: Papa Abdoulaye Seck

Founded: 1974
Agriculture

INSTITUT SÉNÉGALO-BRITANNIQUE D'ENSEIGNEMENT DE L'ANGLAIS
BP 35, rue du 18 juin, Dakar
Tel: +221 224-023

Founded: 1976

Programmes
English

Sierra Leone

INSTITUTION TYPES AND CREDENTIALS

Types of higher education institutions:

University
University College
Technical Institute
Teacher Training College

School leaving and higher education credentials:

Senior School Certificate Examination
General Certificate of Education Advanced Level
Certificate
Diploma
Higher Teacher's Certificate
Bachelor's Degree
Bachelor Honours Degree
Postgraduate Diploma in Education
Master's Degree
Doctor's Degree

STRUCTURE OF EDUCATION SYSTEM

Pre-higher education:

Structure of school system:

Primary
Type of school providing this education: Primary School
Length of programme in years: 6
Age level from: 6 to: 12
Certificate/diploma awarded: National Primary School Examination

Junior Secondary
Type of school providing this education: Junior Secondary School
Length of programme in years: 3
Age level from: 12 to: 15
Certificate/diploma awarded: Basic Education Certificate Examination (BECE)

Senior Secondary
Type of school providing this education: Senior Secondary School
Length of programme in years: 3
Age level from: 15 to: 18
Certificate/diploma awarded: Senior School Certificate Examination

School education:

In the 6-3-3-4 education system, primary education lasts for six years followed by secondary education which is divided into two three-year cycles. The first leads to the Basic Education Certificate Examination and the second to the Senior School Certificate Examination which gives access to higher education. Candidates may also sit for the General Certificate of Education Ordinary Level/Cambridge Overseas School Certificate and the General Certificate of Education Advanced Level/Cambridge Overseas School Certificate, which is conferred after five years of lower secondary education and two years of sixth form.

Higher education:

Higher education is offered by one university (comprising Institutes) and its constituent colleges, teacher training colleges and a technical institute. They come under the jurisdiction of the Ministry of Education, Science and Technology. The University is governed by the Court, composed of non-university and university members, and the Senate, which is composed of academic members and is responsible for academic matters.

Main laws/decrees governing higher education:

Decree: University of Sierra Leone Act   Year: 1972

Academic year:

Classes from: October *to:* June

Long vacation from: 1 July *to:* 7 October

Languages of instruction:

English

Stages of studies:

Non-university level post-secondary studies (technical/vocational type):

Higher vocational and technical education is provided by technical institutes which train technicians and clerks and prepare candidates for examinations of the City and Guilds of London Institute, the Royal Society of Arts and the United Kingdom Ordinary National Diploma in technical studies.

University level studies:

University level first stage: Undergraduate:

The first stage of higher education leads, after a period of three years (or four, in the case of not sufficiently qualified entrants), to the Bachelor's Degree (general). A Bachelor's Degree with Honours is awarded after four years' study. A Diploma in Engineering is conferred after three years' study at undergraduate level. A Certificate in Agriculture and Home Economics is awarded after two years' study at undergraduate level. These are professional qualifications.

University level second stage: *Graduate*:

The Master's Degree is awarded one year following the Bachelor's Degree with Honours and two years following a general degree.

University level third stage: *Doctor of Philosophy*:

The Ph.D. is conferred after a minimum of three years' study following upon the Bachelor's Degree, and the submission of a thesis. A Postgraduate Diploma in Education is awarded after one year's postgraduate study.

Teacher education:

Training of pre-primary and primary/basic school teachers

Primary school teachers are trained in teacher training colleges in three years after junior secondary school. They are awarded the Teacher's Certificate (TC).

Training of secondary school teachers

Junior secondary school teachers are trained at teacher's colleges where studies lead to a Higher Teachers' Certificate. Senior secondary school teachers hold a four-year Bachelor Degree. The Faculty of Education at Njala University College offers a four-year course leading to a BA in Education, and a BSc in Education, Agricultural Education, and Home Economics Education. Fourah Bay College offers a one-year graduate diploma in Education to graduates who have studied at least two subjects taught in secondary schools.

NATIONAL BODIES

Responsible authorities:

Ministry of Education, Science and Technololgy
  Minister: Alpha Wurie
  Director-General (Administration): Edward Kamara
  International Relations: B.I.S. Konneh
  Freetown
  Tel: +232(22) 240-560 +232(22) 235-029
  Fax: +232(22) 235-029

ADMISSIONS TO HIGHER EDUCATION

Admission to university-level studies

Name of secondary school credential required: General Certificate of Education Advanced Level
Minimum score/requirement: Ordinary ('O') level passes in 5 approved subjects, plus 3 approved ('A') level subjects
For entry to: University and College of Medicine and Allied Health Sciences

Name of secondary school credential required: Senior School Certificate Examination

Alternatives to credentials: Provisions are made for entry for mature students with special aptitudes and experience.

Other admission requirements: The choice of subject is based on the type of course students wish to follow in higher education. Faculties have their own special entrance requirements and students are selected from among suitably qualified candidates.

Foreign students admission

Admission requirements: Foreign students should hold qualifications equivalent to the requirements of national students. An orientation programme is provided for all students during the first week of each session.

Language requirements: Proficiency in English is required.

Application procedures:

Apply to individual institution for entry to: University

Application closing dates:

    For university level studies: 31 March

References to further information on foreign student admissions and recognition of studies

Title: Commonwealth Universities Yearbook
Author: Association of Commonwealth Universities
Publisher: ACU

Title: Guide for Prospective Foreign Students
Author: University of Sierra Leone

GRADING SYSTEM

Usual grading system in secondary school
Full Description: For Secondary school leaving certificate A' level: A, B, C, D, E, O (subsidiary pass), F or 1-9 with 1 as maximum.
Highest on scale: A
Pass/fail level: O
Lowest on scale: F

Main grading system used by higher education institutions
Full Description: First Class Honours: A+; Second Class Honours, Upper Division: A-/B+; Second Class Honours, Lower Division: B; Third Class Honours: B-C/+; Pass: C
Highest on scale: A+
Pass/fail level: C
Lowest on scale: F

Other main grading systems

Degrees are classified :
Honours Degrees: Class I, Class II (upper and lower), Class III
Pass Degrees: Division I, II, III; general degrees

NOTES ON HIGHER EDUCATION SYSTEM

Data for academic year: 2002-2003
Source: International Association of Universities (IAU), updated from documentation, 2002

INSTITUTIONS OF HIGHER EDUCATION

UNIVERSITIES

• UNIVERSITY OF SIERRA LEONE
Private Mail Bag, Freetown
Tel: +232(22) 226-859
Vice-Chancellor: Ernest H. Wright (1998-)
EMail: wrighteh@sierratel.sl
Registrar: J.A.G. Thomas

Institutes
Education *Director (Acting)*: Melisa F. Jonah
Library Studies (Administration; Archiving; Documentation Techniques; Information Sciences; Library Science) *Director*: Gladys Sheriff
Public Administration and Management (Accountancy; Business and Commerce; Finance; Management; Public Administration)

History: Founded 1967.
Governing Bodies: Court; Senate
Academic Year: October to June (October-December; January-March; April-June)
Admission Requirements: General Certificate of Education (GCE) with Ordinary ('O') level passes in 5 approved subjects, plus 3 approved ('A') level subjects
Main Language(s) of Instruction: English
Degrees and Diplomas: *Bachelor's Degree*: 3-4 yrs; *Bachelor Honours Degree*: 4-5 yrs; *Master's Degree*; *Doctor's Degree*. Also Diplomas and Certificates, 1-2 yrs.
Student Residential Facilities: For c. 3000 students
Special Facilities: Botanical Garden. Herbarium
Publications: Bulletin of African Studies (quarterly); Journal of Pure and Applied Sciences (annually)
Academic Staff *2001-2002:* Total: c. 45
Student Numbers *2001-2002:* Total: c. 500

COLLEGE OF MEDICINE AND ALLIED HEALTH SCIENCES
Private Mail Bag, Freetown
Tel: +232(22) 240884
Principal: Ahmed M. Taqi (1992-)

Faculties
Basic Medical Sciences (Anatomy; Biochemistry; Dentistry; Haematology; Health Sciences; Medicine; Microbiology; Pharmacy; Physiology) *Dean*: J.K. George
Clinical Sciences (Community Health; Dental Hygiene; Gynaecology and Obstetrics; Medicine; Paediatrics; Surgery) *Dean*: L.G.O. Gordon-Harris
Pharmaceutical Sciences (Pharmacology; Pharmacy) *Dean*: E. Ayiteh-Smith

History: Founded 1988 as a Constituent College of University of Sierra Leone.
Admission Requirements: General Certificate of Education (GCE) with Ordinary ('O') level passes in 5 approved subjects, plus 3 approved ('A') level subjects
Academic Staff *2001-2002:* Total: c. 60
Student Numbers *2001-2002:* Total: c. 165

FOURAH BAY COLLEGE
Mount Aureol, Freetown
Tel: +232(22) 227924
Fax: +232(22) 224260
EMail: fbcadmin@sierratel.sl
Website: http://fbcusl.8k.com
Principal: V.E. Strasser-King (1993-)
EMail: vesking@hotmail.com

Faculties
Arts (Arts and Humanities; Classical Languages; Education; English; History; Linguistics; Modern Languages; Philosophy; Theology) *Dean*: L.E.T. Shyllon
Engineering (Civil Engineering; Electrical Engineering; Electronic Engineering; Engineering; Maintenance Technology; Mechanical Engineering) *Dean*: O.R. Davidson
Pure and Applied Sciences (Botany; Chemistry; Geography; Geology; Mathematics; Natural Sciences; Physics; Zoology) *Dean*: V.E. Godwin
Social Sciences and Law (International Law; Law; Social Sciences) *Dean*: H.M.J. Smart

Institutes
Adult Education and Extramural Studies (INSTADEX) (Environmental Studies; Rural Planning) *Director*: E.D.A. Turay
African Studies *Director*: E. Turay
Library, Information and Communication Studies (Communication Studies; Library Science) *Supervisor*: A.N.T. Deen
Marine Biology and Oceanography (Marine Science and Oceanography) *Director*: E. Ndomahina
Population Studies (Demography and Population; Economics; Statistics) *Director*: Armand C. Thomas

History: Founded 1827 by the Church Missionary Society, became affiliated to University of Durham 1876 and incorporated as independent Institution under Royal Charter 1960. Became Constituent College of University of Sierra Leone 1966.
Academic Year: October to June (October-December; January-March; April-June)
Admission Requirements: General Certificate of Education (GCE) with Ordinary ('O') level passes in 5 approved subjects, including English Language
Main Language(s) of Instruction: English

Degrees and Diplomas: *Bachelor's Degree*: 3-4 yrs; *Master's Degree*: a further 1-2 yrs; *Doctor's Degree*: (PhD), a further 3-4 yrs

Student Residential Facilities: Yes

Libraries: c. 120,000 vols

Publications: Prospectus (biennially); Gazette

Academic Staff *2001-2002*: Total: c. 160

Student Numbers *2001-2002*: Total: c. 1,450

NJALA UNIVERSITY COLLEGE
Private Mail Bag, Freetown
Tel: +232(22) 8788
Website: http://www.nuc-online.com

Principal: A.M. Alghali

Faculties
Agriculture (Agricultural Economics; Agricultural Engineering; Agriculture; Animal Husbandry; Crop Production; Home Economics; Soil Science) *Dean*: E. R. Rhodes
Education (Agricultural Education; Education; Physical Education; Teacher Trainers Education) *Dean*: T.M. Dugba
Environmental Sciences (Biological and Life Sciences; Chemistry; Environmental Studies; Geography; Physics) *Dean*: G. M. T. Robert

Centres
Educational Services (Educational Technology)
Science Curriculum Development *Director*: M.J. Cole

History: Founded 1964. Became a Constituent College of University of Sierra Leone 1966.

Academic Year: October to June (October-December; January-March; April-June)

Admission Requirements: General Certificate of Education (GCE) with Ordinary ('O') level passes in 5 approved subjects, including English Language

Main Language(s) of Instruction: English

Degrees and Diplomas: *Certificate*: Agriculture; *Bachelor's Degree*: 3-4 yrs; *Master's Degree*: a further 3-4 yrs; *Doctor's Degree*: (PhD), a further 3-4 yrs

Student Residential Facilities: Yes

Special Facilities: Herbarium with rare collections

Libraries: c. 50,000 vols

Publications: Education and Agricultural Development in Sierra Leone; Handbook

Academic Staff *2001-2002*: Total: c. 115

Student Numbers *2001-2002*: Total: c. 1,600

OTHER INSTITUTIONS

BO TEACHERS' COLLEGE
PO Box 162, Bo
Founded: 1972
Teacher Training

BUNUMBU TEACHERS' COLLEGE
Private Mail Bag, Kenema
Founded: 1933
Teacher Training

FREETOWN TEACHERS' COLLEGE
PO Box 1049, Freetown
Tel: +232(22) 263010
Founded: 1964
Teacher Training

MAKENI TEACHERS' COLLEGE
Private Mail Bag, Makeni, Northern Provinces
Teacher Training

MILTON MARGAI TEACHERS' COLLEGE
Goderich
Founded: 1960
Teacher Training

PORT LOKO TEACHERS' COLLEGE
Port Loko
Tel: +232(22) 229903
Teacher Training

TECHNICAL INSTITUTE
Congo Cross, Freetown
Tel: +232(22) 31368
Technology

Somalia

INSTITUTION TYPES AND CREDENTIALS

Types of higher education institutions:
University
Institute
Teacher Training College

School leaving and higher education credentials:
Secondary School Leaving Certificate
Bachelor's Degree
Laurea

STRUCTURE OF EDUCATION SYSTEM

Pre-higher education:

Duration of compulsory education:
    Age of entry: 6
    Age of exit: 14

Structure of school system:

    Primary
    Type of school providing this education: Primary School
    Length of programme in years: 8
    Age level from: 6 to: 14

    Secondary
    Type of school providing this education: Secondary School
    Length of programme in years: 4
    Age level from: 14 to: 18
    Certificate/diploma awarded: Secondary School Leaving Certificate

    Technical
    Type of school providing this education: Technical Secondary School
    Length of programme in years: 4
    Age level from: 14 to: 18

School education:

Primary education lasts for eight years. Secondary education lasts for four years. All main subjects are taught. Studies lead to the Secondary School Leaving Certificate. Technical secondary education is offered in technical/vocational secondary schools. The curriculum is being revised.

Higher education:

Higher education is mainly provided by Mogadishu University.

Languages of instruction:

Arabic, English, Italian, Somali

Stages of studies:

Non-university level post-secondary studies (technical/vocational type):

Higher technical and vocational education is offered in specialized institutions which provide courses that last between one and four years in such subjects as Industrial Studies, Public Health, Veterinary Medicine, Telecommunications, and Commerce.

University level studies:

University level first stage: *Bachelor's Degree/Laurea*:
The first stage lasts for four years and leads to the Bachelor's Degree. Students must first spend two years in national service and sit for a competitive entrance examination.

University level second stage: *Master's Degree*:
The University is introducing Master's Degrees.

Teacher education:

Training of pre-primary and primary/basic school teachers
Primary school teachers are trained at Scuole Magistrali one year after completion of secondary education. They are awarded a Diploma.

Training of secondary school teachers
Secondary school teachers are trained in three years at the University or at the Technical Teacher Training College for vocational and technical education. Entrants to the TTTC are selected from among those who have completed three and four years of technical secondary education. Graduates are expected to serve as vocational and/or technical teachers for five years.

Training of higher education teachers
The minimum requirement for the rank of lecturer is a Master's Degree and a minimum of three years' teaching experience. The rank of Professor requires a PhD, scholarly publications and a minimum of five years' service at the University.

NATIONAL BODIES

Responsible authorities:

Ministry of Higher Education
Minister: Mohamud Haji Abdi Zakaria
Mogadishu

ADMISSIONS TO HIGHER EDUCATION

Admission to non university higher education studies

Name of secondary school credential required: Secondary School Leaving Certificate

Admission to university-level studies

Name of secondary school credential required: Secondary School Leaving Certificate

Entrance exams required: Entrance examination.

Other admission requirements: Two years' national youth service.

Foreign students admission

Admission requirements: Foreign students must have completed secondary education and pass the university entrance examination. Services available to foreign students include accommodation, health and teaching facilities. They may also be awarded fellowships.

Entry regulations: Students must hold a resident's permit.

Health requirements: Health certificates are required.

GRADING SYSTEM

Usual grading system in secondary school

Full Description: For the Secondary School Certificate: 0-100%.
Highest on scale: 100%
Pass/fail level: 60%
Lowest on scale: 0

Main grading system used by higher education institutions

Full Description: In the faculties that follow the Italian system all subjects are marked out of a possible maximum of 30 with 18 as the pass mark.
Highest on scale: 30
Pass/fail level: 18
Lowest on scale: 0

NOTES ON HIGHER EDUCATION SYSTEM

Data for academic year: 2002-2003

Source: International Association of Universities (IAU), updated from University's data, 2003

INSTITUTIONS OF HIGHER EDUCATION

UNIVERSITIES

MOGADISHU UNIVERSITY
Mogadishu
Tel: +252 593-4454
Fax: +252 121-6820
EMail: info@mogadishuuniversity.com
Website: http://www.mogadishuuniversity.com
President: Ali Sheikh Ahmed

Faculties
Arts and Humanities (African Studies; Arabic; Arts and Humanities; English; Geography; Grammar; History; Islamic Studies; Linguistics; Literature; Management; Sociology)
Computer Science and Information Technology (Computer Science; Information Technology)
Economics and Management Science (Accountancy; Arabic; Commercial Law; Econometrics; Economics; English; Finance; Human Resources; International Economics; Law; Staff Development)
Education (Arabic; Education; Islamic Studies; Mathematics; Natural Sciences; Physics; Social Sciences)
Shar'ia and Law (Islamic Law; Law)

Institutes
Languages (Modern Languages)
Somali Studies *(ISOS)* (African Studies)

Higher Institutes
Nursing (Anatomy; Dermatology; Gynaecology and Obstetrics; Microbiology; Neurological Therapy; Nursing; Nutrition; Ophthalmology; Paediatrics; Pharmacology; Psychiatry and Mental Health; Psychology; Sociology; Surgery)

History: Founded 1996. A private institution.

Governing Bodies: Board of Trustees, Academic Council

Admission Requirements: Secondary school certificate and entrance examination

Main Language(s) of Instruction: Arabic, English

Degrees and Diplomas: *Bachelor's Degree*: 4 yrs. Also Diploma in Nursing, 3 years, and Postgraduate Diploma in Education.

South Africa

INSTITUTION TYPES AND CREDENTIALS

Types of higher education institutions:

University
University of Technology (former Technikon)
College (Teacher Training, Nursing, Technical Colleges)

School leaving and higher education credentials:

Senior Certificate
Matriculation Endorsement
National Certificate
National Higher Certificate
National Diploma (Ndip)
National Higher Diploma
Bachelor of Technology (Btech)
Bachelor's Degree
Bachelor Honours Degree
Postgraduate Diploma
Master of Technology (Mtech)
Master's Degree
Doctor of Technology (Dtech)
Doctorate

STRUCTURE OF EDUCATION SYSTEM

Pre-higher education:

Duration of compulsory education:

Age of entry: 6
Age of exit: 15

Structure of school system:

Primary
Type of school providing this education: Primary School
Length of programme in years: 6
Age level from: 6 to: 12

Junior Secondary

Type of school providing this education: Junior Secondary School (first year still placed under primary school)

Length of programme in years: 3

Age level from: 12 to: 15

Certificate/diploma awarded: General Education and Training Certificate

Technical Secondary

Type of school providing this education: Technical Level Secondary School

Length of programme in years: 2

Age level from: 15 to: 17

Certificate/diploma awarded: Senior Certificate 1-3 years (depending on N programmes followed)

Senior Secondary

Type of school providing this education: Senior Secondary School

Length of programme in years: 3

Age level from: 15 to: 18

Certificate/diploma awarded: Senior Certificate

School education:

Primary education lasts for six years, divided into junior primary and senior primary. Until now, secondary school lasted for five years, the first year of the junior secondary phase being followed in primary school. At the end of junior secondary (three years), pupils are awarded the General Education and Training Certificate. At the end of the senior secondary phase (lasting three years), pupils sit for the Senior Certificate Examination. The 1996 Constitution confirms the right to basic education and that the Government must progressively make available and accessible through reasonable measures further education (i.e. the senior secondary phase preceding higher education). Compulsory education lasts for nine years (until age 15), followed by non-compulsory further education. In the senior cycle, students may study subjects either at Higher Grade, Standard Grade, or Lower Grade. N-courses are also offered by some technical school and college candidates. A Senior Certificate is awarded by the SA Certification Council after externally moderated examinations on completion of senior secondary school. Technical secondary education is provided by technical centres and secondary and vocational schools. Matriculation endorsements are also offered by this Council to students who have satisfied the ministerially approved overlay on the Senior Certificate. Provision is also made for further education colleges in terms of the Further Education and Training Act. Technical high schools may inter alia offer courses leading to Senior Certificates with matriculation endorsements, which statutorily constitute the minimum general admission requirement for access to universities. Universities of Technology (former Technikons) require Senior Certificates but not necessarily with matriculation endorsements.

Higher education:

The higher education system consists of State Universities, a Technikon (now called Universities of Technology) sector and a College sector. The Higher Education Act (December 1997) provides for the appointment of a Registrar of Private Higher Education Institutions and a number of private institutions have registered or are in the process of registering in terms of these provisions. The South African universities offer Bachelor, Bachelor Honours, Master and Doctorate Degrees, as well as Undergraduate and Postgraduate Diplomas. Course work is structured in modules, with students registering in a unit/credit system. Universities and Universities of Technology, as autonomous institutions, are subsidized by the Department of Education, and provide training at the post senior certificate level. Technikon courses lead to National Diplomas and Certificates and as from 1995 to Degrees with a minimum duration of four years. The Certification Council for Technikons (SERTEC) is responsible for conferring Universities of Technology Diplomas. The Higher Education Act stipulates that higher education at Universities, Universities of Technology and Colleges comes directly under the responsibility of the national government, whilst further education colleges report to the nine provincial governments. The total number of higher education institutions is currently being reduced from 36 to 21. The whole process will be completed in January 2005. It has also recently been planned to reduce the number of Colleges of Education and to incorporate them in the higher education system. In most cases they will be linked to universities and technical institutes.

Main laws/decrees governing higher education:

Decree: Higher Education Act   Year: 1997

Academic year:

Classes from: January *to:* December

Languages of instruction:

Afrikaans, English

Stages of studies:

Non-university level post-secondary studies (technical/vocational type):

Higher technical/vocational studies are provided by Technical Colleges and Technikons. Apprenticeship training for technicians is offered by Technical Colleges. Apprentices study for the National (Technical) Certificate (N training). N-3 courses can also be taken as credits for the Senior Certificate. The programme consists of three parts (N-1, N-2, N-3), each lasting for four months, six months or a year depending on the course concerned. The N-training is a pre-senior Certificate level and the N-3 credits are considered for the Senior Certificate (with pass in English and Afrikaans) for entry to Universities of Technology and National Certificate studies, but not for university studies. Most tertiary-level vocational programmes lead to a three-year National Diploma as basic qualification. Universities of Technology also provide vocationally oriented education and training in a variety of disciplines leading to amongst other Diplomas, first and advanced Degrees. Diplomas at technical-vocational level lead to BTech, MTech and Dtech Degrees. There are other types of specialist colleges, such as Nursing Colleges and Agricultural Colleges, which do not offer Degree studies unless offered in cooperation with Universities or Technikons. In such cases the Degree-awarding institution/authority's name will appear on the Certificate.

University level studies:

University level first stage: First stage:

The Bachelor Degree is awarded both by Universities and Universities of Technology. Universities award the Bachelor Degree after three to six years of study: Humanities, Commerce, Science - 3 years; Agriculture, Law, Engineering, Pharmacy and Education, four years; Veterinary Medicine and Architecture, five years; Dentistry, five-and-a-half years; Medecine and Theology, six years. Students in Humanities, Commerce and Science wishing to proceed to a Master Degree are required to take a Bachelor Honours Degree, which is awarded after a further year's study. Universities of Technology award the Bachelor Degree of Technology (BTech), which is a four-year Degree which includes one year of experiencial training. Universities also confer a Professional Bachelor Degree after four years.

University level second stage: Second stage:
The Master Degree is awarded both by Universities and Universities of Technology. This Degree requires a minimum of one to two years' research after the award of an Honours Degree in the case of universities, and a Bachelor Degree in the case of Universities of Technology. The Master Degree in Technology (MTech) may be obtained at least one year after the BTech. This is an advanced qualification comprising taught subjects and research, or only research. The thesis must relate to an industry specific problem. Some university Master Degrees, e.g. the Master Degree in Business Leadership (MBusAdministration), are partly taught and partly research Degrees, where the thesis must relate to an industry or subject specific problem.

University level third stage: Third stage:
Doctorates and research Degrees are also awarded both by Universities and Universities of Technology. They are conferred to holders of Master Degrees, after a minimum of two years' study. A Doctor in Technology (DTech) is awarded after successful completion of a thesis at Universities of Technology. This degree is research based and studies last at least two years. It comprises an advanced research project.

Teacher education:

Training of pre-primary and primary/basic school teachers
Training Colleges that previously reported to the provinces are currently in the process of transfer to the National Department of Education and certain Universities run three-or four-year Diploma courses qualifying holders to teach in primary schools. This also applies to some universities and universities of technology. The general admission requirement for Diploma studies at any of these colleges is a Senior Certificate with pass marks in one of the two languages of instruction (i.e. English and Afrikaans).

Training of secondary school teachers
Degree-level courses for secondary school teachers are run by all universities and universities of technology. A Senior Certificate with a matriculation endorsement or a Certificate of complete or conditional exemption is required for university study, whilst universities of technology have different requirements (usually Senior Certificates and further requirements as stipulated in their joint statute).

Training of higher education teachers
Forty per cent of academic staff obtained their highest qualification at the University in which they are employed, 30 per cent at another South African University and 30 per cent at a foreign University.

Non-traditional studies:

Distance higher education

Distance teaching, which is mainly by correspondence, provides courses for about 35 per cent of enrolled students. The University of South Africa (UNISA), resulting from the merger of UNISA, Vista University Distance Education Campus and Technikon South Africa, offers correspondence courses, either in English or in Afrikaans, for Bachelor Degree and Postgraduate qualifications, provided such Bachelor Degrees include an in-service training component. Course work is structured in modules. A maximum of ten years is allowed to obtain a Bachelor Degree, an additional year for Bachelor Honours Degree, three years for Postgraduate qualifications, two further years for a Master Degree and two years for a Doctorate. The Degrees are considered to be equivalent in standard to those awarded by other Universities.

NATIONAL BODIES

Responsible authorities:

Department of Education
Minister: A. Kader Asmal
Director-general: Thami Mseleku
International Relations: Ghaleeb Jeppie
Private Bag X9034
Cape Town 8000
Tel: +27(21) 465-7350
Fax: +27(21) 461-4788
EMail: webmaster@educ.pwv.gov.za
WWW: http://education.pwv.gov.za

South African Universities' Vice-Chancellors' Association (SAUVCA)
Chief Executive: Piyushi Kotecha
Director, Administrative Services: Tessa Yeowart
PO Box 27392
Sunnyside
Pretoria 0132
Tel: +27(12) 481-2842
Fax: +27(12) 481-2843
EMail: admin@sauvca.org.za
WWW: http://www.sauvca.org.za

Role of governing body: Umbrella body for South African public universities

Committee of Technikon Principals (CTP)
Executive Director: Dénis Van Rensburg
Executive Officer: Kogie Pretorius
International Relations: Wilna Venter-Mbabama

Private Bag X680
Pretoria 0001
Tel: +27(12) 326-1066 +27(12) 318-6217
Fax: +27(12) 325-7387
EMail: ctpdupre@techpta.ac.za
WWW: http://www.technikons.co.za

Role of governing body: Umbrella for the South African Technikons, recently renamed universities of Technology

Council on Higher Education (CHE)
Chairperson: Saki Macozoma
Chief Executive Officer: Saleem Badat
International Relations: Saleem Badat
PO Box 13354
The Tramshed, Gauteng 0126
Tel: +27(12) 392-9119
Fax: +27(12) 392-9110
EMail: ceo@che.ac.za
WWW: http://www.che.ac.za

Role of governing body: Advises the Minister of Education on strategic issues in higher education, performs quality assurance functions, dissiminates information on higher education.

ADMISSIONS TO HIGHER EDUCATION

Admission to non university higher education studies

Name of secondary school credential required: Senior Certificate
For entry to: Universities of technology, technical colleges, and other colleges.

Alternatives to credentials: Senior Certificate with N-courses obtained at technical colleges or technical high schools.

Admission to university-level studies

Name of secondary school credential required: Senior Certificate
Minimum score/requirement: Pass marks in two Higher Grade languages, two additional Higher Grade subjects, at least a further Standard Grade subject and a minimum aggregate of 45 % for six subjects.
For entry to: Universities.

Alternatives to credentials: Certificate of exemption from the matriculation endorsement required as issued by the Matriculation Board on behalf of SAUVCA or a conditional admission certificate issued by a university of technology

Entrance exams required: Matriculation endorsements are required for admission to first degree studies at university level and senior certificates for first degree studies at university of technology or college level.

Foreign students admission

Admission requirements: Prospective students coming from a non-South African schooling system must for benchmark purposes hold qualifications that must be at least equivalent to the local system. For university studies candidates apply to the university which will forward the application to the Matriculation Board which issues a certificate of exemption in terms of other specified provisions. Conditions must be satisfied on completion of degrees in the case of foreign conditional exemption certificates.

Entry regulations: Students must hold a valid passport, a duly completed application form B1-159 available from the Department of Home Affairs, a standard letter of provisional acceptance to a South African institution, a letter of motivation and proof that the student is in a situation to pay the tuition fees and has adequate means of support.

Language requirements: Students must be proficient in English or Afrikaans.

Application procedures:

Apply to individual institution for entry to: Institutions of higher education

Recognition of studies and qualifications:

Studies pursued in home country (System of recognition/accreditation): A Higher Education Quality Committee (HEQC) functions within the Council on Higher Education (Tel.: +27(12) 392-9132, Fax: +27(12) 392-9120, Email: singh.m@che.ac.za, Website: http://www.che.ac.za). It promotes quality assurance in higher education, audits quality assurance mechanisms and accredits higher education programmes.

Studies pursued in foreign countries (bodies dealing with recognition of foreign credentials):
South African Universities Vice-Chancellors' Association (SAUVCA)
  PO Box 27392
  Sunnyside
  Pretoria 0132
  Tel: +27(12) 481-2842
  Fax: +27(12) 481-2843
  EMail: admin@sauvca.org.za
  WWW: http://www.sauvca.org.za

References to further information on foreign student admissions and recognition of studies

Title: University calendars

STUDENT LIFE

National student associations and unions

South African Students' Representative Council (SAU-SRC)
  Private Bag
  Students' Union. University of Cape Town
  Rondebosch 7700

Tel: +27(21) 650-9111
Fax: +27(21) 650-2138
WWW: http://www.uct.ac.za

Student expenses and financial aid

Student costs:

Home students tuition fees: Minimum: 4,000 (Rand)
Maximum: 25,000 (Rand)

Publications on student services and financial aid:

Title: Guide to Distance Education in South Africa
Publisher: HSRC Publishers

Title: Guide to Higher Education in South Africa
Publisher: HSRC Publishers

Title: Study Abroad 2004-2005, 32nd Edition
Author: UNESCO
Publisher: UNESCO Publishing
Year of publication: 2003

INTERNATIONAL COOPERATION AND EXCHANGES

Principal national bodies responsible for dealing with international cooperation and exchanges in higher education:

South African Universities' Vice Chancellors' Association (SAUVCA)
Chief Executive: Piyushi Kotecha
Director, Administrative Services: Tessa Yeowart
PO Box 27392
Sunnyside, Pretoria 0132
Tel: +27(12) 481-2842
Fax: +27(12) 481-2843
EMail: admin@sauvca.org.za
WWW: http://www.sauvca.org.za

The International Education Association of South Africa (IEASA)
Head: Roshen Kishun
PO Box 65099
Reservoire Hills
Durban 4090
Tel: +27(31) 260-3077
Fax: +27(12) 260-2967
EMail: aieasa@nu.ac.za
WWW: http://www.und.ac.za/und/ieasa

GRADING SYSTEM

Usual grading system in secondary school

Full Description: Marking is alphabetical or expressed as a percentage. The usual pass mark in all higher grade subjects is 40% (with 2 exceptions). The pass mark in all standard grade subjects is 33%.
Highest on scale: A 80-100%
Pass/fail level: E 40-49%
Lowest on scale: F 33-39%

Main grading system used by higher education institutions

Full Description: Classification at some universities: 1st class (75-100%); 2nd class division 1 (70-74); 2nd class division 2 (60-69); 3rd class (50-59); fail (below 50). Other universities only distinguish: Distinction (75-100%); Pass (50-74%).
Highest on scale: 1st class
Pass/fail level: 3rd class
Lowest on scale: F

NOTES ON HIGHER EDUCATION SYSTEM

Data for academic year: 2003-2004
Source: South African Universities Vice-Chancellors' Association (SAUVCA), 2004

INSTITUTIONS OF HIGHER EDUCATION

UNIVERSITIES

• UNIVERSITY OF CAPE TOWN (UCT)
Bremner Bldg., Private Bag, Rondebosch, Cape Town 7701
Tel: +27(21) 650-9111
Fax: +27(21) 650-2138
Telex: 5-22208
EMail: aeshta@bremner.uct.ac.za
Website: http://www.uct.ac.za

Vice-Chancellor: Njabulo S. Ndebele (2000-2004)
Tel: +27(21) 650-2105 Fax: +27(21) 689-2440
EMail: vc@bremner.uct.ac.za

Registrar: Hugh Theodore Amoore Tel: +27(21) 650-2115
Fax: +27(21) 650-2138 EMail: aeshta@bremner.uct.ac.za

International Relations: Lesley Shackleton
Tel: +27(21) 650-2822 Fax: +27(21) 686-5444
EMail: lys@protem.uct.ac.za

Faculties
Commerce (Accountancy; Actuarial Science; Business and
Commerce; Computer Science; Economics; Industrial and Or-
ganizational Psychology; Information Sciences; Law; Manage-
ment; Marketing; Statistics) *Dean:* Douglas Pitt
Engineering and Built Environment (Architecture and Plan-
ning; Building Technologies; Chemical Engineering; Civil Engi-
neering; Computer Engineering; Economics; Electrical and
Electronic Engineering; Engineering; Management; Mechanical
Engineering; Town Planning) *Dean:* C.T O'Connor
Health Sciences (Health Sciences; Medicine; Nursing; Physi-
cal Therapy; Speech Therapy and Audiology; Surgery) *Dean:*
N. Padayachee
Humanities (Arts and Humanities; Dance; Fine Arts; Music;
Performing Arts; Social Sciences) *Dean:* Robin Cohen
Law (Law; Philosophy) *Dean:* H. Corder
Science (Applied Mathematics; Archaeology; Astronomy and
Space Science; Biochemistry; Botany; Chemistry; Computer
Science; Environmental Studies; Geography; Marine Science
and Oceanography; Mathematics; Microbiology; Natural Sci-
ences; Physics; Statistics; Zoology) *Dean:* B. Daya Reddy

Graduate Schools
Business (Business Administration)
Humanities (Arts and Humanities)

History: Founded 1829 as College by local community, acquired official status 1873. Became University by Act of Parliament 1916 and granted Charter 1918. An autonomous
institution receiving financial support (70%) from the State.
Open to all who meet the academic requirements, regardless of
colour, race, sex or religion.

Governing Bodies: University Council; University Senate

Academic Year: February to December (February-April;
April-June; July-September; September-December)

Admission Requirements: Matriculation Certificate or certificate of exemption issued by the Joint Matriculation Board

Main Language(s) of Instruction: English

Degrees and Diplomas: *Bachelor's Degree*: Education (BEd),
1 yr following first degree; Chemical Engineering, 1yr full first
degree; Arts (BA); Commerce (BCom); Laws (LLB); Social Sciences (BSocSc), 3 yrs; Allied Health Professions and Sciences;
Business Science (BBusSc); Library and Information Sciences
(BBibl); Medicine and Surgery (MBChB); Music; Primary Education (BPrimEd), 4 yrs; Electrical Engineering; Electro-Me-
chanical Engineering; Logopaedics and Physiotherapy;
Science (BSc), 4-5 yrs; Civil Engineering; Engineering
(BScEng), 5 yrs; Architecture and Planning (BArch), 6 yrs;
Bachelor Honours Degree: a further yr; *Master's Degree*: a fur-
ther 1-2 yrs; *Doctorate*: 1-2 yrs. The Bachelor (Honours) Degree
is awarded in the same fields of study as the Bachelor's Degree.
Also Undergraduate and Postgraduate Diplomas

Student Services: Academic Counselling, Social Counselling,
Employment Services, Foreign Student Adviser, Cultural Centre, Sports Facilities, Language Programmes, Handicapped Facilities, Health Services, Canteen, Foreign Student Centre

Student Residential Facilities: For c. 4500 students

Special Facilities: Irma Stern Museum (Fine Arts Collection).
Archaeological Museum. P.A. Wagner Museum (Mineralogical
and Geological Specimens). Herbarium

Libraries: J.W. Jagger Library, 7 branch Libraries, total, c. 1m.
vols

Publications: Journal of Energy in Southern Africa (quarterly);
Sea Changes; Social Dynamics (biannually); Centre for African
Studies Communications; Bolus Herbarium Contributions;
Mathematics Colloquium; Oceanography Yearbook; Studies in
History of Cape Town; Jagger Journal; Research Report; Gen-
eral and Faculty Prospectuses; Responsa Meridiane; UCT
News; Acta Juridica (annually)

Academic Staff 2000			TOTAL
FULL-TIME			1,663
PART-TIME			1,000
TOTAL			**2,663**

Student Numbers 2001-2002	MEN	WOMEN	TOTAL
All (Foreign Included)	9,297	8,581	**17,878**
FOREIGN ONLY	–	–	2,260

• UNIVERSITY OF FORT HARE
Private Bag X1314, Alice, Eastern Cape Province 5700
Tel: +27(40) 602-2181
Fax: +27(40) 653-2314
EMail: dmc@ufh.ac.za
Website: http://www.ufh.ac.za

Vice-Chancellor: Derrick Swartz Tel: +27(40) 653-2312
Fax: +27(40) 653-1338
EMail: dbotha@ufh.ac.za;mxoseka@ufh.ac.za

Registrar: A.W. Shaw Tel: +27(40) 602-2181
Fax: +27(40) 653-2314 EMail: ashaw@ufh.ac.za

Head Librarian: Yolisa Soul

Faculties

African and Democracy Studies (African Studies; Afrikaans; Criminal Law; Law; Theology)

Agriculture and Environmental Sciences (Agricultural Economics; Agriculture; Agronomy; Environmental Studies; Geography)

Management, Development and Commerce (Industrial and Organizational Psychology; Management) *Dean*: N. Dladla

Science (Biochemistry; Computer Science; Mathematics; Microbiology; Natural Sciences; Statistics)

Institutes

Government

Further Information: Incorporated East London Campus of Rhodes University 2004

History: Founded 1916 as South African Native College by the United Free Church of Scotland. Affiliated to Rhodes University 1951-1959. Transferred to Department of Bantu Education 1960. Acquired present status 2004 following incorporation of East London Campus of Rhodes University.

Governing Bodies: University Council; University Senate

Academic Year: January to December (January-April; April-June; July-September; September-December)

Admission Requirements: Matriculation Certificate or certificate of exemption issued by the Joint Matriculation Board

Main Language(s) of Instruction: English

International Co-operation: UNESCO "Oliver Tambo" Chair of Human Rights

Degrees and Diplomas: *Bachelor's Degree*: Arts (BA); Commerce (BComm); Financial Law (BProcLaw); Jurisprudence (BJuris); Law (LLB); Nursing (BCur); Pedagogy (BPaed); Science (BSc); Theology (BTheol); *Bachelor Honours Degree*: a further yr; *Master's Degree*: a further 1-2 yrs; *Doctorate*: 1-2 yrs. The Bachelor (Honours) Degree is awarded in the same fields of study as the Bachelor's Degree. Also Undergraduate and Postgraduate Diplomas

Student Residential Facilities: Yes

Special Facilities: F.S. Malan Museum. De Beers Centenary Art Gallery

Libraries: Central Library (Howard Pimm collection of Africana) c. 140,000 vols

Publications: Fort Harian (3 per annum); Papers

Academic Staff *2002-2002*: Full-Time: c. 230 Part-Time: c. 15 Total: c. 245

Student Numbers *2001-2002:* Total: c. 5,520

Evening Students, c. 1,180

*• UNIVERSITY OF KWAZULU-NATAL

Private Bag X54001, King George V Avenue, Glenwood, Durban 4041
Tel: +27(31) 260-2212
EMail: enquiries@ukzn.ac.za
Website: http://www.ukzn.ac.za

Vice-Chancellor: Malegapuru William Makgoba

Faculties

Commerce and Management (Accountancy; Business Administration; Economics; Human Resources; Law; Management; Marketing; Social Sciences)

Communication and Development Disciplines *(Howard College campus)* (Architecture; Development Studies; Nursing; Psychology; Social Sciences; Social Work)

Education *(Edgewood and Pietermaritzburg campuses)*

Engineering *(Howard College campus)* (Agricultural Engineering; Chemical Engineering; Civil Engineering; Computer Engineering; Electrical Engineering; Electronic Engineering; Mechanical Engineering)

Health Sciences *(Medical School campus)* (Health Sciences; Medicine; Surgery)

Human and Management Science *(Pietermaritzburg campus)* (Business Administration; Business and Commerce; Communication Studies; Education; Information Technology; Law; Media Studies; Philosophy; Political Science; Psychology; Social Sciences; Theatre; Theology; Visual Arts)

Human Sciences *(Howard College campus)* (Afrikaans; Ancient Civilizations; Communication Studies; Development Studies; Economics; English; French; German; Greek; History; Labour and Industrial Relations; Latin; Linguistics; Media Studies; Music; Performing Arts; Philosophy; Political Science; Sociology; Theatre)

Humanities (Arts and Humanities; Communication Studies; Education; Journalism; Management; Medical Technology; Medicine; Social Work; Tourism)

Law *(Howard College and Pietermaritzburg Campus)* (Accountancy; Child Care and Development; Commercial Law; Criminology; Economics; Industrial and Organizational Psychology; International Law; Law; Management; Private Law; Public Law)

Management Studies *(Howard College campus)* (Accountancy; Business Administration; Business and Commerce; Finance; Human Resources; Management)

Science *(Howard College campus)* (Actuarial Science; Applied Chemistry; Applied Mathematics; Applied Physics; Biological and Life Sciences; Chemistry; Computer Science; Environmental Studies; Geography; Geology; Mathematics; Physics; Statistics)

Science and Agriculture *(Pietermaritzburg campus)* (Agricultural Business; Agriculture; Botany; Cell Biology; Chemistry; Environmental Studies; Information Technology; Mathematics; Molecular Biology; Physics; Statistics; Zoology)

Further Information: Also Legal Aid Clinic. Advice desk for abused women. Merger of the former University of Durban-Westville and University of Natal

History: Founded 2004 following the merger of the University of Durban-Westville and the University of Natal.

Governing Bodies: University Council

Academic Year: February to December (February-March; April-June; July-September; October-December)

Admission Requirements: Matriculation Certificate or certificate of exemption issued by the Joint Matriculation Board

Main Language(s) of Instruction: English

Degrees and Diplomas: *Bachelor's Degree*; *Bachelor Honours Degree*: a further yr; *Postgraduate Diploma*; *Master's Degree*: a further 1-2 yrs; *Doctorate*: (PhD), 1-2 yrs

• MEDICAL UNIVERSITY OF SOUTHERN AFRICA (MEDUNSA)
PO Box 202, Medunsa 0204
Tel: +27(12) 521-4222 +27(12) 521-4224
Fax: +27(12) 521-4349 +27(12) 560-0274
Telex: 320580 sa
EMail: berndt@medunsa.ac.za
Website: http://www.medunsa.ac.za

Vice-Chancellor: M.F. Ramashala

Registrar (Acting): N.T. Mosia

Director: R.E. More

Faculties
Dentistry (Dentistry; Oral Pathology; Orthodontics; Periodontics; Stomatology) *Dean*: TS Gugushe

Medicine (Anaesthesiology; Anatomy; Cardiology; Clinical Psychology; Community Health; Dermatology; Forensic Medicine and Dentistry; Gastroenterology; Haematology; Medicine; Nursing; Nutrition; Pathology; Pharmacy; Surgery) *Dean (Acting)*: CF Van der Merwe

Science (Applied Mathematics; Biochemistry; Biological and Life Sciences; Biology; Chemistry; Mathematics; Natural Sciences; Physics; Psychology; Statistics; Technology) *Dean*: J. Viljoen Groenewald

Schools
Public Health *(National)* (Nursing; Public Health) *Dean*: Allen A. Herman

Campuses
Polokwane Campus *Dean*: MAF Molehe

History: Founded 1976. An autonomous institution receiving financial support from the Central Government.

Governing Bodies: University Council, comprising 28 members; University Senate, comprising 81 members

Academic Year: January to November (January-June; June-November)

Admission Requirements: Matriculation Certificate or certificate of exemption issued by the Joint Matriculation Board

Main Language(s) of Instruction: English

Degrees and Diplomas: *Bachelor's Degree*: Nursing Science (BCur), 4 1/2 yrs; Nursing Education and Administration (BCur(1and A)); Occupational Therapy (BOccTher); Science (BSc); Science (Medical) (BSc(Med)); Science in Dietetics (BSc(Diet)); Science in Physiotherapy (BSc(Physio)), 4 yrs; Dental Surgery (BChD); Medicine and Surgery (MB ChB);

Veterinary Medicine and Surgery (BVMCh), 6 yrs; *Master's Degree*; *Doctorate*

Student Services: Academic Counselling, Social Counselling, Nursery Care, Cultural Centre, Sports Facilities, Health Services, Canteen, Foreign Student Centre

Student Residential Facilities: For c. 2400 students

Libraries: Medunsa Library, 76,297 vols; 710 periodicals

Publications: Medunsa Yearbook; Principal's Annual Report; Exploration (Medunsa Annual Research Report) (annually); Medunsa Brief; Echo

Academic Staff *2001-2002:* Total: c. 200

Student Numbers *2001-2002:* Total: c. 3,500

*• UNIVERSITY OF THE NORTH
Private Bag X1106, Sovenga 0727
Tel: +27(152) 268-2121
Fax: +27(152) 267-0485
EMail: ndebele-ns@univl.unorth.ac.za
Website: http://www.unorth.ac.za

Principal (Acting): Mahlo Mokgalong (2003-)
Tel: +27(152) 268-2100 Fax: +27(152) 267-0142

Registrar (Acting): P. M. Malgas Tel: +27(152) 268-2407
Fax: +27(152) 268-3048 EMail: malgasp@unin.unorth.ac.za

Faculties
Humanities (Classical Languages; Communication Studies; Educational Sciences; Modern Languages; Social Sciences) *Executive Dean*: L. J. Teffo

Management Sciences and Law (Business Administration; Economics; Law; Leadership; Management) *Executive Dean*: P. E. Franks

Science, Health and Agriculture (Agriculture; Agronomy; Aquaculture; Biological and Life Sciences; Computer Science; Environmental Studies; Geography; Health Sciences; Horticulture; Mathematics; Mathematics and Computer Science; Mineralogy; Molecular Biology; Physics; Plant and Crop Protection; Soil Science) *Executive Dean*: N. M. Mokgalong

Further Information: Also Branches at Qwaqwa and Giyani

History: Founded 1959 as College to serve the Tsonga, Sotho, Vedda, Xitsonga and Tswana communities. Acquired present status and title 1970. An autonomous, non-racial institution receiving financial support from the State.

Governing Bodies: University Council; University Senate

Academic Year: January to December (January-March; April-July; July-December)

Admission Requirements: Matriculation Certificate or certificate of exemption issued by the Joint Matriculation Board

Main Language(s) of Instruction: English

Degrees and Diplomas: *Bachelor's Degree*: Administration (BAdmin); Arts (BA); Commerce (BComm); Jurisprudence (BJuris); Science (BSc), 3 yrs; Agricultural Management (BAgricAdmin); Agriculture in Pedagogy (BAgricPaed); Arts in Pedagogy (BAPaed); Nursing (BCur); Theology (BTh), 3-4 yrs; Arts in Social Work (BA(SW)); Commerce in Pedagogy (BCommPaed); Financial Law (BProcLaw); Library Information

Sciences (BBibl); Optometry (BOptom); Pharmacy (BPharm); Roman Law (LLB(Roman)); Science in Agriculture (BScAgric); Science in Medical Laboratory Sciences (BSc(MedLabSci)), 4 yrs; *Bachelor Honours Degree*: a further yr; *Master's Degree*: a further 1-2 yrs; *Doctorate*. The Bachelor (Honours) Degree is awarded in the same fields of study as the Bachelor's Degree

Student Residential Facilities: Yes

Special Facilities: Biological Museum. Herbarium. Experimental Farm

Libraries: Unin Library, 140,000 vols

Publications: Educationis (biannually); Theologica Viatorum (annually)

Academic Staff *2001-2002:* Total: c. 600

Student Numbers *2001-2002:* Total: c. 9,850

Evening Students, c. 300

• UNIVERSITY OF THE FREE STATE/UNIVERSITEIT VAN DIE VRYSTAAT (UFS/UV)

PO Box 339, Bloemfontein, Free State 9300
Tel: +27(51) 401-9111
EMail: info@stig.uovs.ac.za
Website: http://www.uovs.ac.za

Rector and Vice-Chancellor: Frederick Fourie (2003-)
Tel: +27(51) 401-2114 Fax: +27(51) 444-0740
EMail: gibsonij.rd@mail.ouvs.ac.za

Vice-Rector (Academic Planning) (Acting): Teuns Verschoor

International Relations: H. Barnard Tel: +27(51) 401-2501
EMail: ardp@rs.uovs.ac.za

Faculties

Economic and Management Sciences (Business Administration; Economics; Industrial and Organizational Psychology; Management; Public Administration) *Dean:* Tieniel (M.J.) Crous
Health Sciences (Health Sciences; Medicine; Nursing) *Dean:* L.V.M. Moja
Humanities (African Languages; Afrikaans; Anthropology; Art History; Arts and Humanities; Communication Studies; Criminal Law; Curriculum; Dutch; Education; Educational Administration; English; Fine Arts; French; German; Greek; History; Middle Eastern Studies; Music; Philosophy; Political Science; Psychology; Social Sciences; Social Work; Sociology; Technology; Theatre) *Dean:* Gerhardt de Klerk
Law (Commercial Law; Comparative Law; Criminal Law; Law; Private Law) *Dean:* Johann Henning
Natural and Agricultural Sciences (Agricultural Economics; Agriculture; Animal Husbandry; Applied Mathematics; Architecture; Botany; Chemistry; Computer Science; Crop Production; Electronic Engineering; Entomology; Environmental Management; Geography; Geology; Mathematics; Meteorology; Microbiology; Natural Sciences; Physics; Regional Planning; Soil Science; Statistics; Surveying and Mapping; Town Planning; Zoology) *Dean:* Herman D. van Schalkwyk
Theology (Bible; New Testament; Theology) *Dean (Acting):* Hermie van Zyl

Units

Agricultural Biometrics *(On Campus)* (Statistics) *Head:* Mike D. Fair
Business Ethics (Ethics) *Head:* D.S. Lubbe
Professional Development in Human Sciences (Development Studies; Social Sciences) *Head:* A. Weyers
Small Business Development (Small Business) *Head:* W.J.C. van der Merwe

Programmes

Open Learning Distance Education *(OLDEAP)* *Head:* H.R. Hay

Schools

Management *Director:* H. van Lyl

Institutes

Contemporary History *Director:* A.M. Dippenar
Groundwater Studies (Water Science) *Director:* F.D.I. Hodgson
Research in Educational Planning (Educational Research) *Director:* H.J. van der Linde

Centres

Accountancy *Director:* Dave S. Lubbe
Agricultural Management *(On Campus)* *Director:* Wimpie T. Nell
Business Law (Commercial Law) *Director:* Jozeph J. Henning
Construction Entrepreneurship (Real Estate) *Director:* J.J.P. Verster
Continued Legal Training *(On Campus)* (Law) *Director:* Mouritz C.J. Bobbert
Development Support (Development Studies) *Director:* Lucius C. Botes
Environmental Management *(On Campus)* *Director:* Maitland T. Seaman
Human Rights Studies (Human Rights) *Director:* Jan L. Pretorius
Professional Ethics *(On Campus)* (Ethics) *Director:* Mouritz C.J. Bobbert
Sustainable Agriculture *(On Campus)* (Agriculture) *Director:* Izak B. Groenewald

Research Centres

Farmous *Director:* B.H. Meyer

Further Information: Incorporated Bloemfontein Campus of Vista University 2004

History: Founded 1855 by Sir George Grey and established as University College 1904. Became University 1950. An autonomous institution receiving financial support from the State. Acquired present status 2004 following incorporation of Bloemfontein Campus of Vista University.

Governing Bodies: University Council

Academic Year: February to December (February-March; April-June; July-September; October-December)

Admission Requirements: Matriculation Certificate or certificate of exemption issued by the Joint Matriculation Board

Fees: (Rand): 9000-13,000; graduate, 7800-9000

Main Language(s) of Instruction: Afrikaans, English

Degrees and Diplomas: *Bachelor's Degree*: Education (BEd Hons), 1 yr following first degree; Theology (BTh), 3 yrs following first degree; Accountancy (BAcc); Administration (BAdmin); Agriculture (BAgric); Arts (BA); Commerce (BCom); Economics (BEcon); Financial Law (BProcLaw); Jurisprudence (BJuris); Library Science; Medical Science (BMedSc); Occupational Therapy; Personnel Guidance (BCom (HRM)); Radiography; Science (BSc); Social Sciences (BSocSc), 3-4 yrs; Law (LLB), 4 yrs; Architecture (BArch), 5 yrs; Medicine and Surgery (MBChB), 6 yrs; *Bachelor Honours Degree*: a further yr; *Master's Degree*: a further yr; *Doctorate*: 2 further yrs. The Bachelor (Honours) Degree is awarded in the same fields of study as the Bachelor's Degree. Also Postgraduate Diplomas

Student Services: Academic Counselling, Social Counselling, Employment Services, Foreign Student Adviser, Nursery Care, Cultural Centre, Sports Facilities, Language Programmes, Handicapped Facilities, Health Services, Canteen, Foreign Student Centre

Student Residential Facilities: For maximum 3190 students

Special Facilities: Drama and Theatre Studio. Johannes Stegmann Art Gallery

Libraries: Central Library, c. 436,340 vols. Libraries of: Medicine, Music, Agriculture

Publications: Acta Varia; Acta Academica

Press or Publishing House: University Press

Academic Staff 2001-2002	MEN	WOMEN	TOTAL
FULL-TIME	626	620	1,246
PART-TIME	625	799	1,424
TOTAL	**1,251**	**1,419**	**2,670**
STAFF WITH DOCTORATE			
FULL-TIME	195	66	261
PART-TIME	59	9	68
TOTAL	**254**	**75**	**329**

Student Numbers 2001-2002	MEN	WOMEN	TOTAL
All (Foreign Included)	5,415	6,668	**12,083**
FOREIGN ONLY	–	–	776

• UNIVERSITY OF PORT ELIZABETH/UNIVERSITEIT VAN PORT ELIZABETH (UPE)

PO Box 1600 Summerstrand, Port Elizabeth 6000
Tel: +27(41) 504-2111
Fax: +27(41) 504-2574
EMail: info@upe.ac.za
Website: http://www.upe.ac.za

Vice-Chancellor and Principal: Rolf Stumpf (1994-)
Tel: +27(41) 504-2101 Fax: +27(41) 504-2699

Registrar: Jenny Bishop Tel: +27(41) 504-2108
EMail: samjmb@upe.ac.za

International Relations: Nico J.. Jooste
Tel: +27(41) 504-2572 Fax: +27(41) 504-2333
EMail: international@upe.ac.za

Faculties

Arts (African Languages; Anthropology; Arts and Humanities; English; History; Management; Modern Languages; Music; Philosophy; Political Science; Public Administration; Religious Studies; Sociology) *Dean*: H.M. Thipa

Economic and Building Sciences (Accountancy; Architecture; Building Technologies; Business Administration; Computer Science; Economics; Industrial and Organizational Psychology; Labour and Industrial Relations; Surveying and Mapping) *Dean*: Martheanne Finnemore

Education (Curriculum; Education; Educational Administration) *Dean*: W.E. Morrow

Health Sciences (Health Sciences; Nursing; Pharmacy; Psychology; Social Work; Sociology) *Dean*: N.T. Naidoo

Law *Dean*: C. Van Loggerenberg

Science (Biochemistry; Botany; Chemistry; Computer Science; Geology; Mathematics; Microbiology; Natural Sciences; Physics; Statistics; Textile Technology; Zoology) *Dean*: C.A.B. Ball

Units

Community Development (Social and Community Services) *Head*: J.H. Senekal

Economic Processes (Economics) *Prof.*: André Mueller

Language Education (Modern Languages)

Legal Clinic (Forensic Medicine and Dentistry) *Director*: Rudolf Coetzee

Terrestrial Ecology (Ecology)

Tourism Law (Law; Tourism)

University Clinic *Prof.*: Delores Luiz

Institutes

Environmental and Coastal Management *(SAB)* (Environmental Management; Marine Science and Oceanography) *Director*: G.C. Bate

Social and Systemic Change (Social Sciences) *Director*: Deon Pretorius

Statistical Consultation and Methodology (Statistics) *Director*: D.J.L. Venter

Study and Resolution of Conflicts (Peace and Disarmament; Political Science) *Director*: G.J. Bradshaw

Centres

Advanced Studies (Development Studies; Social Work) *Co-ordinator*: Gysbert Olivier

Applied Business Management (Business Administration) *Prof.*: Johan Bosch

Coastal Resource Management (Regional Studies) *Director*: Brent Newman

Eastern Cape Studies (African Studies)

Human Movement Science (Sports; Sports Medicine) *Prof.*: Rosa Du Randt

Management Development (Management) *Manager*: Helen Hemsley

Research Units

Metal Ion Separation (Physics) *Director*: J.G.H Du Preez

Further Information: Merger with Port Elizabeth Campus of Vista University 2004

History: Founded 1964 by Act of Parliament and financially supported by the State. Acquired present status following merger with Port Elizabeth Campus of Vista University.

Governing Bodies: University Council; University Senate

Academic Year: February to November (February-June; July-November)

Admission Requirements: Matriculation Certificate or certificate of exemption issued by the Joint Matriculation Board

Fees: (Rand): Undergraduate, 4500-10,000 per annum; Honours and postgraduate, 1120-6890 per course

Main Language(s) of Instruction: Afrikaans, English

Degrees and Diplomas: *Bachelor's Degree*: Education (BEd), 1 yr following first degree; Architecture (BArch), 2 yrs; Law (LLB), 2 yrs following first degree; Arts (BA); Commerce (BComm); Jurisprudence (BJuris); Science (BSc), 3 yrs; Physical Education (BPhysEd), 3-4 yrs; Arts in Social Work (BA(SW)); Commerce Education (BCom(Ed)); Financial Law (BProc); Music (BMus); Music Education (BMusEd); Nursing (BCur); Pharmacy (BPharm); Primary Education (BPrimEd); Science in Quantity Surveying (BSc(QS)), 4 yrs; Science in Construction Management (BSc(Man)), 5 yrs; *Bachelor Honours Degree*: a further yr; *Master's Degree*: a further 1-2 yrs; *Doctorate*: Curationis (DCurNursing); Education (DEd); Law (LLD); Literature (DLitt); Music (DMus); Nursing (DCur); Philosophy (DPhil); Science (DSc), 1-2 yrs. The Bachelor (Honours) Degree is awarded in the same fields of study as the Bachelor's Degree. Also Undergraduate and Postgraduate Diplomas.

Student Residential Facilities: For c. 1200 students

Special Facilities: Nature Reserve and Environmental Trail

Libraries: Albert Delport Library, c. 385,000 vols; 1271 periodicals

Publications: UPE Focus (biannually); Building Management Journal; Labour Turnover in Port Elizabeth; Obiter (annually); Publications Series; Institute for Planning Research publications

Academic Staff *2001-2002:* Total: c. 400

Student Numbers *2001-2002*	TOTAL
All (Foreign Included)	**16,243**
FOREIGN ONLY	443

Part-time Students, 283 **Distance Students,** 15,517

• NORTH WEST UNIVERSITY/NOORDWES UNIVERSITEIT

Private Bag X6001, Potchefstroom 2520
Tel: +27(18) 299-2601
Fax: +27(18) 299-2603
EMail: enquiries@nwu.ac.za
Website: http://www.nwu.ac.za

Vice-Chancellor (Acting): Theuns Eloff
Tel: +27(18) 299-2601 Fax: +27(18) 299-2603
EMail: rktsjhvr@puknet.puk.ac.za

Faculties

Arts (Communication Studies; Government; Modern Languages; Music; Social Studies) *Dean*: Annette Combrink
Economic and Management Sciences (Accountancy; Economics; Human Resources; International Business; Management; Marketing; Tourism) *Dean*: G.J. de Klerk
Education Sciences (Education; Educational Administration; Educational Psychology; Educational Research; Educational Sciences; Educational Testing and Evaluation; Mathematics Education; Science Education) *Dean*: HJ. Steyn
Engineering (Chemical Engineering; Electrical and Electronic Engineering; Materials Engineering; Mechanical Engineering; Mining Engineering) *Dean*: J.I.J. Fick
Health Sciences (Behavioural Sciences; Consumer Studies; Health Sciences; Leisure Studies; Nursing; Nutrition; Parks and Recreation; Pharmacy; Physiology; Psychology; Social Work; Sports) *Dean*: HA. Koeleman
Law (Administrative Law; Civil Law; Commercial Law; Criminal Law; Criminology; History of Law; Human Rights; Insurance; International Law; Labour Law; Law; Private Law; Public Law; Taxation) *Dean*: F. Venter
Natural Sciences (Biochemistry; Chemistry; Computer Science; Development Studies; Environmental Studies; Mathematics; Natural Sciences; Physics; Statistics; Technology) *Dean*: DJ. Van Wyk
Theology (Ancient Languages; Bible; Holy Writings; Religious Studies; Theology) *Dean*: Ale R. du Plooy

Units

Adventure and Experimental Learning
Creative Writing *(ATKV)* (Writing)
Environmental Management
Kinderkinetics
Space Research

Schools

Accountancy Sciences (Accountancy; Finance; Management) *Director*: T. Eloff
Biblical Studies and Bible Languages (Ancient Languages; Bible; Greek; Holy Writings; New Testament) *Director*: J.J. Janse van Rensburg
Biokinetics, Recreation and Sports Sciences (Leisure Studies; Parks and Recreation; Sports) *Director*: GL. Strydom
Business *(Potchefstroom)* (Business and Commerce; Management) *Director*: WN. Coetzee
Chemical and Minerals Engineering (Chemical Engineering; Mining Engineering) *Director*: FB. Waanders
Chemistry and Biochemistry (Biochemistry; Chemistry) *Director*: J.J. Pienaar
Communication Studies (Art History; Communication Studies; Graphic Design; Painting and Drawing) *Director*: GF. de J. de Wet
Computer, Statistical and Mathematical Sciences (Applied Mathematics; Computer Science; Mathematics; Statistics) *Director*: JH. Fourie
Ecclesiastical Sciences (Christian Religious Studies; Ethics; History of Religion; Pastoral Studies; Religious Practice; Theology) *Director*: JM. Vorster
Economics, International Trade and Risk Management (Economics; Insurance; International Business; Management) *Director*: JHP. van Heerden
Electrical and Electronical Engineering (Computer Engineering; Electrical and Electronic Engineering) *Director*: ASL. Helberg
Entrepreneurship, Marketing and Tourism Management (Management; Marketing; Tourism) *Director*: LR. Jansen van Rensburg

Environmental Sciences and Development (Botany; Geography; Geology; Microbiology; Regional Planning; Town Planning; Zoology)

Human Resources Sciences (Human Resources; Industrial and Organizational Psychology; Sociology) *Director*: PE. Scholtz

Languages (African Languages; Afrikaans; Ancient Civilizations; Dutch; English; French; German; Latin; Translation and Interpretation; Writing) *Director*: Wam Carstens

Mechanical and Materials Engineering (Materials Engineering; Mechanical Engineering) *Director*: PG. Rousseau

Music (Music; Music Education; Music Theory and Composition; Singing)

Nursing (Health Administration; Health Sciences; Nursing; Public Health) *Director*: M. Greeff

Pharmacy (Chemistry; Pharmacology; Pharmacy) *Director*: CJ. van Wyk

Physics *Director*: H. Moraal

Physiology, Nutrition and Consumer Sciences (Consumer Studies; Dietetics; Nutrition; Physiology) *Director*: NT. Malan

Psycho-Social Behavioural Sciences (Behavioural Sciences; Psychology; Social Work) *Director*: MP. Wissing

Science, Mathematics and Technology Education (Mathematics Education; Science Education; Teacher Trainers Education; Technology Education) *Director*: JJA. Smit

Social and Government Studies (History; Philosophy; Political Science; Public Administration; Sociology) *Director*: WJ. van Wyk

Institutes
Biokinetics
Rugby *(PUK)*
Sports Science and Sports Development (Sports)

Graduate Schools
Education (Civil Security; Consumer Studies; Curriculum; Education; Educational Administration; Educational Psychology; Educational Research; Educational Testing and Evaluation; Mathematics Education; Natural Sciences; Pedagogy; Science Education; Special Education) *Director*: PC. van der Westhuizen

Research Institutes
Industrial Pharmacy (Pharmacy)

Further Information: Merger of Potchefstroom University for Christian Higher Education and incorporation of Sebokeng Campus of Vista University 2004

History: Founded 1869, became Constituent College of University of South Africa 1921, and by Act of Parliament became independent University 1951. An autonomous institution receiving financial support from the State. Acquired present status 2004 following merger with Potchefstroom University for Christian Higher Education and incorporation of Sebokeng Campus of Vista University.

Governing Bodies: University Council; University Senate

Academic Year: January to December (January-April; April-July; July-September; October-December)

Admission Requirements: Matriculation Certificate or certificate of exemption issued by the Joint Matriculation Board

Fees: (Rand): c. 9458 per annum

Main Language(s) of Instruction: Afrikaans, English

Degrees and Diplomas: *National Certificate*: 1-2 yrs; *National Diploma (Ndip)*: 1-3 yrs; *National Higher Diploma*: 4 yrs; *Bachelor's Degree*: Education (BEd); Health Management; Health Sciences (BCur); Arts; Graphic Design; Social Work; Sports; Communication Studies (BA); Commerce; Business Administration; Consumer Studies (BCom); Dietetics (BSc(Dietetics)); Domestic Science; Engineering (BEng); Law; Music (BMus); Pharmacy (BPharm); Psychology; Science; Industrial Science; Information Technology (BSc); Technology, 3-4 yrs; Theology (ThB), 4 yrs following B.A; *Bachelor Honours Degree*: a further yr; *Master's Degree*: a further 1-2 yrs; *Doctorate*: 1-2 yrs following Master's Degree. The Bachelor (Honours) Degree is awarded in the same fields of study as the Bachelor's Degree. Also Advanced and Postgraduate Diplomas

Student Services: Academic Counselling, Cultural Centre, Sports Facilities, Health Services, Canteen, Foreign Student Centre

Student Residential Facilities: For 3850 students in 20 hostels

Special Facilities: PU-Kanamuseum

Libraries: Ferdinand Postma Library, 536,801 vols; 1,649 current periodicals; 123,111 periodical annual vols; 13,930 other materials

Publications: Kampusnuus (bimonthly); Koers, Skriflig, Word and Action (4 per annum); Litterator (3 per annum); PU-kaner Skakelblad (1 per annum)

Academic Staff 2002	MEN	WOMEN	TOTAL
FULL-TIME	320	168	**488**
STAFF WITH DOCTORATE			
FULL-TIME	219	60	**279**

Student Numbers 2002	MEN	WOMEN	TOTAL
All (Foreign Included)	10,552	16,408	**26,960**
FOREIGN ONLY	1,072	1,390	2,462

Part-time Students, 17,797 **Distance Students,** 13,453

Note: include Vaal Triangle Campus students

MAFIKENG CAMPUS
Private Bag X2046, Mmabatho 2735
Tel: +27(18) 389-2111
Fax: +27(18) 392-5775
EMail: rossouwt@uniwest.ac.za
Website: http://www.uniwest.ac.za

Faculties
Agriculture, Science and Technology (Agricultural Economics; Animal Husbandry; Biology; Chemistry; Environmental Studies; Geography; Mathematics; Nursing; Physics; Plant and Crop Protection)

Commerce and Administration (Accountancy; Business and Commerce; Economics; Industrial and Organizational Psychology; Management; Public Administration; Statistics) *Dean*: G.D. Setsetse

Education (Adult Education; Curriculum; Education; Educational Administration) *Dean*: L.M.E.M. Sehlare

Human and Social Sciences (African Languages; Afrikaans; Communication Studies; Demography and Population;

Development Studies; English; History; International Relations; Political Science; Psychology; Social Work; Sociology) *Dean*: R.M. Manyane

Law (Commercial Law; Criminal Law; Law; Private Law; Public Law) *Dean*: R.L. Kettles

MANKWE CAMPUS
Private Bag X1014, Mogwase 0304
Tel: +27(14) 555-5302
Fax: +27(14) 555-5661

VAAL TRIANGLE CAMPUS
PO Box 1174, Vanderbijlpark 1900
Tel: +27(16) 910-3111
Fax: +27(16) 910-3116
EMail: vaal@puk.ac.za
Website: http://www.vaal.puk.ac.za

Vice-Principal: P.J.J. Prinsloo

Schools

Basic Sciences (Bible; History; Management; Philosophy; Public Administration) *Director*: Johann W.N. Tempelhoff
Behavioural Sciences (Behavioural Sciences; Industrial and Organizational Psychology; Psychology; Sociology) *Director*: C. de W. van Wyk
Business School *(Potchefstroom)* (Business Administration)
Economic Sciences (Accountancy; Commercial Law; Economics; Industrial and Organizational Psychology; Management; Psychology; Sociology; Taxation) *Director*: P. Lucouw
Educational Sciences (Curriculum; Educational Administration; Educational Psychology; Educational Sciences; Pedagogy) *Director*: L.M. Vermeulen
Languages (African Languages; Afrikaans; English; Modern Languages) *Director*: M.M. Verhoef
Modelling Sciences (Computer Science; Information Technology; Mathematics; Operations Research; Statistics) *Director*: D.B. Jordaan

History: Founded 1966.
Academic Staff *2002*: Full-Time: c. 50

• UNIVERSITY OF PRETORIA/UNIVERSITEIT VAN PRETORIA (TUKS)
Pretoria 0002
Tel: +27(12) 420-4111
Fax: +27(12) 362-5168
Website: http://www.up.ac.za

Vice-Chancellor and Principal: Carl W.I. Pistorius (2001-)
Tel: +27(12) 420-2900 Fax: +27(12) 420-4530
EMail: rektor@up.ac.za
Registrar: N.J. Grove Tel: +27(12) 420-4273
Fax: +27(12) 420-3696 EMail: njgrove@ccnet.up.ac.za
International Relations: Vinay Rajah Tel: +27(12) 420-3237
Fax: +27(12) 420-2049 EMail: yrajah@ccnet.up.ac.za

Faculties

Economics and Management Sciences (Communication Studies; Computer Science; Economics; Human Resources; Management; Marketing; Statistics; Tourism) *Dean*: Carolina Koornhof
Education (Education; Educational Sciences) *Dean*: J.D. Jansen
Engineering, the Built Environment and Information Technology (Building Technologies; Engineering; Information Technology; Town Planning) *Dean*: R.F. Sanderbergh
Health Sciences (Health Sciences; Pathology; Sports Medicine) *Dean*: T.J. Mariba
Humanities (Arts and Humanities) *Dean*: M.E. Muller
Law (Administrative Law; Civil Law; Comparative Law; Constitutional Law; Criminal Law; History of Law; Human Rights; International Law; Labour Law; Law) *Dean*: D.G. Kleyn
Natural and Agricultural Sciences (Agriculture; Biological and Life Sciences; Mathematics; Natural Sciences; Physics) *Dean*: R.M. Crewe
Theology (Bible; Christian Religious Studies; Missionary Studies; New Testament; Theology) *Dean*: C.J.A. Vos
Veterinary Science (Anatomy; Animal Husbandry; Community Health; Pharmacology; Toxicology; Veterinary Science) *Dean*: N.P.J. Kriek

Schools

Agricultural Sciences (Agricultural Economics; Animal Husbandry; Food Science; Home Economics; Soil Science) *Dean*: J.F. Kirsten
Arts (Music; Visual Arts) *Dean*: M.D. Sauthoff
Biological Sciences (Biochemistry; Biological and Life Sciences; Botany; Entomology; Genetics; Microbiology; Physiology; Plant Pathology; Zoology) *Dean*: T.E. Cloete
Built Environment (Architecture; Interior Design; Landscape Architecture; Regional Planning; Town Planning) *Chairman*: H.M. Siglé
Community Health
Economic Science (Banking; Econometrics; Economics) *Director*: J.H. Van Heerden
Educational Sciences (Teacher Trainers Education)
Engineering (Aeronautical and Aerospace Engineering; Chemical Engineering; Civil Engineering; Computer Engineering; Electrical and Electronic Engineering; Engineering; Food Technology; Industrial Engineering; Mechanical Engineering; Metallurgical Engineering; Mining Engineering) *Dean*: J.L. Steyn
Financial Science (Accountancy; Finance; Taxation) *Dean*: Q. Vorster
Health Care Science (Nursing; Occupational Therapy; Physical Therapy)
Health Systems and Public Health (Community Health; Public Health)
Information Technology (Information Technology; Management) *Dean*: J.D. Roode
Languages (African Languages; Ancient Languages; English) *Dean*: J.H. Potgieter
Management Sciences (Human Resources; Management; Marketing; Public Administration; Tourism) *Dean*: R.S. Rensburg
Mathematical Sciences (Actuarial Science; Applied Mathematics; Mathematics; Statistics)
Medicine (Anaesthesiology; Anatomy; Cardiology; Dermatology; Epidemiology; Forensic Medicine and Dentistry;

Gynaecology and Obstetrics; Medicine; Neurology; Orthopedics; Otorhinolaryngology; Paediatrics; Pharmacology; Physiology; Psychiatry and Mental Health; Radiology; Sports Medicine; Surgery; Urology)
Pathology Sciences (Genetics; Immunology; Pathology)
Physical Sciences (Chemistry; Earth Sciences; Geography; Physics) *Dean*: J.B. Malherbe
Social Sciences (Anthropology; Archaeology; Communication Disorders; Criminology; Cultural Studies; Leisure Studies; Philosophy; Political Science; Psychology; Social Sciences; Social Work; Sports) *Dean*: S.R. Hugo

Centres
Academic Development (Education) *Director*: A.L. De Boer
Augmentative and Alternative Communication (Communication Studies) *Director*: E. Alant
Child Law *Director*: C.J. Davel
Computer Science for Education *(Golgfields)* (Educational Technology) *Director*: J.C. Van Staden
Continued Theological Education (Theology) *Director*: J .H. Le Roux
Education Law and Education Policy *(CELP)* (Educational Administration) *Director*: J.L. Beckmann
Environmental Biology and Biological Control (Biology) *Director*: J.M. Kotze
Equine Research *Director*: A.J. Guthrie
Gender Studies *Director*: M. De Waal
Human Rights *Director*: C.H. Heyns
Information Development (Information Sciences) *Director*: T.J.D. Bothma
Interlanguage Communication (Communication Studies)
Land Development, Housing and Construction (Construction Engineering; Landscape Architecture) *Director*: A.C. Hauptfleisch
Legal Aid (Law) *Director*: F.E. Van der Merwe
Mammal Research (Zoology) *Director*: J.T. Du Toit
Music *Director*: C. Van Niekerk
New Electricity Studies *(CNES)* (Electrical and Electronic Engineering) *Director*: G.J. Delport
Population Studies (Demography and Population) *Director*: J.L. Van Thonder
Science Education *Director*: M.W.H. Braun
Stomatological Research (Dentistry) *Director*: S.J. Botha
Wildlife Research (Wildlife) *Director*: J. du P. Bothma

Bureaux
Economic Politics and Analysis (Political Science) *Head*: N.J. Schoeman
Financial Analysis (Finance) *Director*: T.G. Kruger
Statistics and Methodology *(STATOMET)* (Statistics) *Director*: N.A.S. Crowther

Graduate Schools
Management
Further Information: Incorporated Mamelodi Campus of Vista University 2004

History: Founded 1908 by Transvaal Government, became separate University College 1910 and autonomous University 1930. Financially supported by the State. Incorporated Mamelodi Campus of Vista University 2004.

438

Governing Bodies: University Council, comprising 26 members; University Senate

Academic Year: January to November (January-June; July-November)

Admission Requirements: Matriculation Exemption Certificate. Matriculation subjects passed with at least 50% on the Higher Grade for admission in Science branches. Accessible to members of all race and language groups

Fees: (Rands): c. 7500-12,500 per annum

Main Language(s) of Instruction: Afrikaans, English

Degrees and Diplomas: *Bachelor's Degree*: 3-4 yrs; *Bachelor Honours Degree*: a further yr; *Master's Degree*: a further 2 yrs; *Doctorate*: (PhD), a further 2 yrs. The Honours Degree is awarded in the same fields of study as the Bachelor's Degree. Also, Professional Bachelor Degrees, 4 yrs, and Undergraduate and Postgraduate Diplomas, 1-2 yrs

Student Services: Academic Counselling, Social Counselling, Employment Services, Nursery Care, Cultural Centre, Sports Facilities, Handicapped Facilities, Health Services, Canteen, Foreign Student Centre

Student Residential Facilities: For 6000 students

Special Facilities: Anton van Wouw House Museum. Van Tilburg Collection. Van Gybland-Oosterhoff Collection. Kya Rosa (historical landmark) University Art Collection

Libraries: Academic Information Service, c. 1.1m. vols

Publications: Perdeby, Students' newspapers (name could be translated as "wasp") (1 per week); Annual Report; Research Report, Report on research outputs; Prospectus, Corporate profile; Guide to Expertise, Providing Information on the field of expertise of academic personnel at the University (annually); Tukkievaria, Staff Newsletter (24 per annum); Ad-Destinatum, Commemorative Volumes of the University of Pretoria (3-4 per annum)

Academic Staff *2001-2002*: Full-Time: c. 1,500 Part-Time: c. 980 Total: c. 2,480

Staff with Doctorate: Total: c. 695

Student Numbers *2001-2002*: All (Foreign Included): c. 28,100 Foreign Only: c. 970

Evening Students, c. 6,810

• RAND AFRIKAANS UNIVERSITY/RANDSE AFRIKAANSE UNIVERSITEIT (RAU)
PO Box 524, Auckland Park, Johannesburg 2006
Tel: +27(11) 489-2911
Fax: +27(11) 489-2191
Telex: 424526 sa
Cable: rauniv
EMail: ath@raul.rau.ac.za
Website: http://www.rau.ac.za

Rector and Vice-Chancellor: Theunis Roux Botha (1995-)
Tel: +27(11) 489-3000 Fax: +27(11) 489-2260
EMail: rektor@bestuur.rau.ac.za;trb@bestuur.rau.ac.za

Registrar: P.M.S. Von Staden Tel: +27(11) 489-3008
Fax: +27(11) 489-3057 EMail: regacad@bestuur.rau.ac.za

International Relations: J.H.P. Ellis Tel: +27(11) 489-2417
Fax: +27(11) 489-2632

Faculties

Arts (Arts and Humanities) *Dean*: J.A. Naudé

Economics and Management Sciences (Economic History;
Economics; Management) *Dean*: I.V.W. Raubenheimer

Education and Nursing (Education; Nursing) *Dean (Acting)*:
J.C. Kok

Engineering *Dean*: P. van der Merwe

Law *Dean*: D. van der Merwe

Natural Sciences (Natural Sciences; Optometry) *Dean*: D.D.
Van Reenen

Institutes

Child and Adult Guidance (Social and Community Services)
Director: A. Burke

Centres

Distance Education *Director*: Izak J. Broere

Metropolitan and Regional Administration (Public Administration) *Head*: W. Zybrands

Research Institutes

Energy Studies (Energy Engineering) *Director*: C. Cooper

European Studies *Head*: G.C. Olivier

Further Information: Incorporated the East Rand and Soweto
campuses of Vista University 2004

History: Founded 1966 by Act of Parliament, first students admitted 1968. Financially supported by the State. Incorporated
the East Rand and Soweto campuses of Vista University 2004.

Governing Bodies: University Council; Management Committee; University Senate

Academic Year: January to November (January-June;
July-November)

Admission Requirements: Matriculation Certificate or certificate of exemption issued by the Joint Matriculation Board

Fees: (Rand): 8500 per annum; Honours, 8500; postgraduate,
4200

Main Language(s) of Instruction: Afrikaans, English

International Co-operation: With universities in Europe, USA
and Far Eastern Countries

Degrees and Diplomas: *National Diploma (Ndip)*: Education, 2
yrs; *Bachelor's Degree*: Education (BEd), 1 yr following first degree; Arts (BA); Arts in Law; Commerce (BCom); Information
Science (BInf); Science (BSc), 3 yrs; Commercial Law
(BCom(Law)); Engineering (BIng); Law (LLB); Nursing (BCur);
Optometry (BOptom), 4 yrs; *Bachelor Honours Degree*: a fur-
ther yr; *Postgraduate Diploma*: Information Science, 1 yr follow-
ing Bachelor's Degree; Education; Human Resource
Management; Language and Text Guidance; Transport Eco-
nomics, 1 yr following Bachelor's Degree; *Master's Degree*: Hu-
manities, Natural Sciences, Economics and Management
Sciences, Education, Engineering and Law (MA; MSc;
MMcom; MEd; MIng; LLM; MPhil), a further 1-2 yrs; *Doctorate*:
Humanities, Natural Sciences, Economic and Management

Sciences, Education, Engineering and Law (DLitt; Dcom; DEd;
DIng; LLD; DPhil), 2-4 yrs. The Bachelor (Honours) Degree is
awarded in the same fields of study as the Bachelor's Degree

Student Services: Academic Counselling, Social Counselling,
Employment Services, Foreign Student Adviser, Cultural Cen-
tre, Sports Facilities, Language Programmes, Handicapped
Facilities, Canteen

Special Facilities: Museums: Geology; Zoology and Anthropology. Art Collection

Libraries: 420,448 vols

Publications: Higher Education Bulletin (bimonthly); Quarterly
Econometric Forecast; RAU-Rapport; Ekklesiastikos Pharos
(quarterly); Anvil-Aambeeld: Opinion Journal; Medieval Studies
(biannually);   Communicare,   (Communication   Studies)
(annually)

Academic Staff *2001-2002:* Total: c. 320

Staff with doctorate: Total: c. 190

Student Numbers *2001-2002*: All (Foreign Included): c. 18,830
Foreign Only: c. 300

Evening Students, c. 1,500 **Distance Students,** c. 6,000

• RHODES UNIVERSITY (RU)

POB 94, Drostdy Road, Grahamstown, Eastern Cape 6140
Tel: +27(46) 603-8111
Fax: +27(46) 622-8444
EMail: s.fourie@ru.ac.za
Website: http://www.ru.ac.za

Vice-Chancellor: David R. Woods (1996-)
Tel: +27(46) 603-8148 EMail: d.woods@ru.ac.za

Registrar: S. Fourie Tel: +27(46) 603-8101
Fax: +27(46) 603-8127 EMail: s.fourie@ru.ac.za

International Relations: Sandra L. Stephenson, Director of
Academic Planning Tel: +27(46) 603-8059
Fax: +27(46) 627-8444 EMail: s.stephenson@ru.ac.za

Head Librarian: Margaret Kenyon
EMail: M.Kenyon@ru.ac.za

Faculties

Commerce (Accountancy; Business and Commerce; Commercial Law; Economics; Information Technology; Management;
Statistics) *Dean*: Arthur Webb

Education (Education; Environmental Studies) *Dean*: George
Euvrard

Humanities (African Languages; Afrikaans; Anthropology; Arts
and Humanities; Dutch; English; English Studies; Fine Arts;
French; German; Greek; History; International Relations; Italian; Journalism; Latin; Linguistics; Media Studies; Music; Photography; Political Science; Psychology; Social Work;
Sociology; Theatre)

Law (Commercial Law; Law) *Dean*: R B Mqeke

Pharmacy (Pharmacology; Pharmacy) *Dean*: I. Kanfer

Science (Applied Mathematics; Biochemistry; Biological and
Life Sciences; Botany; Chemistry; Earth Sciences; Economics;
Entomology; Environmental Studies; Ergotherapy; Fishery; Ge-
ography; Geology; Information Sciences; Management; Marine
Biology; Mathematics; Microbiology; Physical Therapy; Phys-
ics; Psychology; Statistics; Zoology) *Dean*: Pat Terry

439

Institutes

Aeronomy *(Herman Ohlthaver) Director:* A.W.V. Poole

Aquatic Biodiversity (Aquaculture) *Director:* P.H. Skelton

Social and Economic Research (Economics; Social Sciences) *Director:* V. Møller

Study of English in Africa (English; Literacy Education; Writing) *Director:* L.S. Wright

Water Research (Water Management) *Director:* J. O'Keefe

Water Research (Water Science) *Director:* J. O'Keeffe

Centres

Crime Prevention Studies (Criminology; Psychology) *Director:* M. Welman

Mathematics Education Projects (Mathematics Education) *Director:* J. Stoker

Research Institutes

Biopharmaceutics (Biology; Pharmacology; Pharmacy)

History: Founded 1904 as University College, became Constituent College of the University of South Africa 1916 and incorporated as independent University 1951. An autonomous institution receiving financial support from the State.

Governing Bodies: University Council; Senate

Academic Year: February to November (February-April; April-June; July-September; September-November)

Admission Requirements: Matriculation Certificate or certificate of exemption issued by the Joint Matriculation Board

Fees: (Rands): 11,500 per annum

Main Language(s) of Instruction: English

Degrees and Diplomas: *Bachelor's Degree:* Education (Bed), 1 yr following first degree; Arts (BA); Arts (Human Movement Studies) (BA); Commerce (Bcom); Economics (Becon); Science (BSc); Social Sciences (BSocSc), 3 yrs; Fine Arts (BFineArt); Journalism and Media Studies (BJourn); Laws (LLB); Music (BMus); Pharmacy (BPharm); Primary Education (BPrimEd), 4 yrs; *Bachelor Honours Degree:* a further yr; *Master's Degree:* a further 1-2 yrs; *Doctorate:* 2 yrs. The Bachelor (Honours) Degree is awarded in the same fields of study as the Bachelor's Degree. Also Undergraduate and Postgraduate Diplomas

Student Services: Academic Counselling, Social Counselling, Employment Services, Foreign Student Adviser, Nursery Care, Cultural Centre, Sports Facilities, Language Programmes, Handicapped Facilities, Health Services, Canteen, Foreign Student Centre

Student Residential Facilities: For 2039 students

Special Facilities: Rhodes University Museum; National English Literary Museum; Albany Museum

Libraries: Central Library, 33,108 vols; Cory Library for Historical Research, 40,000; International Library of African Music

Publications: Rhodes Review (biannually); Statistical Digest; University Calendar (annually)

Academic Staff 2001	MEN	WOMEN	TOTAL
FULL-TIME	208	106	314
PART-TIME	–	–	10
TOTAL	–	–	**324**

Staff with doctorate: Total: **135**

Student Numbers 2001	MEN	WOMEN	TOTAL
All (Foreign Included)	2,640	3,576	**6,216**
FOREIGN ONLY	–	–	1,351

UNIVERSITY OF FORT HARE

50 Church Street, East London, Eastern Cape 5201
Tel: +27(43) 704-7000
Fax: +27(43) 704-7095
EMail: t.marsh@ru.ac.za
Website: http://www.ru.ac.za/eastlondon

Director: T.A. Marsh Tel: +27(43) 704-7008

Departments

Accountancy
African Languages
Afrikaans
Commercial Law
Economics
Education
English
History
Information Systems (Information Technology)
Law
Management
Nursing Sciences (Nursing)
Professional Communication (Communication Studies)
Psychology
Social Work
Sociology and Industrial Sociology (Sociology)
Statistics
Theory of Finance (Finance)

Institutes

Leadership Development *(Johnson and Johnson)*

Social and Economic Research (Economics; Social Studies)

History: Founded 1981.

• UNIVERSITY OF SOUTH AFRICA/UNIVERSITEIT VAN SUID-AFRIKA (UNISA)

PO Box 392, Pretoria, Transvaal 0003
Tel: +27(12) 429-3111
Fax: +27(12) 429-3221
EMail: info@unisa.ac.za
Website: http://www.unisa.ac.za

Vice-Chancellor: Nyamenko Barney Pityana (2004-)
Tel: +27(12) 429-2550 Fax: +27(12) 429-2565
EMail: pityanb@unisa.ac.za;polloja@unisa.ac.za

Pro-Vice-Chancellor: Neo Mathabe

International Relations: Nicolas Bwakira
Tel: +27(12) 429-6918 Fax: +27(12) 429-6239
EMail: bwakin@unisa.ac.za

Faculties

Arts (African Languages; African Studies; Afrikaans; Ancient Civilizations; Anthropology; Archaeology; Archiving; Art History;

Arts and Humanities; Bible; Chinese; Classical Languages; Communication Studies; Criminal Law; Criminology; English; Environmental Studies; French; Gender Studies; Geography; German; Greek; Hebrew; History; Information Sciences; International Studies; Islamic Studies; Italian; Latin; Linguistics; Musical Instruments; Nursing; Philosophy; Political Science; Psychology; Public Administration; Romance Languages; Russian; Social Work; Sociology; Spanish; Visual Arts) *Dean*: W.F. Meyer

Economics and Management (Accountancy; Business Administration; Economics; Industrial and Organizational Psychology; Management; Tourism) *Dean*: M. Shania

Education *Dean*: L.R. MacFarlane

Law (Commercial Law; Law) *Dean*: Johann Neethling

Science (Applied Mathematics; Astronomy and Space Science; Biological and Life Sciences; Chemistry; Computer Science; Geography; Information Sciences; Mathematics; Natural Sciences; Operations Research; Physics; Psychology; Statistics) *Dean*: E.C. Reynhardt

Theology and Biblical Religions (Bible; Missionary Studies; New Testament; Religious Studies; Theology) *Dean*: Johannes N. J. Kritzinger

Institutes

Adult Basic Education and Training (Education)
All African Languages Redevelopment (African Languages)
Continuing Education *Head*: Evelyn Nonyongo
Criminology *Director*: J.H. Prinsloo
Educational Research *Director*: C.H. Swanepoel
Foreign and Comparative Law (Comparative Law) *Director*: A.E.A.M. Thomashausen
Gender Studies *Coordinator*: Jennifer Lemon
Social and Health Sciences (Health Sciences; Peace and Disarmament; Social Sciences) *Director*: Mohamed Seedat
Theology and Religion (Religion; Theology) *Director*: C.W. Du Toit

Centres

Accountancy Studies (Accountancy) *Head*: J.B.J. van Rensburg
Applied Psychology (Psychology)
Applied Statistics (Statistics)
Arts, Culture and Heritage Studies (Cultural Studies; Fine Arts; Heritage Preservation) *Director*: Chris van Vuuren
Bible
Business Law (Commercial Law; Labour Law)
Business Management (Business Administration; Management) *Head*: B.J. Erasmus
Community Training and Development (Social Welfare)
Development Administration (Administration; Development Studies)
Improvement of Mathematics, Science and Technology Education (Mathematics Education; Science Education; Technology Education)
Indigenous Law (Law)
Industrial and Organizational Psychology
Latin American Studies *Head*: Zélia Roelofse-Campbell
Legal Aid *(Clinic)*
Legal Terminology in African Languages (Law)
Peace Education (Peace and Disarmament)

Public Law Studies (Public Law)
Software Engineering

Graduate Schools

Business Leadership (Business Administration)

Further Information: Incorporated Technikon SA and Vista University Distance Education Campus (VUDEC) 2004

History: Founded 1873 as University of Cape of Good Hope. Incorporated by Act of Parliament as the University of South Africa 1916. Since 1951 concerned only with external students for whom it provides tuition by correspondence. Acquired present status 2004 following merger with Technikon SA and Vista University Distance Education Campus (VUDEC).

Governing Bodies: University Council; University Senate

Academic Year: January to December (january-May; June-November)

Admission Requirements: Matriculation Certificate or certificate of exemption issued by the Joint Matriculation Board

Fees: (Rand): Undergraduate, c. 840-1300 per annum; postgraduate, c. 2500-3500

Main Language(s) of Instruction: English, Afrikaans

Degrees and Diplomas: *Bachelor's Degree*: Education (BEd), 1 yr following first degree; Law (LLB), 2-4 yrs following first degree; Divinity (BD), 3 yrs following BA; Accountancy (BCompt); Administration (BAdmin); Arts (BA); Commerce (BCom); Diaconiology (BDiac); Financial Law (BProcLaw); Jurisprudence (BJuris); Library Science (BBibl); Music (BMus); Primary Education (BPrimEd); Science (BSc); Theology (BTh), 3-4 yrs; *Bachelor Honours Degree*: a further yr; *Master's Degree*: a further 1-2 yrs; *Doctorate*: 1-2 yrs. The Bachelor (Honours) Degree is awarded in the same fields of study as the Bachelor's Degree. Also Undergraduate and Postgraduate Diplomas

Student Services: Academic Counselling, Employment Services, Nursery Care, Handicapped Facilities, Health Services, Canteen

Special Facilities: Museums: Anthropology; Theology; Education; Nursing Science. Art Gallery. Archives and Special Collection

Libraries: Central Library, c. 1.5m. vols; 7000 periodicals

Publications: Theologia Evangelica (3 per annum); Unisa English Studies; Educare; Codicillus; Communicatio; Unisa Psychologia; Progressio; Mousaion; Musicus; De Arte; English Usage in South Africa; Politeia (biannually); Ars Nova; Africanus; Dynamica; Kleio (annually)

Press or Publishing House: Unisa Press

Academic Staff *2001-2002:* Total: c. 1,310

Student Numbers *2001-2002*: All (Foreign Included): c. 132,790
Foreign Only: c. 7,875

Note: Also c. 5700 evening students

TECHNIKON SA
Private Bag X6, Florida, Gauteng 1710
Tel: +27(11) 471-2000
Fax: +27(11) 471-2122
EMail: wmaster@tsamail.trsa.ac.za
Website: http://www.tsa.ac.za

Vice-Chancellor and Principal: Neo R. Khutsoane-Mathabe
Tel: +27(11) 471-2552 Fax: +27(11) 471-2554
EMail: nmathabe@tsa.ac.za

Registrar: Tony Links Tel: +27(11) 471-2122
Fax: +27(11) 471-3383 EMail: T.Links@tsa.ac.za

International Relations: Kenneth Mubu
Tel: +27(11) 471-3911 Fax: +27(11) 471-3457
EMail: kmubu@tsa.ac.za

Head Librarian: Judy Henning

Divisions

Applied Community Sciences (Law; Public Administration)
Director: Narend Baijnath

Economics and Management (Accountancy; Business Administration; Economics; Human Resources; Information Technology; Management; Marketing; Real Estate; Tourism)
Director: André Kritsinger

Natural Sciences and Engineering (Agriculture; Engineering; Natural Resources) *Director:* Godfred Humphrey

Public Safety and Criminal Justice (Criminal Law; Police Studies; Public Law) *Director:* Danny Titus

Departments

Research *Director:* Ntabiseng Ogude

History: Founded 1980. Only distance education Technikon in South Africa.

Governing Bodies: Council

Academic Year: January to October (January-March; April-June; August-October)

Main Language(s) of Instruction: English

International Co-operation: With universities in Kenya, Rwanda, Namibia, Lesotho, Swaziland, Zimbabwe, Australia, USA.

Accrediting Agencies: South African Qualifications Authority (SAQA)

Degrees and Diplomas: *National Diploma (Ndip):* Accountancy; Business Management; Engineering; Human Resources; Marketing; Police Studies; Public Management and Development, 3 yrs; *Bachelor of Technology (Btech):* Accountancy; Business Management; Engineering; Human Resources; Marketing; Police Studies; Public Management and Development, 4 yrs

Student Services: Academic Counselling, Employment Services, Foreign Student Adviser, Language Programmes, Handicapped Facilities

Special Facilities: The Allan Boesak Archives

Libraries: Goldfiels Library and Information Centre

VISTA UNIVERSITY DISTANCE EDUCATION CAMPUS
Private Bag X641, Pretoria
Tel: +27(12) 352-4000
Fax: +27(12) 322-3243
Website: http://www.vista.ac.za/VUDEC.html

442

ST AUGUSTINE COLLEGE OF SOUTH AFRICA

PO Box 44782, Linden, Johannesburg 2195
Tel: +27(11) 782-4616
Fax: +27(11) 782-8729
EMail: admin@staugustine.ac.za
Website: http://www.staugustine.ac.za

Vice-Chancellor: Edith Raidt (1999-)
EMail: eraidt@staugustine.ac.za

Registrar: Felicity Eggleston

Head Librarian: Imogen Ndaba

Faculties

Applied Ethics (Ethics) *Dean:* Antony Egan

Culture and Education (Cultural Studies; Education; Educational Administration) *Dean:* Rex Van Vuuren

Philosophy *Dean:* Gerard Walmsley

Religion (Catholic Theology; Pastoral Studies; Religious Education) *Dean:* Stuart Bate

Theology (Canon Law; Christian Religious Studies; Theology) *Dean:* Rodney Moss

History: Founded 1999.

Governing Bodies: Board of Directors; Academic Board

Academic Year: January to December

Admission Requirements: Bachelor Honours

Fees: (Rands) 3500-7200 per annum

Main Language(s) of Instruction: English

International Co-operation: With universities in Australia; Belgium; Netherlands; USA

Accrediting Agencies: State Department of Education

Degrees and Diplomas: *Master's Degree:* Applied Ethics, Culture and Education, Religious Education and Pastoral Ministry, Philosophy, Theology (M Phil), 2 yrs part-time; *Doctorate:* (PhD), 2 yrs full-time (4 yrs part-time)

Student Services: Academic Counselling, Canteen

Student Residential Facilities: Yes

Libraries: c. 7,500 vols

Publications: St Augustine Papers (annually)

Academic Staff 2002	MEN	WOMEN	TOTAL
FULL-TIME	4	2	6
PART-TIME	9	6	15
TOTAL	**13**	**8**	**21**
STAFF WITH DOCTORATE			
FULL-TIME	4	1	5
PART-TIME	9	6	15
TOTAL	**13**	**7**	**20**
Student Numbers 2002	MEN	WOMEN	TOTAL
All (Foreign Included)	63	23	**86**
FOREIGN ONLY	29	1	30

Part-time Students, 86

• UNIVERSITY OF STELLENBOSCH/UNIVERSITEIT VAN STELLENBOSCH

Private Bag X1, Matieland 7602
Tel: +27(21) 808-9111
Fax: +27(21) 808-3800
Telex: 52-0383
EMail: interoff@maties.sun.ac.za;mts@maties.sun.ac.za
Website: http://www.sun.ac.za

Vice-Chancellor and Rector: Chris Brink (2002-)
Tel: +27(21) 808-4490 Fax: +27(21) 808-3714
EMail: chrisbrink@sun.ac.za

Registrar: Johan Aspeling Tel: +27(21) 808-4516
Fax: +27(21) 808-4576 EMail: jaa@sun.ac.za

International Relations: Robert Kotzé
Tel: +27(21) 808-4628 Fax: +27(21) 808-3799
EMail: rk@sun.ac.za

Faculties

Agricultural and Forestry Sciences (Agricultural Economics; Agriculture; Agronomy; Animal Husbandry; Ecology; Entomology; Food Science; Forestry; Genetics; Horticulture; Oenology; Plant Pathology; Soil Science; Viticulture; Water Science; Wood Technology) *Dean:* L. van Huyssteen

Arts (African Languages; Afrikaans; Arts and Humanities; Classical Languages; Dutch; English; Environmental Studies; Fine Arts; Geography; History; Information Sciences; Journalism; Linguistics; Modern Languages; Music; Philosophy; Political Science; Psychology; Religion; Religious Studies; Social Work; Sociology; Theatre) *Dean:* I.J. van der Merwe

Economics and Management (Accountancy; Business Administration; Economics; Industrial and Organizational Psychology; Management; Rural Planning; Statistics; Town Planning; Transport Economics) *Dean (Acting):* J.U. de Villiers

Education (Education; Educational Psychology; Special Education; Sports) *Dean:* T. Park

Engineering (Applied Mathematics; Chemical Engineering; Civil Engineering; Electrical and Electronic Engineering; Engineering; Industrial Engineering; Mechanical Engineering) *Dean:* Arnold Schoonwinkel

Health Sciences *(Tygerberg)* (Anatomy; Biochemistry; Cardiology; Community Health; Dentistry; Dermatology; Forensic Medicine and Dentistry; Gynaecology and Obstetrics; Haematology; Histology; Medicine; Microbiology; Nursing; Nutrition; Occupational Therapy; Oncology; Ophthalmology; Orthopedics; Otorhinolaryngology; Paediatrics; Pathology; Pharmacology; Physical Therapy; Physiology; Plastic Surgery; Psychiatry and Mental Health; Radiology; Speech Therapy and Audiology; Surgery; Urology; Virology) *Dean:* W.L. Van der Merwe

Law (Commercial Law; Law; Private Law; Public Law) *Dean:* J.S.A. Fourie

Military Science *(Saldanha)* *Dean:* D.J. Malan

Science (Biochemistry; Botany; Chemistry; Computer Science; Consumer Studies; Geology; Mathematics; Microbiology; Natural Sciences; Nutrition; Physics; Physiology; Zoology) *Dean:* F.J.W. Hahne

Theology (Bible; Missionary Studies; Religious Studies; Theology) *Dean:* D.J. Louw

Units

Advanced Manufacturing *(SENROB)* (Production Engineering) *Director:* C.J. Fourie

Cranio-Facial Unit *Head:* W.J. Strydom

Drug Research (Toxicology) *Director:* J.R. Joubert

Educational Psychology *(Social Science Psychology)* *Director:* P.J. Normand

Experimental Phonology (Speech Therapy and Audiology) *Director:* J.C. Roux

Mathematics Education *Head:* A.I. Olivier

Perinatal Mortality (Paediatrics; Toxicology) *Director:* H.J. Odendaal

Institutes

Applied Computer Science (Computer Science) *Director:* A.E. Krzesinski

Future Studies Research *(Bellville)* (Futurology) *Director:* A. Roux

Industrial Engineering *Director:* N.D. du Preez

Mathematics and Science Education (Mathematics Education; Science Education) *Director:* J.H. Smit

Oral and Dental Research *(Tygerberg)* (Dentistry) *Director:* P. van der Bijl

Plant Biotechnology (Botany) *Director:* F.C. Botha

Polymer Science (Polymer and Plastics Technology) *Director:* R.D. Sanderson

Sports and Movement Studies (Sports) *Director:* J.H. Malan

Structural Engineering (Building Technologies) *Director:* P.E. Dunaiski

Theoretical Physics (Physics) *Director:* H.B. Geyer

Thermodynamics and Mechanics (Mechanics; Physics) *Director:* A.H. Basson

Transport Technology (Transport Engineering) *Director:* N.J. Theron

Wine Bio-Technology *Director:* I.S. Pretorius

Centres

Afrikaans Usage (Native Language) *Director:* L.G. de Stadler

Applied Ethics (Ethics) *Director:* A.A. van Niekerk

Bible Translation (Bible; Translation and Interpretation) *Director:* C.H.J. van der Merwe

Care and Rehabilitation of the Disabled (Rehabilitation and Therapy)

Cost-Effective Medicine *Director:* J.R. Joubert

Educational Development (Educational Sciences) *Director:* Y. Waghid

Electrical and Electronic Engineering *Director:* J.G. Lourens

Geographical Analysis (Geography) *Director:* J.H. van der Merwe

Global Competitiveness *Director:* N.D. du Perez

Higher and Adult Education (Adult Education; Higher Education) *Director:* C.A. Kapp

Interdisciplinary Studies *Director:* J. Mouton

International and Comparative Labour and Social Security Law (International Studies; Labour and Industrial Relations) *Director:* G. Giles

International and Comparative Politics (Comparative Politics; International Studies) *Director:* H.J. Kotzé

International Business *Director (Acting):* M. Leibold

Military Studies *(Saldanha)* (Military Science) *Director:* L. du Plessis

Molecular and Cellular Biology *(Tygerberg)* (Cell Biology; Molecular Biology) *Director:* P.D. van Helden

Theatre and Performance Studies (Performing Arts; Theatre) *Director:* T. Hauptfleisch

Bureaux

Bioengineering *(Tygerberg) Head:* J.F. Coetzee

Chemical Engineering *Director:* J.H. Knoetze

Continuing Theological Training and Research (Theology) *Director:* C.W. Burger

Economic Research (Economics) *Director:* B.W. Smit

Industrial Mathematics (Mathematics and Computer Science) *Head:* B.M. Herbst

History: Founded 1866 as College, became independent University 1918. An autonomous Institution receiving financial support from the State.

Governing Bodies: University Council; University Senate

Academic Year: February to December (February-March; April-June; July-September; October-December)

Admission Requirements: Matriculation Certificate or Certificate of Exemption issued by the Joint Matriculation Board

Fees: (Rand) Tuition, 10,000 - 25,000 per annum

Main Language(s) of Instruction: Afrikaans, English

International Co-operation: With universities in Germany; Netherlands; Belgium; USA; Gabon; Eritrea

Accrediting Agencies: Ministry of Education

Degrees and Diplomas: *Bachelor's Degree:* Education (BEd), 1 yr following first degree; Law (LLB), 2 yrs following first degree; Agricultural Management (BAgricManagement); Military Science (BMil); Science (BSc), 3 yrs; Accountancy (BAcc); Arts (BA); Commerce (Bcomm); Economics (BEcon); Music (BMus), 3-4 yrs; Consumer Science (BScConsumerSc); Drama (Bdram); Engineering (Beng); Food Science (BScFoodSc); Forestry (BScFor); Law (LLB); Nursing (BNursing); Occupational Therapy (BOccTher); Primary Education (BPrimEd), 4 yrs; Theology (BTh), 4-5 yrs; Dentistry (BChD), 5 1/2 yrs; Medicine and Surgery (MBChB), 6 yrs; *Bachelor Honours Degree:* a further yr; *Master's Degree:* a further 1-2 yrs; *Doctorate:* at least 2 yrs. The Bachelor (Honours) Degree is awarded in the same fields of study as the Bachelor's Degree. Also Undergraduate and Postgraduate Diplomas

Student Services: Academic Counselling, Social Counselling, Employment Services, Foreign Student Adviser, Sports Facilities, Language Programmes, Handicapped Facilities, Health Services, Canteen, Foreign Student Centre

Student Residential Facilities: For 6100 students

Special Facilities: University Museum; John R. Ellerman Museum (Zoology). University Gallery. Botanical Garden

Libraries: J.S. Gericke Library, total, 955,466 vols

Publications: University of Stellenbosch Annales; Matieland; Research Report; Annual Report

Academic Staff *2001-2002:* Full-Time: c. 800

Student Numbers *2001-2002*

	TOTAL
All (Foreign Included)	**22,713**
FOREIGN ONLY	1,165

UNIVERSITY OF TRANSKEI/UNIVERSITEIT VAN TRANSKEI (UNITRA)

Private Bag X1, Unitra, Umtata 5117
Tel: +27(47) 531-2267
Fax: +27(47) 502-2970
EMail: postmaster@getafix.utr.ac.za
Website: http://www.utr.ac.za

Principal and Vice-Chancellor: Nicholas Ishmail Morgan
EMail: dhunraj@getafix.utr.ac.za

Registrar: Peggy Luswazi

Faculties

Arts (African Languages; Afrikaans; Anthropology; Classical Languages; Criminology; English; Geography; History; Industrial and Organizational Psychology; Information Sciences; Modern Languages; Philosophy; Political Science; Psychology; Religious Studies; Social Work; Sociology) *Dean:* N. Mijere

Economic Science (Accountancy; Economics; Industrial and Organizational Psychology; Information Technology; Management; Public Administration) *Dean:* M. Mahabir

Education (Adult Education; Business and Commerce; Continuing Education; Education; Educational Research; Mathematics Education; Music Education; Science Education) *Dean:* S. V. S. Ngubentombi

Health Sciences (Anaesthesiology; Anatomy; Biomedicine; Cardiology; Community Health; Dermatology; Embryology and Reproduction Biology; Gynaecology and Obstetrics; Haematology; Health Education; Nursing; Ophthalmology; Orthopedics; Otorhinolaryngology; Paediatrics; Pharmacology; Physiology; Pneumology; Psychiatry and Mental Health; Radiology; Surgery) *Dean:* E. L. Mazwai

Law (Commercial Law; Criminal Law; History of Law; Law; Private Law; Public Law) *Dean:* V. Dlova

Science (Applied Mathematics; Botany; Chemistry; Computer Science; Mathematics; Physics; Statistics; Zoology) *Dean:* T. V. Jacobs

History: Founded 1976 as branch of the University of Fort Hare and acquired present status 1977.

Governing Bodies: Council

Academic Year: February to November (February-June; July-November)

Admission Requirements: Matriculation Certificate of exemption issued by the Joint Matriculation Board

Main Language(s) of Instruction: English

Degrees and Diplomas: *Bachelor's Degree:* 3 yrs; Laws (LLB), 3 yrs following first degree; Medicine and Surgery (BM), 6 yrs; *Bachelor Honours Degree:* a further yr; *Master's Degree:* a further 2-3 yrs; *Doctorate.* The Bachelor (Honours) Degree is awarded in the same fields of study as the Bachelor's Degree

Student Residential Facilities: For c. 1850 students

Academic Staff *2001-2002:* Total: c. 240

Student Numbers *2001-2002:* Total: c. 6,800

• UNIVERSITY OF VENDA FOR SCIENCE AND TECHNOLOGY

Private Bag X5050, Thohoyandou, Northern Province 0950
Tel: +27(15) 962-8000
Fax: +27(15) 962-4749
EMail: prd@univen.ac.za
Website: http://www.univen.ac.za

Vice-Chancellor: Gessler Moses Nkondo
Tel: +27(15) 962-4756 Fax: +27(15) 962-4742
EMail: gnkondo@univen.ac.za

Registrar: J.N. Matidza

Head Librarian: S.A. Brink EMail: brinkb@univen.ac.za

Faculties

Health, Agriculture and Rural Development (Agricultural Economics; Agricultural Engineering; Agriculture; Animal Husbandry; Food Science; Forestry; Health Sciences; Horticulture; Nursing; Nutrition; Physical Therapy; Plant and Crop Protection; Psychology; Public Health; Rural Studies; Soil Science; Sports) *Dean*: N.S. Shai-Mahoko

Humanities, Law and Management Sciences (Accountancy; African Languages; Anthropology; Business Administration; Commercial Law; Criminal Law; Economics; Educational Administration; English; History; Hotel Management; Human Resources; Human Rights; International Law; Labour and Industrial Relations; Linguistics; Mathematics; Music; Philosophy; Political Science; Private Law; Psychology; Public Administration; Public Law; Science Education; Social Sciences; Social Work; Theology; Tourism) *Dean*: M.D.R. Ralebipi-Simela

Natural and Applied Sciences (Biochemistry; Biological and Life Sciences; Botany; Chemistry; Earth Sciences; Engineering; Environmental Studies; Geological Engineering; Mathematics; Microbiology; Mining Engineering; Physics; Rural Planning; Statistics; Town Planning) *Dean*: P.H. Omara-Ojungu

History: Founded 1982. Acquired present title 1996.

Governing Bodies: Council, comprising 28 members

Academic Year: February to December (February-March; April-June; July-September; September-December)

Admission Requirements: Matriculation Certificate or certificate of exemption issued by the Joint Matriculation Board

Fees: (Rand): Tuition, undergraduate, c. 4490-5430 per annum; postgraduate, c. 4220-5040

Main Language(s) of Instruction: English

Degrees and Diplomas: *Bachelor's Degree*: Education (BEd), 1 yr following first degree; Laws (LLB), 2 yrs following first degree; Administration (BAdmin); Agriculture (BAgric); Arts (BA); Commerce (BCom); Economics (BEcon); Jurisprudence (BJuris); Science (BSc), 3-4 yrs; *Bachelor Honours Degree*: a further yr; *Master's Degree*: a further 1-2 yrs; *Doctorate*: 1-2 yrs. The Bachelor (Honours) Degree is awarded in the same fields of study as the Bachelor's Degree. Also Undergraduate and Postgraduate Diplomas

Student Residential Facilities: For c. 1100 students

Special Facilities: Experimental Farm

Libraries: University of Venda Library, c. 80,000 vols; 900 periodicals

Academic Staff *2001-2002:* Total: c. 250

Student Numbers *2001-2002:* Total: c. 6,200

UNIVERSITY OF THE WESTERN CAPE/UNIVERSITEIT VAN WES-KAAPLAND (UWC)

Private Bag X17, Bellville, Western Cape 7535
Tel: +27(21) 959-2111
Fax: +27(21) 951-3126
EMail: abjosephs@uwc.ac.za
Website: http://www.uwc.ac.za

Rector and Vice-Chancellor: Brian O'Connel (2000-)
Tel: +27(21) 959-2101 Fax: +27(21) 959-2973
EMail: rector@uwc.ac.za

Registrar: Ingrid Muller EMail: imiller@uwc.ac.za

Faculties

Arts (Afrikaans; Anthropology; Arts and Humanities; English; Gender Studies; Geography; History; Information Sciences; Library Science; Linguistics; Native Language; Philosophy; Religion; Sociology; Theology; Women's Studies) *Dean*: Stanley Ridge

Community and Health Sciences (Community Health; Dietetics; Ecology; Health Sciences; Nursing; Occupational Therapy; Physical Education; Physical Therapy; Psychology; Public Health; Social Work; Sports) *Dean*: Ratie Mpofu

Dentistry (Community Health; Dentistry; Oral Pathology; Orthodontics; Periodontics; Radiology) *Dean*: Mohamed Moola

Economics and Management Sciences (Accountancy; Computer Science; Economics; Industrial and Organizational Psychology; Management; Political Science; Public Administration) *Dean*: Chris Tapscott

Education (Adult Education; Computer Education; Continuing Education; Education; Educational Sciences; Mathematics Education) *Dean*: Dirk A. Meerkotter

Law (Civil Law; Commercial Law; Comparative Law; Constitutional Law; Criminal Law; Human Rights; Labour Law; Law; Private Law) *Dean*: Najma Moosa

Science (Anatomy; Biology; Biomedicine; Biotechnology; Botany; Chemistry; Computer Science; Earth Sciences; Environmental Studies; Geology; Mathematics; Natural Sciences; Pharmacy; Physics; Physiology; Statistics; Zoology) *Dean*: Jan van Beverdonker

Further Information: Incorporated the School of Dentistry of the University of Stellenbosch 2004

History: Founded 1959 as University College of the University of South Africa, became independent University 1984. Acquired present status 2004, following incorporation of the School of Dentistry of the University of Stellenbosch. An autonomous institution receiving financial support from the State.

Governing Bodies: University Council, comprising the Rector, 2 Vice-Rectors, 8 members appointed by the State President, 2 elected by the Senate, 4 elected by Convocation, 1 elected by Donors, 1 nominated by the City Council of Bellville, 2 elected by Principals of secondary schools

Academic Year: February to December (February-July; July-December)

Admission Requirements: Matriculation Certificate or certificate of exemption issued by the Joint Matriculation Board

Fees: (Rands): Tuition, undergraduate, c. 6300-6900 per annum; foreing students,c. 9100-9500

Main Language(s) of Instruction: English, Afrikaans

Degrees and Diplomas: *Bachelor's Degree*: Education (BEd), 1 yr following first degree; Law (LLB); Theology (BTh), 3 yrs following first degree; Administration (BAdmin); Arts (BA); Commerce (BComm); Economics (BEcon); Financial Law (BProcLaw); Jurisprudence (BJuris); Library Science (BBibl); Pharmacy (BPharm); Science (BSc), 3-4 yrs; Nursing (BCur), 4 1/2 yrs; Dental Surgery (BChD), 5 1/2 yrs; *Bachelor Honours Degree*: a further yr; *Master's Degree*: a further 1-2 yrs; *Doctorate*: by thesis. The Bachelor (Honours) Degree is awarded in the same fields of study as the Bachelor's Degree. Also Diplomas

Student Residential Facilities: For c. 3120 students

Special Facilities: Cape Flats Nature Reserve. Archives. Mayibuye Historical and Cultural Centre

Libraries: Central Library and specialized libraries, total, 263,059 vols; 1314 periodicals

Publications: UWC News; Campus Bulletin

Press or Publishing House: Publications Committee (in association with David Philip, Publisher)

Academic Staff *2001-2002:* Total: c. 660

Student Numbers *2001-2002:* All (Foreign Included): c. 21,470 Foreign Only: c. 2,210

Part-time Students, c. 8,520

*• UNIVERSITY OF THE WITWATERSRAND

Private Bag 3, Wits 2050
Tel: +27(11) 717-1000
Fax: +27(11) 339-7620
EMail: studysa@atlas.wits.ac.za
Website: http://www.wits.ac.za

Vice-Chancellor and Principal (Acting): Loyiso Nongxa (2001-) Tel: +27(11) 717-1101 Fax: +27(11) 339-8215 EMail: nongxal@vco.wits.ac.za

Registrar (Academic): Derek K. Swemmer
EMail: registrar@registrar.wits.ac.za

International Relations: Sharon Groenemeyer-Edigheji
Tel: +27(11) 717-1052 Fax: +27(11) 403-1385
EMail: edighejis@international.wits.ac.za

Faculties

Commerce, Law and Management (Accountancy; Business and Commerce; Development Studies; Economics; Information Technology; Law) *Dean*: N. Garrod

Engineering and the Built Environment (Aeronautical and Aerospace Engineering; Architecture and Planning; Civil Engineering; Construction Engineering; Electrical Engineering; Environmental Engineering; Industrial Engineering; Information Technology; Materials Engineering; Mechanical Engineering; Mining Engineering) *Dean*: R. Nkado

Health Sciences (Anatomy; Health Education; Health Sciences; Medicine; Oral Pathology; Pathology; Public Health) *Dean*: Max Price

Humanities (Education; Fine Arts; Humanities and Social Science Education; Linguistics; Literature; Social Sciences)

Science (Actuarial Science; Animal Husbandry; Applied Mathematics; Archaeology; Biological and Life Sciences; Cell Biology; Computer Science; Earth Sciences; Environmental Studies; Geography; Geology; Geophysics; Mathematics; Mathematics and Computer Science; Molecular Biology; Natural Sciences; Physics; Plant and Crop Protection; Statistics) *Dean*: Colin J. Wright

Further Information: Also 80 Research Units, Institutes, Groups and Programmes

History: Founded 1896 as School of Mines at Kimberley. Incorporated in Transvaal Technical Institute 1904, renamed South African School of Mines and Technology 1910. Became University College 1920 and University 1922. An autonomous institution receiving financial support from the State.

Governing Bodies: University Council; University Senate

Academic Year: February to November (February-June; July-November)

Admission Requirements: Matriculation Certificate or certificate of exemption issued by the Matriculation Board

Fees: (Rands): First year, 4320-16,550

Main Language(s) of Instruction: English

Degrees and Diplomas: *Bachelor's Degree*: Education (BEd), 1 yr following first degree; Laws (LLB), 2-3 yrs following first degree; Arts (BA); Commerce (BCom); Economic Science (BEconSc); Engineering (BSc(Eng)); Financial Law (BProcLaw); Music (BMus); Pharmacy (BPharm); Primary Education (BPrimEd); Science (BSc), 3-4 yrs; Dental Science, 5 1/2 yrs; Accountancy (BAcc); Architecture (BArch), 5 yrs; Medicine and Surgery (MBBCh), 6 yrs; *Bachelor Honours Degree*: a further yr; *Master's Degree*: a further 1-2 yrs; *Doctorate*: 1-2 yrs. The Bachelor (Honours) Degree is awarded in the same fields of study as the Bachelor's Degree. Also Undergraduate and Postgraduate Diplomas

Student Services: Academic Counselling, Social Counselling, Employment Services, Nursery Care, Cultural Centre, Sports Facilities, Handicapped Facilities, Health Services, Canteen, Foreign Student Centre

Student Residential Facilities: For c. 3100 students

Special Facilities: Adler Museum of the History of Medicine; Archaeology Museum; Bleloch Museum (Geology); Brebner Museum (Surgery); Robert Broom Museum (Sterkfontein Caves); Dental Museum; Hunterian Museum (Anatomy); Museum of Obstetrics and Gynaecology; Palaeontology Museum; Social Anthropology Museum; Sutherland Strachan Museum (Pathology); Museum of Wireless, Radio and Electronics; Zoology Museum. Gertrude Posel Gallery. Standard Bank Collection of African Art. Planetarium. Moss Herbarium

Libraries: Wartenweiler Library, total 1m vols

Publications: Urban Forum; English Studies in Africa (biannually); Palaeontologia Africana (annually)

Press or Publishing House: Wits University Press

Academic Staff *2001-2002:* Total: **2,970**

Student Numbers *2001-2002*
	TOTAL
All (Foreign Included)	**19,407**
FOREIGN ONLY	900

UNIVERSITY OF ZULULAND/UNIVERSITEIT VAN ZULULAND (UNIZUL)
Private Bag X1001, Kwa-Dlangezwa, KwaZulu-Natal 3886
Tel: +27(35) 902-6000
Fax: +27(35) 902-6311
EMail: cvillier@pan.uzulu.ac.za
Website: http://www.uzulu.ac.za

Vice-Chancellor and Rector: Rachel Gumbi (2003-)
Tel: +27(35) 902-6624 EMail: kadlam@pan.uzulu.ac.za

Registrar (Acting): Ernst Doëseb Tel: +27(35) 902-6177

Faculties
Arts (African Languages; Afrikaans; Arts and Humanities; Communication Studies; Criminology; Development Studies; English; History; Library Science; Linguistics; Music; Nursing; Philosophy; Psychology; Social Work; Sociology; Theatre; Tourism) *Dean:* L.Z.M Khumalo

Commerce and Administration *(Umlazi Campus)* (Accountancy; Business Administration; Economics; Political Science; Public Administration) *Dean:* Nico Smith

Education *(Umlazi Campus)* (Education; Educational Administration; Educational Psychology; Educational Sciences) *Dean:* N.V Magi

Law *Dean:* R. Soni

Science (Agriculture; Animal Husbandry; Biochemistry; Botany; Chemistry; Computer Science; Consumer Studies; Geography; Hydraulic Engineering; Mathematics; Microbiology; Natural Sciences; Physics; Zoology) *Dean:* M.F. Coetsee

Theology and Religious Studies (Bible; Ethics; Religious Practice; Theology) *Dean:* J.A. Loubser

History: Founded 1959 as University College for Zulu and Swazi students. Became University 1970. An autonomous institution receiving financial support from the State.

Governing Bodies: Council; Senate

Academic Year: February to December (February-June; July-December)

Admission Requirements: Matriculation Certificate or certificate of exemption issued by the Joint Matriculation Board

Fees: (Rand): 13,792 (without accommodation); 24,092 (accommodation inclusive) per annum

Main Language(s) of Instruction: English

International Co-operation: With universities in the USA.

Degrees and Diplomas: *Bachelor's Degree:* Education (BEd), 1 yr following first degree; Laws (LLB), 2 yrs following first degree; Arts (BA); Commerce (BCom); Financial Law (BProcLaw); Jurisprudence (BJuris); Library Science (BBibl); Pedagogy (BPaed); Science (BSc); Theology (BTh), 3-4 yrs; *Bachelor Honours Degree:* a further yr; *Master's Degree:* a further 1-2 yrs; *Doctorate:* 1-2 yrs. The Bachelor (Honours) Degree is awarded in the same fields of study as the Bachelor's Degree. Also Undergraduate and Postgraduate Diplomas

Student Services: Academic Counselling, Social Counselling, Cultural Centre, Sports Facilities, Language Programmes, Health Services, Canteen

Libraries: c. 95,000 vols

Publications: Paedonomia; Journal of Psychology (biannually); Unizulu (annually)

Academic Staff *2001:* Total: **445**

Student Numbers *2001:* Total: **5,100**

TECHNIKONS

BORDER TECHNIKON
Private Bag 1421, East London 5200
Tel: +27(403) 708-5200
Fax: +27(403) 708-5331
EMail: bormain@indlovu.bortech.ac.za
Website: http://www.bortech.ac.za

Rector: L.R. Brunyee Fax: +27 (043) 7085335
EMail: lbrunyee@indlovu.bortech.ac.za

Registrar: J. Bhana Fax: +27(403) 63-1165

Faculties
Applied Technology (Civil Engineering; Construction Engineering; Electrical Engineering; Engineering; Fine Arts; Information Technology; Mathematics; Mechanical Engineering; Physics; Technology; Tourism) *Dean:* N. Mpako

Human Sciences (Accountancy; Communication Studies; Finance; Human Resources; Management; Marketing; Secretarial Studies) *Dean:* C. Novukela

History: Founded 1988.

Degrees and Diplomas: *National Certificate*; *National Diploma (Ndip)*; *Bachelor of Technology (Btech)*

Student Residential Facilities: Yes

CAPE TECHNIKON
PO Box 652, Cape Town 8000
Tel: +27(21) 460-3911
Fax: +27(21) 460-3695
Website: http://www.ctech.ac.za

Rector and Vice-Chancellor: Marcus Malusi (2002-)
Tel: +27(21) 460-3352 Fax: +27(21) 460-3700
EMail: balintulo@ctech.ac.za

Registrar: A.J. Van Gensen Tel: +27(21) 460-3395
EMail: vangensena@ctech.ac.za

International Relations: Alwyn Van Gensen

Faculties
Applied Sciences (Agricultural Management; Agriculture; Analytical Chemistry; Applied Chemistry; Applied Mathematics; Applied Physics; Environmental Studies; Food Technology; Health Sciences; Horticulture; Landscape Architecture; Nursing; Ophthalmology) *Dean:* Lionel Slammert

Built Environment and Design (Architecture; Fashion Design; Graphic Design; Industrial Design; Interior Design; Jewelry Art; Regional Planning; Surveying and Mapping; Town Planning) *Dean*: Mel Hagan

Business Informatics (Accountancy; Business Computing; E-Business/Commerce; Finance; Information Technology; Taxation) *Dean*: Geoff Erwin

Education (Education; Educational Administration)

Engineering (Chemical Engineering; Civil Engineering; Electrical Engineering; Engineering; Industrial Engineering; Marine Engineering; Mechanical Engineering; Packaging Technology; Production Engineering; Surveying and Mapping) *Dean*: Nico Beute

Management (Business Administration; Cooking and Catering; Hotel Management; Human Resources; Library Science; Management; Marketing; Public Administration; Public Relations; Retailing and Wholesaling; Sports Management; Tourism) *Dean*: Mohamed Bayat

History: Founded 1923, acquired present title 1979. Granted degrees 1995.

Governing Bodies: Council

Academic Year: January to December

Main Language(s) of Instruction: English, Afrikaans

Accrediting Agencies: Certification Council for Technikon Education (SERTEC)

Degrees and Diplomas: *National Diploma (Ndip)*; *National Higher Diploma*; *Bachelor of Technology (Btech)*; *Master of Technology (Mtech)*

Student Services: Academic Counselling, Social Counselling, Employment Services, Cultural Centre, Sports Facilities, Language Programmes, Health Services, Foreign Student Centre

Student Residential Facilities: Yes

Libraries: Central Library

Academic Staff 2001-2002	MEN	WOMEN	TOTAL
FULL-TIME	232	119	351
PART-TIME	96	84	180
TOTAL	**328**	**203**	**531**
STAFF WITH DOCTORATE			
FULL-TIME	27	7	34
PART-TIME	–	–	2
TOTAL	**–**	**–**	**36**

Student Numbers 2001-2002	MEN	WOMEN	TOTAL
All (Foreign Included)	6,611	6,627	**13,238**
FOREIGN ONLY	479	313	792

Part-time Students, 2,799

DURBAN INSTITUTE OF TECHNOLOGY

PO Box 953, Durban, Kwa-Zulu Natal 4000
Tel: +27(31) 204-2056
Fax: +27(31) 204-2663
EMail: vice-chancellor@dit.ac.za
Website: http://www.dit.ac.za

Vice-Chancellor: Daniel J. Ncayiyana (2002-)

Registrar: David Hellinger Tel: +27(31) 204-2517
EMail: davidh@dit.ac.za

International Relations: Harold Reddy, Assistant Registrar Tel: +27(31) 204-2052 Fax: +27(31) 204-2188
EMail: harold@dit.ac.za

Faculties

Arts (Communication Studies; Education; English; Fashion Design; Fine Arts; Graphic Arts; Jewelry Art; Journalism; Music; Photography; Textile Design; Textile Technology; Theatre; Translation and Interpretation; Video) *Dean*: Rosethal Loli Makhubu

Commerce (Accountancy; Business Administration; Business Education; Cooking and Catering; Economics; Food Science; Government; Human Resources; Law; Library Science; Management; Marketing; Public Relations; Sports Management; Statistics; Taxation; Tourism) *Dean*: Malcolm Wallis

Engineering and Science (Architecture; Biotechnology; Building Technologies; Chemical Engineering; Chemistry; Civil Engineering; Clothing and Sewing; Electrical Engineering; Electronic Engineering; Food Technology; Marine Engineering; Mathematics; Mechanical Engineering; Paper Technology; Physics; Surveying and Mapping; Textile Technology) *Dean*: Darren Lortan

Darren Lortan

Health (Biology; Biomedical Engineering; Child Care and Development; Chiropractic; Health Sciences; Homeopathy; Medical Technology; Nursing; Radiology; Stomatology) *Dean*: Greg Bass

Centres

Higher Education Development (Higher Education)

Further Information: Also branches in Pietermaritzburg and Gamalakhe

History: Founded 2002 through the merger of Technikon Natal and M.L. Sultan Technikon.

Governing Bodies: Technikon Council

Academic Year: January to December

Admission Requirements: South African Senior Certificate/British A levels

Fees: (ZAR) 10,000

Main Language(s) of Instruction: English

International Co-operation: With institutions in Europe and USA

Accrediting Agencies: South African Qualifications Authority; National and International Professional Boards

Degrees and Diplomas: *National Certificate*: (N.Cert), 1 yr; *National Higher Certificate*: (N.H. Cert), 1 yr; *National Diploma (Ndip)*: 1 yr; *National Higher Diploma*: (NHDip), 1 yr; *Bachelor of Technology (Btech)*: 1 yr; *Master of Technology (Mtech)*: 1 yr; *Master's Degree*; *Doctor of Technology (Dtech)*: 1 yr

Student Services: Academic Counselling, Social Counselling, Employment Services, Nursery Care, Sports Facilities, Language Programmes, Health Services, Canteen

Student Residential Facilities: Yes

Special Facilities: Art Gallery

Libraries: Yes

EASTERN CAPE TECHNIKON

Private Bag X 3182, Butterworth, Eastern Cape 4960
Tel: +27(474) 401-2000
Fax: +27(474) 492-0735
EMail: vido@garfield.tktech.ac.za
Website: http://www.tktech.ac.za

Principal and Vice-Chancellor: Q.T. Mjoli
Fax: +27 (047) 4920721 EMail: mjoli@garfield.tktech.ac.za

Vice-Principal (Academic): Alfred Bomvu

International Relations: Andrew Christoffels

Head Librarian: P.P. Matshaya

Faculties

Applied Technology (Cooking and Catering; Education; Fashion Design; Technology) *Dean:* M. Sarpong

Business Science (Accountancy; Communication Studies; Human Resources; Law; Management; Public Administration; Secretarial Studies) *Dean:* C.J. Posthumus

Engineering (Civil Engineering; Construction Engineering; Electrical Engineering; Engineering; Information Technology; Mathematics; Mechanical Engineering) *Dean:* S.P.K. Boni

Further Information: Also branches in East London, Queenstown and Umtata

History: Founded 1981.

Degrees and Diplomas: *National Diploma (Ndip)*; *Bachelor of Technology (Btech)*

Libraries: Yes

MANGOSUTHU TECHNIKON

PO Box 12363, Jacobs 4026
Tel: +27(31) 907-7111
Fax: +27(31) 907-2892
EMail: principal@julian.mantec.ac.za
Website: http://www.mantec.ac.za/

Vice-Chancellor and Principal: A.M. Ndlovu (1997-)
Fax: +27 (031) 9061166 EMail: principal@julian.mantec.ac.za

Registrar: E.C. Zingu

International Relations: A. M. Ndulovu

Head Librarian: E.L. Ndaki

Faculties

Engineering
Management Sciences (Management)
Natural Sciences

History: Founded 1979.

Degrees and Diplomas: *National Diploma (Ndip)*; *Bachelor of Technology (Btech)*

Libraries: MC O'Dowd Resource Centre

PENINSULA TECHNIKON

PO Box 1906, Symphony Way, Bellville 7530
Tel: +27(21) 959-6911
Fax: +27(21) 951-5617
EMail: postmaster@pentech.ac.za
Website: http://www.pentech.ac.za

Principal and Vice-Chancellor: Brian Figaji (1995-)
Fax: +27 (021) 9515422 EMail: figajib@mail.pentech.ac.za

Vice-Rector (Administration): A.M. Slabbert

International Relations: Vuyisa Mazwi-Tanga

Faculties

Business (Accountancy; Business Administration; Human Resources; Management; Marketing; Public Administration; Retailing and Wholesaling) *Dean:* Norman Jacobs

Engineering (Building Technologies; Civil Engineering; Clothing and Sewing; Construction Engineering; Electrical Engineering; Fashion Design; Graphic Design; Information Technology; Journalism; Mechanical Engineering; Multimedia; Photography; Textile Technology) *Dean:* Oswald Franks

Science (Analytical Chemistry; Chemical Engineering; Chemistry; Dental Technology; Education; Food Technology; Health Sciences; Horticulture; Management; Natural Sciences; Nursing; Radiology; Technology) *Dean:* Dhiro Gwhala

Centres
Continuing Education

History: Founded 1967, acquired present status and title 1979.

Degrees and Diplomas: *National Diploma (Ndip)*; *National Higher Diploma*; *Bachelor of Technology (Btech)*; *Master of Technology (Mtech)*

PORT ELIZABETH TECHNIKON (PE TECH)

Private Bag X6011, Port Elizabeth, Eastern Cape Province 6000
Tel: +27(41) 504-3911
Fax: +27(41) 533-3644
EMail: info@petech.ac.za
Website: http://www.petech.ac.za

Rector and Vice-Chancellor: Hennie Snyman (1989-)
Tel: +27(41) 504-3211 Fax: +27(41) 583-1558

Registrar: Hugo Grimbeek Tel: +27(41) 504-3370
EMail: grimbeek@ml.petech.ac.za

International Relations: George De Lange
Tel: +27(41) 504-3541 Fax: +27(41) 504-3167
EMail: george@petech.ac.za

Faculties

Applied Science (Biomedicine; Chemistry; Health Sciences; Mathematics; Radiology) *Dean:* D.W. Sharwood

Art and Design (Ceramic Art; Design; Fashion Design; Fine Arts; Glass Art; Graphic Design; Photography; Textile Design) *Dean:* N.P.L. Allen

Civil Engineering, Building, Architecture and Agriculture (Agricultural Management; Agriculture; Architecture; Building Technologies; Business Administration; Civil Engineering; Interior Design) *Dean:* J.J. Van Wyk

Commerce and Governmental Studies (Business and Commerce; Economics; Government; Law; Management; Marketing; Public Administration; Sports Management; Tourism; Transport Management) *Dean*: H.F. Wissink

Communication and Educational Studies (Administration; Adult Education; Business and Commerce; Education; Information Sciences; Journalism; Library Science; Modern Languages; Natural Sciences; Public Relations; Telecommunications Services) *Dean*: M.A. Fouché

Computer Studies (Business Computing; Computer Science; Information Technology) *Dean*: E.F. du Preez

Electrical Engineering (Electrical Engineering; Electronic Engineering; Power Engineering)

Management (Accountancy; Business Administration; Finance; Human Resources; Management) *Dean*: N.J. Dorfling

Mechanical Engineering (Engineering Management; Industrial Design; Industrial Engineering; Mechanical Engineering) *Dean*: H.L.T. Jeffery

Units
Catalysis Research/Chemquest (Chemistry) *Head*: Ben Zeelie

Chemical Technology/Materials Resource (Chemistry; Materials Engineering) *Head*: Ben Zeelie

Furntech (Furniture Design)

Institutes
Building Research and Support *(IBRS)* (Building Technologies)

Research Centres
Manufacturing Technology (Metal Techniques; Technology) *Head*: Eugene du Preez

History: Founded 1882, this tertiary institution offers both formal and non-formal career-oriented courses in nine Faculties located across three campuses. Long recognized for its partnerships with industry and other Eastern Cape institutions of higher education, the PE Technikon continues to maintain a reputation for research, cooperative education, and community service.

Governing Bodies: Council

Academic Year: January to December

Admission Requirements: Matriculation Certificate or School Leaving Certificate issued by the Joint Matriculation Board

Main Language(s) of Instruction: English

International Co-operation: With universities in Germany; France; China

Degrees and Diplomas: *National Higher Certificate*: Computer Studies: Foundation Studies- Information Technology; *National Diploma (Ndip)*: Applied Sciences: Analytical Chemistry, Biomedical Technology, Environmental Health, Fire Service Technology, Rubber Technology, Radiography (Diagnostic); Art and Design: Ceramic Design, Fashion, Fine Arts, Graphic Design, Photography, Textile Design and Technology; Civil Engineering: Agricultural Management, Architectural Technology, Building, Interior Design; Commerce and Governmental Studies: Inventory and Stores Management, Marketing, Public Management, Purchasing Management, Sports Administration and Management, Tourism; Communication and Educational Studies: Commercial Administration, Journalism, Library and Information Studies, Public Relations Management, Adult Basic Education and Training, Education-Commerce, Education-Natural Sciences, Education-Post School; Computer Studies: Information Technology; Electrical Engineering; Management: Cost and Management Accountancy, Financial Information System, Human Resources Management, Internal Auditing, Management; Mechanical Engineering: Industrial Engineering, Mechanical Engineering, Metallurgical Engineering, Production Management, Safety Management; *National Higher Diploma*: Applied Science: Fire Service Technology (NHDip); Communication and Educational Studies: Technical Education (NHDip); *Bachelor of Technology (Btech)*: Applied Sciences: Biomedical Technology, Environmental Health, Chemistry, Radiography; Art and Design: Ceramic Design, Fashion, Fine Arts, Graphic Design, Photography, Textile Design and Technology; Civil Engineering: Agricultural Management, Architectural Technology, Construction Management , Quantity Surveying,; Commerce and Governmental Studies: Marketing, Public Management, Tourism; Communication and Educational Studies: Commercial Administration, Library and Information Studies, Public Relations Management, Commerce, Natural Sciences, Continuing Education; Computer Studies: Information Technology; Electrical Engineering; Management: Business Administration, Cost and Management Accountancy, Financial Information System, Human Resources Management, Internal Auditing; Mechanical Engineering: Quality Engineering, Industrial Engineering, Mechanical Engineering, Production Management; *Master of Technology (Mtech)*: Applied Sciences: Biomedical Technology, Chemistry, Environmental Health; Art and Design: Fashion, Fine Arts, Graphic Design, Photography, Textile Design and Technology; Civil Engineering: Agriculture, Architectural Technology, Business Administration, Construction Management, Quantity Surveying; Commerce and Govermental Studies: Logistics, Marketing, Public Management; Communication and Educational Studies: Library and Information Studies, Public Relations Management, Education; Computer Studies: Information Technology; Electrical Engineering; Management: Business Administration, Human Resources Management; Mechanical Engineering: Industrial Engineering, Mechanical Engineering, Production Management; *Doctor of Technology (Dtech)*: Applied Science: Chemistry, Environmental Health; Art and Design: Fine Arts, Photography; Civil Engineering: Agriculture, Architectural Technology, Construction Management, Quantity Surveying; Commerce and Govermental Studies: Logistics, Marketing, Public Management; Communication and Educational Studies: Library and Information Studies, Public Relations Management, Education; Computer Studies: Information Technology; Electrical Engineering; Management: Human Resources Management, Business Administration; Mechanical Engineering: Industrial Engineering, Mechanical Engineering, Production Management

Student Services: Academic Counselling, Employment Services, Foreign Student Adviser, Sports Facilities, Language Programmes, Health Services, Canteen, Foreign Student Centre

Student Residential Facilities: Yes

Libraries: Central Library and two branch Libraries

Publications: Impetus, General Liaison Magazine; Annual Report (annually)

Academic Staff 2001-2002	MEN	WOMEN	TOTAL
FULL-TIME	172	102	274
PART-TIME	117	66	183
TOTAL	**289**	**168**	**457**
STAFF WITH DOCTORATE			
FULL-TIME	24	8	32
PART-TIME	1	–	1
TOTAL	**25**	**8**	**33**

Student Numbers 2001-2002	MEN	WOMEN	TOTAL
All (Foreign Included)	5,301	4,385	**9,686**
FOREIGN ONLY	370	95	465

Part-time Students, 2,833

TECHNIKON FREE STATE

Private Bag X20539, 20 President Brand Street, Bloemfontein 9300
Tel: +27(51) 507-3911
Fax: +27(51) 507-3199
EMail: gvgensen@tfs.ac.za
Website: http://www.tfs.ac.za

Principal and Vice-Chancellor: A.S. Koorts (1996-)
Tel: +27(51) 507-3001 Fax: +27(51) 507-3310
EMail: askoorts@tfs.ac.za

Registrar: M.J. du Plooy Tel: +27(51) 507-3053
Fax: +27(51) 507-3199 EMail: mduplooy@tfs.ac.za

International Relations: H.S. Wolvaardt
Tel: +27(51) 507-3554 Fax: +27(51) 507-3315
EMail: manie@tfs.ac.za

Faculties

Engineering (Applied Mathematics; Building Technologies; Civil Engineering; Computer Engineering; Electrical Engineering; Engineering; Mechanical Engineering) *Executive Dean:* G. D. Jorrie Jordaan

Health and Environmental Sciences (Agriculture; Environmental Studies; Health Sciences) *Executive Dean:* Barry Frey

Human Sciences (Communication Studies; Design; Teacher Training; Visual Arts) *Executive Dean:* Edward Sedibe

Management Sciences (Accountancy; Business Administration; Government; Information Technology; Management; Secretarial Studies; Sports; Tourism) *Executive Dean:* Piet Le Roux

Further Information: Incorporated Welkom Campus of Vista University 2004

History: Founded 1981. Incorporated Welkom Campus of Vista University 2004.

Governing Bodies: Technikon Council

Academic Year: January to November

Admission Requirements: School leaving certificate and specific subject requirements

Main Language(s) of Instruction: English, Afrikaans

International Co-operation: With universities in Sweden; Netherlands; Germany; United Kingdom; China; Belgium; New Zealand; Australia; United States

Accrediting Agencies: Certification Council for Technikon Education

Degrees and Diplomas: *National Certificate*; *National Diploma (Ndip)*; *Bachelor of Technology (Btech)*; *Master of Technology (Mtech)*; *Doctor of Technology (Dtech)*

Student Services: Academic Counselling, Social Counselling, Employment Services, Foreign Student Adviser, Cultural Centre, Sports Facilities, Language Programmes, Health Services, Canteen

Student Residential Facilities: For women and men students

Special Facilities: Art gallery

Libraries: Main Library, c. 60000 vols; four branch libraries

Publications: Gratia (biannually); Annual Report (annually)

Academic Staff 2001-2002	MEN	WOMEN	TOTAL
FULL-TIME	107	75	182
PART-TIME	210	168	378
TOTAL	**317**	**243**	**560**
STAFF WITH DOCTORATE			
FULL-TIME	20	6	**26**

Student Numbers 2001-2002	MEN	WOMEN	TOTAL
All (Foreign Included)	3,694	3,439	**7,133**
FOREIGN ONLY	–	–	430

Part-time Students, 765 **Evening Students,** 765

TSHWANE UNIVERSITY OF TECHNOLOGY

Private Bag X680, Pretoria, Gauteng 0001
Tel: +27(12) 318-5911
Fax: +27(12) 318-5114
Cable: techpret
EMail: vschale@techpta.ac.za
Website: http://www.techpta.ac.za

Rector and Vice-Chancellor: R.L. Ngcobo (2001-)
Tel: 27(12) 318-4112 Fax: +27(12) 318-5422

Registrar: N.J. vdM Stofberg Tel: +27(12) 318-5180
Fax: +27(12) 318-5181

International Relations: Elsa-Marie Van Schalkwyk, Director
Tel: +27(12) 318-5353 Fax: +27(12) 318-4424
EMail: vschale@techpta.ac.za

Faculties

Agriculture, Horticulture and Nature Conservation (Agricultural Management; Animal Husbandry; Crop Production; Environmental Studies; Farm Management; Horticulture; Landscape Architecture) *Dean:* Kobus Botha

Arts (Arts and Humanities; Dance; Fashion Design; Fine Arts; Graphic Design; Music; Opera; Photography; Textile Design; Theatre) *Dean:* Eric Dinkelmann

Economics (Accountancy; Economics; Human Resources; Industrial Engineering; Management; Marketing; Production Engineering; Public Administration) *Dean:* Maynard van der Merwe

Engineering (Architecture; Engineering; Mechanical Engineering; Polymer and Plastics Technology; Surveying and Mapping) *Dean:* Kobus Vorster

Health Sciences (Dentistry; Health Sciences; Nursing; Paramedical Sciences; Pharmacy; Sports) *Dean:* M.M.J. Lowes

Information Sciences (Advertising and Publicity; Business Administration; Information Sciences; Information Technology; Journalism; Radio and Television Broadcasting; Systems Analysis; Teacher Training; Tourism) *Dean*: S. Imenda

Natural Sciences (Analytical Chemistry; Biomedical Engineering; Ceramics and Glass Technology; Chemical Engineering; Chemistry; Environmental Management; Fire Science; Food Technology; Geology; Metallurgical Engineering; Natural Sciences; Veterinary Science; Water Management) *Dean*: PJJG Marais

Institutes

Clothing, Design and Interior Design *(CLODEC)* (Clothing and Sewing; Fashion Design; Interior Design)

Quality Management and Statistics *(TIQMS)* (Statistics)

Centres

Agro-Industry Training (Agricultural Business)

Business (Business Administration; Business and Commerce)

Dental Technology (Dental Technology; Dentistry)

Drama (Theatre)

Entrepreneurship (Business Administration)

Food Service Management (Food Science)

Human and Animal Molecular Health (Molecular Biology)

Industrial Health and Safety (Safety Engineering)

Information Technology

Language and Leadership Dynamics (Leadership)

Marketing Research and Development (Development Studies; Marketing)

Occupational Health and Safety (Occupational Health)

Outdoor Development Training and Leisure Activities (Leisure Studies; Sports)

Polymer Technology (Polymer and Plastics Technology)

Sports Science (Sports)

Training and Development

Further Information: Merger of Technikon Northern Gauteng, Technikon North-West and Technikon Pretoria 2004

History: Founded 2004 following merger of Technikon Northern Gauteng, Technikon North-West and Technikon Pretoria.

Governing Bodies: Council

Academic Year: January to December

Admission Requirements: Matriculation Certificate or Certificate of Exemption issued by the Joint Matriculation Board

Fees: (Rand): 10,000-17,000 per annum

Main Language(s) of Instruction: English, Afrikaans

International Co-operation: With universities in Africa, Europe, Asia, Australia, USA.

Accrediting Agencies: Education Department, South African Government

Degrees and Diplomas: *Bachelor of Technology (Btech)*: 4 yrs; *Master of Technology (Mtech)*: a further 2 yrs; *Doctor of Technology (Dtech)*: a further 3 yrs following MTech

Student Services: Academic Counselling, Social Counselling, Employment Services, Foreign Student Adviser, Nursery Care, Sports Facilities, Language Programmes, Handicapped Facilities, Health Services, Canteen, Foreign Student Centre

Student Residential Facilities: Yes

Publications: Annual Report (annually)

Academic Staff *2001-2002*	MEN	WOMEN	TOTAL
FULL-TIME	543	377	920
PART-TIME	13	12	25
TOTAL	**556**	**389**	**945**
STAFF WITH DOCTORATE			
FULL-TIME	67	25	92
PART-TIME	–	–	17
TOTAL	**–**	**–**	**109**

Student Numbers *2001-2002*	MEN	WOMEN	TOTAL
All (Foreign Included)	17,492	17,165	**34,657**
FOREIGN ONLY	1,507	730	2,237

Part-time Students, 3,115 **Evening Students,** 3,115 **Distance Students,** 7,331

TECHNIKON NORTH-WEST
Private Bag X31, Rosslyn, North West 0200
Tel: +27(12) 31166 +27(12) 5210500
Fax: +27(12) 31166 +27(12) 7031166
Website: http://www.tnw.ac.za

Principal and Vice-Chancellor: S.J. Molefe
Tel: +27(12) 5210680 EMail: sjmolefe@mweb.co.za

Registrar: R. Maphai EMail: rose-mary.maphai@tnw.ac.za

International Relations: Susan Mahlangu
Tel: +27(12) 3245003 Fax: +27(12) 3255004

Faculties

Economics and Management (Accountancy; Communication Studies; Economics; Education; Human Resources; Management; Marketing; Public Administration; Tourism) *Dean*: Mario Scerri

Science and Engineering (Analytical Chemistry; Chemistry; Engineering) *Dean*: Itumeleng Selala

Technology and Design (Computer Engineering; Computer Science; Fashion Design; Information Technology; Social Sciences; Systems Analysis; Technology; Tourism) *Dean*: Glen Mius

History: Founded 1975, acquired present status and title 1986.

Governing Bodies: Council

Admission Requirements: Matriculation Certificate (grade 12)

Fees: (Rand): 828 per annum

Main Language(s) of Instruction: English

Student Services: Academic Counselling, Social Counselling, Foreign Student Adviser, Sports Facilities, Health Services, Canteen

Student Residential Facilities: Yes

Special Facilities: Computer Centre. Laboratories. Media Centre

Libraries: Central Library

Publications: TNW News, International Newsletter (quarterly); Vice-Chancellor's Annual Report, Highlights of the Year

Academic Staff *2001-2002*	MEN	WOMEN	TOTAL
FULL-TIME	50	80	130
PART-TIME	33	18	51
TOTAL	**83**	**98**	**181**

Staff with doctorate: Total: **11**

Student Numbers *2001-2002:* Total: **5,080**

TECHNIKON NORTHERN GAUTENG
Private Bag X07, Pretoria North 0116
Tel: +27(12) 799-9000
Fax: +27(12) 793-0966
Website: http://www.tng.ac.za/

Principal: C.S.K. Lenyai (1994-) Fax: +27 (012) 7930975
EMail: glenyai@tnt.ac.za

Vice-Principal: M.A. Mashego

International Relations: C.H.J. vander Westheizen

Faculties

Commerce (Accountancy; Computer Science; Information Technology; Management)

Engineering (Analytical Chemistry; Architecture; Building Technologies; Chemical Engineering; Chemistry; Civil Engineering; Electrical Engineering; Engineering; Mechanical Engineering; Physics)

Health and Social Sciences (Biomedicine; Education; Educational Administration; Journalism; Nursing; Occupational Health; Social Sciences; Tourism)

Management (Human Resources; Labour and Industrial Relations; Marketing; Public Administration; Retailing and Wholesaling)

History: Founded 1979.

Degrees and Diplomas: *National Diploma (Ndip)*; *Bachelor of Technology (Btech)*; *Master of Technology (Mtech)*

TECHNIKON WITWATERSRAND (TWR)
PO Box 17011, Doornfontein 2028
Tel: +27(11) 406-2911
Fax: +27(11) 402-0475
EMail: amanda@twrinet.twr.ac.za
Website: http://www.twr.ac.za

Vice-Chancellor and Principal: Connie Mogale (1998-)
Tel: +27(11) 406-2501 Fax: +27(11) 402-7575

Deputy Registrar: Phineas Mabetoa Tel: +27(11) 426-2656

International Relations: Jonathan Stead
Tel: +27(11) 406-2126 Fax: +27(11) 406-2197
EMail: jstead@twrinet.twr.ac.za

Faculties

Art, Design and Architecture (Architecture; Ceramic Art; Clothing and Sewing; Design; Fashion Design; Fine Arts; Graphic Design; Interior Design; Jewelry Art) *Dean*: Eugene Hön

Business Management (Accountancy; Banking; Business Administration; Finance; Food Technology; Information Technology; Management; Marketing; Public Relations; Retailing and Wholesaling; Tourism) *Dean*: Krishna Govender

Engineering (Analytical Chemistry; Building Technologies; Chemical Engineering; Civil Engineering; Computer Engineering; Construction Engineering; Electrical Engineering; Electronic Engineering; Engineering; Geology; Industrial Engineering; Mechanical Engineering; Metallurgical Engineering; Mining Engineering; Real Estate; Regional Planning; Town Planning) *Dean*: Fred Otiend

Health Sciences (Biotechnology; Chiropractic; Food Technology; Health Sciences; Homeopathy; Nursing; Occupational Therapy; Optometry; Podiatry; Radiology; Stomatology) *Dean*: Vic Exner

History: Founded 1925 as Technical College. Acquired present status 1993.

Governing Bodies: Council; Senate

Academic Year: January to November

Admission Requirements: School-leaving certificate (Grade 12) and specific programme requirement

Main Language(s) of Instruction: English

Degrees and Diplomas: *National Diploma (Ndip)*: Art; Business; Engineering; Health, 3 yrs; *Bachelor of Technology (Btech)*: Art; Business; Engineering; Health, 1 yr following Diploma; *Master of Technology (Mtech)*; *Doctor of Technology (Dtech)*

Student Services: Academic Counselling, Social Counselling, Foreign Student Adviser, Sports Facilities, Handicapped Facilities, Health Services, Canteen

Student Residential Facilities: Yes

Libraries: Yes

Academic Staff *2001-2002*			TOTAL
FULL-TIME			961
PART-TIME			777
TOTAL			**1,738**

Student Numbers *2001-2002*	MEN	WOMEN	TOTAL
All (Foreign Included)	7,751	6,867	**14,618**

Evening Students, 1,118

VAAL UNIVERSITY OF TECHNOLOGY
Private Bag X021, Vanderbijlpark 1900
Tel: +27(16) 950-9000
Fax: +27(16) 950-1203
EMail: webmaster@nt.tritek.ac.za
Website: http://www.tritek.ac.za

Vice-Chancellor and Rector: A.T Mokadi (1996-)
Tel: +27(16) 950-9215 Fax: +27(16) 950-9800
EMail: michelle@tritek.ac.za

Vice-Rector (Administration): Prakash Naidoo

Faculties

Applied and Computer Science (Analytical Chemistry; Biological and Life Sciences; Chemistry; Community Health; Computer Science; Information Technology; Mathematics; Physics; Software Engineering) *Dean*: B.R. Mabuza

Engineering (Building Technologies; Chemical Engineering; Civil Engineering; Electronic Engineering; Engineering; Industrial Engineering; Metallurgical Engineering; Power Engineering; Production Engineering) *Dean*: Henk de Jager

Humanities (Arts and Humanities; Ceramic Art; Clothing and Sewing; Fine Arts; Food Science; Graphic Design; Photography; Tourism) *Dean*: G. B. Koen

Management Sciences (Accountancy; Business Administration; Law; Management; Marketing; Public Relations; Retailing and Wholesaling; Staff Development; Tourism) *Dean*: M. Mahabir

Units
Lifelong Learning (Continuing Education)

History: Founded 1966 as Vaal Triangle College for Advanced Technical Education. Acquired present title 2004.

Degrees and Diplomas: *National Diploma (Ndip)*; *Bachelor of Technology (Btech)*

OTHER INSTITUTIONS

ANN LATSKY COLLEGE OF NURSING
Private Bag 40, Auckland Park 2006
Tel: +27(11) 726-3170/8
Nursing

BARAGWANATH NURSING COLLEGE
Private Bag X05, Bertsham 2013
Tel: +27(11) 933-1535
Nursing

B.G. ALEXANDER COLLEGE OF NURSING
Private Bag X43, Johannesburg 2000
Tel: +27(11) 488-3219
Fax: +27(11) 643-1036
Founded: 1961
Nursing

BLOEMFONTEIN COLLEGE
Private Bag X20542, Bloemfontein 9301
Tel: +27(51) 448-1525
Fax: +27(51) 447-0486
EMail: info@bfncol.co.za
Website: http://www.connix.co.za/bfncol/

Faculties
Adult and Community Service (Communication Studies; Computer Science)
Business Studies (Accountancy; Business Administration; Economics; Secretarial Studies)
Continuing Education
Engineering *Head*: C. Botha
General Studies (Ceramic Art; Computer Graphics; Cooking and Catering; Cosmetology; Fashion Design; Jewelry Art; Music; Painting and Drawing; Textile Design; Weaving)
Management (Human Resources; Management; Marketing; Public Administration)
Secondary Commercial Studies (Business and Commerce)

BONALESEDI NURSING COLLEGE
Private Bag X1001, Luipaardsvlei 1743
Tel: +27(11) 410-1402
Nursing

BUSINESS MANAGEMENT TRAINING COLLEGE OF SOUTHERN AFRICA
8 Rhodes Street Kensington B, Randburg
Tel: +27(11) 886-4098
Fax: +27(11) 886-4245
EMail: bmtc@businesscollege.co.za
Website: http://www.businesscollege.co.za
Founded: 1973

Courses
Business English (English)
Business Management (Business Administration)
Entrepreneurship/Marketing (Business Administration; Marketing)
Financial Management (Finance)
Human Resource Management (Human Resources)
Labour Relations (Labour and Industrial Relations)

History: Founded 1973 in association with the Institute of Business Management.

Degrees and Diplomas: Diplomas in Business Management, Financial Management, Human Resource Management and Business English

CARINUS NURSING COLLEGE
Private Bag XI, Groote Schuur 7937
Tel: +27(21) 404-6151 +27(21) 404-6152
Fax: +27(21) 404-4400
Nursing

CEDARA COLLEGE OF AGRICULTURE
Private Bag X 9059, Pietermaritzburg 3200
Tel: +27(331) 355-9100
Fax: +27(33) 355-9303
EMail: college@dae.kzntl.gov.za
Website: http://agriculture.kzntl.gov.za
Principal: Alison van Niekerk (1997-)
EMail: vanniekerka@dae.kzntl.gov.za

Founded: 1905

Colleges
Agriculture *Director*: Alison Van Niekerk
Academic Year: January to November
Admission Requirements: Senior certificate
Main Language(s) of Instruction: English
Accrediting Agencies: Certification Council for Technikon Education (SERTEC)

Degrees and Diplomas: *National Higher Certificate*: Agriculture, 2 yrs; *National Diploma (Ndip)*: Agriculture, 3 yrs

Student Services: Sports Facilities

Student Residential Facilities: For 150 students

Special Facilities: Farm

Libraries: Central Library

Academic Staff 2001-2002: Full-Time: c. 15 Part-Time: c. 10 Total: c. 25

Student Numbers 2001-2002: Total: c. 120

CISKEI COLLEGE OF NURSING
Private Bag 13003, Cambridge 5206
Tel: +27(403) 611-802
Fax: +27(403) 611-158

Nursing

POTCHEFSTROOM COLLEGE OF AGRICULTURE
Private Bag X804, Potchefstroom, Northwest 2520
Tel: +27(18) 299-6556
Fax: +27(18) 293-3925
EMail: oplkirk@potchli.agric.za

Founded: 1909

Faculties

Agriculture (Agricultural Education; Agricultural Engineering; Agricultural Management; Agriculture; Agronomy; Animal Husbandry; Cattle Breeding; Crop Production; Farm Management; Soil Science; Vegetable Production)

Admission Requirements: Senior Certificate or equivalent

Main Language(s) of Instruction: Afrikaans

Accrediting Agencies: Certification Council for Technikon Education (SERTEC)

Degrees and Diplomas: *National Diploma (Ndip)*: Agriculture, 3 yrs

Student Services: Academic Counselling, Social Counselling, Foreign Student Adviser, Sports Facilities, Canteen

Student Residential Facilities: Yes

Special Facilities: Computer Centre

Libraries: Central Library

Academic Staff 2001-2002: Total: c. 40

Student Numbers 2001-2002: All (Foreign Included): c. 350 Foreign Only: c. 10

CORONATION COLLEGE OF NURSING
Private Bag X01, Newclare 2112
Tel: +27(11) 470-9000
Fax: +27(11) 673-4256

Principal: M. Nizamdin
Registrar: R.C. Pugin

Nursing

EASTERN CAPE COLLEGE OF NURSING
Sharley Cribb Campus, Private Bag X6047, Port Elizabeth 6000
Tel: +27(41) 343-000
Fax: +27(41) 332-614

Head: E.P. du Perez

Nursing

EASTERN CAPE COLLEGE OF NURSING, CHARLOTTE SEARLE CAMPUS
Private Bag, Korsten 6014
Tel: +27(41) 405-2150

Nursing

EDENDALE NURSING COLLEGE
Private Bag X 9099, Pietermaritzburg 3200
Tel: +27(331) 95-4161
Fax: +27(331) 81-721

Nursing

ELSENBURG AGRICULTURAL COLLEGE
PO Box 54, Elsenburg 7607
Tel: +27(21) 808-5450
Fax: +27(21) 884-4319
Website: http://www.elsenburg.com

Principal: M.J. Paulse
Vice-Principal: G.J.O. Marincowitz
International Relations: A. Marais, Head

Founded: 1898
Agriculture

EXCELSIUS NURSING COLLEGE
Private Bag A 19, Klerksdrop 2570
Tel: +27(18) 462-1030
Fax: +27(18) 462-1030

Nursing

FORT COX AGRICULTURAL COLLEGE (FCC)
PO Box 2187, King William's Town, Eastern Cape 5600
Tel: +27(40) 653-8034
Fax: +27(40) 653-8336

455

Departments

Agriculture and Natural Resources Management (Agriculture; Forestry; Natural Resources) Richard Awumey

Crop Production and Community Forest (Agricultural Business; Cattle Breeding; Crop Production; Forest Management)

History: Founded in 1930, acquired present status and title 1993.

Governing Bodies: Board of Governors; Academic Council

Academic Year: January to December

Admission Requirements: Grade 12 with one Science subject

Main Language(s) of Instruction: English

Accrediting Agencies: Certification Council for Technikon Education (SERTEC)

Degrees and Diplomas: *National Diploma (Ndip)*: Agriculture; Community Forest, 3 yrs. Also Diplomas, 1 yr

Student Services: Academic Counselling, Social Counselling, Sports Facilities, Canteen

Student Residential Facilities: Yes

Libraries: Central Library, c. 5000 vols; Audio Visual Centre

Academic Staff *2001-2002:* Full-Time: c. 20 Part-Time: c. 5 Total: c. 25

Student Numbers *2001-2002:* Total: c. 240

FRERE NURSING COLLEGE

Private Bag X9023, East London 5200
Tel: +27(43) 709-1136
Fax: +27(43) 743-4265
EMail: frerenc@iafrica.com

Founded: 1975

Nursing (Midwifery; Nursing; Psychiatry and Mental Health) *Director:* Penelope Bellad-Ellis

History: Founded 1975

Governing Bodies: Senate; Council

Academic Year: January to November

Admission Requirements: Senior Certificate

Main Language(s) of Instruction: English

Accrediting Agencies: South African Nursing Council

Degrees and Diplomas: *National Higher Diploma*: Nursing, 4 yrs. Diploma in Midwifery; Diploma in Psychiatric Nursing Science

Student Services: Academic Counselling, Social Counselling, Health Services

Libraries: Local Health Resource Centre

Academic Staff *2001-2002:* Total: c. 30

Student Numbers *2001-2002:* Total: c. 480

GA-RANKUWA COLLEGE

Private Bag X 422, Pretoria 0001
Tel: +27(12) 529-3111

Nursing

456

GERMISTON COLLEGE

Corner of Sol Street and Driehoek Road, Germiston 1401
Tel: +27(11) 825-3524
Fax: +27(11) 873-1769
EMail: gercoll@global.co.za
Website: http://www.home.global.co.za

Rector: H. Pelser

Founded: 1928

Departments

Business Studies (Business Administration; Marketing)

Engineering Studies (Electrical Engineering; Engineering; Mechanical Engineering)

History: Established 1928. The Germiston Technical Institution was one of the 12 branches of the Witwatersrand Technical College. The College was granted autonomy in 1983. It now caters for more than 3000 students and the number of registrations per year is close to 10,000.

GLEN AGRICULTURAL COLLEGE

Private Bag X 01, Glen 9360
Tel: +27(51) 861-1256
Fax: +27(51) 861-1122

Programmes

Agriculture

Farming (Farm Management)

GOLD FIELDS NURSING COLLEGE

Private Bag XII, Westonaria 1783
Tel: +27(11) 752-1145
Fax: +27(11) 752-1109

Nursing *Head:* Louise Wienard

Academic Year: January to December

Admission Requirements: Senior school certificate (English)

Main Language(s) of Instruction: English

Accrediting Agencies: South African Nursing Council

Degrees and Diplomas: *National Diploma (Ndip)*: Nursing, 4 yrs. Also Diploma in Nursing (bridging course), 2 yrs

Student Services: Academic Counselling, Social Counselling

Student Residential Facilities: None

Libraries: Central Library

GROOTFONTEIN COLLEGE OF AGRICULTURE

Private Bag X 529, Middelburg 5900
Tel: +27(49) 842-1113
Fax: +27(49) 842-1477
Website: http://gadi.agric.za/college/

Founded: 1911

Departments

Agricultural Management and Extension (Agricultural Management)
Animal Production (Animal Husbandry)
Crop Production and Agricultural Engineering (Agricultural Engineering; Crop Production)
Environmental Management and Computer Training (Computer Science; Environmental Management)

GROOTHOEK COLLEGE OF NURSING

Private Bag X 1122, Sovenga 0727
Nursing

HENRIETTA STOCKDALE NURSING COLLEGE

Private Bag X5051, Kimberley 8300
Tel: +27(531) 81-4659
Fax: +27(531) 81-4346
Nursing

INTEC COLLEGE

PO Box 19, Cape Town 8000
Tel: +27(21) 460-6700
Fax: +27(21) 447-9569
EMail: info@intec.edu.za
Website: http://www.intec.edu.za
Founded: 1906

Divisions

Business Studies (Accountancy; Business and Commerce; Human Resources; Management; Marketing; Public Relations)
Computer Studies (Computer Science; Data Processing; Information Management; Software Engineering)
Creative Studies (Cosmetology; Fashion Design; Graphic Arts; Journalism; Psychology; Sports)
Technical Studies (Architectural and Environmental Design; Chemistry; Civil Engineering; Construction Engineering; Electrical Engineering; Electronic Engineering; Mechanical Engineering)
Vocational Studies (Business Administration; Child Care and Development; Cooking and Catering; Health Education; Hotel and Restaurant; Safety Engineering; Tourism)

History: Founded 1906, INTEC specializes in Distance Education, also known as correspondence study or home study. Specialist tutors provide guidance and support to students.

LEBONE COLLEGE OF NURSING

Private Bag X 751, Pretoria 0001
Tel: +27(12) 373-8452
Fax: +27(12) 373-8607
Nursing

LOWVELD AGRICULTURAL COLLEGE

Private Bag X 11283, Nelspruit 1200
Tel: +27(13) 753-3064
Fax: +27(13) 753-1110
Founded: 1991
Agriculture

MADZIVHANDILA AGRICULTURAL COLLEGE

Private Bag X2377, Hohoyandou 0950
Tel: +27(159) 21-109
Fax: +27(159) 31-414
EMail: madzivha@mweb.co.za
Founded: 1982
Agriculture

MANGAUNG NURSING COLLEGE

Private Bag X 20556, Bloemfontein 9300
Tel: +27(51) 405-1397
Fax: +27(51) 432-4402
Nursing

MPUMALANGA COLLEGE OF NURSING

Pte Bag X1005, Kabokweni 1245
Tel: +27(13) 7961-352 to 355
Fax: +27(13) 7961-342
Founded: 1974, 1986

Colleges

Nursing *(Kabokweni)* (Community Health; Midwifery; Nursing; Psychiatry and Mental Health) *Director*: B. Patricia Mkwanazi

History: Founded 1974, acquired present status and title 1986.

Governing Bodies: Senate; Council; Students' Representative Council

Admission Requirements: Matriculation certificate

Main Language(s) of Instruction: English

International Co-operation: Links with institutions in Sweden

Accrediting Agencies: South African Nursing Council

Degrees and Diplomas: *National Higher Diploma*: Nursing, 4 yrs. Also Bridging Diploma in Nursing, 2yrs; Diploma in Midwifery, 1 yr

Student Services: Academic Counselling, Social Counselling, Employment Services, Cultural Centre, Sports Facilities, Health Services

Student Residential Facilities: For 228 Students

Special Facilities: Clinical Laboratory; Model Room

Libraries: Central Library

Academic Staff *2001-2002:* Total: c. 30

NATAL COLLEGE OF NURSING
Grey's Campus, Private Bag 9001, Pietermaritzburg 3200
Tel: +27(331) 95-2689
Fax: +27(331) 42-6744
Nursing

NGWELEZANA NURSING COLLEGE
Private Bag X20016, Empangeni 3880
Tel: +27(351) 94-2570
Nursing

NICO MALAN NURSING COLLEGE
Private Bag, Surwell 7762
Tel: +27(21) 637-1313
Fax: +27(21) 638-6988
Nursing

NORTHERN PROVINCE COLLEGE OF NURSING, GIYANI CAMPUS
Private Bag X 9658, Giyani 0826
Tel: +27(158) 20-330
Fax: +27(158) 20-330
Founded: 1983, 1996

Colleges
Nursing (Anatomy; Applied Chemistry; Applied Physics; Biology; Community Health; Midwifery; Nursing; Physiology; Psychiatry and Mental Health; Social and Community Services)
Director: Rachel Cecilia Tlakula

History: Founded 1983, acquired present status and title 1996.

Governing Bodies: Senate; Council

Admission Requirements: Matriculation Exemption Certificate issued by the Joint Matriculation Board. Higher Grade in English or in Biology

Main Language(s) of Instruction: English

Accrediting Agencies: South African Nursing Council

Degrees and Diplomas: *National Higher Diploma:* Nursing, 4 yrs

Student Services: Academic Counselling, Sports Facilities, Health Services

Student Residential Facilities: Yes

Libraries: Central Library

NURSING COLLEGE OF THE FREE STATE
Private Bag X20520, Bloemfotein 9300
Tel: +27(51) 405-2345
Fax: +27(51) 30-6469
Nursing

458

OTTO DU PLESSIS NURSING COLLEGE
Private Bag 7, Tygerberg 7505
Tel: +27(21) 938-4118
Fax: +27(21) 938-4269
Founded: 1957
Nursing

History: Founded 1957

OWEN SITHOLE AGRICULTURAL COLLEGE
Private Bag X 20013, Empangeni 3830
Tel: +27(35) 795-1345
Fax: +27(35) 795-1379
Founded: 1968
Agriculture

QWA-QWA NURSING COLLEGE
Private Bag X883, Witzieshoek 9870
Tel: +27(58) 713-1881
Fax: +27(58) 713-0660
Nursing

SAMS NURSING COLLEGE
Private Bag X1022, Voortrekkerhoogte 0143
Tel: +27(12) 314-0999
Fax: +27(12) 71-3333
Nursing

SARICH DOLLIE NURSING COLLEGE
Private Bag X14, Tygerberg 7505
Tel: +27(21) 938-4313
Fax: +27(21) 938-4314
Nursing

S.G. LOURENS COLLEGE OF NURSING
Private Bag X755, Pretoria 0001
Tel: +27(12) 329-4817
Fax: +27(12) 329-4822
Nursing

TAUNG AGRICULTURAL COLLEGE
PO Box 458, Hartswater 8570
Tel: +27(053) 994-1832
Fax: +27(053) 994-1130
Principal (Acting): L. Kirkland
Registrar: E. Coetzee

Faculties
Agriculture (Agriculture; Cattle Breeding; Crop Production; Farm Management; Fruit Production; Meat and Poultry; Vegetable Production)

TOMPI SELEKA AGRICULTURAL COLLEGE
Private Bag X9619, Marble Hall 0450
Tel: +27(013) 268-9300
Fax: +27(013) 268-9309
Manager: M.H. Ramabofa (1999-)
Administrative Officer: E.M. Buys
International Relations: M.J. Dladla

Founded: 1960
Agriculture

History: Founded 1960.

VENDA NURSING COLLEGE
Private Bag X919, Shayandima 0945
Tel: +27(159) 41-516

Nursing

Note: The whole merger plan in South Africa is to reduce the number of higher education institutions from 36 to 21. This will result in three different kinds of institutions: Traditional Universities, Universities of Technology (former Technikons) and Comprehensive Institutions (offering both university of technology courses and traditional university courses). There will also be one dedicated Distance teaching university which is called Unisa (resulting from a merger between Unisa, Vudec and Technikon SA). Vista University does not exist anymore and its infrastructure has been distributed to the nearest university in that province. The process will be completed in January 2005.

Sudan

INSTITUTION TYPES AND CREDENTIALS

Types of higher education institutions:

University
Institute
College

School leaving and higher education credentials:

Sudan School Certificate
Technician's Diploma
Diploma
Bachelor's Degree
Bachelor Honours Degree
Postgraduate Diploma
Master's Degree
Doctor of Philosophy
Higher Doctorate

STRUCTURE OF EDUCATION SYSTEM

Pre-higher education:

Duration of compulsory education:

Age of entry: 6
Age of exit: 14

Structure of school system:

Basic
Type of school providing this education: Basic School
Length of programme in years: 8
Age level from: 6 to: 14
Certificate/diploma awarded: Basic Education Certificate Examination

Secondary
Type of school providing this education: General Secondary School
Length of programme in years: 3
Age level from: 14 to: 17
Certificate/diploma awarded: Sudan School Certificate Examination

Vocational
Type of school providing this education: Technical and Vocational School
Length of programme in years: 3
Age level from: 14 to: 17
Certificate/diploma awarded: Sudan School Certificate Examination

School education:

Basic education lasts for eight years and is compulsory. It leads to the Basic Education Certificate Examination. General (academic) secondary education lasts for three years leading to the Sudan School Certificate Examination. In the first two years, students follow the same curriculum. In the final year, they choose between arts and science streams. The technical secondary schools include Industrial, Commercial and Agricultural schools for boys and some Home Economics schools for girls. They offer three-year courses leading to the Sudan Secondary School Certificate. Vocational Training Centres offer two-year vocational courses. Admission is based on completion of basic education. Admission to higher education is based on the results of the Sudan School Certificate Examination.

Higher education:

Higher education is provided by universities, both public and private, and institutes and colleges of technical and professional education. All universities are autonomous and government financed. The National Council of Higher Education is the government body responsible for higher education. Since 1990, many government universities have been created, mostly in the provinces. A few private tertiary institutions have also opened.

Main laws/decrees governing higher education:

Decree: Higher Education Act   Year: 1990
Concerns: Higher Education goals and programmes

Academic year:

Classes from: July *to:* March
Long vacation from: 1 April *to:* 30 June

Languages of instruction:

Arabic, English

Stages of studies:

Non-university level post-secondary studies (technical/vocational type):

Specialized higher education institutions offer courses in music, hygiene, nursing, radiography and mechanical engineering.

University level studies:

University level first stage: Bachelor's Degree:
The first year of university studies is devoted to basic studies and the major stage is reached with the award of the Bachelor's Degree in science, humanities and social sciences after another three years. A more specialized Bachelor's Degree with Honours requires a further year of study. Professional qualifications need five to six years' study.

University level second stage: *Master's Degree*:

This stage represents an in-depth knowledge at a certain degree of specialization and requires individual research; it is reached after two to three years' study. A Postgraduate Diploma is also offered in certain disciplines, following one or two years' study after the Bachelor's Degree.

University level third stage: *Doctor of Philosophy*:

The PhD may be reached after at least three years' study following the Master's Degree and requires individual research work and the presentation of a thesis.

University level fourth stage: *Higher Doctorate*:

It is awarded in humanities, law and science at the University of Khartoum only, in respect of published work contributing significantly to the advancement of knowledge.

Teacher education:

Training of pre-primary and primary/basic school teachers

Basic education teachers are trained in colleges of basic education teachers that are affiliated to the Faculties of Education of the universities. Successful secondary school-leavers who wish to join the teaching profession at the basic level follow a two-year programme. Those who successfully complete the course are awarded the intermediate diploma and, after a period of practice in basic schools, they return to the college for another two-year period to obtain the BA or BSc degree.

Training of secondary school teachers

Secondary-school teachers are trained at colleges for secondary school teachers or at the Faculties of Education of the universities. Graduates are awarded a BEd Degree. Since 1990, a postgraduate Diploma in Teaching English at Secondary Level (DIPTEASL) has been offered in Khartoum North.

Non-traditional studies:

Distance higher education

The University of Khartoum has a School of Extramural Studies and there is also a private Open University.

NATIONAL BODIES

Responsible authorities:

Ministry of Higher Education and Scientific Research
    Minister: Mubarak Mohammed Al Maghzoub
    PO Box 2081
    Khartoum
    Tel: +249(11) 779-312
    Fax: +249(11) 779-312
    WWW: http://www.moe-sd.com

National Council for Higher Education
    President: Ibrahim Ahmed Omar
    Under-Secretary: Hassan Mohamed Salih

International Relations: Mirghani Yousif Mohammed Ahmed
PO Box 2081
Khartoum
Tel: +249(11) 779-312
Fax: +249(11) 779-312

Role of governing body: Planning, coordinating and financing higher education.

The Association of Sudanese Universities
c/o University of Khartoum, P.O. Box 321
Khartoum
Tel: +249(11) 772-601
Fax: +249(11) 780-295
EMail: info@uofk.edu

ADMISSIONS TO HIGHER EDUCATION

Admission to non university higher education studies

Name of secondary school credential required: Sudan School Certificate
Minimum score/requirement: 50%

Admission to university-level studies

Name of secondary school credential required: Sudan School Certificate
Minimum score/requirement: 73% for the University of Khartoum; 88% for the medical faculty

Foreign students admission

Admission requirements: Foreign students seeking admission as undergraduates to higher education institutions should have a minimum of 5 credits (45%) in the Sudan School Certificate or equivalent and must fulfil the admission requirements of the University of Khartoum. Only foreign students residing in the Sudan and foreign scholarship holders are accepted in Sudanese universities.

Entry regulations: Students must obtain a visa.

Language requirements: Good knowledge of either Arabic or English. Orientation programme arranged by universities.

Recognition of studies and qualifications:

Studies pursued in foreign countries (bodies dealing with recognition of foreign credentials):
Committee for the Evaluation and Equivalency of Diplomas and Academic Degrees, Ministry of Education and Scientific Research
PO Box 2081
Khartoum
Tel: +249(11) 772-515   +249(11) 779-312
Fax: +249(11) 779-312
Telex: 22115QRANT

Deals with credential recognition for entry to: University and Profession

Multilateral agreements concerning recognition of foreign studies

Name(s) of agreement(s): UNESCO Convention on the Recognition of Studies, Certificates, Diplomas, Degrees and Other Academic Qualifications in Higher Education in the African States
Year of signature: 1981

UNESCO Convention on the Recognition of Studies, Diplomas and Degrees in Higher Education in the Arab States
Year of signature: 1978

References to further information on foreign student admissions and recognition of studies

Title: Annual Admissions Guide
Publisher: National Council of Higher Education

STUDENT LIFE

Main student services at national level

Department of Foreign Cultural Relations, National Council for Higher Education
PO Box 2081
Khartoum
Tel: +249(11) 779-312
Fax: +249(11) 779-312

Category of services provided: Special services/Centre for foreign students

Student expenses and financial aid

Student costs:

Foreign students tuition fees: Minimum: 1,500 (US Dollar)
Maximum: 3,000 (US Dollar)

Bodies providing information on student financial aid:

Department of Foreign Relations and Training, Ministry of Higher Education and Scientific Research
PO Box 2081
Khartoum
Tel: +249(11) 772-515
Fax: +242(11) 779-312
Telex: 22115QRANT

Deals with: Grants
Category of students: Students knowing Arabic, aged 19 to 26 from various countries in Europe, Asia and Africa. Scholarship awarded according to cultural agreements.

GRADING SYSTEM

Usual grading system in secondary school

Full Description: Sudan School Certificate: A: 80-100%; B: 70-79%; C: 60-69%; D: 50-59%; F: 49-0 fail:
Highest on scale: 100
Pass/fail level: 50
Lowest on scale: 0

Main grading system used by higher education institutions

Full Description: A+-F
The Bachelor of Arts is graded: 80-100: Division I; 60-79: Division II; 40-59: Division III
Highest on scale: A+
Pass/fail level: C
Lowest on scale: F

NOTES ON HIGHER EDUCATION SYSTEM

Data for academic year: 2002-2003
Source: International Association of Universities (IAU), updated from IBE website, 2003
(www.ibe.unesco.org/International/Databanks/Wde/profilee.htm)

INSTITUTIONS OF HIGHER EDUCATION

UNIVERSITIES

PUBLIC INSTITUTIONS

• AL FASHIR UNIVERSITY
Jameat Al-Fashir
PO Box 125, Darfoor
Tel: +249(527) 43394
Fax: +249(527) 43111

Vice-Chancellor: Abd Elbagi Mohammed Kabir
Tel: +249(527) 43394

Faculties
Education
Environmental Studies and Natural Resources (Environmental Studies; Natural Resources)
Medicine and Health Science (Health Sciences; Medicine)

Centres
Scientific Research and Documentation (Documentation Techniques)
Society Development and Extramural Studies (Social Studies)

History: Founded 1975.

*• AL-NEELAIN UNIVERSITY
Jameat Al-Neelain
PO Box 12702, Khartoum 12702
Tel: +249(11) 780-055
Fax: +249(11) 776-338
Website: http://www.neelain.8m.net/ARABIC2.htm

Vice-Chancellor: Awad Haj Ali Ahmed (1997-)
Tel: +249(11) 777-643 EMail: awadha@sudanmail.net

Faculties
Agriculture, Animal Production and Fisheries (Agriculture; Animal Husbandry; Cattle Breeding; Fishery)
Arts (Arabic; Archaeology; Arid Land Studies; Art Education; Art History; Art Management; Arts and Humanities; Comparative Religion; English; Geography; History; Library Science; Meteorology; Middle Eastern Studies; North African Studies; Philosophy; Sociology)
Commerce and Socio-Economic Studies (Accountancy; Administration; Administrative Law; African Studies; Anthropology; Automation and Control Engineering; Banking; Behavioural Sciences; Business Administration; Business and Commerce; Business Computing; Business Education; Commercial Law; Communication Arts; Cultural Studies; Data Processing; Economic and Finance Policy; Economics;

Educational Administration; Educational Technology; Engineering Management; Finance; Human Resources; Industrial and Organizational Psychology; Industrial and Production Economics; Industrial Management; Information Management; Information Sciences; Institutional Administration; Insurance; International Business; Labour and Industrial Relations; Leadership; Management; Management Systems; Marketing; Mathematics; Political Science; Private Administration; Public Administration; Rural Planning; Rural Studies; Safety Engineering; Sales Techniques; Secretarial Studies; Small Business; Social Studies; Sociology; Store Management; Systems Analysis; Transport Economics; Transport Management; Welfare and Protective Services)
Engineering (Computer Engineering; Electronic Engineering; Engineering; Technology; Telecommunications Engineering)
Graduate Studies (Arts and Humanities; Natural Sciences)
Law (Air and Space Law; Civil Law; Commercial Law; Comparative Law; Constitutional Law; Criminal Law; Criminology; Fiscal Law; History of Law; International Law; Islamic Law; Justice Administration; Labour Law; Law; Maritime Law; Private Law; Public Law)
Medicine (Anaesthesiology; Anatomy; Biochemistry; Cardiology; Dermatology; Embryology and Reproduction Biology; Gastroenterology; Gynaecology and Obstetrics; Haematology; Health Administration; Health Education; Immunology; Medicine; Microbiology; Neurology; Occupational Health; Ophthalmology; Pharmacology; Physiology; Public Health; Radiology; Surgery; Urology; Venereology; Virology)
Optometry and Visual Sciences (Anatomy; Arabic; Biochemistry; Biology; Chemistry; English; Islamic Studies; Ophthalmology; Optics; Optometry; Pharmacology; Physics; Physiology)
Science and Technology (Actuarial Science; Agricultural Engineering; Aquaculture; Astrophysics; Automation and Control Engineering; Automotive Engineering; Biochemistry; Biological and Life Sciences; Biology; Biophysics; Biotechnology; Botany; Cell Biology; Chemical Engineering; Chemistry; Coastal Studies; Computer Science; Crop Production; Earth Sciences; Ecology; Electrical Engineering; Electronic Engineering; Energy Engineering; Engineering; Entomology; Environmental Studies; Farm Management; Fire Science; Fishery; Food Science; Forestry; Genetics; Geography; Geology; Geophysics; Graphic Arts; Handicrafts; Harvest Technology; Heating and Refrigeration; Heritage Preservation; Homeopathy; Horticulture; Hydraulic Engineering; Industrial Design; Irrigation; Laboratory Techniques; Landscape Architecture; Laser Engineering; Limnology; Maintenance Technology; Marine Biology; Marine Science and Oceanography; Mathematics; Mathematics and Computer Science; Measurement and Precision Engineering; Medical Technology; Meteorology; Microelectronics; Mineralogy; Mining Engineering; Molecular Biology; Mountain Studies; Multimedia; Museum Studies; Music Theory and Composition; Natural Resources; Natural Sciences; Nuclear Physics; Optical Technology; Parasitology; Peace and Disarmament; Petrology; Physics; Radio and Television Broadcasting; Radiology; Safety Engineering; Soil Science; Statistics; Surveying and Mapping;

Technology; Telecommunications Engineering; Textile Technology; Thermal Physics; Town Planning; Tropical Agriculture; Waste Management; Water Science; Wildlife; Wood Technology)

Statistical, Population Studies and Information Technologies (Accountancy; Computer Graphics; Computer Science; Demography and Population; Economic and Finance Policy; Economics; Information Technology; Mathematics; Operations Research; Software Engineering; Statistics; Systems Analysis)

Centres
Computer (Computer Science)

Research Centres
Nile Basin Studies (Arts and Humanities; Natural Sciences; Regional Studies)

History: Founded 1955 as Khartoum Branch of Cairo University. Acquired present status and title 1993.

Academic Year: July to April (July-October; November-April)

Admission Requirements: Secondary school certificate (passes in 7 subjects) or recognized foreign equivalent

Main Language(s) of Instruction: Arabic

Degrees and Diplomas: *Bachelor Honours Degree*: 4 yrs; *Master's Degree*: a further 2 yrs; *Doctor of Philosophy*: (PhD), a further 3-4 yrs. Also High Diploma, 1 yr; General Diploma (Undergraduate)

Student Services: Academic Counselling, Social Counselling, Employment Services, Nursery Care, Cultural Centre, Sports Facilities, Health Services, Canteen

Special Facilities: Al-Neelain University Theatre

Libraries: Central Library, Libraries of the Faculties of Science and Technology, Arts, Law, Commerce, Optometry, Visual Science Engineering and Medicine, Graduate College Library, English Language Library, Computer Centre Library

Press or Publishing House: Al-Neelain University Press

Academic Staff *2001-2002*: Full-Time: c. 210 Part-Time: c. 60 Total: c. 270

Staff with Doctorate: Total: c. 115

Student Numbers *2001-2002:* Total: c. 36,000

*• AL-ZAIEM AL-AZHARI UNIVERSITY
Jameat Al-Ziem Al-Azhari (AAU)
PO Box 1432, Khartoum North 13311
Tel: +249(13) 344-522
Fax: +249(13) 344-510
EMail: itnc@alazhari-unv.net
Website: http://www.alazhari-unv.net

Vice-Chancellor: Ali El Sayed Ali (2003-)
Tel: +249(13) 344-511
EMail: casein@sudanmail.net.sd;casein11@hotmail.com

Principal: Hassan Kamal Eltahir Tel: +249(13) 344-516
EMail: itnc@alazhari-unv.net

Faculties
Agriculture *(Bashir)* (Agriculture; Food Technology)
Economics and Administration (Administration; Economics)

Education
Engineering
Medical Laboratory Sciences (Laboratory Techniques)
Medicine (Anaesthesiology; Health Sciences; Medicine)
Nursing
Physiotherapy (Physical Therapy)
Political Science and Strategic Studies (Military Science; Political Science)
Public and Environment Health (Environmental Studies; Public Health)
Radiological Science and Medical Imaging (Medical Technology; Radiology)
Shari'a and Law (Islamic Law; Law)
Technology and Development Studies (Development Studies; Technology)
Urban Sciences (Urban Studies)

History: Founded 1993.

Governing Bodies: University Council

Admission Requirements: Secondary school certificate

Fees: (US Dollars): International Students, undergraduate 3000-4000; graduate 4000-6000

Main Language(s) of Instruction: Arabic, English

Degrees and Diplomas: *Diploma*: 2-3 yrs; *Bachelor's Degree*: 4-5 yrs; *Bachelor Honours Degree*: 5 yrs

Student Residential Facilities: For 800 students

Academic Staff *2001:* Total: **239**

Student Numbers *2001:* Total: **5,109**

• BAHR-AL-GHAZAL UNIVERSITY
Jameat Bahr Al-Ghazal (U.B.G.)
P.O. Box 10739, Khartoum, West Bahr-Al Gazal 10739
Tel: +249(11) 224-629
Fax: +249(11) 223-015
EMail: ubgzal@sudanmail.net

Vice-Chancellor: Aduol Mathew Atem (1997-)
EMail: maaduol@sudanmail.net

Principal: Marial Paul Dot Tel: +249(11) 226-290

International Relations: Monytooc Monywiir Deng, Academic Secretary Tel: +249(11) 232-664

Colleges
Economics and Rural Studies (Development Studies; Economics; Rural Studies) *Dean:* Madut Aballiaak Them
Education *Dean:* Alamin Alfateh Mustafa
Medicine and Health Sciences (Medicine) *Dean:* Abdel Latif Jubara Mahmoud
Veterinary Science *Dean:* Ali Hassan Ahmed

Institutes
Public and Environmental Health Studies (Environmental Studies; Public Health) *Director:* Bol Anyuat Angui

History: Founded 1991.

Governing Bodies: University Council; University Senate; Dean's Board; College Boards

Admission Requirements: Secondary school certificate or foreign equivalent

Main Language(s) of Instruction: Arabic, English

International Co-operation: With universities in Egypt, Iraq, Syria

Degrees and Diplomas: *Diploma*: Public Health and Environmental Health Studies (DPPEH), 3 yrs; Rural Studies (DPRS), 4 yrs; *Bachelor's Degree*: Education (BEd); Science (Economics) (BSc), 4 yrs; Veterinary Science (BVS), 5 yrs; Medicine and Surgery (MBBS), 6 yrs

Student Services: Academic Counselling, Social Counselling, Employment Services, Sports Facilities, Health Services

Libraries: Central Library

Publications: The Pioneer, Publication of the College of Education (biannually)

Academic Staff 2001-2002	MEN	WOMEN	TOTAL
FULL-TIME	148	61	209
PART-TIME	36	28	64
TOTAL	**184**	**89**	**273**
STAFF WITH DOCTORATE			
FULL-TIME	98	49	147
PART-TIME	30	24	54
TOTAL	**128**	**73**	**201**

Student Numbers 2001-2002	MEN	WOMEN	TOTAL
All (Foreign Included)	594	919	**1,513**
FOREIGN ONLY	–	–	4

BAKHET EL-RUDDA UNIVERSITY
Jameat Bakhet El-Rudda
PO Box 1311, Khartoum, Eldewaym/White Nile
Tel: +249(531) 22440
Fax: +249(531) 20548

Vice-Chancellor: Anaas A. El-Hafeez

Executive Director: Mohamed Musa

Faculties
Agriculture and Natural Resources (Agriculture; Natural Resources) *Dean*: Ghanim Sabih
Economics and Administration (Administration; Economics) *Dean*: Ilham Saadallah
Education *Dean*: Salih Nourin
Medicine *Dean*: Yousif Sultan

Programmes
Postgraduate Studies (Agriculture; Economics; Education) *Dean*: Mahmoud Hassan

History: Founded 1997.

Admission Requirements: Secondary school certificate

Fees: (Sudanese Dinars): 17,500-20,000 per annum

Main Language(s) of Instruction: Arabic, English

Accrediting Agencies: Ministry of Higher Education

Degrees and Diplomas: *Diploma*: Administration, Accountancy, Computer, 3 yrs; *Bachelor's Degree*: Agriculture, Education, Economics, Medicine, 4-5 yrs. Master's Degree and Doctor of Philosophy planned for 2003

Student Services: Academic Counselling, Social Counselling, Nursery Care, Cultural Centre, Sports Facilities, Language Programmes, Health Services, Canteen

Student Residential Facilities: Yes

Special Facilities: Museum, Art Gallery

Academic Staff 2001-2002	MEN	WOMEN	TOTAL
FULL-TIME	120	31	151
PART-TIME	45	2	47
TOTAL	**165**	**33**	**198**
STAFF WITH DOCTORATE			
FULL-TIME	14	1	15
PART-TIME	–	–	33
TOTAL	**–**	**–**	**48**

Student Numbers 2001-2002	MEN	WOMEN	TOTAL
All (Foreign Included)	1,370	2,665	**4,035**
FOREIGN ONLY	–	–	7

Evening Students, 568 **Distance Students,** 1,360

BLUE NILE UNIVERSITY
Jameat Al-Neel Alazarg
PO Box 143, Damazeen, Blue Nile
Tel: +249(11) 785-614

Vice-Chancellor: Mohammed El-Hassan Abdul El-Rahman

Faculties
Education
Engineering

Centres
Extramural Studies and Continuing Education

History: Founded 1995.

DONGOLA UNIVERSITY
Jameat Dongola
PO Box 47, Dongola
Tel: +249(241) 21519
Fax: +249(241) 21514

Vice-Chancellor: Mohammed Osman Ahmed

Faculties
Agriculture
Arts (Arts and Humanities)
Education
Law and Islamic Law (Shari'a) (Islamic Law)
Medicine
Mining and Earth Sciences (Earth Sciences; Mining Engineering)

History: Founded 1994.

EL-DALANG UNIVERSITY
Jameat El-Dalang
El-Dalang, South Kordofan
Tel: +249(11) 785-614

Vice-Chancellor: Kamess Kago Kunda (1993-)

Faculties
Agriculture
Education
Social Development (Social Studies)
Teacher Training

Centres
Computer Science (Computer Education)
Peace Studies (Peace and Disarmament)

History: Founded 1990.

EL-GADARIF UNIVERSITY
Jameat El-Gadarif (G.U.)
P.O. Box 449, El-Gadarif 32211
Tel: +249(441) 43668
Fax: +249(441) 43120
EMail: unged@sudanmail.net

Vice-Chancellor: Omer Kurdi (2002-2005)
Tel: +249(1230) 3829 EMail: omekur@hotmail.com

Principal: Ali Rajab Tel: +249(441) 43964

Faculties
Agricultural and Environmental Sciences (Agricultural Engineering; Agronomy; Horticulture; Zoology) *Dean:* Abdel-Aziza Taha
Economics and Administrative Sciences (Administration; Economics) *Dean:* El-Guzoli Mohamad
Education (Arabic; Biology; Chemistry; Education; Physics) *Dean:* Sultan Nour
Medicine and Medical Sciences (Medicine) *Dean:* El-Dirdiry Salah

Centres
Computer and Information Technology (Computer Engineering; Information Technology)
Contuing Education (Continuing Education)
Languages of the Horn of Africa (African Languages)
Women's Studies

History: Founded 1990, acquired present status 1994.

Governing Bodies: University Council, Senate, Dean's Council, Faculty Boards

Admission Requirements: Secondary school certificate or equivalent

Fees: (Sudanese Dinars): 10,000 per semester

Main Language(s) of Instruction: Arabic, English

International Co-operation: With universities in South Africa.

Degrees and Diplomas: *Diploma:* Accountancy; Banking Studies; Business Administration; Computer Sciences; Information Technology, 2 yrs; *Bachelor's Degree:* Islamic and Koranic Sciences (BIKSc), 4 yrs; *Bachelor Honours Degree:* Economic and Administrative Sciences (BSc (Hons)); Education, Science (BSc (Hons)), 4 yrs; Agricultural and Environmental Sciences (BSc (Hons)), 5 yrs; *Master's Degree:* Medicine, Surgery (MB/BS), 6 yrs

Student Services: Academic Counselling, Social Counselling, Foreign Student Adviser, Nursery Care, Cultural Centre, Sports Facilities, Language Programmes, Health Services, Canteen, Foreign Student Centre

Student Residential Facilities: Yes

Libraries: Main Library; Electronic Library; Internet

Academic Staff 2001-2002	MEN	WOMEN	TOTAL
FULL-TIME	73	23	96
PART-TIME	57	1	58
TOTAL	**130**	**24**	**154**
STAFF WITH DOCTORATE			
FULL-TIME	21	1	22
PART-TIME	29	1	30
TOTAL	**50**	**2**	**52**

Student Numbers 2001-2002	MEN	WOMEN	TOTAL
All (Foreign Included)	1,497	2,348	**3,845**
FOREIGN ONLY	–	–	41

Evening Students, 880

EL-IMAM EL-MAHDI UNIVERSITY
Jameat El-Imam El-Mahdi
PO Box 209, Kosti 11588
Tel: +249(571) 22545; +249(571) 22002
Fax: +249(571) 22222
EMail: abdosm@sudanmail.net

Vice-Chancellor: Abdelrahim Osman Mohammed (2002-)
EMail: abdelrahim_osman@yahoo.com

Principal: Mohamed Haj Eltom

Faculties
Arabic and Islamic Sciences (Arabic; Islamic Studies)
Arts (Arts and Humanities)
Engineering and Technical Studies (Engineering; Technology)
Law and Islamic Law (Shari'a) (Islamic Law; Law)
Medicine and Health Sciences (Health Sciences; Laboratory Techniques; Medicine; Nursing; Public Health)

Centres
Computer Studies (Computer Engineering; Computer Science)
Extramural Studies

History: Founded 1993.

KASSALA UNIVERSITY
Jameat Kassala
Kassala 266
Tel: +249(411) 22095
Fax: +249(411) 23501

Vice-Chancellor: Mustafa Ali Abasher (1998-)

Faculties
Agriculture and Natural Resources (Agriculture; Natural Resources)
Economics and Administration (Administration; Economics)
Education
Medicine and Health Sciences (Medicine)

History: Founded 1990.

• KORDOFAN UNIVERSITY
Jameat Kordofan
PO Box 160, El Obeid, North Kordofan 517
Tel: +249(611) 23119
Fax: +249(611) 23108 +249(611) 23119
Telex: 6001
EMail: korduniv@yahoo.com

Vice-Chancellor: Osman Adam Osman (1994-)

Faculties
Education
Engineering and Technical Science (Engineering; Technology)
Medicine and Health Sciences (Health Sciences; Medicine)
Natural Resources
Science and Humanities (Humanities and Social Science Education; Natural Sciences)

Centres
Arabic Gum (Rubber Technology)
Further Education

History: Founded 1990.

• NILE VALLEY UNIVERSITY
Jameat Wadi Al-Neel
PO Box 52, Eldamer 163
Tel: +249(211) 24433
Fax: +249(211) 22644 +249(211) 26953
EMail: nilevu@sudanmail.net

Vice-Chancellor: Faisal Abdallah Elhag

Faculties
Agriculture
Commerce and Business Administration (Business Administration; Business and Commerce)
Education
Engineering and Technology (Engineering; Technology)
Islamic and Arabic Studies (African Studies; Islamic Studies; Middle Eastern Studies)
Islamic Law (Shari'a) and Law (Islamic Law; Law)
Medicine (Health Sciences; Medicine)
Postgraduate Studies
Science, Technology and Community Development (Development Studies; Natural Sciences; Technology)

Colleges
Teacher Training

Centres
Extramural Studies

Research Centres
Archaeology
Date Palms and Date

History: Founded 1990, incorporating two existing faculties.
Governing Bodies: University Council, comprising 50 members
Academic Year: April to December
Admission Requirements: Secondary school certificate or equivalent
Main Language(s) of Instruction: Arabic, English (subsidiary)
Degrees and Diplomas: *Bachelor's Degree*; *Bachelor Honours Degree*; *Postgraduate Diploma*; *Master's Degree*; *Doctor of Philosophy*. Also Diploma
Libraries: c. 16,000 vols
Academic Staff *2001-2002:* Total: c. 120
Student Numbers *2001-2002*: All (Foreign Included): Men: c. 1,200 Women: c. 500 Total: c. 1,700

• NYALA UNIVERSITY
Jameat Nyala
PO Box 155, Nyala, South Darfur
Tel: +249(711) 33122
Fax: +249(711) 33123
EMail: nyalauni@hotmail.com

Vice-Chancellor: Adam Hassan Sulaiman

Faculties
Economics and Commerce (Business and Commerce; Economics)
Education
Engineering
Veterinary Science

Centres
Extramural Studies
Peace Studies (Peace and Disarmament)

History: Founded 1994.

• OMDURMAN ISLAMIC UNIVERSITY
Jameat Omdurman Islamiah
PO Box 382, Omdurman
Tel: +249(11) 511-524 +249(11) 784-375
Fax: +249(11) 775-253
Telex: (0984) 22527 oui sd

President: Mohammed Osman Salih (2001-)

Faculties
Agriculture
Al-Da'awah Al-Islamia (Islamic Studies)
Arabic Language (Arabic)
Arts (Arts and Humanities)
Business Administration
Economics and Political Science (Economics; Political Science)
Education
Engineering (Educational Sciences; Engineering)
Further Education

Islamic Law (Shari'a) and Law (Islamic Law; Law)
Islamic Principles (Islamic Studies)
Medicine and Health Sciences (Health Sciences; Medicine)
Pharmacy
Science (Natural Sciences)

Centres
Further Education

Further Information: Branches in Damascus and Elginan

History: Founded 1912 as Islamic Institute, became College 1924 and University 1965. Acquired present status 1975. A State Institution under the jurisdiction of and financially supported by the National Council for Higher Education.

Governing Bodies: University Council; Senate; Faculty Boards

Academic Year: July to April (July-November; December-April)

Admission Requirements: Secondary school certificate or recognized equivalent

Main Language(s) of Instruction: Arabic

International Co-operation: UNESCO Chair in Water Resources

Degrees and Diplomas: *Bachelor's Degree*: Arts (BA); Law (LLB); Science (BSc), 4 yrs; *Postgraduate Diploma*: Education, 1 yr; *Master's Degree*: Arts (MA), a further 2-3 yrs; *Doctor of Philosophy*: (PhD), 3 yrs. Also Diplomas in Education; Islamic Economics, 1 yr.

Student Residential Facilities: For c. 1500 students

Libraries: Central Library, c. 90,000 vols; Girls College, c. 10,000 vols

Publications: Journals of the Faculties

Press or Publishing House: The University Press

Academic Staff *2001-2002:* Total: c. 200

Student Numbers *2001-2002:* Total: c. 4,000

RED SEA UNIVERSITY
Jameat Al-Bahar Al-Ahmar
PO Box 24, Port Sudan, Red Sea
Tel: +249(311) 21928
Fax: +249(311) 27778

Vice-Chancellor: Abdel Gadir Dafalla Elhag (1994-)
Registrar: Alsir Ahmed Babiker

Faculties
Applied Sciences (Natural Sciences)
Earth Sciences
Economics and Administration (Administration; Economics)
Education
Engineering (Chemical Engineering; Civil Engineering; Engineering; Mechanical Engineering)
Marine Science and Fisheries (Fishery; Marine Science and Oceanography)
Maritime Transport Economics (Economics; Marine Transport)
Medicine and Health Sciences (Health Sciences; Medicine)
Teacher Training *(Primary Level)*

Units
Continuing Education

Institutes
Oceanography (Marine Science and Oceanography)

History: Founded 1994.

Governing Bodies: University Council; Senate; Faculty Boards

Academic Year: September to June (September-December; March-June)

Admission Requirements: Secondary school certificate

Main Language(s) of Instruction: Arabic, English

Degrees and Diplomas: *Bachelor's Degree*: Arts; Science, 4 yrs; *Bachelor Honours Degree*: 5 yrs; *Postgraduate Diploma*: 3 yrs

Student Residential Facilities: For c. 25 students

Libraries: c. 1550 vols Marine Science; Faculty Libraries

Academic Staff *2001-2002*: Full-Time: c. 50 Part-Time: c. 30 Total: c. 80

Student Numbers *2001-2002:* Total: c. 800

SHENDI UNIVERSITY
Jameat Shendi
PO Box 142, Shendi, River Nile
Tel: +249(261) 721-84
Fax: +249(261) 725-09
Website: http://www.shendiuniversity.net

Vice-Chancellor and President: Ali Abdel Abdel Rahman Barri (1994-) EMail: ali-barri@hotmail.com

Deputy Vice-Chancellor: Yahia Fadulalla Mukhtar
Fax: +249(261) 73988

Faculties
Arts (African Languages; Arabic; Archaeology; Arts and Humanities; English; Hotel Management; Modern Languages; Tourism)
Community Development *(Taybat Al Khawad)* (Development Studies; Gender Studies; Social Studies; Women's Studies)
Education for Basic Level Teacher Training (Arabic; Educational Sciences; English; Geography; History; Mathematics; Natural Sciences; Primary Education; Religious Studies; Social Sciences; Teacher Training; Theology) *Dean*: Malik Mohd-Kheir
Islamic Law (Shari'a) and Law *(Al Matama)* (Islamic Law; Law; Private Law; Public Law)
Medicine and Health Sciences (Health Sciences; Laboratory Techniques; Medicine; Nursing; Public Health; Surgery)

Institutes
Meroitic Studies (Writing)

Centres
Adult Education and Extramural Studies (Preschool Education)
Al-Fatih Islamic Studies (Information Management; Islamic Studies)

471

Crops Studies *(Misaktab)* (Crop Production)

Education Development and Continuing Education *(Ahmed Idirs Al Arbab)* (Curriculum; Educational Sciences)

Further Information: Also Teaching Hospitals

History: Founded 1990 as Faculties of Wadi Elneel University, acquired present status and title 1994.

Governing Bodies: University Council; Senate; Faculty Boards

Admission Requirements: Secondary school certificate or equivalent as required by the National Board of Administration

Main Language(s) of Instruction: Arabic, English

Degrees and Diplomas: *Bachelor's Degree*: 8 Semesters; *Master's Degree*: Medicine and Surgery, 12 semesters; *Doctor of Philosophy*. Also Intermediate Diplomas and Higher Diplomas

Student Services: Social Counselling, Cultural Centre, Sports Facilities, Health Services, Canteen

Student Residential Facilities: Yes

Special Facilities: Movie Studio

Libraries: 6 Libraries and Internet

Publications: Journal of Shandi University (bi-annually)

Academic Staff *2001-2002*: Full-Time: c. 135 Part-Time: c. 80 Total: c. 215

Staff with doctorate: Full-Time: c. 20 Part-Time: c. 30 Total: c. 50

Student Numbers *2001-2002*	TOTAL
All (Foreign Included)	**3,700**
FOREIGN ONLY	50

SINAR UNIVERSITY
Jameat Sinar
Sinar
Tel: +249(561) 785-614
Fax: +249(561) 730-697
Telex: 22115

Faculties
Agriculture
Arabic and Islamic Sciences (Arabic; Islamic Studies)
Education
Engineering
Medicine
Natural Resources and Environment (Environmental Studies; Natural Resources)

Centres
Da'wah
Extramural Studies

History: Founded 1977, acquired present status 1995.

472

*• SUDAN UNIVERSITY OF SCIENCE AND TECHNOLOGY
Jameat El-Sudan I'Leloom Wal Technologia (SUST)
PO Box 407, Khartoum
Tel: +249(11) 772-508
Fax: +249(11) 774-559
Cable: technology
EMail: sust@sudanet.net
Website: http://www.sustech.edu

Vice-Chancellor: Izzeldin Mohammed Osman (1994-)
Tel: +249(11) 775-292 EMail: izzeldin@acm.org

General-Secretary: Ali Abdel-Rahman Ali
Tel: +249(11) 771-839

International Relations: Isam M. Abdulmajid
Tel: +249(11) 770-319

Colleges

Agricultural Studies *(Shambat)* (Agricultural Business; Agricultural Equipment; Agriculture; Agronomy; Food Technology; Horticulture; Rural Planning) *Dean*: Abd Elaziz Mackawi

Business Studies (Accountancy; Banking; Business Administration; Business and Commerce; International Business) *Dean*: Ali Abdalla Adam

Education (Art Education; Education; English; French; Mathematics; Technology Education) *Dean*: Ahmed Saad Masaod

Engineering (Aeronautical and Aerospace Engineering; Architecture; Civil Engineering; Electrical Engineering; Electronic Engineering; Engineering; Mechanical Engineering; Petroleum and Gas Engineering; Surveying and Mapping; Textile Technology) *Dean*: Ahmed El Tayeb

Fine and Applied Arts (Ceramic Art; Fine Arts; Graphic Design; Handicrafts; Industrial Design; Painting and Drawing; Printing and Printmaking; Sculpture; Textile Design) *Dean*: Ali Mohamed Osman

Forestry (Ecology; Forest Biology; Forest Management; Forestry) *Dean*: Mahir Salih Solieman

Medical Radiological Sciences (Radiology; Radiophysics) *Dean*: Bushra Hussein Ahmed

Music and Drama *(HIMD)* (Music; Music Theory and Composition; Musical Instruments; Musicology; Theatre) *Dean*: Ahmed Abdela'al Ahmed

Physical Education (Physical Education; Sports) *Dean*: Eldarouti Sharafeldin

Postgraduate Studies (Agriculture; Business Administration; Business and Commerce; Education; Engineering; Fine Arts; Forestry; Veterinary Science) *Dean*: Sabir Mohamed Salih

Science (Chemistry; Computer Science; Laboratory Techniques; Natural Sciences; Physics; Statistics) *Dean*: Hajou Ahmed Mohamed

Technology and Human Development *(THD)* (Agriculture; Business Administration; Business and Commerce; Development Studies; Education; Engineering; Information Technology; Technology) *Dean*: Tagel Asfiya Alaagib

Veterinary Science and Animal Production (Animal Husbandry; Cattle Breeding; Veterinary Science) *Dean*: Osman Saad

Institutes

Earth Sciences *(WAIESC, Wad El Magboul) Dean*: Abdulbagi Abdurahman Gorashi

Centres

Women Development (Women's Studies) *Director*: Fatima Abdel Mahmoud

Research Centres

External Relations (International Relations) *Director*: Isam Mohamed Abdelmajid

Further Information: Also National Research Institute. English Language Unit; Arabic Language Unit; Arabic as foreign language

History: Founded 1950 as Khartoum Technical Institute. Became Khartoum Polytechnic 1975. Acquired present status and title 1990 incorporating previously existing higher Technical Institutes and specialized Colleges.

Governing Bodies: University Council; Senate

Academic Year: September to June

Admission Requirements: Secondary school certificate or equivalent

Fees: According to student's family financial ability; foreign students, (US Dollars): c. 2000-3000

Main Language(s) of Instruction: Arabic, English

Degrees and Diplomas: *Diploma*: 2-3 yrs; *Bachelor's Degree*: (BSc; BA), 4-5 yrs; *Postgraduate Diploma*: 2 yrs; *Master's Degree*: a further 2 yrs; *Doctor of Philosophy*: (PhD), 3 yrs

Student Services: Academic Counselling, Social Counselling, Sports Facilities, Language Programmes, Health Services, Canteen

Student Residential Facilities: Yes

Libraries: Total, c. 66,000 vols

Publications: Journal of Science and Technology (biannually)

Press or Publishing House: Sudan University Printing Press and Distribution House

Academic Staff 2000	TOTAL
FULL-TIME	700
PART-TIME	130
TOTAL	**830**

Student Numbers 2000	TOTAL
All (Foreign Included)	**22,185**
FOREIGN ONLY	470

*• UNIVERSITY OF GEZIRA

Jameat Al-Gezira
PO Box 20, Wad Medani 2667
Tel: +249(511) 41355
Fax: +249(511) 40466
Telex: (0984) 50009 txowd sd
Website: http://www.gezirauniversity.net

Vice-Chancellor: Ismail Hassan Hussein (2001-)
Tel: +249(511) 43174 Fax: +249(511) 772-062

Principal: Kamal Norain Ibrahim Tel: +249(511) 42464
Fax: +249(511) 40466 EMail: eptsam@yahoo.com

Faculties

Agricultural Sciences (Agriculture)

Animal Husbandry

Communication Sciences (Communication Studies)

Economics and Rural Development (Economics; Rural Planning)

Education

Health and Environmental Sciences (Environmental Engineering; Health Sciences)

Mathematics and Computer Science

Medical Sciences (Health Sciences)

Pharmacy

Postgraduate

Science and Technology (Natural Sciences; Technology)

Textile Engineering (Textile Technology)

Centres

Agriculture and Natural Resources (Agriculture; Natural Resources)

Biological Technology (Biology; Technology)

Cereal Oil Manufacturing (Crop Production)

Demographic Studies (Demography and Population)

Development of Horticultural Exports (Horticulture)

Islamic Knowledge (Islamic Studies)

Neurological Medicine (Neurological Therapy)

Small Scale Industries and Technology (Small Business)

Sugar Research (Food Science)

Technological and Biological Sciences (Biological and Life Sciences; Technology)

Transfer

Water and Irrigation Management (Irrigation; Water Management)

History: Founded 1975. An autonomous State Institution.

Governing Bodies: Council, comprising 29 members; Senate, 3 members

Academic Year: October to June (October-January; February-June)

Admission Requirements: Secondary school certificate

Main Language(s) of Instruction: English

Degrees and Diplomas: *Bachelor's Degree*: Agriculture (BSc (Agric.)); Economics (BSc (Econ.)); Technology (BSc (Tech.)), 5 yrs; Medicine and Surgery (MBN, BCh), 6 yrs; *Master's Degree*: Philosophy (MPhil); Science (MSc); *Doctor of Philosophy*: (PhD)

Student Residential Facilities: Yes

Libraries: c. 7550 vols

Academic Staff 2001-2002: Total: c. 150

Student Numbers 2001-2002: Total: c. 1,100

• UNIVERSITY OF HOLY QU'RAN AND ISLAMIC SCIENCES

Jameat El-Quraan El-Kareem Wa El-Iloom El-Shamia
PO Box 1459, Omdurman
Tel: +249(15) 559-594
Fax: +249(15) 559-175
Telex: 78012
EMail: quranunv@quranunv.net

Vice-Chancellor: Ahmed Khalid Babiker (1991-)

Faculties
Arabic Language (Arabic)
Community Development *(Juba)* (Development Studies)
Da'wah and Media (Media Studies)
Education *(Malakal)*
Educational Sciences
Holy Qu'ran (Koran)
Islamic Law (Shari'a) and Law (Islamic Law; Law)

Centres
Women's Studies

History: Founded 1990.

*• UNIVERSITY OF JUBA

Jameat Juba
PO Box 321, Khartoum Centre, Juba, Baher Elgebal 82
Tel: +249(11) 222-136   +249(11) 451-352
Fax: +249(11) 222-142
Telex: (0984) 22738 kupsd
Cable: jubasity juba
EMail: jucs@sudanet.net

Vice-Chancellor: Fathi Mohamed Ahmed Kaleel (2001-)
Tel: +249(11) 227-986 EMail: jucs@sudanet.net
Deputy Vice-Chancellor: Venansio T. Muludiang

Faculties
Arts and Humanities
Business Administration
Education
Engineering
Law
Medicine
Social and Economic Studies (Accountancy; Arts and Humanities; Management; Political Science; Public Administration; Social Sciences; Sociology)

Centres
Computer Studies (Computer Science)
Languages and Translation (Modern Languages; Translation and Interpretation)
Peace Studies (Peace and Disarmament)

History: Founded 1975. First students accepted 1977. An autonomous State Institution.

Governing Bodies: University Council; Senate

Academic Year: March to December (March-July; August-December)
Admission Requirements: Secondary school certificate or foreign equivalent
Main Language(s) of Instruction: English
Degrees and Diplomas: *Bachelor's Degree*: Arts (BA); Science (BSc), 4 yrs; *Bachelor Honours Degree*: 5 yrs; *Master's Degree*: 1-2 yrs; *Doctor of Philosophy*: (PhD), 2-3 yrs. Also Diploma, 3 yrs.
Student Residential Facilities: Yes
Libraries: c. 50,000 vols
Publications: Juvarsity (monthly)
Press or Publishing House: Juba University Printing Unit
Academic Staff *2001-2002*: Full-Time: c. 300 Part-Time: c. 100 Total: c. 400
Student Numbers *2001-2002:* Total: c. 800

*• UNIVERSITY OF KHARTOUM

Jameat El-Khartoum
PO Box 321, Khartoum 11115
Tel: +249(11) 771-290
Fax: +249(11) 780-295
EMail: info@uofk.edu
Website: http://www.sudan.net/uk

Vice-Chancellor: Abdel Malik Mohammed Abdel Rahman (2000-) EMail: elzubairbashi@hotmail.com
Secretary for Academic Affairs: Abu Buker Ali Abu Goukh
Tel: +249(11) 779-526 Fax: +249(11) 771-203
EMail: abugoukh@hotmail.com
Library: Mohammed Noury Al-Amin

Faculties
Agriculture *(Shambat)* (Agricultural Economics; Agricultural Engineering; Agriculture; Biochemistry; Botany; Crop Production; Horticulture; Soil Science) *Dean*: Gaafer Mohammed Al-Hassan
Animal Husbandry (Animal Husbandry; Dairy; Genetics; Meat and Poultry) *Dean*: Al-Fadil Ahmed Al-Zubier
Arts (Arabic; Archaeology; Arts and Humanities; Chinese; English; French; Geography; German; History; Information Sciences; International Relations; Islamic Studies; Library Science; Linguistics; Philosophy; Psychology; Russian) *Dean*: Majzoub Salim Bur
Dentistry (Dentistry; Orthodontics; Periodontics; Surgery) *Dean*: Ibrahim Ahmed Gandour
Economics and Social Studies (Anthropology; Development Studies; Econometrics; Economics; Political Science; Social Studies) *Dean*: Arbab Ismail Babikir
Education *(Omburman)* (Arabic; Biology; Chemistry; Curriculum; Education; Educational Psychology; Educational Technology; English; Family Studies; French; Geography; History; Mathematics; Pedagogy; Physics) *Dean*: Bashir Mohammed Osman Haj Al-Tom
Engineering and Architecture (Agricultural Engineering; Architecture; Chemical Engineering; Civil Engineering; Electrical Engineering; Mechanical Engineering; Mining Engineering;

Petroleum and Gas Engineering; Surveying and Mapping) *Dean*: Al-Nima Ibrahim Al-Nima

Forestry *(Shambat)* (Forest Management; Forestry) *Dean*: Hashim Ali Al-Ataa

Law (Commercial Law; International Law; Islamic Law; Law; Private Law; Public Law) *Dean*: Awad Abdallah Abu Bukr

Mathematics (Applied Mathematics; Computer Science; Mathematics; Statistics) *Dean*: Mohamed Abdel Moniem Ismail

Medicine (Anaesthesiology; Anatomy; Biochemistry; Community Health; Gynaecology and Obstetrics; Medicine; Microbiology; Orthopedics; Pathology; Physiology; Psychiatry and Mental Health; Surgery) *Dean*: Al Daw Mukhtar Ahmed Mukthar

Pharmacy (Pharmacology; Pharmacy) *Dean*: Idris Babiker Al-Tayib

Public and Environmental Health (Environmental Studies; Epidemiology; Food Science; Health Sciences; Hygiene) *Dean*: Bashir Mohammed Al-Hassan

Science (Botany; Chemistry; Geology; Natural Sciences; Physics; Zoology) *Dean*: Osman Ibrahim Osman

Veterinary Science *(Shambat)* (Anatomy; Biochemistry; Gynaecology and Obstetrics; Medicine; Microbiology; Pathology; Pharmacology; Physiology; Surgery; Toxicology; Veterinary Science) *Dean*: Mohammed Taha Abdel Alla Shgadi

Colleges
Graduate *Dean*: Sidig Ahmed Ismail

Schools
Higher Nursing (Nursing) *Director*: Rugaia Abu Al-Gasim Abdel Rahim

Management Studies (Accountancy; Finance; Management) *Dean*: Ismail Al Khalipa Suliman

Institutes
African and Asian Studies (African Studies; Asian Studies; Folklore; Native Language Education) *Director*: Madeni Mohammed Mohammed Ahmed

Building and Roads Research (Building Technologies; Construction Engineering; Road Engineering; Soil Science) *Director*: Mohammed Ahmed Osman

Desertification Studies (Arid Land Studies)

Endemic Diseases (Entomology; Immunology; Microbiology)

Environmental Studies (Environmental Studies; Meteorology) *Director*: Youssif Babikir Abu Gidari

Extramural Studies and Community Development *Director*: Al Tayib Ahmed Al Mustafa Haiaty

Centres
Computer (Computer Science) *Director*: Hashim Al-Amin Mustafa

Development of Health Professions (Health Sciences)

Urban Studies

Research Centres
Camel

Further Information: Also Teaching Hospital

History: Founded 1951 as University College of Khartoum incorporating Gordon Memorial College, established 1902, and the Kitchener School of Medicine, established 1924. Became University 1956. An autonomous Institution financed by the State.

Governing Bodies: University Council, comprising 29 members; Academic Senate, composed entirely of members of the academic staff

Academic Year: July to April (July-September; October-December; January-April)

Admission Requirements: Secondary school certificate

Main Language(s) of Instruction: English. Arabic in Departments of Islamic Law, of Islamic History, and of Arabic

Degrees and Diplomas: *Bachelor's Degree*: Law (Civil), 3 yrs; Accountancy; Arts (BA); Business Administration; Economics; Economics and Social Studies; Engineering; Law (Islamic); Political Science; Science (BSc); Social Anthropology; Social Studies; Statistics, 4 yrs; Architecture; Pharmacy (BPharm), Veterinary Science (BVSc), 5 yrs; Medicine (MB, BS), 6 yrs; *Bachelor Honours Degree*: Agriculture, 4 yrs; 5 yrs; *Postgraduate Diploma*; *Master's Degree*; *Doctor of Philosophy*

Student Residential Facilities: Yes

Special Facilities: Natural History Museum

Libraries: Main Library, c. 300,000 vols; Engineering and Architecture, c. 8500 vols; Medicine and Pharmacy, c. 9000 vols; Agriculture and Veterinary Science, c. 28,000 vols; Law, c. 5000 vols

Publications: Gazette (3 per annum); Research Committee Report (annually)

Press or Publishing House: University of Khartoum Press

Academic Staff *2001-2002:* Total: **1,016**

Student Numbers *2001-2002:* Total: c. 23,000

UNIVERSITY OF WEST KORDOFAN

Jameat Gareb Kordofan
PO Box 20, En Nahoud, West Kordofan
Tel: +249(11) 785-614

Vice-Chancellor: Ibrahim Musa Tibin

Faculties
Economics and Community Development (Economics) *Dean*: Ibrahim Husein

Education *Dean*: Mohammed Haroun

Islamic Studies and Arabic (Arabic; Islamic Studies) *Dean*: Ibrahim M. Ibrahim

Medicine and Health Sciences (Health Sciences; Medicine)

Natural Resources and Environmental Studies (Environmental Studies; Natural Resources) *Dean*: Saleh Fadlaseed

Petroleum (Petroleum and Gas Engineering)

History: Founded 1997.

• UNIVERSITY OF ZALENGEI

Jameat Zalengei
Zalengei, West Darfur 6
Tel: +249(713) 22013
Fax: +249(723) 22013
EMail: uzal@student.net

Vice-Chancellor: Ahmed Mohamed Abaker (1995-)
Tel: +249(713) 22109 EMail: mohdabaker@hotmail.com

Principal: Suliman Adam Ahmed Tel: +249(213) 22062

International Relations: Ahmed Idris Ahmed
Tel: +249(213) 22109

Faculties
Agriculture *Dean*: Kumal Ibrahim Adam
Education *Dean*: Abdoul Mutalib Moh. Khatir

Institutes
Holy Koran and Islamic Studies (Islamic Studies; Koran)
Dean: Abdoul Mutalib Moh. Khatir

Centres
Computer and Information Science (Computer Science) *Director*: Mohammed El Amin Ibrahim
Peace and Development (Development Studies; Peace and Disarmament) *Director*: Musa Adam Ismali

History: Founded 1994.

Governing Bodies: University Council; University Senate; Board of Deans

Admission Requirements: Sudan Secondary School Certificate or equivalent

Fees: (Sudanese Dinars) 200,000-500,000 per annum

Main Language(s) of Instruction: Arabic

Accrediting Agencies: Council for Higher Education and Scientific Research, Ministry of Higher Education and Scientific Research

Degrees and Diplomas: *Bachelor Honours Degree*: Arabic Language and Islamic Studies; Geography and History; Biology and Chemistry; Mathematics and Physics; English Language and Geography (BSc(Hons)), 4 yrs; Crop Sciences; Horticulture; Rural Economics; Animal Husbandry; Crop Protection; Agricultural Engineering (BSc (Hons)), 5 yrs

Student Services: Academic Counselling, Social Counselling, Sports Facilities, Health Services

Libraries: Central Library

Academic Staff 2001-2002	MEN	WOMEN	TOTAL
FULL-TIME	80	10	90
PART-TIME	14	1	15
TOTAL	**94**	**11**	**105**
STAFF WITH DOCTORATE			
FULL-TIME	10	1	11
PART-TIME	2	–	2
TOTAL	**12**	**1**	**13**

Student Numbers 2001-2002	MEN	WOMEN	TOTAL
All (Foreign Included)	576	673	**1,249**

Distance Students, 57

• UPPER NILE UNIVERSITY

Jameat Al-Neel
PO Box 1660, Khartoum, Ali Elneel
Tel: +249(11) 483-856   +249(11) 222-174
Fax: +249(11) 484-937

Vice-Chancellor: Joshua Otor Akol (1998-)
EMail: jakol48@hotmail.com

Faculties
Agriculture
Animal Production (Animal Husbandry)
Education
Engineering and Technical Studies (Engineering; Technology)
Forestry
Medicine and Health Studies (Health Sciences; Medicine)
Natural Resources and Environmental Studies (Environmental Studies; Natural Resources)

History: Founded 1991.

PRIVATE INSTITUTIONS

• AHFAD UNIVERSITY FOR WOMEN

Jameat Al-Ahfad Llbanat
PO Box 167, Omdurman
Tel: +249(15) 579-112
Fax: +249(15) 553-363
Telex: (0984) 22271 medt
EMail: ahfad@sudanmail.net
Website: http://www.ahfad.org

Vice-Chancellor: Gasim Yousif Badri (1966-)
Fax: +249(15) 579-111 EMail: gasimbadri@hotmail.com

Vice-President: Awatif Mustafa Abdel Halim
Tel: +249(15) 560-050 Fax: +249(15) 564-401
EMail: awatifhalim@usa.net

Head Librarian: Asia M. Makawi

Schools
Family Sciences (Family Studies; Food Science; Social and Community Services)
Management (Business Administration; Management)
Medicine
Pharmacy
Psychology and Pre-School Education (Child Care and Development; Preschool Education; Psychology)

History: Founded 1966. Acquired university status 1995.

Main Language(s) of Instruction: English

Degrees and Diplomas: *Bachelor's Degree*; *Master's Degree*: Gender Studies; Nutrition

*• INTERNATIONAL UNIVERSITY OF AFRICA

Jamitu Ifriqya Al-Alamiyyah (IUA)

PO Box 2469, Khartoum
Tel: +249(11) 223-839 +249(11) 223-880
Fax: +249(11) 223-854
EMail: admin@iua-unv.net
Website: http://www.iua-unv.net

Vice-Chancellor: Omar Elsammani Elsheikh (2000-2004)
Tel: +249(11) 223-840 Fax: +249(11) 223-841
EMail: afriua@sudanmail.net

Registrar: Mahjub Mohammed Al Hussein
Tel: +249(11) 223-846

International Relations: Abdel Hameed Al Bushra, Executive Director

Faculties

Arabic Language *(For non-Arabic Speakers)* *(Arabic) Dean*: V. Al Khalifa
Computer Science *Dean*: Ibrahim Gasm Elseed
Economics, Administration and Political Sciences (Business and Commerce; Economics; Political Science; Public Administration) *Dean*: S. Ahmed Eisa
Education and Humanities (Arabic; Arts and Humanities; Education; English; French; Social Sciences) *Dean*: A. Tahir
Islamic African Studies (Curriculum; Distance Education; Education; Teacher Training) *Dean*: M. Obeid
Islamic Law (Shari'a) and Islamic Studies (Islamic Law; Islamic Studies; Law; Mass Communication) *Dean*: Ismaïl Hanafi
Medicine and Health Sciences (Health Sciences; Medicine) *Dean*: A. Mustafa
Pure and Applied Sciences (Biology; Chemistry; Geology; Mathematics; Natural Sciences; Physics) *Dean*: Ahmed Mahmoud
Research and African Studies (African Studies; Economics; Environmental Studies; Geography; Modern Languages; Political Science; Religion; Statistics) *Dean*: Hasan Mekki

History: Founded 1977 as the Islamic African Centre. University Colleges affiliated to Omdurman Islamic University founded 1985. Acquired present status and title 1991. An independent international organization governed by its Constitution.

Governing Bodies: Board of Trustees

Academic Year: August to May

Admission Requirements: Secondary school certificate or equivalent

Fees: (US Dollars): 1500 per annum

Main Language(s) of Instruction: Arabic

Degrees and Diplomas: *Bachelor's Degree*: Computer Science; Information System; Economics; Administration; Education; Law; Islamic Studies; Mass Communication; Medicine; Surgery; Physics; Mathematics; Geology; Chemistry; Microbiology, 4 yrs; *Master's Degree*: African Studies; Arabic Language; Education; Islamic Studies, a further 2 yrs; *Doctor of Philosophy*: (PhD), a further 3 yrs

Student Residential Facilities: Yes

Special Facilities: Audiovisual and T.V. Unit

Libraries: Main Library, 50,000 vols

Publications: Risalat Ifriqya, Africa Message, News magazine (monthly); Dirasat Ifriqiya, African Studies, Research Journal (biannually)

Press or Publishing House: Printing Press

Academic Staff *2002*: Full-Time: c. 210 Part-Time: c. 130 Total: c. 340

Staff with Doctorate: Total: c. 160

Student Numbers 2002	MEN	WOMEN	TOTAL
All (Foreign Included)	3,397	1,877	**5,274**
FOREIGN ONLY	–	–	2,157

Evening Students, 1,314

KHARTOUM INTERNATIONAL INSTITUTE FOR ARABIC LANGUAGE

Mahad El-Khartoum Eldawally Lil Lugha Elarabia

PO Box 26, El Diyum al Shargiyyah, Khartoum
Tel: +249(11) 223-721
Fax: +249(11) 223-722
Telex: 24065 lugha sd
EMail: lugha@sudanmail.net
Website: http://http//www.alecsolugha.org

Director: Uztaz Abed Elraheem Ali
EMail: aalbrahim@alecsolugha.org

Programmes

Modern Languages and Arabic (Arabic; Modern Languages)

History: Founded 1974.

Governing Bodies: Academic Board

Academic Year: August-May

Admission Requirements: Secondary school certificate

Main Language(s) of Instruction: Arabic

Accrediting Agencies: Ministry of Higher Education; ALECSO

Degrees and Diplomas: *Bachelor's Degree*: Arabic (BA), 4 yrs; *Master's Degree*: Arabic, a further 2 yrs

Student Services: Academic Counselling, Social Counselling, Sports Facilities, Language Programmes, Canteen

Student Residential Facilities: Yes

Special Facilities: Language Laboratory. Audiovisual Unit

Libraries: Central Library

Publications: Majallat al Dirasat al Lughawiyyah (biannually)

Academic Staff 2001-2002	MEN	WOMEN	TOTAL
FULL-TIME	4	2	6
PART-TIME	17	–	17
TOTAL	**21**	**2**	**23**
STAFF WITH DOCTORATE			
FULL-TIME	4	1	5
PART-TIME	17	–	17
TOTAL	**21**	**1**	**22**

Student Numbers 2001-2002	MEN	WOMEN	TOTAL
All (Foreign Included)	200	85	**285**
FOREIGN ONLY	45	20	65

• OMDURMAN AHLIA UNIVERSITY

Jameat Omdurman Ahlia

PO Box 786, Omdurman, Khartoum
Tel: +249(15) 566-116 +249(15) 566-117
Fax: +249(15) 553-447

Vice-Chancellor: Mohamed Ahmed Khalifa
Tel: +249(15) 571-127
EMail: khalifamohamedahmed@yahoo.com

Deputy Vice-Chancellor: Abd El Rahman El Nasri
Tel: +249(15) 556-503

International Relations: Mohamed Saad El Amin
Tel: +249(15) 556-493

Faculties

Applied and Computer Sciences (Computer Science; Engineering; Mathematics; Physics) *Dean*: Ahmed Khogali

Applied Studies (Design; Industrial Design; Interior Design) *Dean*: Mohamed Mirgani

Arts (Arabic; Communication Studies; English; French; Library Science; Modern Languages) *Dean*: Hussein Bayomi

Economics and Administrative Sciences (Accountancy; Administration; Economics; Management) *Dean*: Hassan Sanossie

Environmental Sciences (Environmental Engineering; Environmental Management; Environmental Studies) *Dean*: Awad El Bieli

Health Sciences (Health Sciences; Laboratory Techniques) *Dean*: Ibrahim Kaddam

Technology and Development Studies (Development Studies; Distance Education; Management; Technology) *Dean*: Idris El Niel

Departments

Accountancy *Head*: Idris Bashir

Arabic Language (Arabic) *Head*: Muddasri El-Hagaz

Banking and Insurance (Banking; Insurance) *Head*: Ahmed Osman

Communication and Media Sciences (Mass Communication; Media Studies) *Head*: Salah ElDin El-Fadil

Computer Engineering *Head*: Moawia Ahmed

Computer Science *Head*: Moawia Ahmed

Economics *Head*: Hassan Sanossie

English Language (English) *Head*: Philip Yona Jambi

French Language (French) *Head*: Mohamed Tahir

Library Science (Documentation Techniques; Library Science) *Head*: Abd El-Rhaman El-Nasri

Management *Head*: Saiff Fadi-Alla

Physics and Mathematics (Mathematics; Physics) *Head*: Sarra Nugdalla

Secretariat and Office Management (Management; Secretarial Studies) *Head*: Bothayna Elghorasany

Centres

Sudanese Studies (African Studies; Regional Studies) *Head*: Ibrahim Abd-El-galil

History: Founded 1986, acquired present status 1995.

478

Governing Bodies: Board of Founders; Board of Trustees; Academic Council; University Council; Financial and Administrative Committee

Admission Requirements: Secondary school certificate or foreign equivalent

Fees: (Sudanese Dinars): 80,000-450,000

Main Language(s) of Instruction: Arabic, English

International Co-operation: Association of African Universities and Association of Arabic Universities cooperation programmes

Degrees and Diplomas: *Technician's Diploma*: 3 yrs; *Bachelor's Degree*: Science (BSc), 4 yrs; *Postgraduate Diploma*: 1yr

Student Services: Academic Counselling, Social Counselling, Nursery Care, Cultural Centre, Sports Facilities, Language Programmes, Health Services, Canteen

Student Residential Facilities: Yes (For Volunteers and Expatriates only)

Special Facilities: Theatre

Libraries: University Library

Publications: Sudanese Studies (4 per annum); Mar-Hawir, Social, cultural, economic and political issues (biannually)

Press or Publishing House: Ahlia Press

Academic Staff 2002	MEN	WOMEN	TOTAL
FULL-TIME	74	24	**98**
STAFF WITH DOCTORATE			
FULL-TIME	22	1	**23**

Student Numbers 2002: Total: **2,201**

OTHER INSTITUTIONS

PRIVATE INSTITUTIONS

AFRICA COLLEGE

Koliat Africa El-Jamia

PO Box 3493, Alreiad Street No.12, Khartoum
Tel: +249(11) 224-090

Founded: 1991

Divisions

Accounting and Management (Accountancy; Management)

Home Economics and Social Development of Women (Development Studies; Home Economics; Women's Studies)

COLLEGE OF AVIATION SCIENCES

Koliat Uloom Altyaran

PO Box 714, Azhari Street Bahri, Khartoum-Bahari
Tel: +249(11) 613-163
Telex: 24212 Satco ASD

Dean: Osman Ahmed Eisa (1991-)

Secretary-General: Mohammed Alsafy Hassan Alzain

Founded: 1991

Programmes
Aviation Studies (Air Transport)
Commerce (Business and Commerce)

COLLEGE OF TECHNICAL SCIENCES
Koliat Uloom Altgina
PO Box 30, Omdurman
Tel: +249(11) 555-769

Vice-Chancellor: Muttaz Mohammed Ahmed El-Birair

Registrar: Awad Alkarim Yousif

Founded: 1995

Programmes
Computer Engineering
Computer Science
Dentistry
Engineering and Architecture (Architecture; Engineering)
Medical Laboratory Science (Laboratory Techniques)
Medicine
Pharmacy
Science (Natural Sciences)

COMPUTER MAN COLLEGE FOR COMPUTER STUDIES
Koliat Elhasibat Elalia
PO Box 10553, Khartoum
Tel: +249(11) 428-543
Fax: +249(11) 428-551
Website: http://www.cmc-web.net

Dean: Mustafa Abu-Baker (1991-)

Founded: 1991

Schools
Architecture, Interior Design and Fine Arts (Architecture; Fine Arts; Interior Design)
Communication Engineering
Computer Engineering
Computer Science

Departments
Information Technology

EAST NILE COLLEGE
Koliat Shark El-Neel
PO Box 1087, Omdurman
Tel: +249(11) 550-631

Dean: Al Tahir Mohamed Ali (1991-)

Secretary-General: Altigani Ahmed Abu Algasim

Founded: 1991

Programmes
Education
Engineering and Energy (Energy Engineering; Engineering)
Laboratory Technology (Laboratory Techniques)

ELNASR TECHNICAL COLLEGE
Koliat Elnasr Elitagania
PO Box 744, Omdurman
Tel: +249(11) 54469

Founded: 1990

Programmes
Architecture
Banking
Building (Building Technologies)
Commerce (Business and Commerce)

HIGHER INSTITUTE FOR BANKING AND FINANCIAL STUDIES
El-Maahad El-Ali Lederasat El-Masrafia Walmalia
PO Box 1880, Jama'A Street, Khartoum, Khartoum
Tel: +249(11) 770-564
Fax: +249(11) 780-913

Director: Awatif Yousif (1998-) Tel: +249(11) 780-913

Secretary of Academic affairs: Mohamed. O.M Abdellah Tel: +249(11) 788-942

Founded: 1963, 1993

Departments
Accounting (Accountancy)
Computer (Computer Science) *Head*: Abubaker Abdel Rahman
Law and Islamic Studies (Islamic Studies; Law) *Head*: Mohamed.S. Hussen
Management Studies (Management)
Research and Economics (Banking; Economics) *Head*: Isam Ellaythey

History: Founded 1963, upgraded into higher Institute 1993.

Governing Bodies: Board of Trustees and Board of Directors

Academic Year: August to May

Admission Requirements: Sudan School Certificate or equivalent

Main Language(s) of Instruction: Arabic, English

Degrees and Diplomas: *Bachelor's Degree*: Banking, 4 yrs; *Postgraduate Diploma*: Banking, 3 yrs. Training Diplomas

Student Services: Academic Counselling, Foreign Student Adviser, Sports Facilities, Language Programmes, Canteen

Special Facilities: Computer Lab and Internet Lab

Publications: Banking and Financial Studies Journal, Academic Research Journal (2 per annum); Training Courses Program Publication, Time and contents of the year training program (1 per annum)

Academic Staff *2001-2002*: Full-Time: c. 15 Part-Time: c. 45 Total: c. 60

Staff with Doctorate: Total: c. 25

Student Numbers *2001-2002:* Total: c. 2,230

Evening Students, c. 670

Note: Evening students are Bank staff studying for BSc or Diploma Degree

ISLAMIC INSTITUTE OF TRANSLATION
Mahad Elitergma Elislami
Central PO Box 44755, Khartoum

Director: Altigani Ismeel Elgizoli (1998-)

Founded: 1994

Programmes
Translation and Interpreting (Translation and Interpretation)

KHARTOUM COLLEGE FOR APPLIED STUDIES
Koliat Khartoum Al-Tatpigia
PO Box 3887, Khartoum
Tel: +249(11) 223-135

Founded: 1990

Programmes
Architectural Drawing and Decoration (Architectural and Environmental Design; Design)
Management

KHARTOUM TECHNICAL COLLEGE
Koliat El-Khartoum Eltigania
PO Box 15027, Khartoum-Elamarrat

Dean: Mohammed Osman Abusag

Founded: 1992

Programmes
Commerce (Business and Commerce)
Engineering and Architecture (Architecture; Engineering)

PORT SUDAN ALHIA COLLEGE
Koliat Port Sudan Ahlia
Port Sudan
Tel: +249(11) 23899

Dean: Mustafa Baasher

Founded: 1995

Programmes
Computer Science
Medical Laboratory Sciences (Laboratory Techniques; Treatment Techniques)

SUDAN UNIVERSITY COLLEGE FOR GIRLS (SUC)
Koliat Sudan Alijamia
PO Box 1176, Building No. 8 Block 17, Ryadh Town
Khartoum
Tel: +249(11) 224-265
Fax: +249(11) 77844
Telex: 22657 vtco SD

Director: Fadwa Abd El-Rahman Ali Taha (1990-)

Founded: 1990

Programmes
Business Administration
Computer Science
Economics and Social Sciences (Economics; Social Sciences)
Languages and Translation (Modern Languages; Translation and Interpretation)
Mass Communication
Nutrition and Food Sciences (Food Science; Nutrition)

• WAD MEDANI AHLIA COLLEGE
Koliat Wad Medani Ahlia
PO Box 402, Wad Medani
Tel: +249(511) 47294
Fax: +249(511) 47296
EMail: wahlia@sudanmail.net

Rector: Isam Abdelrahman Elboushi (1993-)
EMail: i_elboushi@yahoo.com

Programmes
Home Economics

Schools
Administration (Accountancy; Administration; Business Administration)
Applied Psychology (Psychology)

Computer Science and Information Technology (Computer Science; Information Technology)
Foreign Languages (English; Modern Languages)

History: Founded 1992.

Degrees and Diplomas: *Diploma*: Accountancy; Business Administration; Information Technology; Computer Science; *Bachelor's Degree*: Accountancy; Business Administration; English; Applied Psychology; Computer Science (BA/BSc), 4 yrs

Libraries: Central Library, c. 3000 vols, 15 periodical subscriptions

Academic Staff *2002-2003*	TOTAL
FULL-TIME	19
PART-TIME	31
TOTAL	**50**

Staff with doctorate: Total: **2**

Student Numbers *2002-2003:* Total: **1,232**

Swaziland

INSTITUTION TYPES AND CREDENTIALS

Types of higher education institutions:
University
College
Institute

School leaving and higher education credentials:
General Certificate of Education 'O' Level
Certificate
Diploma
Bachelor's Degree
Master's Degree

STRUCTURE OF EDUCATION SYSTEM

Pre-higher education:

Structure of school system:

Primary
Type of school providing this education: Primary School
Length of programme in years: 7
Age level from: 6 to: 13
Certificate/diploma awarded: Swaziland Primary School Certificate

Junior Secondary
Type of school providing this education: Junior Secondary School
Length of programme in years: 3
Age level from: 13 to: 16
Certificate/diploma awarded: Junior Certificate

Second Cycle Secondary
Type of school providing this education: Senior Secondary School
Length of programme in years: 2
Age level from: 16 to: 18
Certificate/diploma awarded: General Certificate of Education "O" level

School education:

Primary education lasts for seven years, leading to the Swaziland Primary Certificate. Secondary education is divided into a three-year cycle leading to the Junior Certificate and a two-year cycle preparing pupils to the General Certificate of Education 'O' Level which gives access to higher education.

Higher education:

Higher education is provided by the University of Swaziland established as a National Institution in 1982. The University is governed by the Council which consists of members appointed by the Chancellor from among academic members. The Senate is responsible for academic matters and consists of deans from each faculty. The government contributes about 60% of the recurrent budget of the university and study loans to about 80% of the Swazi students enrolled. Other institutions of higher education include teacher training Colleges, which are affiliated to the University, and specialized institutes.

Main laws/decrees governing higher education:

Decree: University of Swaziland Act (Act N° 2)   Year: 1983
Concerns: Establishment of the University

Academic year:

Classes from: August *to:* May
Long vacation from: 1 June *to:* 31 July

Languages of instruction:

English

Stages of studies:

Non-university level post-secondary studies (technical/vocational type):

The Swaziland College of Technology (SCOT) offers courses for those holding the Cambridge Overseas School Certificate in such fields as Electrical Engineering, Mechanical Engineering, Construction Studies, Hotel and Catering, and Teacher Training in technical fields. There is also a Management Centre and an Institute of Management and Public Administration, as well as a Nursing College and an Institute of Health Sciences.

University level studies:

University level first stage: Bachelor's Degree:
Courses leading to the Bachelor of Arts (BA), the Bachelor of Science (BSc) and other Bachelor's Degrees (Education, Commerce, Nursing, Agriculture etc..) last for four years. In law, the LLB lasts for five years.

University level second stage: Master's Degree:
Courses lead to the award of a Master of Arts (MA), a Master of Science (MSc), or a Master of Education (MEd). after a minimum of two years' study beyond the Bachelor's Degree. In Education, the Master's Degree is awarded after a minimum of two years' study beyond the Bachelor of Education Degree and at least two years' professional experience. A thesis is usually required for Master Degrees.

Teacher education:

Training of pre-primary and primary/basic school teachers
Primary school teachers are trained in three years at teacher training colleges. They are awarded the Primary Teachers Diploma. The University also offers a four-year Bachelor of Education Degree in primary education.

Training of secondary school teachers
A three-year course for holders of the GCE "O" levels leads to the Secondary Teachers Diploma. The University of Swaziland trains teachers in four years. They can obtain a Bachelor's Degree in Education and in various subjects. The University also offers a Postgraduate Diploma in Education for in-service teachers and a Master's Degree in Education.

Non-traditional studies:

Other forms of non-formal higher education
The extra-mural services of the University offer evening classes and short in-service training in Adult Education Skills. It also offers courses leading to a Certificate or Diploma in Adult Education and a Certificate in Accounting and Business Studies.

NATIONAL BODIES

Responsible authorities:

Ministry of Education
    Minister: Ntonzima Dlamini
    Principal Secretary: Jabulani G. Kunene
    International Relations: Dorothy Littler
    PO Box 39
    Mbabane
    Tel: +268 404-2491/2
    Fax: +268 404-3880
    WWW: http://www.gov.sz

ADMISSIONS TO HIGHER EDUCATION

Admission to university-level studies

Name of secondary school credential required: General Certificate of Education 'O' Level
Minimum score/requirement: At least 6 passes (including English) obtained at no more than two sittings
For entry to: The University of Swaziland

Foreign students admission

Admission requirements: Foreign students seeking admission to the University of Swaziland as undergraduates should hold a minimum of six passes at GCE Ordinary "O" level, including English (grade C or above) and at least five other relevant subjects.

Entry regulations: Students from certain countries need a visa.

Language requirements: A good knowledge of English is essential for all university courses.

Application procedures:

Application closing dates:

> *For university level studies:* 1 April
> *For advanced/doctoral studies:* 1 April

Recognition of studies and qualifications:

Studies pursued in foreign countries (bodies dealing with recognition of foreign credentials):
Ministry of Education
> PO Box 39
> Mbabane
> Tel: +268 404-2491/2
> Fax: +268 404-3880
> WWW: http://www.gov.sz

Multilateral agreements concerning recognition of foreign studies

Name(s) of agreement(s): Convention on the Recognition of Studies, Certificates, Diplomas, Degrees and Other Academic Qualifications in Higher Education in the African States
Year of signature: 1981

References to further information on foreign student admissions and recognition of studies

Title: University of Swaziland Prospectus
Publisher: University of Swaziland

STUDENT LIFE

Main student services at national level

Dean of Student Affairs, University of Swaziland
> Private Bag 4
> Kwaluseni M201
> Tel: +268 518-4011
> Fax: +268 518-5276
> EMail: kwaluseni@uniswa.sz
> WWW: http://www.uniswa.sz

> Category of services provided: Social and welfare services

Student expenses and financial aid

Student costs:

> Home students tuition fees: Minimum: 4,300 (Emalangeni)
> Maximum: 8,300 (Emalangeni)

Foreign students tuition fees: Minimum: 13,400 (Emalangeni)
Maximum: 20,400 (Emalangeni)

INTERNATIONAL COOPERATION AND EXCHANGES

Principal national bodies responsible for dealing with international cooperation and exchanges in higher education:

University of Swaziland
  Vice-Chancellor: Cisco M. Magagula
  Registrar: Samuel Vilakati
  International Relations: Dinisile Matse
  Private Bag 4
  Kwaluseni M201
  Tel: +268 518-4011
  Fax: +268 518-5276
  Telex: 2807 wd
  EMail: kwaluseni@uniswa.sz
  WWW: http://www.uniswa.sz

GRADING SYSTEM

Usual grading system in secondary school

Full Description: Individual subjects are marked as follows: 75-100% (1), 65-74% (2), 60-64% (3), 55-59% (4), 50-54% (5), 45-49% (6), 40-44% (7), 35-39% (8), 34-0% (9).
Highest on scale: 1
Lowest on scale: 9

Main grading system used by higher education institutions

Full Description: A (80-100%) excellent; B (70-79%) very good; C (60-69%) good; D (50-59%) pass; E (40-49%) fail, but student can take a supplementary examination; F (below 39%) complete fail.
Highest on scale: A
Pass/fail level: D
Lowest on scale: F

Other main grading systems

Bachelor degrees are classified: 1st class (B average) 2nd class first division (C average) 2nd class lower division (D average) pass (E, F average) fail

NOTES ON HIGHER EDUCATION SYSTEM

Data for academic year: 2002-2003

Source: International Association of Universities (IAU), updated from IBE website, 2003 (www.ibe.unesco.org/International/Databanks/Wde/profilee.htm)

INSTITUTIONS OF HIGHER EDUCATION

UNIVERSITIES

• UNIVERSITY OF SWAZILAND (UNISWA)

Private Bag 4, Kwaluseni M201
Tel: +268 518-4011
Fax: +268 518-5276
Telex: 2807 WD
EMail: vc@admin.uniswa.sz
Website: http://www.uniswa.sz

Vice-Chancellor (Acting): Cisco M. Magagula
Tel: +268 518-5656

Registrar: Samuel S. Vilakati Tel: +268 518-4730
EMail: vilakati@isdu.uniswa.sz

International Relations: Qinisile Z. Matse

Head Librarian: M.R. Mavuso

Faculties

Agriculture (Agricultural Economics; Agricultural Education; Agricultural Management; Agriculture; Animal Husbandry; Crop Production; Home Economics; Management) *Dean*: G.N. Shongwe

Commerce (Accountancy; Business Administration; Business and Commerce) *Dean*: M.A. Khan

Education (Adult Education; Curriculum; Education; Educational Administration; Pedagogy; Primary Education) *Dean*: J.C.B. Bigala

Health Sciences (Community Health; Health Sciences; Midwifery; Nursing; Occupational Health; Psychiatry and Mental Health) *Dean*: P.S. Dlamini

Humanities (African Languages; Arts and Humanities; Communication Studies; English; French; History; Journalism; Mass Communication; Religion; Religious Studies; Theology) *Dean*: H.L. Ndlovu

Postgraduate Studies (Agricultural Education; Agriculture; Chemistry; Crop Production; Curriculum; Education; Educational Administration; Environmental Studies; History) *Dean*: E.C.L. Kunene

Science (Biology; Chemistry; Electronic Engineering; Engineering; Environmental Studies; Geography; Mathematics and Computer Science; Physics) *Dean*: V.S.B. Mtetwa

Social Sciences (Demography and Population; Economics; Law; Political Science; Sociology; Statistics) *Dean*: A.A. Teraifi

Institutes

Distance Education (Accountancy; Adult Education; Arts and Humanities; Business and Commerce; French; Law) *Director*: C.V.S. Sukati

Research in Traditional Medicine, Medicinal and Indigenous Food Plants (*Swaziland*)

Further Information: Also Luyengo and Mbabane Campuses

History: Founded 1982, the University was formerly University College of Swaziland, a Constituent College of the University of Botswana, Lesotho and Swaziland (founded 1976).

Governing Bodies: Council

Academic Year: August - April (August-December; January-April)

Admission Requirements: General Certificate of Education (GCE) 'O' level with at least 6 passes (including English), obtained at no more than two sittings.

Fees: (Emalangeni): Tuition, undergraduate, 4300-4600 per annum; postgraduate, 6200-8300; foreign students, undergraduate, 13,400-13,600; postgraduate, full time, 6200-8300; foreign students, 19,000-20,400; part time undergraduate, 900-3,300; part time postgraduate, 3,300-4,300; foreign students, 9,400-10,100

Main Language(s) of Instruction: English

Degrees and Diplomas: *Bachelor's Degree*: 4 yrs; *Master's Degree*: a further 2 yrs (or 3 yrs part-time)

Student Services: Academic Counselling, Sports Facilities, Canteen

Student Residential Facilities: For 1600 students

Libraries: c. 178,000 vols; c. 1500 periodicals

Publications: UNISWA Briefings (monthly); UNISWA News (quarterly); UNISWA Journal of Agriculture, Science and Technology; Uniswa Research Journal (biannually); Calendar; Swaziland National Bibliography; Prospectus; Vice-Chancellor's Report; Uniswa Research Journal of Agriculture (annually); Serialsin Swaziland University Libraries; Science and Technology

Academic Staff *2001-2002*	MEN	WOMEN	TOTAL
FULL-TIME	184	97	**281**

Student Numbers *2002-2003*	MEN	WOMEN	TOTAL
All (Foreign Included)	1,601	1,503	**3,104**

Part-time Students, 1,353

NAZARENE NURSING COLLEGE

PO Box 14, Manzini
Tel: +268 505-4636
Fax: +268 505-5077

Principal: W.M. Nhlengethwa

Programmes
Nursing

NAZARENE TEACHER TRAINING COLLEGE

PO Box 14, Manzini
Tel: +268 505-4636
Fax: +268 505-5077

Principal: Z.M. Mavuso

Departments

Agriculture

Arts and Crafts (Crafts and Trades)

Education

English and Siswati (English; Native Language)

Home Economics

Music and Physical Education (Music; Physical Education)

Science and Mathematics (Mathematics; Natural Sciences)

Social Studies

History: Founded 1933.

NGWANE TEACHER TRAINING COLLEGE
PO Box 474, Nhlangano
Tel: +268 207-8466
Fax: +268 207-8112

Principal: Peterson Dlamini

Departments

Agriculture

Arts and Crafts (Crafts and Trades)

Education

English and Siswati (English; Native Language)

Home Economics

Music and Physical Education (Music; Physical Education)

Science and Mathematics (Mathematics; Natural Sciences)

Social Studies

History: Founded 1982.

WILLIAM PITCHER TRAINING COLLEGE
PO Box 87, Manzini
Tel: +268 505-2081
Fax: +268 505-4690

Principal: P. Magagula

Departments

Education

English and Religious Knowledge (English; Religious Studies)

English and Siswati (English; Native Language) *Principal*: P.L. Magaula

History and Geography (Geography; History)

Science and Mathematics (Mathematics; Natural Sciences)

History: Founded 1962.

OTHER INSTITUTIONS

INSTITUTE OF DEVELOPMENT AND MANAGEMENT
PO Box 1534, Mbabane
Tel: +268 422-0734
Fax: +268 422-0733
EMail: idm@realnet.co.sz

Director (Acting): Nonhlanhla Dlamini

Founded: 1979

Departments

Development Management (Development Studies; Management)

LUTHERAN FARMER TRAINING CENTRE
Private Bag, Piggs Peak
Tel: +268 437-1168

Departments

Farming (Agriculture)

MANANGA CENTRE FOR REGIONAL INTEGRATION AND MANAGEMENT DEVELOPMENT
PO Box 20, Mhlume
Tel: +268 416-3155
Fax: +268 416-3158
EMail: info@mananga.sz
Website: http://www.mananga.sz

Founded: 1972, 1998

Departments

Agricultural Management, Training and Consultancy (Agricultural Management)

History: Founded 1972, acquired present status 1998.

MLALATINI DEVELOPMENT CENTRE
PO Box 547, Mbabane
Tel: +268 416-1171

Founded: 1970

Departments

Development Studies

SWAZILAND COLLEGE OF TECHNOLOGY (SCOT)

PO Box 69, Mbabane H100
Tel: +268 404-2681 to +268 404-2683
Fax: +268 404-4521
EMail: scot@africaonline.co.sz
Founded: 1946, 1975

Faculties

Building and Civil Engineering (Building Technologies; Civil Engineering) *Dean:* C. Dube

Business Administration (Accountancy; Business Administration; Cooking and Catering; Hotel and Restaurant; Secretarial Studies) *Dean:* V. Nhlabatsi

Education and Technical Teaching (Business Education; Education; Technology Education; Vocational Education) *Dean:* T.P Sukati

Engineering and Science (Automotive Engineering; Computer Science; Electrical and Electronic Engineering; Engineering; Mechanical Engineering) *Dean:* M Maseko

History: Founded 1946, acquired present status and title 1975.

Academic Year: August to June

Admission Requirements: Cambridge Overseas School Certificate (COSC) in approved subjects, such as English, Mathematics, Science, Accountancy

Main Language(s) of Instruction: English

Accrediting Agencies: AAT, City & Guilds, University of Swaziland

Degrees and Diplomas: *Diploma:* 3 yrs

Student Services: Academic Counselling, Social Counselling, Sports Facilities, Health Services, Canteen

Student Residential Facilities: Yes

Special Facilities: Micro Teaching Studio

Libraries: Central Library, c. 17,500 vols

Publications: College Prospectus (annually)
Academic Staff *2001-2002:* Total: c. 60
Student Numbers *2001-2002:* Total: c. 480
Evening Students, c. 200

SWAZILAND INSTITUTE OF MANAGEMENT AND PUBLIC ADMINISTRATION (SIMPA)

PO Box 495, Mbabane 4100
Tel: +268 422-0740
Fax: +268 422- 0742
EMail: simpa@realnet.co.sz
Founded: 1965

Departments

Financial Management (Accountancy; Advertising and Publicity; Finance; Management; Marketing; Public Relations) *Head:* K Mmemma

General Management (Communication Studies; Human Resources; Management) Masilela Siboniso

Information Technology *Head:* Stephen Magongo

Public Administration

History: Founded 1965.

Academic Year: January to December

Main Language(s) of Instruction: English

Accrediting Agencies: ACCA London

Student Services: Sports Facilities, Health Services, Canteen

Student Residential Facilities: Yes

Special Facilities: Computer and Language laboratories

Libraries: Central Library, c. 10,000 vols

Academic Staff *2001-2002:* Full-Time: c. 20 Part-Time: c. 5 Total: c. 25

Student Numbers *2001-2002:* Total: c. 60
Evening Students, c. 30

Tanzania

INSTITUTION TYPES AND CREDENTIALS

Types of higher education institutions:

University
University College
Institute
Open University

School leaving and higher education credentials:

Advanced Certificate of Secondary Education
Diploma
Advanced Diploma
Bachelor Degree
Doctor
Master Degree
Postgraduate Diploma
Doctor of Philosophy

STRUCTURE OF EDUCATION SYSTEM

Pre-higher education:

Duration of compulsory education:

Age of entry: 7
Age of exit: 14

Structure of school system:

Basic First Stage
Type of school providing this education: Primary School (Lower Stage)
Length of programme in years: 4
Age level from: 7 to: 11

Basic Second Stage
Type of school providing this education: Primary School (Upper Stage)
Length of programme in years: 3
Age level from: 11 to: 14
Certificate/diploma awarded: Primary School Leaving Certificate

Lower Secondary
Type of school providing this education: Lower Secondary School
Length of programme in years: 4
Age level from: 14 to: 18
Certificate/diploma awarded: Certificate of Secondary Education (CSE) or East Africa General
Certificate of Education (GCE) "O" levels

Upper Secondary
Type of school providing this education: Upper Secondary School
Length of programme in years: 2
Age level from: 18 to: 20
Certificate/diploma awarded: Advanced Certificate of Secondary Education (ACSE)

School education:

Primary education lasts for seven years, divided into two stages of four and three years respectively and leads to the Primary School Leaving Certificate which is primarily used for secondary school selection purposes. Secondary school is divided into six Forms. Lower secondary school includes Forms I-IV and culminates in a national examination. Those who pass obtain the Certificate of Secondary Education (CSE) or GCE "O" Levels. The curriculum is divided into four tracks: Agriculture, Commerce, Technical Skills, and Home Economics. The 1992 curriculum reform introduced three subjects into each stream: Social Studies, Computer Science and Unified Science. Unified Science is taught as an alternative to Biology, Chemistry and Physics, whereas Social Studies is offered as an alternative to Geography, History and Political Science. At the high school level, pupils study subject combinations of their choice, depending on their results in the examinations at the end of the first cycle of secondary education. Upper secondary school includes Forms V-VI and culminates in a national examination. Those who pass obtain the Advanced Certificate of Secondary Education (ACSE). Students must choose three principal subjects from the following: Languages, Arts and Social Sciences, Sciences and Mathematics, Commercial Subjects, and Military Science and Technology. The fourth subject is Political Education and is compulsory. Some secondary schools are technically oriented. The ACSE gives access to higher education. Students successfully completing the Certificate of Secondary Education may continue their studies at technical colleges which offer Certificate and Diploma level training.

Higher education:

Higher education is provided by universities, university colleges and several training colleges and institutes. In addition there are several training centres designed primarily for Form VI-leavers. All higher education institutions are under the supervision of the Ministry of Science, Technology and Higher Education. The universities are semi-autonomous and manage their own affairs under the Vice-Chancellor, who is appointed by the President of Tanzania. Their running costs are subsidized by the Government.

Main laws/decrees governing higher education:

Decree: Education Act N°25   Year: 1978
Concerns: Education system

Academic year:

Classes from: September *to:* July

Languages of instruction:

English

Stages of studies:

Non-university level post-secondary studies (technical/vocational type):

In the last decade, the number of technical, vocational, and professional schools has increased substantially. They are the responsibility of the relevant Government Ministry under which they fall. The schools which award Certificates, Diplomas, Advanced Diplomas and Postgraduate Diplomas are categorized according to the type of programme offered. Diploma programmes, which last for two years, require Form VI and work experience. Certificates require two to three years' study. The Technician's Certificate requires two years of study. The Full Technician's Certificate requires three years of study. Advanced Diploma programmes, which lasts for three years, require Form VI and work experience.

University level studies:

University level first stage: Undergraduate level:
The first phase leads to a Bachelor's Degree. It usually lasts for three years, except in Pharmacy, Nursing, Veterinary Science and Engineering, which take four years, and Medicine, which takes five years. At the Open University courses generally last for six years.

University level second stage: Graduate level:
A further one to three years' study leads to a Master's Degree. Postgraduate Diplomas require a Bachelor's Degree for admission and, generally, one year of study.

University level third stage: Postgraduate level:
A minimum of a further two years' original research and submission of a thesis lead to a PhD.

Teacher education:

Training of pre-primary and primary/basic school teachers
The Grade C Certificate entitles the holders to teach in the first two grades of primary education. The Grade B Certificate is obtained by promotion or by successfully completing a four-year course at a teacher training college after grade 7. The Grade A Certificate is obtained on successful completion of a two-year course for students who have passed the CGE "O" levels at division II level and entitles the holder to teach in all seven grades of primary education.

Training of secondary school teachers
A two-year Diploma of Education at a Teacher Training College after passing the ACSE is required to teach at lower secondary level. Teachers for upper secondary level should hold a Bachelor of Education or a Postgraduate Diploma in Education. Opportunities for in-service training have increased with the creation of village-based teacher training programmes.

Non-traditional studies:

Distance higher education
Distance education is offered by the Open University of Tanzania which opened in 1993 in

Dar-es-Salaam. It provides courses in Law, Science, Arts, and Education leading to Bachelors, Masters and PhD degrees. Distance teacher training programmes for untrained teachers have been developed.

Lifelong higher education

There are over 300 institutions offering specialist training at post-Form IV (or Form VI) level, leading to Certificates or Diplomas at semi-professional level in a wide variety of disciplines.

NATIONAL BODIES

Responsible authorities:

Ministry of Science, Technology and Higher Education
  Minister: Ng'wandu Pius
  Permanent Secretary: Ruth Mollel
  International Relations: Augustino Kajigili
   PO Box 2645, Jamhuri Street
  Dar es Salaam
  Tel: +255(22) 211-2546   +255(22) 211-6331
  Fax: +255(22) 211-2805
  WWW: http://www.tanzania.go.tz/science.htm

Committee of Vice-Chancellors and Principals in Tanzania
  Chairman: Matthew Luhanga
  University of Dar es Salaam
  PO Box 33091
  Dar es Salaam
  Tel: +255(22) 241-0700
  Fax: +255(22) 241-0078
  EMail: vc@admin.udsm.ac.tz
  WWW: http://www.udsm.ac.tz

Role of governing body: To foster cooperation between the universities and colleges by advising university councils and other organs, including government, on policy matters of common interest to the member institutions.

ADMISSIONS TO HIGHER EDUCATION

Admission to non university higher education studies

Name of secondary school credential required: Advanced Certificate of Secondary Education
For entry to: Diploma and Advanced Diplomas at postsecondary,vocational/technical/professional schools

Alternatives to credentials: Certificate of Secondary Education (11 years of primary and secondary school study) for Full Technician Certificate and Nurse Grade A Diploma.

Admission to university-level studies

Name of secondary school credential required: Advanced Certificate of Secondary Education
Minimum score/requirement: Plusplus 2 credit passes in certificate of Secondary Education Examination or passes in 5 approved subjects in Certificate of Secondary Education
For entry to: University studies.

Alternatives to credentials: Mature Age Entry Examination Scheme.

Foreign students admission

Admission requirements: Foreign students should have qualifications equivalent to the Advanced Certificate of Secondary Education (plus 2 credit passes in Certificate of Secondary Education) or the East African General Certificate of Education (GCE) with 2 Advanced ("A") levels and 5 Ordinary ("O") levels.

Language requirements: Students must be fluent in English.

Application procedures:

Apply to: Ministry of Science, Technology and Higher Education
 PO Box 2645, Jamhuri Street
 Dar es Salaam
 Tel: +255(22) 211-2546
 Fax: +255(22) 211-2805
 WWW: http://www.tanzania.go.tz/science.htm

Recognition of studies and qualifications:

Studies pursued in home country (System of recognition/accreditation): The Higher Education Accreditation Council accredits institutions of higher education.

Studies pursued in foreign countries (bodies dealing with recognition of foreign credentials): Higher Education Accreditation Council
 PO Box 2645
 Dar es Salaam
 Tel: +555(22) 213-7585
 Fax: +555(22) 212-9584
 EMail: heac@interafrica.com
 WWW: http://www.heac.go.tz

Multilateral agreements concerning recognition of foreign studies

Name(s) of agreement(s): Convention on the Recognition of Studies, Certificates, Diplomas, Degrees and Other Academic Qualifications in Higher Education in the African States
Year of signature: 1981

References to further information on foreign student admissions and recognition of studies

Title: Tanzania education website: www.tanedu.org/index.asp

STUDENT LIFE

Student expenses and financial aid

Student costs:

Home students tuition fees: Minimum: 900,000 (Tanzanian Shilling)
Maximum: 1,600,000 (Tanzanian Shilling)

Publications on student services and financial aid:

Title: Study Abroad 2004-2005, 32nd Edition
Author: UNESCO
Publisher: UNESCO Publishing
Year of publication: 2003

INTERNATIONAL COOPERATION AND EXCHANGES

Principal national bodies responsible for dealing with international cooperation and exchanges in higher education:

Ministry of Science, Technology and Higher Education
Principal Education Officer: Augustino Kajigili
PO Box 2645, Jamhuri Street
Dar es Salaam
Tel: +255(22) 211-2546   +255(51) 211-6331
Fax: +255(22) 211-2805
WWW: http://www.tanzania.go.tz/science.htm

GRADING SYSTEM

Usual grading system in secondary school

Full Description: A-E principal passes; S subsidiary pass; F fail
Highest on scale: A
Pass/fail level: S
Lowest on scale: F

Main grading system used by higher education institutions

Full Description: Degrees are classified: 1st class Honours; 2nd class Honours (upper); 2nd class Honours (lower); pass

NOTES ON HIGHER EDUCATION SYSTEM

Data for academic year: 2002-2003

Source: International Association of Universities (IAU) updated from IBE website, 2003 (www.ibe.unesco.org/International/Databanks/Wde/profilee.htm)

INSTITUTIONS OF HIGHER EDUCATION

UNIVERSITIES AND UNIVERSITY COLLEGES

HUBERT KAIRUKI MEMORIAL UNIVERSITY (HKMU)
PO Box 65300, 322 Regent Estate, Dar es Salaam
Tel: +255(22) 270-0021 +255(22) 270-0024
Fax: +255(22) 277-5591
EMail: info@hkmu.ac.tz
Website: http://www.angelfire.com

Vice-Chancellor: Esther Mwaikambo (1999-)
EMail: info@hkmu.ac.tz

Senior Administrative Officer: Raphael Zakayo

Faculties
Medicine (Anatomy; Behavioural Sciences; Biochemistry; Communication Studies; Community Health; Computer Science; Epidemiology; Ethics; Gynaecology and Obstetrics; Medicine; Microbiology; Molecular Biology; Orthopedics; Paediatrics; Parasitology; Pathology; Pharmacology; Physiology; Psychiatry and Mental Health; Radiology; Stomatology; Surgery) *Dean*: Paul Ndile
Nursing (Behavioural Sciences; Child Care and Development; Community Health; Gynaecology and Obstetrics; Microbiology; Nursing; Nutrition; Parasitology; Philosophy; Psychiatry and Mental Health; Psychology; Rehabilitation and Therapy) *Dean*: Paulina Mella

Schools
Nursing (Community Health; Leadership; Management; Midwifery; Nursing; Psychiatry and Mental Health; Psychology; Surgery) *Director*: Paulina Mella

History: Founded 1997, acquired present status 2000.

Governing Bodies: Board of Trustees: Council, Senate

Academic Year: September to August

Admission Requirements: 'A' Level with 2 principal passes, or 'O' Level with 3 credits and Diploma

Fees: (Tanzanian Shillings): 6,448,000 to 7,263,000 per annum; (US Dollars): foreign students,11,240 to 12, 090 per annum

Main Language(s) of Instruction: English

International Co-operation: With univerities in USA, Canada, Norway, Germany, United Kingdom

Accrediting Agencies: Higher Education Accreditation Council (HEAC)

Degrees and Diplomas: *Diploma*: Nursing, 6 yrs; *Bachelor Degree*: Nursing (BSc), 4 yrs; Medicine (MD), 6 yrs; *Master Degree*: Obstetrics, Gynaecology, Medicine, Surgery, Paediatrics; Research, Development Studies, Fundamentals of Nursing, Biostatistics, Educational Psychology, Teaching, Advanced Concepts, Pharmacology, Nutrition, Microbiology, Parasitology, Nursing, Leadership, Counseling, 3 yrs

Student Services: Academic Counselling, Sports Facilities, Health Services

Student Residential Facilities: Yes

Special Facilities: Dissecting Laboratory, Research Laboratory

Libraries: Electronic Library, Internet

Academic Staff *2001-2002*	MEN	WOMEN	TOTAL
FULL-TIME	19	11	30
PART-TIME	19	2	21
TOTAL	**38**	**13**	**51**
STAFF WITH DOCTORATE			
FULL-TIME	2	1	3
PART-TIME	–	–	5
TOTAL	**–**	**–**	**8**

Student Numbers *2001-2002*	MEN	WOMEN	TOTAL
All (Foreign Included)	35	48	**83**
FOREIGN ONLY	4	8	12

INTERNATIONAL MEDICAL AND TECHNOLOGICAL UNIVERSITY (IMTU)
PO Box 77594, Saruji Complex, New Bagamoyo Road, Dar es Salaam
Tel: +255(22) 264-7035
Fax: +255(22) 264-7038
EMail: imtu@afsat.com
Website: http://www.imtu.edu

Vice-Chancellor: H.D. Ballal

Departments
Dermatology *Head*: Murali Mohan Pasumarthy
General Surgery (Surgery) *Head*: H.D. Ballal
Gynaecology and Obstetrics *Head*: Richard Seth Massana Lema
Medicine (Anatomy; Forensic Medicine and Dentistry; Gynaecology and Obstetrics; Medicine; Ophthalmology; Paediatrics; Pathology; Pharmacology; Physiology; Surgery) *Head*: S.H. Verma
Ophthalmology *Head*: Soumendra Sahoo
Otorhinolaryngology

History: Founded 1995.

MZUMBE UNIVERSITY
Chuo Kikuu Mzumbe
PO Box 1, Mzumbe, Morogoro
Tel: +255(56) 4380
Fax: +255(56) 4382
EMail: idm@raha.com

Vice-Chancellor: Moses D. Warioba
Registrar: H. Mahigi

Faculties

Commerce (Accountancy; Banking; Business Administration; Business and Commerce; Finance; Management; Marketing) *Dean*: D.M.L. Kasilo

Law (Administrative Law; Commercial Law; Constitutional Law; Criminal Law; International Law; Law) *Dean*: Eleuter G. Mushi

Science and Technology (Information Technology; Production Engineering; Statistics) *Dean*: D.S.R.M. Muna

Social Sciences (Communication Studies; Demography and Population; Economics; Modern Languages; Social Sciences) *Dean*: Joseph T. Nagu

Institutes

Development Studies (Development Studies; Environmental Studies; Gender Studies; Rural Planning) *Director*: L. Shio

Public Administration (Government; Human Resources; Public Administration) *Director*: Montanus C. Milanzi

History: Founded 1972 as Institute of Development Management (IDM). Acquired present status 2001.

Degrees and Diplomas: *Diploma*; *Advanced Diploma*; *Bachelor Degree*; *Master Degree*; *Postgraduate Diploma*

Libraries: 37,000 vols; 300 periodical subscriptions

*• THE OPEN UNIVERSITY OF TANZANIA

Chuo Kikuu Huria Cha Tanzania (OUT)
PO Box 23409, Dar es Salaam
Tel: +255(22) 266-8445
Fax: +255(22) 266-8759
EMail: dvcout@raha.com

Vice-Chancellor: Geoffrey R.V. Mmari (1998-2004)
Tel: +255(22) 266-8455 EMail: vcout@raha.com

Registrar: Uswege Minga Tel: +255(22) 266-8992
EMail: registrarout@raha.com

International Relations: Gaetan D. Msungu, Assistant to Vice-Chancellor Tel: +255(22) 266-8992
EMail: msunguout@raha.com

Faculties

Arts and Social Sciences (African Languages; Arts and Humanities; Business Administration; Business and Commerce; Economics; English; Geography; History; Linguistics; Literature; Philosophy; Religious Studies; Social Sciences) *Dean*: Arnold Temu

Education (Adult Education; Child Care and Development; Curriculum; Education; Educational Psychology; Philosophy of Education; Preschool Education; Special Education; Teacher Trainers Education) *Dean*: E.B.N.K. Babyegeya

Law *Dean*: M.C. Mukoyogo

Science, Technology and Environmental Studies (Biology; Botany; Chemistry; Environmental Studies; Home Economics; Mathematics; Physics; Zoology) *Dean*: C.A. Kiwanga

Institutes

Continuing Education *Director*: D.Y. Kinshaga
Educational Technology *Director*: S.T. Mahenge

Further Information: Also Regional Centres in: Arusha, Bukoba, Dar-Es-Salaam, Dudoma, Dringa, Kibaha, Kigoma, Lindi, Mbeya, Moroguro, Moshi, Mtwara, Musoma, Mwanza, Ruwma, Stimyanga, Singuda, Sumbawanga, Tabora, Tanga, Zanzibar

History: Founded 1992.

Governing Bodies: University Council, comprising 22 members

Academic Year: January to November (January-March; March-June; June-August; August-November)

Admission Requirements: Advanced Certificate of Secondary Education Examination, or equivalent, plus 3 credits of passes in Certificate of Secondary Education Examination

Fees: (Tanzanian Shillings): 120 per annum for Tanzanian students and (US Dollars) 1265 for foreign students

Main Language(s) of Instruction: English, Kiswahili

Accrediting Agencies: The Higher Education Accreditation Council

Degrees and Diplomas: *Bachelor Degree*: Arts (BA); Arts in Education (BEd); Law (LLB); Science (BSc), 6 yrs; *Master Degree*: 2-5 yrs following first Degree; *Postgraduate Diploma*: (PGDE); Law (PDGL), 3 yrs; *Doctor of Philosophy*: (PhD), 6 yrs

Student Services: Academic Counselling, Handicapped Facilities

Publications: Huria, Journal of the Open University of Tanzania (biannually); Convocation Newsletter (2 per annum)

Academic Staff 2002	MEN	WOMEN	TOTAL
FULL-TIME	66	13	79
PART-TIME	121	11	132
TOTAL	**187**	**24**	**211**
STAFF WITH DOCTORATE			
FULL-TIME	13	2	15
PART-TIME	70	5	75
TOTAL	**83**	**7**	**90**

Student Numbers 2002	MEN	WOMEN	TOTAL
All (Foreign Included)	9,090	1,787	**10,877**

• SOKOINE UNIVERSITY OF AGRICULTURE

Chuo Kikuu Cha Sokoine Cha Kilimo (SUA)
PO Box 3000, Chuo Kikuu, Morogoro 23
Tel: +255(23) 260-3511 +255(23) 260-3514
Fax: +255(23) 260-4651
Telex: 55308 univmo tz
EMail: vc@sua.ac.tz
Website: http://www.suanet.ac.tz

Vice-Chancellor: Anselm Biseko Lwoga (1988-)
Tel: +255(23) 260-4651 EMail: ablwoga@suanet.ac.tz

Registrar: H.O. Dihenga Tel: +255(23) 260-4653
Fax: +255(23) 260-4573 EMail: registra@suanet.ac.tz

Head Librarian: F.W. Dulle

Faculties

Agriculture (Agricultural Business; Agricultural Economics; Agricultural Education; Agricultural Engineering; Agriculture; Agronomy; Animal Husbandry; Crop Production; Food Science; Food Technology; Horticulture; Soil Science) *Dean*: N.A. Urio

Forestry and Nature Conservation (Ecology; Forestry) *Dean*: G.C. Monela

499

Science (Natural Sciences) *Dean*: R.L.B Kurwijila
Veterinary Medicine (Veterinary Science) *Dean*: D.M. Kambarage

Institutes
Continuing Education *Director*: A. Isinika
Development Studies *Director*: D.S. Kapinga
Research and Postgraduate Studies *Director*: W.S. Abeli

Centres
Computer (Computer Science) *Director*: R.R. Kazwala
Pest Management *Director*: R.S. Machangu
Sustainable Rural Development (Rural Planning) *Director*: A.Z. Mattee

Further Information: Also Mazimbu Campus (Morogoro) and Olmotonyi Campus (Arusha).

History: Founded 1984. Previously Faculty of Agriculture, Forestry and Veterinary Sciences of the University of Dar es Salaam.

Governing Bodies: University Council, comprising 45 members

Academic Year: August-July

Admission Requirements: Certificate of Secondary Education Examination, or East African Certificate of Education Ordinary ('O') level, or equivalent, with passes in 5 approved subjects obtained prior to sitting Advanced Certificate of Secondary Education examination, or East African Certificate of Education Advanced ('A') level, or equivalent. Two principal passes at 'A' level with a total of not less than 4 points

Fees: (Tanzanian Shillings): 42,000 per annum

Main Language(s) of Instruction: English

Accrediting Agencies: Higher Education Accreditation Council

Degrees and Diplomas: *Bachelor Degree*: Agricultural Economics, Agribusiness (BSc); Agricultural Education and Extension (BSc); Agronomy (BSc); Animal Science and Production (BSc); Environmental Sciences and Management (BSc); Food Science, Technology (BSc); Forestry, Wildlife Management (BSc); Home Economics, Nutrition (BSc); Horticulture (BSc), 3 yrs; Agricultural Sciences (BSc), 3-4 yrs; Agricultural Engineering, Land Planning (BSc), 4 yrs; Veterinary Sciences (BSc), 5 yrs; *Master Degree*: Agricultural Sciences, a further 2 yrs; *Doctor of Philosophy*: Agricultural Sciences (PhD), 4-6 yrs

Student Services: Academic Counselling, Social Counselling, Employment Services, Foreign Student Adviser, Nursery Care, Cultural Centre, Sports Facilities, Language Programmes, Health Services, Canteen

Student Residential Facilities: Yes

Special Facilities: Botanical Garden, University Television (SUA)

Libraries: Central Library, 75,000 vols

Publications: SUA Newsletter; SUASA Newsletter (quarterly); Research Newsletter (2 per annum); University Prospectus; Convocation Newsletter; Annual Report (annually); University Calendar

Press or Publishing House: Sokoine University of Agriculture Printing Press

500

Academic Staff *2001-2002*: Full-Time: c. 245
Staff with doctorate: Full-Time: c. 198

Student Numbers *2001-2002*	MEN	WOMEN	TOTAL
All (Foreign Included)	1,473	578	**2,051**

ST. AUGUSTINE UNIVERSITY OF TANZANIA (SAUT)
PO Box 307, Mwanza
Tel: +255(28) 255-2727
Fax: +255(28) 255-0167
EMail: saut@africa.online.co.tz
Website: http://www.saut.ac

Vice-Chancellor: Charles Kitima Tel: +255(28) 255-0560
EMail: saut@africaonline.co.tz

Faculties
Business Administration (Accountancy; Business Administration; Finance; Health Administration; Human Resources; Management; Marketing) *Dean (Acting)*: Ildefons Chonya
Humanities and Mass Communication (Arts and Humanities; Journalism; Mass Communication; Media Studies) *Dean (Acting)*: Fr. Joseph Mlacha

History: Founded 1960 as Nyegezi Social Training Centre . Acquired present status and title 1998.

Governing Bodies: Board of Trustees; University Council; Senate

Academic Year: October to June

Admission Requirements: Certificate of secondary education (CSEE). For undergraduate and advanced diploma, minimum 2 principal ('A') level passes in the advanced certificate of secondary education examination (ACSEE)

Fees: (Tanzanian Shillings): Degree courses, 1,600,000; Advanced Diploma courses, 1,300,000; Certificate courses, 1,000,000

Main Language(s) of Instruction: English

Accrediting Agencies: Higher Education Accreditation Council

Degrees and Diplomas: *Advanced Diploma*: Accountancy, Journalism, Materials Management (ADA, ADJ, ADMM), 3 yrs; *Bachelor Degree*: Accountancy and Finance, Marketing, Human Resources Management, Materials Management (BBA); Print Media, Electronic Media, Public Relations and Advertising, 3 yrs

Student Services: Academic Counselling, Social Counselling, Nursery Care, Sports Facilities, Health Services, Canteen

Student Residential Facilities: For 490 students

Special Facilities: SAUT Radio Station; Video Centre; Computer Centre. Photo Laboratory

Libraries: 15,000 volumes and 30 periodical titles

Academic Staff *2001-2002*	MEN	WOMEN	TOTAL
FULL-TIME	31	5	36
PART-TIME	7	1	8
TOTAL	**38**	**6**	**44**

STAFF WITH DOCTORATE
FULL-TIME ... 3
PART-TIME ... 2
TOTAL ... **5**

Student Numbers *2001-2002*	MEN	WOMEN	TOTAL
All (Foreign Included)	201	203	**404**
FOREIGN ONLY	12	26	38

Academic Staff *2001-2002*	MEN	WOMEN	TOTAL
FULL-TIME	119	18	137
PART-TIME	6	2	8
TOTAL	**125**	**20**	**145**

STAFF WITH DOCTORATE

	MEN	WOMEN	TOTAL
FULL-TIME	25	5	**30**

Student Numbers *2001-2002*	MEN	WOMEN	TOTAL
All (Foreign Included)	560	229	**789**
FOREIGN ONLY	15	9	24

TUMAINI UNIVERSITY (TU)

PO Box 2200, Moshi
Tel: +255(27) 275-2291
Fax: +255(27) 275-3612
EMail: kcmcadmin@kcmc.ac.tz
Website: http://www.kcmc.ac.tz

Chancellor: Samson Mushemba
Tel: +255(27) 250-8853 +255(27) 250-8857
Fax: +255(27) 254-8858

Vice-Chancellor: John F. Shao

International Relations: Marystella Katemana

History: Founded 1997. Acquired present status 2001.

Governing Bodies: Board of Trustees; Council; Senate

Academic Year: September to August

Admission Requirements: Advanced Certificate of secondary education examination (ACSEE) , plus 2 credit passes in certificate of secondary education examination

Main Language(s) of Instruction: English

Accrediting Agencies: Higher Education Accreditation Council

Degrees and Diplomas: *Diploma*: Therapy; Health Sciences (DipOth), 3 yrs; Theology; Religion (DipTh), 4 yrs; *Bachelor Degree*: Business Administration (BBA); Dental Technology; Orthodontics (BScP/BScO); Journalism (BAJ); Law (LLB); Mathematics Education (BE (Maths)); Nursing; Health Sciences (BSc); Prosthetics; Orthodontics (BScProth/Orth); Theology; Religion (BD, BTh), 3 yrs; *Doctor*: Health Sciences; Medicine (MD), 5 yrs; *Master Degree*: Orthopaedics; Surgery; Anaesthesiology; Otorhinolaryngology; Radiology; Paediatrics; Internal Medicine; Obstetrics; Gynaecology; Dermatology; Venereology; Ophthalmology, 4 yrs; Health Sciences (MSc); Theology (MTh), a further 2 yrs; Urology; Health Sciences (MScUrol), a further 3 yrs; Medicine (MMed); Public Health (MPH), a further yr; *Postgraduate Diploma*: Education (PdiPEd), 1-3 yrs following Bachelor's Degree

Student Services: Academic Counselling, Social Counselling, Nursery Care, Cultural Centre, Sports Facilities, Health Services, Canteen

Student Residential Facilities: Yes

Libraries: Libraries of the constituent colleges

Publications: Tumaini Hill, Newsletter (quarterly); Tumaini University Prospectus, Bochure (annually)

Press or Publishing House: Radio Habari Maalum Press, Arusha, Tanzania

IRINGA UNIVERSITY COLLEGE

PO Box 200, Iringa
Tel: +255(26) 272-0900
Fax: +255(26) 272-0904
EMail: iuco1993@yahoo.com
Website: http://www.tumaini.com

Provost: Nicolas Bangu

Faculties

Arts and Social Sciences (Arts and Humanities; Education; Journalism; Social Sciences) *Dean:* Samuel Mshana
Business and Economics (Business Administration; Business and Commerce; Economics) *Dean:* George Mpelumbe
Education (Education; Mathematics)
Law *Dean:* Andrew Mollel
Theology *Dean:* Festo Bahendwa

History: Founded as a Lutheran Seminary 1993. Acquired present status 2001.

Accrediting Agencies: Accreditation Council of the Tanzania Ministry of Science, Technology and Higher Education

Degrees and Diplomas: *Diploma*; *Bachelor Degree*

KILIMANJARO CHRISTIAN MEDICAL COLLEGE

PO Box 2240, Moshi
Tel: +255(27) 275-3616
Fax: +255(27) 275-4381
EMail: kcmcadmin@kcmc.ac.tz
Website: http://www.kcmc.ac.tz

Provost: Egbert M. Kessi EMail: ddtsec@kcmc.ac.tz

Faculties

Medicine *Dean:* Augustine L. Mallya
Nursing *Dean:* Marcelina H. Msuya
Rehabilitation Sciences (Health Sciences; Rehabilitation and Therapy) *Dean:* Harold G. Shangali

Institutes

Allied Health Sciences (Health Sciences) *Director:* Henning Grossman
Postgraduate Studies (Health Sciences) *Director:* Wilhelmus Dolmans
Research and Consultancies (Health Sciences) *Director:* Franklin Mosha

History: Founded 1971. Acquired present status 2001.

MAKUMIRA UNIVERSITY COLLEGE
PO Box 55, Usa River, Arusha
Tel: +255(27) 255-3634 +255(27) 255-3635
Fax: +255(27) 255-3493
EMail: academic@makumira.ac.tz
Website: http://www.makumira.ac.tz

Provost: Gwakisa Mwakagali

Departments
Biblical Theology (Bible; Theology) *Chairman:* Ernest Mhando
Pastoral Theology and Liberal Arts (Pastoral Studies; Theology)
Systematic and Historical Theology (Theology)

Institutes
Postgraduate Studies and Research (Religion) *Director:* Mika Jahakangas

History: Founded 1947. Acquired present status 2001.

Degrees and Diplomas: *Diploma:* Theology; Religion (DipTh), 4 yrs; *Bachelor Degree:* Bachelor of Theology, Divinity (BTh), 4 yrs; Theology; Religion (BTh), 5 yrs; *Master Degree:* Theology; Religion (MTH), a further 2 yrs

THE UNIVERSITY OF BUKOBA (UOB)
PO Box 1725, Bukoba
Tel: +255(28) 222-0691
Fax: +255(28) 222-2341 +255(28) 222-1356
EMail: uobtz@yahoo.com
Website: http://uobtz.tripod.com

Vice-Chancellor: M. Hodd

Registrar: Samuel L. Mutasa Tel: +255(741) 505-927

Deputy Vice-Chancellor: Israel K. Katoke
EMail: katokeisrael@yahoo.com

International Relations: Gregory J. Vogl
Tel: +255(28) 222-0862 EMail: gregvogl@yahoo.com

Faculties
Commerce and Management (Accountancy; Business and Commerce; Finance; Human Resources; Management; Marketing) *Dean:* Joseph Mwabuki
Social and Natural Sciences (Education; Information Technology; Natural Sciences; Social Sciences) *Dean (Acting):* Christopher Rwiza

History: Founded 1999.

Governing Bodies: Board of Trustees; University Council; Senate

Academic Year: October to June (October-February; February-June)

Admission Requirements: ('A') levels

Fees: (Tanzanian Shillings): 1,200,000 per annum

Main Language(s) of Instruction: English

Accrediting Agencies: Higher Education Accreditation Council (HEAC)

Degrees and Diplomas: *Bachelor Degree:* Education; Computer Science; Natural Sciences; Accountancy; Finance; Human Resources; Marketing (BSc, BA, BCom)

Student Residential Facilities: None

Libraries: Central Library

Academic Staff 2001-2002	MEN	WOMEN	TOTAL
FULL-TIME	10	5	15
PART-TIME	5	–	5
TOTAL	**15**	**5**	**20**
STAFF WITH DOCTORATE			
FULL-TIME	1	1	**2**

Student Numbers 2001-2002	MEN	WOMEN	TOTAL
All (Foreign Included)	25	25	**50**

Part-time Students, 25

*• UNIVERSITY OF DAR ES SALAAM (UDSM)
PO Box 35091, Dar es Salaam
Tel: +255(22) 241-0500 +255(22) 241-0508
Fax: +255(22) 241-0078
Cable: University of Dar es salaam
EMail: cado@admin.udsm.ac.tz
Website: http://www.udsm.ac.tz

Vice-Chancellor: Matthew L. Luhanga (1991-)
Tel: +255(22) 241-0700 +255(22) 211-3654
EMail: vc@admin.udsm.ac.tz

Chief Administrative Officer: J.S. Mshana
Tel: +255(22) 241-0394 EMail: cado@admin.udsm.ac.tz

International Relations: P.N. Materu
Tel: +255(22) 241-0169 EMail: caco@admin.udsm.ac.tz

Head Librarian: E. Kiondo

Faculties
Arts and Social Sciences (Administration; Agriculture; Anthropology; Arts and Humanities; Development Studies; Economics; Environmental Studies; Fine Arts; Geography; History; Industrial Management; International Relations; Literature; Performing Arts; Political Science; Public Administration; Regional Planning; Rural Studies; Social Sciences; Social Studies; Sociology; Statistics; Water Science) *Dean:* A. Lihamba
Civil Engineering and Built Environment (Civil Engineering; Construction Engineering)
Commerce and Management (Accountancy; Business and Commerce; Finance; Management; Marketing) *Dean:* E.S. Kaijage
Education (Adult Education; Curriculum; Education; Educational Administration; Educational Psychology; Educational Sciences; Physical Education; Sports) *Dean:* W.L. Lugoe
Electrical and Computer Systems Engineering (Computer Engineering; Electrical and Electronic Engineering)
Law (Administrative Law; Civil Law; Criminal Law; International Law; Law) *Dean:* I.H. Juma
Mechanical and Chemical Engineering (Chemical Engineering; Mechanical Engineering)
Science (Botany; Chemistry; Computer Science; Geology; Marine Biology; Mathematics; Microbiology; Natural Sciences; Physics; Zoology) *Dean:* R.T. Kivaisi

Institutes

Development Studies *Director*: B.S. Mlawa
Kiswahili Research (Native Language) *Director*: M. M Mulokozi
Marine Science (Marine Science and Oceanography)
Production Innovation (Production Engineering) *Director*: O. Kaunde
Resource Assessment (Agriculture; Demography and Population; Environmental Studies; Food Science; Natural Resources; Nutrition; Regional Planning; Water Management) *Director*: R.B.B. Mwalyosi

History: Founded 1961 as University College, Dar es Salaam. Acquired present status and title 1970.

Governing Bodies: University Council

Academic Year: September to August (September-December; December-March; March-June; June-August)

Admission Requirements: Completion of form 6 at Tanzanian Schools in previous year. Candidates must also complete basic military training (National Service)

Fees: (Tanzanian Shillings): Tuition, c. 900,000 per annum

Main Language(s) of Instruction: English

Degrees and Diplomas: *Bachelor Degree*: Arts (BA); Commerce (Bcomm); Law (LLB); Science (BSc); Science in Computer Science (BScComp); Science in Electronics, Science and Communication (BScElectrSc & Comm), 3 yrs; Education (BEd); Pharmacy (BPharm); Science in Engineering (BSc(Eng)); Science in Nursing (BScNurs), 4 yrs; Lands and Architecture (BSc), 5-4 yrs; Arts in Education (BAEd); Science in Education (BScEd), a further 1 term; *Doctor*: Dentistry (DDS); Medicine (MD), 5 yrs; *Master Degree*: a further 2 yrs; *Doctor of Philosophy*: (PhD), 6 yrs

Student Services: Academic Counselling, Social Counselling, Employment Services, Foreign Student Adviser, Nursery Care, Cultural Centre, Sports Facilities, Language Programmes, Handicapped Facilities, Health Services, Canteen, Foreign Student Centre

Student Residential Facilities: Yes

Special Facilities: University Flower Nursery; Botanical Garden

Libraries: Main Library, c. 500,000 vols

Publications: Research Bulletin (biannually); Calendar; Annual Report

Press or Publishing House: DUP (1996) Ltd

Academic Staff *2001-2002:* Total: c. 570
Staff with doctorate: Total: c. 490

Student Numbers *2001-2002:* Total: c. 6,200

MUHIMBILI UNIVERSITY COLLEGE OF HEALTH SCIENCES
PO Box 65001, Dar es Salaam
Tel: +255(22) 215-0331
Fax: +255(22) 215-0465
EMail: dfmed@muchs.ac.tz
Website: http://www.muchs.ac.tz/
Principal: K. J. Pallangyo

Schools

Dentistry *Dean*: K. Mabelya
Medicine *Dean*: C.A. Mkony
Nursing *Dean*: H.I. Lugina
Pharmacy (Pharmacy; Toxicology) *Head*: O. Ngassapa
Public Health and Social Sciences (Public Health; Social Sciences) *Director*: M.T. Leshabari

Institutes

Allied Health Sciences (Health Sciences) *Director*: I. Mauga
Development Studies *Director*: A.D. Kiwara
Primary Health Care and Continuing Health Education (Health Education) *Director*: F.D.E. Mtango
Traditional Medicine (Medicine) *Director*: M.J. Moshi

History: Founded 1991. Formerly Faculty of Medicine, University of Dar es Salaam.

UNIVERSITY COLLEGE OF LAND AND ARCHITECTURAL STUDIES
PO Box 35176, Dar es Salaam
Tel: +255(22) 275-004
Fax: +255(22) 277-539
Cable: ardhichuo
EMail: uclas@uclas.ac.tz
Principal: Idris Kikula

Faculties

Architecture, Quantity Surveying and Urban and Rural Planning (Architecture; Rural Planning; Surveying and Mapping; Town Planning)
Housing Studies and Building Research (Construction Engineering; Town Planning)
Land Surveying, Land Management and Valuation and Environmental Engineering (Environmental Engineering; Rural Planning; Surveying and Mapping)

Centres
Continuing Education

History: Founded 1996. Acquired present status and title 1970.

ZANZIBAR UNIVERSITY

Chuo Kikuu Cha Zanzibar (ZU)
PO Box 2440, Zanzibar, Central District
Tel: +255(24) 223-2642
Fax: +255(24) 223-2642
EMail: zanvarsity@yahoo.co.uk
Website: http://www.zanvarsity.ac.tz

Vice Chancellor (Acting): Mustafa Roshash
EMail: roshash@hotmail.com

General Supervisor (Acting): Elmi Nur
Tel: +255(24) 223-0094 Fax: +255(24) 223-0094
EMail: ngeddicad@hotmail.com

International Relations: Gharib Gharib, Public Relations Officer EMail: zanvarsity@yahoo.co.uk

Faculties

Business Administration (Accountancy; Finance; Marketing) *Dean*: Elmi Nur

Law and Shariah (Islamic Law; Law) *Dean*: Mustafa Roshash

History: Founded 1997.

Governing Bodies: Council; Senate

Admission Requirements: Secondary school certificate, with two A-level passes

Fees: (Tanzanian Shilling): 2m.

Main Language(s) of Instruction: English

Accrediting Agencies: Higher Education Accreditation Council

Degrees and Diplomas: *Bachelor Degree*: Business Administration, 3 yrs; Law, 4 yrs

Student Services: Academic Counselling, Social Counselling, Employment Services, Foreign Student Adviser, Cultural Centre, Sports Facilities, Language Programmes, Handicapped Facilities, Health Services, Canteen

Student Residential Facilities: Yes

Libraries: Yes

Academic Staff 2002-2003			TOTAL
FULL-TIME			17
PART-TIME			7
TOTAL			**24**

STAFF WITH DOCTORATE			
FULL-TIME			3
PART-TIME			5
TOTAL			**8**

Student Numbers 2002-2003	MEN	WOMEN	TOTAL
All (Foreign Included)	261	132	**393**
FOREIGN ONLY	62	10	72

OTHER INSTITUTIONS

CO-OPERATIVE COLLEGE OF MOSHI (CCOM)
PO Box 35176, Moshi
Tel: +255 (22) 215-0176
Fax: +255 (22) 150-178

Principal: S.A. Chambo

Founded: 1963, 1964

History: Founded 1963.

COLLEGE OF AFRICAN WILDLIFE MANAGEMENT, MWEKA
PO Box 3031, Moshi
Tel: +255 (27) 275-6451
Fax: +255 (27) 275-6414
EMail: mweka@mwekawildlife.org
Website: http://www.mwekawildlife.org/

Principal: D.M. Gamassa Tel: +255(27) 783-887
EMail: dgamassa@twiga.com

Founded: 1963

Divisions

Wildlife Management (Teacher Training; Wildlife) *Director*: Wilfred Foya

Governing Bodies: Drawing members from various African countries and International Conservation organizations

Academic Year: July to June

Main Language(s) of Instruction: English

Degrees and Diplomas: *Diploma*: 2 yrs; *Advanced Diploma*: 1 yr; *Postgraduate Diploma*: 1 yr

Student Services: Academic Counselling, Social Counselling, Sports Facilities, Language Programmes, Health Services, Canteen

Student Residential Facilities: Yes

Special Facilities: Collection of Wildlife Specimens

Libraries: Central Library, c. 12,000 vols

Publications: News at Mweka (bi-annual)

Academic Staff 2001-2002: Total: c. 20

Student Numbers 2001-2002: All (Foreign Included): c. 160 Foreign Only: c. 100

COLLEGE OF BUSINESS EDUCATION
PO Box 1968, Dar es Salaam
Tel: +255(51) 31056

Principal: G.A.M. Chale

Founded: 1965

Departments

Business Administration (Business Administration; Business Education)

COLLEGE OF EDUCATION ZANZIBAR (CEZ)
PO Box 1933, Zanzibar
Tel: +255(22) 275-004
Fax: +255(22) 754-48
EMail: alfeo@uclas.ud.co.tz

Education

COLLEGE OF NATIONAL EDUCATION
PO Box 533, Dar es Salaam

Principal: F.D. Ntemo

Departments
Education

DAR ES SALAAM INSTITUTE OF TECHNOLOGY (DIT)
PO Box 2958, Dar es Salaam
Tel: +255(22) 215-0174
Fax: +255(22) 215-2504
EMail: principal@dit.ac.tz
Website: http://www.dit.ac.tz/

Principal: John W.A. Kondoro

Director, Finance and Administration: Mhina M. Setebe

Founded: 1957

Departments
Civil and Building Engineering (Building Technologies; Civil Engineering; Road Engineering) *Head*: E.L. Meliara
Computer Engineering *Head*: G.R. Lushaka
Electrical Engineering *Head*: Mashauri A. Kusekwa
Electronics and Telecommunications Engineering (Electronic Engineering; Telecommunications Engineering) *Head*: N.G. Nzowa
General Studies (Communication Studies; Mathematics) *Head*: R.H.A. Kajwaula
Mechanical Engineering *Head*: M.Y. Kiluswa
Science and Laboratory Technology (Laboratory Techniques; Natural Sciences; Photography) *Head*: S.W. Momburi

History: Founded 1957 as Dar es Salaam Technical Institute.

DAR ES SALAAM SCHOOL OF ACCOUNTANCY (DSA)
PO Box 9522, Dar es Salaam
Tel: +255(22) 285-1035
Fax: +255(22) 851-036
Accountancy

EASTERN AND SOUTHERN AFRICAN MANAGEMENT INSTITUTE
PO Box 3030, Arusha
Tel: +255(57) 8383
Fax: +255 (57) 8285
EMail: esami_arusha@marie.grn.org

Director-General: Bonard Mwape

Founded: 1974, 1980

Programmes
Agriculture, Energy and Environment
Corporate Management and Entrepreneurship (Business Administration)

Finance and Banking (Banking; Finance)
Gender, Development and Entrepreneurship Management (Business Administration; Development Studies; Gender Studies)
Health Management (Health Administration)
Human Resource Management (Human Resources)
Information Technology
Policy Analysis and Public Sector (Political Science)
Transport and Infrastructure Development (Transport and Communications)

Schools
Business (Business Administration; Management; Public Relations; Secretarial Studies; Transport Management)

History: Founded 1974, acquired present status and title 1980.

INSTITUTE OF ACCOUNTANCY ARUSHA (IAA)
PO Box 2798, Arusha
Tel: +255(27) 250-1416
Fax: +255(27) 250-8421
EMail: iaa@habari.co.tz
Website: http://www.iaa.ac.tz/

Programmes
Accountancy
Business Administration
Finance
Information Technology
Tax Administration (Taxation)

Degrees and Diplomas: *Advanced Diploma*; *Postgraduate Diploma*. Also Certificates
Libraries: Yes

INSTITUTE OF COMMUNITY DEVELOPMENT TENGERU (ICDT)
PO Box 1006, Tengeru, Arusha
Development Studies; Urban Studies

INSTITUTE OF FINANCE MANAGEMENT (IFM)
PO Box 3918, Shaaban Robert Street, Dar es Salaam
Tel: +255(51) 112-931 +255(51) 112-9314
Fax: +255(51) 112-935
Telex: 41969 IFM TZ
Cable: INSFINANCE
EMail: ifm@twiga.com
Website: http:/www.ifm.ac.tz

Principal: J. Doriye **Tel:** +255(51) 114-817

Director of Studies (Acting): P.K.D. Mugoya
Tel: +255(51) 123-468 **EMail:** ifm@twiga.com

Founded: 1972

Departments

Banking *Head*: S.K. Gamba

Computer Science and Information Technology (Computer Science; Information Technology) *Head*: Elias Otaigo

Executive Development, Research and Consultancy *(Short Courses)* (Management)

Graduate Studies (Accountancy; Banking; Finance; Insurance; Taxation) *Head (Acting)*: F.A. Mkombo

Insurance and Social Security Administration (Insurance; Public Administration) *Head*: J. Mkini

Professional Accountancy (Accountancy) *Head*: S.P. Sadiki

Tax Management (Taxation) *Head*: S.P. Senzige

Further Information: Global Distance Learning Centre (GDLC)

History: Founded 1972 by Act n°3 of Parliament. Offers courses at both undergraduate and postgradute levels, undertakes research and provides consultancy services in finance and related subjects. IFM has established, over the years, an international reputation for the quality of its courses. It has attracted students from Uganda, Ethiopia, Ghana, Kenya, Lesotho, Mozambique, Namibia, Sierra Leone, South Africa, Swaziland, Zambia and Zimbabwe.

Governing Bodies: Council

Academic Year: October to September

Admission Requirements: Completion of form 6 ('A') level or equivalent with 2 principal level passes and at least 2 years of relevant working experience. Or completion of form 4 ('O') level or equivalent with 5 credit passes including English and Mathematics plus at least 4 years of relevant working experience

Main Language(s) of Instruction: English

Accrediting Agencies: Higher Education Accreditation Council

Degrees and Diplomas: *Advanced Diploma*: Information Technology (ADIT); Accountancy (ADA); Banking (ADB); Computer Science (ADCS); Insurance (ADI); Social Security (ADSSA); Taxation (ADTM), 3 yrs; *Master Degree*: Finance (MScFin); *Postgraduate Diploma*: Finance (PGDFM); Taxation (PGDTM), 1 yr; Accountancy (PGDA), 1yr

Student Services: Academic Counselling, Social Counselling, Nursery Care, Health Services, Canteen

Student Residential Facilities: For 700 students

Special Facilities: Function Hall. Global Teleconference Centre. 2 Lecture Theatres

Libraries: Central Library, c. 15,000 vols

Publications: IFM newsletter, provides institutional news (quarterly); The African Journal of Finance and Management, provides a scholarly forum for professionals and academics in these disciplines (bi-annual)

Academic Staff *2001-2002*: Full-Time: c. 60 Part-Time: c. 20 Total: c. 80

Staff with doctorate: Total: c. 5

Student Numbers *2001-2002*: All (Foreign Included): c. 820 Foreign Only: c. 20

Evening Students, c. 400

INSTITUTE OF RURAL DEVELOPMENT PLANNING (IRDP)
PO Box 138, Dodoma
Tel: +255(26) 230-2147

Rural Planning

KIVUKONI ACADEMY OF SOCIAL SCIENCES
PO Box 9193, Dar es Salaam
Tel: +255(51) 820-019

Principal: John M.J. Magotti

Founded: 1961

Departments
Economics
Political Studies (Political Science)
Social Studies

NATIONAL INSTITUTE OF TRANSPORT
PO Box 705, Dar es Salaam
Tel: +255(51) 48328
EMail: nit@intafrica.com

Departments
Transport Studies (Transport and Communications)

NATIONAL SOCIAL WELFARE TRAINING INSTITUTE
PO Box 3375, Dar es Salaam
Tel: +255(51) 74443
EMail: nswti@twiga.com

Principal: T.F. Ngalula

Founded: 1974
Social Welfare

TANZANIA SCHOOL OF JOURNALISM (TSJ)
PO Box 4067, Dar es Salaam
Tel: +255(22) 270-0236
Fax: +255(22) 700-239
EMail: habari@tsj.tznet
Website: http://www.tznet.tsj.net/

Journalism

Togo

INSTITUTION TYPES AND CREDENTIALS

Types of higher education institutions:

Université (University)
Ecole supérieure (Higher School)
Institut (Institute)

School leaving and higher education credentials:

Baccalauréat
Capacité en Droit
Diplôme de Technicien supérieur (DTS)
Diplôme universitaire de Technologie (DUT)
Diplôme universitaire d'Etudes générales (DUEG)
Diplôme universitaire d'Etudes littéraires (DUEL)
Diplôme universitaire d'Etudes scientifiques (DUES)
Diplôme d'Ingénieur de Travaux
Licence
Licence d'Enseignement
Certificat d'Aptitude au Professorat de l'Enseignement secondaire (CAPES)
Diplôme d'Ingénieur de Conception
Doctorat en Médecine
Maîtrise
Agrégation
Certificat d'Etudes spécialisées (CES)
Diplôme d'Etudes approfondies (DEA)
Diplôme d'Etudes supérieures (DES)
Doctorat d'Ingénieur
Doctorat de Spécialité de Troisième Cycle
Doctorat unique

STRUCTURE OF EDUCATION SYSTEM

Pre-higher education:

Duration of compulsory education:

Age of entry: 5
Age of exit: 15

Structure of school system:

Primary
Type of school providing this education: Ecole primaire (Enseignement du premier degré)
Length of programme in years: 6
Age level from: 5 to: 11
Certificate/diploma awarded: Certificat d'Etudes du premier Degré (CEPD)

First Cycle Secondary
Type of school providing this education: Collège d'enseignement général (Enseignement du Second Degré)
Length of programme in years: 4
Age level from: 11 to: 15
Certificate/diploma awarded: Brevet d'Etudes du Premier Cycle du Second Degré (BEPC)

Technical Secondary
Type of school providing this education: Collège d'enseignement technique (CET)
Length of programme in years: 4
Age level from: 11 to: 15
Certificate/diploma awarded: Certificat d'Aptitude Professionnelle (CAP) or Brevet d'Etudes professionnelles (BEP)

Second Cycle Secondary
Type of school providing this education: Lycée d'enseignement général (Enseignement du Troisième Degré)
Length of programme in years: 3
Age level from: 15 to: 18
Certificate/diploma awarded: Baccalauréat de l'Enseignement secondaire (2 parts)

Technical
Type of school providing this education: Ecole secondaire technique ou Enseignement Technique Cycle Long
Length of programme in years: 3
Age level from: 15 to: 18
Certificate/diploma awarded: Baccalauréat de l'Enseignement secondaire (2 parts)

School education:

Primary school (enseignement du premier degré) lasts for six years and leads to the Certificat d'Etudes du premier Degré. Pupils are streamed at the end of primary schooling for entry to the first cycle of secondary education. This cycle of lower secondary education (called enseignement du deuxième degré) lasts for four years (6ème, 5ème, 4ème, and 3ème) after which students take the examination for the Brevet d'Etudes du Premier Cycle du Second Degré. Students are then streamed again and oriented towards vocational or training institutions or enter the Lycée. This second cycle lasts for three years and is called enseignement du troisième degré (2ème, 1ère and terminale). The Baccalauréat (1ère partie) is taken on completion of the '1ère'. On completion of this cycle, pupils take the examinations for the Baccalauréat 2ème partie. The Certificat de Fin d'Etudes secondaires, which represents class attendance in the last year of secondary school, is not equivalent to the Baccalauréat.

Higher education:

Higher education in Togo is provided by the Université du Bénin, recently renamed Université de Lomé, with several faculties, higher schools (including an Ecole normale supérieure) and institutes (including a recently founded National Institute of Educational Sciences) and several private schools and institutes. A second university, the Université de Kara, has been founded recently. Education and scientific research in Togo is the responsibility of the Ministry of National Education and Research.

Main laws/decrees governing higher education:

Decree: Constitution de la IV ème République (article 35)   Year: 1992

Academic year:

Classes from: October *to:* June

Long vacation from: 1 July *to:* 30 September

Languages of instruction:

French

Stages of studies:

Non-university level post-secondary studies (technical/vocational type):

Two private institutes offer short cycle studies in commercial and computer science fields.

University level studies:

University level first stage: Premier Cycle:

The first two-year cycle leads, in the Science Faculty, to the Diplôme universitaire d'Etudes scientifiques (DUES), and, in the Arts Faculty, to the Diplôme universitaire d'Etudes littéraires (DUEL) or the Diplôme d'Etudes universitaires générales (DEUG).

University level second stage: Deuxième Cycle:

In Arts and Humanities, Science, Law, Economics and Management, a second stage corresponding to second-cycle studies leads, after one year, to the Licence. Students then have to obtain a Certificat de Maîtrise and submit a short thesis. In Science, the Maîtrise may be obtained without holding a Licence. The course takes one year from Licence (Humanities) or two years from DUES (Science). A Diplôme d'Ingénieur de Conception is awarded in Agriculture and Engineering after five years' study.

University level third stage: Troisième Cycle:

The Diplôme d'Etudes supérieures spécialisées (DESS) and the Diplôme d'Etudes approfondies (DEA) represent completion of a further one or two years of academic studies beyond the Maîtrise. The Doctorat de Spécialité de Troisième Cycle requires one or two years' further study beyond the DES or DEA. It is now being replaced by the Doctorat unique, awarded two or three years after the DEA and the presentation of a major thesis. In Medicine, the professional qualification of Docteur en Médecine is awarded to candidates who have undertaken seven years' study. The Doctorat d'Ingénieur requires three years' study beyond the Diplôme d'Ingénieur.

Teacher education:

Training of pre-primary and primary/basic school teachers
Primary school teachers must hold the Baccalauréat and follow a one-year course at a teacher training institution called Ecole Normale d'Instituteurs (ENI). Studies lead to the Certificat de Fin d'Etudes Normales des Instituteurs (CFEN-ENI).

Training of secondary school teachers
Secondary school teachers are mostly trained at the University (Ecole normale supérieure). At lower secondary level, teachers must hold a three-year degree after the Baccalauréat or a DEUG plus one year. A one-year course is open to practising teachers. Teachers at the upper secondary level must hold a Maîtrise and a Diplôme de Formation pédagogique. Moreover, in public education, access to teaching positions normally requires the passing of a competitive examination, the Certificat d'Aptitude à l'Enseignement secondaire (CAPES).

Training of higher education teachers
Teachers at this level must theoretically hold the Doctorat de troisième Cycle. However, owing to a shortage of Doctorats, many university lecturers are temporary lecturers (Vacataires). The Agrégation de l'Enseignement du second Degré and the Agrégation de l'Université are certificates of outstanding proficiency in teaching and are obtained by examination before a committee. The Agrégation is not in itself a degree and requires no specific course or research qualification.

NATIONAL BODIES

Responsible authorities:

Ministry of National Education and Research (Ministère de l'Education nationale et de la Recherche)
    Minister: Charles Kondi Agba
    Secretary-General: Adji Otèth Ayassor
    BP 398 or BP 12195
    Lomé
    Tel: +228(221) 24-73 +228(221) 09-93
    Fax: +228(221) 07-83

Ministry of Technical Education and Professional Training (Ministère de l'Enseignement technique et de la Formation professionnelle)
    Minister: Edoh K. Maurille Agbobli
    Secretary-General: Yawo Amouzouvi
    BP 398
    Lomé
    Tel: +228(221) 85-17
    Fax: +228(221) 89-34

Chancellerie des Universités du Togo
    Recteur-Chancelier: Ampah G. Johnson
    Vice-Recteur: Osséni Tidjani

Chargé de Mission: Kofi-Lumo Kodjo
International Relations: Koffi A. Akibode
BP 1296
Lomé
Tel: +228(221) 12-16
Fax: +228(221) 53-65
EMail: apa.g.johnson@ids.tg

ADMISSIONS TO HIGHER EDUCATION

Admission to university-level studies

Name of secondary school credential required: Baccalauréat
Minimum score/requirement: 10/20
For entry to: All institutions

Name of secondary school credential required: Capacité en Droit
For entry to: Only for registration in first year of Faculty of Law

Alternatives to credentials: Special entrance examination for those who do not hold the Baccalauréat or obtain between 10 and 12/20 in the Capacité en Droit examination

Entrance exams required: Every faculty organizes its own test every year

Numerus clausus/restrictions: No

Foreign students admission

Definition of foreign student: Students who do not have Togolese nationality

Quotas: Foreign student quotas are fixed each year for technical studies

Admission requirements: Foreign students must hold a Baccalauréat or an equivalent qualification. Students who do not hold the Baccalauréat must sit for an entrance examination for the faculties of Letters, Law, Science, Economics and Management.

Entry regulations: Foreign students must have a visa (except for students from CEDEAO countries) and a residence permit.

Health requirements: Students must have a health certificate.

Language requirements: Students must have a good knowledge of French. Courses are organized by the Village du Bénin to become proficient in French.

Application procedures:

Apply to: Université de Lomé
   B.P. 1515
   Lomé
   Tel: +228(221) 30-27
   Fax: +228(221) 87-84

Telex: 5258 ubto
WWW: http://www.ub.tg

Recognition of studies and qualifications:

Studies pursued in home country (System of recognition/accreditation): There is a university equivalence commission that examines the dossiers of foreign or Togolese students who wish to change courses. There is no system of evaluation of courses.

Studies pursued in foreign countries (bodies dealing with recognition of foreign credentials): Direction de l'Information des Relations Externes et de la Coopération Internationale

Director: Koffi Akibodé
BP 1515
Lomé
Tel: +228(221) 51-13
Fax: +228(221) 85-95
WWW: http://www.ub.tg

Deals with credential recognition for entry to: Profession
Services provided and students dealt with: Meets every three months to study Diplomas for professional purposes

Multilateral agreements concerning recognition of foreign studies

Name(s) of agreement(s): Conseil africain et malgache de l'Enseignement supérieur (CAMES)

Convention on the Recognition of Studies, Certificates, Diplomas, Degrees and Other Academic Qualifications in Higher Education in the African States
Year of signature: 1981

STUDENT LIFE

Main student services at national level

Centre national des Oeuvres universitaires (CNOU)
B.P. 1515
Lomé
WWW: http://www.ub.tg

Category of services provided: Social and welfare services

Direction des Affaires académiques et de la Scolarité, Université de Lomé
B.P. 1515
Lomé
Tel: +228(225) 48-44
Fax: +228(221) 87-84
WWW: http://www.ub.tg/

Category of services provided: Academic and career counselling services

Health/social provisions

Social security for home students: No

Social security for foreign students: No

Special student travel fares:

By road: No
By rail: No
By air: No

Student expenses and financial aid

Student costs:

Home students tuition fees: Minimum: 200,000 (CFA Franc)
Maximum: 500,000 (CFA Franc)
Foreign students tuition fees: Minimum: 200,000 (CFA Franc)
Maximum: 500,000 (CFA Franc)

Bodies providing information on student financial aid:

Direction des Bourses et Stages
Lomé
398
Tel: +228(221) 49-91
Fax: +228(221) 57-98

INTERNATIONAL COOPERATION AND EXCHANGES

Principal national bodies responsible for dealing with international cooperation and exchanges in higher education:

Direction de l'Information des Relations Externes et de la Coopération Internationale
Director: Koffi Akibodé
BP 1515
Lomé
Tel: +228 225-01-50
Fax: +228 221-85-95
WWW: http://www.ub.tg

Direction des Etudes et Programmes de l'Université de Lomé
Director: Ananivi Doh
B.P. 1515
Lomé
Tel: +228-225-08-37
Fax: +228-221-85-95
Telex: 5258 ubto
WWW: http://www.ub.tg

GRADING SYSTEM

Usual grading system in secondary school

Full Description: The grading system is as follows: 16-20: très bien (very good), 14-16: bien (good), 12-14: assez bien (quite good), 10-12: passable (average).
Highest on scale: 20
Pass/fail level: 10
Lowest on scale: 0

Main grading system used by higher education institutions

Full Description: Grading is usually on a scale of 0-20 (maximum): 16-20: très bien (very good), 14-16: bien (good), 12-14: assez bien (quite good), 10-12: passable (average).
Highest on scale: 20
Pass/fail level: 10
Lowest on scale: 0

Other main grading systems

Très bien; Bien; Assez bien; Passable; Refusé

NOTES ON HIGHER EDUCATION SYSTEM

Data for academic year: 2002-2003
Source: Université de Lomé, updated by the International Association of Universities (IAU) from IBE website, 2003 (www.ibe.unesco.org/International/Databanks/Wde/profilee.htm)

INSTITUTIONS OF HIGHER EDUCATION

UNIVERSITIES

UNIVERSITY OF KARA

Université de Kara
BP 43, Kara
Tel: +228(660) 12-74
Fax: +228(660) 12-74

Président: Aïssa Agbetra
Vice-Président: Koffi Ahadzi-Nonou
International Relations: Koffi A. Akibode

Faculties
Arts and Humanities (Arts and Humanities; Social Sciences)
Economics and Management (Economics; Management)
Law

History: Founded 2004.

*• UNIVERSITY OF LOMÉ

Université de Lomé (UL)
BP 1515, Lomé
Tel: +228(221) 53-61
Fax: +228(221) 85-95
EMail: cafmicro@ub.tg;contact_rectorat@ub.tg
Website: http://www.ub.tg

Recteur: Nicoué L. Gayibor (2004-) Tel: +228(221) 52-41
Fax: +228(221) 52-41 EMail: ub-lome@tgrefer.org
Vice-Président: Thiou T.K. Tchamie
International Relations: Koffi A. Akibode

Faculties
Arts and Humanities *(FLESH)* (Anthropology; Arts and Humanities; English; Geography; German; History; Linguistics; Philosophy; Social Sciences; Sociology; Spanish)
Economics and Management *(FASEG)* (Accountancy; Computer Science; Economics; Management; Mathematics; Statistics)
Law *(FDD)* (Administrative Law; Constitutional Law; International Law; Law; Public Law)
Medicine and Pharmacy *(FMMP)* (Medicine; Pharmacy)
Science *(FDS)* (Chemistry; Mathematics; Natural Sciences; Physics)

Higher Schools
Agriculture *(ESA)* (Agricultural Economics; Agricultural Engineering; Agriculture; Animal Husbandry; Rural Planning; Rural Studies)
Biological and Food Techniques (Biological and Life Sciences; Environmental Studies; Food Technology; Water Management; Water Science)

Engineering *(ENSI)* (Civil Engineering; Computer Engineering; Electrical Engineering; Engineering; Mechanical Engineering)
Medical Assistants *(EAM)* (Health Sciences)
Secretarial Studies *(ESSD)*

Institutes
Educational Sciences *(INSE)* (Education; Educational Sciences; Teacher Training)
Management Technology *(IUT)* (Management; Technology)

Centres
Computer *(CIC-CAFMICRO)* (Computer Engineering; Computer Science; Information Technology; Microelectronics; Systems Analysis)
Distance Learning Education *(CFAD)* (Educational Sciences; Law)

Research Units
Demography *(URD)* (Demography and Population)

History: Founded 1970 as University of Benin replacing former Centre d'Enseignement supérieur, established 1962 with sections in Dahomey and Togo under an agreement between the Governments of the two countries and Government of France. A State Institution enjoying academic and financial autonomy. Acquired present name 2001.

Governing Bodies: Grand Conseil, comprising 13 members; Conseil de l'Université, comprising 21 members

Academic Year: October to July (October-February; March-July)

Admission Requirements: Secondary school certificate (baccalauréat) or equivalent

Fees: (Francs CFA): foreign students, 200,000

Main Language(s) of Instruction: French

Degrees and Diplomas: *Capacité en Droit*: Law, 2 yrs; *Diplôme de Technicien supérieur (DTS)*: Laboratory Techniques, 3 yrs; *Diplôme universitaire de Technologie (DUT)*: Business Administration; Engineering, 3 yrs; *Diplôme universitaire d'Etudes générales (DUEG)*: 2 yrs; *Diplôme universitaire d'Etudes littéraires (DUEL)*: Arts and Humanities, 2 yrs; *Diplôme universitaire d'Etudes scientifiques (DUES)*: Science, 2 yrs; *Diplôme d'Ingénieur de Travaux*: 3 yrs; *Licence*: Arts and Humanities; Economics; Educational Sciences; Law; Science, 3 yrs; *Diplôme d'Ingénieur de Conception*: Agronomy; Civil Engineering; Electrical Engineering; Mechanical Engineering, 5 yrs; *Doctorat en Médecine*: 7 yrs; *Maîtrise*: 1 yr after Licence; *Certificat d'Etudes spécialisées (CES)*: Paediatrics; Surgery; *Diplôme d'Etudes approfondies (DEA)*: Science; *Doctorat d'Ingénieur*: 3 yrs; *Doctorat de Spécialité de Troisième Cycle*. Also Assistant médical, Paramedicine, 3 yrs.

Student Residential Facilities: For c. 2990 students

Libraries: Central Library, 70,000 vols; Specialized libraries

Publications: Annuaire de l'Université du Bénin; Annales de l'Université du Bénin; Actes des Journées Scientifiques (annually)

Press or Publishing House: Presses de l'Université du Bénin

Academic Staff *2001-2002:* Full-Time: c. 390 Part-Time: c. 260 Total: c. 650

Student Numbers *2001-2002:* Total: c. 15,000

OTHER UNIVERSITY LEVEL INSTITUTIONS

NATIONAL SCHOOL OF ADMINISTRATION
Ecole nationale d'Administration
BP 64, Lomé
Tel: +228 21-35-29
Website:
http://www.tg.refer.org/togo_ct/edu/sup/ena/accueil.htm

Programmes
Administration
Diplomacy (International Relations)
Economics and Finance (Economics; Finance)
Magistracy and Legal Careers (Justice Administration; Law)

History: Founded 1958 as École Togolaise d'Administration. Acquired present name and status 1979.

OTHER INSTITUTIONS

AFRICAN SCHOOL OF ARCHITECTURE AND TOWN PLANNING
Ecole africaine des Métiers de l'Architecture et de l'Urbanisme (EAMAU)
BP 2067, 422, rue des Balises, Quartier Doumassesse, Lomé
Tel: +228(221) 62-53
Fax: +228(222) 06-52
EMail: eamau@cafe.tg

Directeur général: N'Da N' Guessan Kouadio (1997-)
Tel: +228(225) 31-96 EMail: kouadio07@yahoo.com

International Relations: Gabriel Yabo Ogalama
Tel: +228(221) 70-79 EMail: gogalama@tg.refer.org

Founded: 1976
Architecture; Town Planning (Architecture; Town Planning; Urban Studies)

History: Founded 1976.

ADVANCED TEACHERS' TRAINING SCHOOL ATAKPAMÉ
Ecole normale supérieure d'Atakpamé (ENS)
BP 7, Atakpamé, Ogou
Tel: +228(440) 00-61

Directeur: Adji Sardji Aritiba (2000-)

Directeur des Etudes: Koffi Séto Notokpe

Founded: 1968, 1983

Departments
Art and Science Education (Art Education; Science Education) *Head:* Tohonon Gbeasor

English (Education; English; French; Linguistics) *Head:* Ms Degboe

French (Civics; Education; French; Linguistics) *Head:* M. Djabare

History and Geography (Civics; Education; Geography; History) *Head:* Nadjombé Notokpe

Mathematics (Chemistry; Education; Mathematics; Physics) *Head:* M. Sewonou

Natural Sciences (Chemistry; Education; Natural Sciences; Physics) *Head:* M. Akpagnonité

Physics and Chemistry (Chemistry; Education; Mathematics; Physics) *Head:* M. Mensah

History: Founded 1968 with financial aid from PNUD, UNESCO and UNICEF, acquired present status and title 1983.

Academic Year: September to June

Admission Requirements: Secondary school certificate (baccalauréat)

Fees: None (students are granted monthly allowances)

Main Language(s) of Instruction: French

Degrees and Diplomas: *Certificat d'Aptitude au Professorat de l'Enseignement secondaire (CAPES):* English; French; History; Geography (CFENS); Mathematics; Natural Sciences; Physics; Chemistry (CFENS), 3 yrs

Student Services: Sports Facilities, Canteen

Student Residential Facilities: Yes

Libraries: Main Library and Department Libraries

Academic Staff *2001-2002:* Full-Time: c. 15 Part-Time: c. 20 Total: c. 35

Staff with Doctorate: Total: c. 25

Student Numbers *2001-2002:* Total: c. 240

Tunisia

INSTITUTION TYPES AND CREDENTIALS

Types of higher education institutions:

Université (University)
Institut supérieur (Higher Institute)
Ecole supérieure (Higher School)
Institut supérieur des Etudes technologiques (Higher technological Institute)

School leaving and higher education credentials:

Baccalauréat
Certificat d'Aptitude
Diplôme universitaire de Technologie (DUT)
Technicien supérieur
Certificat de Capacité
Diplôme d'Etudes universitaires de Premier Cycle (DEUPC)
Diplôme universitaire d'Etudes littéraires (DUEL)
Diplôme universitaire d'Etudes scientifiques (DUES)
Diplôme
Licence
Diplôme d'Ingénieur
Maîtrise
Diplôme d'Architecte
Diplôme d'études supérieures spécialisées (DESS)
Mastère spécialisé
Diplôme de Recherches approfondies
Diplôme d'Etudes approfondies (DEA)
Mastère
Doctorat

STRUCTURE OF EDUCATION SYSTEM

Pre-higher education:

Duration of compulsory education:

Age of entry: 6
Age of exit: 16

Structure of school system:

> *Primary*
> Type of school providing this education: Ecole de Base (Premier Cycle)
> Length of programme in years: 6
> Age level from: 6 to: 12
>
> *Primary*
> Type of school providing this education: Ecole de Base (Second Cycle)
> Length of programme in years: 3
> Age level from: 12 to: 15
> Certificate/diploma awarded: Diplôme de Fin d'Etudes de l'Enseignement de Base
>
> *Secondary*
> Type of school providing this education: Ecole secondaire
> Length of programme in years: 4
> Age level from: 15 to: 19
> Certificate/diploma awarded: Baccalauréat

School education:

Basic education lasts for nine years, divided into two cycles of six and three years respectively. It culminates in the Diplôme de Fin d'Etudes de l'Enseignement de Base. Secondary education lasts four years and is divided into two stages (two years of general education and two years of pre-specialized education). It leads to the Baccalauréat in Arts, Mathematics, Experimental Sciences, Technology, Economy and Management. Vocational studies are available for those who have completed basic education. They lead to a vocational/ technical qualification. Students who have obtained 12 out of 20 or students who have completed the first cycle of secondary education may apply to study for a vocational/technical non-university level diploma.

Higher education:

Higher education is mainly provided by universities and their numerous higher institutes and schools. Institutions of higher education come under the responsibility of the Ministry of Higher Education, Scientific Research and Technology or the Ministry most appropriate to their speciality. The Conseil supérieur de l'Education, set up in 1988, is presided over by the Prime Minister and composed of all ministers having an interest in education and higher education. It is called upon to give its opinion on all major matters including financial policy. The Comité national d'Evaluation, created in 1995, evaluates higher education and university research as well as project results. Twenty new institutions opened in the year 2002-2003.

Main laws/decrees governing higher education:

Decree: Loi n° 2000-67   Year: 2000
Concerns: Modifies Law n° 89-70 of 1989

Decree: Loi n° 2000-73   Year: 2000
Concerns: Private higher education

Decree: Arrêté du Ministère de l'Enseignement supérieur   Year: 1996
Concerns: Composition of the Comité national d'Evaluation

Decree: Décret n °95-470   Year: 1995
Concerns: Comité national d'évaluation

Decree: Loi n° 90-72   Year: 1990
Concerns: Higher agricultural education

Decree: Loi n° 89-70   Year: 1989
Concerns: Organization of Higher Education

Academic year:

Classes from: September *to:* June

Long vacation from: 1 July *to:* 15 September

Languages of instruction:

Arabic, French

Stages of studies:

Non-university level post-secondary studies (technical/vocational type):

Higher technical education is mainly offered in higher institutes of technological studies (Instituts supérieurs des Etudes technologiques) where studies last for two-and-a-half years. Admission is on a competitive basis.Training is also offered in such fields as Agriculture, Nursing, Transport, Communications and Journalism. Studies come under the responsibility of the relevant ministries. A vocational/technical diploma is awarded after three years.

University level studies:

University level first stage: *First Cycle*:
The first cycle of university studies lasts for two years and leads to the Diplôme d'Etudes universitaires du 1er Cycle. In Engineering, studies start with two years in a preparatory institute, after which candidates must sit for a competitive examination. Engineering studies last for five years and lead to the Diplôme national d'Ingénieur.

University level second stage: *Second Cycle*:
The second cycle lasts for a further two years and leads to the award of the Maîtrise or Licence. In Engineering, studies last for three years after the two preparatory years and lead to the Diplôme d'Ingénieur. The Ministry is introducing a Diplôme des Etudes supérieures technologiques. The Diplôme d' Etudes supérieures spécialisées (DESS) is conferred after one year's study following upon the Maîtrise. There is a reform of studies leading to the Maîtrise in Engineering.

University level third stage: *Third Cycle*:
The third cycle leads to a Mastère (Master) after a further two or three semesters' study and to the Doctorat. The Doctorat de 3ème Cycle and the Doctorat d'Etat have been replaced by a single Doctorate. A Doctorate in Agricultural Sciences was introduced in 1993. In Medicine, the professional title of Docteur en Médecine is conferred after seven years.

Teacher education:

Training of pre-primary and primary/basic school teachers
Primary school teachers are trained in higher institutes (Instituts supérieurs de Formation des Maîtres) where they study for two years. They must hold the Baccalauréat.

Training of secondary school teachers
Secondary school teachers are usually university graduates in the arts and sciences. On-site training and formal retraining through continued education are also provided. A Doctorat en Sciences de l'Education, a Certificat d'Enseignement supérieur en Sciences de l'Education et en Pédagogie and a Maîtrise d'Education civique have been created for the teachers of the second cycle of basic education and secondary education.

Training of higher education teachers
The Maîtres-Assistants must hold the new Doctorate. Assistants must hold the Master and have started work on their doctoral thesis. Maîtres de conférence must hold a university research degree. In some disciplines, there exists a Tunisian form of Agrégation which is awarded after taking a competitive examination.

Non-traditional studies:

Distance higher education
A Virtual University was launched in 2001. Its objective is to provide 20% of courses through e-learning by 2006.

Lifelong higher education
Tunisia now has an Institute of Education and Continued Education which caters for primary and secondary school teachers. Lifelong training is also offered in Agriculture. Students can then become Technical Assistants, Assistant Engineers and Works Engineers. Nine institutions offer this kind of training. Lifelong education caters for mid-career professionals who seek further degree training in specialized and autonomous cycles.

Other forms of non-formal higher education
Supplementary education aims at enhancing the outgoing students' job prospects by training them in second competences and skills.

NATIONAL BODIES

Responsible authorities:

Ministry of Higher Education, Scientific Research and Technology (Ministère de l'Enseignement supérieur, de la Recherche et de la Technologie)
Minister: Sadok Chaâbane
Adminsitrative Officer: Sadok Korbi
International Relations: Noomane Ghodbane
Avenue Ouled Haffouz
1030   Tunis
Tel: +216(71) 784-170

Fax: +216(71) 786-711
Telex: 1380 minsup tn
EMail: mes@mes.tn
WWW: http://www.mes.tn

ADMISSIONS TO HIGHER EDUCATION

Admission to non university higher education studies

Name of secondary school credential required: Baccalauréat
For entry to: Higher Institutes for Technological Studies

Admission to university-level studies

Name of secondary school credential required: Baccalauréat
For entry to: All university institutions

Foreign students admission

Definition of foreign student: Non-national students.

Admission requirements: Foreign students must hold the Baccalauréat or an equivalent qualification. For some faculties, an entrance examination is also required. Students are entitled to social and welfare services and to grants and scholarships.

Entry regulations: A visa is necessary

Language requirements: Students must have a good knowledge of French and in some cases of Arabic (Theology, Arts, Law and Economics). A preparatory course in Arabic is organized at the Institut Bourguiba des Langues vivantes.

Recognition of studies and qualifications:

Studies pursued in foreign countries (bodies dealing with recognition of foreign credentials): Commission nationale d'Equivalence et d'Agrément des Ecoles techniques, Ministère de l'Enseignement supérieur
Rue Ouled Haffouz
Tunis
Tel: +216(71) 784-170
Fax: +216(71) 786-711
Telex: 1380 minsup tn
EMail: mes@mes.tn
WWW: http://www.mes.tn

Multilateral agreements concerning recognition of foreign studies

Name(s) of agreement(s): Convention on the Recognition of Studies, Diplomas and Degrees in Higher Education in the Arab States
Year of signature: 1978

References to further information on foreign student admissions and recognition of studies

Title: Guide du bachelier en langue française
Publisher: Office national des Oeuvres universitaires

STUDENT LIFE

Main student services at national level

Office national des Oeuvres universitaires (ONOU)
    57 rue de Palestine
    Tunis

    Category of services provided: Social and welfare services

National student associations and unions

Union générale des Etudiants tunisiens
    13 rue Essadikia
    Tunis

Student expenses and financial aid

Student costs:

    Average living costs: 4,000 (Tunisian Dinar)

Bodies providing information on student financial aid:

Direction de la Coopération internationale et des Relations extérieures, Ministère de l'Enseignement supérieur
    Avenue Ouled Haffouz
1030   Tunis
    Tel: +216(71) 786-300
    Fax: +216(1) 791-424

    Category of students: Students from all countries having a Secondary School Leaving Certificate (French or Arabic compulsory)

Office national du Tourisme tunisien
    1, avenue Mohamed-V
    Tunis
    Tel: +216(71) 835-844
    Fax: +216(71) 350-997
    WWW: http://www.tourismtunisia.com

    Category of students: Students from Francophone and Arab countries in the field of hotel management and tourism

Publications on student services and financial aid:

    Title: Study Abroad 2004-2005, 32nd Edition
    Author: UNESCO

Publisher: UNESCO Publishing
Year of publication: 2003

GRADING SYSTEM

Usual grading system in secondary school

Full Description: 0-20; 16-20 très bien; 14-15 bien; 12-14 assez bien; 10-12 passable; 0-9 insuffisant.
Highest on scale: 20
Pass/fail level: 10
Lowest on scale: 0

Main grading system used by higher education institutions

Full Description: 0-20; 16-20 très bien; 14-15 bien; 12-14 assez bien; 10-11 passable; 0-9 insuffisant.
Très bien is rarely awarded.
Highest on scale: 20
Pass/fail level: 10-11
Lowest on scale: 0

NOTES ON HIGHER EDUCATION SYSTEM

Data for academic year: 2002-2003
Source: Ministère de l'Enseignement supérieur, Tunis, 2003

INSTITUTIONS OF HIGHER EDUCATION

UNIVERSITIES

PUBLIC INSTITUTIONS

EZZITOUNA UNIVERSITY TUNIS

Université Ezzitouna Tunis
21, rue Sidi Jelizi , Place Maâkel Ezzaïm, Montfleury, 1008
Tunis
Tel: +216(71) 575-514
Fax: +216(71) 576-151
Website: http://www.mes.tn/u_zitouna/

Président: Boubaker El Khzouri **Tel:** +216(71) 575-870

Secrétaire général: Mohamed Dhelfani

International Relations: Khira Chibani

History: Founded 987.Acquired present status 1995.

Academic Year: September to June

Admission Requirements: Secondary school certificate
(baccalauréat)

Main Language(s) of Instruction: Arabic, French

Degrees and Diplomas: *Maîtrise*: Religion, 4 yrs; *Diplôme de
Recherches approfondies*: 2 yrs; *Doctorat*: 4 yrs

Student Services: Academic Counselling, Social Counselling,
Cultural Centre, Sports Facilities, Handicapped Facilities,
Health Services, Foreign Student Centre

Libraries: Bibliothèque centrale de l'Université, c. 40,000 vols

Publications: Al Mickat (annually)

Academic Staff *2001-2002*: Full-Time: c. 75 Part-Time: c. 10 Total:
c. 85

Student Numbers *2001-2002:* Total: c. 1,200

CENTRE FOR ISLAMIC STUDIES, KAIROUAN
CENTRE D'ETUDES ISLAMIQUES DE KAIROUAN
BP 209, Rue Beït el Hikma, 3100 Kairouan
Tel: +216(77) 232-669
Fax: +216(77) 234-844

Président: Harrath Bouallagui

Secrétaire général: Mohamed Badreddine

Programmes
Islamic Studies (Islamic Law; Islamic Studies; Islamic Theology; Koran)

History: Founded 1989.

HIGHER INSTITUTE OF ISLAMIC CIVILIZATION STUDIES,
TUNIS
INSTITUT SUPÉRIEUR DE LA CIVILISATION ISLAMIQUE
DE TUNIS
11, rue Jamaâ El Hawa, Place Maâkel Ez-Zaïm, Montfleury,
1088 Tunis
Tel: +216(71) 569-233
Fax: +216(71) 574-575

Directeur: Mehrez Hamdi **Tel:** +216(71) 569-237

Secrétaire général: Allala Maamouri

Programmes
Islamic Civilization Studies (Ancient Civilizations; Islamic
Studies)

History: Founded 1987.

HIGHER INSTITUTE OF THEOLOGY, TUNIS
INSTITUT SUPÉRIEUR DE THÉOLOGIE DE TUNIS
4, avenue Abou Zakaria El Hafsi, Montfleury, 1008 Tunis
Tel: +216(71) 575-870
Fax: +216(71) 576-555

Directeur: Salem Bouyahya **Tel:** +216(71) 569-237

Secrétaire général: Rachid Zaafrane

Programmes
Islamic Theology (Heritage Preservation; Islamic Studies; Islamic Theology; Koran; Multimedia; Theology)

History: Founded 1995.

LA MANOUBA UNIVERSITY, TUNIS

Université de La Manouba, Tunis
6, rue Sanaa, Cité Al Amal, 2010 Tunis
Tel: +216(71) 562-700
Fax: +216(71) 524-873
Website: http://www.mutan.org

Président: Moncef Hergli

Secrétaire général: Naceur Oueslati

Faculties
Letters (Arabic; English; French; Geography; German; History;
International Business; International Relations; Italian; Multime-
dia; Spanish; Translation and Interpretation) *Dean*: Mohamed
Ali Drissa

History: Founded 2001 from Faculty of Letters of Université
des Lettres, des Arts et des Sciences humaines (Tunis 1).

Governing Bodies: Ministry of Higher Education

Admission Requirements: Baccalauréat de l'Enseignement
secondaire

Main Language(s) of Instruction: Arabic, French

Degrees and Diplomas: *Maîtrise:* Languages, History, Geography, 4 yrs; *Diplôme d'Etudes approfondies (DEA):* Languages, History, Geography (DEA), 6 yrs

Student Residential Facilities: Yes

Libraries: Yes

Publications: Cahiers de Tunisie (annually); Revue des Langues

Academic Staff *2001-2002*	MEN	WOMEN	TOTAL
FULL-TIME	220	120	340
PART-TIME	38	12	50
TOTAL	**258**	**132**	**390**
STAFF WITH DOCTORATE			
FULL-TIME	137	39	176
PART-TIME	25	15	40
TOTAL	**162**	**54**	**216**

Student Numbers *2001-2002*	MEN	WOMEN	TOTAL
All (Foreign Included)	3,126	6,908	**10,034**
FOREIGN ONLY	5	14	19

HIGHER INSTITUTE OF ACCOUNTANCY AND BUSINESS ADMINISTRATION
INSTITUT SUPÉRIEUR DE COMPTABILITÉ ET D'ADMINISTRATION DES ENTREPRISES
4, rue des Entrepreneurs, Zone industrielle Charguia II, 2035 Tunis
Tel: +216(71) 701-018
Fax: +216(71) 701-270

Directeur: Samir Ghazouani Tel: +216(71) 940-480
Fax: +216(71) 941-170 EMail: samir.ghazouani@fsegt.rnu.tn

Departments
Accountancy *Head:* M. Bouattour
Economics and Quantitative Methods (Economics; Mathematics; Statistics) *Head:* Fatine Maghrebi
Law (Administrative Law; Commercial Law; Law) *Head:* Mohamed Kobbi
Management (Computer Science; Management; Systems Analysis) *Head:* Mougi Ben Ferjani

History: Founded 1988 as Ecole supérieure de Comptabilité, acquired present title 1995.

Academic Year: September to July (September-January; February-July)

Academic Staff *2001-2002:* Full-Time: c. 140 Part-Time: c. 40 Total: c. 180

Student Numbers *2001-2002:* Total: c. 2,500

HIGHER INSTITUTE FOR THE ADVANCEMENT OF THE DISABLED
INSTITUT SUPÉRIEUR DE PROMOTION DES HANDICAPÉS
2, rue Jabran Khalil Jabran, 2010 Manouba
Tel: +216(71) 520-588
Fax: +216(71) 521-267
EMail: iph@iph.org.tn

Directeur: Sarra Jarraya Tel: +216(71) 523-575

Programmes
Special Education Teacher Training (Education of the Handicapped; Psychology; Psychometrics; Social Psychology; Special Education; Teacher Trainers Education) *Director:* Tahar Midouni

History: Founded 1983, acquired present status and title 1990.

HIGHER INSTITUTE OF ARTS AND CRAFTS, TUNIS
INSTITUT SUPÉRIEUR DES ARTS ET MÉTIERS DE TUNIS
Ed Dendane, 2011 Tunis
Tel: +216(71) 610-700
Fax: +216(71) 610-750

Directeur: Raïf Malek (2000-)

Departments
Environmental Design (Architectural and Environmental Design; Design; Interior Design)
Graphic Design (Advertising and Publicity; Graphic Design)
Industrial Design (Crafts and Trades; Industrial Design; Packaging Technology)

History: Founded 2000.

Main Language(s) of Instruction: Arabic, French

HIGHER INSTITUTE OF DOCUMENTATION, TUNIS
INSTITUT SUPÉRIEUR DE DOCUMENTATION DE TUNIS
Campus universitaire, La Manouba, 2010 Tunis
Tel: +216(71) 601-550
Fax: +216(71) 600-200
EMail: isd@isd.rnu.tn

Directeur: Khaled Miled Tel: +216(98) 360-227
EMail: khaled.miled@flm.rnu.tn

Departments
Documentation (Archiving; Documentation Techniques; Library Science)

History: Founded 1981.

HIGHER INSTITUTE OF MULTIMEDIA ARTS, LA MANOUBA
INSTITUT SUPÉRIEUR DES ARTS DU MULTIMÉDIA DE LA MANOUBA
Campus universitaire, La Manouba, 2010 Tunis, Manouba
Tel: +216(71) 602-050
Fax: +216(71) 601-070

Directeur: Moncef Gafsi EMail: moncef.gafsi@ensi.rnu.tn

Programmes
Audio-visual Arts (Cinema and Television; Sound Engineering (Acoustics)) *Director:* Moncef Gafsi
Multimedia Arts (Graphic Design; Multimedia) *Director:* Moncef Gafsi

History: Founded 2001.

HIGHER INSTITUTE OF PHYSICAL EDUCATION AND SPORTS, KSAR SAÏD
INSTITUT SUPÉRIEUR D'EDUCATION PHYSIQUE ET DES SPORTS DE KSAR SAÏD

ISEPS Ksar Saïd Manouba, 2010 Tunis
Tel: +216(71) 508-416
Fax: +216(71) 513-425
EMail: crd@issep-ks.rnu.tn
Website: http://www.mes.tn/issep/default.htm

Directeur: Kamel Benzarti Tel: +216(71) 513-298

Secrétaire général: Salem Boughattas

Departments

Biological Sciences (Biological and Life Sciences) *Head*: Ridha Layouni
Educational Sciences and Pedagogy (Educational Sciences; Pedagogy) *Head*: Mongi Chabir
Physical Education and Sports *(collective level)* (Physical Education; Sports) *Head*: Daghbagi Gomri
Physical Education and Sports *(individual level)* (Physical Education; Sports) *Head*: Laâbidi Saï

History: Founded 1957 as Institut national d'Education physique et sportive, moved to Ksar Saïd 1959. Reorganized 1980 as Ecole normale supérieure de l'Education physique et du Sport. Acquired present status 1992 as Institut supérieur du Sport et de l'Education physique de Ksar Saïd, and present title 2001.

Governing Bodies: Conseil scientifique

Admission Requirements: Secondary school certificate (Baccalauréat) and entrance examination

Main Language(s) of Instruction: Arabic, French

HIGHER INSTITUTE OF THE PRESS AND INFORMATION SCIENCES
INSTITUT SUPÉRIEUR DE LA PRESSE ET DES SCIENCES DE L'INFORMATION

Campus universitaire, La Manouba, 2010 Tunis
Tel: +216(71) 600-980
Fax: +216(71) 600-465
EMail: ipsi@ipsi.rnu.tn

Directeur: Mustapha Hassen (1995-) Tel: +216(71) 600-981

Departments

Communication Studies
Fundamental Training (Information Sciences; Journalism)
Newspaper and Audioviual Press (Journalism)

History: Founded 1967 within Faculty of Letters of University of Tunis I, became autonomous institution 1973.

HIGHER SCHOOL OF COMMERCE, TUNIS
ECOLE SUPÉRIEURE DE COMMERCE DE TUNIS

4, rue des Entrepreneurs, Zone industrielle , Charguia II, 2035 Tunis
Tel: +216(71) 710-751
Fax: +216(71) 710-856

Directeur: Mohamed Zouaoui Tel: +216(71) 703-767

Secrétaire général: Habib Habouria

Departments

Banking
General Studies
Hospital Management (Health Administration)
International Trade (International Business)
Tourism Management (Tourism)

History: Founded 1987.

Academic Year: September to July (September-January; February-July)

Academic Staff *2001-2002:* Full-Time: c. 110 Part-Time: c. 30 Total: c. 140

Student Numbers *2001-2002:* Total: c. 2,010

INSTITUTE OF THE NATIONAL MOVEMENT
INSTITUT SUPÉRIEUR D'HISTOIRE DU MOUVEMENT NATIONAL

Campus Universitaire, La Manouba, 2010 Tunis
Tel: +216(71) 600-950
Fax: +216(71) 600-277
EMail: ishmn@ishmn.rnu.tn
Website: http://www.ishmn.rnu.tn

Directeur: Mohamed Lotfi Chaïebi

Secrétaire général: Mohamed Riadh Khammassi

Programmes

African Studies
Contemporary History (Contemporary History; History)

History: Founded 1990.

NATIONAL SCHOOL OF COMPUTER SCIENCE
ECOLE NATIONALE DES SCIENCES DE L'INFORMATIQUE

Campus universitaire, La Manouba, 2010 Tunis
Tel: +216(71) 706-267
Fax: +216(71) 706-297
EMail: a.benyoussef@ensi.rnu.tn

Directeur: Abdelhamid Ben Youssef Tel: +216(71) 600-224

Secrétaire général: Naceur Mrabet

Programmes

Computer Science (Computer Engineering; Computer Networks; Computer Science; Software Engineering; Systems Analysis)

History: Founded 1985.

NATIONAL SCHOOL OF VETERINARY MEDICINE, SIDI THABET
ECOLE NATIONALE DE MÉDECINE VÉTÉRINAIRE DE SIDI THABET

Sidi Thabet, 2020 Ariana
Tel: +216(71) 552-200
Fax: +216(71) 569-692

Directeur: Atef Malek

Departments

Animal Husbandry (Animal Husbandry; Zoology) *Head*: Jamel Rekhis

Clinical Sciences (Surgery; Veterinary Science; Zoology) *Head*: Nourredine Ben Chehida

Fundamental Sciences (Animal Husbandry; Veterinary Science; Zoology) *Head*: Abdelhamid Matoussi

History: Founded 1974.

* UNIVERSITY OF THE CENTRE, SOUSSE

Université du Centre, Sousse

BP 526, Avenue Khelifa Elkaroui Sahloul IV, 4002 Sousse
Tel: +216(73) 368-000 +216(73) 234-011
Fax: +216(73) 368-126 +216(73) 234-013
EMail: universite.centre@uc.rnu.tn
Website: http://www.universites.tn/univ_centre/index.htm

Président: Mohamed Ali Hamza (2002-)
Tel: +216(73) 368-125 EMail: President.U.Centre@uc.rnu.tn

Secrétaire général: Béchir Bel Hadj Yahya
Tel: +216(73) 239-344 Fax: +216(73) 234-013

Faculties

Arts and Humanities (Arabic; Education; English; French; Geography; History) *Dean*: Hédi Jatlaoui

Arts and Humanities *(Kairouan)* (Arabic; Archaeology; English; French; Philosophy) *Dean*: Mohamed Essahbi Allani

Dentistry *(Monastir)* (Dental Technology; Dentistry) *Dean*: Khaled Bouraoui

Economics and Management *(Mahdia)* (Economics; Management) *Dean*: Ali Fraj

Law, Economics and Political Science (Commercial Law; Economics; Finance; Fiscal Law; International Economics; Law; Management; Political Science; Private Law; Public Law) *Dean*: Ali Frej

Medicine (Community Health; Gynaecology and Obstetrics; Medicine; Nursing; Paediatrics; Surgery) *Dean*: Béchir Bel Hadj Ali

Medicine *(Monastir)* (Community Health; Gynaecology and Obstetrics; Medicine; Nursing; Paediatrics; Surgery) *Dean*: Habbib Sabbah

Pharmacy *(Monastir)* (Animal Husbandry; Biochemistry; Biology; Botany; Cell Biology; Haematology; Immunology; Microbiology; Parasitology; Pharmacology; Pharmacy; Physiology; Toxicology) *Dean*: Rached Azaiez

Science *(Monastir)* (Analytical Chemistry; Applied Mathematics; Biological and Life Sciences; Chemistry; Computer Science; Earth Sciences; Electronic Engineering; Mathematics; Natural Sciences; Physics) *Dean*: Mongi Ben Amara

History: Founded 1986 as Université de Monastir pour le Centre. Acquired present title 1999.

Governing Bodies: University Senate, comprising the President, the Secretary-General and the Deans and delegates of the University

Academic Year: September to July (September-February; February-July)

Admission Requirements: Secondary school certificate (baccalauréat)

Main Language(s) of Instruction: Arabic, French, English

Degrees and Diplomas: *Technicien supérieur*: Engineering; Information Technology; Transport and Communication; Horticulture; Marine Transport; Science, 2-3 yrs; *Diplôme d'Etudes universitaires de Premier Cycle (DEUPC)*: Arts and Humanities; Economics; Law; Management, 2 yrs; *Diplôme*: Pharmacy, 5 yrs; *Diplôme d'Ingénieur*: Engineering; Horticulture; *Maîtrise*: Accountancy; Arts and Humanities; Economics; Law; Management; Science, 4 yrs; *Diplôme d'études supérieures spécialisées (DESS)*: Medicine; Pharmacy; Science; *Diplôme d'Etudes approfondies (DEA)*: Law; Pharmacy; Science (DA); Engineering, 5-6 yrs; *Mastère*: Engineering; *Doctorat*: Pharmacy; Science; Dentistry, 6 yrs; Medicine, 7 yrs

Student Residential Facilities: Yes

Publications: Publications of the faculties

Academic Staff *2002-2003:* Total: **1,832**

Staff with doctorate: Total: **1,494**

Student Numbers *2002-2003:* Total: **58,252**

HIGHER INSTITUTE OF APPLIED LANGUAGES FOR BUSINESS AND TOURISM, MOKNINE

INSTITUT SUPÉRIEUR DES LANGUES APPLIQUÉES AUX AFFAIRES ET AU TOURISME DE MOKNINE
Avenue des Martyrs, Route de Jammel, 5050 Moknine
Tel: +216(73) 437-100
Fax: +216(73) 437-100

Directeur: Mansour Mhenni (2001-)

Secrétaire général: Younes Ghorbali

Programmes

Applied Languages (Applied Linguistics; Arabic; Business and Commerce; English; Italian; Modern Languages; Spanish; Tourism; Translation and Interpretation)

History: Founded 2001.

HIGHER INSTITUTE OF APPLIED SCIENCES AND TECHNOLOGY, SOUSSE

INSTITUT SUPÉRIEUR DES SCIENCES APPLIQUÉES ET DE TECHNOLOGIE DE SOUSSE
Cité Taffala, Ibn Khaldoun, 4003 Sousse
Tel: +216(73) 332-657
Fax: +216(73) 333-658

Directeur: Younès Bouazra (2001-) Tel: +216(73) 333-659
Fax: +216(73) 332-656

Secrétaire général: Fethi Khayri

Departments
Electronic Engineering
Information Technology
Mechanical Engineering

History: Founded 1998.

HIGHER INSTITUTE OF BIOTECHNOLOGY, MONASTIR
INSTITUT SUPÉRIEUR DE BIOTECHNOLOGIE DE
MONASTIR
Boulevard de l'environnement, 5000 Monastir
Tel: +216(73) 505-405
Fax: +216(73) 505-404

Directeur: Ahmed Noureddine Helal (2001-)

Secrétaire général: Abderrazak Hachana

Programmes
Biotechnology

History: Founded 2001.

INSTITUTE OF HIGHER COMMERCIAL STUDIES
INSTITUT DES HAUTES ETUDES COMMERCIALES DE
SOUSSE
Rue Abd-Elaziz Elbahi, Sousse
Tel: +216(73) 332-976
Fax: +216(73) 331-491

Directeur: Lotfi Belkacem

Secrétaire général: Mohamed Naceur Kahla

Programmes
Accountancy
Commerce (Business and Commerce)
Finance

HIGHER INSTITUTE OF COMPUTER SCIENCE AND
COMMUNICATION TECHNOLOGY, HAMMAM-SOUSSE
INSTITUT SUPÉRIEUR D'INFORMATIQUE ET DES
TECHNIQUES DE COMMUNICATION DE
HAMMAM-SOUSSE
5 bis, rue du 1er juin 1955, 4089 Hammam-Sousse
Tel: +216(73) 364-410
Fax: +216(73) 364-411

Directeur: Rafik Brahem (2001-)

Secrétaire général: Chiheb Belkhiria

Programmes
Communication Technology (Information Technology)
Computer Science

History: Founded 2001.

HIGHER INSTITUTE OF COMPUTER SCIENCE AND
MANAGEMENT, KAIROUAN
INSTITUT SUPÉRIEUR D'INFORMATIQUE ET DE GESTION
DE KAIROUAN
Rue Assad Ibn El Fourat, Kairouan
Tel: +216(77) 236-571
Fax: +216(77) 236-543

Directeur: Abdessatar Elbarrek

Secrétaire général: Nacer Ayari

Programmes
Economics and Management (Economics; Management)

HIGHER INSTITUTE OF COMPUTER SCIENCE AND
MATHEMATICS, MONASTIR
INSTITUT SUPÉRIEUR D'INFORMATIQUE ET DE
MATHÉMATIQUES DE MONASTIR
BP 24, Monastir
Tel: +216(73) 274-373
Website: http://www.mes.tn/isim_mo/index.htm

Directeur: Habib Youssef

Secrétaire général: Chicheb Ben Ali

Programmes
Mathematics and Computer Science (Applied Mathematics;
Computer Networks; Information Sciences; Mathematics; Sta-
tistics; Telecommunications Engineering)

History: Founded 2002.

Degrees and Diplomas: *Technicien supérieur; Maîtrise*

HIGHER INSTITUTE OF CRAFTS AND TRADES,
KAIROUAN
INSTITUT SUPÉRIEUR DES ARTS ET METIERS DE
KAIROUAN
Avenue Kortouba
Tel: +216(77) 237-812
Fax: +216(77) 237-812

Directeur: Amor Kraiem

Secrétaire général: Mohamed Jaouadi

Programmes
Design
Furniture Design
Graphic Arts

HIGHER INSTITUTE OF FASHION TRADES, MONASTIR
INSTITUT SUPÉRIEUR DES MÉTIERS DE LA MODE DE
MONASTIR
Voie El-kornich -Stah Jaber, Monastir
Tel: +216(73) 504-534
Fax: +216(73) 461-423

Directeur: Faten Elskhiri

Secrétaire général: Abdelfattah Elsakli

Programmes
Fashion Design
Retailing (Retailing and Wholesaling)
Textile Design

HIGHER INSTITUTE OF FINANCE AND FISCALITY,
SOUSSE
INSTITUT SUPÉRIEUR DE FINANCE ET DE FISCALITE DE
SOUSSE
Avenue Abou Elkassem Elchabi, Sousse
Tel: +216(73) 671-230
Fax: +216(73) 222-700

Directeur: Néjib Belaid

Secrétaire général: Abdel Majid Elmasoudi

Programmes
Finance

HIGHER INSTITUTE OF FINE ARTS, SOUSSE
INSTITUT SUPÉRIEUR DES BEAUX ARTS DE SOUSSE
Place de la Gare, 4000 Sousse
Tel: +216(73) 214-333
Fax: +216(73) 214-334

Directrice: Aziza Mrabet (2000-) Tel: +216(73) 214-334
Secrétaire général: Lotfi Chouri

Programmes
Computer-Aided Design (Computer Graphics; Painting and Drawing; Visual Arts)
Fine Arts (Fine Arts; Painting and Drawing; Sculpture)
Interior Design

History: Founded 2000.
Main Language(s) of Instruction: Arabic, French
Degrees and Diplomas: *Diplôme d'Etudes universitaires de Premier Cycle (DEUPC)*

HIGHER INSTITUTE OF MANAGEMENT, SOUSSE
INSTITUT SUPÉRIEUR DE GESTION DE SOUSSE
Rue Abed Aziz El Bahi, 4000 Sousse
Tel: +216(73) 332-976
Fax: +216(73) 332-978

Directeur: Fayçal Mansouri Tel: +216(73) 332-977
Secrétaire général: Salem Mahjoub

Departments
Accountancy and Finance (Accountancy; Finance)
Economics (Economics; International Business)
Law (Commercial Law; Law; Private Law; Public Law)
Management (Management; Management Systems)
Quantitative Methods and Information Technology (Information Technology; Management Systems)

History: Founded 1995.
Main Language(s) of Instruction: Arabic, French, English
Degrees and Diplomas: *Technicien supérieur; Maîtrise; Diplôme d'études supérieures spécialisées (DESS)*

HIGHER INSTITUTE OF MUSIC, SOUSSE
INSTITUT SUPÉRIEUR DE MUSIQUE DE SOUSSE
Avenue Abou Kacem Chebbi, 4000 Sousse
Tel: +216(73) 239-555
Fax: +216(73) 239-555

Directeur: Mohamed Zinelabidine (2000-)
Tel: +216(73) 239-554

Programmes
Music (Music; Music Theory and Composition; Musical Instruments; Musicology)

History: Founded 1999.
Degrees and Diplomas: *Maîtrise*

HIGHER INSTITUTE OF TRANSPORT MANAGEMENT, SOUSSE
INSTITUT SUPÉRIEUR DU TRANSPORT ET DE LA LOGISTIQUE DE SOUSSE
12, rue Abdallah Ibn Ezzoubeïr, 4000 Sousse
Tel: +216(73) 226-365
Fax: +216(73) 226-211
Website: http://www.mes.tn/istls

Directeur: Mustapha Belhareth (2001-)
Secrétaire général: Moncef Sougir

Programmes
Transport Management
Transports (Transport and Communications)

History: Founded 2001.
Degrees and Diplomas: *Technicien supérieur; Maîtrise*

HIGHER SCHOOL OF HEALTH SCIENCES AND TECHNIQUES, MONASTIR
ECOLE SUPÉRIEURE DES SCIENCES ET TECHNIQUES DE LA SANTÉ DE MONASTIR
Rue Ibn Sina, 5000 Monastir
Tel: +216(73) 462-477
Fax: +216(73) 464-599

Directeur: Habib Hassine Tel: +216(73) 460-482
Secrétaire général: Mohamed Lamjed Saâd

Departments
Anaesthesiology
Dental Prosthetics (Dental Technology)
Human Biology (Biology)
Obstetrics (Gynaecology and Obstetrics)
Radiology and Radiotherapy (Radiology)
Rehabilitation (Rehabilitation and Therapy)

History: Founded 1990.
Main Language(s) of Instruction: Arabic, French

HIGHER SCHOOL OF HORTICULTURE, CHOTT-MERIEM
ECOLE SUPÉRIEURE D'HORTICULTURE DE CHOTT-MERIEM
Chott-Meriem, 4042 Sousse
Tel: +216(73) 348-546
Fax: +216(73) 348-691

Directeur: Mohamed Habib Mahjoub Tel: +216(73) 348-544
Secrétaire général: Ridha Rouis

Departments
Biological Sciences (Animal Husbandry; Biochemistry; Biological and Life Sciences; Botany; Cattle Breeding; Chemistry; Food Technology; Plant and Crop Protection; Plant Pathology; Zoology)
Economics and Social Sciences (Agricultural Economics; Economics; Management; Mathematics; Rural Planning; Social Sciences; Statistics)
Horticulture (Crop Production; Fruit Production; Horticulture; Landscape Architecture; Plant and Crop Protection; Plant Pathology)

Plant Protection (Entomology; Parasitology; Plant and Crop Protection; Plant Pathology)
Soil, Water and Environment (Agricultural Engineering; Agronomy; Environmental Studies; Mechanics; Meteorology; Natural Resources; Physics; Soil Science; Water Science)

History: Founded 1975.

HIGHER SCHOOL OF HEALTH SCIENCES AND
TECHNIQUES, SOUSSE
ECOLE SUPÉRIEURE DES SCIENCES ET TECHNIQUES
DE LA SANTÉ DE SOUSSE
BP103 - La Poste Sahloul, Sousse
Tel: +216(73) 369-308

Directeur: Rafiaa Nouira
Secrétaire général: Rajaa Beltaief

Programmes
Health Sciences (Nursing; Rehabilitation and Therapy; Secretarial Studies; Surgery)

History: Founded 2001.
Degrees and Diplomas: *Technicien supérieur*

HIGHER INSTITUTE OF APPLIED STUDIES IN THE
HUMANITIES OF MAHDIA
INSTITUT SUPÉRIEUR DES ETUDES APPLIQUÉES EN
HUMANITÉS DE MAHDIA
Route Rajech-Mahdia, Sousse
Tel: +216(73) 693-501
Fax: +216(73) 693-518

Directeur: Hachemi Bannour Tel: +216(73) 226-211

Programmes
Arts and Humanities

History: Founded 1968.
Main Language(s) of Instruction: Arabic, French

NATIONAL SCHOOL OF ENGINEERING, MONASTIR
ECOLE NATIONALE D'INGÉNIEURS DE MONASTIR
Rue Ibn El Jazzar, 5000 Monastir
Tel: +216(73) 500-244
Fax: +216(73) 500-514
EMail: enim@rnrt.tn

Directeur: Sassi Ben Nasrallah Tel: +216(73) 500-405
Secrétaire général: Mohamed Fekri Kraïem

Departments
Electrical Engineering (Electrical Engineering; Electronic Engineering; Systems Analysis)
Energy Engineering (Energy Engineering; Environmental Engineering; Thermal Engineering)
Mechanical Engineering (Industrial Design; Industrial Engineering; Mechanical Engineering)
Textile Engineering (Chemical Engineering; Polymer and Plastics Technology; Textile Technology)

History: Founded 1987.

Main Language(s) of Instruction: Arabic, French

PREPARATORY INSTITUTE FOR ENGINEERING STUDIES,
MONASTIR
INSTITUT PRÉPARATOIRE AUX ETUDES D'INGÉNIEURS
DE MONASTIR
Route de Kairouan, 5000 Monastir
Tel: +216(73) 500-273
Fax: +216(73) 500-512

Directeur: Bechir Ben Hassine Tel: +216(73) 500-277
Secrétaire général: Jamelleddine Boudriga

Departments
Mathematics and Physics (Mathematics and Computer Science; Physics)
Physics and Chemistry (Chemistry; Mechanical Engineering; Mechanics; Physics)
Technology (Engineering; Natural Sciences; Technology)

History: Founded 1992.
Main Language(s) of Instruction: Arabic, French

UNIVERSITY OF JENDOUBA
Université de Jendouba
8110 Tabarka
Tel: +216(78) 670-542
Fax: +216(78) 670-471

Président: Mustapha Nasraoui

Faculties
Law, Economics and Management *Dean:* Hassouna Fdhila

Higher Institutes
Applied Languages and Computer Science *(Béja)* (Computer Science; Modern Languages) *Directeur:* Imed Ben Ammar
Applied Studies in the Humanities *(du Kef)* (Arts and Humanities) *Directeur:* Youssef Othmani
Humanities *(Jendouba)* (Arts and Humanities) *Directeur:* Mohamed Raja Rahmouni

History: Founded 1970.

FORESTRY INSTITUTE
INSTITUT SYLVO-PASTORAL DE TABARKA
8110 Tabarka
Tel: +216(78) 670-542
Fax: +216(78) 670-471

Directeur: Lamjed Toumi

Programmes
Forestry

History: Founded 1970.

HIGHER INSTITUTE OF PHYSICAL EDUCATION OF LE KEF
INSTITUT SUPÉRIEUR D'EDUCATION PHYSIQUE DU KEF
Cité Eddir, 7100 Le Kef
Tel: +216(78) 224-240
Fax: +216(78) 224-251

Directeur: Youssef Boussaidi

Secrétaire général: Mohamed Sdiri

Programmes
Physical Education

History: Founded 1990.

HIGHER SCHOOL OF AGRICULTURE OF LE KEF
ECOLE SUPÉRIEURE D'AGRICULTURE DU KEF
7119 Le Kef
Fax: +216(78) 223-137

Directeur: Nasraoui Bouzid

Secrétaire général: Mohamed Snoussi

Programmes
Agriculture

History: Founded 1981.

HIGHER SCHOOL OF RURAL ENGINEERING, MEDJEZ EL BAB
ECOLE SUPÉRIEURE DES INGÉNIEURS DE L'EQUIPEMENT RURAL DE MEDJEZ EL BAB
Route du Kef km 5, 9070 Medjez El Bab
Tel: +216(78) 562-300
Fax: +216(78) 561-700

Directeur: Tijani El Mehouachi

Secrétaire général: Abed El Melak El Hechemi

Schools
Agricultural Engineering
Rural Engineering (Rural Planning)

History: Founded 1976.

• UNIVERSITY OF 7TH NOVEMBER AT CARTHAGE
Université du 7 novembre à Carthage
29 rue Asdrubal, 1002 Tunis
Tel: +216(1) 787-502
Fax: +216(1) 788-768
Website: http://www.univ7nc.rnu.tn

Président: Taïeb Hadhri (2001-) Tel: +216(71) 788-768

Secrétaire général: Mohamed Ameur Ismaïl
Tel: +216(71) 841-353

International Relations: Kaouther Hedhly
Tel: +216(71) 841-353 EMail: Kaouther.hedly@tun3.rnu.tn

Faculties
Economics and Management *(Nabeul)* (Economics; International Economics; Management; Social Policy) *Dean:* Ezzeddine Zouari

Law, Political and Social Sciences (Commercial Law; Criminal Law; Law; Political Science; Public Administration; Public Law; Social Sciences) *Dean:* Mohamed Saleh Ben Aissa

Science *(Bizerte)* (Biology; Chemistry; Computer Science; Electronic Engineering; Food Technology; Industrial Chemistry; Information Technology; Mathematics and Computer Science; Natural Sciences; Physics; Telecommunications Engineering) *Dean:* Chaabane Chefi

History: Founded 1987, reorganized 1989 as Université de Droit, d'Economie et de Gestion (Tunis III), and acquired present title 2001.

Academic Year: September to June (September-January; February-June)

Admission Requirements: Secondary school certificate (baccalauréat)

Fees: (Dinars): c. 30-100 per annum

Main Language(s) of Instruction: French, Arabic, English

International Co-operation: With universities in France; Italy; Canada; United Kingdom; Japan; Russia; Austria; Belgium; USA

Accrediting Agencies: AUF; AUA

Degrees and Diplomas: *Diplôme d'Etudes universitaires de Premier Cycle (DEUPC):* Accountancy; Administration; Commerce; Economics; Labour Studies; Law; Management; Social Studies, 2 yrs; *Diplôme:* Hotel Management; Tourism; *Maîtrise:* Accountancy; Administration; Economics; Labour Studies; Law; Management; Social Studies, 4 yrs; *Diplôme d'études supérieures spécialisées (DESS):* Commerce; Economics; Management, a year following Maîtrise; *Diplôme d'Etudes approfondies (DEA):* Economics; Labour Studies; Law; Management, a further 1-2 years following Maîtrise; Accountancy, a further 1-2 yrs following Maîtrise; *Doctorat:* Economics; Law; Management. Also courses towards the Certificat d'Etudes Spécialisées (CES) awarded in Accountancy by the University of Law, Economics and Management (Tunis III)

Student Services: Social Counselling, Sports Facilities, Handicapped Facilities, Canteen

Student Residential Facilities: Yes

Libraries: University Library

Academic Staff *2001-2002:* Total: **2,003**

Student Numbers 2001-2002	MEN	WOMEN	TOTAL
All (Foreign Included)	14,532	16,058	**30,590**

CENTRE FOR LAW AND JUSTICE STUDIES
CENTRE D'ETUDES JURIDIQUES ET JUDICIAIRES
2, rue de l'Artisanat, Zone industrielle, La Charguia, 2035 Tunis
Tel: +216(71) 707-992
Fax: +216(71) 702-896

Directrice: Saida Jaouida Guiga

Programmes
Law and Justice Studies (Law)
Main Language(s) of Instruction: Arabic, French

HIGHER INSTITUTE OF EXECUTIVES FOR YOUTH
INSTITUT SUPÉRIEUR DES CADRES DE L'ENFANCE
26, avenue Taïeb Mhiri, 2016 Carthage
Tel: +216(71) 730-436
Fax: +216(71) 733-215
EMail: isce@email.ati.tn
Directeur: Tahar Abid

Programmes
Teacher Trainers Education (Arts and Humanities; Communication Studies; Environmental Studies; Health Education; Music Education; Native Language Education; Preschool Education; Primary Education; Statistics; Teacher Trainers Education; Teacher Training)

History: Founded 1989.
Main Language(s) of Instruction: Arabic, French

HIGHER INSTITUTE OF FINE ARTS, NABEUL
INSTITUT SUPÉRIEUR DES BEAUX-ARTS DE NABEUL
Avenue Ali Belhaouane, 8000 Nabeul
Tel: +216(72) 232-210
Fax: +216(72) 232-144
EMail: ipein@ipein.rnu.tn
Website: http://www.mes.tn/ipein/index.htm
Directeur: Hayet Tlili Tel: +216(72) 232-144

Departments
Arts and Communication (Communication Studies; Graphic Design; Visual Arts)
Plastic Arts (Ceramic Art; Fine Arts; Glass Art; Painting and Drawing; Sculpture)

History: Founded 2000.

HIGHER INSTITUTE OF FISHERY AND AQUACULTURE, BIZERTE
INSTITUT SUPÉRIEUR DE PÊCHE ET D'AQUACULTURE DE BIZERTE

Programmes
Fishing and Aquaculture (Aquaculture; Fishery)

History: Founded 2003.

HIGHER INSTITUTE OF LANGUAGES, TUNIS
INSTITUT SUPÉRIEUR DES LANGUES DE TUNIS
14 Ibn Maja, Cité El Khadra, 1003 Tunis
Tel: +216(71) 773-813
Fax: +216(71) 770-134
Directeur: Mohamed Miled Tel: +216(71) 772-460

Departments
Arabic and Translation (Arabic; English; Translation and Interpretation) *Head*: Taoufik Hamdi

English *Head*: Nourreddine Fgair
French *Head*: Mohamed Naceur Bouguatef
Languages (Modern Languages) *Head*: Mourad Ben Abderrak
Specialized English (English)

History: Founded 1968. Acquired present status 1999.

Main Language(s) of Instruction: Arabic, French

HIGHER INSTITUTE OF STATISTICS AND INFORMATION ANALYSIS
INSTITUT SUPÉRIEUR DES STATISTIQUE ET DE L'ANALYSE DE L'INFORMATION
1080 Tunis
Tel: +216(71) 703-717
Fax: +216(71) 704-329
Directeur: Mekki Ksouri Tel: +216(71) 703-746
Fax: +216(71) 708-559 EMail: Mekki.Ksouri@iisetr.mu.tn

Departments
Information Analysis (Computer Science; Econometrics; Information Sciences) *Head*: Nacef Elloumi
Statistics (Applied Mathematics; Statistics) *Head*: Nacef Elloumi

History: Founded 2001.

HIGHER SCHOOL OF AGRICULTURE, MATEUR
ECOLE SUPÉRIEURE D'AGRICULTURE DE MATEUR
7030 Mateur
Tel: +216(72) 465-565
Fax: +216(72) 468-088
Directeur: Abdelhak Ben Younes Tel: +216(71) 703-103
EMail: Abdouli.hedi@iresa.agrinet
Secrétaire général: Tahar Mazlout

Departments
Agriculture (Agricultural Engineering; Agriculture)

History: Founded 1981.

HIGHER SCHOOL OF AGRICULTURE, MOGRANE
ECOLE SUPÉRIEURE D'AGRICULTURE DE MOGRANE
1121 Mograne-Zaghouan
Tel: +216(72) 660-283
Fax: +216(72) 660-563
EMail: souissi.abderrazaki@iresa.agrinet.tn
Directeur: Abderrazak Souissi

Departments
Agriculture (Agricultural Engineering; Agriculture)

History: Founded 1981.

HIGHER SCHOOL OF COMMUNICATION, TUNIS
ECOLE SUPÉRIEURE DES COMMUNICATIONS DE TUNIS
Route de Raoued Km. 3,5, Cité El Gharella, 2083 Ariana
Tel: +216(71) 857-000
Fax: +216(71) 856-829

Directeur: Naceur Ammar
EMail: naceur.ammar@supcom.rnu.tn

Departments
Applied Mathematics, Signals and Communication (Applied Mathematics; Telecommunications Engineering) *Head:* Ziad Belhaj
Computer Science and Networks (Computer Networks; Computer Science) *Head:* Hamza Rached
Physics, Electronics and Propagation (Electronic Engineering; Physics) *Head:* Adel Ghazel

History: Founded 1974. Acquired present status 1998.

HIGHER SCHOOL OF FOOD INDUSTRIES, TUNIS
ECOLE SUPÉRIEURE DES INDUSTRIES ALIMENTAIRES
DE TUNIS
58, rue Alain Savary, El Khadra, 1003 Tunis
Tel: +216(71) 799-680
Fax: +216(71) 286-437
Website: http://www.mes.tn/esiat/index.htm

Director: Abdelkader Chérif
EMail: cherif.abdelkader@iresa.agrinet.tn

Departments
Basic Science (Natural Sciences)
Food Processing (Food Technology)
Food Technology

History: Founded 1976.

INSTITUTE OF HIGHER BUSINESS STUDIES,
CARTAGENA
INSTITUT DES HAUTES ETUDES COMMERCIALES DE
CARTHAGE
2016 Carthage
Tel: +216(71) 774-720
Fax: +216(71) 775-944
Website: http://www.mes.tn/ihec/

Directeur: Mohamed Goaïed Tel: +216(71) 703-103

Departments
Accountancy
General Studies
Management Studies (Business and Commerce; Economics; Law; Management; Marketing; Mathematics)
Tourism and Hotel Management (Hotel Management; Tourism)

History: Founded 1942.
Academic Year: September to June (September-January; February-June)
Academic Staff *2001-2002:* Full-Time: c. 120 Part-Time: c. 20 Total: c. 140
Student Numbers *2001-2002:* Total: c. 2,350

NATIONAL AGRICULTURAL INSTITUTE, TUNIS
INSTITUT NATIONAL AGRONOMIQUE DE TUNIS
43, avenue Charles Nicolle , Cité Mahrajène, Le Belvédère,
2002 Tunis
Fax: +216(71) 287-110
Telex: +276(71) 799-391

Director: Fethi El Lebdi Tel: +216(71) 840-270

Programmes
Agronomy (Agriculture; Agronomy) *Head:* Moncef Harrabi

History: Founded 1970, acquired present status 1989.

NATIONAL AGRICULTURAL RESEARCH INSTITUTE OF
TUNIS
INSTITUT NATIONAL DE RECHERCHES AGRONOMIQUES
DE TUNIS
Rue Hédi Karray, 2049 Ariana
Tel: +216(71) 230-739
Fax: +216(71) 752-897

Directeur: Netij Ben Mchila (2001-) Tel: +216(71) 230-024

Institutes
Crop Production and Small Ruminants Research (Agricultural Economics; Agronomy; Animal Husbandry; Botany; Cattle Breeding; Crop Production; Laboratory Techniques; Plant Pathology; Zoology)
Further Information: Also 18 Research stations nation-wide

History: Founded 1913, acquired present status and title 1964.
Main Language(s) of Instruction: Arabic, French

NATIONAL INSTITUTE OF APPLIED SCIENCES AND
TECHNOLOGY
INSTITUT NATIONAL DES SCIENCES APPLIQUÉES ET DE
TECHNOLOGIE
BP 676, Centre urbain nord, 2035 Tunis
Tel: +216(71) 703-627
Fax: +216(71) 704-329
EMail: webmaster@insat.rnu.tn
Website: http://www.mes.tn/insat/index.htm

Director: Mekki Ksouri (1999-) Tel: +216(71) 703-746
EMail: mekki.ksouri@isetr.rnu.tn

Departments
Biological and Chemical Engineering (Applied Chemistry; Applied Mathematics; Applied Physics; Bioengineering; Biological and Life Sciences; Chemical Engineering; Natural Sciences; Technology) *Head:* Mokhtar Hamdi
Mathematics and Computer Engineering (Computer Engineering; Mathematics and Computer Science) *Head:* Hedi Amara
Physical and Measurement Engineering (Measurement and Precision Engineering; Physical Engineering)

History: Founded 1996.
Governing Bodies: Conseil d'administration; Conseil scientifique et pédagogique
Main Language(s) of Instruction: Arabic, French

NATIONAL INSTITUTE OF LABOUR AND SOCIAL STUDIES
INSTITUT NATIONAL DU TRAVAIL ET DES ETUDES
SOCIALES
BP 692, 44, rue de l'Artisanat, 2035 La Charguia II Z I
Tel: +216(71) 706-207
Fax: +216(71) 703-464
EMail: intes@intes.rnu.tn
Website: http://www.intes.rnu.tn
Directeur: Abdessatar Moualhi Tel: +216(71) 703-103

Departments
Continuing Education (Social Studies; Statistics) *Head:* Ali Belhadj
Labour Sciences (Labour and Industrial Relations) *Head:* Lofti Bennour
Social Studies (Economics; Social Studies; Statistics) *Head:* Lassad Laabidi

History: Founded 1983.
Academic Year: September to July (September-January; February-July)
Main Language(s) of Instruction: Arabic, French
Academic Staff *2001-2002:* Full-Time: c. 110 Part-Time: c. 75 Total: c. 185
Student Numbers *2001-2002:* Total: c. 1,600

NATIONAL RESEARCH INSTITUTE OF RURAL, WATER
AND FORESTRY ENGINEERING
INSTITUT NATIONAL DE RECHERCHES EN GÉNIE
RURAL, EAUX ET FORÊTS
BP 10, 2080 Ariana
Tel: +216(71) 718-055
Fax: +216(71) 717-952
Director: Mohamed Néjib Rejeb (1996-)
Tel: +216(71) 709-033 EMail: rejeb.nejib@iresa.agrinet.tn
Secrétaire générale: Khalifa Gharsallah

Departments
Regional Planning

Institutes
Rural, Water and Forestry Engineering (Agricultural Engineering; Agricultural Equipment; Forest Management; Forestry; Irrigation; Rural Planning; Soil Conservation; Water Management; Water Science) *Director:* Mohamed Nejib Rejeb

History: Founded 1996.
Main Language(s) of Instruction: Arabic, French

NATIONAL SCHOOL OF ARCHITECTURE AND TOWN
PLANNING, TUNIS
ECOLE NATIONALE D'ARCHITECTURE ET D'URBANISME
DE TUNIS
Rue El Kodes, 2026 Sidi Bou Saïd
Tel: +216(71) 729-197 +216(71) 729-198
Fax: +216(71) 729-264
Directeur: Mouldi Chaabani Tel: +216(71) 729-263
Fax: +216(71) 729-264

Departments
Architecture *Head:* Faouzi Chabchoub
Town Planning *Head:* Abdelmajid Kolsi

History: Founded 1973. Acquired present status 1995.

POLYTECHNIC SCHOOL OF TUNISIA
ECOLE POLYTECHNIQUE DE TUNISIE
BP 743, 2078 La Marsa
Tel: +216(71) 774-611
Fax: +216(71) 748-843
Directeur: Jmaiel Ben Ibrahim (2001-)

Departments
Applied Mathematics and Computer Science (Applied Mathematics; Mathematics and Computer Science) *Director:* Riadh Robbana
Economics *Director:* Adel Dhif
Electricity (Electrical Engineering) *Director:* Abdelaziz Samet
Languages and Communication (Communication Studies; Modern Languages) *Director:* Bechir Bouaicha
Mechanics (Mechanical Engineering; Mechanics) *Director:* Lamia Guellouz

History: Founded 1991 as Branch of Université de Tunis El Manar, became Branch of Université du 7 novembre à Carthage 2001.

PREPARATORY INSTITUTE FOR ENGINEERING STUDIES
OF BIZERTE
INSTITUT PRÉPARATOIRE AUX ETUDES D'INGÉNIEUR
DE BIZERTE

Programmes
Engineering (Biology; Engineering; Geology)

History: Founded 2003.

PREPARATORY INSTITUTE FOR ENGINEERING STUDIES,
MATEUR
INSTITUT PRÉPARATOIRE AUX ETUDES D'INGÉNIEURS
DE MATEUR
Route de Tabarka, 7030 Mateur
Tel: +216(72) 466-481
Fax: +216(72) 466-044
Directeur: Abdelhak Ben Younes Tel: +216(72) 448-544

Institutes
Engineering (Chemistry; Engineering; Mathematics; Physics; Technology) *Director:* Radhouane Tarhouni

History: Founded 1995 as Branch of Université Tunis El Manar, became Branch of Université du 7 Novembre à Carthage 2001.
Main Language(s) of Instruction: Arabic, French

PREPARATORY INSTITUTE FOR ENGINEERING STUDIES, NABEUL

INSTITUT PRÉPARATOIRE AUX ETUDES D'INGÉNIEURS DE NABEUL

Campus Universitaire Merazka, 8000 Nabeul

Tel: +216(72) 220-033

Fax: +216(72) 220-181

EMail: ipein@ipein.rnu.tn

Website: http://www.mes.tn/ipein/index.htm

Directeur: Abdelghani Ben Hadj Amor Tel: +216(72) 220-091

Departments

Mathematics and Physics (Mathematics; Physics) *Head*: Slaheddine El Mokthar

Physics and Chemistry (Chemistry; Physics) *Head*: Nourddine Yacoubi

Technology (Engineering; Technology) *Head*: Habib Bougezzala

Research Units

Physics and Chemistry (Chemistry; Materials Engineering; Optics; Physics; Thermal Engineering) *Head*: Nourddine Yacoubi

History: Founded 1986 as Branch of Université de Tunis El Manar, became Branch of Université du 7 Novembre à Carthage 2001.

Governing Bodies: Conseil scientifique

Accrediting Agencies: Ministère de l'Enseignement Supérieur

PREPARATORY INSTITUTE FOR SCIENTIFIC AND TECHNICAL STUDIES, LA MARSA

INSTITUT PRÉPARATOIRE AUX ETUDES SCIENTIFIQUES ET TECHNIQUES DE LA MARSA

BP 51, 2035 La Marsa

Tel: +216(71) 740-048

Fax: +216(71) 746-551

EMail: webmaster@insat.rnu.tn

Website: http://www.mes.tn/insat/index.htm

Directeur: Hassen Maaref (2001-) Tel: +216(71) 741-836

EMail: hassen.maaref@fsm.rnu.tn

Departments

Preparatory Studies for the Agrégation (Chemistry; Mathematics; Physics) *Head*: Hikmet Smida

Preparatory Studies for the Competitive Entrance Examination to Schools of Engineering (Chemistry; Mathematics; Mathematics and Computer Science; Physics; Technology) *Head*: Chokri Mrabet

History: Founded 1991.

UNIVERSITY OF SFAX FOR THE SOUTH

Université de Sfax pour le Sud (USS)

Route de l'Aéroport Km. 0,5, 3029 Sfax

Tel: +216(74) 240-678

Fax: +216(74) 240-913

EMail: sodki.triki@uss.rnu.tn

Website: http://www.mes.tn/uss/index.htm

Président: Hamed Ben Dhia Tel: +216(74) 240-986

EMail: hamed.bendhia@uss.rnu.tn

Secrétaire général: Mohamed Mahfoudh

Tel: +216(74) 240-200 Fax: +216(74) 240-200

Faculties

Arts and Humanities (Arabic; Arts and Humanities; English; French; Geography; Heritage Preservation; History; Philosophy; Sociology; Tourism; Translation and Interpretation) *Dean*: Mohsen Dhieb

Economics and Management (Accountancy; Business and Commerce; Business Computing; Economics; Finance; Human Resources; Management; Management Systems; Marketing) *Dean*: Ali Chkir

Law (Commercial Law; International Law; Law; Private Law; Public Law) *Dean*: Ahmed Omrane

Medicine (Biology; Biophysics; Community Health; Embryology and Reproduction Biology; Gender Studies; Genetics; Gynaecology and Obstetrics; Haematology; Histology; Medicine; Microbiology; Neurosciences; Paramedical Sciences; Sports Medicine; Urology) *Dean*: Adnane Hammami

Science (Biology; Computer Science; Earth Sciences; Mathematics; Natural Sciences; Physics; Telecommunications Engineering) *Dean*: Abdelhamid Ben Salah

Science *(Gabès)* (Biological and Life Sciences; Chemistry; Earth Sciences; Mathematics; Natural Sciences; Physics) *Dean*: Mohamed Mars

Science *(Gafsa)* (Biological and Life Sciences; Chemistry; Computer Science; Earth Sciences; Mathematics; Natural Sciences; Physics) *Dean*: Elaïd Belkhiri

History: Founded 1986.

Governing Bodies: Conseil de l'Université, comprising 42 members

Academic Year: September to July (September-January; February-July)

Admission Requirements: Secondary school certificate (baccalauréat)

Main Language(s) of Instruction: French, Arabic

International Co-operation: With Institutions in Mauritania, Morocco, Algeria, Libya, France, Belgium, Italy, Egypt, Saudi Arabia

Degrees and Diplomas: *Technicien supérieur*: Engineering; Health Sciences; Management; Technology, 2 yrs; Biotechnology; Business Computing; Computer and Telecommunications Engineering; Computer Engineering; Computer Science; Computer Science and Multimedia; Computer Systems Maintenance; Music, Musicology; Production Management; Safety Engineering; Software Engineering, 3 yrs; *Diplôme d'Etudes universitaires de Premier Cycle (DEUPC)*: Arts and Humanities; Economics; Management; Science, 2 yrs; *Diplôme*: Arts;

Physical Education, 2 yrs; *Diplôme d'Ingénieur*: 4-6 yrs; Biotechnology; Computer Engineering and Telecommunications Engineering; Computer Science, 5 yrs; *Maîtrise*: Accountancy; Arts and Humanities; Business and Commerce; Business Computing; Economics; Finance; French, English, Spanish; Law; Music; Physical Education; Production Management; Safety Engineering; Science; Software Engineering; Taxation, 4 yrs; *Diplôme d'études supérieures spécialisées (DESS)*: Business Administration; Engineering; Medicine; *Diplôme d'Etudes approfondies (DEA)*: Economics; Arts and Humanities; Business Administration; Engineering; Fine Arts; Law; Mathematics and Computer Science; Natural Sciences; Science; Technology and Computer Science, a further 2 yrs following Maîtrise; *Doctorat*: Economics; Engineering; Law; Mathematics and Computer Science; Natural Sciences; Science; Technology; Medicine, 7 yrs. Thèse d'Université, 3 yrs. Habilitation: Economics, Law, Mathematics and Computer Science, Natural Sciences, Engineering

Libraries: Total, c. 215,500 vols

Publications: UnivEchos

Academic Staff *2001-2002:* Total: **2,357**

Student Numbers *2001-2002*	TOTAL
All (Foreign Included)	**46,216**
FOREIGN ONLY	471

HIGHER INSTITUTE OF FINE ARTS, SFAX
INSTITUT SUPÉRIEUR DES ARTS ET MÉTIERS DE SFAX
34, avenue du 5 Août, 3002 Sfax
Tel: +216(74) 299-593
Fax: +216(74) 297-286

Directeur: Noureddine El Heni Tel: +216(74) 299-511

Secrétaire général: Mouncef Kossentini

Programmes

Design (Design; Fashion Design; Industrial Design; Interior Design; Textile Design)
Plastic Arts (Ceramic Art; Engraving; Handicrafts; Painting and Drawing; Sculpture; Visual Arts; Weaving)

History: Founded 1995.

Main Language(s) of Instruction: Arabic, French

BIOTECHNOLOGY CENTRE, SFAX
CENTRE DE BIOTECHNOLOGIE DE SFAX
BP 358, Route de la Sokra Km. 4, 3038 Sfax
Tel: +216(74) 274-110
Fax: +216(74) 275-970
EMail: ellouz@cbs.rnrt.tn

Directeur: Radhouane Ellouz (1988-)

Units

Bioenergy (Biotechnology)
Cell Biology
Metabolites (Biotechnology; Cell Biology)
Sugar (Food Technology)
Vegetal Biotechnology (Biotechnology; Genetics; Microbiology)

History: Founded 1988.

Main Language(s) of Instruction: Arabic, French
Academic Staff: Total: c. 20

HIGHER INSTITUTE FOR APPLIED SCIENCES AND TECHNOLOGY, GABÈS
INSTITUT SUPÉRIEUR DES SCIENCES APPLIQUÉES ET DE TECHNOLOGIE DE GABÈS
Route de Médenine, 6029 Gabès
Tel: +216(75) 392-108
Fax: +216(75) 392-390

Directeur: Mohieddine Alaoui (1992-) Tel: +216(75) 392-404

Secrétaire général: Hassen Trabelsi

Departments

Chemistry (Biological and Life Sciences; Chemistry) *Director*: Farhat Habachi
Mathematics and Computer Science *Director*: Jilani Alaya
Physics and Technology (Physics; Technology) *Director*: Romdhane Ben Slama

History: Founded 1992.

Main Language(s) of Instruction: Arabic, French

Academic Staff *2001-2002:* Total: c. 65

Student Numbers *2001-2002:* Total: c. 800

HIGHER INSTITUTE OF APPLIED STUDIES IN HUMANITIES, GAFSA
INSTITUT SUPÉRIEUR DES ETUDES APPLIQUÉES EN HUMANITÉS DE GAFSA
Cité des Jeunes, 2133 Gafsa
Tel: +216(76) 224-328
Fax: +216(76) 211-051

Directeur: Ibrahim Jadla (2001-) Tel: +216(76) 211-051

Programmes

Arts and Humanities (Arts and Humanities; Heritage Preservation; Photography; Tourism)

History: Founded 2001.

Main Language(s) of Instruction: Arabic, French

HIGHER INSTITUTE OF ARTS AND CRAFTS, GABÈS
INSTITUT SUPÉRIEUR DES ARTS ET MÉTIERS DE GABÈS
Avenue Aboul Elkacem Echabbi, 6000 Gabès
Tel: +216(75) 273-522
Fax: +216(75) 273-499

Directeur: Mohamed Mohsen Zeraï

Secrétaire général: Mohamed Hfidhi

Programmes

Arts and Crafts (Ceramic Art; Crafts and Trades; Fine Arts; Graphic Arts; Interior Design; Weaving)

History: Founded 2001.

Main Language(s) of Instruction: Arabic, French

HIGHER INSTITUTE OF BIOTECHNOLOGY, SFAX
INSTITUT SUPÉRIEUR DE BIOTECHNOLOGIE DE SFAX
Route M'harza Km 1, Sfax
Tel: +216(74) 247-560
Fax: +216(74) 247-560

Directrice: Besma Hentati

Programmes
Biotechnology

History: Founded 2002.

HIGHER INSTITUTE OF BUSINESS ADMINISTRATION,
GAFSA
INSTITUT SUPÉRIEUR DE GESTION DES ENTREPRISES
DE GAFSA
Gafsa

Programmes
Business Administration
Finance, Banking and Insurance (Banking; Finance; Insurance)

History: Founded 2003.

HIGHER INSTITUTE OF BUSINESS ADMINISTRATION,
SFAX
INSTITUT SUPÉRIEUR D'ADMINISTRATION DES
AFFAIRES DE SFAX
Route de Mharza Km 1, 3018 Sfax
Tel: +216(74) 452-350
Fax: +216(74) 452-640

Directeur: Abdelwaheb Rebaï (2001-) Tel: +216(74) 452-640
Secrétaire général: Raouf Turki

Programmes
Business Administration (Administration; Business Administration; Management; Management Systems)

History: Founded 2001.

Main Language(s) of Instruction: Arabic, French

HIGHER INSTITUTE OF ELECTRONICS AND
TELECOMMUNICATION TECHNOLOGY, SFAX
INSTITUT SUPÉRIEUR D'ELECTRONIQUE ET DE
TECHNOLOGIE DE TÉLÉCOMMUNICATION DE SFAX
Route Menzel Chaker Km 1, Sfax
Tel: +216(74) 247-498

Directeur: Lotfi Kamoun (2002-)

Programmes
Electronic Engineering
Telecommunications Engineering

History: Founded 2002.

NATIONAL SCHOOL OF ENGINEERING, SFAX
ECOLE NATIONALE D'INGÉNIEURS DE SFAX
Route de la Soukra Km. 4, 3038 Sfax
Tel: +216(74) 274-088
Fax: +216(74) 275-595

Directeur: Boubaker El Euch (1998-) Tel: +216(74) 274-409
Secrétaire général: Moncef Abida

Departments
Applied Mathematics and Computer Science (Applied Mathematics; Mathematics; Mathematics and Computer Science) *Director*: Fahti Ghribi
Biological Engineering (Bioengineering; Environmental Engineering) *Director*: Youssef Talel Gargouri
Electrical Engineering *Director*: Lofti Kammoun
Geological Engineering (Geological Engineering; Natural Resources) *Director*: Mohamed Jamel Rouis
Materials Engineering (Chemistry; Materials Engineering) *Director*: Mohieddine Fourati
Mechanical Engineering (Automation and Control Engineering; Industrial Engineering; Mechanical Engineering) *Director*: Chedli Bradai

History: Founded 1983.

Main Language(s) of Instruction: Arabic, French

HIGHER INSTITUTE OF COMPUTER SCIENCE AND
MULTIMEDIA, SFAX
INSTITUT SUPÉRIEUR D'INFORMATIQUE ET DE
MULTIMÉDIA DE SFAX
Route de Mharza Km. 1.5, 3000 Sfax
Tel: +216(74) 452-632

Directeur: Abdelmajid Ben Hamadou (2001-)
Secrétaire général: Hamda Kamoun

Programmes
Computer Science
Multimedia Studies (Multimedia)

History: Founded 2001.

Main Language(s) of Instruction: Arabic, French

HIGHER INSTITUTE OF INDUSTRIAL MANAGEMENT,
SFAX
INSTITUT SUPÉRIEUR DE GESTION INDUSTIELLE DE
SFAX
Route Sidi Mansour, Sfax
Tel: +216(74) 272-980
Fax: +216(74) 272-980

Directeur: Habib Chabchoub (2002-)

Departments
Management

History: Founded 2002.

537

HIGHER INSTITUTE FOR INFORMATICS AND
MULTIMEDIA, GABÈS
INSTITUT SUPÉRIEUR D'INFORMATIQUE ET DE
MULTIMÉDIA, GABÈS
Complexe Universitaire Cité Erriadh Zrik, 6072 Gabès
Tel: +216(75) 394-229
Fax: +216(75) 394-309
Directeur: M. Abdelrazzak Jdai (2002-)

Departments
Computer Science

History: Founded 2002.

HIGHER INSTITUTE OF LANGUAGES, GABÈS
INSTITUT SUPÉRIEUR DES LANGUES DE GABÈS
6029 Gabès
Tel: +216(75) 274-244
Fax: 216(75) 274-522
Directeur: Noureddine Lammouchi (2000-)
Tel: +216(75) 274-344
Secrétaire général: Mohamed Zekri

Departments
English
French
Services and Communication Studies (Administration; Administrative Law; Arabic; Communication Studies; Geography; German; Italian; Labour Law; Secretarial Studies; Sociology; Tourism; Translation and Interpretation)

History: Founded 2000.
Main Language(s) of Instruction: Arabic, French

HIGHER INSTITUTE OF LEGAL STUDIES, GABÈS
INSTITUT SUPÉRIEUR DES ETUDES JURIDIQUES DE
GABÈS
Gabès

Programmes
Business Law (Commercial Law)
Fiscal Studies (Fiscal Law)
Legal Affairs (Law)

HIGHER INSTITUTE OF MANAGEMENT, GABÈS
INSTITUT SUPÉRIEUR DE GESTION DE GABÈS
Avenue Habib Jilani, 6002 Gabès
Tel: +216(75) 270-096
Fax: +216(75) 270-686
Directeur: Jilani Alaya (1998-) Tel: +216(75) 272-280
Secrétaire général: Sahbi Souaissa Tel: +216(75) 276-090

Departments
Economics
Finance
Management (Accountancy; Management)
Quantitative Methods (Management Systems)

History: Founded 1998.

Governing Bodies: Conseil scientifique
Main Language(s) of Instruction: Arabic, French

HIGHER INSTITUTE OF MUSIC, SFAX
INSTITUT SUPÉRIEUR DE MUSIQUE DE SFAX
Rue Maghreb Arabe - B.P. 143, 3049 Sfax
Tel: +216(74) 225-545
Fax: +216(74) 220-610
Directeur: Mourad Siala (1999-) Tel: +216(74) 220-610
Secrétaire général: Mohamed Triki

Programmes
Music (Music; Music Theory and Composition; Musical Instruments)
Music and Musicology (Music; Musicology)
Musicology (Folklore; Musicology; Oriental Studies)

History: Founded 1999.
Admission Requirements: Secondary school certificate (Baccalauréat) and entrance examination
Main Language(s) of Instruction: Arabic, French

HIGHER INSTITUTE OF PHYSICAL EDUCATION AND
SPORTS, SFAX
INSTITUT SUPÉRIEUR DU SPORT ET D' EDUCATION
PHYSIQUE DE SFAX
Route de l'Aéroport Km 3.5, 3023 Sfax
Tel: +216(74) 278-504
Fax: +216(74) 278-502
Directeur: Jalel Miladi Tel: +216(74) 278-505
Secrétaire général: Noureddine Mnif

Departments
Physical Education and Sports (Physical Education; Sports)

History: Founded 1989.
Main Language(s) of Instruction: Arabic, French

HIGHER SCHOOL OF COMMERCE, SFAX
ECOLE SUPÉRIEURE DE COMMERCE DE SFAX
Route de l'Aérodrome Km. 4,5, 3018 Sfax
Tel: +216(74) 279-620
Fax: +216(74) 278-630
Directeur: Abdelkader Chaâbane Tel: +216(74) 279-410
Secrétaire général: Abdelmajid Torjmène
Tel: +216(74) 278-870

Departments
Accountancy
Business and Commerce (Business and Commerce; Management)
Finance (Finance; Management Systems)
International Business (International Business; International Relations; Management)

History: Founded 1995.
Main Language(s) of Instruction: Arabic, French

HIGHER SCHOOL OF HEALTH SCIENCES AND
TECHNIQUES, SFAX
ECOLE SUPÉRIEURE DES SCIENCES ET TECHNIQUES
DE LA SANTÉ DE SFAX
Avenue Majida Boulila, 3003 Sfax
Tel: +216(74) 241-971
Fax: +216(74) 246-821

Directrice: Mongia Hachicha Tel: +216(75) 241-923
Secrétaire général: Abdelwaheb Mseddi
Tel: +216(74) 241-902

Departments
Health Sciences and Technology (Alternative Medicine;
Anaesthesiology; Biology; Gynaecology and Obstetrics; Health
Sciences; Medical Technology; Physical Therapy; Psychiatry
and Mental Health; Radiology)

History: Founded 1989.

Main Language(s) of Instruction: Arabic, French

INSTITUTE OF ARID ZONE STUDIES, MÉDENINE
INSTITUT DES RÉGIONS ARIDES DE MÉDENINE
4119 Médenine
Tel: +216(75) 633-121
Fax: +216(75) 633-006

Directeur: Houcine Khattali Tel: +216(75) 633-122
Secrétaire général: Jilani Ezzemzmi

Laboratories
Agronomy
Animal Husbandry (Animal Husbandry; Environmental
Management)
Environmental Studies (Arid Land Studies; Environmental
Studies)
Pastoral Ecology (Ecology; Environmental Management)
Rural Planning (Environmental Studies; Natural Resources;
Rural Planning; Rural Studies)

History: Founded 1976.

Main Language(s) of Instruction: Arabic, French

INSTITUTE FOR HIGHER COMMERCIAL STUDIES, SFAX
INSTITUT DES HAUTES ETUDES COMMERCIALES DE
SFAX
Route Sidi Mansour Km10, Sfax
Tel: +216(74) 272-980
Fax: +216(74) 272-980

Directrice: Faika Scander Charfi

History: Founded 2002.

NATIONAL SCHOOL OF ENGINEERING, GABÈS
ECOLE NATIONALE D'INGÉNIEURS DE GABÈS
Route de Medenine, 6029 Gabès
Tel: +216(75) 393-100
Fax: +216(75) 392-190
EMail: contact@enig.rnu.tn
Website: http://www.mes.tn/enig/index.htm

Directeur: Abdelatif El Gadri Tel: +216(75) 392-257
Secrétaire général: Malek Ezzammouri
Tel: +216(75) 392-257

Departments
Automation and Electrical Engineering (Automation and
Control Engineering; Electrical Engineering; Power
Engineering)
Chemical Engineering (Analytical Chemistry; Applied Mathe-
matics; Chemical Engineering; Computer Science; Industrial
Chemistry; Thermal Engineering)
Civil Engineering (Applied Mathematics; Arabic; Architecture;
Civil Engineering; Computer Science; Construction Engineer-
ing; Electronic Engineering; English; French; Geology; Materi-
als Engineering; Road Engineering; Town Planning; Water
Management)

Centres
Computer Science (Mathematics and Computer Science;
Statistics)

History: Founded 1975.

Main Language(s) of Instruction: Arabic, French

PREPARATORY INSTITUTE FOR ENGINEERING STUDIES,
SFAX
INSTITUT PRÉPARATOIRE AUX ETUDES D'INGÉNIEURS
DE SFAX
Route Menzel Chaker Km. 0,5, 3018 Sfax
Tel: +216(74) 241-403
Fax: +216(74) 246-347

Directeur: Fathi Laadhar Tel: +216(74) 241-733
Secrétaire général: Ridha Triki

Departments
Biology *Director:* Fayçel Turki
Chemistry *Director:* Samir Djemel
Mathematics and Computer Science *Director:* Ameur
Ch'hayder
Physics *Director:* Hassiba B. Halima Ketata

History: Founded 1992.

Main Language(s) of Instruction: Arabic, French
Academic Staff *2001-2002:* Total: c. 80
Student Numbers *2001-2002:* Total: c. 1,250

ZITOUNA INSTITUTE, SFAX
INSTITUT DE L'OLIVIER DE SFAX
BP 1087, Route de l'Aéroport Km. 1,5, 3029 Sfax
Tel: +216(74) 241-589
Fax: +216(74) 241-033

Directeur: Taieb Jardak Tel: +216(74) 241-240

Programmes
Olive Research (Agricultural Economics; Agronomy; Arid Land
Studies; Biology; Food Science; Harvest Technology; Physiol-
ogy; Plant and Crop Protection; Technology; Vegetable
Production)

History: Founded 1981.

Main Language(s) of Instruction: Arabic, French

UNIVERSITY OF TUNIS
Université de Tunis
92, avenue du 9 avril 1938, 1007 Tunis
Tel: +216(71) 567-322
Fax: +216(71) 560-633
Website: http://www.utunis.rnu.tn

Président: Abderraouf Mahbouli Tel: +216(71) 562-700
Secrétaire général: Lamjed Messoussi

Faculties

Humanities and Social Sciences (Arabic; Arts and Humanities; Civics; English; French; Geography (Human); History; Philosophy; Psychology; Social Sciences; Sociology) *Dean:* Habib Dlala

History: Founded 1988. Acquired present status 2001.

Governing Bodies: Councils of the University and its constituent faculties and schools

Academic Year: October to June (October-February; February-June)

Admission Requirements: Secondary school certificate (baccalauréat) or foreign equivalent

Main Language(s) of Instruction: Arabic, French, English

Degrees and Diplomas: *Technicien supérieur:* Commerce, 2 yrs; Economics and Management, a further 2 yrs following Licence; *Diplôme universitaire d'Etudes littéraires (DUEL):* 2 yrs; *Diplôme universitaire d'Etudes scientifiques (DUES):* 2 yrs; *Licence; Maîtrise:* Commerce; Economics and Management; Law; Letters, 4 yrs; *Diplôme d'Etudes approfondies (DEA):* Science (DEA), a further 1-2 yrs following Maîtrise; *Mastère:* History, Geography, Philosophy, Sociology, a further 1-2 yrs following upon Maîtrise; *Doctorat:* Arabic Language and Literature; Medicine, 6 yrs; Letters; Science, a further 2-3 yrs following DEA

Student Services: Cultural Centre, Sports Facilities, Health Services

Libraries: Total, c. 186,000 vols

Publications: Cahiers de Tunisie (quarterly); Revue géographique

Academic Staff *2000:* Total: **1,280**

Student Numbers *2000:* Total: **32,000**

CENTRE FOR ECONOMIC AND SOCIAL STUDIES AND RESEARCH
CENTRE D'ETUDES ET DE RECHERCHES ÉCONOMIQUES ET SOCIALES
23, rue d'Espagne, 1000 Tunis
Tel: +216(71) 244-810
Fax: +216(71) 343-237

Directeur: Hachmi Labaïed

Programmes
Economics and Social Studies (Economics; Social Studies)

HIGHER INSTITUTE OF APPLIED STUDIES IN HUMANITIES, TUNIS
INSTITUT SUPÉRIEUR DES ETUDES APPLIQUÉES EN HUMANITÉS DE TUNIS
23, avenue Hédi Saidi, El Omrane, 1005 Tunis
Tel: +216(71) 899-006
Fax: +216(71) 899-118

Directeur: Jamel Ben Tahar (2000-)
Secrétaire général: Abdellah Belarbi

Programmes
Culture and Civilization (Cultural Studies; Painting and Drawing; Psychology; Sociology; Sports)
Languages (Arabic; English; French)
Plastic Arts (Fine Arts)
Techniques (Communication Studies; Computer Education; Documentation Techniques)

History: Founded 2000.
Main Language(s) of Instruction: Arabic, French

HIGHER INSTITUTE OF CULTURAL STUDIES AND HERITAGE PROFESSIONS OF TUNIS
INSTITUT SUPÉRIEUR DES SCIENCES CULTURELLES ET MÉTIERS DU PATRIMOINE DE TUNIS
10, rue Kelibia, 1002 Tunis
Tel: +216(71) 286-224
Fax: +216(71) 285-978

Directeur: Habib Baklouti
Secrétaire général: Mohamed Salah Ben Miled

Programmes
Cultural Studies
Heritage (Cultural Studies; Heritage Preservation)
Main Language(s) of Instruction: Arabic, French

HIGHER INSTITUTE OF DRAMA
INSTITUT SUPÉRIEUR D'ART DRAMATIQUE
16, rue Mikhaïl Nouaima, El Omrane, 1005 Tunis
Tel: +216(71) 891-333
Fax: +216(71) 289-612

Directeur: Mohamed El Mediouni (1995-)
Secrétaire général: Faouzi Mahmoud

Programmes
Dramatic Art (Acting; Performing Arts; Theatre)

History: Founded 1982.

HIGHER INSTITUTE OF EDUCATION AND CONTINUING EDUCATION
INSTITUT SUPÉRIEUR DE L'EDUCATION ET DE LA FORMATION CONTINUE
43, rue de la Liberté, Le Bardo, 2000 Tunis
Tel: +216(71) 563-170
Fax: +216(71) 568-954

Directeur: Mohamed Kameleddine Gaha (1995-)
Tel: +216(71) 564-727 EMail: malika.trabelsi@isefc.rnu.tn

Departments

Arabic Language and Literature (Arabic; Arts and Humanities; Modern Languages)
Education
Foreign Languages (Modern Languages)
Humanities (Arts and Humanities; Social Sciences)
Mathematics
Natural Sciences
Physics and Technology (Physics; Technology)

History: Founded 1982.

Main Language(s) of Instruction: Arabic, French

HIGHER INSTITUTE OF FINE ARTS, TUNIS
INSTITUT SUPÉRIEUR DES BEAUX ARTS DE TUNIS
Route de l'Armée nationale, El Omrane, 1005 Tunis
Tel: +216(71) 898-447
Fax: +216(71) 568-291

Directeur: Mohamed Ben Taher Guiga
Tel: +216(71) 898-441

Departments

Plastic Arts (Fine Arts)
Science and Technology of Arts (Fine Arts; Technology)

History: Founded 1995.

HIGHER INSTITUTE OF MANAGEMENT, TUNIS
INSTITUT SUPÉRIEUR DE GESTION DE TUNIS
41, rue de la Liberté, Cité Bouchoucha, Le Bardo, 2000 Tunis
Tel: +216(71) 560-378
Fax: +216(71) 568-767

Directeur: Abdelwahed Trabelsi (2001-)
Tel: +216(71) 560-313

Secrétaire général: Jellali Noureddine

Departments

Applied Computerized Management (Business Computing; Management)
Finance and Accountancy (Accountancy; Finance)
Management, Human Resources and Law (Commercial Law; Human Resources; Law; Management)
Marketing, International Business and Languages (English; French; German; International Business; Marketing; Modern Languages; Spanish)
Quantitative Methods and Economics (Economics; Management Systems)

History: Founded 1969.

Academic Year: September to June (September-January; February-June)

Academic Staff *2001-2002*: Full-Time: c. 215 Part-Time: c. 80 Total: c. 295

Student Numbers *2001-2002:* Total: c. 3,300

HIGHER INSTITUTE OF MUSIC, TUNIS
INSTITUT SUPÉRIEUR DE MUSIQUE DE TUNIS
20, avenue de Paris, 1000 Tunis
Tel: +216(71) 255-577
Fax: +216(71) 245-575

Directeur: Mustapha Aloulou (1982-) Tel: +216(71) 257-526
Secrétaire général: Mondher Kalaï

Programmes

Music (Music; Music Theory and Composition; Musical Instruments; Musicology)

History: Founded 1982.

Main Language(s) of Instruction: Arabic, French

HIGHER INSTITUTE FOR YOUTH AND CULTURE
INSTITUT SUPÉRIEUR DE L'ANIMATION POUR LA JEUNESSE ET LA CULTURE
Bir El Bey, 2055 Tunis
Tel: +216(71) 420-075
Fax: +216(71) 420-608

Directeur: Moncef Jazzar (1995-) Tel: +216(71) 420-090
Secrétaire général: Abdeljelil Bourgou

Departments

Animation Techniques (Leisure Studies)
General Training (Leisure Studies)

History: Founded 1968, merged with the Institut supérieur de l'Animation culturelle 1995. Acquired present status and title 1995.

HIGHER SCHOOL OF ECONOMICS AND COMMERCE, TUNIS
ECOLE SUPÉRIEURE DES SCIENCES ÉCONOMIQUES ET COMMERCIALES DE TUNIS
4, rue Abou Zakaria El Hafsi, Montfleury, 1008 Tunis
Tel: +216(71) 330-266
Fax: +216(71) 333-518

Directeur: Chokri Mamoghli Tel: +216(71) 334-190
Secrétaire général: Fethi Ben Echeikh

Programmes

Economics and Commerce (Business and Commerce; Economics)

TUNIS COLLEGE OF SCIENCE AND TECHNIQUES
ECOLE SUPÉRIEURE DES SCIENCES ET TECHNIQUES DE TUNIS
5, avenue Taha Hussein, Montfleury, 1008 Tunis
Tel: +216(71) 496-066
Fax: +216(71) 391-166
EMail: mail@esstt.rnu.tn
Website: http://www.mes.tn/esstt

Directeur: Jilani Lamloumi Tel: +216(71) 392-591

Departments

Civil Engineering *Head*: Mohamed Ali Komiha
Electrical Engineering *Head*: Abdelkader Chaari

Mathematics and Computer Science *Head*: Jounaidi Abdeljaoued

Mechanical Engineering *Head*: Mohamed Tmar

Physics and Chemistry (Chemistry; Physics) *Head*: Mohamed Daoud

History: Founded 1973, acquired present status and title 1994.

HIGHER TEACHER TRAINING SCHOOL, TUNIS
ECOLE NORMALE SUPÉRIEURE DE TUNIS
8, place aux Chevaux, El Gorjani, Montfleury, 1008 Tunis
Tel: +216(71) 562-305
Fax: +216(71) 562-998
Website: http://www.mes.tn/ens

Directeur: Mabrouk El Mannaï

Secrétaire générale: Hmaida El Hedfi

Departments

Arts and Humanities (Arabic; Arts and Humanities; English; French; Geography; History; Mathematics; Physics; Psychology; Social Sciences; Teacher Training)

Main Language(s) of Instruction: Arabic, French

NATIONAL INSTITUTE OF HERITAGE
INSTITUT NATIONAL DU PATRIMOINE
4, place du Kaser, Bab Menara, 1008 Tunis
Tel: +216(71) 561-693
Fax: +216(71) 562-452

Directeur: Béji Ben Mami Tel: +216(71) 561-622

Secrétaire général: Taieb El Oussaï

Programmes

Heritage Studies (Heritage Preservation; Museum Management; Museum Studies; Restoration of Works of Art)

History: Founded 1957.

PREPARATORY INSTITUTE FOR ENGINEERING STUDIES, TUNIS
INSTITUT PRÉPARATOIRE AUX ETUDES D'INGÉNIEURS DE TUNIS
2, rue Jawaher Lel Nahrou, Montfleury, 1008 Tunis
Tel: +216(71) 336-641
Fax: +216(71) 337-323

Directeur: Mohamed Abedelmanaf Ben Abdrabou
Tel: +216(71) 336-653

Secrétaire général: Mohamed Sakly

Programmes

Engineering (Engineering; Technology)

History: Founded 1995.

UNIVERSITY OF TUNIS EL MANAR
Université de Tunis El Manar
Campus universitaire, 2092 Tunis
Tel: +216(71) 873-366 +216(71) 889-085
Fax: +216(71) 872-055
EMail: unitumanar@tun2.rnu.tn

Président: Youssef Alouane (2001-) Tel: +216(71) 871-567
Fax: +216(71) 889-085 EMail: yousef.alouane@tun2.rnu.tn

Secrétaire général: Ismaïl Khalil
EMail: ismail.khalil@tun2.rnu.tn

Faculties

Economics and Management *(Tunis)* (Accountancy; Economics; Finance; Management; Management Systems; Marketing) *Dean*: Mohamed Haddar

Law and Political Science (Criminal Law; Fiscal Law; Political Science; Private Law; Public Law) *Dean*: Chafik Saïd

Mathematics, Physics and Natural Sciences (Applied Mathematics; Biological and Life Sciences; Biotechnology; Chemistry; Computer Science; Earth Sciences; Electronic Engineering; Environmental Engineering; Mathematics; Natural Sciences; Physics) *Dean*: Chedli Touibi

Medicine (Acupuncture; Cardiology; Education of the Handicapped; Genetics; Gerontology; Neurological Therapy; Rehabilitation and Therapy; Social and Preventive Medicine; Sports Medicine; Toxicology) *Dean*: Rachid Mechmech

Schools

Engineering *(Tunis)* (Civil Engineering; Electronic Engineering; Industrial Engineering; Mechanical Engineering) *Dean*: Khalifa Halaal

History: Founded 1988 incorporating existing faculties.

Academic Year: September to June

Admission Requirements: Secondary School Certificate

Fees: (Tunisian Dinars): 30-200 per annum

Main Language(s) of Instruction: French, Arabic, English

International Co-operation: With universities in: Canada, France, Germany, Italy, Japan, the Netherlands, Turkey, United Kingdom, USA

Degrees and Diplomas: *Diplôme universitaire de Technologie (DUT)*: Civil Engineering; Electrical Maintenance, 2 yrs; *Technicien supérieur*: Engineering (DTS); Forestry; Health Sciences, 2 yrs; *Diplôme universitaire d'Etudes scientifiques (DUES)*: Science, 2 yrs; *Diplôme*: Computer Engineering; Technology; Veterinary Medicine; *Diplôme d'Ingénieur*: Agriculture; Agronomy; Computer Engineering; Engineering; Geology, 4 yrs; *Maîtrise*: Engineering; Science; Technology, 4 yrs; *Diplôme d'Etudes approfondies (DEA)*: Computer Engineering; Engineering; Mathematics; Natural Sciences; Physics; Technology, a further 2 yrs following Maîtrise; *Doctorat*: Biology; Chemistry; Computer Science; Geology; Mathematics; Medicine; Physics; Veterinary Medicine; Engineering, 6 yrs

Publications: Revue de l'Université, reports casual activities (bimonthly)

Academic Staff *2001:* Total: c. 2,735

Student Numbers *2001:* Total: c. 22,530

BOURGUIBA INSTITUTE OF MODERN LANGUAGES
INSTITUT BOURGUIBA DES LANGUES VIVANTES
47, avenue de la Liberté, 1002 Tunis
Tel: +216(71) 835-885
Fax: +216(71) 833-684
Website: http://www.iblv.rnu.tn

Directeur: Abed El Majid El Bedoui Tel: +216(71) 833-393

Secrétaire général: Mohamed Mouldi Ben Amara

Departments
Arabic and Translation (Arabic; Translation and Interpretation)
English
French
Hebrew
Italian
Japanese
Spanish
Turkish

History: Founded 1964.

Main Language(s) of Instruction: Arabic, French

'EL KHAWARIZMI' COMPUTER CENTRE
CENTRE DE CALCUL 'EL KHAWARIZMI'
Campus Universitaire, 1060 Tunis
Tel: +216(71) 873-756
Fax: +216(71) 871-032
EMail: cck@cck.rnu.tn
Website: http://www.cck.rnu.tn

Directrice: Henda Hadjami Ben Ghezala (2000-)
Tel: +216(71) 873-740

Programmes
Computer Science (Computer Science; Mathematics and Computer Science; Statistics)

History: Founded 1976.

Main Language(s) of Instruction: Arabic, French

HIGHER INSTITUTE OF APPLIED BIOLOGY
INSTITUT SUPÉRIEUR DES SCIENCES BIOLOGIQUES APPLIQUÉES

Departments
Biology

HIGHER INSTITUTE OF COMPUTER SCIENCE, EL MANAR
INSTITUT SUPÉRIEUR D'INFORMATIQUE D'EL MANAR
2, rue Abou Raihan El Bayrouni, 2080 Ariana
Tel: +216(71) 706-317
Fax: +216(71) 706-164

Directeur: Samir Ben Ahmed (2001-)

Secrétaire général: Salah Kamoun

Programmes
Computer Science (Computer Networks; Mathematics and Computer Science; Statistics)

History: Founded 2001.

HIGHER INSTITUTE OF HUMANITIES
INSTITUT SUPÉRIEUR DES SCIENCES HUMAINES DE TUNIS
26, avenue Darghouth Bacha, 1007 Tunis
Tel: +216(71) 561-439
Fax: +216(71) 571-911

Directeur: Mohamed Mahjoub Tel: +216(71) 569-499

Secrétaire général: Abdelhay Manaï

Departments
Applied Languages (Modern Languages)
Arabic *Head*: Mohamed El Bahri
English *Head*: Khaled El Kenani
French *Head*: Mohamed Kameleddine Gharha
Psychology *Head*: Mohamed Bensassi
Sociology *Head*: Michel Belajouza

Main Language(s) of Instruction: Arabic, French

Degrees and Diplomas: *Diplôme d'Etudes universitaires de Premier Cycle (DEUPC)*; *Maîtrise*; *Mastère*

HIGHER INSTITUTE OF MEDICAL TECHNOLOGY
INSTITUT SUPÉRIEUR DES TECHNOLOGIES MÉDICALES DE TUNIS
9, rue Zouheir Safi, 1006 Tunis
Tel: +216(71) 563-710
Fax: +216(71) 563-710

Directrice: Fatma Hila (2001-)

Secrétaire général: Mehdi Badreddine

Programmes
Electronic Systems (Electronic Engineering)
Medical Technology

History: Founded 2001.

HIGHER SCHOOL OF HEALTH SCIENCES AND TECHNOLOGY, TUNIS
ECOLE SUPÉRIEURE DES SCIENCES ET TECHNIQUES DE LA SANTÉ DE TUNIS
BP 176, Bab Saadoun, 1006 Tunis
Tel: +216(71) 562-455
Fax: +216(71) 570-062

Directeur: Mohamed Habib Jaâfoura

Secrétaire général: Faycel El Gheriani

Programmes
Health Sciences and Technology (Anaesthesiology; Biology; Ergotherapy; Gynaecology and Obstetrics; Health Sciences; Hygiene; Nursing; Nutrition; Paediatrics; Radiology; Secretarial Studies; Speech Therapy and Audiology)

Departments
Biological Sciences (Biological and Life Sciences) *Head*: Ersia Ben Hssine
Medical Imagery and Radiology (Radiology) *Head*: Mohamed Habib Daghfous

History: Founded 1990.

NATIONAL SCHOOL OF ENGINEERING, TUNIS
ECOLE NATIONALE D'INGÉNIEURS DE TUNIS
BP 37, Le Belvédère, Campus Universitaire, 1060 Tunis
Tel: +216(71) 874-700
Fax: +216(71) 872-729
Telex: 15051
EMail: enit.info@enit.rnu.tn

Directeur: Bahri Rezig Tel: +216(71) 872-880

Secrétaire général: Tahar Friâa

Departments
Civil Engineering (Civil Engineering; Construction Engineering; Environmental Engineering; Hydraulic Engineering) *Head*: Mounir Bouanida
Electical Engineering (Computer Engineering; Electrical Engineering; Telecommunications Engineering) *Head*: Rabeh Attia
Industrial Engineering *Head*: Mohamed Baklouda
Mechanical Engineering *Head*: Jaleleddine Briki

History: Founded 1969.

NATIONAL UNIVERSITY CENTRE FOR SCIENTIFIC AND
TECHNICAL DOCUMENTATION
CENTRE NATIONAL UNIVERSITAIRE DE
DOCUMENTATION SCIENTIFIQUE ET TECHNIQUE
BP 85, 1, avenue de France, 1002 Tunis
Tel: +216(71) 336-708
Fax: +216(71) 354-216

Directrice: Fatma Chammam-Ben Abdallah

Programmes
Scientific and Technical Documentation (Documentation Techniques; Information Technology; Library Science)

Main Language(s) of Instruction: Arabic, French

PASTEUR INSTITUTE
INSTITUT PASTEUR
13, place Pasteur, 1002 Tunis
Tel: +216(71) 783-022
Fax: +216(71) 791-833

Directeur: Koussai Dellagi Tel: +216(71) 845-452

Programmes
Biological Research (Biological and Life Sciences; Biology; Immunology; Microbiology; Pharmacology)

History: Founded 1893.

PREPARATORY INSTITUTE FOR ENGINEERING STUDIES,
EL MANAR
INSTITUT PRÉPARATOIRE AUX ETUDES D'INGÉNIEURS
D'EL MANAR
Campus universitaire, 1060 Tunis
Tel: +216(71) 872-330
Fax: +216(71) 872-729

Directeur: Mohamed Abaab (2001-)

Secrétaire général: Abderraouf Chaouch

Programmes
Engineering (Engineering; Technology) *Head*: Mohameda Soula
Physics and Chemistry (Chemistry; Physics) *Head*: Abdlah Hamdi

History: Founded 2001.

VETERINARY RESEARCH INSTITUTE, TUNIS
INSTITUT DE RECHERCHE VÉTÉRINAIRE DE TUNIS
Rue Jabal El Akdah Errabta, 1006 Tunis
Tel: +216(71) 562-602
Fax: +216(71) 569-692

Directeur: Malek Ezzrelli Tel: +216(71) 564-321

Research Institutes
Veterinary Science (Animal Husbandry; Biotechnology; Veterinary Science)

PRIVATE INSTITUTIONS

CENTRAL PRIVATE UNIVERSITY OF BUSINESS ADMINISTRATION AND TECHNOLOGY
Université Centrale Privée d'Administration des Affaires et de Technologie
16, Rue Ibn Tafarjine, 1002 Tunis Belvédère
Tel: +216(71) 796-679
Fax: +216(71) 796-493
EMail: infucaat@planet.tn
Website: http://www.ucaat.ens.tn

Departments
Commerce (Business and Commerce; Finance)
Computer Science Applied to Management (Computer Science; Management)
Technology (Mathematics; Physics; Technology)

History: Founded 2001.

Degrees and Diplomas: *Maîtrise*; *Mastère*. Also preparation courses for schools of engineering.

"EL AMEL" PRIVATE UNIVERSITY OF HIGHER EDUCATION
Université privée d'Enseignement supérieur 'El Amel'
3, rue El Imam Ibn Arafa Megrine, Ben Arous
Tel: +216(71) 295-233
Fax: +216(71)432-443
EMail: upes@gnet.tn

Departments

Computer Science Applied to Management (Computer Science; Management)

Economics and Management (Banking; Business Administration; Economics; Finance; Hotel Management; International Business; Management; Marketing; Tourism)

Degrees and Diplomas: *Technicien supérieur; Maîtrise*

FREE UNIVERSITY OF THE SOUTH

Université Libre du Sud

Avenue 5 Août Rue Saïd Abou Baker No 74, 3002 Sfax
Tel: +216(74) 225-665
EMail: uls_tn@yahoo.com

Departments

Computer Science Applied to Management (Computer Science; Management)

Economics and Management (Business and Commerce; Economics; Finance; International Business; Management; Marketing)

Engineering (Automation and Control Engineering; Computer Engineering; Data Processing; Electronic Engineering; Engineering; Industrial Engineering)

Law

Tourism and Hotel Management (Cooking and Catering; Hotel Management; Tourism)

History: Founded 2001.

FREE UNIVERSITY OF TUNIS

Université libre de Tunis (ULT)

30, avenue Khéreddine Pacha, 1002 Tunis
Tel: +216(71) 841-411
Fax: +216(71) 782-260
EMail: intac.ult@planet.tn
Website: http://www.ult.ens.tn

Recteur: Sadok Belaid

Président: Mohamed Bouebdelli Tel: +216(71) 890-393
EMail: intac.ult@planet.tn

Vice-présidente: Madeleine Bouebdelli
EMail: mbouebdelli@yahoo.fr

International Relations: Mehdi Bouebdelli
Tel: +216(71) 841-411 Fax: +216(71) 841-411
EMail: Kbouebdelli@yahoo.fr

Faculties

Law, Economics and Management (Accountancy; Commercial Law; Computer Science; Criminal Law; Economics; Finance; Hotel Management; Human Resources; International Business; Law; Management; Marketing; Private Law; Public Law; Tourism) *Dean:* Samy Ben Naceur

Literature, Arts and Humanities (Architecture; Education; Fashion Design; Fine Arts; Graphic Arts; Industrial Design; Interior Design; Journalism; Literature; Modern Languages; Painting and Drawing; Sculpture; Translation and Interpretation)

Institutes

Polytechnic (Agronomy; Biochemistry; Bioengineering; Biology; Chemical Engineering; Chemistry; Civil Engineering; Computer Engineering; Data Processing; Electrical Engineering; Energy Engineering; Food Science; Industrial Engineering; Mathematical Physics; Mechanical Engineering; Natural Sciences; Statistics; Telecommunications Engineering; Town Planning)

Centres

Correspondence Education and Training *(CIFED)* (Economics; Engineering; Law; Management; Modern Languages) *Director:* Mehdi Bouebdelli

History: Founded 1992 by the merging of the Ecole d'Electronique et d'Automatisme and the Institut des Technologies avancées et des Etudes commerciales. Acquired present status 2001. A private institution.

Governing Bodies: Conseil d'Administration; Conseil scientifique; Conseil des Etudes et de la Vie universitaire; Conseil de Parrainage

Admission Requirements: Secondary school certificate (Baccalauréat) or equivalent, and entrance examination

Fees: (Dinars) 3280-4330 per annum; Faculty of Pharmacy 9550 per annum

Main Language(s) of Instruction: Arabic, French

International Co-operation: With universities in France; Canada; Ukraine

Degrees and Diplomas: *Certificat d'Aptitude:* Arabic, 1 yr; *Diplôme universitaire de Technologie (DUT):* Chemical Engineering; Civil Engineering and Town Planning; Electrical Engineering and Industrial Computing, Mechanical and Energy Engineering, 3 yrs; *Diplôme d'Etudes universitaires de Premier Cycle (DEUPC):* Business Computing; Communication; Economics; Law; Management; Plastic Arts, 2 yrs; *Diplôme:* Pharmacy, 5 yrs; *Diplôme d'Ingénieur:* Chemical Engineering; Civil Engineering and Town Planning; Computer Engineering; Electrical Engineering and Industrial Computing; Mechanical Engineering and Energy Engineering; Physics Engineering, 5 yrs; *Maîtrise:* Accountancy; Business Computing; Commercial Law; Communication and Media; Design and Fashion Design; Economics; Finance; Graphic Design; Human Resources; International Tourism and Hotel Management; International Trade; Management; Marketing; Modern Languages; Operations Research, Econometrics, Finance and Banking, International Economics, Economics and Industrial Strategy; Plastic Arts; Private Law; Public Law, 4 yrs; Interior Design; Product Design, 5 yrs; *Diplôme d'Architecte:* Architecture, 5 yrs; *Mastère spécialisé:* Law, Economics, Management, Engineering, 2 yrs following Maîtrise with mémoire; *Mastère:* Law, Economics, Management, Engineering, 6 months following Maîtrise

Student Services: Academic Counselling, Social Counselling, Employment Services, Foreign Student Adviser, Cultural Centre, Sports Facilities, Language Programmes, Health Services, Canteen, Foreign Student Centre

Student Residential Facilities: Yes

Special Facilities: Studies and Research Centre, Computer Laboratories, Language Laboratories

Libraries: Central Library (2 centres)

Academic Staff *2003-2004*   TOTAL
FULL-TIME   38
PART-TIME   77
TOTAL   **115**

Staff with doctorate: Total: **93**

Student Numbers *2002-2003:* Total: c. 1,460

INTERNATIONAL UNIVERSITY OF TUNIS

Université internationale de Tunis (UIT)
Rue 8301, Immeuble Nozha, Cité Montplaisir, 1002 Tunis
Tel: +216(71) 951-499
Fax: +216(71) 951-567
EMail: admin@uit.ens.tn
Website: http://www.uit.ens.tn

Higher Schools
Applied Sciences (Automation and Control Engineering; Computer Engineering; Industrial Engineering; Measurement and Precision Engineering)
Commerce (Business and Commerce; Business Computing; Finance; Hotel Management; International Business; Management; Marketing; Tourism)
Hotel Management (Hotel Management; Tourism)

History: Founded 2002.

Degrees and Diplomas: *Diplôme universitaire de Technologie (DUT):* 3 yrs; *Diplôme d'Ingénieur:* a further 2 yrs; *Maîtrise:* a further 2 yrs; *Mastère*

PRIVATE ARAB SCIENCE UNIVERSITY

Université privée arabe des Sciences
34, rue Cyrus le Grand, 1002 Tunis
Tel: +216(71) 336-023
Fax: +216(71) 334-897

Departments
Architecture
Business Computing
Economics and Management (Banking; Economics; Finance; Insurance; International Business; Management; Marketing)
Engineering (Civil Engineering; Computer Engineering; Electrical Engineering; Engineering; Industrial Engineering; Mechanical Engineering)
Fine Arts (Fine Arts; Graphic Arts; Interior Design)
French Literature (Literature)
Journalism and Communication (Communication Studies; Journalism)
Law
Technology (Civil Engineering; Instrument Making; Maintenance Technology; Mechanical Engineering; Technology; Telecommunications Engineering)
Tourism and Hotel Management (Hotel Management; Tourism)

History: Founded 2001.

Degrees and Diplomas: *Diplôme universitaire de Technologie (DUT);* *Technicien supérieur;* *Maîtrise*

PRIVATE INFORMATION TECHNOLOGY AND BUSINESS ADMINISTRATION UNIVERSITY

Université privée de Technologies de l'Information et de Management de l'Entreprise
45, Avenue Mohamed V, Montplaisir, 1002 Tunis
Tel: +216(71) 951-194
Fax: +216(71) 951-171
EMail: info@time.ens.tn
Website: http://www.time.ens.tn

Higher Schools
Computer Science (Computer Networks; Computer Science; Software Engineering)
Management (Business and Commerce; Computer Science; Finance; Management; Marketing)

History: Founded 2002.

Degrees and Diplomas: *Mastère*

PRIVATE TECHNOLOGICAL UNIVERSITY

Université privée de Technologie
22, Avenue de Madrid, 1000 Tunis
Tel: +216(71) 336-888
Fax: +216(71) 343-302

Departments
Computer Science Applied to Management (Computer Science; Management)
Management

History: Founded 2001.

PRIVATE UNIVERSITY OF SCIENCE, ARTS AND TECHNOLOGY, SOUSSE

Université privée des Sciences, Arts et Techniques de Sousse
Avenue Commandant Bejaoui, 4000 Sousse
Tel: +216(73) 236-122
Fax: +216(73) 236-123
EMail: upsat@topnet.tn

Departments
Arts and Crafts (Communication Studies; Crafts and Trades; Fine Arts; Interior Design)
Computer Science Applied to Management (Computer Science; Management)

Economics and Management (Accountancy; Economics; Hotel Management; International Business; Management; Tourism)
Law (Commercial Law; Law)
Optics (Optical Technology; Optics)

History: Founded 2001.

TUNIS CARTHAGE PRIVATE UNIVERSITY
Université privée Tunis Carthage (UTC)
Avenue Fattouma Bourguiba, La Soukra, 2036 Tunis
Tel: +216(71) 868-145
EMail: admission@utc.ens.tn
Website: http://www.utc.ens.tn

Units
Applied Languages (Modern Languages)
Architecture and Fine Arts (Architecture; Fine Arts)
Computer Science
Economics and Management (Accountancy; Economics; Finance; Human Resources; International Business; Management; Marketing)

Departments
Continuing Education
Information Technology

History: Founded 2001.
Degrees and Diplomas: *Maîtrise*; *Mastère*

OTHER INSTITUTIONS

PUBLIC INSTITUTIONS

HIGHER INSTITUTE OF TECHNOLOGICAL STUDIES, CHARGUIA
Institut supérieur des Etudes technologiques de Charguia (ISET Charguia)
Rue des Entrepreneurs, Charguia II, 2035 Tunis
Tel: +216(71) 704-405
Fax: +216(71) 940 370
Directeur: Habib Zenguer
Secrétaire général: Ahmed Ktari

Programmes
Engineering
Technology
Main Language(s) of Instruction: Arabic, French

HIGHER INSTITUTE OF TECHNOLOGICAL STUDIES, DJERBA
Institut supérieur des Etudes technologiques de Djerba (ISET Djerba)
Zône Henchir Bargou, 4116 Midoun Djerba
Tel: +216(75) 733-110
Fax: +216(75) 733-111
Directeur: Béchir Bachouel Tel: +216(75) 603-110
Secrétaire général: Béchir Mehdaoui

Programmes
Engineering
Technology
Main Language(s) of Instruction: Arabic, French

HIGHER INSTITUTE OF TECHNOLOGICAL STUDIES, GABÈS
Institut supérieur des Etudes technologiques de Gabès (ISET Gabès)
Cité El Manara, 6029 Gabès
Tel: +216(75) 282-353
Fax: +216(75) 280-041
Directeur: Ridha Ben Abedennour Tel: +216(75) 280-651
Secrétaire général: Farhat Mjaïed

Founded: 1995

Programmes
Engineering
Technology

History: Founded 1995.
Main Language(s) of Instruction: Arabic, French

HIGHER INSTITUTE OF TECHNOLOGICAL STUDIES, GAFSA
Institut supérieur des Etudes technologiques de Gafsa (ISET Gafsa)
Cité des Jeunes, 2119 Gafsa
Tel: +216(76) 211-081
Fax: +216(76) 211-080
Directeur: Jalel Kdhiri Tel: +216(76) 211-040
Secrétaire général: Mechri Kaabachi Tel: +216(76) 211-041

Founded: 1995

Programmes
Engineering (Engineering; Industrial Engineering; Mining Engineering)

History: Founded 1995.
Main Language(s) of Instruction: Arabic, French
Student Numbers *2001-2002:* Total: c. 770

HIGHER INSTITUTE OF TECHNOLOGICAL STUDIES, KAIROUAN

Institut supérieur des Etudes technologiques de Kairouan (ISET Kairouan)
Avenue Assad Ibn El Fourat, 3100 Kairouan
Tel: +216(77) 323-300
Fax: +216(77) 323-320

Directeur: Sayed Laatar

Programmes
Engineering
Technology

Main Language(s) of Instruction: Arabic, French

HIGHER INSTITUTE OF TECHNOLOGICAL STUDIES, KEBILI

Institut supérieur des Etudes technologiques de Kebili
Nozel Borj Ennaem, 4200 Kebili
Tel: +216(75) 494-000
Fax: +216(75) 491-000

Directeur: Ali Beltaïef
Secrétaire général: Fethi Bousif

Programmes
Commercial Techniques (Business and Commerce; Sales Techniques)
Technology

HIGHER INSTITUTE OF TECHNOLOGICAL STUDIES, KSAR HELLAL

Institut supérieur des Etudes technologiques de Ksar Hellal (ISET Ksar Hellal)
Rue Hadj Ali Soua, 5070 Ksar Hellal
Tel: +216(73) 475-900
Fax: +216(73) 475-163

Directeur: Faouzi Sakli Tel: +216(73) 475-900
Secrétaire général: Mustapha Khouja

Founded: 1995

Programmes
Textile Technology

History: Founded 1995.
Main Language(s) of Instruction: Arabic, French

548

HIGHER INSTITUTE OF TECHNOLOGICAL STUDIES, MAHDIA

Institut supérieur des Etudes technologiques de Mahdia (ISET Mahdia)
Avenue Mourouj 5111, Hiboum, 5111 Mahdia
Tel: +216(73) 672-400
Fax: +216(73) 672-399

Directeur: Hamadi Ben Naceur (2001-)
Secrétaire général: Ridha Ben Nasr

Founded: 2001

Programmes
Engineering
Technology
Main Language(s) of Instruction: Arabic, French

HIGHER INSTITUTE OF TECHNOLOGICAL STUDIES, NABEUL

Institut supérieur des Etudes technologiques de Nabeul (ISET Nabeul)
Campus Universitaire Mrezgua, 8000 Nabeul
Tel: +216(72) 220-051
Fax: +216(72) 220-033

Directeur: Mohamed Chokri Chaouachi
Tel: +216(72) 220-035
Secrétaire général: Monsor Turki

Founded: 1995

Programmes
Civil Engineering
Electrical Engineering
Maintenance Technology
Materials Engineering
Surveying (Surveying and Mapping)
Main Language(s) of Instruction: Arabic, French

HIGHER INSTITUTE OF TECHNOLOGICAL STUDIES, RADÈS

Institut supérieur des Etudes technologiques de Radès (ISET Radès)
Rue El Kods, 2080 Radès
Tel: +216(71) 460-100
Fax: +216(71) 442-322

Directeur: Naceur Hadj Braïek Tel: +216(71) 461-610
Secrétaire général: Béchir Bedday

Founded: 1992

Programmes
Engineering
Technology

Main Language(s) of Instruction: Arabic, French

HIGHER INSTITUTE OF TECHNOLOGICAL STUDIES, SFAX

Institut supérieur des Etudes technologiques de Sfax (ISET Sfax)
BP 88a, Route de Medhia Km. 2,5, El Bosten, 3002 Sfax
Tel: +216(74) 237-425
Fax: +216(74) 237-386

Directeur: Slimène Gabsi Tel: +216(74) 237-493

Secrétaire général: Abdellatif Yangui Tel: +216(74) 237-495

Founded: 1992

Programmes
Engineering
Technology

Main Language(s) of Instruction: Arabic, French

HIGHER INSTITUTE OF TECHNOLOGICAL STUDIES, SIDI BOUZID

Institut supérieur des Etudes technologiques de Sidi Bouzid
9100 Sidi Bouzid
Tel: +216(76) 632-842

Directeur: Mohamed Seghaïr Zâafouri

Secrétaire général: Ezzeddine Hessimi

Programmes
Agricultural Engineering
Food Processing (Food Technology)
Technology

HIGHER INSTITUTE OF TECHNOLOGICAL STUDIES, SILIANA

Institut supérieur des Etudes technologiques de Siliana
Avenue 13 Août, 6100 Siliana
Tel: +216(78) 874- 600
Fax: +216(78) 874-699

Directeur: Mohamed Mansi

Secrétaire général: Saleh Zoghlemi

Programmes
Business Administration
Technology

HIGHER INSTITUTE OF TECHNOLOGICAL STUDIES, SOUSSE

Institut supérieur des Etudes technologiques de Sousse (ISET Sousse)
Cité Erriadh, 4032 Sousse
Tel: +216(73) 307-960
Fax: +216(73) 307-963

Directeur: Khaled Bouzouita Tel: +216(73) 307-961

Secrétaire général: Abdessattar Ben Dhia

Founded: 1992

Programmes
Engineering
Technology

Main Language(s) of Instruction: Arabic, French

HIGHER INSTITUTE OF TECHNOLOGICAL STUDIES, ZAGHOUAN

Institut supérieur des Etudes technologiques de Zaghouan
Mogren, 1121 Zaghouan
Tel: +216(72) 660-300
Fax: +216(72) 670-420

Directeur: Ahmed Ben Nsirr

Secrétaire général: Mohamed Tlili

Programmes
Technology

HIGHER INSTITUTE OF TECHNOLOGICAL STUDIES IN COMMUNICATION, TUNIS

Institut supérieur des Etudes technologiques en Communications de Tunis (ISET'COM)
Route de Raoued Km. 3,5, Cité El Ghazala, 2083 Ariana
Tel: +216(71) 857-000
Fax: +216(71) 857-555
EMail: couriel@isetcom.rnu.tn
Website: http://www.isetcom.mincom.tn

Directeur: Lofti Ammar Tel: +216(71) 857-788

Secrétaire général: Abdelhamid Meddeb

Founded: 1998

Departments
Postal Services
Telecommunications Services (Telecommunications Engineering; Telecommunications Services)

Main Language(s) of Instruction: Arabic, French

PRIVATE INSTITUTIONS

PRIVATE FACULTY OF MANAGEMENT AND INTERNATIONAL TRADE
Faculté privée de Management et de Commerce international
Rue 8300 Montplaisir, 1002 Tunis
Tel: +216(71) 791-300
Fax: +216(71) 794-415
EMail: fmciinfo@fmci.ens.tn
Website: http://www.fmci.ens.tn

Dean: Mohamed Hedi Chedly

Founded: 2001

Departments
Computer Science Applied to Management (Computer Science; Management)

Economics and Management (Accountancy; Business and Commerce; Economics; Finance; Hotel Management; International Business; Management; Marketing; Taxation; Tourism)
Law

PRIVATE INSTITUTE OF HIGHER STUDIES
Institut privé des Hautes Etudes
3, rue Jughurta Mutuelleville, Tunis, 1002
Founded: 2001

Departments
Computer Science Applied to Management (Computer Science; Management)
Economics and Management (Accountancy; Economics; Finance; Hotel Management; International Business; Management; Marketing; Tourism)

Note: Also 6 Instituts supérieurs de Formation des Maîtres in Gafsa, Kairouan, Korba, Le Kef, Sbeitla and Sousse

Uganda

INSTITUTION TYPES AND CREDENTIALS

Types of higher education institutions:

University
Polytechnic
Technical College
Teachers' College

School leaving and higher education credentials:

Uganda Advanced Certificate of Education
Grade III Teachers' Certificate
Grade IV Teachers' Certificate
Ordinary Diploma in Electrical Engineering
Ordinary Technician's Diploma
Grade V Teachers' Certificate
Higher Diploma in Electrical Engineering
Higher Technician's Diploma
Certificate
Diploma
Bachelor's Degree
Postgraduate Diploma
Master's Degree
Doctor's Degree

STRUCTURE OF EDUCATION SYSTEM

Pre-higher education:

Structure of school system:

Primary
Type of school providing this education: Primary School
Length of programme in years: 7
Age level from: 6 to: 13

Lower Secondary
Type of school providing this education: Lower Secondary School
Length of programme in years: 4

Age level from: 13 to: 17
Certificate/diploma awarded: Uganda Certificate of Education

Technical Secondary
Type of school providing this education: Technical Secondary School
Length of programme in years: 3
Age level from: 13 to: 16
Certificate/diploma awarded: Uganda Junior Technical Certificate

Upper Secondary
Type of school providing this education: Upper Secondary School
Length of programme in years: 2
Age level from: 17 to: 19
Certificate/diploma awarded: Uganda Advanced Certificate of Education

School education:

Primary education lasts for seven years, leading to the Primary School Leaving Certificate. Secondary education is divided into two cycles: lower secondary and upper secondary. Lower secondary education lasts for four years. At the end of Form 4 pupils sit for the examinations for the Uganda Certificate of Education. Upper secondary education lasts for two years and leads to the Uganda Advanced Certificate of Education at the end of Form 6. Technical secondary schools offer three-year full-time courses to pupils who successfully pass the Primary School Leaving Examination. Students sit for the Uganda Junior Technical Certificate at the end of the course. Qualifying students who do very well can enter the technical institutes. Agriculture is compulsory in all secondary schools.

Higher education:

Higher education is provided by universities, both public and private, a polytechnic, teachers' colleges and technical colleges. The key body which is responsible for planning university education is the University Council in consultation with the appropriate government agencies such as the Ministry of Education and Sports. The University Council acts as the main governing body and has a joint membership of both academic staff and representatives of society. It is assisted by a Senate which is responsible for all academic concerns.

Main laws/decrees governing higher education:

Decree: Universities and other Tertiary Institutions Act   Year: 2001
Concerns: Institutions of Higher Education

Academic year:

Classes from: October *to:* July

Languages of instruction:

English

552

Stages of studies:

Non-university level post-secondary studies (technical/vocational type):

Higher technical and vocational education is provided by technical colleges which offer two-year courses leading to the Ordinary Technician's Diploma to holders of the Uganda Advanced Certificate of Education with at least one principal pass in Physics and a subsidiary pass in Mathematics or vice versa. A further two years lead to the Higher Technician's Diploma. A full-time three-year course at the Uganda Polytechnic leads to the Ordinary Diploma in Electrical Engineering. Requirements for entry are at least two principal passes in Mathematics, Chemistry or Physics and one subsidiary pass in any of them. The Higher Diploma in Electrical Engineering is conferred at the end of a two-year full-time course. Students must hold an Ordinary Diploma pass with grade passes 1-2 and 3-6. They must also have completed one year's practical work experience.

University level studies:

University level first stage: Certificate, Diploma, Bachelor's Degree:
Certificates are awarded after six months in Librarianship and after one year in Theology. Diplomas are conferred in Music, Dance and Drama after two years and an entrance examination. The Bachelor's Degree is conferred after studies lasting between three (Arts, Science, Law), four (Engineering, Agriculture, Forestry, Agricultural Engineering) and five years (Medicine, Pharmacy, Engineering).

University level second stage: Diploma, Master's Degree:
In Education, a Diploma is conferred after one year's postgraduate education or two years after the Post-Higher School Certificate. The Master's Degree is conditional upon the student's being resident in the University and is awarded after eighteen months' study following upon the Bachelor's Degree in Fine Arts, Arts, Science, Agriculture, Education and Surgery. Candidates must submit a thesis and, in some cases, must do course work as well. In Medicine, three years' research work and courses are required. An advanced professional qualification, the Diploma, is awarded in Education and Medicine (Paediatrics, Public Health and Obstetrics) one year after the Bachelor's Degree.

University level third stage: Doctor's Degree:
The Doctor's Degree is conferred by some universities after a minimum of two to three years' research subsequent to the Master's Degree. Candidates must submit a thesis. In Medicine, the Doctor's Degree is a professional title (Doctor of Medicine, MD) awarded at least one year after the Bachelor's Degree upon submission of a thesis.

Teacher education:

Training of pre-primary and primary/basic school teachers
Primary school teachers are trained at Grade III primary teachers colleges. For lower primary school, candidates who have completed four years of secondary education follow a two-year course leading to the Grade III Teachers Certificate. Upper primary school teachers who hold the Uganda Certificate of Education follow a one-year course leading to the Grade IV Teachers Certificate.

Training of secondary school teachers
Secondary school teachers are trained at the National Teachers' Colleges, the University and the Institute of Teacher Education, Kyambogo. Courses last two years. There is also a three-year

upgrading course for grade IV teachers leading to the Grade V Teachers Certificate. To teach in Form 6, teachers must hold a Bachelor of Education Degree.

Non-traditional studies:

Distance higher education

Distance education is offered by the Centre for Adult and Continuing Education of Makerere University. It provides university type instruction in various parts of the country by correspondence and via the press, radio and television.

Lifelong higher education

The Centre for Continuing Education of Makerere University organizes a one-year full-time course for adults leading to a certificate and a special course which prepares mature students for higher studies.

NATIONAL BODIES

Responsible authorities:

Ministry of Education and Sports
    Minister of Education and Sports: Edward Kiddu Makubuya
    Minister of State for Higher Education: Betty Akech Okullu
    Commissioner for Higher Education: Yeko Acato
    International Relations: Aggrey David Kibenge
    PO Box 7063
    Kampala
    Tel: +256(41) 257-200
    Fax: +256(41) 230-437
    EMail: kibenge@hotmail.com
    WWW: http://www.education.go.ug

Role of governing body: Oversees teacher training, technical and commercial education. Plans and monitors standards for university education in conjunction with the university councils and the National Council for Higher Education. The latter is established under The Universities and Other Tertiary Institutions Act, 2001

Uganda National Council for Higher Education
    Executive Director: A.B. Kasozi
    PO Box 76
    Kyambogo
    Kampala
    Tel: +256(31) 262-140 +256(31) 262-145
    Fax: +256(41) 230-658

Role of governing body: Established by the Universities and other Tertiary Institutions Act to review higher education institutions and their programmes.

ADMISSIONS TO HIGHER EDUCATION

Admission to non university higher education studies

Name of secondary school credential required: Uganda Advanced Certificate of Education
Minimum score/requirement: Two principal passes in Maths, Physics or Chemistry and one subsidiary pass in any of them.
For entry to: Uganda Polytechnic

Name of secondary school credential required: Uganda Advanced Certificate of Education
Minimum score/requirement: One principal pass in Physics and a subsidiary pass in Maths or vice versa.
For entry to: Technical Colleges

Admission to university-level studies

Name of secondary school credential required: Uganda Advanced Certificate of Education
Minimum score/requirement: Six passes in approved subjects at Uganda Certificate of Education and two at Advanced Certificate level.

Foreign students admission

Admission requirements: Foreign students wishing to study in Ugandan universities should possess 2 principal passes at the Ugandan Advanced Level Certificate or an equivalent qualification.

Entry regulations: Students should obtain a visa from the Ugandan Embassy in their country.

Health requirements: Health Certificate.

Language requirements: Students must be proficient in English.

Recognition of studies and qualifications:

Studies pursued in home country (System of recognition/accreditation): The Uganda National Council for Higher Education reviews higher education institutions and their programmes.

Studies pursued in foreign countries (bodies dealing with recognition of foreign credentials):
Uganda National Council for Higher Education
    Executive Director: A.B. Kasozi
    PO Box 76
    Kyambogo
    Kampala
    Tel: +256(31) 262-140
    Fax: +256(41) 230-658

References to further information on foreign student admissions and recognition of studies

Title: Makerere University Calendar
Publisher: Makerere University

Title: Prospectus
Publisher: Uganda Martyrs University

STUDENT LIFE

Student expenses and financial aid

Student costs:

Home students tuition fees: Minimum: 2,500,000 (Uganda Shilling)
Maximum: 4,200,000 (Uganda Shilling)
Foreign students tuition fees: Minimum: 1,700 (US Dollar)
Maximum: 3,500 (US Dollar)

Bodies providing information on student financial aid:

Central Scholarships Committee, Ministry of Education and Sports
PO Box 7063, Crested Towers
Kampala
Tel: +256(41) 234-451
Fax: +256(41) 345-994
Deals with: Grants

Publications on student services and financial aid:

Title: Study Abroad 2004-2005, 32nd Edition
Author: UNESCO
Publisher: UNESCO Publishing
Year of publication: 2003

GRADING SYSTEM

Usual grading system in secondary school

Full Description: A-F; 1-9; 1-2 very good (distinction); 3-6 credit pass; 7-8 pass grade; 9 fail.
Highest on scale: A 1
Pass/fail level: 7-8
Lowest on scale: F 9

Main grading system used by higher education institutions

Full Description: Bachelor's degree: class I top honours; class II(i) honours upper; class II(ii) honours lower; pass general pass; fail

NOTES ON HIGHER EDUCATION SYSTEM

Data for academic year: 2002-2003
Source: International Association of Universities (IAU), updated from documentation, 2003

INSTITUTIONS OF HIGHER EDUCATION

UNIVERSITIES

PUBLIC INSTITUTIONS

GULU UNIVERSITY
Gulu

Programmes
Business Administration
Development Studies
Education

History: Founded 2002.

KYAMBOGO UNIVERSITY (KYU)
PO Box 1, Kampala
Tel: +246(41) 285-001
Fax: +246(41) 220-464
EMail: itek@starcom.co.ug
Website: http://www.kyambogo.ac.ug

Vice-Chancellor (Acting): A.J. Lutalo-Bosa

Registrar (Acting): A. A. Cula

Faculties
Art and Social Sciences (Economics; Geography; History; Literature; Modern Languages; Music; Religious Studies; Social Sciences) *Dean*: Filda L. Ojok
Education (Distance Education; Education; Educational Administration; Educational Psychology; Special Education; Teacher Training) *Dean*: E.L. Gumisiriza
Engineering (Civil Engineering; Construction Engineering; Electrical and Electronic Engineering; Mechanical Engineering; Production Engineering) *Dean*: M. Mugisha
Science (Biology; Chemistry; Computer Science; Mathematics; Physics; Sports) *Dean*: A. Wanyama
Special Needs Education and Rehabilitation
Vocational Studies (Agriculture; Business and Commerce; Fine Arts; Food Technology; Home Economics; Industrial Design; Technology) *Dean*: Habib Kato

History: Founded 2001 following merger of Uganda Polytechnic Kyambogo, Institute of Teacher Education, Kyambogo and Uganda National Institute of Special Education.

Degrees and Diplomas: *Certificate*; *Diploma*; *Bachelor's Degree*; *Postgraduate Diploma*; *Master's Degree*

Student Numbers *2003-2004:* Total: c. 9,000

• MAKERERE UNIVERSITY (MAK)
PO Box 7062, Kampala
Tel: +256(41) 532-631   +256(41) 542-803
Fax: +256(41) 541-068   +256(41) 531-288
EMail: postmaster@muk.ac.ug
Website: http://www.makerere.ac.ug

Vice-Chancellor: John P.M. Ssebuwufu (1993-)
EMail: vc@admin.mak.ac.ug

Academic Registrar: Sebastian M. Ngobi
Tel: +256(41) 532-752 Fax: +256(41) 533-640
EMail: acadreg@acadreg.mak.ac.ug

University Secretary: Sam Byanagwa
Tel: +256(41) 533-332 EMail: unisec@admin.mak.ac.ug

Faculties
Agriculture (Agricultural Business; Agricultural Economics; Agricultural Engineering; Agriculture; Animal Husbandry; Crop Production; Food Science; Food Technology; Soil Science; Technology) *Dean*: E.N. Sabiiti
Arts (Art History; Arts and Humanities; Dance; English; Geography; History; Literature; Mass Communication; Modern Languages; Music; Philosophy; Printing and Printmaking; Religious Studies; Sculpture; Theatre) *Dean*: O. Ndoleriire
Forestry and Nature Conservation (Ecology; Forest Biology; Forest Management; Forestry; Natural Resources; Wood Technology) *Dean*: J.R.S Kaboggoza
Law (Commercial Law; Comparative Law; Human Rights; Law; Peace and Disarmament; Public Law) *Dean*: J. Oloka-Onyango
Medicine *Dean*: N.K. Sewankambo
Science (Botany; Chemistry; Geology; Mathematics; Natural Sciences; Physics; Zoology) *Dean*: L.S. Luboobi
Social Sciences (Political Science; Public Administration; Social Sciences; Social Work; Sociology; Women's Studies) *Dean*: Joy Kwesiga
Technology (Architecture; Civil Engineering; Electrical Engineering; Mathematics and Computer Science; Mechanical Engineering; Surveying and Mapping; Technology) *Dean*: B. Nawangwe
Veterinary Medicine (Embryology and Reproduction Biology; Microbiology; Parasitology; Pathology; Physiology; Public Health; Social and Preventive Medicine; Surgery; Veterinary Science) *Dean*: E.R. Katunguka

Schools
Business (Accountancy; Business and Commerce; Business Computing; Finance; Management; Marketing) *Principal*: Waswa Balunywa
Education (Education; Natural Sciences; Technology Education) *Dean*: C. J. Sekamwa
Graduate
Industrial and Fine Arts *(Margaret Trowell)* (Art History; Ceramic Art; Computer Graphics; Fashion Design; Fine Arts; Furniture Design; Industrial Design; Jewelry Art; Painting and

Drawing; Printing and Printmaking; Sculpture; Textile Design; Weaving) *Director*: P.K. Kwesiga

Library and Information Science *(EASLIS)* (Information Sciences; Library Science) *Director*: S.A.H. Abidi

Institutes

Adult and Continuing Education (Communication Studies) *Director*: Nuwa Sentongo

Computer Science *Director*: J.N. Mulira

Economics *Director*: J. Ddumba Ssentamu

Environment and Natural Resources (Environmental Studies; Natural Resources; Surveying and Mapping; Town Planning) *Director (Acting)*: P. Kasoma

Social Research (Social Studies) *Director*: B. Nakanyike Musisi

Statistics and Applied Economics and Psychology (Demography and Population; Economics; Psychology; Rural Planning; Statistics) *Director*: M. Mugisha

Further Information: Also Teaching Hospital

History: Founded 1922 as Makerere College and became Makerere University College 1949. Acquired present status 1970 and title 1975.

Governing Bodies: Council, comprising 37 members; Senate, comprising 99 members

Academic Year: October to September (October-February; March-July;July-September)

Admission Requirements: Uganda Certificate of Education (UCE) or equivalent with at least 6 passes in approved subjects, and 2 passes in approved subjects at the same sitting of Uganda Advanced Certificate of Education (UACE) or equivalent

Main Language(s) of Instruction: English

Degrees and Diplomas: *Bachelor's Degree*: 3-5 yrs; *Postgraduate Diploma*: 1 yr; *Master's Degree*: a further 1-3 yrs; *Doctor's Degree*: (PhD), at least 2 yrs

Student Services: Academic Counselling, Social Counselling, Sports Facilities, Language Programmes, Health Services, Canteen

Student Residential Facilities: For 4780 students

Special Facilities: Art Gallery (Margaret Trowell School of Industrial and Fine Arts). Botany and Zoology Biodiversity Data Bank

Libraries: Main Library, c. 550,000 vols

Publications: Annual Report (annually); University Calendar; Handbook

Press or Publishing House: Makerere University Press

Academic Staff *2000-2001*	TOTAL
FULL-TIME	988
PART-TIME	200
TOTAL	**1,188**

Student Numbers *2000-2001:* Total: **22,000**

• MBARARA UNIVERSITY OF SCIENCE AND TECHNOLOGY (MUST)

PO Box 1410, Kabale Road, Mbarara
Tel: +256(485) 20-785
Fax: +256(485) 20-782
EMail: mustmed@infocom.co.ug;vcmust@inform.co.ug
Website: http://www.must.ac.ug

Vice-Chancellor: Frederick I.B. Kayanja (1988-)
Tel: +256(485) 20-783

Registrar: S.B.. Bazirake

International Relations: Jane L. Kibirige

Faculties

Development Studies (Computer Science; Development Studies) *Dean*: Pamela Mbabazi

Medicine *Dean*: E.K. Mutakooha

Science Education (Biology; Chemistry; Mathematics; Physics; Science Education) *Dean*: J. Barranga

Institutes

Tropical Forest Conservation (Forestry) *Director*: Richard Malenky

History: Founded 1989.

Governing Bodies: Council

Academic Year: October to August (October-December; January-March; April-August)

Admission Requirements: Uganda Certificate of Education or equivalent, or at least 2 principal passes of the Uganda Advanced Certificate of Education or its equivalent

Fees: (Uganda Shillings): 1m.-2.12m. per annum; foreign students, (US Dollars), 1700-3500

Main Language(s) of Instruction: English

Degrees and Diplomas: *Bachelor's Degree*: Computer Science; Development Studies; Science Education, 3 yrs; Medicine, 5 yrs; *Master's Degree*: Science, 2 yrs; Development Studies, a further 2 yrs; Medicine, a further 3 yrs; *Doctor's Degree*: Basic Sciences (Anatomy, Microbiology), Development Studies, Science Education (Biology) (PhD), 4 yrs

Student Services: Academic Counselling, Social Counselling, Sports Facilities, Health Services, Canteen

Student Residential Facilities: For 450 students

Libraries: Total, 17,169 vols

Publications: Science with Education Journal; Mbarara Medical School Journal (annually)

Academic Staff *2001-2002*	MEN	WOMEN	TOTAL
FULL-TIME	121	27	148
PART-TIME	–	–	4
TOTAL	–	–	**152**

Staff with doctorate: Total: **11**

Student Numbers *2001-2002*	MEN	WOMEN	TOTAL
All (Foreign Included)	519	266	**785**
FOREIGN ONLY	–	–	15

Evening Students, 9

PRIVATE INSTITUTIONS

BUGEMA UNIVERSITY (BU)

PO Box 6529, Luwero, Kampala
Tel: +256(75) 706-529
Fax: +256(41) 345-597
EMail: registrar_bu@yahoo.com
Website: http://www.bugemauniv.ac.ug

Vice-Chancellor: Sampson Kenneth Twumasi (2000-)
Tel: +256(77) 410-335

Registrar: Paul Katamba   Tel: +256(77) 561-152

Schools

Business (Accountancy; Business and Commerce; Finance; Management; Marketing) *Head*: Gladness Mtango Kwizera
Computer Science
Education (Education; Preschool Education; Primary Education; Secondary Education) *Head*: Yona Balyage
English Language (English; English Studies; Literacy Education; Literature; Mass Communication) *Head*: Vinita Gaikwad
Humanities and Social Sciences (Arts and Humanities; Development Studies; Economics; Social Sciences; Social Work) *Head*: Paul Mukasa
Science and Technology (Automation and Control Engineering; Technology)
Theology and Religion (Religion; Theology) *Head*: Reuben Mugerwa

History: A private Institution

Governing Bodies: Seventh Day Adventist Church of Uganda Union

Admission Requirements: Uganda Certificate of Education or equivalent

Fees: (US Dollars): 2000 per annum

Main Language(s) of Instruction: English

International Co-operation: With universities in USA, United Kingdom, Australia

Accrediting Agencies: Adventist Accrediting Association; Uganda Government

Degrees and Diplomas: *Certificate*; *Diploma*; *Bachelor's Degree*: 3 yrs; *Postgraduate Diploma*; *Master's Degree*

Student Services: Academic Counselling, Social Counselling, Foreign Student Adviser, Sports Facilities, Health Services, Canteen

Student Residential Facilities: Yes

Libraries: Main Library

Publications: Bugema Times (quarterly)

Academic Staff 2001-2002	MEN	WOMEN	TOTAL
FULL-TIME	15	10	25
PART-TIME	4	5	9
TOTAL	**19**	**15**	**34**
STAFF WITH DOCTORATE			
FULL-TIME			3
PART-TIME			3
TOTAL			**6**

Student Numbers 2001-2002	MEN	WOMEN	TOTAL
All (Foreign Included)	393	307	**700**
FOREIGN ONLY	200	210	410

Part-time Students, 20

BUSOGA UNIVERSITY

PO Box 154, Iganga
Tel: +256(43) 242-502
Fax: +256(43) 242-345
EMail: adminbugosauniversity@gyename.com
Website: http://bugosauniversity.gyename.co.uk

Vice-Chancellor: Joseph M. Ngobi-Igaga
Registrar: Nathan Ba. K. Muyobo

Faculties

Agriculture, Science and Technology (Agriculture; Animal Husbandry; Environmental Studies; Fishery; Horticulture; Rural Planning)
Architecture, Fine Art and Industrial Design (Architecture; Fine Arts; Industrial Design)
Business and Management Studies (Business Administration; Business and Commerce; Management)
Education (Education; Educational and Student Counselling; Primary Education; Secondary Education)
Social, Cultural and Development Studies (Development Studies; Social Work)

Schools

Law and Professional Studies *(Grotious)* (Business Administration; Journalism; Law)

History: Founded 1999.

Degrees and Diplomas: *Diploma*; *Bachelor's Degree*

• ISLAMIC UNIVERSITY IN UGANDA

PO Box 2555, Mbale
Tel: +256(45) 33-502
Fax: +256(45) 34-452 +256(45) 34-461
Telex: 66176isluniv ug
EMail: iuiu@infocom.co.ug
Website: http://www.iuiu.ac.ug

Rector: Mahdi Adamu (1994-)

University Secretary: Haruna Chemisto

Faculties

Arts and Social Sciences (Arts and Humanities; Economics; English; Environmental Studies; French; Geography; History; Literature; Modern Languages; Political Science; Social Sciences) *Dean*: Umar Labdo
Education (Curriculum; Education; Educational Administration; Educational Psychology; Educational Sciences) *Dean*: Victoria Mukibi
Islamic Studies and Arabic Language (Arabic; Islamic Law; Islamic Studies; Sociology) *Dean (Acting)*: Abodulqadir Bolande
Management Studies (Management; Public Administration) *Dean*: Haroonah Nsubuga

559

Science (Botany; Chemistry; Computer Science; Mathematics; Natural Sciences; Physics; Zoology) *Dean*: Shaaban Okurut

Programmes
Remedial Studies (Arabic; Biology; Chemistry; Economics; English; History; Islamic Studies; Physics) *Director*: Hassan

Centres
Postgraduate Studies *(CPS)* (Education; Islamic Studies; Management; Natural Sciences; Social Sciences) *Director*: Umar Labdo

History: Founded 1988, acquired present status and title 1990.

Governing Bodies: Organization of Islamic Conference

Academic Year: October to June (October-December; January-March; April-June)

Admission Requirements: Uganda Certificate of Education, or equivalent, with 2 passes at Advanced ('A') Level

Fees: (US Dollars): 600 per annum; postgraduate degrees, 900

Main Language(s) of Instruction: English, Arabic (for Faculty of Islamic studies)

Degrees and Diplomas: *Bachelor's Degree*: Arabic Language; Business Studies; Education; Islamic Studies; Public Administration; Science, 3 yrs; *Postgraduate Diploma*: Education, a further yr; *Master's Degree*: 2 yrs; *Doctor's Degree*: Philosophy, 3 yrs

Student Services: Academic Counselling, Social Counselling, Sports Facilities, Health Services

Student Residential Facilities: Yes

Publications: Islamic University Journal (biannually)

Academic Staff 2001-2002			TOTAL
FULL-TIME			77
PART-TIME			54
TOTAL			**131**
STAFF WITH DOCTORATE	MEN	WOMEN	TOTAL
FULL-TIME	–	–	18
PART-TIME	–	12	12
TOTAL	–	–	**30**

Student Numbers *2001-2002*: All (Foreign Included): Men: c. 820 Women: c. 325 Total: c. 1,145

KAMPALA INTERNATIONAL UNIVERSITY (KIU)
PO Box 20000, Ggaba Road, Kansanga, Kampala
Tel: +256(41) 266-813
Fax: +256(41) 501-974
EMail: admin@kiu.ac.ug
Website: http://www.kiu.ac.ug

Deputy Vice-Chancellor (Academic Affairs): Mohammed Nduala

Faculties
Education (Education; Educational Administration) *Dean*: M. Nsereko
Health Sciences (Community Health; Health Sciences; Nursing) *Dean*: Gerald Amandu Matua
Social Sciences and Law (Development Studies; Environmental Management; Law; Mass Communication; Public Administration; Social Sciences; Social Work) *Dean*: A.G.G. Gingyera Pinycwa

Schools
Business and Management (Business Administration; Cooking and Catering; Hotel Management; International Business; Secretarial Studies; Statistics; Tourism) *Dean*: John Muhumuza
Computer Science (Computer Engineering; Computer Science; Information Technology) *Dean*: Edmund Katiti

History: Founded 2001.

Admission Requirements: 2 'A' levels

Degrees and Diplomas: *Certificate*; *Diploma*: 2-3 yrs; *Bachelor's Degree*: 3-4 yrs; *Postgraduate Diploma*; *Master's Degree*: 2 yrs

KAMPALA UNIVERSITY
PO Box 25454, Kampala
Tel: +256(41) 258-219
EMail: kunir@swiftuganda.com

NAMASAGALI UNIVERSITY
PO Box 219, Kamuli
Tel: +256(77) 861-961
EMail: namasagaliuniv@teacher.com
Website: http://www.namasagali.com
Arts and Humanities; Business Administration; Computer Science; Education

Further Information: Also Jinja Campus.

History: Founded 1975 with the assistance of London University as a department of Namasagali College to promote education for women . Expanded in 1991.

NDEJJE UNIVERSITY
PO Box 7088, Kampala, Central Province
Tel: +256(41) 610-058
Fax: +256(41) 245-597

Vice-Chancellor: Michael Senyimba

Schools
Business Administration and Computer Science (Accountancy; Business Administration; Computer Science; Finance; Management; Marketing)
Education

History: Founded 1992 by the Luwero/Namirembe Dioceses of the Anglican Church of Uganda. Acquired present status 1995.

Governing Bodies: University Council

Academic Year: October to August (October-January;February-May; May-August)

Admission Requirements: Uganda Certificate of Education or equivalent

Main Language(s) of Instruction: English

Degrees and Diplomas: *Diploma*: 1-2 yrs; *Bachelor's Degree*: 2-3 yrs

Student Residential Facilities: For c. 300 students

Libraries: Main Library, c. 40,000 vols

NKUMBA UNIVERSITY (NU)
PO Box 237, Entebbe Road, Entebbe
Tel: +256(41) 320-134
Fax: +256(41) 321-448
EMail: nkumbaun@infocom.co.ug
Website: http://www.nkumbauniversity.ac.ug
Vice-Chancellor: William Senteza Kajubi (1994-)
Tel: +256 (41) 320-283 Fax: +256 (41) 320-134

Academic Registrar: Samuel Busulwa
Tel: +256 (41) 320-283

International Relations: Eric K. Kigozi, Director, University Relations and Consultancy Services Tel: +256 (41) 320-537

Schools
Business Administration (Business Administration; Computer Science; Economics; Statistics) *Dean*: Eric Mugerwa
Commercial, Industrial Art and Design (Business Education; Computer Education; Computer Engineering; Industrial Design; Painting and Drawing; Printing and Printmaking; Textile Technology) *Dean*: Francis Musangogwantamu
Education, Humanities and Social Sciences (Accountancy; Business Education; Management; Secretarial Studies) *Dean*: Grace Kyeyune
Hospitality and Environmental Sciences (Cooking and Catering; Environmental Studies; Hotel Management; Tourism) *Dean*: Eric Edroma

History: Founded 1951, acquired present status and title 1994.

Governing Bodies: Board of Trustees; University Council

Academic Year: January to December (January-April; May-August; September-December)

Admission Requirements: Uganda Advanced Certificate of Education or equivalent

Fees: (Uganda Shillings): 690,000 per term

Main Language(s) of Instruction: English

Accrediting Agencies: National Council for Higher Education

Degrees and Diplomas: *Certificate*: Hotel Management and Institutional Catering; Commercial, Industrial Art and Design; Office Management and Secretarial Studies; Wildlife Management; Home Economics, 1 yr; *Diploma*: Development Studies; Political Science; Sociology and Development; Office Management and Secretarial Studies; Environment Management; Wildlife Management; Home Economics and Nutrition; Marketing; Purchasing and Supplies Management; Computer Science; Banking, Finance and Management; Accountancy; Business Management; Hotel Operations; Tourism; Commercial, Industrial Art and Design, 2 yrs; *Bachelor's Degree*: Development Studies; Political Science; Sociology and Development; Office Management and Secretarial Studies; International Relations and Diplomacy; Community Based Development; Education; Business Education; Hotel Operations; Tourism; Wildlife Management; Home Economics and Nutrition; Environmental Studies; Business Administration (BBA); Business Law (BBL); Commercial, Industrial Art and Design (BA(CIAD)); Information Technology (BIT); Public Administration and Management (BA(PAM)), 3 yrs; *Master's Degree*: Education; Educational

Administration; Curriculum Development; Educational Management and Planning (MEd); Public Administration and Management; Development Studies; Community Based Development (MA); Accountancy and Finance; Human Resources; Marketing; Purchasing and Supplies Management (MSc); Accountancy; Finance; Human Resources; Marketing; Purchasing and Supplies; Management (MBA), a further 15 mths; Environment Management; Tourism; Commercial, Industrial Art and Design; International Relations and Diplomacy (MSc), a further 2 yrs

Libraries: Nkumba University Library, 8966 vols; 8997 journal subscriptions

Publications: Nkumba University Business Journal (annually)

Academic Staff 2002	MEN	WOMEN	TOTAL
FULL-TIME	61	9	70
PART-TIME	16	5	21
TOTAL	77	14	91
STAFF WITH DOCTORATE			
FULL-TIME	12	1	13
PART-TIME	–	–	1
TOTAL	–	–	14
Student Numbers 2002	MEN	WOMEN	TOTAL
All (Foreign Included)	1,204	1,276	2,480
FOREIGN ONLY	53	34	87

Evening Students, 492

UGANDA CHRISTIAN UNIVERSITY (UCU)
PO Box 4, Bishop Tucker Campus, Mukono, Church
Tel: +256(41) 290-231
Fax: +256(41) 290-139
EMail: ucu@africaonline.co.ug
Website: http://www.ucu.ac.ug
Vice-Chancellor: Stephen Noll

Academic Registrar: Alex Kagume Mugisha

International Relations: Stephen Noll

Faculties
Divinity and Theology (Religion; Theology) Edison Kalengyo
Law Lilian Tibatemwa
Management, Business and Development (Business Administration; Business and Commerce; Development Studies; Management) Joseph Owor
Mass Communication
Technology (Computer Science; Information Technology; Technology)

Departments
Education John Bwanuki
Social Sciences (Development Studies; Social Sciences; Social Work) Benon Musinguzi

History: Founded 1997.

Governing Bodies: University Council

Fees: (Uganda Shillings): 570,000-1,200,000 per annum

Main Language(s) of Instruction: English

International Co-operation: International Christian Medical Institute, Trinity Episcopal, Pennsylvania

Accrediting Agencies: National Council for Higher Education; Ministry of Education and Sports

Degrees and Diplomas: *Diploma*; *Bachelor's Degree*; *Master's Degree*

Student Services: Academic Counselling, Social Counselling, Employment Services, Sports Facilities, Language Programmes, Health Services, Canteen, Foreign Student Centre

Student Residential Facilities: Yes

Libraries: c. 50,000 vols, 70 periodicals, Internet facilities, Audio-visual

Publications: Anvil, Student newspaper (monthly)

Academic Staff 2001-2002	MEN	WOMEN	TOTAL
FULL-TIME	26	6	32
PART-TIME	31	11	42
TOTAL	**57**	**17**	**74**

STAFF WITH DOCTORATE			
FULL-TIME			4
PART-TIME			4
TOTAL			**8**

Student Numbers 2001-2002	MEN	WOMEN	TOTAL
All (Foreign Included)	871	694	**1,565**
FOREIGN ONLY	38	9	47

Part-time Students, 111 **Evening Students,** 204

UGANDA MARTYRS UNIVERSITY (UMU)

PO Box 5498, Kampala
Tel: +256(38) 410-611
Fax: +256(38) 410-100
EMail: umu@umu.ac.ug
Website: http://www.fiuc.org/umu

Vice-Chancellor: Michel Lejeune (1992-)
Tel: +256(38) 410-603 EMail: mlejeune@umu.ac.ug

Registrar: Marie-Esther Haflett Tel: +256(38) 410-606
EMail: mehaflett@umu.ac.ug

International Relations: Michel Lejeune

Faculties

Agriculture *Dean*: Charles Ssekyewa
Building Technology and Architecture (Architectural and Environmental Design; Architecture; Building Technologies) *Dean*: Simon Kisasa
Business Administration and Management *(Nkozi)* (Accountancy; Business Administration; Commercial Law; Finance; Management; Marketing) *Dean*: Simeon Wanyama
Education *Dean*: Emurwon Olupot
Science *(Nkozi)* (Computer Science; Economics; Mathematics; Natural Sciences; Statistics) *Dean*: Tom Muyanja

Institutes

Ethics and Development Studies *(Nkozi)* (African Studies; Development Studies; Ethics) *Director*: Deirdre Carabine

Centres

African Research and Documentation *(ARDC/CARD)* (African Studies; Peace and Disarmament) *Director*: Peter Kanyandago

Note: Also Polytechnic and Management Institute

Extramural Studies *(Nkozi)* (Finance; Human Resources; Management) *Director*: Martin O'Reilly
Good Governance and Civil Society *(International)* (Government; Sociology) *Director*: Deirdre Carabine

History: Founded 1989, first academic year 1993. A private institution under the supervision of the Catholic Church in Uganda.

Governing Bodies: Governing Council; Senate; Advisory Board

Academic Year: October to June (October-January; February-June)

Admission Requirements: Uganda Advanced Certificate of Education or equivalent

Fees: (Uganda Shillings): 3.6m. per annum; postgraduate, 4.2m.

Main Language(s) of Instruction: English

Accrediting Agencies: National Council for Higher Education

Degrees and Diplomas: *Diploma*: Health Services Management (Dip.(HSM)); Human Resources Management (Dip(HRM)), 1 yr; *Bachelor's Degree*: Building Design and Technology (BSc (BT&A)); Business Administration and Management (BBAM); Education (BEd); Ethics and Development Studies, 3 yrs; Agriculture (BSc (Agric)), 4 yrs (Distance learning); *Master's Degree*: Management, Finance and Banking, a further yr; Ethics and Development Studies (MA (DS)); Health Services Management; Information Systems, a further yr. Also 2-yr Associate Bachelor's Degree (Distance Learning) in Micro Finance; Democracy and Development Studies; Human Rights and Good Governance

Student Services: Academic Counselling, Nursery Care, Sports Facilities, Health Services, Canteen

Student Residential Facilities: For 460 students

Special Facilities: Museum of African Art

Libraries: University Library, c. 20,000 vols

Publications: Mtafiti Mwafrika; UMU Studies in Contemporary Africa (biannually)

Press or Publishing House: UMU Press.

Academic Staff 2002-2003	MEN	WOMEN	TOTAL
FULL-TIME	38	19	57
PART-TIME	18	4	22
TOTAL	**56**	**23**	**79**

STAFF WITH DOCTORATE			
FULL-TIME	8	2	10
PART-TIME	2	–	2
TOTAL	**10**	**2**	**12**

Student Numbers 2002-2003	MEN	WOMEN	TOTAL
All (Foreign Included)	213	246	**459**
FOREIGN ONLY	29	50	79

Part-time Students, 17 **Evening Students,** 79 **Distance Students,** 1,567

Zambia

INSTITUTION TYPES AND CREDENTIALS

Types of higher education institutions:

University
Technical and Vocational College
Institute

School leaving and higher education credentials:

General Certificate of Education
Zambian School Certificate
Certificate
Diploma
Bachelor's degree
Master's degree
Doctorate

STRUCTURE OF EDUCATION SYSTEM

Pre-higher education:

Duration of compulsory education:

Age of entry: 7
Age of exit: 14

Structure of school system:

First Cycle Primary
Type of school providing this education: Lower Primary School
Length of programme in years: 4
Age level from: 7 to: 11

Second Cycle Primary
Type of school providing this education: Upper Primary School
Length of programme in years: 3
Age level from: 11 to: 14
Certificate/diploma awarded: Certificate of Primary Education

Junior Secondary
Type of school providing this education: Junior Secondary School
Length of programme in years: 2

Age level from: 14 to: 16
Certificate/diploma awarded: Junior Secondary School Certificate

Senior Secondary
Type of school providing this education: Senior Secondary School
Length of programme in years: 3
Age level from: 16 to: 19
Certificate/diploma awarded: Zambian School Certificate Examination or General Certificate of Education "0" Levels

School education:

Primary education lasts for seven years, divided into two parts, and leading to the Certificate of Primary Education. The secondary school system is also divided into two parts: Junior Secondary consisting of Grades 8 and 9, and Senior Secondary consisting of Grades 10-12. To proceed from Grade 9 to 10, one has to sit for an examination, the Junior Secondary School Certificate Examination. At the end of senior secondary education, students sit for the Zambian School Certificate or the General Certificate of Education "O" Levels.

Higher education:

Higher education is provided by two universities under the Ministry of Education, and by various specialized technical and vocational institutions controlled by the Ministry of Science, Technology and Vocational Training. The highest administrative body of the constituent universities is the Council on which serve members of the Government, students, teaching staff, graduates and representatives of outside bodies. The highest academic body is the Senate.

Main laws/decrees governing higher education:

Decree: The University of Zambia Act   Year: 1987
Concerns: University

Decree: Technical Education and Vocational Training Act   Year: 1973
Concerns: Technical Education and Vocational Training

Decree: Education Act   Year: 1966
Concerns: Basic framework for education system

Academic year:

Classes from: February *to:* December

Languages of instruction:

English

Stages of studies:

Non-university level post-secondary studies (technical/vocational type):

At this level, a Craft Certificate is offered in two years, plus one year of industrial practice. A Technician Diploma is offered in two years and four months. Certificates and Diplomas in non-Technical subjects require two years of study. Diplomas underwritten by the University of Zambia also require two years.

University level studies:

University level first stage: *Bachelor's Degree*:
The first stage consists of university level degrees taking from four to seven years. Degree courses are the following: BA, BSc, BSc Education, BA Library Studies, BA Education, Bachelor of Social Work, Bachelor of Law, BSc in Nursing, Bachelor of Accounting, Bachelor of Business Administration, four years; Bachelor of Mineral Science, Bachelor of Agriculture, Bachelor of Engineering, Bachelor of Architecture, BSc in Building, five years; Bachelor of Veterinary Medicine, six years; Bachelor of Medicine, seven years. Undergraduate Certificates and Diplomas are the following: Certificate in Law, Certificate in Adult Education, one year; Diploma in Adult Education, two years; Diploma in Social Work and Technology Diploma, three years.

University level second stage: *Master's Degree*:
This stage consists of courses leading to a qualification at Masters' level. Studies generally last for two years. The following Master's courses are offered: Law (15 months); Business Administration (18 months); Agronomy, Education, Engineering, Economics, Educational Psychology, Political Science, Sociology, Public Administration, Veterinary Medicine, MSc (all two years); Medicine (four years).

University level third stage: *Doctorate*:
This stage leads to PhD qualifications which are offered in a limited number of specializations. The course takes up to four years to complete.

Teacher education:

Training of pre-primary and primary/basic school teachers
Primary school certificate teachers follow a two-year training course at any of the eleven primary school teacher colleges. There is no specialization per se for this pre-service programme, as teachers are expected to teach all subjects offered at primary school. Primary school diploma teachers are trained at the National In-service Training College after completing the initial training from a primary school teacher college and having served in schools for some years. Primary school diploma teachers may obtain a diploma in special education from the Lusaka College for Teachers of the Handicapped.

Training of secondary school teachers
Secondary school diploma teachers are trained at Nkrumah Teacher College, Copperbelt Secondary Teacher College, and Luanshya Technical and Vocational Teacher College. The latter is run by the Ministry of Science and Technology. They are qualified to teach at the junior secondary education level. There is another category of secondary school diploma teachers who follow a three-year course in agriculture science at the Natural Resources Development College, belonging to the Ministry of Agriculture, Food and Water Development. This category is qualified to teach agriculture science up to the senior secondary school level.
Secondary school degree teachers are trained at the University of Zambia and are qualified to teach up to the senior secondary level. They can also teach at the teacher training colleges and as staff development fellows. During their study they take two teaching subjects and professional courses in education.

Non-traditional studies:

Distance higher education
This type of education is offered by technical and vocational colleges and the University of Zambia. Entrance requirements are lower than for those who enter a full-time course. The duration of studies is also much longer since students do not take all the courses for a given year at one time.

NATIONAL BODIES

Responsible authorities:

Ministry of Education
    Minister: Andrew Mulenga
    PO Box 50093
    Lusaka
    Tel: +260(1) 227-636 +260(1) 227-639
    Fax: +260(1) 222-396
    Telex: 42621

Ministry of Science, Technology and Vocational Training
    Minister: Abel M. Chambeshi
    Permanent Secretary: Geoffrey P. Mukala
    International Relations: Paul Zambezi
    PO Box 50464
    Lusaka
    Tel: +260(1) 252-053 +260(1) 252-099
    Fax: +260(1) 252-951 +260(1) 252-954
    Telex: 40406
    EMail: momstvt@zamtel.zm
    Role of governing body: Coordinates Technical Training Institutions

ADMISSIONS TO HIGHER EDUCATION

Admission to university-level studies

Name of secondary school credential required: General Certificate of Education
Minimum score/requirement: Pass in at least 5 subjects at GCE 'O' level
For entry to: University admission

Name of secondary school credential required: Zambian School Certificate
Minimum score/requirement: Passes at credit level in five approved subjects.
For entry to: University

Alternatives to credentials: A two-year Diploma from a college which has a special relationship with the University.

Numerus clausus/restrictions: Dependent upon the number of places available.

Other admission requirements: Students not entering university directly from school are required to sit for a mature age examination.

Foreign students admission

Quotas: 5 per cent quota for foreign student admission at university level

Entry regulations: Foreign students have to obtain a study permit for entry into the country and have full financial support. Admission is facilitated if they are part of an established inter-university exchange agreement.

Health requirements: The applicant has to undergo a medical examination, and is admitted only if declared fit by a Medical Doctor.

Language requirements: Foreign students must be proficient in English.

Application procedures:

Apply to individual institution for entry to: All Higher Education Institutions.

Apply to: Senior Assistant Registrar (for University of Zambia)
The University of Zambia
PO Box 32379
Lusaka
WWW: http://www.unza.zm

Recognition of studies and qualifications:

Studies pursued in home country (System of recognition/accreditation): Credentials are recognized by the State and the Professional Bodies

Studies pursued in foreign countries (bodies dealing with recognition of foreign credentials):
Ministry of Science, Technology and Vocational Training
PO Box 50464
Lusaka
Tel: +260(1) 252-053
Fax: +260(1) 252-951 +260(1) 252-954
Telex: 40406
Deals with credential recognition for entry to: University

Other information sources on recognition of foreign studies: Universities

Special provisions for recognition:

For access to non-university post-secondary studies: They should be equivalent to local qualifications

For access to university level studies: They should be equivalent to national entry requirements

For access to advanced studies and research: First degree or equivalent

For the exercise of a profession: This is left to individual professions and the Ministries under which a given profession falls. The Law Assocation of Zambia has its own rules and regulations for Law credentials.

Multilateral agreements concerning recognition of foreign studies

Name(s) of agreement(s): Convention on the Recognition of Studies, Certificates, Diplomas, Degrees and Other Academic Qualifications in Higher Education in the African States
Year of signature: 1981

References to further information on foreign student admissions and recognition of studies

Title: Handbooks and Calendars produced by individual institutions

STUDENT LIFE

Main student services at national level

Department of Human Resource Development, Public Service Management Division, Office of the President
　PO Box 50340
　Lusaka
　Tel: +260(1) 252-704 +260(1) 252-015
　Fax: +260(1) 253-958 +260(1) 254-231
　EMail: dhr@zamtel.zm

National student associations and unions

National Student Union
　PO Box 32379
　Great East Road
　Lusaka
10101
　Tel: +260(1) 293-058
　Fax: +260(1) 253-952

Health/social provisions

Social security for home students: No

Special student travel fares:

By road: No
By rail: No
By air: No
Available to foreign students: No

Student expenses and financial aid

Student costs:

　Home students tuition fees: Maximum: 2,500,000 (Zambian Kwacha)

INTERNATIONAL COOPERATION AND EXCHANGES

Principal national bodies responsible for dealing with international cooperation and exchanges in higher education:

Department of Human Resource Development, Public Management Division, Office of the President
  Head of Department, Director: Marcharligne Nkhuwa
  Assistant Director (Terp): Stella C. Chishimba
  PO Box 50340
  Lusaka
  Tel: +260(1) 252-704 +260(1) 252-015
  Fax: +260(1) 253-958 +260(1) 254-231
  EMail: dhr@zamtel.zm

GRADING SYSTEM

Usual grading system in secondary school

Full Description: The grading system is expressed in points which are also represented in percentages. The Zambian School Certificate is graded 1-9, 9 being a fail.
Highest on scale: 1
Pass/fail level: 7-8
Lowest on scale: 9

Main grading system used by higher education institutions

Full Description: Letters grading system is represented by A,B,C,D,and E: A+=90, A=80, B+=75, B=65, C+=55, C=45, D=35 and below
Highest on scale: A+
Pass/fail level: C
Lowest on scale: E

NOTES ON HIGHER EDUCATION SYSTEM

Data for academic year: 2002-2003
Source: University of Zambia, Lusaka, updated by the International Association of Universities (IAU) from IBE website, 2003 (www.ibe.unesco.org/International/Databanks/Wde/profilee.htm)

INSTITUTIONS OF HIGHER EDUCATION

UNIVERSITIES

PUBLIC INSTITUTIONS

• COPPERBELT UNIVERSITY (CBU)

PO Box 21692, Jambo Drive, Riverside, Kitwe, Copperbelt
Tel: +260(2) 212-066
Fax: +260(2) 212-469
Telex: (0902) 53270 cbu za
Cable: cbu kitwe
EMail: cbu@zamnet.zm

Vice-Chancellor: John Lungu (1999-) Tel: +260 (2) 228-797
Fax: +260 (2) 228-319 EMail: lunguj@cbu.ac.zm

Registrar: K.K. Kapika Tel: +260(2) 223-015
EMail: kkk@cbu.ac.zm

International Relations: M.K. Chilufya, Dean of Students
Tel: +260(2) 220-552

Schools

Architecture and Land Economy and Civil Engineering (Agricultural Economics; Architecture; Building Technologies; Civil Engineering; Regional Planning; Town Planning) *Dean*: Gibson Ngoma

Business (Accountancy; Business Administration; Business and Commerce; Industrial and Production Economics) *Dean*: F.P. Tailoka

Forestry and Wood Science (Ecology; Forestry; Wildlife; Wood Technology) *Dean*: Peter Fushike

Technology (Chemical Engineering; Computer Science; Electrical and Electronic Engineering; Technology) *Dean*: Felix Kanungwe

Departments

Built Environment Research (Building Technologies; Town Planning) *Head*: Binwell N. Dioma

Business Research *(ICAR)* (Business Administration; Business and Commerce) *Head*: Davison Chilipamushi

Technological Research *(ICAR)* (Computer Science; Electrical and Electronic Engineering; Metallurgical Engineering; Mining Engineering; Surveying and Mapping; Technology) *Head*: Mulemwa Akombelwa

Institutes

Applied Research and Extension Studies *Director*: Kamona Maseka

Environmental Management *Director*: Julius Kanyembo

Centres

Lifelong Education *(ICAR)* (Accountancy; Business and Commerce; Human Resources; Marketing) *Director*: Emmanuel Chunda

History: Founded 1987. Previously University of Zambia at Ndola, a Constituent institution of the University of Zambia. Acquired present status 1989

Governing Bodies: Council; Senate

Academic Year: March to December (March-May; June-August; August-December)

Admission Requirements: Zambian School Certificate with passes at credit level in 5 approved subjects, or General Certificate of Education (GCE) with passes in 5 approved subjects at Ordinary ('O') level

Fees: (Kwacha): 3.5m. per annum

Main Language(s) of Instruction: English

Degrees and Diplomas: *Bachelor's degree*: 4 yrs; Engineering, 5 yrs; *Master's degree*: Business Administration (MBA), a further 1 1/2 yrs

Student Services: Academic Counselling, Social Counselling, Employment Services, Nursery Care, Sports Facilities, Health Services, Canteen

Student Residential Facilities: For c. 1800 students

Libraries: University Library, c. 25,000 vols

Publications: Journal of Business (2 per annum)

Academic Staff *2002:* Total: **140**

Student Numbers *2000:* Total: **2,670**

• UNIVERSITY OF ZAMBIA (UNZA)

PO Box 32379, Lusaka
Tel: +260(1) 291-777
Fax: +260(1) 253-952
EMail: unza@unza.za.
Website: http://www.unza.zm

Vice-Chancellor: Elizabeth Mumba Tel: +260(1) 250-871
Fax: +260(1) 250-871 EMail: vc@unza.zm

Head Librarian: H. C. Mwacalimba

Schools

Agricultural Sciences (Agricultural Economics; Agricultural Education; Agriculture; Animal Husbandry; Crop Production; Education; Soil Science) *Dean*: Faustin Mwape

Education (Educational Administration; Library Science; Mathematics; Psychology; Science Education; Social Sciences; Sociology; Special Education) *Dean*: D. M. Mwansa

Engineering (Agricultural Engineering; Civil Engineering; Electrical Engineering; Electronic Engineering; Engineering; Mechanical Engineering; Mining Engineering; Surveying and Mapping) *Dean*: Alvert N. Ng'andu

Humanities and Social Sciences (Arts and Humanities; Development Studies; Economics; History; Humanities and Social Science Education; Literature; Mass Communication; Modern Languages; Philosophy; Political Science; Psychology; Social Sciences) *Dean*: John D. Chileshe

Law (International Law; Law) *Dean*: F. Ng'andu

Medicine (Anatomy; Community Health; Gynaecology and Obstetrics; Medicine; Microbiology; Nursing; Paediatrics; Pathology; Physiology; Psychiatry and Mental Health; Surgery) *Dean*: L. Munkonge

Mines (Geology; Metallurgical Engineering; Mineralogy; Mining Engineering) *Dean*: Francis Tembo

Natural Sciences (Biochemistry; Biology; Chemistry; Computer Science; Geography; Mathematics; Natural Sciences; Physics) *Dean*: I. E. Mumba

Veterinary Science (Biomedicine; Veterinary Science) *Dean*: K.L. Samui

Institutes

Economic and Social Research (Economics; Government; Health Sciences; Rural Planning; Social Sciences; Urban Studies) *Director*: O. Saasa

Centres

Creative Arts (Fine Arts) *Director*: M. Mapopa
Distance Education *Director*: R.C.M. Siaciwena
Research and Postgraduate Studies *Director*: G. Lungwangwa

History: Founded 1965.

Governing Bodies: Council; Senate

Academic Year: February to December (February-June; July-December)

Admission Requirements: Certificate with passes at credit level in 5 approved subjects, or General Certificate of Education (GCE) with passes in 5 approved subjects at Ordinary ('O') level

Fees: (Kwacha): c. 2m.-3m. per annum.

Main Language(s) of Instruction: English

Degrees and Diplomas: *Bachelor's degree*: Arts (BA); Arts in Education (BAEd); Arts in Library Science (BALS); Laws (LLB); Mass Communication (BMassComm); Science (BSc); Science in Education (BScEd); Science in Human Biology (BScHB); Science in Nursing (BScN); Social Work (BSW), 4 yrs; Agricultural Science (BAgSc); Engineering (BEng); Mineral Sciences (BMinSc), 5 yrs; Veterinary Medicine (BVetMed), 6 yrs; Medicine and Surgery (MB ChB), 7 yrs; *Master's degree*: Arts (MA); Education (MEd); Engineering (MEng); Laws (LLM); Medicine (MMEd); Mineral Sciences (MMinSc); Public Administration (MPA); Science (MSc); Veterinary Medicine (MVM), a further 2-4 yrs; *Doctorate*: (PhD), up to a further 4 yrs. Also undergraduate and postgraduate Certificates and Diplomas

Student Residential Facilities: Yes

Special Facilities: UNZA Nursery (for plants/horticulture)

Libraries: Main Library, c. 251,750 vols; Medical Library; Veterinary Medicine Library

Academic Staff *2001-2002*: Full-Time: c. 430 Part-Time: c. 60 Total: c. 490

Staff with Doctorate: Total: c. 230

Student Numbers *2001-2002:* Total: c. 3,500

COPPERBELT SECONDARY TEACHERS' COLLEGE
PO Box 20382, Kitwe
Tel: +260 711-202

Colleges
Teacher Training (Home Economics Education; Mathematics Education; Science Education; Teacher Training)

GEORGE BENSON CHRISTIAN COLLEGE
Namwianga
Tel: +260(32) 324-304
Principal: F. Chona

Programmes
English
Mathematics
Religious Education

LUANSHYA TECHNICAL AND VOCATIONAL TEACHERS'
COLLEGE
PO Box 90199, Luanshya
Tel: +260(2) 512-244
Principal: G.D. Zulu

Colleges
Teacher Training (Vocational Education)

History: Founded 1976.

NKRUMAH TEACHERS' COLLEGE
PO Box 80404, Kabwe
Tel: +260 221-525
Principal: S.B. Mpundu

Teacher Training (Secondary Education; Teacher Training; Technology Education; Vocational Education)

History: Founded 1967.

OTHER INSTITUTIONS

PUBLIC INSTITUTIONS

EVELYN HONE COLLEGE OF APPLIED ARTS AND COMMERCE
PO Box 30029, Lusaka
Tel: +260(1) 211-752
EMail: ehcbs@zamnet.zm

Principal: Edrick A.Y. Mwambazi (1995-)
Tel: +260(1) 225-127 Fax: +260(1) 225-127
Registrar: Aaron P. Chitsulo Tel: +260(1) 222-387

Founded: 1963

Departments
Academic and Applied Sciences (Natural Sciences)
Business Studies (Business and Commerce)
Comunication Skills (Communication Studies)
Education

Media Studies
Paramedical Studies (Paramedical Sciences)
Secretarial Studies

NATIONAL INSTITUTE OF PUBLIC ADMINISTRATION
PO Box 31990, Lusaka
Tel: +260(1) 228-802
Fax: +260(1) 227-113

Principal: M.C. Bwalya (1998-) Tel: +260(1) 222-480
Registrar: R. Mwambu Tel: +260(1) 228-802, Ext 102

Divisions
Accountancy and Financial Management Training (Accountancy; Business Education; Finance; Management)
Legal Training (Law)
Management and Administration Training (Administration; Business Education; Management)
Research, Consultancy and Development (Development Studies; Educational and Student Counselling) *Head*: T.D.C. Syamunyangwa

Further Information: Also Burma Road Campus.

History: Founded 1963. A semi-autonomous institution.

NATURAL RESOURCES DEVELOPMENT CENTRE
PO Box 310099, Lusaka
Founded: 1965
Agricultural Education; Agricultural Engineering; Agriculture; Fishery; Natural Resources; Nutrition; Water Science

NORTHERN TECHNICAL COLLEGE
PO Box 250093, Chela Road, Ndola
Tel: +260(2) 680-141
Fax: +260(2) 680-423

Head: Godfrey Mwango Kapambwe (1995-)
Tel: +260(2) 680-739

Founded: 1961
Automotive Engineering; Business and Commerce; Communication Studies; Electrical Engineering; Mechanical Engineering; Technology

Zimbabwe

INSTITUTION TYPES AND CREDENTIALS

Types of higher education institutions:

University
Polytechnic
Technical College
Teacher Training College

School leaving and higher education credentials:

General Certificate of Education 'O' Level
Cambridge Higher School Certificate (HSC)
General Certificate of Education 'A' Level
National Certificate
Diploma
Bachelor Degree
Bachelor Honours Degree
Master Degree
Graduate Certificate
Master of Philosophy
Doctorate

STRUCTURE OF EDUCATION SYSTEM

Pre-higher education:

Duration of compulsory education:

Age of entry: 6
Age of exit: 13

Structure of school system:

Primary
Type of school providing this education: Primary School
Length of programme in years: 7
Age level from: 6 to: 13
Certificate/diploma awarded: Grade 7 Certificate Examination

Lower Secondary
Type of school providing this education: Secondary School (Forms I to IV)

Length of programme in years: 4
Age level from: 13 to: 17
Certificate/diploma awarded: General Certificate of Education 'O' Level

Upper Secondary
Type of school providing this education: Secondary School (Forms V and VI)
Length of programme in years: 2
Age level from: 17 to: 19
Certificate/diploma awarded: Cambridge Higher School Certificate (HSC)/CGE 'A' Level

School education:

Primary education lasts seven years and children usually enrol at the age of 6. The seven-year cycle is divided into infant grades (I and II) and junior grades (III-VII). At the end of the primary stage, successful pupils are awarded the Grade Seven Certificate.

Secondary education lasts six years and includes: a four-year Ordinary Level cycle where the official entry age is 13 years (there is unimpeded progress to the CGE O-Level cycle, but some schools set selection criteria based on Grade VII examinations); a two-year Advanced Level cycle, which is a restricted cycle since progression is on merit or selection . At the end, students take the Cambridge Higher School Certificate (HSC) or CGE 'A' Level Certificate.

Higher education:

Tertiary education in Zimbabwe is offered at State and private universities, university colleges, teacher training colleges and technical colleges, including two polytechnics. After CGE 'O' or 'A' levels, students can be awarded Diplomas in Teaching, Agriculture, Nursing and follow several technical courses. With good 'A' level passes, a student can enrol at University for undergraduate studies.

Main laws/decrees governing higher education:

Decree: Manpower Planning and Development Act (Amended)   Year: 1994
Concerns: Tertiary education and training

Academic year:

Classes from: August *to:* June

Languages of instruction:

English

Stages of studies:

Non-university level post-secondary studies (technical/vocational type):

The following Diplomas and Certificates (National Certificate) are offered after 'O' or 'A' level Certificates: Library and Information Science; Teaching; Nursing, Agriculture, Business Studies, etc. Studies leading to these qualifications last between two and three years. These studies are offered in: Agricultural Colleges, Nursing Schools attached to Hospitals, Polytechnics and Teacher Training Colleges. Students with good grades at the Diploma level may apply to the University to undertake undergraduate studies.

University level studies:

University level first stage: Undergraduate studies:

On completion of undergraduate studies, students obtain Bachelor Degrees in Arts, Science, Commerce, Engineering, Education, Social Studies, Agriculture, Veterinary Science and Medicine. Studies vary in length from three years for the Bachelor of Arts Degree to five years for the Bachelor of Medicine and Bachelor of Surgery Degrees.

University level second stage: Graduate studies:

This stage comprises two types of Degrees. The Master Degree by coursework and dissertation; and the Master of Philosophy by research. The length of study varies from one to three years.

University level third stage: Doctorate:

The third stage requires a minimum of three years' specialization and research and the presentation of a thesis. It leads to the Degree of Doctor of Philosophy, (PhD), which is conferred by all faculties.

University level fourth stage:

A Higher Doctorate is awarded in Law (LLD), Humanities (DLitt) and Science (DSc) after submission of published work and after at least eight years' study following upon the first Degree.

Teacher education:

Training of pre-primary and primary/basic school teachers

Students intending to train as primary school teachers must hold at least five "O" levels credits including English Language. The training offered in teacher training colleges lasts for three years. Studies include theoretical and practical courses. Primary school teacher training colleges require each student to study all the subjects offered in the primary school curriculum, including theory of education and one main subject. Most of the training colleges are now affiliated with the University of Zimbabwe Faculty of Education. Students, on completion of their studies, obtain a University of Zimbabwe Diploma in Education. Good grades in Mathematics and Science are required.

Training of secondary school teachers

Secondary School Teachers are trained at two levels. The first level is open to students who hold full 'O' and 'A' level Certificates. Courses last for three years (two years for "A" levels holders). Studies consist of compulsory courses in Education after which students specialize in the subjects they will teach. The second level of training is for students who have completed a Bachelor Degree and a one-year Postgraduate Certificate in Education at the University of Zimbabwe Faculty of Education. These teachers will also teach subjects which they studied for the Bachelor's Degree.

Training of higher education teachers

Higher education teachers are those who teach Undergraduate and Postgraduate programmes at university. Most hold Master and Doctoral Degrees. Normally the University selects students with First Class passes at the Bachelor Degree level for advanced training at the Master and Doctoral levels at any good University. When students complete their studies they return to the University to teach.

Non-traditional studies:

Higher education training in industry
Training in industry covers many kinds of skills and qualifications. There are private Colleges which train individuals in Banking, Personnel and Manpower Training, Motor Mechanics, Insurance, etc...

NATIONAL BODIES

Responsible authorities:
Ministry of Higher and Tertiary Education
    Minister: S.T. Mombeshora
    Permanent Secretary: Washington T. Mbizvo
    International Relations: Josiah Mhlanga
    PO Box UA 275
    Old Mutual Centre, Union Avenue
    Harare
    Tel: +263(4) 796-740 263(4) 730-051
    Fax: +263(4) 790-923 263(4) 728-730
    EMail: thesecretarymhet@mhet.ac.zw
    WWW: http://www.mhet.ac.zw/index.html

    Role of governing body: Financing, development and co-ordination of higher education in Zimbabwe

National Council for Higher Education
    Chairman: Christopher Chetsanga
    Executive Secretary: Felicity Joyce Mkushi
    International Relations: Felicity Joyce Mkushi
    PO Box UA 94
    Union Avenue
    Harare
    Tel: +263(4) 796-441
    Fax: +263(4) 728-730
    EMail: mkushij@mhet.gov.zw
    WWW: http://www.mhet.ac.zw/index.html

    Role of governing body: Created in1990, it facilitates the establishment of universities and university colleges, accreditation and standardization of programmes.

Zimbabwe Universities' Vice-Chancellors' Association
    Chairperson: Ngwabi Bhebe
    International Relations: E.D. Shoko
    PB 9055
    Gweru
Midlands
    Tel: +263(54) 60753

Fax: +263(54) 60753

EMail: msuvcoffice@yahoo.com

Role of governing body: To provide a means whereby universities can take counsel together on matters of mutual concern; to formulate advice to governing bodies to take other appropriate action whenever it believes this could be useful and to collect and disseminate to universities information on matters of mutual interest

ADMISSIONS TO HIGHER EDUCATION

Admission to non university higher education studies

Name of secondary school credential required: General Certificate of Education 'O' Level
Minimum score/requirement: Passes in five subjects
For entry to: Polytechnics etc...

Admission to university-level studies

Name of secondary school credential required: General Certificate of Education 'A' Level
Minimum score/requirement: Two or three subjects with C or better

Name of secondary school credential required: Cambridge Higher School Certificate (HSC)
Minimum score/requirement: Two or three subjects with C or better

Alternatives to credentials: Holders of Diplomas in Education, Nursing, Agriculture, Business studies can enter undergraduate studies. Provisions for special and mature student entry with approval from the University of Zimbabwe Senate.

Other admission requirements: Experience relevant to the subject is also used as an entry criterion for students who do not hold Advanced ("A") levels.

Foreign students admission

Admission requirements: Foreign students must have qualifications equivalent to the GCE with 5 Ordinary ('O') level passes plus 2 Advanced ('A') level. Some provision is made for special and mature students entry with approval from the University Senate. Admission is directed to the Admission Office of each University.

Entry regulations: Student permits are normally provided on arrival in Zimbabwe with proof of acceptance to the University

Language requirements: English

Application procedures:

Apply to individual institution for entry to: Universities
Apply to: Admissions Office

Recognition of studies and qualifications:

Studies pursued in foreign countries (bodies dealing with recognition of foreign credentials): National Council for Higher Education

Chairman: Christopher Chetsanga
Executive Secretary: Joyce Mkushi
PO Box UA 94 Union Ave
Harare
Tel: +263(4) 796-441
Fax: +263(4) 728-730
EMail: mkushij@mhet.gov.zw
WWW: http://www.mhet.ac.zw/index.html

Deals with credential recognition for entry to: University and Profession
Services provided and students dealt with: Holders of Diplomas and Degrees

References to further information on foreign student admissions and recognition of studies

Title: Prospectus (Annual publication)
Author: Students Enquiries Office
Publisher: University of Zimbabwe

STUDENT LIFE

Student expenses and financial aid

Student costs:

Home students tuition fees: Minimum: 1,500 (Zimbabwean Dollar)
Maximum: 2,400 (Zimbabwean Dollar)
Foreign students tuition fees: Minimum: 1,450 (US Dollar)
Maximum: 8,000 (US Dollar)

GRADING SYSTEM

Usual grading system in secondary school
Full Description: A-F for Ordinary ("O") Level and Advanced ("A") Level.
Highest on scale: A
Pass/fail level: E for"A" Level and D for "O" Level.
Lowest on scale: F

Main grading system used by higher education institutions
Full Description: 80%+ =1 (First Division); 70%-79%=2.1 (Upper Second Division); 60%-69% =2.2 (Lower Second Division); 50%-59%= 3(Third Division); Below 50%= Fail. (used by University of Zimbabwe for undergraduate and masters degrees by coursework)
Highest on scale: 80%+= 1 (First Division)
Pass/fail level: 50%= 3 (Third Division)
Lowest on scale: below 50%

Other main grading systems

80%+= Distinction; 70%-79%= Merit; 50%-69%= Pass; Below 50%= Fail.(used by University of Zimbabwe for all certificates and diplomas).

NOTES ON HIGHER EDUCATION SYSTEM

Data for academic year: 2002-2003

Source: National Council for Higher Education, Harare, updated by the International Association of Universities (IAU) from IBE website, 2003 (www.ibe.unesco.org/International/Databanks/Wde/profilee.htm)

INSTITUTIONS OF HIGHER EDUCATION

UNIVERSITIES

PUBLIC INSTITUTIONS

Academic Staff *2001-2002*	MEN	WOMEN	TOTAL
FULL-TIME	37	5	**42**
STAFF WITH DOCTORATE			
FULL-TIME	3	2	**5**
Student Numbers *2001-2002*	MEN	WOMEN	TOTAL
All (Foreign Included)	390	125	**515**

• BINDURA UNIVERSITY OF SCIENCE EDUCATION (BUSE)
Private Bag 1020, Bindura, Mashonaland Central
Tel: +263(71) 75-32 +263(71) 75-36
Fax: +263(71) 75-34
Website: http://www.buse.ac.zw

Vice-Chancellor (Acting): Saba Abel Tswana (2002-)
Tel: +263(71) 76-21 Fax: +263(71) 75-52
EMail: tswana@mailhost.buse.ac.zw

Registrar: Elliot Dzaramba Tel: +263(71) 76-21
EMail: dzaramba@mailhost.buse.ac.zw

International Relations: James J. Gutura
Tel: +263(71) 76-21 Fax: +263(71) 75-34
EMail: gutura@mailhost.buse.ac.zw

Faculties
Agriculture and Environmental Science (Agricultural Economics; Agricultural Management; Environmental Studies; Forestry; Soil Science)
Science Education (Biology; Chemistry; Geography; Mathematics; Physics; Science Education) *Dean:* Mashack Matshazi

History: Founded 1995 as University of Zimbabwe College, acquired present title and status 2000.

Governing Bodies: Bindura University of Science Education Council; Ministry of Higher Education and Technology

Academic Year: Fully semesterized with new intakes in March and August

Admission Requirements: General Certificate of Education with at least 2 ('A') level passes

Fees: (Zimbabwe Dollars) 30,000 per annum

Main Language(s) of Instruction: English

Accrediting Agencies: Ministry of Higher Education and Technology

Degrees and Diplomas: *Bachelor Degree*: Science Education (BScEd); Agriculture (BScAgric), 3 yrs; *Bachelor Honours Degree*: Environmental Science (BESc (Hons)), 4 yrs

Student Services: Academic Counselling, Social Counselling, Sports Facilities, Health Services, Canteen

Student Residential Facilities: For 398 students

Libraries: Central Library, 8660 vols, 86 journal titles, 235 maps, access to Internet

Publications: University Prospectus (annually)

GREAT ZIMBABWE UNIVERSITY
PO Box 1460, Masvingo
Tel: +263(39) 62-028
Fax: +263(39) 62-028

Vice-Chancellor (Acting): Hilda Matarira
EMail: hmatarira@healthnet.zw

History: Founded 2001.

MIDLANDS STATE UNIVERSITY (MSU)
Private Bag 9055, Gweru
Tel: +263(54) 607-53
Fax: +263(54) 603-11
EMail: msuvcoffice@yahoo.com

Vice-Chancellor: Ngwabi Bhebe (1999-2004)
EMail: nbhebe@zarnet.ac.zw;bheben@msu.ac.zw

Registrar (Acting): G.T. Gurira Tel: +263(54) 605-86
Fax: +263(54) 603-11

Faculties
Arts (Arts and Humanities)
Commerce (Business and Commerce)
Education
Natural Resources Management and Agriculture (Agriculture; Natural Resources)
Science (Natural Sciences)
Social Sciences

History: Founded 1999.
Libraries: c. 50,850 vols
Academic Staff *2001-2002:* Total: c. 160
Student Numbers *2001-2002:* Total: c. 2,380

• NATIONAL UNIVERSITY OF SCIENCE AND TECHNOLOGY (NUST)
PO Box 346, Bulawayo, Matabeleland
Tel: +263(9) 282-842
Fax: +263(9) 286-803
EMail: mkariwo@esanet.zw
Website: http://www.nust.ac.zw

Vice-Chancellor: Phineas M. Makhurane (1991-)
Fax: +263(9) 289-651 EMail: pmmakhurane@nust.ac.zw

Registrar: Michael N. Kariwo Tel: +263(9) 286-803
Fax: +263(9) 289-057 EMail: mtkariwo@nust.ac.zw
International Relations: Felix F. Moyo
EMail: ffmoyo@nust.ac.zw

Faculties

Applied Sciences (Biochemistry; Biology; Chemistry; Computer Science; Mathematics; Physics) *Dean:* Maclean M. Bhala
Architecture and Surveying (Architecture and Planning; Surveying and Mapping) *Dean:* Samson Ik. Umenne
Commerce (Accountancy; Banking; Business and Commerce; Finance; Insurance; Management) *Dean:* T. Nkomo
Communication and Information Sciences (Communication Studies; Information Sciences)
Environmental Sciences (Environmental Studies; Forest Management; Wildlife) *Dean (Acting):* M.M. Bhala
Humanities (Arts and Humanities; Teacher Training)
Industrial Technology (Chemical Engineering; Civil Engineering; Electronic Engineering; Industrial Engineering; Textile Technology; Water Science) *Dean:* Mqhele E. Dlodlo

Centres

Research and Development

History: Founded 1991, following the establishment in 1988 of a Commission of Inquiry into the establishment of a second University in Zimbabwe. A State Institution.

Governing Bodies: University Council; Senate

Academic Year: August to May (August-December; January-May)

Admission Requirements: General Certificate of Education (GCE) with either passes at Ordinary ('O') level and 2 at Advanced ('A') level, or passes in 4 subjects at 'O' and minimum 3 passes at 'A' level. A pass in English Language at 'O' level and general paper at 'A' level or equivalent compulsory. Details of approved subjects shown in General Information and Registration Handbook

Fees: (Zimbabwe Dollars) 36,000,000

Main Language(s) of Instruction: English

International Co-operation: With universities in the United Kingdom, South Africa, Bulgaria, United States

Accrediting Agencies: Council for Higher Education

Degrees and Diplomas: *Bachelor Degree:* Architecture and Quantity Surveying (BAQS), 5 yrs; *Bachelor Honours Degree:* Applied Sciences; Biology and Biochemistry; Chemistry; Physics; Mathematics; Computer Science (HAS); Commerce; Accountancy; Actuarial Science; Finance; Banking; Marketing; Insurance and Risk Management (Hcom), 4 yrs; Engineering; Chemical Engineering; Civil and Water Engineering; Electronic Engineering; Industrial Engineering; Textile Technology (HEN), 5 yrs

Student Services: Academic Counselling, Social Counselling, Employment Services, Nursery Care, Health Services, Foreign Student Centre

Student Residential Facilities: Yes

Libraries: Central Library, 23,000 vols

Publications: NUST Newsletter (bimonthly); NUST Yearbook (annually)

Academic Staff *2001-2002*: Full-Time: c. 440 Part-Time: c. 90 Total: c. 530

Student Numbers *2001-2002:* Total: c. 1,820

• UNIVERSITY OF ZIMBABWE (UZ)

PO Box MP 167, Mount Pleasant, Harare
Tel: +263(4) 303-211
Fax: +263(4) 333-407
EMail: ghill@adminiuz.ac.zw
Website: http://www.uz.ac.zw

Vice-Chancellor: Levy M. Nyagura Tel: +263(4) 333-493
Fax: +263(4) 334-018 EMail: nyagura@admin.uz.ac.za
Registrar: Wilfred Mukondiwa Tel: +263(4) 308-941
EMail: wililpaul@icon.co.zw
International Relations: Margaret S. Murandu
Tel: +263(4) 333-676

Faculties

Agriculture *Dean:* Otis A. Chivinge
Arts (Arts and Humanities) *Dean:* Gilbert Pwiti
Commerce (Business and Commerce) *Dean:* Tracey Mutaviri
Education *Dean:* C. Dyanda
Engineering *Dean:* Eustace Wright
Law *Dean:* Arthur J. Monase
Medicine *Dean:* Sam Tswana
Science (Natural Sciences) *Dean:* Teddy .A. Zengeni
Social Studies *Dean:* C. Mumbengegwi
Veterinary Science *Dean:* Samson Mukaratirwa

Colleges

Teacher Education (Teacher Training) *Dean:* J.E.N. Bourdillan

Departments

Family Science, Food and Nutrition (Family Studies; Food Science; Nutrition) *Chairman:* A.N. Mutukumira

Institutes

Development Studies *Director:* D.P. Chimanikire
Environmental Studies *Director:* S.F. Feresu
University Lake Kariba Research Station (Water Science) *Director:* J. Chimbari
Water and Sanitation (Sanitary Engineering; Water Science) *Director:* P. Taylor

Centres

Computer (Computer Science) *Director:* G. Hapanyengwi
Development Technology (Technology) *Director:* T. Rukuni
Human Resources *Director:* F. Zindi
University Teaching and Learning (Higher Education Teacher Training; Pedagogy) *Director:* C.T. Nziramasanga

History: Founded 1955 as University College of Rhodesia in Nyasaland. Acquired present title 1980 and present status 1982.

Governing Bodies: Council

Academic Year: March to November (March-June; August-November)

Admission Requirements: General Certificate of Education (GCE) or equivalent at Advanced ('A') level

Fees: (Zimbabwe Dollars): Undergraduate: 25,000-35,000 per annum; Postgraduate: 20,000-176,000 per annum

Main Language(s) of Instruction: English

International Co-operation: With universities in the United States, United Kingdom, Belgium, Norway, Sweden, South Africa, Netherlands

Degrees and Diplomas: *Bachelor Degree*: Agriculture, Arts and Humanities, Business Administration, Education, Engineering, Health Sciences, Natural Sciences, Law, Social Sciences, 3-5 yrs; *Master Degree*: Agriculture, Arts and Humanities, Business Administration, Education, Engineering, Health Sciences, Natural Sciences, Law, Social Sciences, a further 1-2 yrs; *Master of Philosophy*: Agriculture, Arts and Humanities, Business Administration, Education, Engineering, Health Sciences, Natural Sciences, Law, Social Sciences, 2-6 yrs; *Doctorate*: Agriculture, Arts and Humanities, Business Administration, Education, Engineering, Health Sciences, Natural Sciences, Law, Social Sciences (Dphil), 3-8 yrs. Also Certificates and Diplomas, 2 yrs

Student Services: Academic Counselling, Social Counselling, Sports Facilities, Handicapped Facilities, Health Services, Canteen, Foreign Student Centre

Student Residential Facilities: For 4002 students

Special Facilities: Audiovisual Teaching Unit. Drug and Toxicology Information Service

Libraries: 450,000 vols

Publications: The Central African Journal of Medicine (CAJM) (monthly); Zimbabwe Journal of Education Research (3 per annum); Journal of Applied Social Sciences in Africa (JASSA) Zimbazia (biannually)

Press or Publishing House: University of Zimbabwe Publications

Academic Staff *2001-2002*: Full-Time: c. 990

Student Numbers *2001-2002*: All (Foreign Included): Men: c. 7,130 Women: c. 3,160 Total: c. 10,290

ZIMBABWE OPEN UNIVERSITY (ZOU)

PO Box MP 1119, Mount Pleasant, Harare
Tel: +263(4) 333-452
Fax: +263(4) 307-136

Vice-Chancellor (Acting): Primrose Kurasha
Tel: +263(4) 333-452 Fax: +263(4) 303-151
EMail: pkurasha@mweb.co.zw;Kurasha@ecoweb.co.zw

Registrar: M. Mhasvi Tel: +263(4) 307-145

International Relations: Chawawa Morgen

Head Librarian: L. Maenzanise

Faculties
Education and Humanities *Dean*: Matthew Izuagie
Science and Applied Social Sciences *Dean*: Robert Chimedza

History: Founded 1996 as University College of Distance Education, acquired present status and title 1999.

582

PRIVATE INSTITUTIONS

AFRICA UNIVERSITY (AU)
PO Box 1320, Mutare
Tel: +263(20) 60-026
Fax: +263(20) 61-785
EMail: africa@africau.uz.zw
Website: http://www.africau.edu

Vice-Chancellor: Rukudzo Murapa (1998-)
Tel: +263(20) 60-075 Fax: +263(20) 63-284
EMail: vc@syscom.co.zw

Deputy Vice-Chancellor: Edward A. Baryeh
Tel: +263(20) 64-912

International Relations: Frank Chikanga, Registrar
Tel: +263(20) 61-611 EMail: aureg@syscom.co.zw

Faculties
Agriculture and Natural Resources (Agriculture; Natural Resources) *Dean*: Anathanius Mphuru
Education *Dean*: James Quarshie
Humanities and Social Sciences (Arts and Humanities; Social Sciences) *Dean*: Robson Silitshena
Management and Administration (Administration; Management) *Dean*: Cyprian Eboh
Theology *Dean*: Kekumba Yemba

History: Founded 1992. A private Institution linked to the United Methodist Church, acquired present status and name 1994.

Governing Bodies: Board of Directors

Academic Year: August to May (August-December; January-May)

Admission Requirements: General Certificate of Education (GCE) with passes at Advanced ('A') level in relevant subjects and passes in 5 subjects at Ordinary ('O') level

Fees: (US Dollars): 3618 per annum; Postgraduate, 5175

Main Language(s) of Instruction: English

International Co-operation: With universities in United States and South Africa.

Degrees and Diplomas: *Bachelor Degree*: Agriculture (BSc); Arts (BA); Divinity (BD), 3 yrs; Education (BEd); Fine Arts; Education (BAEd); Management; Economics; Marketing; Accountancy (BSc); Natural Sciences; Agriculture (BScAgric); Natural Sciences; Education (BScEd), 4 yrs; *Master Degree*: Management; Administration; Finance (MBA); Theology (MTS), 1 1/2 yr; Management; Administration; Finance (EMBA), 2 yrs; Agriculture (MSc/MPhil), 2-3 yrs

Student Services: Academic Counselling, Social Counselling, Sports Facilities, Language Programmes, Health Services, Canteen

Student Residential Facilities: For 900 students

Libraries: Africa University Library, c. 40,000 vols

Press or Publishing House: Africa University Press

Academic Staff 2002-2003	MEN	WOMEN	TOTAL
FULL-TIME	47	16	63
PART-TIME	12	9	21
TOTAL	**59**	**25**	**84**
STAFF WITH DOCTORATE			
FULL-TIME	17	2	**19**

Student Numbers 2002-2003	MEN	WOMEN	TOTAL
All (Foreign Included)	597	528	**1,125**
FOREIGN ONLY	179	76	255

Part-time Students, 54

CATHOLIC UNIVERSITY IN ZIMBABWE (CUZ)

PO Box CY 3442, Causeway, Harare
Tel: +263(4) 705-368
Fax: +263(4) 706-911
EMail: cocuz@mango.zw

Rector: S. Nondo (1999-) Tel: +263(4) 570-169
Fax: +263(4) 573-973
Administrative Officer: A. Mukeredzi Tel: +263(4) 570-570

History: Founded 1999.

• SOLUSI UNIVERSITY

Private Bag T5399, Bulawayo
Tel: +263(9) 83226 -8
Fax: +263(9) 83229
EMail: solusi@esanet.zw

Vice-Chancellor: Norman Maphosa (1992-)
Tel: +263(9) 83267 Fax: +263(9) 83229
EMail: vchancellor@solusi.ac.zw;prof_maphosa@yahoo.com
Registrar: Richard Sithole Tel: +263(9) 83383

Faculties
Arts and Science (Arts and Humanities; Natural Sciences) *Dean:* Tommy Nkungula
Business (Business and Commerce) *Dean:* Ropafadzo Maphango
Theology and Religious Studies (Religious Studies; Theology) *Dean:* Zacchaeus Mathema

Departments
Accountancy *Head:* Davison Mwanahiba
Computer Management and Information Systems (Computer Engineering; Information Management; Systems Analysis) *Head (Acting):* Nation Madikiza
Education *Head:* Eunice Mgeni
English *Head:* Betty Mkwinda-Nyasulu
Family and Consumer Sciences (Consumer Studies; Family Studies; Nutrition; Textile Technology) *Head:* Lloyd Makamure
Fine Arts (Fine Arts; Music) *Head:* Lesley Hall
History *Head:* Meshack Zimunya
Management (Business Administration; Economics; Finance; Management) *Head:* Daniel Bwonda
Mathematics and Natural Sciences (Agriculture; Biology; Chemistry; Electronic Engineering; Mathematics; Natural Sciences; Physics) *Head:* Gertahun Merga

Centres
Research Information and Publications (Documentation Techniques; Publishing and Book Trade)

History: Founded 1894, acquired present status and title 1994.
Governing Bodies: University Council
Academic Year: August to May (August-December; January-May)
Admission Requirements: General Certificate of Education passes at Ordinary 'O' level and a pass in English language at 'A' level
Fees: (Zimbabwe Dollars): c. 46,960 per semester
Main Language(s) of Instruction: English
Accrediting Agencies: National Council for Higher Education
Degrees and Diplomas: *Bachelor Degree:* 3 yrs; *Master Degree:* 2 yrs (full-time), 4 yrs (part-time); *Graduate Certificate:* Education, 1 yr
Student Services: Nursery Care, Sports Facilities, Health Services, Canteen
Student Residential Facilities: For c. 600 students
Special Facilities: Solusi Museum
Libraries: Solusi Library, c. 45 000 vols
Publications: Solusi Echo (3 per annum); Solusi University News; Solusi University of Research (biannually)
Academic Staff 2001-2002: Total: c. 50
Student Numbers 2001-2002: Total: c. 800

OTHER INSTITUTIONS

PUBLIC INSTITUTIONS

BULAWAYO POLYTECHNIC (BYO POLY)

PO Box 1392 , CNR Park Road/12th Avenue, Bulawayo, Matabele Land
Tel: +263(9) 631-81
Fax: +263(9) 711-65

Principal: A. Mwadiwa (1997-) Tel: +263(9) 778-53
EMail: mwadiwa@hotmail.com
Vice-Principal: H.M. Talukder EMail: talukder@mweb.co.zw
International Relations: M. Vimbai Tel: +263(9) 631-83

Founded: 1961, 2000

Institutes
Adult and Continuing Education *Director:* P.C. Moyo
Applied Arts and Design (Design; Fine Arts; Graphic Arts) *Director:* C. Craven
Business Studies (Accountancy; Business Administration; Management; Marketing; Secretarial Studies) *Director:* B. J Ndlovu

Engineering (Automotive Engineering; Civil Engineering; Construction Engineering; Electrical Engineering; Engineering; Mechanical Engineering) *Director*: Edmond Jaya

Hospitality and Tourism (Cooking and Catering; Hotel Management; Tourism) *Director*: Margaret Nyamuda

Science and Technology (Applied Chemistry; Food Science; Health Sciences; Laboratory Techniques; Metallurgical Engineering; Natural Sciences; Polymer and Plastics Technology; Rubber Technology; Technology) *Director*: Andrew Sibanda

History: Founded 1961. Acquired present status and title 2000.

GWERU TEACHERS COLLEGE (GTC)
Private Bag 9055, Gweru
Teacher Training

HARARE POLYTECHNIC
Causeway, PO Box 8074, Harare
Tel: +263(4) 705-951
Fax: +263(4) 720-955

Principal: C. Chivanda (1988-) Tel: +263(4) 794-880

Deputy Principal and Director: Stephen T. Raza
Tel: +263(4) 753-029

International Relations: B.A. Mapondera, Registrar

Founded: 1927

Departments
Adult and Continuing Education (Clothing and Sewing)

Business and Secretarial Studies (Business Administration; Secretarial Studies)

Electrical Engineering *Head*: Irene Olga Mbwanda

Engineering and Construction (Architecture; Architecture and Planning; Civil Engineering; Construction Engineering; Interior Design; Landscape Architecture; Painting and Drawing; Regional Planning; Surveying and Mapping; Urban Studies; Wood Technology) *Head (Acting)*: Joseph Ruzive

Graphic and Design (Design; Graphic Arts)

Mass Communication

Printing and Printmaking (Graphic Design; Packaging Technology; Photography; Printing and Printmaking) *Head*: Samson Moyo

Science and Technology (Natural Sciences; Technology) *Head*: Eldah Matikiti

History: Founded 1927.

Governing Bodies: Advisory Council

Main Language(s) of Instruction: English

Accrediting Agencies: Higher Education Examination Council